EVERYDAY LIFE

Everyday Life

Theories and Practices from Surrealism to the Present

MICHAEL SHERINGHAM

OXFORD

UNIVERSITY PRESS

OXFORD
UNIVERSITY PRESS

Great Clarendon Street, Oxford OX2 6DP

Oxford University Press is a department of the University of Oxford.
It furthers the University's objective of excellence in research, scholarship,
and education by publishing worldwide in

Oxford New York

Auckland Cape Town Dar es Salaam Hong Kong Karachi
Kuala Lumpur Madrid Melbourne Mexico City Nairobi
New Delhi Shanghai Taipei Toronto

With offices in

Argentina Austria Brazil Chile Czech Republic France Greece
Guatemala Hungary Italy Japan Poland Portugal Singapore
South Korea Switzerland Thailand Turkey Ukraine Vietnam

Oxford is a registered trade mark of Oxford University Press
in the UK and in certain other countries

Published in the United States
by Oxford University Press Inc., New York

© Michael Sheringham 2006

The moral rights of the author have been asserted
Database right Oxford University Press (maker)

First published 2006

British Library Cataloguing in Publication Data

Data available

Library of Congress Cataloging in Publication Data

Data available

Typeset by SPI Publisher Services, Pondicherry, India
Printed in Great Britain
on acid-free paper by
Biddles Ltd., King's Lynn, Norfolk

ISBN 978–0–19–927395–9

5 7 9 10 8 6 4

In memory of my mother
Yvette Habib Sheringham
(1912–1967)

Acknowledgements

I am grateful to the French department at Royal Holloway University of London for providing a stimulating and supportive environment during the composition of much of this book, and to the Warden and Fellows of all Souls College and my colleagues in the French sub-faculty at Oxford for their encouragement in the final stages. Many of the ideas were tested and enhanced in debate with students on my special subject course, 'Exploring the Every-day', at Royal Holloway, as well as at the universities of Paris VII-Jussieu in 1995–6, Bordeaux-III in 2000, Paris IV-Sorbonne in 2002, and the Institute of French Cultural Studies at Dartmouth College in July 2005. I profited enormously from questions raised after talks in universities in the UK, France, and the US and would like to thank the various organisers for making this possible. For research leave and support I thank Royal Holloway University of London, the Arts and Humanities Research Board, the British Academy, and the University of London Central Research Fund. I have much appreciated the contribution of colleagues at Oxford University Press, especially Tom Per-ridge, Jacqueline Baker, Andrew McNeillie, and Sophie Goldsworthy. I also thank the anonymous readers of my manuscript for their helpful suggestions.

Earlier versions of some sections of this book have appeared in the following places: *French Studies, Paragraph, Cross-Cultural Poetics*, in Diana Knight (ed.), *Critical Essays on Roland Barthes* (New York: G. K. Hall, 2000), Johnnie Gratton and Michael Sheringham (eds.), *The Art of the Project* (Oxford: Berghahn, 2005), Charles Forsdick and Andy Stafford (eds.), *The Modern Essay in French* (Bern: Peter Lang, 2005), Michel Murat and Gilles Leclerq (eds.), *Le Romanesque* (Paris: Presses de la Sorbonne Nouvelle, 2004), Elisa-beth Cardonne-Arlick and Dominique Viart (eds.), *Effractions de la poésie, Écritures contemporaines*, no. 7 (Paris: Minard, 2003). I am grateful to the relevant editors and publishers for permission to reproduce this material.

One of the pleasures of working on everyday life is that everyone has a view on the matter. It is not possible to thank them all personally, but I owe an immense debt to the numerous friends who have shared their ideas with me. Priscilla, with whom I share my own everyday life, has benevolently tolerated its disruption by this project: to her I express my loving gratitude.

List of Illustrations

Contents

Introduction

Browsing in the Bibliothèque Georges Perec, a wonderful archive hidden away at the back of the Arsenal library in Paris, I came across an official-looking exhibition catalogue, dating from 1981. Sponsored by a government planning department, the exhibition was called *Construire pour habiter* (Building for Living), and the brief preface was by Paul Delouvrier, the civil servant commissioned by de Gaulle in 1961 to modernize the Paris area. The 'Plan Delouvrier' with its famous 'Schéma directeur' led to the construction of innumerable tower blocks and 'grands ensembles', changing the face of Paris and introducing the new RER railway to link the capital with its surrounding 'Villes nouvelles'. Pilloried in Jean-Luc Godard's 1967 film about Paris, *2 ou 3 choses que je sais d'elle*, Delouvrier had come to incarnate the functionalist *urbanisme* repeatedly attacked by more progressive architects and thinkers.[1] It was therefore a surprise to see that, after Delouvrier, the first author in the catalogue's opening section—'Habiter'—was Georges Perec. Perec's contribution was a two-page meditation on ways of telling someone where you live. Making characteristically subtle distinctions between cases where one would simply indicate the country or city, as opposed to specifying the street or giving precise details of one's address, Perec paid close attention to the discourse of 'saying where you live', amusing his readers with offbeat humour while at the same time prompting them to think about their everyday lives. As we shall have ample opportunity to observe in the course of this book, Perec's piece, titled 'De quelques emplois du verbe habiter' (On some uses of the verb to inhabit)[2] reflected a central concern of his work: to rescue the everyday from

[1] On Delouvrier see Bernard Marchal, *Paris: Histoire d'une ville, 19e–20e siècle* (Paris: Seuil, 1993), and Eduard Welch 'Experimenting with Identity: People, Place and Urban Change in Contemporary French Photography', in Johnnie Gratton and Michael Sheringham (eds.), *The Art of the Project* (Oxford: Berghahn Books, 2005).

[2] Georges Perec *Penser/Classer* (Paris: Hachette, 1981), 13–16. In all instances of citation in this volume, the page number belongs to the French edition and the translations are my own.

the neglect and oblivion to which it is customarily consigned. The invitation to write a piece for the exhibition catalogue no doubt stemmed from the notoriety he had achieved with the huge success in 1978 of his *La Vie mode d'emploi*, a compendium of everyday things conjured up by the description of an imaginary Parisian apartment block. Equally striking however was the choice of other contributors, for not only did they include two other figures who will be at the centre of this book—Henri Lefebvre and Michel de Certeau—but others, including Luce Giard, Michel Maffesoli, Pierre Sansot, and Paul Virilio, whose contribution to thinking about the *quotidien* will in some cases be discussed at length in the chapters that follow.

At the turn of the 1980s *Construire pour habiter* signalled the coming of age of a set of ideas—very different from those that had informed Delouvrier's planning—about the central importance of the everyday. These ideas had been progressively elaborated in the two previous decades. The exhibition and its catalogue display official (if possibly superficial) recognition that there is a kind of thinking about everyday life that goes beyond narrow functionalism and gives importance to different styles and priorities—to spaces, rhythms, objects, and practices. They acknowledge that the verb 'habiter' refers to human needs (as Perec's title suggested) but also that it can be declined in different moods and tenses, that living has its grammar, and life its 'mode(s) d'emploi'. Certeau's piece in the catalogue is about 'inhabiting' as an art; Giard's is on the bodily investment of lived spaces, and the histories inscribed through physical gestures; Maffesoli's and Sansot's are concerned with the social meanings articulated in modes of dwelling, while Virilio considers what can be learnt from aberrant or bizarre solutions to the question of where and how to live. Jean-François Augoyard, whose work on the 'language' of urban itineraries had impressed Certeau,[3] reflected on the place of imagination in the everyday, while Michel Butor, like Perec the author of a book about a single apartment block (*Passage de Milan*, 1954), provided some thoughts on what it means to live in a house. *Construire pour habiter* acknowledges the everyday, but just as importantly it recognizes that by this point in French cultural history, the turn of the 1980s, a body of ideas and a set of discourses on the *quotidien*, associated with Perec, Lefebvre, Certeau, and others, were available to articulate and inspire new insights into everyday life.[4]

---

[3] See Michel de Certeau, *L'Invention du quotidien*, I, *Arts de faire* (1980; Paris: Gallimard Folio, 1990), 151–2.

[4] The phrase 'everyday life' will be used to designate the overall sector or framework with which the writers, artists and thinkers discussed in this book are concerned, while the terms 'the everyday'

A central contention of this book is that if we look back from that point we can see that the quarter-century or so leading up to the 1980s saw the elaboration of a cluster of closely-knit ways of thinking about and exploring everyday life that planted the question of the everyday at the heart of French culture in the last two decades of the twentieth century and into the new millennium. Since 1980 investigations and explorations of the *quotidien*, in a considerable range of media and genres, have enjoyed remarkable prominence in France and elsewhere. This ties in with the decline of the novel in the 1980s and 1990s in favour of hybrid works exploiting the documentary impulse in such modes as autobiography, biography, the journal, historical writing, travel writing, and the essay. In a climate that saw the end of the structuralist embargo on subjectivity and reference, and favoured new ways of looking at the concrete human subject at grips with experience, these modes, often involving fusions between different media, including film, photography, theatre, and reportage, tended to incorporate a self-reflexive awareness of their methods and status.[5] The referential and the fictional, for example, tended no longer to be viewed as polar opposites but as interactive elements. Hard-nosed objectivity in the human sciences came to seem illusory, as did art's severance from experiential reality. As France became increasingly in-clined to revisit its troubled recent history, and to address its late-twentieth-century physiognomy, the investigation of individual and collective memory, and the realignment of the ethnographic gaze to focus on the near at hand rather than the exotic, became key impulses behind a plethora of cultural activities.[6] All these currents tended to converge on ordinary, everyday experi-ence, leading to the explorations and investigations of the *quotidien* we find in such varied works as Marc Augé's *Un Ethnologue dans le métro*, Pierre Sansot's *Les Gens de peu*, François Maspero's *Les Passagers du Roissy-Express*, Annie Ernaux's *Journal du dehors*, the 'Théâtre du quotidien' of Michel Vinaver and Michel Deutsch, François Bon's *Paysage fer*, Jacques Réda's *La Liberté des rues*, the novels of Echenoz, Toussaint, Oster and Daeninckx, Christian

---

and 'the *quotidien*' will be used as synonyms for the dimension of lived experience that is involved in everyday life. Popularized by Henri Lefebvre, 'everyday life' tends to have distinct political and sociological connotations; more neutral and indeterminate, 'the everyday' has become increasingly prevalent and will generally be preferred here.

[5] On the return of the subject, see Paul Gifford and Johnnie Gratton (eds.), *Subject Matters: Essays on Subject and Self in French Literature from Descartes to the Present* (Amsterdam: Editions Rodopi, 2000).

[6] See for example, Pierre Nora (ed.), *Les Lieux de mémoire*, 3 vols. (1984–92; Paris: Gallimard Quarto, 1997), and the discussion of 'anthropology at home' in Ch. 8 below.

Boltanski's installations, Sophie Calle's projects, Cédric Klapisch's film *Chacun cherche son chat*, and so on. Yet however much they reflect the spirit of their times, these approaches to the everyday all draw significantly on ideas and practices elaborated in the years prior to 1980.

At the core of this book is a close study of four major figures: Henri Lefebvre (1901–91), Roland Barthes (1916–80), Michel de Certeau (1925–86), and Georges Perec (1936–82). I argue that the contributions and interactions of these writers elaborated, in the 1960s and 1970s, a set of interconnecting discourses on the everyday that played an essential role in French culture over the following two decades. To be sure, Lefebvre's seminal notion of a 'critique de la vie quotidienne' had not only crystallized in an earlier period (the original *Critique* was written in 1945 just after the Liberation) but drew on a range of ideas about the everyday at large in Marx, Freud, Lukács, Heidegger, Surrealism, Bataille, Leiris, Queneau, and Benjamin: these figures will all therefore have their place in this book, and I will return to them in a moment. But it is important to recognize that it was the creative interaction, from the mid 1950s onwards, between Lefebvre, Barthes, Perec, and Certeau (and of course between them and other figures including the Situationists, Edgar Morin, Jean-Luc Godard, Pierre Bourdieu, Michel Foucault) that transformed a disparate set of often contradictory intuitions into a relatively cohesive, if still far from homogeneous body of theories and practices that could then impact significantly on cultural production in France and elsewhere through the 1980s and beyond.

Barthes was well acquainted with Lefebvre and his work. As Michael Kelly has argued, Barthes's *Mythologies* (written between 1953 and 1955) can be seen as a natural extension of Lefebvre's original, Marxist-oriented, programme for a *Critique de la vie quotidienne*,[7] and it is clear that, in its turn, *Mythologies* (where Lefebvre gets a mention in passing)[8] fed into the evolution of Lefebvre's project. Yet I will argue in due course that just as Lefebvre's first (1947) critique was rather thin, Barthes's brilliant but essentially negative *Mythologies* (1957) by no means fully represents the importance of the *quotidien* in his subsequent career, from his work on fashion and the city, to his marvellous book on everyday life in Japan, to his last seminars at the Collège de France. Concerted thinking about the everyday arguably gets fully

---

[7] See M. Kelly, 'Demystification: A Dialogue between Barthes and Lefebvre', *Yale French Studies*, 98 (Fall 2000), 79–97

[8] Roland Barthes, *Mythologies, Œuvres complètes*, ed. Eric Marty, I, (Paris: Seuil, 1993), 697–8.

under way at the turn of the 1960s when, firstly, Lefebvre produces the long-awaited second volume of his *Critique* (warmly received in a prescient essay by Maurice Blanchot) and launches a centre for the study of 'la vie quotidienne' with a regular seminar; and, secondly, when Barthes, newly installed at the École des Hautes Études en sciences sociales, decides to devote his first seminar to the signifying processes involving objects in modern society. A number of common factors underlie these two developments—the emergence of the figure of the consumer in the context of rapid modernization (already at the heart of *Mythologies*) and the pervasiveness of a 'functionalist' ideology; the concurrent rise of 'scientific' sociology and of a need to find alternatives to it; the search on the intellectual left for alternatives to Stalinism; the re-emergence, in the Situationists, of a group concerned, like the historic avant-gardes, with revolutionizing everyday life (in 1961 the Situationist Guy Debord contributed to Lefebvre's seminar).[9] This is the climate in which the young Georges Perec visits Henri Lefebvre in the Pyrenees, takes part in meetings of the *Arguments* group while attempting with friends to set up his own journal *La Ligne générale*, and attends Barthes's seminars at the EHESS (where Jean Baudrillard will also be present). Subsequently, in the 1960s, it is to Barthes that Perec sends drafts of *Les Choses*, his exploration of consumerist obsession where *Mythologies* is a key intertext. The Situationists and Lefebvre (then teaching at Nanterre) will be widely cited in the context of the events of May '68, while Michel de Certeau's study of the *événements*, *La Prise de parole* (1968), and his critique of notions of popular culture, may have brought him to the attention of Lefebvre, Barthes, and Perec. At any rate, their ideas are clearly evident (all three are quoted) in *L'Invention du quotidien* (1980), the team project Certeau embarks on in the mid 1970s, when he and Perec contribute to *Traverses*, the interdisciplinary journal of the Centre Pompidou.

Four central chapters of this book are devoted, in turn, to Lefebvre, Barthes, Certeau, and Perec. In each case my concern has been to delineate clearly the place of the *quotidien* in their work, the specific ways in which their ideas contribute to the construction and emergence of a wider set of discourses on the everyday, and how their ideas are specifically linked to later work as well as to each other. A striking testimony to the importance of these four figures is that if the flourishing of the *quotidien*, the ubiquity of this notion in every

---

[9] *Internationale Situationniste*, 1958–1969, édn. angmentée (Paris: Fayard, 1997), 218–25; on avant-gardes, see P. Burger, *The Theory of the Avant-Garde* (Minneapolis: University of Minnesota Press, 1984).

corner of cultural activity, belongs to the 1980s and after, Perec, Certeau, and Barthes (with Lefebvre as *eminence grise*) remain the thinkers constantly cited (for example by Augé, Sansot, or Vinaver) into the new century, despite the fact that Barthes died in 1980, Perec in 1982, Certeau in 1986, and Lefebvre in 1991, none having added significantly, where the *quotidien* is concerned, to what they had written by 1980. As I shall argue throughout, we are dealing here with a real tradition rooted in cultural and intellectual history, where the period between 1960 and 1980 is a phase of active, if often invisible, invention, and the period from 1980 to 2000 (and beyond) a phase of practice, variation, and dissemination.

This active sense of a tradition evolving through a set of discourses and practices, defences and illustrations, is what differentiates the account of the everyday in this book—which consistently plots its course in relation to France even when looking at other bearings—from the 'everyday life' prominent in Anglo-Saxon cultural studies. Ben Highmore, for example, in his excellent *Everyday Life and Cultural Theory* (and accompanying *Everyday Life Reader*) makes it clear that his aim is to draw out from an avowedly eclectic range of sources the lineaments of a future discipline, 'everyday life studies'. This draws inspiration from the pioneering sociological insights of Georg Simmel in the early twentieth century, the Surrealists, the 'trash aesthetics' of Walter Benjamin, the remarkable work of the British Mass Observation movement in the 1930s, as well as the ideas of Lefebvre and Certeau (the *Reader* casts its net even wider to consider work on Japan, Russia, etc.). Rather than 'telling a coherent story of the progressive refinement of an idea' Highmore presents 'a heterogeneous mix of divergent interests', a variety of attempts to tackle from different positions and in different contexts the intractable matter of the everyday.[10] Unlike Highmore's, my aim is to stress the coherence of an intellectual tradition. This does not mean the elaboration of a single monolithic view or doctrine on the everyday, the 'progressive refinement of an idea'. Far from it: throughout I will draw attention to plurality, ramifications, and multiple pathways. What it does mean, however, is exchange, interaction, and emulation, as well as differentiation. Lefebvre's everyday is not the same as Barthes's, Perec's, or Certeau's. But if we identify a specific historical framework, centred on the period 1960–80, we can observe four complex visions of the everyday, each combining theoretical and political acuity with imaginative power and insight, evolving through interaction

---

[10] Ben Highmore, *Everyday Life and Cultural Theory* (London: Routledge, 2002), 18.

rather than in isolation and each sharing a number of contemporary and historical reference points (rapid modernization, May '68, urbanism, Structuralism and its decline, cultural policy, a shift towards collective memory).

As Highmore's example demonstrates, Anglo-American cultural studies tends to appropriate selective aspects of the tradition this book seeks to elucidate (there is also some borrowing in the other direction: Certeau and Sansot cite Richard Hoggart's 'ethnographic' account of British working-class life, as well as the work of Erving Goffman and others, while Certeau was aware of the beginnings of cultural studies in Britain). Cultural studies reappraises Surrealism (often through the prism of Benjamin) via its visual archive, its celebration of the city, and its ethnographic turn (notably in Bataille and Leiris), while Lefebvre and Certeau are constantly cited. In all cases the hazards of translation impact on reception, leading, in Lefebvre's case, to a serious distortion of his thinking on the everyday. The English translation of the first volume of the *Critique de la vie quotidienne* did not appear until 1991 prior to which the main source was the less representative synthesis Lefebvre wrote in 1968, *La Vie quotidienne dans le monde moderne*, immediately translated as *Everyday Life in the Modern World*. Translations of Lefebvre's later work on space and cities also appeared in the 1990s[11] reflecting the renewed interest in his work displayed by contemporary geographers such as Edward Soja.[12] But the absence, until 2002, of an English translation of the second, 1961, volume of Lefebvre's *Critique* means that the full flowering of his thought on the *quotidien* has been ignored by 'cultural studies', impeding understanding of its true relation to the work of Certeau (Highmore sees a 'gulf' between them). Lefebvre and Certeau are often nonetheless linked as pioneers in the field of everyday life studies. Alec McHoul and Toby Miller, for example, see Certeau as drawing on the heritage of Lefebvre and becoming 'the most significant contemporary cultural theorist of the everyday'.[13] These authors, who explore such topics as food, sport, conversation, and self-help therapies, situate the contribution of Lefebvre and Certeau in a wider field including the work of Erving Goffman, Raymond Williams, and Roland Barthes, as well as the Ethnomethodology school of Harold Garfinkel.

---

[11] Henri Lefebvre, *The Production of Space*, trans. Donald Nicholson-Smith (1974; Oxford: Blackwell, 1991), and E. Kofman and E. Lebas (eds.), *Henri Lefebvre: Writings on Cities* (Oxford: Blackwell, 1996).

[12] See Edward Soja, *Postmodern Geographies: The Reassertion of Space in Critical Social Theory*, (London: Verso, 1989).

[13] Alec McHoul and Toby Miller, *Popular Culture and Everyday Life* (London: Sage, 1998), 11.

Susan Willis pays tribute to the 'pioneering work done by Henri Lefebvre and Michel de Certeau towards the development of the concept of "everyday life" ("la vie quotidienne") and its theoretical apprehension' and seeks 'to preserve their focus on mundane social life and practice while situating it in a more properly US and suburban [as opposed to urban] context'.[14] More critically, Laurie Langbauer invokes Lefebvre and (to a lesser degree) Certeau in her critique of the essentialism and gender politics of British cultural studies, notably in Raymond Williams.[15] Rita Felski, for her part, in a wide-ranging and thought-provoking article, queries some of the common assumptions underlying 'cultural studies' approaches to the everyday, and seeks to bring these into dialogue with perspectives from feminism and phenomenology.[16] She argues that there are other ways of overcoming negative views of the quotidian than celebrating urban resistance or the energies of nomadic displacement. By focusing on the spheres of repetition, home, and habit, Felski argues that 'repetition can signal resistance as well as enslavement',[17] that home can involve more than banal home-making, and that habitual actions can be an authentic way of experiencing the world. Certeau and Perec would certainly have agreed.

Thanks in part to the author's North-American connections, Michel de Certeau's *L'Invention du quotidien, I, Arts de faire* appeared rapidly in translation as *The Practice of Everyday Life*, and has been widely influential. But the second volume, mainly comprising analyses based on the empirical investigations of Luce Giard into culinary practices and Pierre Mayol into neighbourhoods, was only translated in 1999. Despite the wide dissemination of Certeau's book, the complexity of his thought, along with other factors such as the necessity to see it in the context of other contributions, such as those of Lefebvre, mean that the true nature and particularly the range and subtlety of his study of the everyday have yet to be fully recognized or exploited.[18] As I seek to demonstrate, Certeau's concept of everyday practice is best understood when explored in connection with the ideas of Lefebvre, Barthes, Perec, and others. Since their deaths in the early 1980s Barthes's and Perec's contributions to thinking on the everyday have begun to be recognized although they still

---

   [14] Susan Willis, *A Primer for Daily Life* (London: Routledge, 1991), 'Author's note'.
   [15] Laurie Langbauer, 'Cultural Studies and the Politics of the Everyday', *Diacritics*, 22 (Spring 1992), 47–65.
   [16] Rita Felski, 'The Invention of Everyday Life', *New Formations*, 39 (1999–2000), 15–31.
   [17] Ibid., 21.
   [18] See however J. Ahearne, *Michel de Certeau: Interpretation and its Other* (Cambridge: Polity Press, 1995), and I. Buchanan, *Michel de Certeau: Cultural Theorist* (London: Sage, 2000).

await full exploration.[19] This book tries especially to give Perec his due place alongside such recognized theoreticians as Lefebvre and Certeau.

Whilst in no way asserting the homogeneity of their thinking on the everyday, I argue that between 1960 and 1980 the evolving ideas of Lefebvre, Barthes, Perec, and Certeau fed into and drew on each of the others and, for reasons to be considered presently, made this a vital period in the emergence of the everyday as a paradigm. But one of the features that does make them different from one another (whilst enhancing the collective power of their contributions) is that these authors emerged from different intellectual traditions and therefore stood in different relationships to the earlier thinking on the everyday they appropriated selectively (in the same way that their contributions were appropriated selectively by 'cultural studies', or by later investigators of the *quotidien* in France and elsewhere). In the broadest of terms, Lefebvre can be associated with humanist Marxism, Barthes with Structuralism and its evolution into post-structuralism and post-modernism, Certeau with history, anthropology, and psychoanalysis, and Perec with the literary experimentalism of the Oulipo group, inaugurated by Raymond Queneau.[20] All of these intellectual orientations can be related in certain ways to Surrealism (more than, say, to Existentialism) and in Chapters 2 and 3 I focus on the category of the everyday in Surrealism, especially the work of Breton and Aragon, and then its transmutations through the 1930s in the hands of such dissident thinkers as Bataille, Leiris, and Queneau. Surrealism, which famously sought to combine Marx, Rimbaud, and Freud, who all reflected importantly on the everyday, provides an ideal context for the consideration of these and other strands in the progressive elaboration of a *quotidien* tradition, including Baudelaire's notion of *modernité* and its legacy in the modernist enthusiasm for urban experience to be found in Romains and Apollinaire, as well as in Surrealism and Walter Benjamin; or Victor Segalen's notion of exoticism which anticipates the ethnographic dimension of Surrealism that will come to the fore in Leiris.[21] Surrealism also provides a context within which to consider parallel instances of thinking on the everyday in the

---

[19] See for example Diana Knight, *Barthes and Utopia: Space, Travel, Writing* (Oxford: Oxford University Press, 1997), and Manet van Montfrans, *Georges Perec: la contrainte du réel* (Amsterdam-Atlanta: Rodopi, 1999). Ben Highmore includes a text by Perec in *The Everyday Life Reader* (London: Routledge, 2002), but does not mention him in his monograph.

[20] On Oulipo see Warren Motte (ed.) *Oulipo: A Primer of Potential Literature* (Lincoln: University of Nebraska Press, 1986).

[21] See Charles Forsdick, *Victor Segalen and the Aesthetics of Diversity: Journeys between Cultures* (Oxford: Oxford University Press, 2000).

thought of Lukács and Heidegger, and subsequently in Benjamin. In writing his first *Critique* in 1945 Lefebvre explicitly rejects Surrealism, Heidegger, and Lukács for having in various ways depreciated the *quotidien*, and advocates an approach based on Marx's early elaboration of his theory of alienation. Like Barthes's, Lefebvre's interpretation of Marxist thought will be inflected in the 1950s by the theatrical practice of Brecht as revealed by the tours of his Berliner Ensemble in the 1950s (Brecht will also be a direct influence on the 'Théâtre du quotidien' of the 1970s and 1980s). After Barthes's discovery of Saussure, semiology becomes the key to his exploration of 'signifying systems' at work in everyday life; the *quotidien* then survives the fading of the structuralist paradigm in the last phase of Barthes's work, governed by a renewed vision of subjectivity rooted in affects and pleasures at large in the everyday. At this stage Barthes acknowledges Surrealism's fascination with the everyday and takes a close interest in one of the heroes in the surrealist pantheon (also admired by Marx): the utopian socialist Charles Fourier. Certeau, partly through the religious aspect of his formation (he trained as a Jesuit priest), will also see the radical inventiveness of utopian thought as an important source of inspiration for understanding the everyday. Perec often noted his debt to Leiris, whose systematic combination of ethnography and autobiography had arisen in the context of his participation in Surrealism and its aftermath.

The remarkable flowering of ways of thinking about the everyday in the period 1960–80 drew on a rich but until then somewhat disparate heritage. Why did it occur at this time, and then inspire a spate of works centred on everyday life in the decades after 1980? In her stimulating *Fast Cars, Clean Bodies: Decolonization and the Reordering of French Culture* (1995) Kristin Ross argues that the concern with the everyday in the 1950s originated in the extraordinarily rapid pace of modernization in France, from the early 1950s to the early 1960s, achieved not only through the embrace of American capitalism but also through accelerated decolonization. Part of this process consisted in the conquest of a new territory, as modernization brought about what Lefebvre and the Situationists called 'the colonization of everyday life'. Developing this insight, Ross looks at such developments as the cult of the automobile and the obsession with domestic space and hygiene, as symptoms of everyday life being submitted to intensive scrutiny and control. Brought under the sway of bureaucratic and functionalist order, everyday life is privatized and de-realized: removed from history and real events, it becomes an essentially imaginary construct, a disembodied space—the world of pure consumption so well evoked in Perec's first novel *Les Choses* (1965).

Ross argues that literature and ideas in the 1950s and early 1960s also fell under the de-realizing spell of modernization: shunning history, the *nouveau roman* presents a world of objects outside time. The major intellectual movement of the period, Structuralism, adopts, according to Ross, the prevalent functionalism by installing the 'linguistic model' and substituting the agentless, synchronic play of structural elements for historical causality. In this perspective, Structuralism is part and parcel of the same process through which the social sciences in France adopted quantitative, statistical methods that were also to have a strong impact on the evolution of the *Annales* historians, away from 'histoire événementielle' to the 'longue durée' where change is so slow as to be barely perceptible, and revolution literally unthinkable. As Ross observes, her charge against Structuralism is in line with the critique spearheaded in the 1960s by Henri Lefebvre, and she places Lefebvre at the centre of an opposing current that also found expression in literature and other media. This current consists, firstly, in theoretical reflection on everyday life, Lefebvre above all, but also the Situationists, Castoriadis, Morin, the Barthes of *Mythologies*, and the Baudrillard of *Le Système des objets* and *La Société de consommation* (although these belong to the late 1960s); and, secondly, a strand of literary and visual work in the 'realist mode': novels by Christiane Rochefort, Elsa Triolet, Simone de Beauvoir, and Georges Perec, films by Jacques Tati and Jacques Demy.[22]

Ross's account is persuasive in the way it associates the rise of the everyday as a central intellectual and artistic preoccupation with a reaction against an all-pervasive functionalism engendered by rapid modernization. Yet the effect of focusing primarily on reactions to modernization is to suggest that the investigation of the everyday was exclusively negative in tenor and 'realist' in its aesthetic mode. To be sure, the writers Ross commends for having chronicled the 'lived, social reality' of the period drew attention to the impoverished everyday of functionalism: Lefebvre's account of 'le temps comprimé' (compressed time); Perec's depiction of the young couple Jérôme and Sylvie, losing all contact with lived reality as they allow their lives to be consumed by an insatiable appetite for conspicuous consumption; Jacques Tati's 'little man' embroiled with gadgets and bureaucratic planning in *Playtime*. Yet in Lefebvre and Perec at least, negative critique is far from the whole story. And when we follow the evolution of their long-lived fascination with the everyday beyond

---

[22] Kristin Ross, *Fast Cars, Clean Bodies: Decolonization and the Reordering of French Culture* (Cambridge, MA: MIT Press, 1996), 13.

the early Sixties it becomes apparent that this body of ideas and investigative practices evolved not simply by positing an alternative, 'realist', picture of everyday life, involving, say, a return to history, agency, and lived experience, but by finding ways of teasing out the complex imbrication of the positive and the negative, alienation and freedom, within the weave of everyday life itself. This had been Lefebvre's project since the first volume of the *Critique* where, as throughout his work, a central insight, deriving from early Marx, is that everyday life harbours within itself the possibility of its own existential or ontological transformation. Banality, in other words, has a benign as well as a malignant side, and the role of critique is maieutic in that it seeks to give birth to what is already there in embryo. As Lefebvre put it in 1968: 'Ce qui compte n'est pas seulement ce que les forces sociales font de notre vie quotidienne mais ce que nous faisons de ces forces à travers notre manière de les "vivre"' (What counts is not simply what social forces do to our everyday life but what we do with those forces through the way we 'live' them).[23] This is what makes Lefebvre's thought a gateway to that of Certeau and Perec. The critique of everyday life is bound up with apprehending the lived, the 'vécu', within what threatens it, and as such, at the level of both intellectual reflection and artistic representation or enactment, it goes beyond socio-political critique and the realist mode.

By way of illustration let us consider briefly a film from the early 1960s not mentioned by Kristin Ross: *Chronique d'un été* (1961), a documentary about Parisians in the summer of 1960, made collaboratively by the sociologist Edgar Morin and the ethnographic film-maker Jean Rouch. In *L'Esprit du temps* (1962), his pioneering study of popular culture, written immediately after the making of the film, Morin called for a sociology of historical and cultural immersion, based on a 'méthode de la totalité' that would acknowledge and encourage the observer's active participation in the phenomena to be studied, whilst combining a range of techniques and disciplines susceptible of reaching 'l'authenticité du vécu' and avoiding 'le sociologisme abstrait, bureaucratique, du chercheur coupé de sa recherche, qui se contente d'isoler tel ou tel secteur sans essayer de voir ce qui relie les secteurs les uns aux autres' (abstract and bureaucratic sociologizing, where the enquirer is cut off from what he studies, and is content to isolate a particular sector without trying to see what links different sectors).[24] As Charles Forsdick has shown, the ambition to 'plonger

---

[23] Henri Lefebvre, *La Vie quotidienne dans le monde moderne* (Paris: Gallimard 'Idées', 1968), 349.
[24] Edgar Morin, *L'Esprit du temps* (1962; Paris: Livre de poche, 1991), 20.

dans un milieu réel'—diving being a recurrent metaphor for Morin—links *Chronique* to Morin's extraordinarily ambitious 'enquête pluridisciplinaire' centred on the Breton village of Plodémet, the fieldwork for which, involving nearly one hundred researchers, was conducted in 1965.[25] A central ambition in these projects is to reverse the ethnographic gaze by using fieldwork techniques to look at modern France (a move which, as we shall see in Chapter 8, was not to be fully developed until the 1980s). Hence Morin's collaboration with Rouch, the pioneer of 'cinéma-verité', a non-interventionist documentary practice, involving the interaction of observer and observed, which Rouch had developed to study African societies but which, partly influenced by Surrealism, he also applied to European subjects. In every respect *Chronique* is conducted as an experiment, an 'interrogation cinématographique'. Focused on a small group of Parisians, mostly acquaintances of Morin's, the film's initial premises are the questions 'comment vis-tu?' (How do you live?) and 'es-tu heureux'? (Are you happy?) to which the participants respond by recounting and re-staging their daily lives (including work, relationships, ambitions). The film-makers are active participants throughout, and the interactions between themselves, and with other protagonists, create a space of exchange where the *quotidien* is approached from within an individual and collective matrix rather than from the outside. A long discussion with the participants at the end reveals the conflicts between them over methods and results, but these tensions are part of the film, which progressively questions its own procedures, constituting what Morin called 'une expérience vécue par ses auteurs et ses acteurs' (an experiment lived through by its authors and its participants).[26]

Whilst engaging with the conventions of the documentary, the filmic practices of Morin and Rouch push experimentation with genre, structure, and authorship well beyond the scope of anything we would normally associate with realism. The same applies to Perec's *Les Choses*, which can be read as a realist text, as Ross argues,[27] insofar as it attends critically, like the novels of de Beauvoir and Christiane Rochefort, to the realities and contradictions of its historical moment, but which also, through the total suppression of dialogue, the predominance of the conditional mood, the constant use of intrusive and

[25] Charles Forsdick, 'Plonger dans un milieu réel : Edgar Morin in the field', *French Cultural Studies*, 8 (1997), 309–31.

[26] Edgar Morin and Jean Rouch, *Chronique d'un été* (filmscript), (Paris: Inter Spectacles, 1962), 9. See Steven Ungar, 'In the Thick of Things: Rouch and Morin's *Chronique d'un été* Reconsidered', *French Cultural Studies*, 14/1 (2003), 5–22.

[27] Ross, *Fast Cars*, 126.

hidden quotation, and particularly the disjunction produced by the combination of these devices, tends to subvert representation, engendering more circuitous connections between text and world. Yet, whilst it is admirably focused in its presentation of a sealed world, *Les Choses* lacks a number of features that Perec's later everyday-oriented work, like that of Morin and Rouch or Jean-Luc Godard, will possess in abundance: the sense of a total field, direct involvement and experimentation that registers the interaction of subjective experience and objective structures, the need for open-ended questioning. In the 1960s challenges to the way everyday life was being subordinated to narrow functionalism quickly outgrew realism since they called not only for alternatives to the sterility of quantitative sociology, and other bloodless and de-historicized modes of analysis and representation, but also for ways of exploring a complex tissue of lived experience. As Maurice Blanchot perceived in 1962, when he took stock of the remarkable evolution of Lefebvre's thinking about the everyday from the late 1940s to the early 1960s, the *quotidien* needed to be apprehended in the lived complexity of its ambiguity, not least because, as the Surrealists had seen from the start, and as Lefebvre was never to stop saying (both of them influenced by Marx in this respect), to be effective the critique of everyday life had to be the instrument of, and not simply the prelude to, its transformation.[28]

One of the main objectives of this book is chronological and historical. By demonstrating the enduring contribution that Lefebvre, Barthes, Certeau, and Perec made, between around 1960 and 1980, and by exploring the way this involved the revision of an inheritance in which the Surrealist movement was crucial, I want to suggest a genealogy for the remarkable 'explosion' of interest in the everyday that characterized French culture in the 1980s and 1990s. This strand of the argument is developed in the four middle chapters of the book, preceded by two chapters on the Surrealist bequest, and followed by two chapters largely devoted to the period 1980–2000.

Just as important, however, is a second main objective: to raise questions about the dimension of experience addressed by artists and thinkers when they invoke the *quotidien* or related concepts. Does the 'everyday' refer to an objective 'content', defined by a particular kind of (daily) activity, or is it best thought of in terms of such notions as rhythm, repetition, festivity, ordinariness, non-cumulation, seriality, the generic, the obvious, the given? Are there events or acts that are uniquely 'everyday', or is the *quotidien* a way of

---

[28] Blanchot's 'La Parole quotidienne' will be examined in the next chapter.

thinking about events and acts in the 'here and now' as opposed to the longer term? If it makes sense to see the everyday as one of the parameters of our lives, can this parameter ever be disentangled from others? If these are the sorts of issue that seem to be at stake, how are they addressed in works focusing on the everyday? Is it characteristic of such works to depict the everyday, or do they work on us in ways that train attention on our own experience, so that discourse on the everyday is ultimately pragmatic or performative in character? Do specific genres or media have particular virtues in granting access to, or purchase on, the everyday? Or does the everyday seem to slip between the fingers, so to speak, of established genres and, by virtue of an inherent elusiveness, seem to escape the purview of, say, narrative fiction, lyric poetry, drama, film, photography, pictorial art, reportage, thriving rather on the indeterminacy offered by the transgression of generic boundaries?

In consistently addressing such questions this book seeks to contribute, alongside a historical approach, to the epistemology and phenomenology of the everyday. It does so, firstly, by adopting a consistently comparative approach, exploring connections between a broad variety of ways of thinking, staging, or questioning the everyday. Although the main focus is on the contribution of French thinkers and artists, who have been so influential in this sphere, the book encompasses other strands, including the ideas of Heidegger, Heller, and Cavell, or the minimalist tradition in avant-garde art, and so on. Emphasis is also placed on the interdisciplinary character of thinking about the everyday—for example, the dialogue between Certeau and thinkers such as Wittgenstein, Foucault, Bourdieu, or Baudrillard—and the book strives to create a space where connections can be perceived between, say, the photographs of Atget, a film by Godard, a project by Boltanski or Calle, a play by Vinaver, or a best-seller such as Philippe Delerm's *La Première Gorgée de bière et autres plaisirs minuscules*. The second main objective of *Everyday Life* is also articulated, particularly in the last two chapters, through the treatment of key figures and motifs, such as the street name, the urban trajectory, the day, and the project. A central theme here, anticipated in earlier sections, is that of attention. A leitmotif in the introductory chapter—centred on the indeterminacy of the everyday—and in the comparative discussion of different movements and contributions, the question of forms of attention, and of transformations of awareness wrought by paying attention to the *quotidien*, emerges more explicitly in the treatment of Perec, and it lies at the heart of my account, in the final chapter, of some of the key 'figures' through which the *quotidien* has been apprehended and articulated.

1

The Indeterminacy of the Everyday

'THE HARDEST THING TO UNCOVER': BLANCHOT WITH LEFEBVRE

In Maurice Blanchot's essay, 'La Parole quotidienne',[1] which originally appeared in the *Nouvelle Revue française* in June 1962 with the title 'L'Homme de la rue', the everyday is a dimension of human experience rather than an abstract category. Using expressions such as 'in the everyday' and 'the experience of the everyday' (362), Blanchot describes the *quotidien* as a 'niveau de la vie' (level of existence), although one that is characterized by paradox and ambiguity. Indeed, Blanchot sees indeterminacy as the everyday's defining characteristic: 'le quotidien échappe. C'est sa définition' (the everyday escapes: that is its definition) (359); it is the hardest thing to uncover: 'Le quotidien: ce qu'il y a de plus difficile à découvrir' (355). The fact or condition of being 'in' the everyday does not imply cognizance on our part: the *quotidien* is, for Blanchot, 'sans sujet' and 'sans objet', neither subjective nor objective. Participation in daily acts places us in a sphere of anonymity, a fluid, undramatic present. But this does not mean that we can be labelled by our actions: our anonymity in the everyday does not turn us into ciphers or statistics. The experience of the everyday cannot be reduced to its content; it eludes objectification because it consists in perpetual becoming. And it is this 'devenir perpétuel' (363), a mobile indeterminacy and openness, that gives the *quotidien* its radical character.

With its echoes and anticipations of Barthes, Debord, Perec, and Certeau, Blanchot's essay is an invaluable source of thinking about the everyday.[2] Yet it was prompted by the writings of Henri Lefebvre, and particularly the

---

[1] In Maurice Blanchot, *L'Entretien infini* (Paris: Gallimard 1969), 355–66. Page references incorporated in the text.

[2] Cf. Kristin Ross, 'Two Versions of the Everyday', *L'Esprit créateur*, 24 (Fall, 1984), 29–37.

second volume, published in 1961, of Lefebvre's mammoth *Critique de la vie quotidienne* (which registers Lefebvre's encounter with Debord and Situationism).[3] Although Blanchot's reflections are entirely consistent with the evolution of his own thought, particularly with regard to such concepts as the 'neutral', the community, or the 'yet-to-come', 'La Parole quotidienne' is remarkably faithful to the spirit of Lefebvre's analyses. Indeed, there is little in Blanchot that is not to be found in the *Critique*: from Lefebvre's methodologically obsessive and constantly self-revising engagement with the *quotidien* Blanchot distils the essence of the everyday *as* experience. Where Lefebvre brought many strands of modern thought, ranging across Descartes, Hegel, Marx, Surrealism, Existentialism, psychoanalysis, linguistics, sociology, and anthropology, to bear on one unstable object, Blanchot absorbs the *quotidien* into his own thinking. The ambiguity of the everyday is a central theme in Lefebvre, but where he tends to see ambiguity as a symptom of alienation, a sign that the everyday has yet to overcome the contradictions by which it is fissured, Blanchot sees indeterminacy (his preferred term) as central to the everyday's 'puissance de dissolution' (365), its energizing capacity to subvert intellectual and institutional authority.

To trace how Blanchot restates and revises Lefebvre is to encounter recurrent elements in the theorization of the everyday, and grasp how such theorization evolves through intertextual transmission. Blanchot credits Lefebvre with having pinpointed an oblique and elusive dimension that tends to fall outside history but which, by dint of this very marginality, harbours the possibility of its own transformation. The everyday is not just 'la vie résiduelle' (residual life—the idea of the *quotidien* as 'résidu' or left-over is recurrent in Lefebvre)—in other words average mundane existence, an absence of qualities—it is also potentially the present, alive with the force of lived but uncategorizable experience. Blanchot repeatedly uses the word 'mouvement' to convey this active potential, linking the force of the *quotidien* to the way it eludes definition. Even if a variety of 'sciences' might provide tools for studying it (Blanchot lists sociology, ontology, psychoanalysis, linguistics, literature), the *quotidien* is inherently 'inépuisable, irrécusable et toujours inaccompli et toujours échappant aux formes ou aux structures (en particulier celles de la société politique: bureaucratie, rouages gouvernementaux, partis)' (inexhaustible, unimpeachable and always open-ended and always eluding forms or structures, particularly socio-political: bureaucracy, government,

---

[3] On this see Ch. 4 below.

parties) (357). For Blanchot, Lefebvre saw that a sector most at the mercy of legislation and bureaucracy was at the same time refractory to such limitation (Michel de Certeau will make this insight the cornerstone of *L'Invention du quotidien*), and perceived moreover that only a 'faible déplacement d'accent' (357), a minimal shift of focus, separates positive from negative, constrained banality from corrosive freedom. Thus, as Blanchot puts it, 'L'homme [. . .] est à la fois enfoncé dans le quotidien et privé de quotidien' (man is . . . at once submerged in the everyday and deprived of it) (356): the everyday is both too much with us and as yet remote from us, still on the horizon.

Blanchot identifies the connections Lefebvre makes between the way the everyday eludes various forms of reduction or alienation, and the fact that it is, firstly, insignificant ('insignifiant', in the sense that it does not display meanings to which it can be reduced); secondly, uneventful ('sans événement', 363); and thirdly, overlooked ('inaperçu') (a theme Perec will later develop at length). Alluding to Lefebvre's theory of 'needs' (derived partly from Jacques Lacan), as well as Situationist critique, Blanchot observes how mass culture and media meet our need for the everyday by supplying, in the shape of movies, soap operas, fashions, and scandals, substitutes for the 'lived' everyday we fail to recognize all around us, manufacturing an everyday-as-spectacle where the *quotidien* is no longer 'ce qui se vit, mais ce qui se regarde ou se montre, spectacle et description, sans nulle relation active' (what is lived, but what is looked at or shown, spectacle or description, without interaction) (358). This has the effect of further alienating or disguising (and de-politicizing) the everyday in which we actually participate (Blanchot refers here to 'pratique'—a key notion in discussions of the *quotidien*, notably in Certeau).

Similarly, Blanchot takes up Lefebvre's discussions of the 'fait divers' (a theme developed by Barthes and Auclair around this time)[4] and argues that newspapers tend to turn everything that happens into a *fait divers*: a rounded, dramatic, readily assimilated item, with a stable meaning and a clear message, rooted in received opinion. Adopting another Lefebvrian motif, the street, Blanchot contrasts it with the newspaper. Newspapers compensate for their inability to grasp the everyday—as flow or 'process'—by sensationalizing it, replacing the 'nothing happens' side of the *quotidien* with the emptiness of the 'fait divers': 'incapable d'atteindre ce qui n'appartient pas à l'historique mais

---

[4] See Roland Barthes, 'Structure du fait divers', *Œuvres complètes*, ed. Eric Marty, II, (Paris: Seuil, 1993), 442–51; Georges Auclair, *Le Mana quotidien: structures et fonctions de la chronique des faits divers* (2nd edn., Paris: Éditions Anthropos, 1982).

qui est toujours sur le point de faire irruption dans l'histoire, [il] s'en tient
à l'anecdote et nous retient par des histoires' (unable to reach what cannot be
historicized yet is always on the brink of irrupting into history, [it] makes do
with anecdotes and beguiles us with stories) (364). In the 'transcribed everyday' of the newspaper, everything is on show: 'tout s'annonce, tout se dénonce,
tout se fait image' (everything is announced, denounced, turned into images)
(363). The street, by contrast, 'n'est pas ostentatrice' (does not show itself off).
In Lefebvre, like the Surrealists and the Situationists, the city street is the
quintessential space of the everyday.[5] Quoting Lefebvre,[6] Blanchot describes
the street as poised between public and private spheres, a space where the
intimate and personal is anonymized through chatter and hearsay. Developing
his own perspective, although drawing partly on the paradoxical attributes of
the Baudelairean 'flâneur'—the man in the street is 'indifférent et curieux,
affairé et inoccupé, instable, immobile' (indifferent, curious, busy and un-
occupied, unstable, immobile) (363)—Blanchot sees 'l'homme de la rue' as a
key avatar of everyday man, ascribing to him a dangerous irresponsibility,
vesting him with a potentially anarchic power, 'une réserve d'anarchie'. If the
everyday cannot be objectified historically, commodified into narratable
events, its dangerous fluidity and non-alignment make it a reservoir of
dissident political energy.

Blanchot goes beyond Lefebvre in his emphasis on anonymity and desub-
jectification. In Lefebvre's scheme of things, inherited from the theory of
alienation in early Marx, political aspiration to a positive everyday is channelled through the notion of critique. Critical understanding or unveiling will
bring about a sea change through which the positive dimension of the
quotidien will predominate over the negative; ambiguity will be superseded
by clarity. For Blanchot, by contrast, indeterminacy is central to the political
power of the everyday, and the key forum of indeterminacy is the human
subject. This is linked to the everyday's uneventfulness: 'rien ne se passe, voilà
le quotidien' (nothing happens, that is the everyday) (360). Blanchot follows
Lefebvre in rejecting Lukács's famous account of the 'chiaroscuro' of everyday
life, which is 'anarchic' (Lukács's word) because deadly dullness is from time to
time alleviated by miraculous moments.[7] As Lefebvre had insisted, such an
analysis fails to engage with the *quotidien*, 'car l'ordinaire de chaque jour ne

  [5] See Ch. 9 below.
  [6] The passage Blanchot quotes on p. 362 is from Henri Lefebvre, *Critique de la vie quotidienne*, II:
Fondements d'une sociologie de la quotidienneté (Paris: L'Arche, 1961) 310.
  [7] Lukács's view of the everyday will be considered later in this chapter.

l'est pas par contraste avec quelque extraordinaire; ce n'est pas le "moment nul" qui attendrait le "moment extraordinaire"' (for the ordinariness of each day is not in contrast to something extraordinary; it is not an 'empty time' that awaits the 'extraordinary moment') (361). Homing in on the 'rien ne se passe' of the everyday, Blanchot asks: for *whom* does nothing happen? In other words, 'Quel est le "qui" du quotidien?' (what is the 'who' of the everyday?) (360). And in seeking to portray the everyday subject he identifies him/her with an almost passive participation in daily activities, where the self dissolves into anonymity. The paradox here turns on questions of will and awareness. Boredom ('ennui') is one way of experiencing the *quotidien*, but when we are conscious of being bored we have, according to Blanchot, parted company with the essence of the everyday, which is to be unspecified. The context of speech, the idle chatter of the street or the neighbourhood (another key theme in Lefebvre), brings us closer to this essence, and to the mode of being that is available in the everyday:

Cette part d'existence inapparente et cependant non cachée, [...] silencieuse, mais d'un silence qui s'est déjà dissipé lorsque nous nous taisons pour l'entendre et que nous écoutons mieux en bavardant, dans cette parole non parlante qui est le doux bruissement humain en nous, autour de nous (361).

(This portion of existence that is not apparent yet not hidden ... silent, but whose silence has already dispersed when we try to listen and that we hear better while we chatter, in the unclamouring speech that is the soft human murmur in us, around us)

The soft buzz of daily speech flowing in and around us, requiring no conscious effort at formulation, epitomizes the ontology of the everyday. On this description, the everyday is a liminal region of experience that we can be aware of only at the fringes of consciousness, since it exists only through our unreflecting participation in the rhythms of existence. Expressing the same paradox, Blanchot refers to the *quotidien*, in the next sentence, as 'le mouvement par lequel l'homme se retient comme à son insu dans l'anonymat humain' (the movement through which man lingers, all but unaware, in human anonymity) (361). 'In' the everyday, personal identity and social affiliation are on hold; we are not wholly present to ourselves or to others but in an interpersonal, communal dimension, a 'présent sans particularités' (a present without qualities), part of common humanity (362). My life in the everyday is that of an 'homme quelconque', 'ni à proprement parler moi ni à proprement parler l'autre' (neither myself, strictly speaking, nor the other) (364). Like a fragile eco-system, the everyday is highly vulnerable to the depredations of invasive, manipulative forces or pressures (both outer and inner), and this is exacerbated by our fear of allowing our lives to be reduced to the everyday, which drives us to flee such vacancy.

Yet the banal everyday contains its own antidote, 'le principe de sa propre critique' (the principle of its own critique), notes Blanchot, using Lefebvre's key term, and rather than flee from it we should try to grasp its 'secrète capacité destructrice' (secret destructive capacity) (365), which derives from 'la force corrosive de l'anonymat humain' (the corrosive force of human anonymity). Rather than positing alternative 'higher' values to combat those that seek to determine our lives, we should have recourse, in the everyday, to 'un niveau où la question de valeur ne se pose pas' (a level where the question of value does not arise) (365). The 'il y a (sans sujet, sans objet)' (the 'there is' (without subject, without object)) of the *quotidien*, in its radicality, its immunity from all origins, its anarchic destruction of all established order, will always provide a basis for the future.

Imbued with his concern for the limits of human experience, shaped by Nietzsche and Georges Bataille, Blanchot's *quotidien* can be seen as an avatar of his central 'myth' concerning the abolition of all origins and determined identities. Yet to observe how closely Blanchot engages with the thought of Lefebvre is to recognize, firstly, that, as later chapters will make clear, the two writers shared a number of key points of reference, including Communism, Surrealism, and Situationism, and other currents of thought where everyday life is at issue. More importantly, however, Blanchot signals key elements in the orientation towards the everyday with which this book is concerned. In different ways, 'La Parole quotidienne' affirms a central paradox: the everyday is all around us, yet we cannot 'arise and go' there, in Yeats's phrase; it is where we already are, although we do not see it. Rather, we only see it when it weighs heavily on us, and we are led to depreciate it; or else when we glorify it into something it usually is not. The *quotidien* is elusive: it is neither objective fact nor subjective fantasy, but a level of lived experience that exists for us to the extent that, rather than treat it with disdain, we find ways of paying it— oblique—attention. We fail to connect with the everyday when we make it an object of 'scientific' knowledge, reducing it to its statistical content, even if it is important to see it as occupying a point where a wide range of 'human sciences' converge; but, equally, we miss out when we lavish too much attention on it, when we invest it with superior qualities, in a redemptive vision for example (to be examined later in this chapter), or when we see it as the context for moments of transcendent illumination. Attention to the everyday involves a tension between knowledge and experience or, to put this another way, the everyday brings out the tension with knowledge inherent in the idea of lived experience (a *topos* that can be traced through a number of key figures, including Benjamin, Breton, and Bataille, as well as Blanchot).

In its insistence on the way everyday experience challenges individual identity ('met [. . .] en question la notion de sujet', 364), Blanchot's meditation draws attention to the key areas of space and language, the city street and idle chatter, that will be of central importance in other investigations of the everyday, and invites us to consider a mode of anonymity that is by no means purely negative. Rather than being reducible to a number of disconnected, repetitious activities (waking, eating, conversing, going to work, shopping)—viewed from the outside—the everyday is perceived as the level of human life at which these diverse activities are 'lived through' in what Blanchot calls a 'mouvement lié' (continuous movement) that never forms a stable and knowable totality, yet links us to the 'ensemble indéterminé des possibilités humaines' (indeterminate ensemble of human possibilities) (364). Rather than simply ambiguous, or conceptually paradoxical—superficial and profound, strange and familiar, monotonous and ever-changing, insignificant and fundamental, outside praxis yet the harbinger of anarchic energies, individual and collective, constrained and free—the *quotidien* manifests our relationship to the fundamental indeterminacy of human possibility. Hegelian in origin, the word 'mouvement' in Blanchot seems to designate the 'living through' that makes the everyday a process, 'en perpétuel devenir' (363)—Perec will talk of grasping the *quotidien* in its 'émergence'.[8] Rather than being a level of experience that is simply amorphous, the everyday's resistance to form (357) signals its opening onto the wider horizon of human realization, and hence to the possibility of a different future. Far from being dominated by sameness, the everyday is an arena of endless difference.

THE AMBIGUITY OF THE EVERYDAY

The everyday is beneath our attention. It is what we overlook. On one view this is as it should be: the everyday is a place of perdition. Why linger on what is merely daily? Our duty is to higher things: we are right to shun the ordinary. Yet, by a different token, we overlook the everyday at our peril. It is the source

---

[8] Perec, *Penser/Classer*, 23.

of our truth; the daily world is our homeland: we alienate ourselves in the extraordinary, not in the ordinary.

The oscillation between positive and negative evaluations is endemic to thinking about the everyday. This means that any appeal to everydayness as interesting or valuable is likely to involve rehabilitation or exhortation: look at what you've overlooked! See the significance of the seemingly insignificant! Yet, in the sphere of the everyday, such zeal is paradoxical. If we go too far, the everyday ceases to be itself: it becomes the exceptional, the exotic, the marvellous. Transfigured, the commonplace is no longer commonplace.[9] In Blanchot and Lefebvre we have seen how an awareness of such tensions and paradoxes becomes crucial to a vision of the everyday as a level of human reality whose very ambiguity and indeterminacy are seen as clues to its importance as a dimension of our lives. But I want now to look more closely at the common constituents of negative and positive evaluations of the *quotidien*.

Let us consider firstly the negative picture, the routine downgrading of what is merely everyday. Look up *quotidien* in a French dictionary, or *quotidian* in an English one, and you will find a range of predominantly negative definitions. Everydayness is more or less exclusively associated with what is boring, habitual, mundane, uneventful, trivial, humdrum, repetitive, inauthentic, and unrewarding. At the everyday level, life is at its least interesting, in opposition to the ideal, the imaginary, the momentous. We submit to the everyday, we tolerate the unremitting round of trivial repetition, because we have no choice; meanwhile, life is elsewhere. Jules Laforgue's exclamation, 'Ah ! que la vie est quotidienne. . . . ' sums this up.[10] A life reduced to the level of the *quotidien* is scarcely worth living. Equally, Michel Leiris's definition, in his personal lexicon based on punning wordplay, brings out a number of negative qualities: 'quotidien—commun et tiède, tel quel demain aussi bien que hier': the everyday is common, in the negative sense of undistinguished; it is lukewarm, stagnant, and affectively bloodless; it denies cumulation: same old thing, day after day.[11] Seen in this way, the *quotidien* is opposed to a range of more positive dimensions of experience. It is a level we must extricate ourselves from if we are to live authentically. Talk of the everyday nearly always invokes questions of 'art de vivre', of how we should conduct our lives. In the everyday

---

[9] Cf. Arthur C. Danto, *The Transfiguration of the Commonplace* (Cambridge, MA: Harvard University Press, 1981).

[10] Jules Laforgue, 'Complainte sur certains ennuis', *Les Complaintes* (1885), *Poésies complètes* (Paris: Livre de poche, 1970), 86.

[11] Michel Leiris, *Langage Tangage ou ce que les mots me disent* (Paris: Gallimard, 1985), 52.

we vacillate, we take things as they come; we are often simply passive victims of fate. Nothing is clear-cut here: hence 'the anarchic chiaroscuro of the every-day', in Georg Lukács's phrase.[12] Frequently associated with the domestic sphere, the everyday can be seen as antithetical to politics and the public domain. Hearth and neighbourhood are its spatial parameters. Real events happen somewhere else—on the regional, national or international stages that are beyond its range (television has obviously changed this, at least at an imaginary or illusory level).[13] In terms of the negative picture, everydayness offers little possibility of true self-realization. Within its narrow constraints, experience is regulated by daily rituals, and human beings live out a common destiny. At worst they are 'all the same', clones of one collective social being (Ionesco's plays capture this well).

The widespread currency of 'the quotidian' as a negative term appears to have a dual ancestry: firstly, in religion and philosophy, and, secondly, in a current of feeling that grew up with industrialization. When Christian doc-trine prizes dailiness, it is primarily as a sphere where the Christian can display recognition of and obedience to God's purpose.[14] In the monastic tradition, the punctuation of the day by regular moments for prayer implies both recognition that daily repetition can have a spiritual dimension that enhances worship, and a sense that the daily round needs to be transcended. In religious thought (e.g. Pascal's notion of 'divertissement') the sphere of daily activities is often associated with dispersion, and hence dissolution, as opposed to the concentration and singleness of mind required by religion. Viewed negatively, the everyday is antithetical to the higher realms of religion, philosophy, and art. Where religious observance is part of the fabric of daily life for given groups and individuals, faith is generally held to illuminate and transcend the daily round, rather than to draw inspiration from it (even if, in some tradi-tions, going about everyday tasks in an appropriate manner is a path to goodness). With regard to philosophy, and abstract (including scientific) thinking generally, the everyday is often seen as unpropitious since, in binding us to habitual, concrete, and short-term activities, it does not favour specu-lative thought and tends to be intellectually conservative. Where art is concerned, if the everyday can be seen as the wellspring of the aesthetic impulse (as attested, for some, by prehistoric cave-painting), the openness

---

12 G. Lukács, *Soul and Form* (1911; London: Merlin Press, 1994), 152.

13 See Roger Silverstone, *Television and Everyday Life* (London: Routledge, 1999).

14 Cf. Charles Taylor on 'the affirmation of ordinary life' in *The Sources of the Self: The Making of Modern Identity* (Cambridge: Cambridge University Press, 1989) discussed below.

and non-functionality of the aesthetic do not express the everyday itself but rather (as in Lukács) the attempt to transcend its horizons. Moreover if 'moments of vision', uniting human self-realization and aesthetic form, such as those evoked by Heidegger in *Being and Time* (1926), belong—by virtue of their momentariness—to the immediate present, their true import lies in the way they break with the temporal order of everydayness. As we shall see presently, Heidegger's negative portrayal of *Alltäglichkeit* is important and influential not least because it construes the everyday as the negative pole in a pair of opposed terms: it pertains to the bareness of the 'ontic' rather than the density of the 'ontological'.[15]

Much historical shading would be required to review how discourses critical of the everyday, from antiquity to the present, have highlighted this or that strand of thought or feeling. Summing up his findings in the context of the five-volume history of private life he co-edited with Georges Duby, Philippe Ariès suggests that the shifting lines of demarcation between different dimensions of existence gave little specificity to what we would now think of as everyday life until at least the rise of mercantile, pre-industrial, and industrial modes of production from the seventeenth century onwards.[16] The 'espace communautaire' of the late Middle Ages placed the individual in a milieu where public and private spaces and spheres were largely indistinguishable. By the mid nineteenth century on the other hand the individual had retreated to 'the bosom of his family', cut off from others. The period in between, and particularly the early eighteenth century, saw a number of shifts that led to new ways of thinking about and organizing everyday activities. The principal causative factors were the new role of state power which led individuals to think more about social appearances; the new habit of silent reading that ensued from the print revolution; and new modes of religion which placed a premium on inner piety and self-reflection.[17]

Ariès notes the impact of these changes on *mentalités* in various fields, including new attitudes to the body (increased 'pudeur'), the rise of diaries and autobiographies, and new ways of embracing both friendship and solitude; and he notes that overall these changes increasingly focused attention on and transformed everyday life. This is reflected in the rise of an art of interior

---

[15] See next section.

[16] P. Ariès, 'Pour une historie de la vie privée', in id. and G. Duby (eds.), *Histoire de la vie privée*, III (Paris: Seuil, 1986), 7–19.

[17] Cf. Charles Taylor, *The Sources of the Self*, discussed below.

furnishing (as reflected in Dutch painting), greater emphasis on daily costume and on the arts of the table. The layout of domestic space was also transformed, with rooms becoming smaller and more specialized (nursery, living room, (with)drawing room) and more intimate. Within this new constellation of material and psychological shifts, Ariès notes key phases. Initially the move is towards the recognition of individual autonomy or intimacy, modulated but not challenged by the rise of 'convivial groups'—salons, academies, clubs, coffee houses, country house parties. But by the end of the eighteenth century the family structure had come to absorb into itself much of what had been evolving. Providing a refuge or haven from public history and demands, and from the eyes of others, the family—with its own set of roles and demarcations (matriarch, paterfamilias, etc.)—came to be the prime forum and focus of everyday life. In this new dispensation, the everyday is set apart from public space and is no longer identified with the anonymous sociability of the street. Restricted, for its home base, to the family circle and the domestic arena, everyday life embraces other dimensions, but discretely: professional life is hived off as something separate, as is the attenuated public life of the citizen.

If we accept Ariès's argument, we can see why daily life, thus privatized and atomized, proved vulnerable to the pressures of modernity, and why it seems reasonable to assert that the sense of a specific dimension of human experience, designated by such expressions as 'la vie quotidienne', 'everyday life' and eventually 'le quotidien' and the everyday, arose precisely at the point when this sector came to be perceived as under threat, and thus acquired the pervasive negative tinge that still often attaches to this sphere. The theory of alienation that dominates Marx's early thinking (and which strongly influenced Lefebvre who translated the 1844 manuscripts in the 1930s)[18] is directly related to an impoverishment of everyday experience as labour came to be treated as a commodity.[19] By imposing the artificial, atomized, and economically contingent cycles of production on human labour, industrialization brought the curse of alienation to the daily round, making the quotidian a byword for tedium and *ennui*. To some degree, Marx's account of the dynamic whereby exchange value comes to predominate over use value imports economic forces into a picture of human reality inherited from strands in Enlightenment thought that employ the image of the machine to

[18] Henri Lefebvre (ed.), *Morceaux choisis de Karl Marx* (Paris: Gallimard, 1934).
[19] Karl Marx, *Economic and Political Manuscripts of 1844* (London: Lawrence and Wishart, 1970), trans. Ben Fowkes (1867: London: Penguin, 1992).

portray human society.[20] But whilst, in the world of the *Encyclopédie* for example, craft and technology are seen as beneficent harbingers of a more civilized everyday life, the industrial era rapidly revealed the dark side of industrial development. And since Marx's time the relationship between mechanization and everyday life has been subject to repeated shifts and reversals of emphasis.[21]

Sometimes the liberating power of technology is uppermost, and the era of trains, radio, and fridges—not to mention inoculations—is celebrated. At other times technology is perceived to be the enemy of authentic existence and a prime agent of alienation. A key strand in European modernism celebrated the new kinds of perception generated by crowds, speed, electricity, flight, and rapid communications, seeing these as harbingers of new forms of everyday life. Yet alongside this was the tendency in Modernist writing to locate authenticity in 'epiphanies' (Joyce), 'moments of being' (Woolf), or experiences of 'mémoire involontaire' (Proust), which were to be cherished because they tore through the veil of mundane experience, even if they originated within that sphere. In Freud's 'psychopathology of everyday life' the incursions of authentic (repressed) material are traced in the fabric of daily existence.[22] Drawing on Freud and Proust, as well as Baudelaire, Walter Benjamin argued that only the discontinuous, momentary shock that bypassed the prevailing order of consciousness could resist the 'atrophy of experience'. 'Experience' (*Erfahrung*) had been dealt a deadly blow by mechanization. Modern techniques of production and reproduction, he claimed, altered the structure of human consciousness, gravely reducing the range of what could be shared and communicated.[23] In the guise of Heidegger's *Alltäglichkeit*, or of what Virginia Woolf would call the 'cotton-wool' of 'non-being', the everyday is, at best, a catalyst for what must transcend it.[24] More broadly, the spectre of a daily existence hijacked by manipulative, quasi-mechanical, forces adopts different guises, coming to be associated less with direct material developments than with economic factors (as envisaged by Marx), ideological pressures (e.g. law and order), social pressures (e.g. conformity, rivalry), or a powerful

[20] See Karl Marx *Capital*, I, ch. 1.

[21] On the ambivalence of modernity, see Marshall Berman, *All That is Solid Melts into Air* (London: Verso, 1983).

[22] Sigmund Freud, *The Psychopathology of Everyday Life* (1901; London: Penguin Classics, 2002).

[23] Walter Benjamin, 'On some Motifs in Baudelaire', *Illuminations*, trans. H. Zohn (London: Jonathan Cape, 1970), 157–202.

[24] See, Virginia Woolf, *Moments of Being* (2nd edn., San Diego: Harvest Books, 1985).

combination of several strands. Yet, threaded through the variety of negative pressures and imaginings—the horrors of the self-enclosed family decried by André Gide, the miseries of the production line and the wage slave, the desert of modern housing and the anomie of routine—the sense of the possibilities of an everyday life invigorated and enriched rather than depleted by modernity persists in many quarters—from the Surrealists through Lefebvre to Barthes and Perec; and in *L'Invention du quotidien* Michel de Certeau will tackle head on the negative view of the everyday with which the modern literary and sociological tradition has often been imbued.

Let us now turn to positive ways of looking at the *quotidien*. A staple constituent of the negative view is the belief that everyday life, once rich and organic, has undergone a negative transformation: elsewhere, or before, in a golden age, everyday life and the higher aspirations of humanity were in harmony. Yet discourses that celebrate everydayness are often equally based on postulates that ultimately deny it any inherent virtues, simply projecting onto the everyday values that are rooted in such non-everyday spheres as art, religion, or philosophy. Pro-everyday discourses, in other words, may ultimately be as negative as those they oppose.

My first example is Colette Nys-Mazure's *Célébration du quotidien*, a series of lyrical 'textes brefs'—a form particularly favoured in contemporary explorations of the everyday[25]—some of which are addressed to a friend dying of cancer, and which are interspersed with free verse poems. Inspired by an exhortation attributed to Brecht: 'beneath the everyday, find the inexplicable | find disquiet in what seems habitual', Nys-Mazure identifies a strong life force in elementary things—the greenness of a salad, the roundness of an apple—which, whilst lacking the force of events that galvanize, provide strength to keep going and to grow.[26] Sounding a note often found in writing on the everyday, she stresses the triple difficulty of apprehending, rendering verbally, and not exaggerating, the essence of the *quotidien*. It is hard to speak of what is just under our noses, the microscopic events that make up a single day, familiar objects and sights, habitual gestures, 'tout ce tissu modeste et sûr du quotidien' (all the modest and certain fabric of the everyday). How can we praise this without hyperbole? At the heart of the matter is the question of paying heed to what we overlook, and more particularly of being present to the full range of our experience: 'Ce n'est pas la répétition des gestes et des mots, l'hallucinante succession des saisons qui nous use mais notre absence à cette marche, notre défaut de présence à ce miracle continu' (It is not the repetition of words and gestures, the dazzling succession of seasons, that wears us down, but our absence from this round, the failure to be present to this unending miracle).[27] Towards the end, the author reveals that it was the death of both her parents when she was seven that triggered her search for the *quotidien*. But she also makes clear that the wisdom she found is rooted in religious faith, in Transfiguration that gives meaning to existence.

Written in the wake both of familiar models of Christian piety and the upsurge in *quotidien* writings in the 1980s, *Célébration du quotidien* endows the everyday with religious meaning. This raises the possibility that all writing that celebrates everydayness may derive from religious ways of thinking about experience, a point we will need to consider later. But here it is important to suggest that making religion the basis for celebrating the *quotidien* can be seen as a betrayal of everydayness itself. In the religious version of the everyday, the here and now is a rehearsal for the hereafter. The light that illuminates the humble things of daily experience does not emanate from them, but is projected by religious faith or longing. Yet Nys-Mazure's Christianity is permeated by an acute sense of loss, and the connections she makes between dying, losing, and clinging to the everyday world, are relevant to very different everyday explorers, including Georges Perec.

Another revealing case, where enthusiastic endorsement of the everyday produces a limited, ideologically circumscribed perspective, is Philippe Delerm's hugely successful *La Première Gorgée de bière et autres plaisirs minuscules* (1997). Charming and beautifully written, this series of prose texts devoted to such daily 'plaisirs' as shelling peas, getting one's *espadrilles* wet, reading on the beach, idling away Sunday evenings, or taking an old train, reflects the spectacular revaluation of the *quotidien* in France in the 1990s.[28] Reading Delerm is like watching a series of advertisements where one is not quite sure what product is on sale. In fact what is on offer is essentially a pre-packaged, commodified everyday, steeped in nostalgia for a pastoral, picture-book lifestyle where one has the time to savour life's little pleasures. Homing in

[27] Ibid., 35.
[28] Delerm followed it up with *La Sieste assassinée*, focused on disruptions to the pleasures of routine, and *Enregistrements pirates*.

on gestures, rituals, and sensations, Delerm's seductive prose consistently hits the mark, provoking authentic shivers of recognition. Yet his Epicureanism isolates experiences, removing them from the stream of existence. However mundane and ordinary these 'plaisirs minuscules' may be, they become special through being singled out in this way, and each island of experience, individually wrapped in its own textual fragment, blots out the rest of life. The text celebrating the pleasure of breakfast reading, the newspaper propped up against the teapot, emphasizes the dissociation from historical events: 'les catastrophes du présent deviennent relatives. Elles ne sont là que pour pimenter la sérénité du rite' (present catastrophes become relative. They are only there to spice up the serenity of the ritual).[29] Any sense of the everyday as a dimension of experience within a wider totality is replaced by a stable, coherent, transient but knowable plenitude.

What is lacking in Delerm is a sense of the openness and indeterminacy of the everyday, the ambiguity of its intermediate status as a dimension within a mobile field of interactions, and its resistance to representation. Here the affirmation of the everyday has the same effect as its repudiation: evanescent moments coagulate into a stable consistency. This suggests that taking a particular stance to the everyday, viewing it as good or bad—as an area to extricate oneself from or to embrace—may not be conducive to grasping it authentically. To opt for positive or negative evaluations is to filter out the tensions that give the everyday its fruitful ambivalence, and above all its status as a sphere of human self-realization.

The next two sections of this chapter pursue the issues of ambiguity and indeterminacy with regard, firstly, to philosophical approaches to the everyday and, secondly, to questions of genre. As we shall see in Chapter 4, the notion of ambiguity is central to the most thoroughgoing attempt to think philosophically about the everyday, Lefebvre's *Critique de la vie quotidienne*. But to explore further the status of ambiguity as a criterion of everydayness I want at this stage to look briefly at Lukács and Heidegger, who provide key bearings for later thinking on the everyday, and then to consider how, in counterpoint to Lefebvre, the philosopher and social theorist Agnes Heller has re-articulated Lukács's thought in directions that are symptomatic of the burgeoning of interest in the *quotidien* from the 1970s onward.

---

[29] Delerm, *La Première Gorgée*, 70.

TYPES OF AMBIGUITY: LUKÁCS, HEIDEGGER, AND HELLER

'L'anarchie du clair-obscur du quotidien' (the anarchy of the chiaroscuro of the everyday): when Michel de Certeau quoted these words by Georg Lukács as the epigraph to the concluding section of his book on the everyday,[30] the context made it clear that he intended the phrase to be interpreted in positive terms. The section—titled 'Indéterminées' (Indeterminacies)—insists on how the practices that make up the *quotidien* subvert functionalist order by inject-ing difference: the anarchic disorder of the everyday enables positive resist-ance.[31] Yet in its original context, his 1909 essay on 'The Metaphysics of Tragedy', Lukács's phrase evocatively sums up the negative pole in an oppos-ition where everyday life is contrasted with a higher existence possessing 'soul' and 'form': '[Everyday] Life is an anarchy of light and dark: nothing is ever fulfilled . . . nothing quite ends . . . nothing ever flowers into real life [which is] always unreal, always impossible'.[32] For the young Lukács there are no channels of mediation between these two forms of life: when glimpsed at rare moments real life penetrates the dark of the everyday: 'something lights up, a lightning flash in the midst of banality . . . chance, great moments, the miraculous'. As is well known, the sharp opposition Lukács drew between everyday life and real life, authenticity and inauthenticity, was transposed a decade later, after his conversion to Marxism (due in particular to the impact of the account of commodity fetishism in *Capital*), into a view where the everyday is dominated by the 'reification of consciousness': in *History and Class Consciousness* (1923) the advent of 'real life', rather than being a matter of moments of illumination, is linked to the fate of the proletariat. Later on, as we shall see, Lukács revisited the category of everyday or ordinary life. But in the immediate aftermath of the account of 'reification', it is in the work of Heidegger that one can find parallels with Lukács, as well as a significant development in thinking about the everyday.[33] Whether it is right to assert,

---

[30] Certeau, *L'Invention du quotidien*, I, 291. On the influence of Lukács on the young Perec see M. van Montfrans, *Georges Perec: la contrainte du réel*.

[31] As noted earlier, Blanchot, commenting on Lefebvre, also sees the *quotidien* in this way.

[32] Lukács, *Soul and Form*.

[33] Georg Simmel is a third figure one could mention here: his 'impressionist sociology', including writings on fashion, the city, the face, etc., also feeds into the tradition of the everyday, and on that account has been widely revisited in both France and the UK in the 1990s. Highmore devotes a chapter to Simmel in *Everyday Life and Cultural Theory*.

with Lucien Goldmann, that *Being and Time* owes much to Lukács,[34] it is clear that the importance of the category of everydayness (*Alltäglichkeit*) in Heidegger, and the negative complexion he gives it, do strongly echo Lukács (and the influence of both figures was crucial to the work of Lefebvre).[35] Lefebvre rightly pointed out, however, in a comparative discussion of Lukács and Heidegger, that the depreciation of everyday life as trivial, meaningless, and antithetical to 'la vraie vie', sprang from Romanticism (particularly German) and he also noted that where Lukács always affirmed the possibility of unity or totality (for which the novel became a prime medium), Heidegger (and then Sartre) developed more radically pessimistic ontologies in which the 'fallen' nature of the everyday was seen as irremediable.[36]

For Heidegger, *Alltäglichkeit* (Everydayness) does pertain to Being (*Dasein*) but to *Dasein* in its 'undifferentiated character' or modality (69).[37] This is everydayness as 'averageness', and it is hard to identify *Dasein* here: Being seems very distant. Yet Heidegger insists on the need to see *Dasein* in this context, where it is ontologically far away. The ontological signification of average everydayness 'is constantly overlooked' and must 'be made accessible by a positive characterization' even if is effectively 'forgetfulness of Being' (69). The essential thing is that when Being *is* 'remembered', it is in the same place, not elsewhere. It has been covered over all the while, for example by the surrender to the sway of 'the they' ('Das Man'): '*Dasein* in its everydayness is disburdened by the "they" '. Yet, given that *Alltäglichkeit* is the kind of Being in which *Dasein* manifests itself 'proximally and for the most part' (69), it is imperative that we identify it here, however unpromising the terrain.

Heidegger stresses the difficulty of delimiting the 'existential meaning of "everydayness" ' (422) and, like subsequent writers in the tradition, he notes that as a rule 'we never pay any heed to it' (423). The key factor is temporality. Having set out the structures of *Dasein* as the mode of Being, Heidegger insists that they need to be thought of in regard to 'this "temporal" stretching-along of *Dasein*'. If *Dasein* involves 'reckoning with time', this

---

[34] See Lucien Goldmann, *Lukács et Heidegger* (Paris: Denoël, 1973).

[35] On this see Michael Trebitsch, 'Preface', in Henri Lefebvre, *Critique of Everyday Life*, I (London: Verso, 1991).

[36] Henri Lefebvre, *Critique de la vie quotidienne*, III: *De la modernité au modernisme (Pour une métaphilosophie du quotidien)* (Paris: L'Arche, 1981), 23–5.

[37] References, incorporated in the text, are to Martin Heidegger, *Being and Time*, trans. J. Macquarrie and E. Robinson (Oxford: Blackwell, 1978).

reckoning (or acknowledgement) has everydayness as its context. And, at bottom, says Heidegger, 'everydayness is nothing but temporality itself'. This is because everydayness manifests the bewildering ambiguity of temporality: its dual manifestations as both cumulative and non-cumulative (Lefebvre will later make this property a key feature of the *quotidien*). On one hand, everydayness is the day-by-day: it is not 'calendrical'; it is not a sum of days. On the other hand, it does have 'an overtone of . . . temporal character'. And this is what enables *Alltäglichkeit* to mean 'the "how" in accordance with which *Dasein* "lives unto the day"' (422). Even though *Dasein* depends on a 'surmounting' of everydayness, it is only within its folds that everydayness can be surmounted. Thus, 'Everydayness is a way *to be*': it comprises both dullness and 'moments of vision' yet if, for the duration of such moments, 'existence can even gain mastery over the "everyday"' . . . it can never extinguish it' (422). As Malcolm Bowie observes, making an illuminating comparison with psychoanalysis: 'For Freud the "everyday" is the erotic force field in which the unconscious makes itself heard; while for Heidegger it is, at one and the same time, the particular, close-at-hand habitation in which *Dasein* has its roots and the "averageness" over and against which *Dasein* achieves its "moments of vision"'.[38] By talking of 'moments of vision' Heidegger does seem to introduce a kind of transcendence, but the whole thrust of his discussion (and it is part of the pessimism of his thought at this stage), underlines how 'moments of vision' cannot be thought of independently of the terrain in which they are immanent. Authentic as well as inauthentic *Dasein* has everydayness as its field. If Being is intermittent and inaccessible it is because it depends on the everydayness that is antithetical to it.

The ambiguity of Heidegger's *Alltäglichkeit* is echoed in many subsequent versions of everydayness where authentic experience is seen to need the everyday as its ground, whilst at the same time being defined in contradistinction to it. Lukács developed this view in his later writings, effecting, relatively speaking, 'reconciliation with the everyday'.[39] In his mature work of the 1930s and 1940s he had championed the 'critical realism' of the novel against both naturalist and modern art which remained tainted by the chaos of the everyday. But in his later aesthetic philosophy (where aesthetics is still

---

[38] Malcolm Bowie, *Psychoanalysis and the Future of Theory* (Oxford: Blackwell, 1993), 22.
[39] Ferenc Feher, 'Lukács in Weimar', in A. Heller (ed.), *Lukács Revalued* (Oxford: Blackwell, 1983), 103.

primordially the realm of unity between subject and object) he sought to give a greater role to the 'recipient' of the artwork, and thus to the 'performative' dimension of art.[40] If art could transcend the everyday it might follow that it could enable the everyday subject to transcend everydayness, not only momentarily but more enduringly. This led to the evolutionist theory that Lukács developed in *The Specificity of the Aesthetic* (1963) where 'the whole edifice of the aesthetic is built up "from below", departing from the daily efforts of man, which were condemned in the 1930s and 1940s to be incurably alienated'.[41] Lukács's formulations of this theory have usually been judged unsatisfactory, but in the more complex and subtle version evolved by one of his followers, Agnes Heller, a view of the everyday as the locus of human self-transformation takes on a complexion that has important resonance for the French tradition, particularly Lefebvre, Foucault, and Certeau. Heller's insistence on the centrality of the everyday, as long as it is seen as a threshold rather than as an end in itself, will introduce links between ethical self-fashioning, *art de vivre*, and everydayness that will recur at other points in the tradition we are studying.

Agnes Heller belongs to a group of Hungarian intellectuals who were close to Lukács in the last decades of his life. Written in Hungarian in 1967–8, and published in Budapest in 1970, her *Everyday Life* is now best known in the revised edition prepared for English publication in 1984. A fellow Marxist (at least until 1956), Heller knew Lefebvre's work, and she quotes the important second volume of his *Critique*, published in 1961. As in Lefebvre's case, a primary stimulus is dissatisfaction with the depreciation of the everyday in the thought of Heidegger and Lukács, coupled with the possibility of discovering in the writings of the young Marx (and notably the 1844 manuscripts which Lefebvre edited and translated in French) ideas and concepts that can illuminate the importance of everyday life. Heller endorses Heidegger's analysis of the limitations of everydayness, but she rebuts the absolute separation he makes between the everyday and the non-everyday. Indeed one of the central contentions of *Everyday Life* is that the full efflorescence of human reality is only attainable via an engagement with everydayness. Even if it must be transcended (this is where Heller will differ from Lefebvre) the everyday is the ineluctable gateway to authentic being.

---

[40] See, Agnes Heller, 'Lukács's later philosophy', in A. Heller (ed.), *Lukács Revalued* (Oxford: Blackwell, 1983), 177–90.

[41] Feher, 'Lukács in Weimar', 104. Lukács's text is as yet untranslated in English.

Deeply imbued with late Lukács, Heller's view of everyday life is inflected by classical moral philosophy. Rather than virtue, her touchstone is the growth of human individuality. Marx's concept of the 'species-essential' (developed in Lukács's *The Specificity of the Aesthetic*), designating what lies beyond particularistic interests and engages the deeper collective or generic needs of human beings, provides the argument with its horizon. Equally important is Heller's 'paradigm of objectification', partly derived from Marx's notion of appropriation and partly from Husserlian phenomenology. In all spheres of activity human beings are 'objectified'. We acquire our particular quality via the ways in which we 'reproduce' ourselves in the multiple contexts where we operate. Heller distinguishes between two main types of objectification—'in-itself' and 'for-itself'—and between two corresponding categories of person: the particular and the individual. We progress from particularity to individuality, she argues, not by asserting our personality but by realizing our 'species-essentiality'. It is accordingly through objectifications of the 'for-itself' variety—those associated with consciousness and freedom—that individuality is attained.

To a large extent the distinctions between particularity and individuality, and 'in-itself' and 'for-itself', coincide with the distinction between the everyday and the non-everyday. The 'in-itself' of everyday life is essentially heterogeneous. In the everyday we constantly 'objectify' ourselves in diverse, *ad hoc* ways, as we are faced with a haphazard array of circumstances. Here we deal primarily with the immediate environment and our particular interests. Inclined to take things as they come, we generally apply a few basic rules of thumb to a plethora of variegated cases. 'Everyday thinking' (a category introduced by Lukács) is therefore often based on bias, prejudice, and unexamined custom, and is at odds with higher forms of thought (scientific innovation, for example). It also tends to be anthropocentric, localized, and tied to the field of perception rather than reflection. A practical relationship to values predominates, associated with concrete rather than abstract norms.

Homogeneity is, by contrast, the touchstone of what lies beyond the everyday. If it is epitomized in such higher spheres as art, science, and philosophy, the essence of the 'for-itself' is the 'process of homogenization'. Whatever the sphere, the sign of a non-everyday attitude is the attempt to achieve synthesis, and this often involves a suspension of ready-made responses. But if homogenization is 'the criterion of the non-everyday' (86),[42]

---

[42] References to *Everyday Life* are incorporated in the text.

it is a process rather than a separate realm. And in the first instance it works on the same *données* that we encounter in everyday life. Just as individuality is achieved by a conscious relationship with values that we place before our own particularity, and which lead us freely to shape and synthesize our experience into a homogeneous unity, so the non-everyday is reached, in the first instance, not by a turn in a different direction but by a different stance towards the same elements. Throughout *Everyday Life* Heller strives to show not only that everyday and non-everyday attitudes co-exist and interpenetrate, but that everyday life provides the essential foundation for what transcends it. To qualify the everyday, abundant use is made of expressions such as 'take-off point', 'pre-condition', 'bedrock', 'indispensable ground structures', 'fundament'. At one point Heller, accounting for the ways in which the 'non-everyday' or higher level of being is immanent within the everyday, refers to a 'gravitational shift within the given structure' (192).

Much of the richness of Heller's work is to be found in her analyses of the 'frontier situations of everyday life' (84), and her attempts to capture the 'undulations between the everyday and what is beyond' (60). In her chapter on 'Everyday Knowledge' the distinction between the everyday and the non-everyday is constantly postulated and constantly undermined. Heller provides a detailed account of everyday thinking, which is seen to involve a bank of passive knowledge that includes snippets of science ('Calcium is good for teeth') or hearsay, and she suggests that when a piece of hearsay is corrected scientifically we move up and out of everyday thinking. Acquired through the constant internalization of experiences and perceptions, everyday thinking remains a 'heterogeneous amalgam' that is totally inseparable from praxis. And yet, imbued with needs, perceptions, and feelings, everyday knowledge, Heller observes at one point, 'is the basis of all non-everyday knowledge' (203). Everyday knowledge is always opinion (*doxa*) rather than truth (*episteme*). And it finds verification in practical, concrete activity rather than in being proved true or false in abstract terms. Yet even when *doxa* is countered by higher thought (*episteme*), its perceptual and emotional aspects cannot as a rule simply be refuted. To know something in everyday life is to know that something works (whether it is right or not by other standards). Like Walter Benjamin's 'Storyteller' (discussed in the next section) Heller's everyday subject possesses a heritage of practical knowledge. The links between the everyday and the domain of practice, which permeate thinking about the *quotidien* (Certeau, following Bourdieu, will insist on it) are clearly in evidence here, even if Heller's view is equivocal.

In fact, rather than simply contrasting everyday and non-everyday modes, Heller's discussion of everyday knowledge keeps eroding the distinction between them, revealing their mutual interdependence and functional insep-arability, but also underlining the primacy of the everyday. And it is striking that Heller often comes close to self-contradiction when she acknowledges the presence of what are (on her terms) non-everyday elements within the every-day. If blind faith pertains to everyday belief, while trust, moral certainty, and responsibility for knowledge belong to the non-everyday, Heller acknowledges that *scepsis*, defined as a local suspension of belief, is a feature of the everyday, even if the attainment of a judicious balance between *scepsis* and belief rests on non-everyday qualities. More tellingly, Heller concedes that contemplation, and a non-pragmatic relation to nature, play a part in everyday life, as does an apprehension of the qualities of phenomena (colour, shape, size) which, whilst pragmatic in origin, goes beyond this. In identifying 'pure non-everyday attitudes which are nevertheless organic components of everyday life and thinking' (212), Heller not only blurs the distinction between these two modes, but further enhances the purview—and the ambiguity—of the every-day itself.

If Heller's dense and eloquent analyses constantly undermine any clear dichotomies, what ultimate valuation does she place on the everyday? At the heart of *Everyday Life* is a basic paradox: the everyday is everything and it is nothing. Against Heidegger, Heller contends that everyday life must not be renounced: it is the indispensable gateway to full human self-realization. And yet, according to a central strand of Heller's argument, it is no more than a gateway, a threshold: the everyday must be transcended. Even if we have to go via the everyday, our destination is beyond and outside it. But it then transpires that the non-everyday is not really beyond; it is virtually present within the everyday. What constitutes the higher realm is in fact the product of a particular way of dealing with the lower one—the everyday. And the question that then arises is whether the higher attitudes are extraneous to the everyday, and brought to bear on it, or whether they are generated by it. Heller's apparent ambivalence on this is crucial. On one hand she tends to present the higher attitudes—synthesis, homogenization, distance—as spe-cifically coming from the outside, like a spark that brings ignition from without, or as if everyday life were some kind of base matter awaiting alchemical transmutation by the 'for-itself' of synthesizing consciousness. On the other hand she often writes as if the everyday itself were capable of generating its own self-transforming dynamism. For example, she observes that if stagnation can reign in all aspects of everyday life, it is nevertheless always open to 'new prehensions' (54). If 'in itself and without remainder, everyday life is objectivation' (47), the modes of appropriation it fosters are innumerable: the everyday not only constrains, it obliges a multifaceted response that produces 'individual life-rhythms'. Nor does it inevitably impose conformity: 'no two people share exactly the same structural system of personal customs' (157). In the field of the everyday itself we may observe what Heller calls 'gravitational shift within the given structure' (192). On this view, which chimes with Certeau's thought, the process of appropriation is what creates energy in the limited system of the everyday, opening it up and releasing its capacity to be self-transcending by virtue of the fact that the generic is virtual within it.

But how can this second view be reconciled with Heller's insistence that the criteria for the non-everyday are synthesis, homogenization, distance, consciousness, the attainment of individuality through the movement 'from the everyday to the generic' (to cite a chapter title), and so on? Throughout *Everyday Life* these features are all categorized as being beyond the everyday. If they must be brought to bear to induce its transformation, then clearly this transformative dynamic comes from outside rather than from within the everyday manifold itself. At some point we encounter aporia: the clash of incompatible scenarios. And ultimately Heller's arguments favour the second. However close she comes to seeing everyday life as capable of engendering appropriations that would make it not only the gateway, but the haven for what initially seems to transcend its horizons (this is the position that will painstakingly be worked out by Lefebvre) Heller ultimately resists this view. To a large extent this seems attributable to her prior and primordial commitment to an ethical perspective based on the classical ideal of the perfected individual. For her, everyday life remains a testing ground, the inescapable forum for the attainment of a mode of being that is not part and parcel of the everyday itself. The values associated with the Individual in Heller's scheme of things are all tinged with the heroic and the Olympian (one of the merits of Foucault's late work on the care of the self is that, while working with Greek and Roman texts, he does away with this). Ultimately, the identification Heller establishes between the generic and the Individual leads not only to her emphasis on transcending everydayness but to a position where such transcendence, however much it is grounded in the dynamics of the everyday, depends on what lies beyond it. It is in this area that Lefebvre as well as other investigators of the everyday, including Perec, will differ markedly from

Heller. For them the prestige of everyday life will lie precisely in its links with the generic level that Heller sees as lying outside its scope. If, like Heller, Lefebvre sees the everyday in terms of a process of appropriation that can lead to its transformation, this process depends for him on the way engagement with the everyday can foster not only, as in Heller, a move away from particularity, but also a profound rapport with the generic, grounded not in a conscious and distanced relationship with 'species-essentiality' but in the experience of immersion.

Yet Heller's work has the great merit of connecting a concern for the everyday with the question of how we live our lives. As will be particularly evident in the work of Certeau and Perec, ethical matters are at the heart of the everyday. And in Chapter 9 we will return to the question of everydayness as a framework for ethical self-fashioning. Heller's own approach to these questions is echoed in Tzvetan Todorov's later work, notably *Éloge du quotidien*, a study of Dutch painting, and his philosophical essay *La Vie commune*. Todorov's central argument is encapsulated in a phrase from Rousseau which had figured two years earlier as the epigraph to Annie Ernaux's *Journal du dehors*, a key book of everyday exploration. Rousseau wrote: 'Notre *vrai* moi n'est pas tout entier en nous' (our *real* self is not entirely within us). For Todorov, human self-realization depends on our recognizing the social nature of human existence: 'la socialité n'est pas maudite, elle est libératrice; il faut se débarasser des illusions individualistes' (social being is not cursed, it is liberating; we must free ourselves from individualistic illusions).[43] This means recognizing, as Heller does, the existence of everyday virtues, 'la voie des vertus quotidiennes'[44] available to a self that is reflective and capable of modification through interaction with others. By opening ourselves to others in the forum of everyday life we renounce inert, archaic images of ourselves, and benefit from the open plasticity of authentic human existence.

GENRE AND THE EVERYDAY: RESISTING THE NOVEL

Until now we have been concerned with general attitudes towards the everyday, rather than the medium through which they are articulated. Historically, however, the emergence of a concern with everydayness is closely linked to the

---

[43] Tzvetan Todorov, *La Vie commune* (Paris: Seuil, 1995), 169.
[44] Ibid., 171.

evolution of styles and genres. For example, Tzvetan Todorov has argued that Dutch painting of the seventeenth century can be seen globally as an 'éloge du quotidien': a paean to the riches of ordinary existence.[45] Yet a significant body of art-historical research points to the range of ideological meanings trans-mitted through an iconography that is far from simply representational: in Dutch painting the presentation of the everyday cannot simply be taken at face value. Acknowledging this, Todorov nonetheless sees the works of the Dutch masters as engaging with everydayness through the attention their work confers on the overlooked: painterly practice, on Todorov's reading, bypasses the problem of representation and, via the spectator's response, opens another channel onto the real world.

Charles Taylor's magisterial account of the evolution of modern western identity, *The Sources of the Self*, establishes connections between modern selfhood, attitudes to everyday life, and the emergence of artistic genres, notably the realist novel. What Taylor calls 'the affirmation of ordinary life' involved an attenuation of the sacred and the assertion of an individual first-person viewpoint tied to a body of experience garnered in the processes of production and reproduction—work and marriage.[46] In its first avatars (not-ably Puritanism) the affirmation of ordinary life was an inflexion of religious feeling, and it sponsored a version of the religious celebration of the everyday that we have already touched on. In tracing its transmutation into more secular forms, via Protestantism, eighteenth-century Deism, and the radical Enlightenment, to the cult of nature which flourished in Romanticism (and was perpetuated, according to Taylor, in such avant-garde movements as Surrealism), *The Sources of the Self* not only emphasizes the historical continu-ity between the religious affirmation of the ordinary and its later versions, but raises the question broached earlier, namely whether all such affirmations must at some level maintain a connection with spirituality.

The rise of the novel has often been linked to the emergence of the individual as a subject placed in a world of things defined by their market value and their place within a wider context of social and economic relation-ships. Taylor argues that in the eighteenth-century novel a wealth of particu-lars—entities and events all placed on the same footing—dislodges established hierarchies and archetypes. Henceforth, in the novel, as in the form of autobiography initiated by Rousseau, 'we have to scrutinize the particular to

---

[45] See TzvetanTodorov, *Éloge du quotidien* (1993; Paris: Seuil Points-Essais, 1997).
[46] Taylor, *The Sources of the Self*, 211–304.

arrive at the general'.[47] The meaning of a series of events derives from the connections and ingredients established by a narrative whose shape is not predetermined by conventions and archetypes. On the face of it, both the realist novel, which emerged in the contexts of the Enlightenment and the Industrial Revolution, and the whole range of non-fictional writings aimed at describing, dissecting, and classifying the world, which can be associated, in the nineteenth century, with the realist project more generally, seem ideally disposed to the exploration of the everyday. The realist writer is an active observer whose mission is to see, to understand, to interpret, and to classify. Like the scientist, he or she seeks to establish laws, to go from the particular (no detail is too insignificant) to the general, devising modes of deduction and inference suited to the objects under scrutiny. As is well known, one of the great innovations of Balzac, Dickens, and Galdos as realists is to focus not only on man as a social and economic being, or on a wide cross-section of social types and levels, but on human beings in their daily lives, attending closely to what we would now call material culture (objects, interior décor, clothes) and to the practices and rituals of daily life—eating, domestic economy, social interaction.

It is possible to argue, however, as in the case of other celebrations of the *quotidien*, that the realist novel often fails to connect with the everyday as a dimension of human experience. Even though it evolved considerably, Lukács's theory of the novel consistently pits the novel against the formlessness of the everyday. His key concepts—'totality', 'typicality', the 'world-histor-ical'—underline the need to go beyond surfaces in order to grasp the com-plexity of social processes; naturalist writing, in his view, fails to identify the typical and thus to create totality. For Lukács the great novel represents the triumph of form over the mess of the everyday. Yet it has become a truism to say that realism, far from offering either a transparent window on reality, innocently relaying a neutral vision, or the 'complex vision' of a sovereign author, is a mode of discourse with its own laws, conventions, and codes: it is by manipulating these, while at the same time failing to acknowledge their existence, that the realist writer achieves his or her effects. Thus the everyday, as constructed in the realist work, becomes part of a wider project where the presentation of everyday reality is clearly subservient to other ends, literary and ideological. For example, furnishings, street names, or body language often connote character. Balzac's settings famously mirror the personalities of

[47] Ibid., 287.

their inhabitants: in *Le Père Goriot* the denizens of the Pension Vauquer are reflected in its grimy pretensions to gentility. To this metaphorical status can be added a metonymic role whereby settings invoke a wider social and historical reality. In fiction, the everyday is often no more than a background. The actions of the protagonists—Rastignac's social ascent, for example—are what really count. However rich and meaningful the details in which their unfolding is embedded, it is the destinies of individual fictional characters that are illuminated.

Modern critical theory has insisted that within the terms of the realist project, description is a form of discourse which presents phenomena as processed by the grammar of its language or the axioms of its logic.[48] As Barthes observed in *S/Z*: 'dépeindre, c'est faire dévaler le tapis des codes, c'est référer, non d'un langage à un référent, mais d'un code à un autre code' (to depict is to spread out the carpet of codes, it is to refer—not by linking language to referent, but one code to another).[49] Descriptions are allusive and intertextual. The unknown is presented in terms of the known. It is clear that realist fiction excels at representing the surfaces of the *quotidien*, and at drawing our attention to a first-level everyday that can be accessed via the eye. Here the everyday is an external spectacle laid on for a privileged viewer. Explained and exposed, it lends itself to judgement and categorization. This perspective is eminently compatible with the various forms of organized knowledge whose rise the novel accompanied and to some degree abetted: history, sociology, anthropology and folklore, economics, psychology, philology. Everyday life is scrutinized, situated, classified, and evaluated. At this level it is possible to typify and compare everydays: those of miners and stevedores, Assyrians and Eskimos, mountain folk and city-dwellers.[50]

Yet, once again, the everyday—as a level of human experience—cannot be reduced to an objectified background on which blanket judgements can be passed. Does this mean that the more complex vision of the everyday, outlined earlier in this chapter, is totally incompatible with the novel? I want to suggest that if the everyday is inherently resistant to being captured in the nets

[48] See Philippe Hamon, *Introduction à l'analyse du descriptif* (Paris: Hachette, 1991); Michael Riffaterre, 'L'Illusion référentielle', in Gérard Genette and Tzvetan Todorov (eds.), *Littérature et réalité* (Paris: Seuil, 1982), 91–118.

[49] Barthes, S/Z, *Œuvres complètes*, II, 555–742.

[50] Cf. the famous series 'La Vie quotidienne au temps de . . .' launched by Hachette in 1938 and still going strong. Reflecting the emergence of *Annales*, the series has had some notable successes, including Jérôme Carcopino on Ancient Rome.

of realism, its elucidation may be compatible with a strain of resistance within the novel itself, a strain we can identify, in the first instance, with the act of narration rather than with the world docketed by the narrator. To explore this I want to look firstly at Walter Benjamin's famous account of 'The Storyteller'.[51] Benjamin contrasts the novel with the tale. The novel is the product of a solitary individual who confronts the perplexities of life. 'The novelist', writes Benjamin 'stands aside. The birthplace of the novel is the solitary individual [who] does not receive advice and does not know how to give any' (87). The novel explains: it identifies causes and reasons, pins down the meaning of events, and passes on information, the low-down. It is the instrument of a social order represented by the individual who cuts himself off in order to organize the real. It is linked to the era of mechanization, when the traces of the human hand are effaced from the fruits of man's labour. By contrast, the tale, according to Benjamin, maintains connection with oral transmission and with the body. The storyteller, or narrator, is a member of the human community. In his role as witness he affirms the 'transferable reality' of a life that comes into view at the hour of death: 'death is the sanction of everything the storyteller can tell' (94). For Benjamin there is a link between the teller and the itinerant tradesman ('storytelling . . . is itself an artisan form of communication' (91)), and thus between his art and the domain of practice which Michel de Certeau will place at the heart of 'pratiques quotidiennes'— the 'practice of everyday life'. According to Benjamin, every authentic tale stems from 'practical interests' and contains something useful: a tip, a piece of advice, a short cut; something that depends on know-how rather than knowledge, and which, rather than offering the explanation for a series of events in its logical unfolding, provides a gloss that helps us to understand how such events have their place in 'the inscrutable course of things' (96). Citing Lukács, Benjamin argues that the novel separates meaning and life, showing how elusive meaning is in the thick of experience (99). The story, on the other hand, remains within the field of experience and derives its meanings from this core. The authority of the teller, a man of 'good counsel', stems from experience.

The concept of experience—*Erfahrung*—plays a key role in Benjamin's thought. Associated with memory and tradition, with synthesis rather than analysis, this mode of being fell victim to the rise of technology, almost to the point of obliteration. Cut off from immediate lived experience (*Erlebnis*—

[51] In Benjamin, *Illuminations*, 83–109 (page references included in the text; some translations modified).

which itself then takes on an air of unreality), *Erfahrung* becomes increasingly incommunicable.[52] For Benjamin, the rise of the novel is a symptom of the increasing incommunicability of experience (86), while the art of the teller, which depends on 'communicability', survives in areas where practice still prevails—in the countryside, in urban trades, and in the army. For Benjamin, the rise of the novel is a response to the 'atrophy of experience'. Through the order it sets in place, the scaled-down and highly organized world it creates, the novel fills a gap. But in remedying a loss it substitutes its own order for that of lived reality. Despite all that links it to modernity, and to the real world of technology, the novel has proved a poor conductor of everydayness, not so much—and this is a key point—because of its fictionality but because of its tendency to abstraction. Of course, as the realist and naturalist currents demonstrate in spectacular fashion, there is nothing like a novel if you want to be served a slice of life! But even when it seems to abstain from ideological comment, resorting to hyperrealism to show us the customs of such and such a sector of humanity, the novel's reliance on the logic of mimesis asserts itself in a number of ways. Meaning in the novel (and the same applies more or less to non-fictional genres such as reportage, testimonies, autobiographical narratives) is a function of such factors as the logic of actions, modes of narration, types of hero. As Barthes, Genette and other narratologists have argued, little escapes the functionalist logic of narrative (we shall see later how functionalism in all its forms is antithetical to the recognition of the everyday).[53] Of course the novel can be an instrument of ideological critique, as the *roman à these* or the concept of critical realism bear out, but here again it is the machinery of narrative that creates meaning, through its panoply of functions regulating the interplay of narrator, hero, setting, and so on. The switch from objectivity to subjectivity in the modernist novel does not necessarily alter this: variations in focus and voice may privilege the lived experience of the individual, but making the mind 'transparent' usually depends just as much as realism does on code and convention.[54] The here and now of the stream of consciousness is a fabrication. The hours of Mrs Dalloway's day are very different from ours.

The novel is good at conveying a sense of the banal, insofar as this can be seen as the projection of a subjective state. According to the psychoanalyst Sami-Ali, banality originates in a form of sensibility 'qui schematise à l'excès le

---

[52] See ibid., 'On some motifs in Baudelaire' (1939), *Illuminations*, 157–202.

[53] See, e.g., Barthes, 'Introduction à l'analyse structurale du récit', *Œuvres Complètes*, II, 74–103, and Génard Genette, 'Vraisemblance et motivation', *Figures*, I (Paris: Seuil, 1966).

[54] See Dorrit Cohn, *Transparent Minds: Narrative Modes for Presenting Consciousness in Fiction* (Princeton: Princeton University Press, 1978).

contenu de l'expérience' (that renders the content of experience excessively schematic).[55] But this 'reality' is not that of the everyday, of that dimension of our lives that always pre-exists any particular attitude we adopt towards it. To render this kind of everydayness the novel needs to cast off some of its familiar attributes. In the modern period (which is not an age of tales) it is by playing with its own conventions and limits that the novel has been able to contribute to the exploration of the *quotidien*. Despite its alleged fluidity, its 'loose baggy monster' quality, observed by Henry James, or what Gide called its 'lawless' side, the novel's habitual bent is towards abstraction and linear coherence.[56] Thus if, in existential terms, the everyday is a dimension that resists the external conditioning of lived experience, there is a dimension of the novel that subverts its own inherent tendency to order. It is often where the artifice of fiction is made most manifest that an effective grasp on the everyday is seemingly achieved: in Joyce's *Ulysses* for example, or the anti-novels of Raymond Queneau, or in the work of more recent writers like Georges Perec and François Bon. Apprehending the everyday calls for particular forms of attention, allied to practices rather than genres. No genre can lay claim to the everyday, but subversive practices that cut across generic divisions have often been productive.

Michel de Certeau's *L'Invention du quotidien* considers the conditions under which narrativity can have a purchase on the everyday. For Certeau the everyday is not a spectacle, to be described, decoded, or explained, but, rather, a field of action. Whatever the sector—knowledge, culture, administration, space, institution—this field or space is always regulated by the other. Yet through his or her 'manières de faire' (ways of doing) the user or participant, whose perspective Certeau adopts almost exclusively, has a capacity to be not only a passive subject but an active agent. In his elaboration of this central paradigm, Certeau strives not only to evoke a range of such 'manières de faire' in order to demonstrate their effectiveness, but also to establish what he calls the 'logic' or 'formality' of practices, in other words the shared mode of operation that is at work in all these different spheres. Among these practices is narration.

The act of narration, telling a story, crops up in several places in *L'Invention du quotidien*. First, the nineteenth-century realist novel is said to constitute a

[55] M. Sami-Ali, *Le Banal* (Paris: Gallimard, 1980).
[56] Henry James, Preface, *The Tragic Muse, Novels, 1886–1890*, (1890; New York: Library of America, 1989) 107; André Gide, *Les Faux-Monnayeurs* (1926; Paris: Gallimard Folio, 1986).

veritable encyclopedia of 'manières de faire'; the novel, says Certeau, is 'le zoo des pratiques quotidiennes'[57] where we can find 'everyone's micro-histories'. This is not by virtue of the representational space constituted by fiction, but because the artistry of telling opens a new space: an 'art de faire' finds its expression in an 'art de dire'. The multiplicity of stories, and the dialogical interplay of narrative performances that features in many novels, create a discursive space. Secondly, the art of saying involves temporality. The efficacy of a narrative often stems from good timing. A narration may derive its effectiveness from a detail in the right place; indeed, in narrative, detail often determines structure. Like Benjamin, Certeau identifies a particular mode of memory at work in the temporality of the narrator's art: not a memory weighed down by accumulated experience, but a light, tactical, and mobile memory 'that shines in the occasion'. Thirdly, the 'récit', as a performance, creates links between spaces. To tell a story is to invent a spatial syntax, to create a route through spaces that bear the mark of the other. 'Tout récit est un récit de voyage—une pratique de l'espace' (Every story is a travel story—a spatial practice) (171). In two shakes of a lamb's tail, as the saying goes, the narrative—and of course notably the tale—springs us from castle to hovel, from city to seaside, from boudoir to gutter. In a flash, the narration transmutes places into spaces. 'Là où la carte découpe, le récit traverse' (What the map cuts up, the story cuts across) (245): narrating is a transversal art. Lastly, narratives derive their capacity to subvert established structures from their connections to the oral, to the 'noises' of the body. And this active and activating dimension of narration finds its parallel in reading, envisaged not as submission to the authority of the written, but as an activity, a form of poaching on the other's territory: 'lire c'est pérégriner dans un système imposé' (to read is to wander through an imposed system) (245). For Certeau, the everyday is linked to a narrativity that prompts an active—and activating— mode of reading (the kind of reading which, according to Paul Ricoeur, 'applies' fiction to the real).[58] Linked to the tale, the 'conte', this type of narrativity—a process of displacement rather than a structure or a representation—sets up resistance, within the novel itself, to the dominant *modus operandi* of narrative. It can be identified as the dimension of the novel, linked

---

[57] Certeau, *L'Invention du quotidien*, I, 120. Subsequent references will be incorporated in the text.

[58] Paul Ricoeur, *Temps et récit*, III (Paris: Seuil, 1983–5), 229–30.

to the act or art of narration, through which the narrator's performance addresses the reader's own relationship to lived reality. In making reading a practice, the narrative text triggers a process of *appropriation* (central to the *quotidien* for both Lefebvre and Certeau) on the part of the reader. This dimension of narrative engages with the receiver's participation in the ways of the world.

In Georges Perec, narrative practice works on these lines. The indication of genre in the subtitle of *La Vie mode d'emploi*—*romans* in the plural, and the epigraph from Jules Verne: 'Regarde de tous tes yeux, regarde!', suggest that what counts is the activity of telling. Confronting the profusion of the everyday, the novel splits into a multiplicity of strands. It is for the reader to appropriate his or her living space by following the leads provided by the teller. The title, with its notion of providing life with a 'user's manual', brings out the idea of appropriation, as does the emphasis on artifice and experimentation. Laying bare the mechanisms of writing breaks with the customary illusion of fiction but liberates fictive material that is attuned to the real. The profusion of stories and characters, which replaces any single plot, also reflects this experimental, interrogative attitude. Perec claimed that the 'romanesque'—'le goût des histoires et des péripéties'—was one of the four main overlapping fields he worked in, another being the *quotidien*.[59] The choice of the term 'romanesque' rather than 'roman', and of the plural—'des histoires'—is important: in this multiplicity of criss-crossing stories we can find the universe of the tale and its modern avatars such as the detective story (Benjamin cites Poe in his essay on the Storyteller). *La Vie mode d'emploi* is full of investigations, residues, clues, and traces.[60] And also of *peripetaia*: incidents and coincidences where narrative pleasure becomes linked to the inexhaustibility of the everyday. The abundance of 'stuff'—documents, things classified, collected, or abandoned—becomes 'romanesque' not by virtue of an 'effet de réel' enabling the novel to simulate reality, nor because of the various objects serving as indexes of character—this is not an alternative mode of storytelling—but because, by dint of being embedded in a web of infinitely interlocking stories, this material draws attention globally to the everyday in which we are enmeshed.

[59] Perec, *Penser/Classer*, 9–12
[60] Cf. Ch. 7 below.

THE ESSAY AND THE EVERYDAY: PEREC WITH ADORNO

Despite the claims of the realist novel, the everyday evades generic pigeonholing, although its hybrid indeterminacy can find outlets in a host of media, visual as well as verbal. Michel de Certeau insists on its subversive or erosive character, the everyday's capacity to disrupt the systems that seek to encapsulate it.[61] The last part of this chapter will examine a genre which, by dint of its own heterodoxy and hybridity, can claim to have marked affinities with the everyday. Since Montaigne, the essay has retained its solidarity with the concrete, run-of-the-mill, experience of the ordinary mortal. Equally, attempts to give voice to the everyday as a level or dimension of experience have often used the essay as a vehicle, or have imported the spirit of essayistic thinking into other genres and media, including film and photography. There is, then, something mutually illuminating about the essay and the everyday. In the succession of his *Essais*, Montaigne makes us privy to the emergence of an attitude towards knowledge and a way of rendering the processes of the mind as it makes sense of the world.[62] In doing so he famously brings in more and more of his day-to-day experience—what he eats, how he sleeps, what he likes, whom he hates. It is not so much as information that these everyday things matter, but as parameters in an approach to knowledge that refuses to efface the embodied, concrete experience of the subject. Interestingly Lukács's *Soul and Form* begins with an encomium for the essay, which is seen as a form that mediates between art and philosophy and expresses a view of the world as experience. Even if, to Lukács's way of thinking, this implies that the everyday transcends the ordinary, the appeal of the essay mode is that it has affinities with the heterogeneous materials it deals in.[63]

Historically, the essay's indeterminacy stems from the fact that it breaks out of the straitjacket of scholasticism and commentary, without wholly embracing the abstract systematizations of science—'the essay [in Montaigne] exists outside any organization of knowledge, whether medieval or modern. In it an open mind confronts an open reality'.[64] Having truck with the everyday reflects the essay's resistance to systematic thought; conversely, the everyday's

---

[61] See Ch. 6 below.

[62] On the everyday in Montaigne see Philippe Desan, *Naissance de la méthode* (Paris: Nizet, 1987).

[63] Lukács, 'The Nature and Form of the Essay', *Soul and Form*, 1–18.

[64] Graham Good, *The Observing Self: Rediscovering the Essay* (London: Routledge, 1988), 4.

resistance to system, the heterogeneous contingency that makes it so hard to pin down, disposes it towards the open-minded, mind-opening essay. The essay and the *quotidien* have in common their vulnerability. The category of the everyday, like the non-knowledge of the essay, is in a sense superfluous. Eating, sleeping, walking, reading, working, resting, buying, conversing, are all things we can have ideas about, abstractly and analytically. They can all be analysed, separately or in various combinations, by innumerable discourses and disciplines. But to try and grasp their everydayness, the experience, rather than the simple fact, of repetition, of the rhythm of things; to try and grasp how it 'all hangs together', for me, here and now, is to forget what we generally think of as knowledge—as the essay characteristically does.

Georges Perec's *Espèces d'espaces*, published in 1974, disdains disciplinary orthodoxy and plays cat and mouse with organized forms and procedures of knowledge. In a succession of brief chapters, often subdivided into numbered sections, we move from a blank sheet of paper to the vastness of 'space' itself, according to a logic of 'emboîtement' where each successive space—bed, room, apartment, building, street, *quartier*, city, country, world—is contained in the next. But rather than indicating subservience to pre-existent systems and ideologies, this logical orderliness flouts them all the more effectively as we recognize its arbitrariness, the way the order adopted merely provides a framework for a play of ideas generated from the interaction between inner needs and exigencies and outer constraints and pressures.

In a preamble on the cover Perec begins by asserting that the space we live in (as opposed to theorize) is not homogeneous or uniform. Spatial experience is discontinuous: we are constantly shuttling between different kinds of space, separated by 'des fissures, des hiatus, des points de friction' (fissures, hiatuses, friction points).[65] Rather than inventing space or reinventing it (there are already many well-meaning agencies ready to 'think' our environment for us), we need to interrogate or, more simply, to read it: to log the experience of negotiating the 'laps d'espaces', the gaps encountered as we constantly shift from one kind of space to another. Approached in this mode, that of the 'diary' of 'un usager de l'espace' (space user), the act of *reading* space is a matter of beginning with elementary observations, and thus counteracting our tendency not to see or to feel our everyday experience: 'car ce que nous appelons quotidienneté n'est pas évidence, mais opacité: une forme de cécité, une manière d'anesthésie' (for what we call everydayness is not obvious but

---

[65] Perec, *Espèces d'espaces*, back cover. References incorporated in the text.

opaque: a kind of blindness or anaesthesia) (cover). The manner of reading and writing enacted in Perec's text is designed not to conceptualize or to create something new, but to reanimate, as one might regain feeling in an anaesthetized limb, a pre-existent ambient reality that needs to find an appropriate form.

One of the central arguments in T. W. Adorno's remarkable discussion of 'The Essay as Form' is that the essay—unlike the treatise, on the one hand, and the poem or novel on the other—'does not begin with Adam and Eve' (152).[66] The essay is not concerned with deduction from first principles, or with 'primeval givens'. Indeed the essay 'uses its relation to its object as a weapon against the spell of beginnings' (166). It might look at first as if, by beginning with the blank page, Perec goes against this, but as the 'Avant-propos' to *Espèces d'espaces* makes clear, he only starts out from abstract, immaterial, notional space in order to insist that, for the human subject, it is never like that. We do not live in infinite space, or Euclidean space. We can, if we wish, create a *tabula rasa*, imagining a time when there was nothing—but what is the point? The problem is not how we got where we are, but recognizing that this is where we have got to (14). It is differences that matter, not origins: 'il y a plein de petits bouts d'espaces [qui] se sont multipliés, morcelés et diversifiés [...] Vivre, c'est passer d'un espace à un autre, en essayant le plus possible de ne pas se cogner' (there are lots of little bits of space that have multiplied and fragmented... To live is to go from one space to another, while trying not to bump into anything) (14). To begin with a blank page is not to begin with abstraction, but with inscription. At the beginning and end of *Espèces d'espaces* writing is seen as a paradigm of orientation (and disorientation) in space, because writing, like moving, mobilizes space: as Perec demonstrates, calligramatically, by placing characters vertically, or in the margin, or leaving blank spaces. If something primordial is involved, it is the act of making an inscription since this is where human, lived space starts.

The idea is developed in two ways in the opening chapter of *Espèces d'espaces*. Firstly, Perec pursues the notion that most of what we do in our daily lives leaves a written trace, from scrawled directions on a cigarette packet, to cheque stubs, form-filling, application letters, tax returns—the whole domain of 'Écritures ordinaires' which, in the wake of Perec, has recently come to be studied by practitioners of 'anthropology at home'.[67] Secondly,

---

[66] T. W. Adorno, 'The Essay as Form' (1958), trans. B. Hullot-Kentor and F. Will, *New German Critique*, 32 (Spring-Summer 1984), 151–71. References incorporated in the text.

[67] See Daniel Fabre (ed.), *Écritures ordinaires* (Paris: POL, 1993).

evoking the inventoried space of the maritime chart, and the illustrated encyclopedia, Perec brilliantly conjures up a page from the *Petit Larousse* where sixty-five geographical terms—*désert, oued, torrent, isthme, archipel, golfe, cratère*, etc.—are captured in one illustrated view of an impossible landscape. A fantasy image, but one that, as Perec observes, answers a profound need for reassurance in the face of the spatial unknown. The generic space of the encyclopedia is soon filled, imaginatively, by a generic cast of characters and actions: a goods train with its puffing locomotive, neat barges loaded with glistening gravel, the postman panting as he goes up the hill. 'Image d'Epinal. Espace rassurant' (23) notes Perec, giving voice, as he will in *La Vie mode d'emploi*, to a strong need to posit, as a bulwark against the ever-present threat of barbarism, a space that is lovingly detailed, individualized, and specific, yet at the same time—because so idealized and generic—unreal. One could say that Perec's way of drawing out these two strands, in numbered sections of his chapter (a recurrent device in the text) is systematic, and thus redolent of the analytical survey rather than the essay. But what makes it essayistic is the way that, just as Paul Klee talked of taking a line for a walk, Perec traces out the ramifications of an idea, in quite different directions, feigning exhaustiveness through his trademark use of long enumerations, and then denying it, with a nonchalant 'et cetera' and an abrupt shift to another facet of an emerging pattern.

Fragmentation is one of the tendencies Adorno perceives in the essay form, which he sees as being radical in its indifference to roots, and its enthusiasm for branches, 'accentuating the fragmentary, the partial rather than the total' (157). Adorno defines the essay as 'the speculative investigation of specific, culturally predetermined objects' and he characterizes the intellectual, and ludic, freedom it deploys as a 'childlike freedom that catches fire, without scruple, on what others have already done' (152). Rather than segregating the technician from the dreamer, and submitting understanding to narrow criteria, the essay risks overinterpretation as it revels in the 'abundance of significations encapsulated within each spiritual phenomenon' (153). But if this gives the essay aesthetic autonomy, it also endows it with its own conceptual character. By refusing to bracket out the 'spontaneity of subjective fantasy' in the name of neutrality, the essay resists 'departmental specialization' and so releases 'the object's expression in the unity of its elements' (153) (just as Perec looks at the multiple facets of lived space). The essay recognizes a qualitative difference between different modes of thought, acknowledging that there are 'little acts of knowledge [. . .] that [. . .] cannot be caught in the net of science' (156).

Adorno insists that the essay, sceptical and unsystematic as it is, has its own epistemology, that it manifests a process of thought, but one that is performed through the formal characteristics of the genre. Lukács had noted that 'the essay is a court, but (unlike in the legal system) it is not the verdict that is important, that sets standards and creates precedents, but the process of examining and judging'.[68] Adorno underlines the essay's experimental bent, often enacted through a ludic, quasi-scientific approach (very clear in *Espèces d'espaces* as in many other writings by Perec). The affinities between Adorno's vision of the essay (itself a highly 'essayistic' construct), and Perec's practice are both related to the matter of the everyday, and our blindness to it which stems from narrowly based modes of thought. The essay's 'desire and pursuit of the whole' echoes the way all thinking about the *quotidien* involves a sense of a whole—not an abstract totality, but a lived manifold of interconnections.

A key aspect here is historicity. For Adorno, the essay refuses 'airtight' concepts and embraces the changing and the ephemeral. The mode of relation to experience (and to aspects of thought) enacted in the essay is rooted in historicity, in becoming (what Perec in *Penser/Classer* calls 'émergence').[69] The way Perec dwells on the multichannelled character of his own engagement with space—for example, when he attempts to recall details of all the bedrooms he had slept in, while at the same time citing and speculating on other people's experience—acknowledges the mediated nature of lived experience. For Adorno the essay acknowledges the 'historically produced': it 'makes reparation' for the abstraction that boils off the accretion of human and historic meanings. The way of the essay is not to seek 'derivations' but to delve into the 'sedimentation', the layers that accrue to phenomena in their intercourse with living subjects.[70] The essay's logic is associative; it refuses to define or fetishize concepts, although it does not reject them out of hand so much as process them as they 'come up', recognizing that the discourses that surround objects are part and parcel of them. In a key passage on the kind of thinking the essayist does, Adorno points to the ways in which 'the reciprocal interaction of [. . .] concepts in the process of intellectual experience' achieves an interweaving and a density of texture that apprehends an open interconnectedness, a wholeness of experience. 'Actually', he observes, 'the thinker does not think, but rather transforms himself into an arena of intellectual experi-

---

[68] Lukács *Soul and Form*, 16.

[69] Perec, *Penser/Classer*, 23.

[70] Certeau underlines the sedimented character of the *quotidien* in *L'Invention du quotidien*, I, 293–5.

ence, without simplifying it'. Proceeding 'methodically unmethodically', the essay 'becomes true in its progress, which drives it beyond itself, and not in a hoarding obsession with fundamentals'(161).

If the essay accepts discontinuity, it is because 'differentiation is its medium'. Recognizing the impossibility of exhaustive knowledge, the essay's experimental complexion revels in small variations. But foregoing abstract totality allows the essay to illuminate another kind of whole, a complexity of relations, a constellation. Foreshadowing Perec's reference to 'fissures' on the back cover of *Espèces d'espaces*, Adorno writes that the essay 'thinks in fragments just as reality is fragmented and gains its unity only *by moving through the fissures* rather than by smoothing them over' (164, emphasis added). Important here—and this parallels a deep-seated tendency in approaches to the *quotidien*—is the small-scale ('little acts of knowledge'), the detail ('the claim of the particular to truth'), and the concrete, experimental stance of the essay. Adorno cites an earlier contribution to the aesthetics of the essay by Max Bense who wrote:

He writes essayistically who writes while experimenting, who turns his object this way and that, who questions it, feels it, tests it, thoroughly reflects on it, attacks it from different angles, and in his mind's eye collects what he has seen, and puts into words what the object allows to be seen under the conditions established in the course of writing (164).

The probing and testing described here, so characteristic of Perec, are allied to a strategy of immersion in cultural phenomena that does not aim at the definitive and the primal, but at exploring the *mediated*, the interaction of the natural and the cultural. And for Adorno, as for Perec, this tactic of mobility is related to a positive attitude to rhetoric, to a kind of discourse, rich in nuance and variation, which is shunned by scientific rationality. In the essay, rhetoric is linked to freedom insofar as it preserves a certain distance, often humorous and ironic, from the object under investigation. Even if, as Perec's writing shows clearly, there is a risk of appearing flippant, whimsical, or self-indulgent, of perpetuating mere 'jeux d'esprit', the endorsement of rhetoric, of rhetorical performance, serves essayistic truth by virtue of a 'freedom *vis-à-vis* the object, freedom that gives the object more of itself than if it were mercilessly incorporated into the order of ideas' (168). At this point Adorno gives a further clue as to how Perec exemplifies the links between the essay and the everyday, when he connects the essay's freedom with happiness, with criteria of well-being and imagined futurity. The essay, he says, rejects 'the hostility to happiness of official thought' (168) which 'seals it off against anything new as well as against curiosity, the pleasure principle of thought' (169). And this is consistent with the musicality of the essay, the way its transitions 'disavow rigid deduction in the interest of establishing internal cross-connections' in a manner that 'verges on the logic of music'. In its constantly self-reflective and self-relativizing progress the essay co-ordinates rather than deduces, and in so doing makes manifest 'that which is blind in its objects'. This chimes with Perec's emphasis on the *cécité* (blindness) that makes the everyday the unseen, endowing it with that opacity that Adorno sees the essay as wishing to 'blow open': the essay, he says, wants to 'polarize the opaque', to unbind powers that are latent within it. And Adorno's essay ends by stressing a transgressive power of negativity at work in the essay that makes it heretical. 'The law of the innermost form of the essay', he concludes, 'is heresy. By transgressing the orthodoxy of thought, something becomes visible in the object which it is orthodoxy's secret purpose to keep invisible' (171).

The connections I have been unearthing in Adorno, between experimentation, variation, rhetoric, difference, happiness, music, and heresy can be illustrated by key features of Perec's approach to space in *Espèces d'espaces*. One obvious example is the use he makes of counterfactual speculation, as a way of opening up the object of his enquiry, exposing the hidden assumptions that disguise it from us. Take for instance the chapter on 'L'appartement'. If this follows on, rationally enough, from 'La chambre', Perec characteristically plays down the logic and fluidity of the transition. Having ended the previous chapter quite arbitrarily, he comes into the topic of the 'appartement' slant-wise, by immediately plunging into the different ways we inhabit our living spaces, recollecting first an old neighbour who never went beyond the landing, where she would occasionally stop people to ask what day it was, or if they would fetch her a slice of ham. He then tells of a friend who had come up with the idea of living for a whole month in a big airport, taking advantage of the way such institutions furnish all our needs. Changing tack again, he offers a series of definitions of the varieties of room, quickly pinpointing the narrow functionalism that determines the conventional distribution of space in an apartment. As a result of the stereotyped lifestyles imagined by designers and architects, we tend to define and inhabit rooms purely according to their function, and the regulated timetable these presuppose: living room, bedroom, utility room, spare room, children's room, etc. Drawing up the 'emploi du temps modèle' (model timetable) implied by the standard design for living, Perec rapidly identifies the ways we submit to the regimentation of imposed lifestyles. To explore further what is at stake here, he adapts one of his favourite devices, ever the stock-in-trade of the essayist, the strategy of 'what if'. What if we stick with functionalism, but imagine a living space divided up according to different priorities?[71] Those of the senses, for example: one room would be a *gustatorium* another an *auditoir*, both easily imagined, but there would also be a *visoir* (presumably the TV room nowadays), an *humoir*, and a *palpoir*. Or, more transgressively, what if the distribution of rooms were based not on circadian rhythms, day and night, but heptadian ones, so that we would have a room for each day of the week—a *lundoir*, a *mardoir*, a *mercredoir*, and so forth. This could be combined with the sort of thematic approach favoured in old-style brothels: the *lundoir* could be like a boat; the *mardoir*, an explorers' base—no heating, thick furs for bedding, tins of corned beef for sustenance; the *mercredoir*, for the children's benefit, would have sugarloaf walls and plasticine furniture.

Through counterfactual speculation, the invention of variations and permutations, comic and rhetorical in tenor, Perec's writing—deploying the power of the essay, on Adorno's model—unsettles systematic thought and scientific data—in this case the priorities of functionalism—exposing the cultural beneath the falsely natural; infiltrating difference into tyrannical similitude. The appeal is not to some lost, original purity or unity, but rather to the variety of human needs and wishes. Historicity, abolished by the functional, is restored: Perec reminds us, for example, that an eighteenth-century *hôtel particulier*, or a fin-de-siècle *appartement bourgeois*, had very different, and often very subtle, distributions of rooms, based on 'variations minimes' (minute variations). In the Perequian 'what if', thought manifests its freedom, not by creation *ex nihilo*, but by addressing a predetermined object (in this case living space), taking it apart, and putting it back together again in new ways that not only remind us of, or awaken us to, the world we actually live in, but remind us also of the needs and desires through which we relate to that world. Simply and indirectly, Perec's ways of attending to the everyday, imbued with the essayistic tradition, draw attention to ends as well as means, to questions of ethics, happiness, and the art of living.

Another key device is that of *travaux pratiques*, exercises where Perec invites the reader to pursue the experimental spirit of his speculations. In the chapter on the street Perec outlines his tactics of observation, designed to overcome the

---

[71] Ariès, 'Pour une histoire de la vie privée', had noted that giving rooms specific functions was a sign of the emergence of attention to the everyday.

blindness that makes our own environment invisible to us. Here verbs of action in the infinitive incite him, and then us, to:

Observer la rue, de temps en temps, peut-être avec un souci un peu systématique.
S'appliquer. Prendre son temps. Noter ce que l'on voit. Ce qui se passe de notable.
Sait-on voir ce qui est notable? [. . .]
Essayer de décrire la rue, de quoi c'est fait, à quoi ça sert [. . .]
Se forcer à épuiser le sujet.
S'obliger à voir plus platement.
Déceler un rythme (70–1).

(Observe the street, from time to time, perhaps in a slightly systematic fashion. Apply yourself. Take your time. Note down what you see. The noteworthy things going on. Do we know how to see what is noteworthy? . . . Try to describe the street, what it's made of, what it's for . . . Try to exhaust the topic. Force yourself to see in a more basic way. Identify a rhythm)

Moving on to 'La ville', Perec notes that if we are to answer the really important questions raised by city-dwelling, we need to speak, and think, 'simplement, évidemment, familièrement. Cesser de penser en termes tout préparés, oublier ce qu'ont dit les urbanistes et les sociologues' (simply, evidently, familiarly. Stop thinking in ready-made terms; forget what the urbanists and sociologists have said) (85). This aspect of Perec's writing articulates the essay's limited, small-scale systematicity, its probing, testing, experimental bent, its orientation toward performance.

Perec's apparent obsession with minute particulars, epitomized by his lists and enumerations, expresses his concern for the everyday and the ordinary, yet does not represent indifference to the big picture. Again in accordance with the impulse of the essay, the particular is seen as a necessary route to the general, a route towards recognition of a totality of relationships, a 'tout' rather than an abstract blueprint. This is borne out by the overall drift of *Espèces d'espaces* which, by a logic of expansion, leads Perec to the fundamental notion, and the word, *espace* itself. Suddenly he confronts the reader with a section titled 'L'inhabitable' (the uninhabitable), in two parts. Firstly, we are given an enumeration, punctuated initially by the anaphoric repetition of the word *espace*, listing things that disfigure and dehumanize space, ecologically, polit-ically, and socially: barbed wire, polluted seas, soulless tower blocks, shanty towns, grey anonymous spaces, cosy private gardens. Secondly, a Nazi docu-ment, quoted from David Rousset, consisting of a memo from an estates officer at Auschwitz, putting in an order for plants to surround the gas chambers with a 'bande de verdure' (herbaceous border). These accounts of the uninhabitable serve to remind us how much is at stake in the question of space, and why we should not leave it to the planners. We all have a stock of images and clichés of idyllic spaces: the 'pays natal' (native land), the 'berceau de ma famille' (bosom of my family), 'le grenier de mon enfance' (childhood attic). But such places do not really exist:

c'est parce qu'ils n'existent pas que l'espace devient question, cesse d'être évidence, cesse d'être incorporé, c'est-à-dire approprié. L'espace est un doute: il me faut sans cesse le marquer, le désigner; il n'est jamais à moi, il ne m'est jamais donné, il faut que j'en fasse la conquête (122)

(it's because they don't exist that space becomes a question, stops being something self-evident, stops being incorporated, in other words appropriated. Space is a doubt: I have endlessly to mark it out, to designate it; it's never mine, I have to conquer it)

The role of writing, of inscription as an always provisional gesture of appropriation, is to counter the fragility of our everyday space.

The common ground with the essay could be further explored in other essays that go to the heart of the everyday such as Baudelaire's 'Le Peintre de la vie moderne', Aragon's *Le Paysan de Paris*, Godard's film-essay *2 ou 3 choses que je sais d'elle*, Roland Barthes's *L'Empire des signes*, Phillipe Jaccottet's *Paysages avec figures absentes*, or indeed Certeau's *L'Invention du quotidien*. Two other areas of convergence can be mentioned in conclusion. Noting its affinity with walking, Graham Good talks of the essay as tending to consist in 'a foray into an open world where almost anything can be encountered'.[72] Walking plays a key role in explorations of the *quotidien*, not just as a handy way of being out and about within it but because many of the attributes of walking match the everyday itself—an activity at ground level geared to the aptitudes of the body, a practice involving rhythm, repetition, non-accumulation, an activity that is concrete, open-ended, private as well as social, limited to the here and now but capable of embracing distant horizons.[73] Accordingly, walking will feature in our later discussion of the Surrealists, of Certeau's famous account of the rhetoric of walking, and of the writings of Jacques Réda, a walker whose prose texts, in *Le Sens de la marche* or *La Liberté des rues*, not only record fascinating incursions into the everyday but display all the features of evolved forms of the essay in France today. Finally, as *Espèces d'espaces* has illustrated, and as we shall

[72] Good, *The Observing Self*, xii.
[73] Cf. Rebecca Solnit, *Wanderlust: A History of Walking* (London: Verso, 2001).

see further in our discussions of Barthes's *L'Empire des signes* or Peter Handke's *Essai sur la journée réussie*, both the essay, in its self-relativizing, freewheeling, multiplicity, and the everyday, as the *tout-ensemble* that is always the same yet ever-changing, connect with *art de vivre*, with the question of how we should live. And in both cases indeterminacy is the key to creative freedom.

2

Surrealism and the Everyday

FROM BAUDELAIRE TO DADA

Surrealism can claim a central place in any discussion of approaches to the everyday. Firstly, because through all its switches of emphasis, and even in its dissident forms, the movement always maintained a commitment to the transformation of daily life, in line with Rimbaud's dictum: 'changer la vie'. Secondly, because in its obsession with precursors, Surrealism retrospectively created a lineage, encompassing German Romanticism, Baudelaire, Rimbaud, Mallarmé, Apollinaire, and Reverdy, in which we can now identify key elements in the valorization and exploration of the *quotidien*. Thirdly, because in absorbing and transforming this lineage Surrealism bequeathed ways of construing, uncovering, and acting on the everyday that have retained their inspirational power until now.

In fact, the surrealist imprint is perceptible in many recent approaches to the everyday that have no immediate connection with Surrealism. As we shall see in Chapter 3, Breton's ideas evolved in the 1930s both in parallel and through interaction with the dissident or anti-Surrealist approaches of such writers as Georges Bataille, Michel Leiris, Raymond Queneau, and Walter Benjamin. Some late-twentieth-century approaches to the *quotidien* are connected to Surrealism via these intermediaries. As Chapter 4 will show, a discussion of Surrealism is the starting point for Henri Lefebvre's 1947 *Critique de la vie quotidienne*, and in the 1950s the Situationists absorbed surrealist practices into their approach to lived experience. In the lead-up to May 1968 and its aftermath, the debates between the 'Situs' and Lefebvre, centred on the fate of the city and the transformation of everyday life, had a direct impact on Barthes, Certeau, and Perec. In the 1980s and 1990s, a generation of 'cultural studies' theorists, new geographers, architects, photographers, and enthusiasts for the city rediscovered the surrealist contribution to the invention and exploration of everyday life through their reading of Lefebvre, Certeau, the Situationists, and Barthes.[1]

Since the 1960s, the masters of surrealist art have attained star status, while advertising, Monty Python, and pop culture have made watered-down Surrealism part of the everyday environment. Yet the desire to bring about a 'revolution of everyday life', by restoring the forces of imagination and desire that had been smothered by rationalism, is often missing here. By contrast, the Surrealism that feeds into thinking about the everyday maintains a vital connection to the central energies of the movement that were deployed in such collective enterprises as the great surrealist reviews, such as *La Révolution surréaliste* and *Minoataure*, where columns were dedicated to such topics as death, encounters, sex, objects, clairvoyance, nursery rhymes, and so on; and in such key texts as Breton's essays and manifestos which articulate a surrealist vision of human possibility rooted in the liberation of desire. This is the Surrealism of chance encounters, mysterious and melancholy streets, of signs and messages; profoundly experiential, it tends towards a 'pure pratique d'existence' (pure existential practice) as Maurice Blanchot put it in the essay he wrote after André Breton's death in 1966.[2] At the same moment, Michel Foucault hailed Breton for having evolved a way of thinking that transgressed the borders between the human sciences—ethnography, linguistics, psychoanalysis, myth, religion, and aesthetics—seeing the human being first and foremost as a subject of experience whose identity is engendered through constant interaction with words, events and representations. Referring to Breton as 'notre Goethe', Foucault credited the surrealist leader with 'la découverte du domaine de l'expérience'.[3]

Surrealism claimed to be a movement that encompassed the totality of 'l'esprit moderne' and its dynamics of influence involved creative appropriation. In some cases, Sade and Lautréamont for example, or Rimbaud, the emphasis was on the assertion of individual freedom against social and literary convention. In the 1924 *Manifeste du surréalisme* Rimbaud is held to have been 'surréaliste dans la pratique de la vie et ailleurs' (surrealist in the practice of life and elsewhere). In other instances the Surrealists seized on artists, including Mallarmé, Huysmans, Apollinaire, Reverdy, and behind them all

---

[1] See, for example, the work of Edward Soja, David Harvey, Fredric Jameson, Peter Wollen.

[2] Maurice Blanchot, 'Le Demain joueur', in id., *L'Entretien infini* (Paris: Gallimard, 1989), 597–619; 597.

[3] 'C'était un nageur entre deux mots', Michel Foucault, *Dits et écrits*, I (Paris: Gallimard Quarto, 2001), 557

Baudelaire, who anticipated the surrealist sensibility in various ways. Baudelaire's notion of 'modernité' is haunted by the desire to grasp the present, which is seen as the point of access to the continuum of experience where past, present, and future flow and commingle. Baudelaire urged the artist to recognize 'le coté épique de la vie moderne' (the epic side of modern life) in which the eternal and the transitory are fused. Anticipating later responses to the everyday he observes that 'Le merveilleux nous enveloppe et nous abreuve comme l'atmosphère; mais nous ne le voyons pas' (the marvellous envelops and sustains us like the atmosphere; but we do not see it).[4] For Baudelaire the city was the quintessential forum of modernity and, as such, the theatre of modern identity. In the 'Lettre–préface' to Arsène Houssaye accompanying a batch of his prose poems, Baudelaire recorded his ambition to find a style of writing 'assez souple et assez heurté pour s'adapter aux mouvements lyriques de l'âme, aux ondulations de la rêverie, aux soubresauts de la conscience' (supple yet striking enough to adapt itself to the lyric movements of the soul, the undulations of reverie, the somersaults of conscience) (292), switches of mood, attention, focus and feeling that mark the everyday experience of those who frequent '[les] villes énormes' and expose themselves to the 'croisement de leurs innombrables rapports'. In 'Le Cygne' (as in other 'Tableaux parisiens' such as 'À une passante', or 'Les Petites Vieilles') the 'fourmillante cité' is a place of constant circulation, brimming with an endless flow of experiences. By providing an infinite supply of objects of attention—particularly for the pedestrian whose itinerary is not predetermined by haste or narrow fixity of purpose—the city offers the opportunity for constant transactions between outer and inner: moments of revulsion, compulsion, desire, and recognition. 'Le Cygne' begins with a moment of disarray when the poet, passing through an area reconstructed under the auspices of Baron Haussmann, finds it all but unrecognizable save for a feature of the scene that suddenly prompts recollection of what the area had looked like before. The role of poetic form is to create a space of interaction and reverberation such that the present is never lost from sight. For in 'Le Cygne' memory does not take us back to a then; it is enfolded or recessed within a now—a present given density by the revelation of the past it incorporates yet conceals (81–3).

Memory is a central theme in Baudelaire's 'Le Peintre de la vie moderne' which, in making Constantin Guys the paradigm of an artist sensitive to

---

[4] Charles Baudelaire, *Œuvres complètes* (Paris: Gallimard, 1961), 952. References to Bandelaire are incorporated in the text.

'modernité'—'le transitoire, le fugitif, le contingent' (1163)—and to 'le fantastique réel de la vie' (1166), focuses at length on the creative process. Crucial to Baudelaire's account of Guys's art is the fact that although his aim is to capture the present he works from memory. Initially, Guys's technique is to plunge into the teeming diversity of the crowd:

La foule est son domaine, comme l'air est celui de l'oiseau, comme l'eau celui du poisson. Sa passion et sa profession c'est d'*épouser la foule*. Pour le parfait flâneur, pour l'observateur passionné, c'est une immense jouissance que d'élire domicile dans le nombre, dans l'ondoyant, dans le mouvement, dans le fugitif et l'infini' (1160).

(The crowd is his domain, like air for birds, and water for fishes. His passion and profession are to *become wedded with the crowd*. For the perfect flâneur, the impassioned observer, it is an immense delight to make his home in the multiple, the undulating, in movement, in the fleeting and the infinite)

Shedding his customary identity, and making himself anonymous (Baudelaire refers to his 'incognito'), the artist makes the crowd his family, becoming a 'kaléiodoscope doué de conscience', or a machine capable of being charged up by the city's 'immense réservoir d'électricité'. But it is when, at nightfall, he returns to his garret that the artist sets to work. With feverish rapidity he seeks to capture 'l'image écrite dans son cerveau', impressions automatically registered by his perceptual apparatus, as if on a photographic plate, that now need to be externalized on paper. At one point Baudelaire notes that Guys fears losing what he calls 'la mémoire du présent'—the present made accessible through its provisional and fragile assimilation into short-term memory, by virtue of sensory receptivity (Baudelaire talks of 'l'estampille [de] la sensation') (1165). If Guys is the paradigm of the modern artist it is not simply because he took the present—fashions, social life, military parades—as his subject matter, but because his method reveals the extent to which art itself—in its relationship to subjectivity—had to do with the present. The 'merveilleux qui nous abreuve mais que nous ne voyons pas', and the 'fantastique réel de la vie' that haunted Guys, are ancestors of the 'merveilleux quotidien' (Aragon) or 'magie quotidienne' (Breton) that the Surrealists will prospect.

   The period between the publication of Baudelaire's *Le Spleen de Paris* in 1869 and Breton's *Manifeste du surréalisme* in 1924 saw an increasing synergy between experiments in poetic prose writing and the project of rendering the everyday experience of modern urban life. In February 1869 the Goncourt brothers claimed in their diary that modern experience might most authentically be reproduced through 'un poème en prose de sensations' (a prose poetry of sensations)[5] and in the 'écriture artiste' of their journal writing and novels of urban working-class life, they attempted to find a style capable of rendering the everyday present. In similar fashion, J.-K. Huysmans, in his *Croquis parisiens* and in such novels as *À vau l'eau*, wrote about drab places and banal activities—such as trying to find a tolerable restaurant—in ways that we can now see as forays into the realm of the *quotidien*. Indeed, André Breton greatly appreciated this aspect of Huysmans and other naturalist writers, commenting enthusiastically on the way they would often make insignificant details predominate over larger concerns.[6] In addition, the vogue for the inventory and the catalogue in fiction reflected the rise of consumerism in the second half of the nineteenth century, as new technologies made a wide range of material goods available to a public anxious to achieve social distinction through interior decor.[7] The recourse to enumeration, at the expense of plot and character, in Flaubert's *Bouvard et Pécuchet* and Huysmans's *À Rebours*, reflects a fascination with the profusion of objects in modern life, and the new logics of circulation, exchange, and reproduction that these engendered.

Recent re-evaluations of these aspects of late-nineteenth-century fiction stem directly from the critical perspectives generated by the upsurge of interest in the notion of the everyday, and particularly consumer culture, in the 1980s and 1990s, deriving from the work of Barthes, Certeau, Baudrillard, Bourdieu, and Perec. The poet Stéphane Mallarmé has also been reappraised in this light. Renewed attention to his prose writings, particularly the strange fashion journal, *La Dernière Mode*, he edited single-handed, has refocused attention on how Mallarmé's writing, which often features everyday objects and gestures, is concerned not only with escaping from the real world, but also with finding ways of capturing what he calls 'la vie, immédiate, chère et multiple, la nôtre avec ses riens sérieux' (life, immediate, clear and multiple, our own with its serious nothings).[8] As Georg Simmel remarked, fashion sharpens our awareness of the present,[9] and Mallarmé's magazine, *La Dernière Mode*, from which the above quotation is taken, and which, as we shall see in Chapter 5, has a significant place in Barthes's later analyses of fashion, is intensely

---

[5] Edmond and Jules Goncourt, *Journal* (1851–96; Paris: Laffont, 2004).

[6] See André Breton, *Œuvres complètes*, II (Paris: Gallimard Pléiade, 1992) 159.

[7] See Janell Watson, *Literature and Material Culture from Balzac to Proust: The Collection and Consumption of Curiosities* (Cambridge: Cambridge University Press, 2000).

[8] Stéphane Mallarmé, *Œuvres complètes* (Paris: Gallimard Pléiade, 1945), 718. See R. Pearson, *Mallarmé and Circumstance: The Translation of Silence* (Oxford: Oxford University Press, 2004).

[9] See G. Simmel, 'La Mode' (1895) in *La Tragédie de la culture*, 103.

concerned with the ephemeral aspects of reality that Baudelaire, another fashion enthusiast, had commended Constantin Guys for capturing in his sketches.

In a famous review of *Alcools* in 1913 Georges Duhamel complained that Guillaume Apollinaire's collection resembled a 'boutique de brocanteur' because it was full of stray objects and recycled styles, juxtaposed without any obvious connection.[10] In retrospect this can be seen as a tribute to the way Apollinaire's route out of symbolism towards an engagement with the modern world involved an art of quotation, parataxis, and blurred identities. An illegitimate alien who longed to be thought as French as his beloved Eiffel Tower, Apollinaire wrote short lyrics and long free-verse poems marked by fragmentation and juxtaposition, enacting his desire to embrace modernity in all its aspects but also to find security in the past as much as the future. His art became increasingly concerned with neutralizing the contradictory pressures of past and future by focusing on the present, the flow of immediate perceptual experience.[11] In Apollinaire, as later for the Surrealists, the zone of present experience, a space that plays host to past and future versions of self, is quintessentially the city street. One of the obsessive concerns of Apollinaire's art criticism, as well as his verbo-visual 'calligrammes', was to render the multichannelled simultaneity of modern experience. In some respects—for example, his obsession with memory, time, and personal identity, and his belief in art's capacity to transmute experience—Apollinaire remained closer to mainstream European modernism than to Surrealism. But the Surrealists cherished Apollinaire for his restless versatility: as the self-styled 'Flâneur des deux rives' who collected the flotsam and jetsam of daily street experience for his review column 'La Vie anecdotique'—visiting a series of municipal depots, including the Hôtel des Haricots at Auteuil, where rows of disused streetlights resembled a primeval forest, or reporting his encounter with an Albanian domiciled in the London suburb of Chingford;[12] as the poet of 'poèmes-conversations', such as 'Lundi Rue Christine',[13] made up of snippets of conversation apparently overheard in a café; as the celebrant of perfume labels, street signs, or locomotives, who sang the praises of a 'jeune rue industrielle'

---

[10] Georges Duhamel, 'Guillaume Apollinaire: *Alcools*', *Mercure de France*, 16 June 1913.

[11] On this see Timothy Mathews, *Reading Apollinaire* (Manchester: Manchester University Press, 1987).

[12] See Guillaume Apollinaire, *Œuvres en prose complètes*, III (Paris: Gallimard Pléiade, 1993) 53–304.

[13] See Id., *Œuvres poétiques* (Paris: Gallimard Pléiade, 1959), 180–2.

with its 'sténo-dactylos', and who once declared: 'les miracles lyriques sont quotidiens';[14] as the writer who through his use of the phrase 'il y a', followed by the presentation of a simple datum, showed how the bare enumeration of the given can go to the heart of our engagement with everyday experience.[15]

By the time Apollinaire died in 1918, Breton, Aragon, and Soupault, the nucleus of the Surrealist group in the early 1920s, had shifted their allegiance to Dadaism. Less naïve than Apollinaire about the powers of art and the wonders of technology, the Dadaists also went much further in abolishing the frontier between art and life. Indifferent to its products, Dada identified art— or anti-art—with acts or gestures, designed to intervene directly in lived experience, whether in the form of performance, as in the Cabaret Voltaire, or the 'ready-made', such as Marcel Duchamp's urinal, spade, and bicycle wheel, or Kurt Schwitters's assemblages which, unlike the collages of the Cubists, were made entirely of recycled detritus. Dada also undertook a radical questioning of language and meaning, comparable to some degree with the work of Ludwig Wittgenstein on 'ordinary language' in the same period (against the same background of World War I). For Breton, whose discovery of Valéry and Rimbaud had in different ways revealed the ability of language to alter the perception of reality, the *tabula rasa* of Dada was primarily a revelation of the power of words, the discovery that meaning could survive the most thoroughgoing assault on language's sense-making capacities.

Years later, Breton remarked that Surrealism had originated in a wide-scale operation on language.[16] But he insisted that the repercussions of the surrealist exploration of the verbal were on the tenor of life itself. In its Parisian version, to which Breton and his friends contributed massively, Dada also involved active intervention in everyday life, as in the 'Visite à Saint-Julien-le-Pauvre', where the public were invited to join the Dadaists at a Paris church at a specific time.[17] Rather than simply anti-bourgeois mystification, this event involved, through its very gratuitousness, the adoption of an experimental, interrogative attitude towards the nature of events themselves.

The visit to Saint-Julien-le-Pauvre connects with 'L'Esprit nouveau', a brief text written by Breton, but originally published anonymously, in 1923.[18] In the flat style of a legal document, 'L'Esprit nouveau' reports on a banal event:

---

14 Ibid., 39.
15 Ibid., 317–76.
16 André Breton, *Manifestes du surréalisme* (Paris: Pauvert, 1972), 311.
17 See M. Sanouillet, *Dada à Paris* (Paris: Pauvert, 1965), 244–5.
18 Breton, *Œuvres Complètes* I, 257–8.

arriving separately at a café in the space of a few minutes, Breton, Aragon, and Derain each report on having been captivated by the behaviour of a young woman in the streets around Saint-Germain des Près: they had each set out to find her but had drawn a blank. As in Edgar Allan Poe's story 'The Man of the Crowd', which had fascinated Baudelaire, the ubiquitous yet evanescent young woman is seen—in a manner that foreshadows *Nadja*—as an eman-ation or gift of the city streets themselves.

'L'Esprit nouveau' and the visit to Saint-Julien-le-Pauvre involve a reorien-tation of Dada negativity, a desire to uncover what subsists when conventional meaning and purpose are stripped away. This attitude was further encouraged when the Surrealists appropriated Freud's techniques, linking the unconscious to the basic level of signification uncovered by Dada, a virgin forest in which the purity of human desire, and hence human possibility, awaited deliverance from the accretions of bourgeois ideology and narrow rationalism. Initially a method designed for provoking the eruption of the unconscious into run-of-the-mill existence, Surrealism can look like pure surrender to the world of dream. But its consistently inquisitive and experimental attitude—encapsu-lated by the opening in 1925 of a 'Bureau de recherches surréalistes'—always sought to break down the barriers between waking life and dream life, the ordinary and the extraordinary. Surrealism involved tapping into the unreal-ized possibilities harboured by the ordinary life we lead rather than rejecting it for another life. As Ferdinand Alquié put it, the Surrealists did not want to lose their reason, they wanted what reason made them lose.[19] This was the basis on which a movement that rejected all fixed canons of taste, logic, and represen-tation, and instead championed hysteria, dreams, the irrational, chance, 'amour fou', 'humour noir', revolution, and convulsive beauty, was (and still is) a vital source of inspiration for thinking about everyday life. To understand this better we need to look at how Surrealism envisaged lived experience and to examine the uses and connotations of the word 'vie' in Breton's writings.

'PLUTÔT LA VIE': SURREALIST VITALISM

In 'Plutôt la vie', a poem from his early collection *Clair de terre* (1923), Breton opposes one set of qualities, redolent of 'la vie', to another set that seems to represent the 'ambience' of surrealist avant-gardism, epitomized in the world

---

[19] Ferdinand Alquié, *Philosophie du surréalisme* (Paris: Flammarion, 1955), 41.

summoned up through automatic writing—'cette mare aux murmures' (this marsh of murmurs), as the poem puts it.[20] Yet where one would expect the poem to endorse the perturbing world of automatism the poet in fact sings the praises of ordinary life, epitomized by 'une petite ville comme Pont-à-Mousson' (a little town like Pont-à-Mousson)—a place-name ubiquitous in daily life because it was—and still is—embossed on wrought-iron manhole covers. 'Plutôt la vie' is the insistent refrain. The bizarreries of surrealist imagery—bits of cloth that sing, squidgy stones, cars made of cold flame, necklaces that serve you at table—are rejected in favour of ordinary life with all its drawbacks. Whilst the poetic world is lurid and dramatic, the 'ordinary' world is inconsistent and frustrating, full of waiting rooms where your turn never comes. However, the poem seems to keep two divergent readings in play: seen ironically, it is a sardonic comment on stay-at-home complacency and playing safe for fear of the unknown; read literally, it is a paean to ordinary life, *malgré tout*. The overall effect is to present the surrealist quest as involving neither an out-and-out embrace of the *jamais vu*, nor a whimsical cosiness, but a dynamic process in which 'la vie de la présence rien que la présence' (the life of presence nothing but presence), however elusive, is always at stake.

Through its role in different contexts in Breton's writings the word *vie* posits a conception of lived experience that articulates the central thrust of Surrealism, encompassing the sphere of the everyday.[21] Never theorized as such, 'la vie' is a plural and unstable notion that embodies the positive aspirations of the surrealist project—the search for the 'vraie vie' that Rimbaud had declared missing. But 'la vie' is also the framework—that of ordinary day-to-day existence—within which a 'true' life can be located. 'La vraie vie' is to be found within 'la vie' not outside it. Neither literary nor political in the first instance, surrealist practice operates in the everyday—the street, the café, the hairdresser's; in speech, desire, and chance. For Surrealism, the possible is contained in the actual; what might be is always already present within what is. The problem is to find a way of grasping it, and this involves both deconditioning: getting round the barriers that have grown up to impede access to our own lives; and active prospecting: the invention of strategies that will propitiate the revelation of what is virtual yet inaccessible. Either way, the surrealist 'practice of existence' (Blanchot) addresses the concrete world of the here and

[20] Breton, *Œuvres Complètes* I, 176.
[21] See Michael Sheringham, ' "Plutôt la vie": Vitalism and the Theory and Practice of Subjectivity in Breton's Writings', in Ramona Fotiade (ed.), *André Breton: The Power of Language* (Exeter: Elm Park Books, 2000), 9–22.

now, the present. The crucial dimension of Surrealism is that of experience. But, as Foucault observed, when he credited Breton with 'la découverte du domaine de l'expérience' (the discovery of the domain of experience), this dimension falls outside the frame of any single kind of knowledge.[22] Hence, the fusion of art, philosophy, psychiatry, ethnology, science, and linguistics instituted by the Surrealists. From Surrealism onwards, creative thinking about everyday life involves a crossing of disciplinary boundaries.

Taking alienation as its starting point, the 1924 *Manifeste du surréalisme* opens with a sentence where the word 'vie' occurs three times. 'Tant va la croyance à la vie, à ce que la vie a de plus précaire, la vie *réelle* s'entend, qu'à la fin cette croyance se perd' (so it goes with our belief in life, in what is most fragile in life, *real* life I mean, that in the end this belief is lost).[23] Breton enumerates a range of factors: positivism, the cult of reason and utilitarianism, habit and routine, the shibboleths of maturity, self-improvement, and 'getting on in life', that conspire to alienate the individual from the possibilities held out by childhood creativity and imagination. Playing with the proverb 'Tant va la cruche à l'eau qu'à la fin elle se casse', Breton's opening sentence identifies a customary mechanism that is destructive of what life has to offer. The proverb means roughly that if you expose yourself to a danger too often you will end up succumbing to it. By analogy, Breton's version says that taking ordinary life for granted, allowing it to become no more than routine ends up being life-denying. Belief in 'la vie *réelle*', Breton specifies, often falls casualty to this tendency, with the result that the individual substitutes 'higher' beliefs—progress, self-improvement, religion—for those inherent in life itself. The Surrealist Manifesto does not begin, as one could have expected, by urging the reader to abandon 'la vie *réelle*' for the imaginary, but by warning us of the fragility of 'ce que la vie a de plus précaire', namely what is simply given. Moreover, it is 'la vie *réelle*'—not dreams, fantasy, or disembodied spirit—that is deemed to be the most precarious dimension of life, the one most easily sacrificed on the altar of ideology. The point is not to equate 'la vie' with a kind of bedrock or material base, but to emphasize that surrealist aspiration is directed towards what is latent but elusive within the everyday co-ordinates of existence rather than what lies outside them. The *Manifeste* begins with a statement about the loss of belief. If we do not believe in real life

---

[22] Foucault, *Dits et écrits*, I, 557.
[23] Breton, *Œuvres Complètes*, I, 311.

we may end up believing in all sorts of other, supposedly better, things. Or, as Michel de Certeau puts it, ending his *L'Invention du quotidien* on this very issue, we will be incapable of believing anything, only of taking things on other people's authority. Too often, 'la capacité de croire' (the ability to believe) falls victim to ideology, to 'la volonté de faire croire' (the wish to convince); as a result, says Certeau, 'le croire s'épuise' (believing expires).[24]

The question of believing in life as it comes recurs in Breton's preface to a new edition of the *Manifeste du Surréalisme* in 1929 where he recounts how, in the midst of despair, the sight of a stray phenomenon—the silky shininess of a polished floor—made him discover that he cherished life ('que je tenais à la vie'): 'j'ai compris que malgré tout la vie était *donnée*, qu'une force indépen-dante [...] présidait, en ce qui concerne un homme vivant, à des réactions d'un intérêt inappréciable dont le secret sera emporté avec lui' (I realized that life after all is *given*, that an independent force lay behind reactions which, for a living person, are extremely precious and whose secret will be taken to the grave).[25] Breton suggests that an individual's unpremeditated 'réactions' to certain phenomena reveal a hidden dimension of identity (a point he develops in *Nadja*). A moment of perception provokes a reaction that reveals a con-nection between life as something given (rather than earned), and individual subjectivity as something virtual rather than circumscribed. Insisting on the non-religious character of these experiences (the revelation involved here is not epiphanic) Breton places the emphasis on perception and representation. This is consistent with the fact that in the early essay on *Le Surréalisme et la peinture* (1926) surrealist visuality is seen in terms of techniques for liberating vision from its habitual enslavement. By presenting us with what are explicitly unreal visions, Ernst jolts the viewer into a renewed perception of the real world:

S'il arrive à Max Ernst, tel ou tel jour de nous faire souvenir plus gravement de *cette vie* et de nous émouvoir d'autant plus qu'il nous en fait souvenir, nous saurons du moins par quel admirable couloir nous y rentrons comme nous rentrerions dans une vie antérieure.[26]

(If, one of these days, with more gravity, Ernst reminds us of *this life*, touching us all the more since it is a reminder, we will at least know via what admirable channel we return as if to a former existence.)

---

[24] Certeau, *L'Invention du quotidien*, I, 260.
[25] Breton, *Œuvres Complètes*, I, 402.
[26] *Le Surréalisme et la peinture*, 30.

Ernst makes no attempt to copy ordinary reality, for that would be to remain in the framework of habitual perception. But in his works we do catch glimpses of *this life* and they are all the more vivid for returning to us via the unfamiliar corridor of the unreal. Beyond representation, we return to our own reality as if to an earlier incarnation; the motif of the 'vie antérieure', derived from Baudelaire, links this to felicity and desire.

Surrealism never parts company with a kind of realism. Breton make this point in an important declaration at the end of *Le Surréalisme et la peinture* as a prelude to a discussion of Hans Arp's woodcuts. In subverting the opposition between depth and surface, or animate and inanimate objects, Arp assaults customary representation, perpetrating the crime of 'lèse-réalité'. But in terms of Breton's vision this does not mean the real has been transcended:

Tout ce que j'aime, tout ce que je pense et ressens, m'incline à une philosophie particulière de l'immanence d'après laquelle la surréalité serait contenue dans la réalité même, et ne lui serait ni supérieure ni extérieure (46).

(Everything I admire, all my thoughts and feelings, incline me towards a philosophy of immanence according to which the surreal is contained in reality itself and is neither superior nor exterior to it.)

Breton holds out for immanence, insisting that the surreal is contained within the real. But then, in order to dispense with any sense of hierarchy, he suggests that the reverse is also true: the surreal contains the real. Adopting the image of 'communicating vessels', he suggests that rather than either one containing the other there is a fluid interplay between the two realms, which, he goes on to argue, can also be seen as those of 'la pensée' and 'la vie'. Breton rejects idealism: thought cannot cut loose from life; but, equally, life is not subordinate to the workings of the mind. Implicitly rejecting psychoanalytical determinism, Breton suggests that the logic here is not one of the manifest and the hidden—'Ce qu'on cache ne vaut ni plus ni moins que ce qu'on trouve' (what one keeps hidden is no more valuable than what one finds)—but of dynamic process. Existence, he seems to suggest, proceeds from the field of forces created by the interplay of two kinds of experience, mental and physical.

As in poetry, experimental practice in the visual domain reveals, and in so doing liberates, life. Rather than a circumscribed set of pathways, 'la vie' is revealed to be a dynamic field of experience, embracing and synthesizing mental and physical, inner and outer, higher and lower. Surrealist experimentation is not confined to aesthetic activity: it operates directly in the realm of lived experience. The everyday is seen as a field of practice and experiment, principally in the areas of love, street life, sense experience, and what Freud called the psychopathology of everyday life. What is so compelling about the surrealist *invention* of the everyday (to borrow Certeau's formulation) is that it cuts across the distinction between everyday and non-everyday. If surrealist narratives such as *Le Paysan de Paris* or *Nadja* seem to report on what is exceptional rather than humdrum in everyday experience, this does not involve a transcendence of the everyday but a revelation of its total field.

IN THE CITY STREETS: EXPERIENCE AND EXPERIMENT

Surrealism approaches everyday life through an experimental attitude bearing on the domain of experience. Breton often uses the word 'expérience', which also means experiment in French, and the term 'surréalisme' initially referred to experimental activity designed to manifest 'le fonctionnement réel de la pensée' (the true mechanisms of thought).[27] In the *Second Manifeste du surréalisme* in 1929 Breton identifies 'l'expérience surréaliste' with the exploration of mental processes (I, 782). In *Nadja* he argues that we need to explore the 'sensations électives'—the nuances of sensory reaction and spontaneous affinity—that make up the subjects's 'lumière propre', the singular, irreducible configuration of an individual subjectivity (I, 652). Elsewhere, Breton observes that subjective reality, our 'true' identity, is not hidden deep inside us so much as scattered around the perceptual world, where we can piece it together from our sensory reactions: 'la vérité particulière à chacun de nous est un jeu de patience dont il lui faut, entre tous les autres, saisir les éléments au vol' (the specific truth of each individual is a game of patience in which we have to grasp the constituents on the wing) (II, 304). Identity is fleeting and must be captured on the wing. Hence, far from seeking to transcend the real, Surrealism comprises 'une volonté d'approfondissement du réel, de prise de conscience toujours plus nette en même temps que toujours plus passionnée du monde sensible' (a desire to deepen the real, and to apprehend ever more clearly and more passionately the world of the senses) (II, 231). The formulation is striking, pointing as it does to the density of the real, and the need to

[27] Breton, *Œuvres Complètes*, I, 328. References to Breton, *Œuvres Complètes* (I–III) are incorporated in the text.

explore its recesses. But, again, Breton insists that this is not a move away from the ordinary world; the surrealist aim is to 'poursuivre toutes fenêtres ouvertes sur le dehors nos investigations propres, de s'assurer sans cesse que les résultats de ces investigations sont de nature à affronter le vent de la *rue*' (pursue our own investigations with all channels to the outside world fully open, making sure at every stage that the results of these investigations are on a par with the wind of the *street*). The street is Breton's true element—'la rue, que je croyais capable de livrer à ma vie ses surprenants detours, la rue avec ses inquiétudes et ses regards, était mon véritable élément: j'y prenais comme nulle part ailleurs le vent de l'éventuel' (the street, which I thought capable of transferring to my life its surprising detours, the street with its anxieties and glances: there, as nowhere else, I felt the wind of possibility) (I, 196). The city street is the true ground of the surrealist adventure.

Experiences in the city street are at the core of Breton's trilogy of prose works: *Nadja*, *Les Vases communicants*, and *L'Amour fou*. Recounting in *Nadja* a series of unsettling encounters and incidents, Breton observes 'J'en arrive à ma propre expérience, à ce qui est pour moi sur moi-même un sujet à peine intermittent de méditations et de rêveries' (I come to my own experience, a subject of almost endless meditations and reveries). By focusing on himself as a subject of experience Breton can make discoveries about his own unconditioned life ('ma vie—*telle que je puis la concevoir hors de son plan organique*' (my life—*that part of it that falls outside any overall plan*) I, 651). But these experiences are often themselves the fruit of a particular 'disponibilité' that is by no means easy or risk-free, partly because it involves putting on hold the usual goal-seeking vectors of purposeful activity. Reporting on a group expedition to the environs of Blois undertaken in 1924, Breton recalled that 'l'absence de tout but' (absence of all aim) rapidly cut the participants off from ordinary reality and encouraged the liberation of fantasy (III, 473). Surrealist experimentation, Breton observes, gives expression to a 'soif d'errer à la rencontre de tout' (appetite for encountering everything) (II, 697). A key parameter of the surrealist construction of the everyday is the sense of totality. Surrealism shares with Marxism a central preoccupation with 'l'homme total'.[28]

---

[28] Cf. Martin Jay, *Marxism and Totality: The Adventures of a Concept from Lukács to Habermas* (Oxford: Blackwell, 1984).

Although the revelation of individual identity is one of the frameworks for the surrealist quest in *Nadja* (which famously opens with the words 'Qui suis-je?'), identity is seen to be located in a wider field of forces and preoccupations. Blanchot once observed that Breton sought 'l'expérience de l'expérience': the experience of experience itself.[29] In other words something immanent to the 'domaine de l'expérience' (Foucault).[30] Breton's accounts of the methods of 'écriture automatique' stress the process or performance rather than the products. The same applies to surrealist 'spatial practices' (Certeau's term) where mental space, textual space, and urban space are conflated.[31] The kinds of experience Breton reports on in *Nadja* are the fruits of an attitude of openness (resembling the 'posture' of automatism) epitomized by that non-utilitarian wandering in urban space that the Situationists would later call *dérive*. Breton talks of his 'après-midis tout à fait désoeuvrés',[32] (utterly leisurely afternoons) and Blanchot will develop this notion of an 'absence d'oeuvre', a secession from purposefulness. What makes Nadja always 'inspirée et inspirante' (inspired and inspiring) is that '[elle] n'aimait qu'être dans la rue, pour elle seul champ d'expérience valable' (she only liked being in the street, for her the only valid field of experience) (I, 716); this dictated her 'manière de se diriger ne se fondant que sur la plus pure intuition et tenant sans cesse du prodige' (way of choosing her direction, based purely on intuition and endlessly prodigious) (I, 718), a disposition earlier ascribed to the young woman in 'L'Esprit nouveau'. Rather than sympathizing with people who accept the servitude of repetitive labour, we should encourage them to throw off their shackles and walk freely. Weaving together metaphors of the chain (emblem of the alienated everyday) and the footstep (emblem of the free everyday), Breton extols the 'merveilleuse suite de pas qu'il est possible à l'homme de faire désenchaîné' (marvellous succession of footsteps a man can make without his chains) (I, 687). If, he tells the reader, you may be sure to find me towards the end of most afternoons going back and forth on the same stretch of the Boulevard Bonne-Nouvelle between the premises of the *Matin* newspaper and the Boulevard de Strasbourg, he does not know why it is there his footsteps take him apart from the obscure feeling that 'c'est là que se passera *cela*(?)' (it is here that *it*(?) will happen) (I, 663). What counts is the feeling of being on the track of something, being orientated.

[29] Blanchot, *L'Entretien infini*, 618.   [30] Foucault, *Dits et écrits*, 557.
[31] Cf. Michael Sheringham, 'City Space, Mental Space, Poetic Space: Paris in Breton, Benjamin and Réda', in id. (ed.), *Parisian Fields* (London: Reaktion, 1996), 85–114.
[32] Breton, *Œuvres Complètes*, I, 683. Page references are incorporated in the text.

In *Nadja* the word 'vie' figures in a number of the work's most resonant and memorable declarations, encompassing a range of different contexts: individual self-identity, the pre-eminence of life over writing, the enigmatic character of certain life events, the opposition between immanence and transcendence, life as the pursuit of long-term goals versus life as it is given minute by minute:

L'événement dont chacun est en droit d'attendre la révélation du sens de sa propre vie (the event from which each of us is entitled to expect the revelation of the meaning of his own life) (I, 681).

La vie est autre que ce qu'on écrit (life is other than what is written) (I, 689).

Il se peut que la vie demande à être déchiffrée comme un cryptogramme (perhaps life needs to be deciphered like a cryptogram) (I, 716).

Qui vive? Est-ce vous, Nadja ? Est-il vrai que *l'au-delà*, tout l'au-delà soit dans cette vie? (Who goes there? Is that you Nadja? Is it true that the beyond, everything beyond is in this life?) (I, 743).

Par ce que je puis être tenté d'entreprendre de longue haleine, je suis trop sûr de démériter de la vie telle que je l'aime et qu'elle s'offre: de la vie *à perdre haleine* (through my long-term undertakings I make myself less deserving of life as it comes, the life I love: life that *takes your breath away*) (I, 744).

All these statements stress expectancy rather than achievement. The mood is consistently interrogative and speculative. 'La vie' is seen as a field of latent possibilities that are too easily left unrealized: by the cult of hard grind; the overvaluation of literature; a failure to look deeply enough into experience, or to see that what is held to be the prize of a transcendent afterlife is in fact available in this life. According to the last quotation, pinning our hopes on long-term projects is an affront to what life has to offer in the here and now.

The ingredients of Aragon's *Le Paysan de Paris* are in many ways similar to those of *Nadja*. The focus is on active exploration, through experimental practice, of lived experience in concrete space. The relationships between subject and object, and between the real and the imaginary, are played out in the context of very specific Parisian locations. Yet as Walter Benjamin observed when he sought to demarcate his own 'Arcades Project' from a text that had been one of its principal sources of inspiration, 'Aragon persists in remaining in the field of dreams'.[33] Seeking to be the mythologist of modern

---

[33] Walter Benjamin, *The Arcades Project*, trans. H. Eiland and K. McLaughlin (Cambridge, MA: Harvard University Press, 1999), 458.

urban everyday life, Aragon tends to become trapped in his own myth-making, rather than use his investigation as the springboard for a more radical perception or transformation.

The reason *Le Paysan de Paris* nonetheless makes such a compelling contribution to the surrealist sense of the everyday is the way it records a live engagement with real space. The photographer Eugène Atget, who was still actively building up an archival record of Parisian topography at the time when Aragon wrote, and whose partial adoption by the Surrealists will be discussed later, inscribed the words 'va disparaître' on some of his images in order to indicate to his clients the forthcoming destruction of a street, building, or architectural feature.[34] Similarly, in the first part of *Le Paysan de Paris*, Aragon conducts a kind of rescue dig, drawing up a thorough inventory of the Passage de l'Opéra which was under threat of destruction when he began writing, and had actually disappeared by the time the work appeared in book form. Like *Nadja*, *Le Paysan de Paris* is a 'livre battant comme une porte'[35] (book ajar like a door): having published part of it in *La Revue européenne* Aragon received entreaties from the syndicate of proprietors who thought his surrealist musings might damage their attempts to have the arcade reprieved![36] Aragon incorporates this feedback into his text, along with transcriptions of many other documents and inscriptions, including lists of drinks, signboards, and announcements, and in the second half of the text, devoted to the Buttes-Chaumont park, the entire contents of a municipal information column.[37] Like the photographs in *Nadja* (to be discussed below) this material, in principle at least, seeks to anchor the movements of subjectivity in concrete reality.

The narrator of *Le Paysan de Paris* also adopts the guise of an ethnographer seeking to piece together the mythology of a society on the basis of close scrutiny of its material culture, and participatory observation in its rituals (notably in the sphere of consumption: eating, drinking, sex, and shopping). The initial premise of the investigation is to suggest that, by analogy with temples or hallowed tribal ground, scrutiny of which would

---

[34] On Atget, see Molly Nesbit, *Atget's Seven Albums* (New Haven and London: Yale University Press, 1992): A. Buisine, *Eugène Atget ou la mélancolie en photographie* (Paris: Jacqueline Chambon, 1994).

[35] Breton, *Œuvres Complètes*, I, 651, 752.

[36] Louis Aragon, *Le Paysan de Paris* (1926; Paris: Gallimard Folio, 1972), 105–6.

[37] The incorporation of such indexical material will be discussed below (Ch. 7) in connection with Perec's *La Vie mode d'emploi*.

give us important insights into the nature of a given society or civilization, we need to find equivalent sites providing access to the myths of our own age. Where does modern life reveal the underlying beliefs and representations that may account for its particular qualities? Influenced by Freud, Aragon takes it as axiomatic that hidden desires fashion human realities, and that these are channelled particularly through places devoted to pleasure and consumption—the cult of the ephemeral is a recurrent theme—rather than in specifically religious practices. He judges that both the arcade and the public gardens can be seen as concretizations of modern mythology, the first relating to culture, the second to nature. Only by participating, if vicariously, in the life of these locales can the mythographer hope to penetrate their hidden, 'sacred', dimension. The narrator therefore chooses to give free rein to his senses: the errors and distortions to which they are prone are seen, like Freudian slips, as evidence of unconscious desires (for Benjamin, the now dilapidated arcades were the concretization of the nineteenth-century 'dream' of capitalism). As manifestations of myth, the different *commerces* of the arcade and the various sections of the artificial garden (laid out on the site of old quarries and featuring a dangerous ravine), must be seen both objectively and subjectively. Microscopic objective description must register in minute detail the precise look and feel of the environment. Detective work is also involved as the observer keeps the denizens of the arcade under covert surveillance, deciphering their secret purposes from details of dress and physiognomy. Just as importantly, however, the mythographer has to succumb to the allure of these spaces, responding to the affective currents beneath the surface. This requires a very different tactic, with its own stylistic exigencies. Rising to the challenge, Aragon not only anticipates many later exercises in cultural phenomenology, but excels at one of the principal arts that will feature prominently in later investigations of the everyday: that of the inventory.

The glaucous half-light of the arcade, and the illicit visit to the park after nightfall (where Aragon is accompanied by André Breton and Marcel Noll), act as reminders that the narrator of *Le Paysan de Paris* perceives these locales as poised between the outer world of material objects and the inner world of dreams and fantasies. Aragon's text is peppered with words such as 'insolite', 'équivoque', 'ambigu', 'glauque', conjuring up the 'vie mystérieuse' of these 'zones mal éclairées de l'activité humaine' (ill-lit zones of human activity) (20). The narrator oscillates between the exercise of his 'don d'observateur' (gift for observation), the ability to size things up from the outside, and his sense that the kind of observation he is practising means that he is exploring his own psyche as much as the external world: the strange proprietress of the shop selling handkerchiefs, and the sugar bowl on the café table become 'des limites intérieures de moi-même, des vues idéales que j'ai de mes lois' (my own inner limits, ideal views of my own laws) (109). When he reaches one end of the arcade, near an exit, he fancies he is on the frontier (liminality is a constant theme) between external reality and the 'subjectivisme du passage'. But this very liminality seems to dissolve both domains so that each becomes a kind of abyss: on one hand, discontinuous banality, on the other the anarchic disorder of 'ses propres abymes' (my own abyss).

A thoroughgoing philosophical idealism constantly threatens to unbalance *Le Paysan de Paris*, pitching it squarely into the realm of dream and unreality. In the garden the narrator observes: 'je me promène dans mes demeures mentales par les moyens de l'écriture' (I wander in my mental territories by means of writing) (185). Increasingly abstract disquisitions, drawing explicitly on German romantic philosophy, are especially prominent in the later pages. For all the narrator's professed ambition to focus on the everyday—'Le quotidien, on n'approchera jamais assez du quotidien' (the everyday, one never gets close enough to the everyday) (188) he exclaims—in order to capture 'le sentiment moderne de l'existence', he tends increasingly to become a victim of his own compulsion to see the real world as a springboard for his imaginative processes. Rather than honing his forensic skills, his chosen environments serve to unleash the intoxicating power of the surrealist image. The prospective phenomenology of urban space gives way to an ultimately rather sterile rhetorical performance as the narrator loses his bearings in the everyday world.

Echoing Baudelaire's sense of modernity, Aragon wonders for how long he will possess 'le sentiment du merveilleux quotidien?' (the feeling of the everyday marvellous) (16). The problem with seeing everyday life in terms of the marvellous is that it tends to start with the idea that there is more to the everyday than usually meets the eye, and ends by foisting the attributes of the marvellous onto mundane realities. As Aragon's example shows, the 'merveilleux quotidien' always risks being an essentially literary rather than an experiential category. What begins as exploration of lived experience ends up as a form of rhetorical intoxication: an illumination of a traditionally romantico-religious kind transcends the 'profane illumination'—a 'materialist, anthropological inspiration'—in which Walter Benjamin saw the more authentic energies of Surrealism.[38] Aragon, we might say, falls into the trap of 'histrionic or fanatical stress on the mysterious side of the mysterious' which, says Benjamin, 'takes us no further; we penetrate the mystery only to the degree that we recognize it in the everyday world, by virtue of a dialectical optic that perceives the everyday as impenetrable, the impenetrable as everyday'.[39] Aragon seems to lose sight of this dialectic, increasingly seeing in the world of the everyday a total interpenetration of subject and object. If Breton, whilst by no means always avoiding the pitfalls of 'magie quotidienne', maintains a better sense that the real mystery of the everyday world resides in its impenetrability, it is partly because, in Benjamin's terms, he also preserved a stronger sense that intractable questions regarding experience are themselves posed at an everyday level. In its resistance to meaning the everyday shows how its mystery is central to our understanding of lived reality.

EVERYDAYNESS AND SELF-EVIDENCE

'Prenons le Boulevard Bonne-Nouvelle et montrons-le' (Let's take the Boulevard Bonne-Nouvelle and show it forth).[40] A key aspect of the surrealist sense of daily life is the idea that the everyday is simply what is there, plainly and evidently, if we could but see it.[41] Breton and Eluard's injunction cited above makes no reference to the Boulevard Bonne-Nouvelle as having a hidden dimension: what is to be revealed is the Boulevard itself. The Boulevard is to be shown forth, demonstrated—as it is, for what it is. Not *my* Boulevard, but *our* Boulevard: everyone's Boulevard. '*Prenons*': take, grasp, get hold of; apprehend, as one takes something in one's hand. This is an invitation to practice phenomenology: locate the Boulevard in the field of your perception, as something you have to grasp with both mind and body. But what is to be shown is the Boulevard, not us. How can it be shown? '*Montrons-le*': Ideally, we would just point; but would anyone else see what we were pointing at?

---

[38] Benjamin, *Illuminations*, 227. On this see Margaret Cohen, *Profane Illumination: Walter Benjamin and the Paris of Surréalist Revolution* (Berkeley, London: University of California Press, 1993).

[39] Ibid., 237.

[40] André Breton and Paul Eluard, *L'Immaculée conception*, in Breton, *Œuvres Complètes*, I, 841.

[41] Cf. Peter Berger and Thomas Luckmann: 'the reality of everyday life is taken for granted as reality. It does not require simple additional verification over and beyond its simple presence. It is simply *there*, as self-evident and compelling facticity', *The Social Construction of Reality: A Treatise in the Sociology of Knowledge* (London: Penguin, 1967), 37.

What if we took a photograph? The idea of photographic revelation does seem to underlie Breton and Eluard's exhortation: the photograph could vouch for the fact that the Boulevard was really there at such and such a time. But if that is important, is it enough? Does it amount to showing it?

Surrealism inherited a fascination with self-evidence from the German Romantics, and also from French Symbolism as it grew out of Baudelaire.[42] An important observation in Baudelaire's *Journaux intimes* points in this direction: 'Dans certains états de l'âme presque surnaturels, la profondeur de la vie se révèle tout entière dans le spectacle, si ordinaire qu'il soit, qu'on a sous les yeux. Il en devient le symbole' (In certain, almost supernatural states of the soul, the depth of life is revealed in the spectacle, however ordinary it is, we have before our eyes. It becomes its symbol).[43] We can link this with Heidegger's insistence in *Being and Time* that authentic *Dasein* only 'shows forth' through the inauthenticity of *Alltäglichkeit*.[44] The evolution of Heidegger's thought steadily involved a greater sense of the positive nature of the everyday: not so much as the ground of authentic *Dasein*, but as offering access to it through its connection to the idea of dwelling. In a famous essay on 'Building, Dwelling, Thinking', learning to dwell, 'habiter', involves living in and through the everyday. And in the concept of *Ereignis*, Heidegger developed a way of thinking of Being as *event*; not so much the fact of the event, but the event as 'happening.'[45] The term *Ereignis* comprises an ostensive dimension: it designates the movement through which something becomes manifest. As in the surrealist account of expectancy and *rencontre*, what is stressed is not what happens but the process or conditions of happening itself, the experience of experience, in Blanchot's phrase.

These connections between lived experience, events, and the showing forth of what simply happens bring us back to surrealist experience and to the demonstration or ostension of the Boulevard Bonne-Nouvelle—not as a spectacle, an object of curiosity, a sociological datum, or a site of 'merveilleux quotidien', but as a living space. Yet the idea of apprehending ordinary things in their self-evidence, as it manifests itself in Surrealism, also fits into the tradition that culminates in the conceptual or minimalist art of the late twentieth century. Since the 1960s, artistic practice has often consisted in

---

[42] Cf. M. Raymond, *De Baudelaire au surréalisme* (1940; Paris: José Corti, 1966), 335–48.

[43] Baudelaire, *Œuvres Complètes*, 1, 257.

[44] See Ch. 1 above.

[45] Martin Heidegger, 'Building, Dwelling, Thinking', in id., *Poetry, Language, Thought*, trans. A. Hofstadter (New York: Harper Colophon Books, 1971).

doing away with the artwork and devising ways of focusing the viewer's attention on 'mere real things'. In a famous phrase, the philosopher Arthur C. Danto called this activity 'The Transfiguration of the Commonplace', where art consists in modifying consciousness and fostering new modes of sensibility. George G. Leonard traces this back to Wordsworth's vision of Paradise as 'a simple produce of the common day', and he retraces the trend of 'natural supernaturalism' in Emerson, Carlyle, and Ruskin, in avant-garde movements such as Futurism, in the *ready-mades* of Marcel Duchamp and in the work of John Cage.[46] For Cage, whose most notorious work, *4′33″*, exposes the audience to the ambient sound during a fixed stretch of silence, the residual purpose of art is 'purposeless play':

This play, however, is an affirmation of life—not an attempt to bring order out of chaos nor to suggest improvements in creation, but simply to wake up to the very life we're living, which is so excellent once one gets one's mind and one's desires out of its way and lets it act of its own accord.[47]

The connection between suspending the purposive ambitions of the mind, and waking up to 'the very life we're living', is similar to the one we traced in Breton's recurrent uses of the word 'vie' (Cage met Breton in New York in 1942). For Leonard, the evolution of 'the art of the commonplace', from the Wordsworthian 'hallowing' of the ordinary to recent conceptual art, with its jettisoning of the art object, has a spiritual orientation. In the 1960s, he argues, 'concept art . . . led inevitably into world ecology and habitability'. Cage went on to develop techniques of composition which aimed, like many surrealist tactics, to neutralize reason and encourage chance and indeterminacy. In this he was influenced by oriental religion and philosophy, and particularly his encounter with the form of Zen Buddhism centred on the idea of satori, expounded in the United States by D. T. Suzuki.[48]

This raises once again the question of whether all modes of thinking that home in on everyday life necessarily partake, if not of a specifically religious impulse, at least of a certain kind of spirituality. The question of epiphany, which has surfaced at a number of points in our discussion, including Heidegger's account of 'moments of vision', is relevant here. According to

---

[46] George C. Leonard, *Into the Light of Things: The Art of the Commonplace from Wordsworth to John Cage* (Chicago: University of Chicago Press, 1994).

[47] Quoted in Calvin Tomkins, *Ahead of the Game* (1962; London: Penguin, 1968).

[48] Cf. D. T. Suzuki, *Zen Buddhism: Selected Writings of D. T. Suzuki*, ed. W. Barrett (1956; New York: Doubleday, 1996); Taisen Deshimaru, *Zen et vie quotidienne* (Paris: Albin Michel, 1985).

Charles Taylor, Modernism involved a rejection of the 'epiphanies of being' through which Romanticism had resisted mechanistic forms of thought. In an 'epiphany of being' the higher reality (Nature for example) shines through external things: self-revelation goes hand in hand with the simple presentation of phenomena. Modernism, on the other hand, says Taylor, involves a turn towards experience rather than the self: 'the epiphanic centre of gravity begins to be displaced from the self to the flow of experience'.[49] In Modernist epiphany it is not the description or presentation of a thing—object or landscape—that makes something appear, but rather a juxtaposition of images or words: 'the epiphany comes from between the words or images, as it were, from the force field they set up between them, and not through a central referent which they describe while transmuting'.[50] What is involved is the creation of a frame around reality, which makes something appear—indirectly—by giving it a structure. Modernist epiphany involves mediation.

Taylor brackets Surrealism and Futurism together as movements that in his view do not take the modernist path because they reject form and retain a belief in unmediated contact with the fullness of life. Yet, as we saw earlier, mediation is by no means alien to Surrealism: the crucial thing is that practices in the linguistic, visual, or experiential spheres, designed to break with customary conventions, are ontologically productive. Breton expressly had the continuity of Romanticism, Symbolism, and Surrealism in mind when he referred to 'une volonté d'émancipation *totale* de l'homme, qui puiserait sa force dans le langage, mais serait tôt ou tard réversible à la vie' (a desire for man's *total* emancipation, which would draw its force from language but sooner or later be transmitted to life itself).[51] It is true that Surrealism, in common with the traditions explored by Leonard, preserves, to some degree, Taylor's 'epiphanies of being'. But the issue is not whether there is mediation: there is always mediation of some sort, if only that of the perceptual apparatus. The issue is that of grasping things in their self-evidence, in the present of their presence, as events rather than forms. 'Prenons le Boulevard Bonne-Nouvelle et montrons-le' expresses one of the least understood facets of Surrealism's engagement with the everyday—the aspiration to apprehend a field of lived experience and one's place in it. Under this dispensation, the artwork can only be an experiment, an activity, its residue or record—*Nadja* is not a work of art but a log-book, the register of an experience. The photographs in Breton's text

---

[49] Taylor, *The Sources of the Self*, 465.   [50] Ibid., 466.
[51] Breton, *Œuvres Complètes*, III, 654.

stand witness to what happened, and the 'ton qui se calque sur celui de l'observation médicale' (tone based on that of medical observation)[52] inaugurates the tactics of the experiment, the document and the inventory that are central to Surrealism's contribution to later explorations of the *quotidien*.

The Surrealism that connects with the everyday as a territory to be uncovered or revealed, aims, through techniques of defamiliarization, dislocation, or disruption, to reveal reality—'ce qui est donné' (what is given)—and to change it by revealing what it is. As Ferdinand Alquié observes, surrealist activity may involve the negation of the real, but this is the better to deliver reality from enslavement to 'l'empire de la connaissance rationnelle et de la logique' (the sway of rational knowledge and logic).[53] In this perspective, Surrealism aims to remove the scales that prevent our eyes from seeing what is there. It is conventional seeing that alters or disfigures the world rather than surrealist techniques. In his writing on art Breton frequently talks of healing a rift between physical perception and mental representation or image. The mind (through the influence of dream and the unconscious, which remain privy to unalienated desire) retains a capacity to see—'l'oeil existe à l'état sauvage' (the eye exists in a savage state)[54]—a visionary capacity that is usually denied by routine perception. By tapping the energies of unconscious vision art can restore the powers perception has lost, bringing about a reunification of perception and representation. What we see comes to conform more closely to what we are able to imagine. In this context the object of perception has no need to be extraordinary; what is extraordinary is the renewal of seeing. Surrealism does not aim to see new things, but to see things anew: to make the act of perception performative rather than merely constative.

Yet the performance of perception, or attention, is actually constative, to the extent that what it renders visible is in fact already there. This paradox, central to the tradition of 'revealing' the everyday, is at the heart of philosophical discussions of self-evidence dating back to William of Occam and Duns Scotus, and leading, via Malebranche and Bayle, to Bergson and Husserl. With regard to a proposition (say the principles of the Declaration of Independence), or a phenomenon (a tree outside our window), an assertion of self-evidence refers to an irrefutable quality that is not vested in logic but in experience: the feeling of self-evidence. The 'force' of conviction reflects a

---

[52] Breton, *Œuvres Complètes*, I, 645.
[53] Ferdinand Alquié *Philosophie du surréalisme* (Paris: Flammarion, 1955), 98.
[54] André Breton, *Le Surréalisme et la peinture* (Paris: Gallimard, 1965), 1.

sense of necessity deriving from the way a mental or physical entity presents itself to us. In his account of self-evidence, Fernando Gil underlines its performative character.[55] The phrase 'la force de l'évidence' recognizes the way self-evidence involves an intensification of the linguistic and sensory data generated in the process of comprehension and perception. The 'work' involved in apprehending something in its self-evidence does not transform the real but grasps and 'marks' its presence. Gil's thesis has a particular relevance to Surrealism since he insists on the hallucinatory character of self-evidence and its link to a primal ('archaic') phase in the evolution of representation. In self-evidence the real comes to us with the force of a hallucination (this archaic level of mental representation has links with what both Breton and Lévi-Strauss called 'la pensée sauvage'). The truth of 'évidence' rests in a sensory experience rather than a logical operation of inference or decoding. But the senses do not serve purely as a receptacle: self-evidence is produced through a process; like Heidegger's *Alltäglichkeit*, it needs time. If it has the character of epiphany it is not because a light shines through but, as in the Thomist speculations of James Joyce's *Stephen Hero*, because the thing simply shows itself forth as what it is.[56]

In the active process of self-evidence (as 'ostension' or 'monstration'), an orientation or posture towards reality, an angle towards phenomena, is intensified through a work of attention. Bergson's view of philosophy as a 'conversion of attention' illuminates the connections we are making between Surrealism and the everyday:

Is philosophy's role not to bring about a fuller perception of reality by a certain reorientation (détournement) of our attention? This would involve directing attention away from (détourner) the practical interests of the world, and returning it to what, in practical terms, has no function. This conversion of attention would be philosophy itself.[57]

We shall see later (Chapter 4) that the idea of 'détournement', derived by the Situationists from Surrealism, feeds into the 'retournement du regard'[58] at the heart of Michel de Certeau's invention of the everyday. But it is also worth noting at this point, since it will have a particular relevance to Georges Perec, that the link to spatial orientation gives attention its embodied character, a

55 Fernando Gil, *Traité de l'évidence* (Grenoble: Jérôme Millon, 1993).
56 James Joyce, *Stephen Hero* (1944; London: Jonathan Cape, 1975).
57 Bergson, quoted in Gil, *Traité de l'évidence*, 84.
58 Luce Giard in Certeau, *L'Invention du quotidien*, II, 219.

connection with somatic processes. Moreover, if attention 'embodies' an 'I', since it depends on a physical orientation and a conscious receptivity towards the given, this 'Je' is not a psychological identity so much as the anonymous avatar of a self that seeks to grasp ('saisir') the world, a 'Moi *en dehors*' to adopt Jean Pfeiffer's phrase about Breton.[59] The 'operation' that engenders a sense of self-evidence takes us away from the individual self to a wider feeling of participation in the course or flow of things, in a totality of relations. Malebranche argues that 'l'attention n'est pas une faculté psychologique, elle signifie l'abord d'une vérité qui sans elle reste cachée' (attention is not a psychological faculty, it means the apprehension of a truth that would otherwise remain hidden).[60] Attention is not epistemophilic—driven by a desire for knowledge or certainty—but oriented towards truth. Attention is performative in that, through a process that remains perceptual and linguistic, it produces self-evidence. Husserl notes that the act of consciousness here does not transform the phenomenon: it is attention that undergoes transmutation as the 'rayon attentionnel' (ray of attention) touches what it is oriented towards. Attention launches the 'dépassement de la pensée vers l'existence qui est le sceau de l'évidence' (the overtaking of thought by existence that is the seal of evidence).[61]

If 'évidence' is something we can behold, its temporal dimension, and its link to language, underlined in the process of attention, may be clarified with reference to hearing rather than vision. Sound, like attention, is always temporal and progressive, and it involves change, flux and *durée*. One can note here Breton's insistence that Surrealism does not exclusively favour vision, and indeed that the 'verbo-auditif', as in the foundational experience of 'phrases de réveil', was as important as the 'verbo-visuel'.[62]

In connection with the performative quality of attention in 'évidence', Fernando Gil makes references to a progressive 'changement d'échelle' (change of scale). In this process the object become layered or stratified, as the present dilates to include the past and the anticipated future. Husserl's account of 'retention', which pays homage to Augustine's thesis about the three dimensions of the present (past, present, and future), further echoed in Baudelaire's 'mémoire du présent',[63] specifies the process through which

---

[59] Jean Pfeiffer, 'Breton, le moi, la littérature', *Nouvelle Revue Française*, 172 (1967), 855–62; 858.
[60] Quoted in Gil, *Traité de l'évidence*, 110.
[61] Quoted in ibid., 113.
[62] Breton, *Œuvres Complètes*, II, 389.
[63] Baudelaire, *Œuvres Complètes*, 1165. Cf., Benjamin, *The Arcades Project*, 833.

attention grasps the unfolding of existence. Self-evidence derives from the 'changement d'échelle' whereby a percept is re-sited as part of a continuum of experiences, including the course of one's life.

Drawing on the psychoanalytical theory of Henri Ey (who took a strong interest in Surrealism) and Wilfrid Bion, as well as Freud, Fernando Gil describes self-evidence as an 'opération hallucinatoire' which, if immobilized, can be pathological. The intensification of perception and signification depends on a 'passage à l'acte' (Bion talks of 'acting out') that can be delusional if the 'présence compulsive' is isolated from the rest of experience (Surrealism will be fascinated by instances of this). But the performative 'passage à l'acte', the channelling of desire through attention (the cathexis of attention), whilst always vulnerable to delusion (as we shall see in Perec's experiments) may simply lead to the 'clarté' or 'éclat' of 'évidence',[64] as the thing perceived appears to signify itself. This process, which we can trace in Baudelaire's remark about 'la profondeur de la vie', runs counter to the analytical act of description. In the context of 'évidence' it is the naïve act of 'constatation' (the plain 'il y a') that operates a conversion of attention; 'la conscience naïve de la donation de la chose y change d'échelle' (the naïve awareness of the thing's being given changes the scale).[65] The result is a process of appropriation rooted in perception (a kind of proprioception) and a 'sentiment de intéllégibilité' (feeling of intelligibility) that brings about a lived experience of truth.

Many features of the philosophy of self-evidence align it with the apprehension of the everyday: the opposition to description and analytical knowledge; the link to the unfolding process of attention; the performativity whereby the everyday, like self-evidence, is produced through the act of attention; the *détournement* or change of scale that does not change the phenomenon but makes it perceptible;[66] the connection with a non-psychological, anonymous experience of self; the importance of flow, *durée*, and totality; the paradox whereby it is the purely constative 'il y a' (whose poetic resources were developed by Apollinaire) that has performative effects; the link to radical naïveté and the deictic language of pure 'constatation'; the connection with desire and habitability; the link via the senses to the body's spatial orientation or proprioception. These features are by no means all equally relevant to Surrealism. But, as we have seen, the philosophy of self-evidence

---

[64] Cf. Barthes's reference to 'la détonation de l'évidence' discussed in Ch. 5 below.
[65] Gil, *Traité de l'évidence*, 250.
[66] Change of scale is a key issue in Barthes—see Ch. 5 below.

chimes with one of Surrealism's deepest ambitions: to reveal what might be at the heart of what is.

THE PHOTOGRAPH AS TRIGGER AND AS TRACE

The Surrealists initially saw photography as a technique for revealing the hidden side of reality, corresponding to unconscious desire rather than narrow reason. Breton linked the revelatory power of photography to the disconnection between act and product. Like the hand that wrote automatically, or cut up and combined visual fragments, the camera was an 'instrument aveugle' (blind instrument) that helped to transform perception. In his preface to an exhibition of Max Ernst collages, in 1921, Breton refers to 'écriture automatique' as 'une véritable photographie de la pensée' (a true photography of thought), and he goes on to claim that we respond to Ernst's collages 'sans sortir du champ de notre expérience' (without leaving the field of our experience). By depriving us of familiar bearings, Ernst's works 'nous dépayse[nt . . .] en notre propre souvenir' (make us all at sea in our own memories).[67]

In the field of photography Man Ray quickly pioneered a range of techniques of distortion, superimposition, solarization, cropping, staging, etc., that made photography a vehicle of surrealist *dépaysement*, on a par with techniques like collage and frottage.[68] As a result, Breton's *Le Surréalisme et la peinture* refers to the 'pouvoir de suggestion' (power of suggestion) of the photographic 'épreuve' (print), and links this to a 'valeur émotive' (emotional value) that makes the photograph a 'precious object of exchange' (32). By virtue of its 'automatic' character the photographic image is credited with an objective and documentary status. But at an individual and collective level, it stimulates what Breton, in a 1929 essay on Dalí, called 'notre pouvoir d'hallucination volontaire' (our power of voluntary hallucination).[69] If the 'surreal' is a function of 'notre volonté de dépaysement complet de tout' (our desire to cut adrift from everything),[70] photography, ideally combining the objective and the subjective, is well placed to be an instrument of its revelation.

[67] Breton, *Œuvres Complètes*, I, 246.

[68] On Man Ray see Emanuelle De L'Ecotais and Alain Sayag, *Man Ray: Photography and its Double* (New York: Gingko Press, 1998).

[69] Breton, *Œuvres Complètes*, II, 309.

[70] Ibid., 305.

Yet, from an early stage, a photographic practice based not on distortion, manipulation or collage within the image, but on the insertion of quite straightforward photographs into unfamiliar contexts, marked an equally striking contribution to photographic culture, and one with major repercussions on the movement's contribution to ways of looking at the everyday. A crucial factor here is the Surrealists' discovery of Eugène Atget who allowed three of his photographs to appear in *La Révolution surréaliste* on condition that his name be suppressed.[71] Atget's photographs are above all documents. Their *raison d'être* is not aesthetic delectation. In fact Atget was content to be an artisan, trundling his camera and plates on a cart in the early hours of the morning, his aim being to record as accurately as possible the phenomena to be 'documented'. Atget worked in series: trade signs, street lights, shop windows, statues, courtyards, vehicles, staircases, cafés, types of labour. Each image derives its significance by representing a particular variety of a given species. The photograph is a specimen and its significance is linked to the exhaustiveness of the project from which it originates. It testifies to the variety but also to the specificity of real things in our daily surroundings. Far from being one-off snapshots, seeking to mark particular moments, Atget's photographs aim to withdraw items from actuality and present them as variants of a basic model. Yet when looked at individually an Atget photograph has a powerful sense of presence and place, underlined by the functional title indicating, as in a catalogue, precise date and location. Walter Benjamin famously claimed that these photographs always look like 'the scene of the crime': the reaction they provoke is strongly heuristic and interpretative.[72] Benjamin provides another clue to the power of Atget when he argues that what is new in photography, its 'valeur magique', has to do with its connection to the real, its 'indexicality' as Rosalind Krauss, borrowing the term from Pierce, has called it.[73] The interest of a painting is inseparable from the artistry of the painter; but confronted by the photograph of a fisherwoman from Newhaven who averts her eyes from the camera, or that of a woman who committed suicide a few days later, the viewer is captivated by an irreducible reality that does not stem from, and indeed may be at odds with, the

---

[71] On Atget and the Surrealists see Nesbit, *Atget's Seven Albums*; Ian Walker, *City Gorged with Dreams: Surrealism and Documentary Photography in Interwar Paris* (Manchester and New York: Manchester University Press, 2002), 88–113.

[72] Walter Benjamin, *One-Way Street and Other Writings*, trans. E. Jephcott and K. Shorter (London: New Left Books, 1979), 256.

[73] Rosalind Krauss, 'Photography at the Service of Surrealism' in id., Jane Livingston, and Dawn Ades, *L'Amour fou: Photography and Surrealism* (New York: Abbeville Press, 2002), 12–53.

photographer's technique. Despite all the photographer's mastery, noted Benjamin,

the viewer feels obliged to scrutinize such a photograph for the little spark of chance, of the Here and Now, thanks to which reality so to speak burnt a hole in the image; he seeks the imperceptible place where, in the singular quality of this minute from long ago, the future still resides.[74]

On this basis, the surrealist project of transforming perception so as to 'reveal' reality finds an alternative path. Rather than creative manipulation akin to collage, it consists in creating a context where a straightforward 'documentary' record of a person, place, or object invites a form of scrutiny that gives it the power not to transcend the real but to make the real visible. [75]

Nowhere is this more effective than in the photographs that form an integral part of *Nadja*, and more specifically the nine photographs that were taken by J.-A. Boiffard, at Breton's request. Using Boiffard's photograph of the Hôtel des Grands Hommes as my focus (Fig. 1)[76] I want to analyse the means by which a banal 'prise de vue' (view), whilst remaining unexceptional, marks a powerful engagement with the real. To facilitate discussion I will distinguish between contextual factors and formal characteristics of the image. Prefacing the revised edition of *Nadja* in 1963 Breton claimed that the role of the 'abondante illustration photographique' was to obviate description and to underscore his ambition that *Nadja* should have the character of a medical or legal report.[77] The photographs do not provide additional information; they attest the objective, concrete reality of places, people, and objects involved in events notable for a high degree of irrationality. Semantically redundant, they have a predominantly performative role, amplified by the captions. Benjamin rightly insists that surrealist writings were not concerned with literature or abstract theories, still less with fantasies: they were 'documents' that related to experiences.[78] In Breton's work the photographic image strips the things it records—streets, squares, and monuments—of their 'banal obviousness', and via the captions, 'injects' into the text the 'original intensity' of the 'events

---

[74] Benjamin, *One-Way Street*, 243 (translation modified).

[75] On the documentary dimension of surrealist photography see Walker, *City Gorged with Dreams*, and John Roberts, 'Surrealism, Photography and the Everyday', in id., *The Art of Interruption: Realism, Photography and the Everyday* (Manchester and New York: Manchester University Press, 1988), 98–113.

[76] In Breton, *Œuvres Complètes*, I, 654.

[77] Ibid. 645.

[78] Benjamin, *One-Way Street*, 227.

Fig. 1. J.-A. Boiffard, 'Je prendrai pour point de départ l'hôtel des Grands Hommes' (I will take the Hôtel des Grands Hommes as my starting point), from André Breton, *Nadja* (Paris: Gallimard, 1928). Collection Lucien Treilland, Paris.

described'. The photograph's power to achieve this lies in its indexicality. Literally partaking, by virtue of the physical nature of a chemical process, of the reality that was before the camera lens, the photograph says 'ça a été': this place really existed, this is what it looks like.[79]

In the case of the Hôtel des Grands Hommes (which is the first photograph in *Nadja*)[80] the caption links to a portion of text that elucidates how, as the site of a series of surprising incidents usually involving an element of coincidence, this location was the starting point for the events relating to Nadja herself. The premonitory incidents include being fixated by a mental image of the wooden sign, and the words 'BOIS CHARBONS', on shops selling winter fuel, and projecting them onto the crown of Rousseau's head on the statue in the Place du Panthéon; and the sudden apparition of Benjamin Péret and Paul Eluard in surprising circumstances (further photographs register these events). Via the relay of the caption, the text provides material that we incorporate into our scrutiny of the image. Without any manipulation a simple 'shot' of the hotel becomes charged with energies that then seem to emanate from the location itself.

Dedicating a copy of *Nadja* to him, Breton thanked Boiffard for having been able, with his photographer's eye, to see the 'true sites' as Breton had seen them with his own eyes.[81] If Breton must have conveyed, presumably by reference to the events in *Nadja*, the kind of significance each location possessed for him, 'l'angle spécial dont je les avais moi-même considérés', the resulting images show these places as seen through the additional prism of Boiffard's own subjectivity. From Breton's point of view the role of the camera as an 'instrument aveugle' is maintained. But the issue is complicated by the fact that it was presumably Breton who oversaw the way the photographs were 'cropped' for inclusion in his book. In the original Boiffard photograph, a greater portion of the houses on either side of the hotel, particularly to the left, and a foreground of empty pavement in front of the railings round the statue, are visible (Fig. 2). But, rather than giving greater prominence to the hotel, the effect of coming in closer is to focus more on the statue of Rousseau: while 'Boiffard's' photograph gives a straightforward 'middle-shot' of the hotel and

[79] On the 'ça a été' of photography see Roland Barthes, *La Chambre Claire, Œuvres Complètes*, III, 1105–1201.

[80] Ibid., 231. For a general discussion see Jean Arrouye, 'La Photographie dans *Nadja', Mélusine*, 4 (1982), 123–51.

[81] Cited by Dawn Ades, 'Photography and the Surrealist Text', 161.

Fig. 2. J.-A. Boiffard, Sans titre (pour *Nadja*), 1928, Collection Lucien Treillard, Paris.

environs, 'Breton's' photograph—the cropped image—homes in on the statue of the 'grand homme' making it more central and closer to the viewer.

Since the photographs do not record events themselves, but documentary testimony or evidence in relation to particular incidents or types of occurrence, the inescapable element of arbitrariness in the document—the fact that such and such just happened to be there—is in fact fairly restricted. The fact that the hotel is photographed, like most of the other locations, at a time when the scene is almost devoid of human presence—as was Atget's practice—is presumably deliberate. The commercial premises on the ground floor of the hotel could clearly not have been omitted, but the element of incongruity in the fact that it is a branch of the well-known (and still extant) 'chain' of undertakers, Henri de Borniol (the name is clearly visible, and the window appears to contain objects resembling gravestones) is underlined by the unattended horse and cart standing by a lamppost in front of the hotel, perhaps ready to deliver a consignment to the gravedigger. The theatrical emptiness and immobility of the square point to the possibility of a future event. The sense of a stage on which something may be about to happen is suggested by the elaborately cos-tumed figure in the statue (Rousseau appears to have a wig and sword), which has the air of an automaton about to burst into action. The position of the head and hands suggests inner contemplation, while the outstretched fingers and the sword create vectors in different directions. Banal as it is, Boiffard's image shows signs of visual construction or opportunism, notably through a number of mirrorings or visual echoes. For example, there are two open windows on the fourth floor (corresponding to Breton's vantage point), one empty (matching another open window on the top floor) whilst at the other we can make out a human figure in profile looking in the same direction as Rousseau. Among other things this parallelism introduces an opposition between the animate and the inanimate, the natural and the cultural. Through a slight tilting of the camera, the image also sets up a parallel between the iron fence in the foreground and the ironwork on various balconies in the hotel façade. This emphasis on the horizontal is then in tension with the strong vertical lines accentuated by the decision—in cropping the image—to show only a small part of the adjacent buildings on either side of the hotel, drawing attention to the drainpipe running down from top to bottom on the left hand side. Another dynamic factor in the image—the back-to-back effect induced by the way Rousseau and the cart-horse face in opposite directions—adds to the features that give Boiffard's image, banal as it is, a strongly semiotic quality which in fact enhances its sense of location. This 'legibility' is further intensified or literalized by the verbal material in the image, including the name of the hotel in large letters, the name of the undertaker's shop at pavement level (along with part of the word *imprimerie*) partly obscured by the statue, as well as indecipherable inscriptions on the plinth of the statue and on a plate beside a door next to the hotel.

I have been seeking to show that Boiffard's shot of the hotel works by setting up a two-way process of interaction. This involves on the one hand *projection*:

the image encourages what is simply seen to stimulate recognition at an unconscious level, to engender a cathexis—a bonding with unconscious drives and memories—through which the image comes to have the aura of a hallucination. On the other hand, the process involves *apprehending* what is already there, making one's psyche permeable to the genius loci, to the ambience, the 'dehors'. As the opening so subtly affirms, *Nadja* is about convergences, in certain places and events, between what haunts us and what we in turn haunt, between what we are magnetically drawn to, and what we inject with energies derived from our own hidden profile: not our hidden depths but the identity that is ours by virtue of interaction with the world we inhabit. Yet if these places and events are special they are also ubiquitous and multiple, in fact they could be anywhere ('ici ou là' as Nadja herself puts it).[82] What counts is expectancy, the sense that it is *here* that something may happen, *here* always being deictic, a shifter, a question mark. In the end there are no special places, only a special kind of relationship to places and events, of which the photograph can be the trigger and the trace.

Another contextual factor shaping our response to these images is their seriality. The subsequent topographic photographs in *Nadja*, and particularly the eight other images by Boiffard—including the Porte Saint-Denis, the Librairie de l'Humanité, the little restaurant in the Place Dauphine, the shop in the arcades of the Palais-Royal, the 'Sphinx-Hotel' on the boulevard Magenta, where Nadja had stayed, the huge poster for Mazda light bulbs with its image of ram's horns (and a little cart in front, a recurrent detail)—display a similar range of features: emptiness, signs, open doors, etc. But this consistency does not simply enhance the thematic or symbolic power of the photographs, it also serves to confirm the hermeneutic moves we make in response to them individually. In other words the effect of the series (as Olivier Lugon has indicated in his excellent account of the 'documentary style' in photography which provides a wider context for surrealist practice),[83] is not so much to provide interpretative clues as to ratify the response that gives the individual everyday image the power to engender an act of recognition. Seriality is one of the means through which we are led to recognize in the banal image not only what is there in the literal sense, but what is there (and what we usually miss) at the more ontological level. In these everyday images the everyday remains

---

[82] Breton, *Œuvres Complètes*, I, 727.
[83] Olivier Lugon, *Le Style Documentaire. D'August Sander à Walker Evans, 1920–1945* (Paris: Macula, 2001).

unexceptional and recognizable; but, through the interactive process we have described, it also manifests itself as worthy of recognition.

The photographic practice I am seeking to characterize positions the everyday as a space of possibility: not the closed realm of empty repetition and routine, nor yet the site of authenticity, but a space whose enigmatic character is revealed little by little, by our homing in on it, rather than delving behind it. The process induced by the photograph is marked by a sense of the trace and the event: the place as the arena of passage. It is therefore centripetal. The photograph removes the film from our eyes, provokes an activity of attention. Breton encapsulated the two-way process involved when, in a 1929 essay on Dalí, he asserted that if we wish to see what lies behind the trees obscuring the view—a dig at conventional realism—we must exploit 'notre pouvoir *d'hallucination volontaire*' (our power of *voluntary hallucination*). And, in a striking formulation, he added: '*Le domaine de l'attention* est, pour peu qu'on y réfléchisse, celui où se font jour tout ce que nous pouvons entretenir de mieux comme sentiments suspects'[84] (emphasis added) (the *domain of attention* is, when one thinks about it, where our most uncanny feelings are manifested). We need to train our sights on as yet unclassified feelings occurring on the fringes of perception. Never losing touch with reality, surrealist practices, however radical in their treatment of familiar appearances, constitute detours aimed at realizing the plenitude of the real. Attention is all.

The banal photographic document, testifying to the verifiable existence of real places, people, and things, has a central place in Surrealism, and particularly in the way of perceiving ordinary, everyday surroundings that is one of the movement's key legacies. But as we shall see in the next chapter, the evolution of Surrealism at the turn of the 1930s, initially in the context of the review *Documents*, edited by Georges Bataille, generated further visions of the everyday that also had a strong influence on later theory and practice. And here, once again, the photographic document, and in the first place its treatment in Bataille's review, is particularly symptomatic. For this reason, the next chapter, on the dissident Surrealism of the 1930s, will begin with discussion of another photograph by J.-A. Boiffard.

---

[84] Breton, *Œuvres Complètes*, II, 309.

3

Dissident Surrealism:
The Quotidian Sacred and Profane

BOIFFARD'S BIG TOES: THE CHALLENGE OF
DOCUMENTS

If Surrealism has remained a rich source of inspiration for later ways of exploring the everyday it is in large part thanks to the dynamic field of interactions between Breton's group and a number of dissident figures including Georges Bataille, Michel Leiris, Raymond Queneau, and Walter Benjamin. When Bataille, Leiris, and others broke with Breton to found the review *Documents* in 1929, they asserted the primacy of the contingent here and now over what they saw as Surrealism's idealist tendencies.[1] Radicalizing the surrealist premium on the experiential, *Documents* maintained, to some extent, a focus on everyday experience. However, in drawing strongly on the ethnographic and primitivist enthusiasms already fostered by Surrealism, *Documents* construed the everyday primarily as the arena of primal fears, taboos, and desires. To understand the forces that reshaped Surrealism's visions of the everyday, enriching its legacies, we need to gauge the interactions between *Documents* and *La Révolution surréaliste*, and between Breton, Bataille, and Leiris.[2] No area is more symptomatic in this regard than the treatment of photography and the poetics of the photographic document.

In the last chapter I focused on J.-A. Boiffard's work for Breton's *Nadja*. Let us now contrast this with an equally famous series of images by the same

---

[1] On *Documents* see Georges Didi-Huberman, *La Ressemblance informe ou le gai savoir visuel de Georges Bataille* (Paris: Macula, 1995).

[2] On this see, Denis Hollier, *Les Dépossédés* (*Bataille, Caillois, Leiris, Malraux, Sartre*) (Paris: Minuit, 1993): David Lomas, *The Haunted Self: Surrealism, Psychoanalysis, Subjectivity* (New Haven and London: Yale University Press, 2000); Hal Foster, *Compulsive Beauty* (Cambridge, MA: MIT Press, 1993)

photographer—the startling close-ups of big toes featured in the sixth issue of *Documents* in 1929. Since the recent promotion of photography to the centre of Surrealism's aesthetic contribution, both series have been seen as quintessential examples of surrealist photography, but there has been a tendency to play down the obvious differences between these images, or to promote the big toe over the banal hotel. I want to argue, however, that these photographs work in very different ways, and that this difference is highly illuminating with regard to the question of Surrealism and the everyday.

Boiffard's three photographs of big toes, two male, one female, were commissioned to accompany an article by Georges Bataille in the sixth issue of *Documents*, published in 1929 (Figs. 3, 4, and 5).[3] These images represent something ordinary, banal and unaesthetic, but their power stems from the way, unlike the photographs in *Nadja*, the image is constructed and manipulated.[4] This is not by dint of distortion or collage. Boiffard's images combine the irrefutable reality of the document with a hallucinatory presence that opens the real to the play of fantasy. The first main device is the use of close-up, combined with enlargement, lighting, and camera angle. Boiffard contrives to focus so closely as to isolate the big toe from everything else, including the foot. As a result, the body part becomes monstrous. The close-up, aided by spotlighting, blots out everything else, framing the big toe so that it emerges from a primal darkness. (In fact, as is clearly shown in a photograph not published in *Documents* (Fig. 6), the foot was also physically manipulated, a finger bends back the toes so as to exclude them from the image.) In the case of the first male toe—captioned, 'sujet masculin, 30 ans' (male subject, age 30), (Fig. 3), anonymity and scientific or medical exactitude adding to the effect— the camera is positioned in front, a little above, and at a slight angle to the toe. The effect is to make it very bulbous, while the nail, cut in a shallow triangle with the apex jutting towards us, catching the light in a different way, gives the image a different texture. In the other photograph of a male toe, (Fig. 4), probably of the same subject since the nail is cut in the same way, the exposure accentuates the harshness of the lighting (which is strongly reflected on the nail) and the view is more or less directly from above. This time we see the entire big toe, which has a distinctly phallic appearance, and a small part

[3] 'Le Gros orteil' will be found in the reprint of *Documents*, D. Hollier (ed.), 2 vols. (Paris: Jean-Michel Place, 1991), vol. 1, 297–302.

[4] For discussions of the Boiffard toes see Dawn Ades, 'Photography and the Surrealist Text' and Rosalind Krauss, 'Corpus delicti', both in Krauss, Livingston, and Ades, *L'Amour fou: Photography and Surrealism*, 153–89 and 54–111.

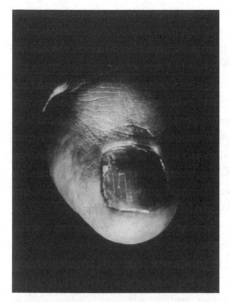

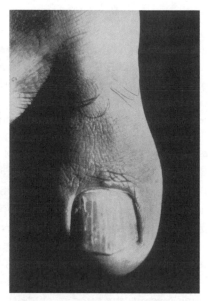

Fig. 3. J.-A. Boiffard, *Gros orteil. Sujet masculin, 30 ans* (Big toe. Male subject, age 30). Musée national d'art moderne, Centre Pompidou, Paris.

Fig. 4. J.-A. Boiffard, *Gros orteil. Sujet masculin, 30 ans* (Big toe. Male subject, age 30). Collection Lucien Treillard, Paris.

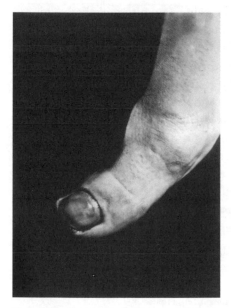

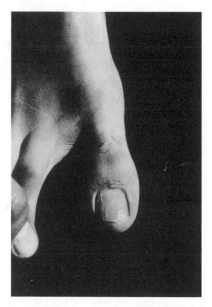

Fig. 5. J.-A. Boiffard, *Gros orteil. Sujet féminin, 24 ans* (Big toe. Female subject, age 24). Collection Lucien Treillard, Paris.

Fig. 6. J.-A. Boiffard, Sans titre (1929). Collection Lucien Treillard, Paris.

of the next one. For the third toe in the series, that of a 'sujet féminin, 24 ans' (female subject, age 24), (Fig. 5), the exposure is particularly harsh and graceless, the light catching both the nail and the surface of the toe, which has a blotchy appearance. Longer, thinner, and without the bulbous end of the others, the female toe is seen at a fairly steep angle and from the side. Part of the foot is shown, but the adjacent toes remains invisible. A second factor is scale. The photographs were reproduced in full page (and the first two as a double-page spread), so that the big toes are in fact four or five times life-size. One effect of this enlargement is to make wrinkles look like furrows, hairs (particularly in the second image) like bits of cord, and nails like slabs of slate. But this also sets up a metaphorical exchange with the kinds of 'subject' that normally appear this size in photographs, notably, as Georges Didi-Huberman points out, the human face in the portrait.[5]

In 'Le Gros orteil', Bataille sees the foot as the embodiment of what, in a subsequent article, he called 'cette matière basse, qui seule [. . .] permet a l'intélligence d'échapper à la contrainte de l'idéalisme'[6] (base matter that, alone, permits the mind to elude the constraints of idealism). The idealism Bataille had in mind was primarily that of the Surrealists, and the role of *Documents* was, in Bataille's mind, to provide a more subversive and above all a more corporeal and material version of surrealist contestation. The article on the big toe ends by rejecting the poetic and the metaphorical (and implicitly the surreal) and affirming 'un retour à la réalité' (a return to reality). This did not, Bataille insisted, imply a new attitude of acceptance but was, rather, a response to the seductive power of things that are base yet have the power to astonish and admonish—such as the big toe.[7] The foot is the most human part of the body because it least resembles the equivalent organ in the hominid ape; but we tend to see it as dirty and ignoble because of its distance from the head and proximity to the ground. Basing his analysis on the opposition between higher and lower, the ideal and the base or abject, Bataille illustrates our disdain for the foot by imagining someone rapt in admiration before a noble national monument, who is suddenly afflicted by a stabbing pain in the foot occasioned by corns: an acute reminder of the 'obscure bassesse' (obscure baseness) we despise (or repress) in ourselves and of the fact that our feet lead, independently of us, an 'ignoble' existence. Being confronted with the 'aspect

---

[5] Didi-Huberman. *La Ressemblance informe*, 54.

[6] Georges Bataille, 'Le Bas Matérialisme et la gnose', *Documents*, ed. Hollier, 302.

[7] Georges Bataille, 'Le Gros Orteil', *Documents*, ed. Hollier, 302.

hideusement cadavérique et en même temps criard et orgueilleux du gros
orteil' (hideous, corpse-like yet at the same time garish and proud look of the
big toe) brings us down from our attempts to flee the 'boue terrestre' (terrestrial mud). Boiffard's images are supposed to make us 'écarquiller les yeux'
(our eyes pop out) as we experience a dizzying to and fro between repulsion
and attraction, fascination and disgust.[8] As Georges Didi-Huberman puts it,
the big toe 'accuse "performativement" les disproportions évoquées par
Bataille' (underlines 'performatively' the disproportions evoked by Bataille)[9].
But how does the photographic image achieve this?

Didi-Huberman argues that Boiffard's photographs directly enact what he
calls disproportion, the otherness and singularity of human phenomena, the
lack of fit between man and world, the incongruity of reality. The 'efficacité
imaginaire' of these images is inherent: their force complements the text, but
does not derive from their relation to it. This performative energy is designed
to call into question our definition of the human by putting the human figure
under pressure—not by distortion but by using excess to highlight difference
(our difference from 'ourselves'). Yet the photographs remain documents, in
other words incontrovertible records of the reality of what was before the lens.
Boiffard's treatment of the shot, as outlined earlier, produces an image that is
'self-disfiguring' through the way it offends canons of taste and aesthetic order.
The handling of the close-up does not isolate a detail from a wider totality, it
makes the organic fragment a totality in itself, and one that is capable: 'comme
"document", comme "réel", comme image de dislocation [de produire] une
image capable de transgresser l'image [. . .] de transgresser ou de déborder
l'imagination elle-même (l'image surréaliste en particulier)' (as 'document',
'reality', image of dislocation [of producing] . . . an image capable of transgressing the image . . . of transgressing or overflowing the imagination itself
(and the surrealist image in particular)) (61). The framing of the toe by close-
up, camera angle and lighting, the uncomfortable proximity, and a number of
contextual factors, including the element of seriality, make the image dynamic. The familiar becomes other, and yet the apparent lack of fakery
maintains the irrefutable reality of what is shown. Thus Boiffard's treatment
of the image gives it the double power of a document and a fantasy: it is at once
a 'vision du réel' and a 'vision de rêve'—'une vision "au ras des choses" qui

[8] Ibid., 302.
[9] Didi-Huberman, *La Ressemblance informe*, 56. Subsequent page references are given in the text.

serait néanmoins une vision toujours au-delà' (a vision 'at the level of things'
that also leads beyond) (313).

What makes the project of *Documents* and its treatment of images continuous with Bretonian Surrealism is precisely the documentary impulse, central
to *La Révolution surréaliste* and to *Nadja*, and its links to experience (a key
word in Bataille's writing) and to the real. Yet it is evident that in countering
Surrealism with something allegedly *more* real, *Documents* sought in fact to
break radically with the everyday experience of the human subject. As in
Nadja, both text and image in *Documents* aim at destabilizing the viewer/
reader, and focusing attention on what is unacknowledged in the familiar. Yet
even when what is pinpointed is immanent within ordinary experience, it is
clear that *Documents* aimed at a different region of experience altogether, one
which radically and definitively unsettled all forms of order, rather than
pointing to a new order. For Didi-Huberman what differentiates Bataille's
project, despite the many things it shared with the surrealist enterprise, is that
his mode of thought required 'un genre particulier de montage figuratif,
constamment réinventé aux fins d'imposer la valeur d'effraction de certains
rapports, de certaines relations, fût-ce au détriment des termes—des objets—
eux-mêmes. Fût-ce au détriment de la signification elle-même' (a particular
kind of figurative montage, constantly reinvented with the sole aim of imposing the subversive power of certain relationships, if necessary to the detriment
of the terms—the objects—themselves. If necessary to the detriment of
meaning itself) (115).

If the 'gallery' of documents in *Nadja*—people, places, objects, printed and
handwritten material, drawings—insists on the heterogeneity of the real, in a
mix that *Documents* will emulate and intensify; and if this heterogeneous
quality draws attention to the alterity of experience, Breton's text also points
in the direction of unity at another level—that of the subject's lost but
recoverable subjectivity: human subjectivity itself as lost but to be refound,
as Breton will put it in *Les Vases communicants*.[10] In *Documents*, on the other
hand, disunity presides over the 'montage figuratif': the juxtaposition of
radically different and incommensurable images—old masters and S/M
gear, monuments and graffiti, Celtic coins and jazz singers, totem poles and
starlets, abattoirs and flowers—insists on relationships that serve to undermine the integrity of the entities caught up in a violent process of dislocation,
rather than pointing to a higher level of interpretation. If another level is

---

[10] See discussion in Ch. 2 above.

posited—that of the base side of human reality—this is in no sense a fixed point, but a pole in a dialectic of high and low, ideal and real, etc., that not only undoes fixed identities (also the goal of *Nadja*) but any kind of coherence, however remote, of subjective identity, or of subject and world.

Commissioned first by Breton, then by Bataille, Boiffard produced two sets of images of ordinary, everyday things. I have been seeking to show that, whilst the image of the hotel and the image of the big toe both work performatively, actively transforming the viewer's perception of the phenomena in front of the lens, they function in quite different ways. In the *Nadja* image, the interplay of the indexical and the semiotic works to produce a process of attention that makes the visible a crossroads of convergent meanings that disclose a density of subjective experience indissolubly linked with specific, real locations. The *Documents* image works, on the other hand, to produce a radical experience of disproportion and disjunction. By insisting on the difference between these images I am seeking, in the context of the surrealist sense of the everyday, to preserve the specificity of the banal, particularly topographic, image, as one of the key legacies of the movement. In this regard my analyses differ from Rosalind Krauss's important and influential account of Surrealism and photography which does not see any essential difference between the explicitly manipulated images of Man Ray—or later Tabard, Cahun, or Ubacs—and the apparently 'straight' images of Boiffard, or later Brassaï.[11] If Surrealism, unlike Dada, avoided photomontage and tended to play down the act of representation and the constructed character of the image, surrealist photography nevertheless, in Krauss's view, always plays with and foregrounds representation through the way it introduces 'espacement' (spacing).

Surrealist techniques sought to preserve the seamless surface of the final print and thus reinforce the sense that this image, being a photograph, documents the reality from which it is a transfer. But at the same time, this image, internally riven by the effects of syntax—of spacing—would imply nonetheless that it is reality that has composed itself as a sign. To convulse reality from within, to demonstrate it as fractured by spacing, became the collective result of all that vast range of techniques to which surrealist photographers resorted and which they understood as producing the characteristics of the sign.[12]

---

[11] See Rosalind Krauss, 'Photography in the Service of Surrealism', in Krauss, Livingston, and Ades, *L'Amour Fou*, 15–56; id., 'Photographie et surréalisme' in *Le Photographique: pour une théorie des écarts* (Paris: Macula, 1990), 110–20.

[12] Id., 'Photography in the Service of Surrealism', 28.

For Krauss, surrealist photography, even when it shuns 'darkroom manipulation' or 'scissors and paste', is never straight:

Surrealist photography is contrived to the highest degree [. . . it] does not admit of the natural, as opposed to the cultural or made, and so all of what it looks at is seen as if already, and always, constructed through a strange transposition of this thing into a different register. We see the object by means of an act of displacement, defined through a gesture of substitution. The object, 'straight' or manipulated, is always manipulated and thus always appears as a fetish. It is this fetishization of reality that is the scandal.[13]

In fact Krauss bases her account of (ostensibly) 'non-manipulated' or 'straight' images not on Boiffard's work in *Nadja* but, firstly, on the big toes, and, secondly, on Brassaï's famous images of nocturnal Paris in the 1930s. Here Krauss shows convincingly how, in Brassaï, an ostensibly unmanipulated, indexical image can convey a 'double vision', both documenting and transforming the real. Through techniques of framing and duplication—often involving the inclusion of mirror images in the photograph, as in the well-known café and brothel scenes—bodies and objects are not so much apprehended in their unity and coherence, as 'opened out' ('éclatés'), in a 'processus qui permet de transformer l'obstination et la rigidité du 'réel' en un champ de représentations' (process that allows the recalcitrant rigidity of the 'real' to be transformed into a field of representations).[14] This is certainly an excellent analysis, but in my view it points to key differences between Brassaï's photographs and those in *Nadja*. Brilliant as they are as evocations of Parisian scenes, Brassaï's images are, as Krauss shows, supremely constructed, and if their effect is indisputably to communicate a certain kind of 'magie quotidienne', a mystery in everyday scenes, it tends to manufacture or project this rather than gather it from the phenomena under scrutiny. The image predominates over the real: or, in the terms of Breton's key 1930 text 'Il y aura une fois', the real becomes imaginary rather than vice versa.[15] As we shall see in the fourth section of this chapter, devoted to *L'Amour fou*, for which Brassaï provided photographs, one of the ways in which the surrealist everyday mutated, in the course of the 1930s, was towards a more ready-made, easily reproducible

13 Krauss, Livingston, and Ades, 'Corpus delicti', *L'Amour Fou*, 91.
14 'Les Noctambules' in *Le Photographique*, 151. See also Marja Warehime, *Brassai: Images of Culture and the Surrealist Observer* (Baton Rouge, LA; London: Louisiana State University Press, 1996).
15 Breton, *Œuvres Complètes*, I, 825.

poetic realism. Krauss rightly draws a parallel between Breton's treatments of reality in *L'Amour fou* (to be discussed below) and the way Brassaï's photographs operate. But if this convergence shows how the surrealist everyday developed—and its evolution is the subject of this chapter—there is no reason to accept its validity in the context of *Nadja*.

THE BENEFICENCE OF DESIRE

By comparison with its 1924 predecessor the *Second Manifeste du surréalisme* (1930) is darker in tone, and its existential dimension is more radical and apocalyptic. Breton responded directly to the challenge of *Documents* by a counter-attack on Bataille's 'vieux matérialisme antidialectique' (old antidialectical materialism) (I, 825) and a reassertion of Surrealism's commitment to throwing out idealism—'en finir avec l'idéalisme'—via fidelity to the historical, yet dialectical, materialism of Marx and Engels. Repudiating Bataille's delectation in baseness, Breton emphasises the purity of Surrealism's aspirations. But he stresses that, far from pure mind, Surrealism is concerned with the interaction of inner and outer: 'la pénétrabilité de la vie subjective par la vie "substantielle"' (the penetrability of subjective life by 'substantial' life); this will be the essence of 'hasard objectif' (I, 826). Numerous allusions to the aims and rituals of alchemy lend the manifesto's formulations of surrealist doctrines a decidedly radical and experiential flavour. The famous passage on Surrealism's aspiration to locate the 'certain point de l'esprit' (certain point in the mind) where contradictions cease to be operative is followed by the claim that 'l'expérience surréaliste' has nothing to do with aesthetics or philosophy but with 'l'anéantissement de l'être en un brillant, intérieur et aveugle, qui ne soit pas plus l'âme de la glace que celle du feu' (the absorption of being into an opaque gem that is no more the soul of glass than that of fire). Inspiration is recognizable by the 'prise de possession totale de notre esprit' (total possession of our mind) that short-circuits the customary mechanisms of thought and illuminates 'la partie non révélée et pourtant révélable de notre être' (the unrevealed yet revealable part of our being) (I, 810). Social revolt, existential angst, and the aura of the 'fait divers' combine in the definition of the simplest surrealist act: shooting at random into a crowd. A darker, more troubled side of Surrealism is also perceptible in Breton's poetry at this time, notably in the poems written at Lyons-la-Forêt in spring 1931. 'L'Union libre' is often read as a paean to the loved one but goes far beyond the Renaissance tradition of the *blason* in fragmenting and fetishizing the female body. Desire in these poems is a transgressive force that threatens identity.[16] In this context, *Les Vases communicants*, which can be seen as a response to *Documents*, represents the attempt to reclaim the beneficent and reparative powers of the unconscious from the darker drives of the human psyche. Significantly, it is of all Breton's texts the one where everyday life is most prominent.

In *Les Vases communicants* the word 'vie' and its cognates, 'vivant', 'vital', 'vivre', 'le vécu' occur repeatedly.[17] Aiming to demonstrate the unity of the real world and the dream world, Breton claims to take a resolutely materialist line, chiding Freud himself for having at times resorted to ambiguous formulations and for lacking any sense of dialectical method. Breton's first tactic is to provide an exhaustive analysis of one of his own dreams, showing that every detail has a function, and underlining the dream's therapeutic efficacy. When he was at a low ebb because a woman had left him for a man with more money, the dream, not only monitory but performative, worked to dissolve mental fixations: 'il [le rêve] m'engage à éliminer et, peut-on dire, élimine pour moi la part consciemment la moins assimilable du passé [. . .] [le rêve] aide l'homme à accomplir le *saut vital*' (the dream commits me to eliminating and, as it were, eliminates for me the elements of the past least capable of being assimilated by the conscious mind . . . it helps man to take the *vital* leap).[18] However, the burden of Breton's demonstration is found in the middle section where, as in the central portion of *Nadja*, he closely scrutinizes a brief period of his own daily life. Modelling his discussion on the earlier dream analysis, he treats occurrences in his waking life over a three-week period, 5–24 April 1931, and particularly the days around 12 April, as if they were the manifest content of a dream. Encounters with women—a German tourist, a young girl from a poor area, and a dancer from the Folies Bergères—feature prominently. Breton seeks to identify, through its traces in his daily life, the process of unconscious choice-making, proceeding inductively from the evidence of particular reactions, modes of attention and decision, to the presumed pathways of unconscious association. He argues that surrendering to the erotic theatre of the city streets may inspire conduct at odds with 'l'amour réciproque' (reciprocal love)—in his case succumbing to the appeal of a number of women in rapid succession—but that this provisional return to disorder and indeterminacy is a

---

[16] See Michael Sheringham 'Éros noir, éros blanc: l'interrogation du désir dans la poésie d'André Breton: 1931–33', *André Breton, Revue des Sciences Humaines*, 237 (1995), 11–27.

[17] Cf. the discussion of surrealist vitalism in Ch. 2 above.

[18] Breton, *Œuvres complètes*, II, 135. Subsequent references to *Les Vases* are given in the text.

route back to individual choice, preference, and monogamy. At stake here is the challenge of returning to 'la vie', which involves thinking of other people as real rather than as projections of one's fantasies (II: 153).

In the case of the working-class girl he meets on the 'Boulevards extérieurs', Breton's attraction is determined by a number of factors, including her eyes and her evident penury, confirmed when she stops to buy gherkins on the way back to the rue Pajol. For Breton the humble 'cornichons' relished by the girl and her mother emblematize 'la vie de tous les jours' (everyday life) with which he is happy to renew contact, and the 'goûts minimes qu'on a, qu'on a pas' (little tastes we have or don't have) (II, 158), reminiscent of the 'sensations électives' in *Nadja*. The girl's poverty enables Breton to reverse the roles in his failed relationship, and to shower her with small luxuries (a red azalea, a large doll), while her gloomy neighbourhood prompts admiring reflections on the descriptive power of naturalist writers, judged to be more poetic than the Symbolists, including Zola, the Goncourts, Huysmans, and Robert Caze, and a paean to detail (II, 159).

The assignation in the Café Batifol on 21 April, when a third woman takes the place of the young girl, is at the heart of the three-day period when Breton's daily life was at its most dream-like, and when the networks of unconscious association linking widely differing aspects and events will in retrospect be most conspicuous. Breton's analysis of this period constitutes an anthology of the ways the unconscious can manifest itself in daily life, including substituted names, jokes, bizarre events, coincidences, found objects, chance encounters. Summing up the experiences he has described in such detail, Breton argues that there is no fundamental difference between the dream state and the one he found himself in for a few days in April 1931 (and, by implication, quite frequently for shorter periods). The fact that in one case he is in bed, while in the other, 'je me déplace réellement dans Paris' (I am really going round Paris) (II, 177), is immaterial. In both contexts Breton is able to perform routine actions (breathing when asleep; walking and talking when awake), while at the same time almost totally absorbed by unconscious processes. In both cases unconscious desire runs the show:

l'éxigence du désir à la recherche de l'*objet* de sa réalisation dispose étrangement des données extérieures, tendant égoïstement à ne retenir d'elle que ce qui peut servir sa cause. La vaine agitation de la rue est devenue à peine plus gênante que le froissement des draps. Le désir est là, taillant en pleine pièce dans l'étoffe pas assez vite changeante, puis laisssant entre les morceaux courir son fil sûr et fragile (II, 177).

(the exigency of desire in quest of the *object* of its realization makes hay with external facts, egotistically retaining only what may serve its cause. The futile activity of the street is scarcely more irksome than tangled bed sheets. Desire is at work, carving up the rapidly changing fabric, then deftly setting its fragile thread to work between the pieces)

Desire cuts and pastes, tears and sews, just as happy with 'choses prises sur le vif'—this woman's eyes, that cartoon, this café—as with memory traces of the previous day's activities. Breton insists that even if unconscious desire plays fast and loose with appearances, it is nonetheless on the side of life, reality, and unity: 'le café Batifol n'est pas un mythe' (the café Batifol is not a myth), he observes (II, 178). The vision of desire being elaborated at this point is essentially positive in its tonality. It holds that human desire acts in concordance with 'la nécéssité naturelle' (natural necessity), a life force serving as a 'bouée de sauvetage' (buoy) against life's adversities. 'Je tentais déséspérément, de toutes mes forces, d'extraire du *milieu*, à l'exclusion de tout le reste, ce qui devait d'abord servir à la reconstitution de ce moi' (I was desperately striving, with all my power, to extract from the *milieu*, to the exclusion of all else, what could contribute to the rebuilding of my self) (II, 179). Despite the negativity of the forces in play—the omnipotence of subjective representations potentially endangering psychic health by sequestering the subject from the real world—the process at work is ultimately beneficent. The world of dreams can be seen as antithetical to real life, but the work of desire in daily life, properly understood, involves a 'passage à vide' that is ultimately restorative. The influence of the role of negativity in Hegel's *Philosophy of Mind*, a key text for Breton at this time, is clearly perceptible here.[19]

In the final section of *Les Vases communicants* the enquiry into the relationship between dreams and waking life turns into a eulogy of 'la nécéssité subjective' (subjective necessity). Arguing for subjectivity's 'revanche éclatante' (dazzling revenge) in the spheres of knowledge and moral consciousness, Breton urges that 'l'étude du moi' be rehabilitated (II, 196). This introduces the famous finale where 'l'essence générale de la subjectivité' (the general essence of subjectivity) is allegorized in a vision of Paris—viewed at dawn from the steps of the Sacré-Coeur basilica—as a giant woman slowly awakening. Breton's peroration turns feminine beauty and nocturnal indeterminacy into figures of subjectivity's absolute sovereignty, incarnated by the city itself (II, 207). But Breton's next move is to evoke a subjectivity currently out of

---

[19] On this see the helpful footnotes in Breton, *Œuvres complètes*, II, 1363.

joint, requiring the commitment of fresh resources if it is to realize its true potential. What subjectivity, in its currently parlous state, does *not* need are 'vies romancées', newly in vogue (presumably thanks to André Maurois), and other 'literary' treatments. What it does need is the subjective testimony of individuals willing to explore their own feelings, seeking to understand:

comment tel individu est affecté par le cours des années de la vie, d'une part, et par l'idée qu'il se fait, d'autre part, du rapport sexuel. Ce sont là, bien entendu toutes recherches que la légèreté commune et l'hypocrisie sociale rendent pratiquement impossibles de façon suivie. Ainsi se perd la dernière chance que nous ayons de disposer, en matière de subjectivité, de documents vivants de quelque prix (II, 207).

(how a particular individual is affected by the successive phases of his life, and by sexuality. These are of course enquiries that the general levity and social hypocrisy tend for the most part to impede. Thus we lose the access we might otherwise have to living documents of great value)

What is needed, in other words, is authentic autobiography. It is arguably no coincidence therefore that, soon after Breton publishes *Les Vases communicants*, Michel Leiris, freshly returned from the Dakar-Djibouti expedition, to which he had been appointed secretary after meeting the ethnologist Marcel Griaule in the context of *Documents*, was settling down in earnest to create his remarkable fusion of surrealist collage and autobiography, *L'Age d'homme* (written 1932–5, published 1939), which is precisely concerned with the areas mentioned by Breton: the transitions between the ages of man, and the question of sexual relations.[20] No more coincidental, perhaps, than the fact that Breton refers to his desiderata as '*documents* vivants'. Just as *Les Vases communicants* was Breton's response to the challenge of Bataille, *L'Age d'homme*, which acknowledges the influence of *Nadja* on its rejection of fiction in favour of documentary authenticity, was Leiris's route out of *Documents*.

If a vitalist current in Breton's thought manifests itself particularly strongly in *Les Vases communicants*, it is partly because Breton centred his demonstration on a period when the reparative character of desire which, 's'il est vraiment vital, ne se refuse rien' (if it is truly vital refuses itself nothing) (II, 181), was most manifest because most needed. Here desire's office is to act as a go-between from the imaginary or fantasmatic to the real, to serve the interests of life by taking on the quality of a life force. Unity and synthesis are certainly predominant in *Les Vases communicants*. Yet it is also possible to identify,

---

[20] Michel Leiris, *L'Age d'homme* (1939; Paris: Gallimard Folio, 1979)

in the picture of 'la vie' which this text offers, a complex and disturbing reality rather than something reassuring or accessible. After all, 'la vie', in Breton's use of the word, far from being associated with the pleasures and pains of the daily round, is associated with intermittence, desire, and unconscious processes, in short with a subjectivity ever in the making rather than with secure identity. Defending the view that far from constituting a pure irrationalism surrealist activity has a direct bearing on life, Breton asserts that the poet's door does not open onto a world elsewhere but in fact brings us back to life: 'il n'y a plus qu'un pas à faire pour, au sortir de la maison vacillante des poètes, se retrouver de plain-pied dans la vie' (only one further step and, emerging from the poet's shuddering door, we are reinstated in real life). A phrase in the preceding sentence provides a gloss on this. If one can show that the dream world and the world of reality can be reconciled, Breton argues, then one helps bring about 'la conversion de plus en plus nécessaire [...] de l'imaginé au vécu ou plus exactement au devoir-vivre' (the increasingly necessary conversion ... of the imagined into the lived or more exactly into life as it should be) (II, 104). By being convertible into 'life', the imaginary exhibits both exchange value and use value: what it helps to instate is not only 'le vécu', in the sense of routine lived experience, but 'le devoir-vivre', in other words the aspect of 'la vie' that is elusive, future-oriented, yet to come.

MICHEL LEIRIS AND THE SACRED IN EVERYDAY LIFE

On 24 April 1933 Michel Leiris's diary recorded his dissatisfaction with Breton's attempt to demonstrate, in *Les Vases communicants*, that the world of dreams was continuous with and almost entirely reducible to the world of waking life.[21] What made dreams precious for Leiris was precisely their alterity, the way their occasional incursions into everyday life brought intensity to an amorphous *quotidien*. Five years later, Leiris's 'Le Sacré dans la vie quotidienne'—delivered as a lecture to the Collège de Sociologie—seems to make the same point: the instances of 'sacred' experience with which it is concerned are held to be 'séparé du monde courant' (separate from the ordinary world), 'sans commune mesure avec le reste' (incommensurate

---

[21] Michel Leiris, *Journal 1922–1989*, ed. Jean Jamin (Paris: Gallimard, 1992), 214–15.

with the rest).[22] Yet Leiris's desire to track down sacred experience at the level of 'des faits très humbles et situés en dehors de ce qui constitue aujourd'hui le sacré' (very humble facts situated outside what today we call the sacred)[23] is symptomatic of an ambiguity, running right through his discussion, which makes his text significant in the context of later ethnographies of the everyday that take daily rituals and objects as their focus.[24]

Leiris's preoccupation with 'le sacré' reflects the central place this notion came to have for the dissident Surrealists of the 1930s, in the aftermath of *Documents* and notably in the context of the Collège de Sociologie, founded by Bataille, Leiris, and Caillois in 1937.[25] By the early 1930s 'le sacré' was the key concept of the French ethnographic school, to which Leiris became closely affiliated through his participation in the 'Mission Djakar-Djibouti' in 1931–3 under the leadership of Marcel Griaule who had been a contributor to *Documents*. The opposition between the sacred and the profane played a central role in Emile Durkheim's *Les Formes élémentaires de la vie religieuse* (1912), but his account of 'moments d'effervescence' had posited two heterogeneous dimensions of experience: one individual, the other collective.[26] Marcel Mauss's *Essai sur le don* (1925) had focused on ritual practices where the polarity between sacred and profane, whilst fundamental, operated within the field of social exchange, and his work inspired, notably in Griaule, a rigorously codified practice of 'participant-observation' through which the fieldworker aimed progressively to understand the imbrications of sacred and profane in myths and rituals. Rudolph Otto's influential *Das Heilige*, 1929 (the Holy, or in French 'le sacré'), had given the sacred/profane polarity a more experiential character, contrasting and classifying different states and contexts, giving considerable prominence to sacred places. Meanwhile, Caillois, Leiris, and others adopted a key distinction, originally made by Roger Hertz, between a 'sacré droit' corresponding to an aspiration towards disembodied purity, and a 'sacré gauche' reflecting the way sacred experience is often rooted in fear and awe, as Otto had insisted, but also in disgust, horror, and transgression.[27]

---

[22] Ibid., 'Le Sacré dans la vie quotidienne' in id., *La Règle du jeu*, ed. Denis Hollier, (1946–66; Paris: Gallimard, 2003), 1115.

[23] Ibid., 1110.

[24] See Ch. 8 below.

[25] On this see Denis Hollier, *Le Collège de sociologie 1937–39* (Paris: Gallimard Folio, 1995).

[26] See Michèle Richman, 'L'Altérité sacrée chez Durkheim', in C.W. Thompson (ed.), *L'Autre et le sacré: surréalisme, ethnographie, cinéma* (Paris: L'Harmattan, 1995).

[27] On Hertz, see Hollier, *Le Collège de sociologie*, 105.

For Bataille, 'le sacré' was above all 'gauche'. Insisting on 'le caractère essentiellement répugnant des choses sacrées' (the essentially repugnant character of sacred realities),[28] Bataille associated the 'sacré' with transgression, taboo, and limit experiences, notably in the domain of eroticism and suffering. As Denis Hollier has argued, the Collège de Sociologie, a project involving the collaboration of Bataille, Caillois, and Leiris, first outlined in July 1937,[29] presented itself, beyond literature and politics, as a scientific venture aimed at identifying the vital currents in society. 'Sacred sociology' analysed modern urban society with the concepts evolved in the study of so-called primitive societies, studying concrete social existence in those of its manifestations 'où se fait jour la présence active du sacré' (where the active presence of the sacred is felt).[30] The Collège launched a cycle of public lectures, of which Leiris's, delivered on 8 January 1938, was the fourth. In November 1938 Caillois gave a lecture on 'L'ambiguité du sacré', the second chapter of his *L'Homme et le sacré* published in 1939, giving particular prominence to the opposition of 'gauche' and 'droit', and the polarities of attraction and repulsion on which Bataille had lectured earlier in the series.[31]

The 'droit/gauche' polarity is at the heart of Leiris's *Miroir de la tauroma-chie*, published just before the foundation of the *Collège*. Here the bullfight mirrors a category of experiences where customary limits are transcended and we find ourselves, albeit briefly, at a tangent to the world and to our customary identity:

Certains sites, certains événements, certains objets, certaines circonstances très rares nous donnent, en effet, le sentiment [. . .] que leur fonction dans l'ordre général des choses est de nous mettre en contact avec ce qu'il y a au fond de nous de plus intime, en temps ordinaire de plus trouble.[32]

(Certain places, events, objects and very rare circumstances make us feel . . . that their function in the general run of things is to put us in touch with what is most intimate to us and in terms of ordinary duration most troubling)

Leiris insists on momentariness—a 'bref paroxysme, qui ne dure pas plus qu'un éclair' (a brief paroxysm that is over in a flash)—whose force stems from its vivid contrast with the placid surface of ordinary existence and from its

---

[28] Hollier, *Le Collège de sociologie*, 21.
[29] Ibid., 17–29.
[30] On Hertz, see Hollier, *Le Collège de sociologie*, 27. Cf. Mass-Observation in Britain.
[31] Both lectures are included in Hollier, *Le Collège de sociologie*.
[32] Michel Leiris, *Miroir de la tauromachie* (Montepellier: Fata Morgana, 1981), 25.

intermittent nature, which sets up a rhythm of sacralization and desacraliza-
tion. But he also insists on its ambivalence, linking this to the two dimensions
of the 'sacré' that such 'expériences cruciales' manifest. Here the 'élément
gauche' is constituted by the very brevity and negativity of the experience,
the fact that, by disappointing the promise of plenitude, it opens a void or
abyss which confirms that total fusion can only occur at the moment of death.

'Le Sacré dans la vie quotidienne' (The Sacred in Everyday Life) seems to
conform to the tenets of the Collège de Sociologie. At first sight Leiris brings
the notion of the 'sacré'—with its two modalities—to bear on everyday life, in
conformity with the *Collège*'s ambition to address modern society. But what
makes Leiris's lecture far more valuable as a contribution to thinking about the
everyday is that, in significant ways, it breaks with the prevailing model,
including *Miroir de la tauromachie*, and anticipates more recent ethnographies
of the everyday in, say, Barthes, Perec, Ernaux, or Augé, and more generally the
'proximate ethnography' of the 1980s.[33] What is striking when we read it
today is how Leiris avoids such terms as 'perte', dépense', 'déchirure', and the
climate of transgression and taboo surrounding the sacred in Bataille or
Caillois.[34] Indeed, what now seems provocative in 'Le Sacré dans la vie
quotidienne' is not the 'sacralization' of everyday life, so much as the 'quoti-
dianization' of the sacred.[35]

Leiris's first move is to locate the sacred in the everyday world: objects,
places, events. He sets out to establish the particular consistency ('couleur') of
his personal 'sacré'. His strategy resembles Breton's when in *Nadja* he enumerates a series of encounters—with objects, places, and events—that gave
him the feeling of being a participant in a network of coincidences and signals
in which a hidden side of his identity was at stake.[36] But, in Leiris's case,
routing the quest for the sacred through autobiographical space involves
delving into childhood memories so as to establish the founding framework
of the individual's world, insofar as it is marked by a fundamental opposition
between sacred and profane. If the psychological sign of this polarity is
ambivalence—a mixture of fear and attraction, danger and desire, respect
and horror—the detour via childhood locates this border area amidst very

---

[33] See Ch. 8 below.

[34] Hollier indicates that Leiris seems consistently to have a certain distance from the activities of
the Collège.

[35] Jean Jamin discerns a 'banalization' of the *sacré* in Leiris's essay, and argues that Leiris never fully
embraced the ideology of the Collège. See Jamin's 'Quand le sacré devint gauche', *L'Ire des vents*, 3–4
(1981), 98–120.

[36] Breton, *Œuvres complètes*, I, 652.

ordinary objects, places, and circumstances (the categories are the same as *Miroir*, but the emotional temperature is quite different). In fact Leiris repeatedly insists on the minor mode, using words like 'humble', 'menu', 'minime', a trait that will be central to the 'écriture du quotidien' from Barthes and Perec onwards, as is the recourse to enumeration. The decision to call up memories provokes a recapitulative inventory.[37] Firstly, objects, and initially those symbolizing paternal authority: his father's top hat, revolver, and purse (a 'coffre-fort bijou'), but also the 'Radieuse', a household boiler with its female effigy. Secondly, places: both indoor, notably the toilet, where Leiris and his brother devised complex mythologies based on their enthusiasm for sport and adventure; and outdoor, notably the 'espace mal qualifié' around the Auteuil racecourse, a kind of no-man's-land outside established boundaries, and the racecourse itself with its radiant jockeys and arcane rituals of gambling and etiquette. Thirdly, 'circonstances' or events; above all 'certains faits de langage': words or combinations of words that had a quasi-magical aura, like the phrase 'maison vide' which Leiris and his brother applied to an outcrop of rocks near their holiday home; and instances where the sudden discovery of correct pronunciation ('heureusement' not ' . . . reusement'), or usage, made language a territory where the tiniest difference can have vast repercussions.

Rather than focusing on the moment of transition, the perturbing experience of the sacred itself, Leiris's deadpan enumerations locate the otherness of the 'sacré' within the everyday framework of the individual's relation to self and world. If it is heterogeneous and other, otherness and heterogeneity are located within the coordinates of individual, everyday identity. Yet Leiris makes subtle use of ethnological concepts to bring out their wider significance or typicality. The brothers' clubby confabulations in the lavatory evoke the 'maison des hommes' of Polynesian islanders, and the droit/gauche polarity is used to differentiate the 'official' sacred of the living room from that of the toilets. The no-man's-land round the race track is compared to the 'brousse' (scrubland) outside the native village, associated with the supernatural, and the prowess of the sporting hero is compared to that of the shaman. In the sphere of language, Leiris and his brother, with their private nomenclature, distinguishing *sablonnière* (big sandpit) from *sablière* (small sandpit), or two types of paper aeroplane, are said to behave in the manner of 'ritualists' for whom the sacred is based on minute distinctions.[38]

---

[37] Leiris, *La Règle du jeu*, 1111–12.
[38] Ibid, 1112–13.

Although it pays lip-service to the contemporary discourse on the 'sacré' (including his own contribution to this in *Miroir de la tauromachie*) Leiris's lecture has different orientations. Whereas, in the context of the *Collège* lecture series, one would have expected to see the 'sacré' annexing the territory of the everyday, here the everyday infiltrates the preserve of the 'sacré'. If Leiris maintains the idea that the sacred is a radically other world, 'aussi différent du monde profane que le feu l'est de l'eau' (as different from the profane world as fire is from water), in focusing his attention on its more attenuated manifestations, on 'menus faits' and minimes découvertes', and by referring less to key moments than to 'le glissement d'un état profane à un état sacré' (the slide from a profane state to a sacred one), he points to a far more diffuse and pervasive presence of the sacred, more akin to the Freudian psychopathology of everyday life and its surrealist applications. This is consistent with the emphasis on autobiography, which associates the sacred with the survival and return of childhood experiences.

The distancing from the *Collège* is confirmed by a notebook, titled 'L'Homme sans honneur' (Man without Honour), that Leiris kept before, during, and after the composition of his lecture. Conceding that the sacred can only exist 'par *instants*' (momentarily),[39] that it involves the transcendence of limits, Leiris sees these as the narrow confines of individual experience that sever us from the world of others. The sacred, like childhood, is that from which we feel distant. In sacred experience we do not break with ordinary humanity, but are brought (albeit briefly) into communion with it. We must seek it like a missing link 'à partir de quoi l'on peut s'insérer à nouveau dans le monde' (from which we can again be united with the world) (1124). Associated with poetry and with language, it unites us with a lost but desired totality: 'C'est dans le sacré qu'on est à la fois le plus soi et le plus hors-de-soi. Parce qu'on se meut, alors, sur le plan de la totalité' (It is in the sacred that one is both most oneself and the furthest away from oneself. Because there we are at the level of totality) (1135). Ideally, therefore, poetic creation should not seek discontinuous illuminations, relating to special circumstances, but 'un système constant de représentation du monde, une série continue de perceptions poétiques' (a regular system of representation, a continuous series of poetic perceptions) (1135). Rather than the consecration or trigger of special moments, poetry (and the sacred) would be 'une sorte de *dimension* de la pensée

---

[39] M. Leiris, 'L'Homme sans honneur: notes pour "Le Sacré dans la vie quotidienne" ', in *La Règle du jeu*, 1119–54. Other page references are incorporated in the text.

(au même titre que l'espace, le temps, la causalité)' (a sort of *dimension* of thought (like space, time or causation)) (1135). This option for continuity, community, and totality makes Leiris's 'sacré' very different from that of Bataille, *Documents*, and the Collège de Sociologie, where the only continuity affirmed is with the primal, anthropological roots of the human organism.

For Leiris the 'sacré *par excellence*' arises when one is simultaneously 'parfaitement soi' and 'parfaitement hors de soi', (1145) and hence it is, paradoxically, a mode of communication. This is borne out in '.... reuse-ment', the famous text at the start of *Biffures* where Leiris enlarges on one of the 'faits de langage' (matters of language) broached in 'Le Sacré dans la vie quotidienne'. The toy soldier that survives intact after being dropped, prompting the interjection '...reusement' (...'ortunately), and the well-meant but traumatic restitution of the correct word, 'fortunately', that ensues, is an instance of the sacred, not because it provides access to the 'monde à part [...] surajouté au quotidien' (world apart, added on to the everyday), the closed, sacred world of childhood, but because it reveals the border between that world and the world of others: language ceases to be the property of the sacred band of brothers and is revealed to be everybody's: 'de chose propre à moi il devint chose commune et ouverte'.[40] If this means that the sacred is revealed just at the point when it is lost, Leiris also suggests that it should be identified with neither pole but with the passage from the one to the other: the movement of communication itself, which aligns 'soi' and 'hors de soi'. What is sacred is the connection: 'je parle du lien lui-même, qui seul constitue le sacré, dont l'objet n'est que le support'[41] (I refer to the link itself, which alone constitutes the sacred, the object being only the vehicle); and so: 'le sacré reste fluide, n'est jamais substantialisé' (the sacred remains fluid, is never substanti-fied).

By locating it in an everyday context, not as what takes us away from the ordinary but as an experience that reveals it, Leiris alters the bearings of the 'sacré'. Identifying the sacred with fluidity, communication, and totality, he turns it away from the momentary spasm and locates it in a dimension of subjective experience itself. In this, as in its link to the autobiographical, to the minimal, and to the pertinence of ethnological paradigms in the investigation of ordinary, near-at-hand experience, Leiris's lecture is a major step in the direction of later ethnologies of the everyday.

---

[40] Leiris, *La Règle du jeu*, 6.
[41] 'L'Homme sans honneur' in *La Règle du jeu*, 1146.

ANDRÉ BRETON AND THE 'MAGIQUE-CIRCONSTANCIELLE'

In its very insistence on the category of the 'sacré' Leiris's contribution to the Collège de Sociologie remains dissident with respect to Surrealism. Yet Leiris's lecture represented a move away from Bataille towards new forms of autobiographical writing, often exploring events or series of events that seemed to manifest the inner workings of the psyche. In *L'Age d'homme* and *Biffures* this tendency to find allegories of inner experience in the unfolding of outer occurrences is more often than not censured as illusory, but in *Fourbis*, where it is classified as 'le mythe vécu', and in *Fibrilles*, Leiris is more charitable towards a fundamentally poetic strategy based on real desire for convergence between microcosm and macrocosm. In *Frêle bruit*, the rehabilitation of this way of seeing, and its assimilation to the category of the 'merveilleux', with its explicitly surrealist antecedents, is all but complete.[42]

The Leirisian 'mythe vécu' has clear affinities with the concept of 'le magique-circonstantielle' (the magical-circumstantial) outlined and explored by André Breton in a series of articles mainly published in the review *Minotaure* between 1933 and 1936 and brought together to form *L'Amour fou* in 1937. This work is often seen (notably by Breton himself) as the third part of a trilogy, comprising *Nadja* and *Les Vases communicants*, focused on the close documentation and quasi-scientific investigation of real experiences in the streets of Paris. But the orientation of Breton's scrutiny of chance events and strange convergences, which had already shifted between the first two volumes, has a different complexion in *L'Amour fou*, and this has significant implications for the evolution of the surrealist everyday.

Although he uses it sparingly, notably in the programmatic opening text, the phrase 'magique-circonstantielle' embraces a range of experiences, including those Breton will label by the more abstract term 'hasard objectif' (objective chance), that exhibit a 'magical' convergence between the inner, subjective desires of the individual and the seemingly independent pathways of causation determining circumstances in the outer, objective world. Where the analyses of *Les Vases communicants* showed how, in daily life, desire shaped lived experi-

---

[42] On this see Michael Sheringham, *French Autobiography: Devices and Desires* (Oxford: Oxford University Press, 1993), 246–87. (*Biffures, Fourbis, Fibrilles,* and *Frêle bruit* are constituent parts of *La Règle du jeu*.)

ence in the interests of psychic reparation, *L'Amour fou* will go further, focusing
on instances—special moments—when the realization of desire produces
special kinds of event. The 'magique-circonstantielle' is introduced as one of
the three components of 'convulsive beauty' (a concept adumbrated at the end
of *Nadja*),[43] but it is manifestly the core element since the others are essentially
criteria attesting the authenticity of the experiences concerned. Thus, Breton is
indifferent to spectacles or works that fail to affect him physically and quasi-
erotically (this criterion is called 'érotique-voilée' (erotic-veiled)), inducing a
sensation he compares to a breath of air brushing his temple. Another constituent of beauty is the combination of movement and stasis, process and form,
epitomized by crystals that are perfectly shaped but are also the product of a
spontaneous, undirected process of formation, and which display both density
and transparency—this criterion, labelled 'explosante-fixe' (explosive-fixed), is
illustrated by a magnificent Man Ray photograph of a flamenco dancer's
swirling skirts.[44] As the hyphens indicate, each of these categories is dialectical
and dynamic, and each implies the two others. Thus, in the 'magique-circonstantielle' the conjunction of chance and necessity enacts a combination of
formal harmony and open-endedness liable to induce a *jouissance* that is
dizzying and erotically charged. What prompts this is the feeling that an
event or series of events in the course of one's daily life depends not only on
an evident chain of outer causation, but on a hidden chain rooted in the
workings of unconscious desire. At the core of 'le magique-circonstantiel' is the
'trouvaille' (lucky find)—a powerful sense that external reality has in some way
lent itself to the articulation of inner feeling, gifting an unforeseeable 'solution'
(this word is recurrent) to a psychic conjuncture that is made manifest, and
often reconfigured, in the process. Breton describes the *trouvaille* as 'le merveilleux précipité du désir' (the marvellous precipitate of desire),[45] noting that
'la vie quotidienne abonde [. . .] en menues découvertes de cette sorte' (everyday life abounds in tiny discoveries of this kind), and he singles out once more
the modalities of attention. Attention—the 'attention flottante' (floating
attention) of psychoanalysis—is the antenna that registers what is grist to the
mill of unconscious desire (II, 685).[46] In the second chapter, on 'la rencontre'

[43] Breton, *Œuvres complètes*, I, 753.
[44] Breton did not include another Man Ray photograph, of a naked Meret Oppenheim, which
illustrated 'érotique-voilée' in *Minotaure*. By and large, the photographs in *L'Amour fou*, of excellent
artistic quality—notably those by Brassaï—have a conventional illustrative role and are not integral
to the text as in *Nadja*.
[45] Breton, *Œuvres complètes* II, 682.
[46] On 'attention flottante' see previous chapter and Ch. 9 below.

(meeting), Breton states that his aim in *L'Amour fou* will be to conduct a rigorous analysis designed to highlight the 'lumière de l'anomalie' (anomalous light) emanating from 'quelques-uns des faits à première vue les plus humbles [aussi bien] que les plus significatifs de ma vie' (some of the, at first sight, most humble . . . as well as most significant occurrences in my life) (II, 696).

After two theoretical chapters Breton focuses on four instances where an encounter in the everyday world—with an object at the flea market, a new love, a 'good' place, and a 'bad 'place'—turned out to have been conditioned by inner desire, or human and logical, as opposed to purely natural, necessity. In each case the encounter in the real world reveals itself, on analysis, to be a mirror or screen revealing the pathways and ruses of desire as it seeks to make itself known to the conscious mind (II, 696). Thus, in chapter 3, the 'trouvailles' of a strange mask and an oddly handled spoon by Breton and Giacometti at the Marché aux puces are shown to have had a catalytic effect, externalizing and 'solving' problems lying dormant in the unconscious.

The account, in chapter 4 of *L'Amour fou*, of how a walk through Paris, on the night Breton met the woman who was to become his second wife, had matched, in its topography and many other details, a scenario 'predicted' in a poem he had written ten years earlier, offers a far more complex, and, as Breton acknowledges, less inherently plausible, demonstration of the capacity of subjective desire to shape the path of external events. But Breton's detailed account, modelled as he insists (as in *Nadja*) on 'l'obversation médicale' (medical observation) (Breton had received training in psychiatry), and paying particular heed to what he calls the 'état émotionnel du sujet au moment où se produisirent de tels faits' (the subject's emotional state at the moment when the events occurred) (II, 710), makes most sense if we underline the parallelism between the composition of the poem and Breton's state of mind on the 'nuit du tournesol' (night of the sunflower). He insists that the poem, titled 'Tournesol', snatches of which had come back to him while he was shaving a day or two after the nocturnal walk, had been the product of automatic writing and that it had puzzled and irritated him ever since. Equally, as in the case of the period analysed in detail in *Les Vases communicants*, Breton claims that his state of mind on 29 May 1934 inclined him to 'take things as they come', to surrender as far as possible to the course of events. So much so that, in retrospect, he scarcely recognizes himself: 'Je me perds presque de vue, il me semble que j'ai été emporté' (I lose sight of myself, I think I was transported) (II, 715). These circumstances explain how the real world lent itself the more readily to the needs of the unconscious. By surrendering Breton had in effect adopted the 'comportement lyrique' (lyrical behaviour), akin to the 'dés-oeuvrement' (idleness) celebrated in *Nadja*—a non-determinative 'dérive' (drifting) as the Situationists will call it—which he sees as one of the main 'divinatory' strategies of Surrealism (II, 722). It is as if, in the events of the 'Nuit du tournesol', and by dint of Breton's 'comportement', a virtual scen-ario, long held on ice, had found circumstances favourable to its realization, its irruption into actuality. The poem, written 'automatically', had been the receptacle for Breton's desiring subjectivity, and it is this desire, of which the poem is the reservoir, that finds its expression in a sequence of real events ten years later, through the 'projection du poème dans la vie réelle' (projection of the poem onto real life) (II, 730). Breton's analysis is designed to provide a 'document [...] probant' (convincing document) testifying to the 'condi-tionnement purement spirituel' (purely spiritual conditioning) of a series of events that looked as if they were conditioned by contingent, objective factors (II, 733). A walk apparently determined by contingent circumstances—for example the location of his partner's dwelling—turns out to have been in conformity with the script of inner desire, promulgated by Breton's 'compor-tement lyrique'.

Chapter 5 recreates the ascent of the Pic du Teide volcano in Tenerife by Breton and his new wife, Jacqueline. Here it is the landscape that takes on the status of an 'objet trouvé' (found object) and serves, via numerous, primarily botanical and geological, details as a 'révélateur' of inner desire. In this instance the landscape of desire that doubles the physical one is not so much Breton's subjective unconscious as the general realm of human subjectivity itself, and specifically its manifestation in *amour-passion*. Turning the scrutiny of the landscape into a 'leçon de choses', Breton derives universal principles from his personal experience: 'Seul compte l'effet universel, éternel: je n'existe qu'autant qu'il est réversible à moi' (Only the universal effect counts: I only exist insofar as it applies to myself) (II, 752). Key passages focus on points during the ascent when visibility was restricted and vision gave way to projection. On the first occasion Breton notes the way the rapid withdrawal of visual plenitude had rallied the forces of subjectivity, the capacity of the 'moi' to recreate the world (II, 739). On the second occasion, vision is impeded by what Breton, with a sideways glance at Bataille, refers to as 'l'informe par excellence' (the formless *par excellence*): a cloud.[47] For Breton, however, the *informe* is also the profusion of changing shapes and, as in

---

[47] Bataille celebrated the 'informe' in *Documents* and elsewhere.

Gestalttheorie, the interaction of mind and form can serve to externalize, through projection, the powers and riches of inner subjective vision. Citing Shakespeare's Polonius, Baudelaire's poem 'Le Voyage' and his prose poem 'L'Étranger', and Leonardo da Vinci's famous exhortation to his pupils to take inspiration from old stretches of wall, Breton develops the idea that external reality provides a whole variety of 'écrans' (screens) that can serve to bring inner desire into the open, solving the 'problème du passage de la subjectivité à l'objectivité' (the problem of the passage from subjectivity to objectivity) (II, 752–3). Anything can provide such a screen, including a snatch of song or a passage of everyday experience: 'un de ces ensembles homogènes de faits d'aspect lézardé, nuageux [que comporte toute vie]' (one of those homogeneous sets of facts, which every life has, that have a cloudy, or fissured appearance) (II, 784).

The sovereign power of human subjectivity, rooted in inner necessity and desire, the tragedy of its repression, and the drama of its revelation and externalization are at the heart of *L'Amour fou*. A Romantic, Wordsworthian cult of the power of mind (the Pic du Teide echoes the Snowdon of *The Prelude*), rethought in terms of Freud and other branches of psychology, tends to make the world of reality primarily a sounding board for the inner world. Of course Surrealism had always been concerned with the inner world, but by the mid 1930s, the interaction of inner and outer seems increasingly in Breton's thought to have favoured the projection of the former onto the latter. As the writing of place, in his essays on Mexico, and of course in *Arcane 17*, comes to predominate in Breton's writing, the outer becomes above all the mirror of the inner.[48] As in Leiris, what is sought is a 'gage d'accord' (bond of concord)[49] between the self and the world. Even if the last major chapter of *L'Amour fou* redresses the balance somewhat, in its account of an experience in which the negative resonance of a place where a murder had taken place is claimed to have cast a temporary shadow on the relationship between Breton and his lover, so that here it is outer that impinges on inner, subjectivity is still in the centre of the frame (II, 764–77).

Increasingly lacking, however, is that sense of the enigmatic density of the real that led Surrealism to focus with such intensity on the everyday. Admirable as it often is, Breton's desire to rescue subjectivity—encapsulated increas-

---

[48] See Michael Sheringham, 'André Breton et l'écriture du lieu', in C. Bommerz and J. Chénieux Gendron (eds.), *Regards/mises en scéne dans le surréalisme et les avant-gardes* (Leuven: Peeters, 2002), 133–48.
[49] Leiris, *La Règle du jeu* (ed. Hollier), 245.

ingly in love and the feminine, and in exceptional places, rather than in the street and the text—leads to a utopian confidence in its powers. If, nonetheless, Bretonian Surrealism never quite parts company with the everyday, it is because 'le magique-circonstantielle' remains closely linked to a particular attitude or 'comportement', a particular availability to experience. In a superb passage at the beginning of the chapter on the 'trouvaille' Breton expresses his solidarity with imminence rather than realization. Surrealism, he says, does not favour the prey over the shadow, or vice versa, but aims at 'ce qui n'est déjà plus l'ombre et n'est pas encore la proie' (what is already no longer the shadow and not yet the prey). And he affirms: 'Aujourd'hui encore je n'attends rien que de ma seule disponibilité, que de cette soif d'errer *à la rencontre* de tout [. . .] Indépendamment de ce qui arrive, n'arrive pas, c'est l'attente qui est magnifique' (Still today all my expectations spring from my availability, my errant desire to encounter everything . . . Regardless of what happens or does not happen, it is the waiting that is magnificent) (II, 697). Crucial here is the idea that an attitude of openness and availability puts one in tune with a totality, a 'tout' that becomes palpable not only in real encounters but through the sense of the possible and the virtual induced by the climate of expectancy itself. 'Errance', 'disponibilité', 'attente'—and a sense of the mystery of the event, any event: 'ce qui arrive'—remain fundamental to *L'Amour fou* and to the legacy Surrealism bequeaths to the Situationists and other later prospectors of the everyday.

This view is confirmed by the poet Yves Bonnefoy's account of the way Breton's predilection for the *conte* over the *récit* does not represent the triumph of fantasy over reality, but the repudiation of a diminished reality in recognition of the human needs articulated in the tale as opposed to the novel. Even if Breton's poems and narratives, such as *Nadja* and *L'Amour fou*, assert the primacy of a liberated subjectivity, endowed with an infinite power of self-transformation, they are at the same time attentive to the ordinary contexts of human existence. In Breton the surreal is a weapon against the fantasies of rationality itself: transgressing reason, it is, according to Bonnefoy, 'intensément orient[é] vers l'exister quotidien' (intensely oriented towards everyday existence).[50] Where the *récit*, like the novel for Walter Benjamin, in its functional logic, remains complicit with the world as it has become, the *conte*, seemingly committed to the unreal, remains in fact attuned to the world that could be, to the lost world of the everyday.

[50] Yves Bonnefoy, *Breton à l'avant de soi* (Tours: Farrago, 2001), 84.

QUENEAU AND THE *QUOTIDIEN*

France's political, social, economic, and cultural upheavals in the 1930s produced massive changes in daily living. Many of the rhythms and pursuits of everyday life, as it was experienced well into the later twentieth century—mass production, mass media, mass communications: radio, advertising, illustrated magazines full of gossip and lurid 'faits divers', the weakening of gender divisions, mass entertainment dominated by America, tourism and organized leisure—were established at this time. Yet the escalation of violent social and ideological conflict, both nationally and internationally, the crisis of parliamentary democracy, and the depth of economic recession, produced an atmosphere of constant crisis and division. Only with the post-war economic recovery of the mid 1950s would the question of the everyday, placed firmly on the agenda by Henri Lefebvre after the Liberation, be explicitly addressed in a variety of socio-cultural contexts.

Yet a concern for the everyday lives of ordinary people, especially the working classes and the petite bourgeoisie, is a key theme in French culture in the 1930s, before and after the short-lived Front populaire government put the conditions of 'la vie quotidienne' at the heart of its programme. The dissident Surrealism of a Jacques Prévert, a Robert Desnos (who quickly exploited the resources of the new medium of radio), or a Pierre MacOrlan (with his notion of a 'fantastique social') were in tune with the popular front ethos, while Breton's group, having initially placed itself 'au service de la révolution', underwent further political mutations: Aragon and Eluard remained faithful to Moscow, while Breton (and Bataille) participated in a range of revolutionary and anti-fascist groupings. If, as I have emphasized, Surrealism was often strongly vitalist—'Plutôt la vie'—writers and intellectuals of many tendencies questioned the claims of art and disinterested thought and chose to enter the fray of life. Eluard embraced *La Rose publique*, moving 'de l'horizon d'un homme à l'horizon de tous' (from the horizon of one individual to the horizon of all);[51] during the Spanish Civil War Malraux organized a fighter squadron, and wrote *L'Espoir*; Picasso painted *Guernica*. The desire to 'prendre contact avec la vie réelle' (make contact with real life) that led Simone Weil to work on the Renault assembly line, so as to experience

---

[51] Paul Eluard, *Œuvres complètes*, I (Paris: Gallimard Pléiade, 1968), 417–51.

at first hand the soul-destroying monotony of factory piece-work, was emblematic of the period.[52]

Surrealism, populism, philosophy, and formal play are the main currents running through Raymond Queneau's *Le Chiendent*, published in 1933, and this unlikely convergence inaugurated a body of work, including a dozen or so 'anti-novels', that contrive to be highly artificial and anti-realist and yet communicate, indirectly and obliquely a profound concern for lived experience at the level of everyday life. Queneau's novels illustrate perfectly the view, outlined in Chapter 1, that if fictional realism often purports to make the everyday accessible and knowable, it is in fact indirection and obliquity, often produced via the friction and fusion of genres, that give more grip on a dimension of existence that is inherently elusive and indeterminate. Georges Perec acknowledged Queneau as his mentor, and Perec's work will display a similar combination of encyclopedic curiosity, literary experimentation based on the use of formal constraints, apparent flippancy disguising deeply rooted concerns and convictions, and a profound sense of wonder at the ostensibly unremarkable. Basing my discussion primarily on a reading of *Le Chiendent*, I want to argue that if a concern for the everyday is at the heart of Queneau's project this is articulated, indirectly, through the interplay and tension between different strands in his writing.

Centred on the Parisian suburbs linked to the Gare du Nord by the 'train de banlieue' (commuter train), *Le Chiendent* builds a fictional world out of the daily routines of office workers, the rituals of the petit bourgeois household, the cynical secrecy of adolescents, the vacuous worldly wisdom of the aged, the déclassement of young men in search of adventure, the rapacity and gullibility of impecunious cafetiers and serving girls, and so forth. This is seemingly the terrain of the *roman populaire* of the late Twenties and Thirties: Emmanuel Bove, Henri Poulaille, Louis Guilloux, Henri Calet, Eugène Dabit's *Hôtel du Nord*. But like Céline (whose *Voyage au bout de la nuit* was also published in 1933), and inspired partly by Gide and Joyce, Queneau subverts the *roman populaire* model through a host of devices. In Queneau's case the mimetic illusion is totally dispelled. Whether or not we recognize the particular formal patterns he used—for example, the division of each chapter into thirteen sections—we are never likely to 'believe' in the world he invents. Yet the prevalence of comic devices and the use of popular speech patterns do not annul the work's philosophical orientations. A plethora of intertextual allu-

---

[52] See Simone Weil, *La Condition ouvrière* (1951; Paris: Gallimard 'Idées': 1976), 34.

sions, often parodic, give the novel a strange aura of philosophical and spiritual resonance. Indeed the submerged presence of spiritual questions is possibly the most elusive, but in the context of the everyday not the least significant, aspect of Queneau's fiction. Since the posthumous publication of his *Journal*, evidence of Queneau's life-long quest for illumination through esoteric and particularly oriental forms of wisdom has added a new dimension to the reception of his texts.[53] In *Le Chiendent* this is still linked to the features that had drawn him to Surrealism, notably the need to challenge orthodox rationality in the quest for an order behind conventional experiences. But Queneau's surrealist apprenticeship also equipped him with a sense of the anarchic power of comedy and derision. As in Perec and Beckett (another admirer) laughter does not serve to provide a consensual vantage point, but to maintain fluidity, ambiguity, and obliquity.

Queneau's strategies for avoiding any definitive view of his fictional world can be linked to the way everyday life is explicitly approached in *Le Chiendent* via two central motifs: firstly that of observing the everyday in a quasi-experimental fashion, and secondly that of a shift in the perception of everyday experience that leads to existential transformation. The first chapter is structured round the interplay between Pierre le Grand's close observation of the office worker Etienne Marcel, and the latter's rapid transformation as he becomes aware of his relationship with his daily environment. The novel's topography is estab-lished by Pierre's journeys on the suburban line to Obonne in pursuit of Etienne, intercut with the journeys of another young man, Narcense, in pursuit of Etienne's wife. Much of the subsequent action will stem from these and other acts of observing, spying, eavesdropping, and intercepting.

The early parts of *Le Chiendent*[54] feature a number of highly intertextual variations on the figure of the urban 'observateur'. In an essay published in the *Nouvelle Revue Française* in 1969 Queneau corrected an earlier statement regarding the genesis of *Le Chiendent* by claiming that the 'observateur' who features at the beginning derived from his abandoned attempt to translate J. W. Dunne's *An Experiment with Time*.[55] In Dunne's investigation of premoni-tory dreams, the observer's scrutiny of everyday situations and newspaper reports (including the 'faits divers' that feature prominently in *Le Chiendent*) supposedly provides evidence for rethinking the nature of time, breaking

---

[53] See Raymond Queneau, *Journal, 1914–1964* (Paris: Gallimard, 1996). Cf Ch. 8 below.
[54] Raymond Queneau, *Œuvres complètes*, II, *Romans*, I (Paris: Gallimard Pléiade, 2002), 3–247.
[55] Ibid., 1443.

down the barriers between past, present, and future. Pierre le Grand's scrutiny of passers-by, from the vantage point of a café situated opposite the bank where Etienne is employed, initially has a quasi-scientific slant, as in the opening paragraph where Etienne, as yet unidentified, is a mere silhouette: 'Détachée du mur, la silhouette oscilla bousculée par d'autres formes, sans comportement individuel visible, travaillée en sens divers, moins par ses inquiétudes propres que par l'ensemble des inquiétudes de ses milliers de voisins' (detached from the wall the silhouette trembled, buffeted by other forms, without any visible individuating features, badgered in various ways, not by his own anxieties but by the overall anxieties of his thousands of neighbours) (3). Here the neutral gaze of the anonymous 'buveur quotidien' (everyday drinker) (5) does apprehend something of the rhythms of the urban crowd, but if the 'observateur' (observer) (6) thinks he is involved in disinterested experimental activity we soon find out that he is a wealthy dilettante, irritated when his usual seat in the café is taken. Before he mutates into the fictional protagonist Pierre le Grand, the 'observateur' is presented as a composite figure embodying elements of the Gidean 'acte gratuit' and various strands of surrealist 'disponibilité'. The quasi-ethnographic stance of Aragon's Parisian 'paysan' is adumbrated, but if the notion of 'la vie française de café' crosses Pierre's mind, 'il ne s'attarda pas à ces considérations ethnographiques et s'assit au hasard' (he did not linger on these ethnographic considerations and sat down at random) (4). When, 'sans le faire exprès' (unintentionally), he notices a woman's worn shoes, he conjures up the idea of a 'civilisation de souliers éculés, une culture de talons ébréchés, une symphonie de daim et de box-calf...' (civilization of worn shoes, a culture of scuffed heels, a symphony of suede and box-calf...) (4) but the vision, reminiscent of certain passages in *Le Paysan de Paris*, is short-lived and clearly based on class snobbery. Although his decision to follow Etienne is in the tradition of Poe's 'Man of the Crowd', as developed by Baudelaire, the 'observateur' will, to great comic effect, undergo a 'voyage au bout de la nuit' when he is initiated into the grimy horrors of Obonne and Blagny. Disgusted by the filthy cutlery and vile habitués of the café where he is forced to spend the night, he is amazed to find that his views are not shared by another interloper. Narcense, who has arrived in Obonne in pursuit of Etienne's wife, is lyrical about Hipolyte's establishment:

N'est-ce pas étonnant ce petit bistrot de banlieue? [...] comme ça, de temps en temps, une chose vulgaire me paraît belle et je voudrais qu'elle fût éternelle. Je voudrais que ce bistrot et cette lampe Mazda poussiéreuse et ce chien qui rêve sur le marbre et cette nuit même—fussent éternels. Et leur qualité essentielle, c'est précisément de ne pas l'être (17–18).

(Is it not surprising this little suburban bistro? . . . From time to time, out of the blue, something vulgar strikes me as beautiful and I want it to be eternal. I wish this bistro and this dusty Mazda lamp and this dog dreaming on the marble and this night itself—could be eternal. But their essential quality is precisely that they are not)

The Mazda light is probably an allusion to Breton's *Nadja*, but the paradox of the transitory and the eternal is Baudelairean. Narcense's desire to make the café as exotic as the far-off places the drunken sailor in the corner forever mumbles about reveals that, like the 'observateur', he views the everyday 'banlieue' (suburbs) through the veil of his own obsessions. In his way he is no less self-interested or deluded than Mme Cloche who, having fortuitously witnessed the sad demise of Narcense's friend Potice in an 'accident de la circulation' (traffic accident) near the Gare du Nord, decides to place herself daily at the same café table in the hope of witnessing further bloody 'faits divers' (40–1).

Early in *Le Chiendent* Queneau, no doubt with the Surrealists principally in mind, exposes the limitations of the experimental stance of the would-be 'observateur' who views the world from the outside. Through the figure of Etienne Marcel he opens another perspective—that of someone who undergoes an inner transformation in relation to his own everyday life. Bearing the name of a historical personage, a Paris street and a metro station, Etienne Marcel is indeed a cipher—even his wife addresses him as 'Untel' (A. N. Other) (8). Initially 'sans comportement individuel visible' (without visible individual features), his daily routines are brilliantly evoked. At lunchtime he is caught in the 'filet inexplicable' (inexplicable net) that sweeps thousands of citizens in successive waves into the same 'bouillon' (cheap restaurant). His afternoons at work, his daily train rides, and his evenings at home in his half-finished villa ('Obonne, villas, villas, et revillas' (99)) are conveyed through descriptions of mundane gestures. Change is signalled by a momentary departure from routine when Etienne's attention is suddenly attracted by a shop window display where toy ducks floating in water demonstrate the waterproof properties of a hat. Initially, the consequences of Etienne's deviation are seen from the outside perspective of the 'observateur': the birth of self-awareness is comically assimilated to morphology: Etienne's 'modification de structure' (structural modification) leads him by stages from the status of 'silhouette', through that of 'être plat, être doué de quelque consistance, être doué de quelque réalité' (flat being, being endowed with some substance, being endowed with a certain reality) (11), 'être de moindre réalité' (being of lesser reality) (22), 'être de consistance réduite' (being with reduced consistency) (24), être de réalité minime' (being with minimal reality), to his apotheosis in 'la réalité tridimensionelle' (three-dimensional reality) (44).

Etienne's second deviation involves a sudden fascination with a café bearing a large sign saying FRITES that he sees every day when his train stops at Blagny. He visits the café the following Saturday, and although he finds the atmosphere grotesque he is gripped by the conviction that life is here: 'C'est ça la vie, c'est ça la vie, c'est ça la vie' (This is life!) (27). Despite the obvious parody of populist enthusiasm for proletarian life, Etienne's naïvety, and the fact that he is responding to a sea change of which he is largely the passive subject, set him apart from the more knowing characters. Etienne's 'transformation' has a number of phases. The discovery that both stations on his daily journey have forty-seven steps, and the new-found fascination with household gadgets that leads him to purchase a device for slicing hard-boiled eggs, lead to a feeling that the world is 'plein de mystères': 'il m'a suffi de tourner la tête à droite au lieu de le tourner à gauche [. . .] et j'ai découvert des choses à côté desquelles je passais chaque jour, sans les voir' (full of mysteries . . . I only had to turn my head to the right instead of to the left . . . and I discovered things I'd walked past every day, without seeing them) (42). Horrified at what he has hitherto failed to notice in his everyday surroundings, Etienne begs Pierre le Grand to tell him what he is missing in the 'bouillon' where they have lunch. But Le Grand, appalled at the inedible food, sees nothing: 'Pierre regarde autour de lui. Il ne remarque rien. Rien. Il sent qu'il devrait remarquer quelque chose: que *tout* dépend de cette remarque' (Pierre looks around him. He notices nothing. Nothing. He feels he should notice something: that *everything* depends on it) (45); the italicization probably parodies one of Breton's stylistic tics.

Convinced that he is beginning to exist for the first time, Etienne meditates on thinking and existing (another intertext, Descartes's *Discours de la méthode*, which Queneau had considered 'translating' into colloquial French, is perceptible here). But the dialectic of ordinary and extraordinary, and the idea of perceiving what one had previously overlooked, still predominate. Etienne observes that when you live through the same things every day you no longer see anything, and hence do not really exist: 'lorsque j'ai regardé le monde j'ai commencé à exister' (when I looked at the world I started existing) (65). This leads him to wonder if directing our attention in certain ways allows us to transcend the banality of 'la vie quotidienne': 'il me suffit de regarder comme ça de travers pour ainsi dire et me voilà sorti' (I just need to look slantwise so to speak and I'm out of it) (66). But the experiences that give Etienne the impression of shifting out of the everyday and of feeling that he exists are in fact everyday ones. What they are departures *from* is the predictable run of banal experiences that we misguidedly think of as the whole of 'la vie quotidienne'.

Another facet of the same paradox is that what seems very complicated is in fact very simple: the moment one looks at things disinterestedly a change comes about: 'C'est bien évident et c'est cela qui rend difficile l'évidence de ce qui se présente d'emblée. Ne pas tenir compte de la destination d'un objet, quelle étrange activité!' (it's all evident and that what makes the obviousness (évidence) of what is just straightforwardly there very difficult. Not to bear in mind the purpose of an object, what a strange activity!) (102). Simple *évidence*—the plain fact of existing, of being there and being thus—is at once the most basic and the most recondite aspect of 'la quotidienneté'.[56] But as the hapless Etienne demonstrates, it is extremely difficult to hold on to this perception without complicating it out of existence. Various branches of philosophy—aesthetics, epistemology, philosophy of language—offer succour, but at the price of sacrificing simplicity. Etienne experiences different forms of wonder: at things without words and words without things, at what Sartre will call 'la contingence', and at his own loss of identity as his existence seems to slip out of the range of available concepts. If his evolution anticipates that of the hero of Sartre's (more or less contemporaneous) *La Nausée*, Etienne ends up in a state of utter confusion: 'même un mégot, on ne sait pas ce que c'est [. . .] JE NE SAIS PAS! cria-t-il' [. . .] et moi-même, hein, qui suis-je?' (even a fag-end, you don't know what that is . . . I DON'T KNOW! he shouted . . . And me, eh, who am I?) (123).

Like the posture of the 'observateur', the notion of individual transformation brought about by a reorientation towards the ordinary and the everyday is handled ironically in *Le Chiendent*. But rather than simply debunking the idea Queneau seems to draw attention to the everyday as a dimension of experience, whilst undermining the view that it is intrinsically marvellous, mysterious, enigmatic, or whatever. In different ways, Etienne, Pierre le Grand, and the others are drawn to investigate what is all around them; but it is precisely this enveloping all-aroundness, in which their lives are steeped, that makes it impossible to grasp the *quotidien* other than obliquely. As in the

---

[56] See Ch. 2 above.

case of Père Taupe's door—the central focus of the novel's rudimentary plot—
the mistake with the *quotidien* is to think that there is something behind it. In
Le Chiendent and subsequent novels (including *Un Rude hiver*, *Pierrot mon
ami*, *Loin de Rueil*, and *Le Dimanche de la vie*) centred on the 'banlieue' and the
'petit peuple', Queneau repeatedly found ways of making the everyday at once
intensely present and consistently elusive. In addition to the issues of genre,
narration, and intertextuality we have touched on, four other features need
briefly to be broached: character and language; the generic; the 'fait divers'; the
wisdom of ignorance.

By consistently privileging the microlevel of social exchange Queneau
locates the real action of his fictions in the linguistic behaviour of his characters—in the realm of speech acts, and their complex embedding in gesture,
cultural knowledge, the dynamics of gender, age, and life experience.[57] It is
here that an ethos which contributes to an overall vision of everyday life is
perceptible. In verbal action Queneau's characters display a versatility and
creativity that belie or transcend local contexts and motivations. Whatever the
status, with regard to the evolution of the spoken language, of Queneau's
experiments in *néo-français* this is indisputably the medium of the speech
community in his novels, but also crucially that of the narrative voice or
voices. As, in rapid succession, Queneau's people are funny, nasty, laconic,
pedantic, stupid, learned, aggressive, scheming, or affectionate, their language
locates them in a remarkably fluid and creative medium marked by a rejection
of authority, established boundaries and hierarchies, by a capacity to adapt,
graft, generate, and fuse, and by an overwhelming sense of the infinite variety
even the most circumscribed world has to offer. This dimension of Queneau,
with its basis in orality, anticipates Certeau's notion of the 'invention' of
everyday life.

The generic is essential to the *quotidien*. As the work of Perec will show
unmistakably, to focus on the everyday is to pull back from the perceived
world just enough to be able to see generically—patterns, rhythms, repetitions—but not so far as to analyse, delimit, or pigeon-hole. On one side, a
world of specifics: this house, this street, this bus, this neighbour. On the other
side, abstract, scientific knowledge—social anthropology, sociology, sociolin-
guistics, psychology. *Between* these poles is our awareness of the street, the
house, the bus, not as analysable phenomena, nor simply as purely localized

---

[57] See Christopher Shorley, *Queneau's Fiction: An Introductory Study* (Cambridge, New York:
Cambridge University Press, 1985).

one-off experiences, but as constituent parts of a rhythm, a series, an order of repetitions. Queneau's everyday universe is local, specific, detailed, and individualized, and at the same time profoundly generic. In *Le Chiendent* the presentation of people and places is often handled generically, perhaps the most striking examples being the recurrent passages that conjure up the world of the suburban railway, through evocations of passengers patrolling the platforms or jockeying for seats, gestures with newspapers, varieties of conversation or pastime, or the numerous passages concerning eating and drinking. But there are also brief 'vues de banlieues', like this 'nocturne':

Des trains sifflaient de temps à autre et des chiens hurlaient de temps en temps. [...] Derrière les palissades fragiles, les jardins potagers dormaient paisiblement [...] Vers Paris il y avait une grande lueur parce que c'est une grande ville, avec beaucoup de réverbères et d'affiches lumineuses. De l'autre côté de la rivière, assez loin, une usine restait illuminée [...] Par instants, tout tombait dans des gouffres de silence pour en ressortir traîné par le sifflet d'un train ou l'aboiement d'un chien ou le chant d'un coq ou le ronflement d'une auto (176).

(Trains whistled from time to time and dogs growled now and then ... Behind fragile fences kitchen gardens slept peacefully ... Towards Paris was a large gleam because it's a big city, with many lamp posts and luminous signs. Over the river, in the distance, a factory was still lit up ... Intermittently everything was plunged into silence and then dragged out again by a train's whistle, a dog's bark, a cock's crow or the purring of a car engine)

The generic everyday world is on the margins—between country and city, nature and culture, the organic and the artificial. By no means immune from time, it is dislocated from history. Everything here is on the same level: trains, dogs, cocks, onions, lettuces and tomatoes, rivers and factories, lights and sounds. There is no set rhythm or externally sanctioned harmony; heterogeneous percepts and events seem to exist in a homogeneous medium. Strongly anthropomorphic, even animistic, this way of looking at the world risks preciosity or sentimentality, a danger partially averted—in both Queneau and Perec—by the leavening of humour and irony.

The 'fait divers' is the generic label for a fairly diffuse category of newspaper item that is either brief, local and minor, or, if on a larger scale, interesting by dint of weird, aberrant, or lurid detail. One of its roles is to represent the claims of the individual and the little world against the wider forces of society.[58] A character in *Pierrot mon ami* expresses this succinctly: 'Foutaises,

---

[58] For discussions of the 'fait divers' see Auclair, *Le Mana quotidien*; Barthes, 'Structure du fait divers', *Œuvres complètes*, I, 1309–16; David H. Walker, *Outrage and Insight: Modern French Writers and the 'fait divers'* (Oxford: Berg, 1995).

ami Paul! Foutaises que tout cela! La politique, les guerres, les sports: aucun intérêt. Ce qui me botte, moi, c'est le fait divers et les procès. La grosse bête Société: connais pas' (Nonsense, Paul, my friend! All nonsense! Politics, war, sport: of no interest. Me? I like 'faits divers' and trials. Society, that big beast: never heard of it).[59] The 'fait divers' is a one-off, heterogeneous occurrence that tends 'systematically to commemorate the recurrent, rather than ongoing, patterns in current affairs [including] the curious accidents and paradoxes of everyday life', as David Walker puts it.[60] A whole sequence (137–40) of *Le Chiendent* consists of a catalogue of 'faits divers' in italic type where Queneau succeeds brilliantly in mimicking the characteristic tone of local news items relating to outbreaks of dog biting, a schoolboy finding a rusty knife, a brutal murder 'rewarded' by recruitment in the army, a 'vin d'honneur' to mark the retirement of a postman called Rude Agricole, a girl who swallows a whole tube of aspirins—without opening the tube!, Count Adhémar de Rut informing local maidens of his intention to exercise his 'droit de cuissage', a cosmetic potion that will guarantee your bones are presentable in the event of being disinterred, and so forth.

The question of the everyday is central to Queneau's preoccupations but as something that has to be approached obliquely, questioningly, and tentatively. Irony, parody, and humour are omnipresent in all the modes we have touched on, as they were in his use of the figure of the 'observateur' and in the experience of Etienne's philosophical awakening in *Le Chiendent*. But the effect of these diverse and to some extent mutually inconsistent approaches is to deny any specific discourse or idiom special legitimacy, and to leave space for a sense of the everyday that preserves an aura not of mystery or wonder— those are simply partial ways of looking at it—but of profound ambiguity. In a multiplicity of ways Queneau's strategies forestall any direct moves to pin down the *quotidien*, while keeping it very much on the reader's mind. In *Le Chiendent* this tactic of neutrality and ignorance—or nescience—has its hero in le Père Taupe, owner of the door that harbours no secret. Taupe is a quietist: 'rester dans son trou, voilà le bonheur' (stick in your hole, there's happiness) (74), he advises. He thinks it best to live without ambitions or possessions and he sings the praises of invisibility: 'ça m'épate un peu de disparaître' (disappearing excites me) (172). Taupe is a comic character but the attitude he expresses, a potpourri of western mysticism and oriental philosophy, has

---

[59] Queneau, *Œuvres complètes*, II, *Romans*, I, 1210.
[60] Walker, *Outrage and Insight*, 89.

important ramifications in Queneau. It finds a different expression in a happy-go-lucky character like Pierrot, for whom the enigma of the Poldavian chapel, on which *Pierrot mon ami* hinges, is of no more concern than the next pretty girl or 'jambon beurre' sandwich accompanied by a 'petit blanc' and a well-thumbed copy of *Le Rire*. Like many other Queneau characters Pierrot has a proclivity to make his mind a blank and to enjoy withdrawal from the clamour for understanding that comes to afflict Etienne Marcel. Spirituality became increasingly central, though in typically oblique and diffuse ways, to Queneau's approach to everyday experience, as expressed, for example in *Morale élémentaire*, his last collection of poems that will be referred to in Chapter 8. Spirituality is absent from *Le Chiendent*, but the means by which Queneau resists finality and definition anticipate a later emphasis on the achievement of a contemplative state of attunement to the rhythms of the everyday.

CODA: WALTER BENJAMIN AND THE EVERYDAY LEGACIES OF SURREALISM

Walter Benjamin's 'microcosmic attention to the elements of everyday life', noted by his friend Gershom Scholem,[61] found renewed inspiration in Surrealism. The moment he read *Le Paysan de Paris* in 1927 Benjamin felt a strong affinity with the Surrealists, and this encounter shaped his *magnum opus*, the *Passagenwerk* or *Arcades Project*, on which he worked throughout the 1930s, during which time he had exchanges with both Breton and Bataille, and participated in the Collège de sociologie.[62] Through the posthumous publication, and translation into French and English, of the *Arcades Project*, and the rise in Benjamin's reputation, particularly in the 1990s, his ideas contributed to the rise of cultural and philosophical investigations of the everyday, and in some contexts inflected the understanding of Surrealism's contribution to this discursive framework.[63] Overall, recognition of Benjamin's importance enhances the place of Surrealism in the context of explorations of the everyday.

What astounded Benjamin in *Le Paysan de Paris* was the way Aragon's modern mythography lay bare the unconscious substratum of modern Paris.

---

[61] Gershom Scholem, *Walter Benjamin: Story of a Friendship* (New York: New York Review Books, 2003).

[62] In Spring 1939 Benjamin offered to give a lecture on fashion but Bataille declined. See Hollier, *Le Collège de sociologie*, 609.

[63] See Cohen, *Profane Illumination, passim*.

In his 1929 essay on Surrealism Benjamin credits the movement with having understood 'the revolutionary energies of the outmoded'.[64] What he admired in Surrealism was the energy of appropriation (or 'détournement'). Benjamin could see that there was nothing up-to-date about the 'oneiric kitsch'[65] of cluttered umbrella shops, seedily lubricious hotels and theatres, old-fashioned signboards, horses and carts, flea market bric-a-brac and the like in *Le Paysan de Paris* and *Nadja*, any more than in Atget's photographs. But Benjamin also knew that the Surrealists' vision was no more nostalgic than it was techno-logical. The achievement of Surrealism was, firstly, to reveal the hidden desires legible in the everyday environment; and secondly, on the basis of authentic ethical and political aspirations, to identify what was creative or moribund in both material and immaterial culture. The identification of the past in the present—Baudelaire's 'mémoire du présent'—and the capacity (which Cer-teau will emphasize) to impinge on the present by apprehending its layers, chimed with Benjamin's deepest intuitions. Surrealism revealed that the 'outmoded' becomes revolutionary when the trace of desire is located in fashion, style, design, objects, space, gesture, and appetite, and when fresh energies are committed at strategic points in this field of forces. Benjamin will develop the perception that the material space of the city figures the reification of its citizens, locked in the nineteenth-century phantasmagoria of the com-modity. Surrealism showed that the act of appropriation, of making the city the space of individual and collective desire, could be a path of liberation, even if some aspects of the movement—including features of *Le Paysan* and *Nadja*—showed that true 'awakening', as Benjamin conceived it, might not result. The surrealist city, not to be confused, Breton insisted, with 'la forme d'une ville' about which one could be nostalgic, but rather 'la vraie ville distraite et abstraite de celle que j'habite par la force d'un élément qui serait à ma pensée ce que l'air passe pour être à la vie' (the true city distracted and abstracted from the one I live in by the force of an element which would be to my thoughts what air is claimed to be for my life),[66] is a site of future-oriented experiences, a springboard for new raids of desiring fantasy. Like Heidegger, the Surrealists perceived what Breton called the 'dearth of reality',[67] and Benjamin termed 'the atrophy of experience' induced by modernity; but to Heidegger's conservative pessimism, Benjamin, imbued with Marxist and

---

[64] Benjamin, *One-Way Street*, 229.

[65] This was the title of an earlier version of his essay on Surrealism.

[66] Breton, *Œuvres complètes*, I, 749.

[67] See his 'Introduction au discours sur le peu de réalité', *Œuvres complètes*, II, 265–80.

messianic thought, preferred the Surrealists' belief in a revolution of consciousness to be brought about through the subjective appropriation of concrete reality and everyday life.[68] For Benjamin, as for Surrealism, everyday life and concrete material reality were the real terrain of revolutionary change. And, as his writing on photography indicated, Benjamin also shared the surrealists' sense of the work of art as pragmatic or performative, enshrining cognitive acts that transform reality.[69]

It would be wrong to assimilate Benjamin's project entirely to Surrealism or to limit Surrealism to Benjamin's perspective on it. But the area where the two converge is a nodal point for investigations of the everyday, through their parallel focus on the city, appropriation and transformation, the unconscious, objects, details, small things, collecting, street names,[70] urban wandering and, in the broadest sense, 'the domain of experience'—a key term in Benjamin— as both lost and to be refound.[71] Benjamin provided a new lens through which to view Surrealism. In many respects his vision matches the picture elaborated in the last two chapters, where Surrealism has not been seen as a fixed doctrine but, in connection with the everyday, as an evolving set of intuitions, projects, modes of scrutiny and transformation, ramifying in the 1930s into dissident versions (Bataille, Leiris, Queneau, Benjamin—but also Prévert, Brassaï, Desnos) that have provided a reservoir still able to irrigate new fields of attention. We now need to look at how the interdisciplinary fertility of Surrealism combined with new paradigms in the 'sciences humaines' to inform the work of four pioneering figures who together shaped the intellectual landscape in which Surrealism remains central to the varied discourses that constitute our sense of the everyday.

---

[68] See Benjamin, *Arcades Project*, 544–5.
[69] See Ch. 2 above.
[70] See below, Ch. 9.
[71] See Howard Caygill, *Walter Benjamin: The Colour of Experience* (London: Routledge, 1998).

4

Henri Lefebvre: Alienation and Appropriation in Everyday Life

THE 1947 *CRITIQUE DE LA VIE QUOTIDIENNE*

The first *Critique de la vie quotidienne* was a slim volume of barely 150 pages written in the summer and autumn of 1945, and published in 1947. Its central message was the pressing need, at a time of national renewal, and in the context of first-hand accounts of the Nazi death camps, for a rehabilitation of everyday life as the essential ground of human existence: 'l'homme sera quotidien ou ne sera pas' (man's only future is in the everyday) (I, 140).[1] The burden of the argument was that Christianity had depleted the richness of everyday life by identifying ritual and festivity ('la fête') with particular institutions—Sunday rather than every day. The modern literary and philosophical tradition had then further depreciated the everyday by highlighting privileged experiences at the expense of the ordinary. In the face of this, Lefebvre argued, Marxist critique, and particularly the theory of alienation and the idea of man as totality, had the capacity to provide the foundations for the kind of critical understanding of the everyday that might lead to its revaluation. For this to happen, Marxist dialectic needed to be supplemented and developed in new directions. In specifying potential revisions, extensions, and applications of Marxist critique, as they might bear on everyday life, Lefebvre embarked on the kinds of methodological investigation into the everyday that would occupy him on and off for the next forty years.

Lefebvre's initial target was the literary onslaught on the everyday mounted by those who depreciate it (Flaubert, the existentialists) and those who appear to celebrate it. Chief culprits in the latter category are the Surrealists. For

---

[1] References (incorporated in the text and designated I, II and III) are to the three vols. of Henri Lefebvre's *Critique de la vie quotidienne* (Paris: Éditions de l'Arche, 1947, 1962, and 1981).

Lefebvre, who had participated in the movement in the 1920s,[2] the surrealist 'merveilleux' is always based on the exceptional and the extraordinary, on an 'envers de la vie quotidienne' (obverse of everyday life) associated with privileged moments. Lefebvre rejects the 'merveilleux moderne' and the surrealist vision of the city in *Nadja* and *Le Paysan de Paris*, arguing that it is always easier to transmute than to apprehend. The error of the poetic tradition is in fact overintellectualization: 'cherchant à penser le sensible et le quotidien au lieu de les percevoir' (seeking to think the sensory and the everyday rather than to perceive them) (I, 120). The quest for the surreal undermines and depreciates daily existence. In rejecting Surrealism Lefebvre shows no desire to oppose it with social realism or existentialism. Before turning to the conceptual framework of Marxism, he looks to the burgeoning 'sciences humaines' and in particular to the 'new history' of the *Annales* school where what impressed him, as in psychoanalysis and Bachelard's then recent work on space,[3] was the emergence of new kinds of detail which, once identified, reveal how, in a Hegelian axiom Lefebvre quoted more than once, and saw as central to the project of knowing the everyday, 'le familier n'est pas pour cela connu' (the familiar is not necessarily the known) (I, 145).[4] These new orientations in contemporary thought helped Lefebvre appreciate how far Marx and Engels, as philosophers and historians, had established the basis for a 'connaissance critique de la vie quotidienne' (critical knowledge of everyday life). If daily life is the level at which man realizes his humanity ('que s'accomplit l'humain'), alienation is the generic term for the obstacles to that realization. In such contexts as labour, where the worker's efforts are cut off from their outcome, alienation lies in severance from the concrete, in the abstractions that lead the individual 'à effacer son existence' (to efface his own existence) (I, 180). To scrutinize and diagnose alienation is to understand how specific acts, gestures, or other manifestations deny the individual, substituting 'l'être factice [...] que l'on a suscité en moi pour que je ne sois plus moi-même' (the factitious being... produced in me so that I should no longer be myself) (I, 180). But this means that it is only through an awareness of their alienation that human beings can realize their potential. Hence, paradoxically and ambiguously, the

---

[2] For biographical information on Lefebvre see Rémi Hess, *Henri Lefebvre, une aventure dans le siècle* (Paris: A. M. Métailié, 1988); Rob Shields, *Henri Lefebvre: Love and Struggle—Spatial Dialectics* (London: Routledge, 2000); Michel Trebitsch, 'Preface' in Henri Lefebvre, *Critique of Everyday Life*, I (London: Verso, 1991).

[3] See Gaston Bachelard, *La Poétique de l'espace* (Paris: PUF, 1961).

[4] On *Annales* and the everyday see Alice Kaplan and Kristin Ross (eds.) 'Introduction', *Everyday Life, Yale French Studies*, 73 (1987), 1–4.

individual 'se réalise à travers son aliénation' (finds realization through alienation). And hence the dual privilege of the everyday as both the place of
alienation—it is only at the level of daily life that we can register it—and the
place of its potential abrogation. Janus-faced, the everyday is ambiguous:
'L'ambiguité est une catégorie [essentielle] de la vie quotidienne' (ambiguity
is an essential category of everyday life) (I, 26). For Lefebvre, Marxism
provided a spirit and a rationale for approaching the everyday, but new lines
of enquiry, deriving from such concepts as alienation, fetishism,
and mystification needed urgently to be developed. Such was human complexity that understanding its reality required a multiplicity of forms of
knowledge. Far more than just an abstract category alienation had to be seen
as a lived reality, an experience of dispossession that occurs in the very moment
of imagined possession: in hit songs, verses learnt at school, financial transactions, shopping, posters (I, 197).

At this point Lefebvre suggests that a critique of daily life should generate a
comprehensive investigation of contemporary mores to be titled 'Comment
on vit' (How we live) (I, 209). Using the interview methods evolved in
contemporary sociology such an investigation would focus on the 'real life'
of selected individuals, concentrating on such areas as work and marriage, and
prioritizing what Lefebvre saw as relatively unknown sectors of social life such
as the lives of women. Detail would be of paramount importance, and
Lefebvre suggests that one type of enquiry might home in on a single ordinary
day, 'telle ou telle journée [. . .] d'un individu. Une journée banale' (such and
such a day... for an individual. A banal day) (I, 210).[5] He also suggests that
the enquiry should encompass 'l'art de vivre', the relatively new territory of
individual lifestyles that give expression to human needs, presupposing that
the individual envisages his or her way of living not simply as the means to
attain something beyond it, but as its own end. In conceiving of life as a work
of art, 'l'art de vivre' implies the end of alienation, and thus actively contributes to this end.[6]

These concrete proposals are one of the most significant features of the
Critique de la vie quotidienne, and they will be reiterated frequently in
Lefebvre's later work. Yet, characteristically, Lefebvre does not implement
them here but moves on to recount a visit to the church in his local village

---

[5] The importance of the day for explorations of the *quotidien* will be examined in Ch. 9.

[6] 'L'art de vivre' will be a constant preoccupation in the *quotidien* tradition: see below, Ch. 5 on
Barthes and the discussion of Foucault in Ch. 8.

in the south-west of France, and to analyse it in the manner of an *Annales* historian, as the concrete embodiment of an ideology which, in driving a wedge between 'la fête' and 'le quotidien', brought about the depreciation of everyday life in western culture. In the concluding chapter Lefebvre stresses that 'la vie quotidienne' is not immutable, forever condemned to greyness and repetition, alleviated from time to time by special moments. Insisting that the everyday is subject to change—for better or worse—he emphasizes that its current 'déchéance', despite the material progress of the twentieth century, needs to be understood in terms of the failure to realize the plenitude of human possibility expressed in the notion of 'l'homme total'. For Lefebvre, qualitative improvement in the sphere of everyday life is the prime measure of the achievement of this goal. Citing the testimonies, including that of David Rousset,[7] of those who had survived the Nazi death camps, Lefebvre argues that the inhumanity of Auschwitz, however extreme, should not be set apart as pertaining to a separate 'universe'. Rather, it gives hyperbolic expression to the abstract rationality of capitalism and is therefore of a piece with an everyday life reduced to banality. In the face of a purely quantitative approach, what is called for is a change in the way human beings regard themselves.

THE 1958 'AVANT-PROPOS'

Along with his many other activities, Lefebvre persevered through the late Forties and early Fifties with the project of a critique of everyday life. But the need to confront the scepticism of many communist intellectuals, and to keep abreast with new currents in the social sciences that sought to analyse mass society in the post-war world, led to constant difficulties and delays. Following the loss of a substantial draft for a second volume Lefebvre was led, in 1956–7, to provide an interim update on his thinking in the form of a substantial (111-page) 'Avant-propos' to a second edition of the *Critique de la vie quotidienne* which was published in 1958 (volume II would appear three years later, in 1961).

This emphasis on method probably owed something to the way Sartre, in his contemporaneous 'Existentialisme et Marxisme' (subsequently *Questions de méthode*), had derived his 'progressive-regressive method' from a 1953

---

7 David Rousset, *L'Univers concentrationnaire* (1946; Paris: Hachette, 1993).

article on rural sociology by Lefebvre.[8] Like Lefebvre, Sartre was concerned to blend 'living Marxism' with other currents of thought, in the context of a general account of concrete human reality (in Sartre's case the relation between the individual and the group takes the place of the everyday) designed to maintain the claims of freedom and praxis against those of socio-economic determinism. The following year, in *La Somme et le reste* (1959), an autobiographical meditation on his career to date, Lefebvre noted Sartre's appropriation of one of his key ideas; in the new 'Avant-propos' to his *Critique de la vie quotidienne*—Lefebvre's own 'Questions de méthode'—he puts it to use himself.

Lefebvre begins by arguing that, in response to rapid changes in lifestyles and living conditions, recent developments in a number of fields, including history, ethnography, philosophy, sociology, and literature, have developed new ways of looking at everyday life. Seeking to attain a quality that is 'mal définissable et cependant essentielle et concrète' (hard to define yet essential and concrete), these diverse approaches underline the richness and multiplicity but also the elusiveness of 'le concret humain' as it manifests itself in everyday life. This insistence on the concrete, and on multifaceted unity, will be key themes in Lefebvre's discussion, and they lead him to focus initially on Brechtian epic theatre, recently revealed in France by the visits of the *Berliner Ensemble* which had a huge impact on many French intellectuals including the Situationists, Roland Barthes, and Michel Vinaver. For Lefebvre, Brecht's great achievement was to avoid the pitfalls of realist or mythological presentations of the everyday by placing the spectator, as in the famous 'street scene', in the midst of the ambiguity of everyday life. Brecht's art acknowledges Hegel's 'Was ist bekannt ist nicht erkannt' (What is familiar is not known)—'formule condensée qui pourrait servir d'épigraphe à la *Critique de la vie quotidienne*' (a dense formulation that could stand as epigraph to the *Critique*) (I, 22)—and strips away the veil of familiarity masking the everyday. In opposition to Sartre, Lefebvre refuses to identify the perception of ambiguity with bad faith, as indicative of the inability to choose. Brecht's theatre makes manifest the real contradictions, and the real ambiguity, of the everyday through situations that reveal it as a place of both illusion and truth, power and powerlessness: the everyday is seen as the 'intersection du secteur que l'homme domine et du secteur que l'homme ne domine pas' (intersection of the

---

[8] The essay subsequently became the introduction to Sartre's *Critique de la raison dialectique*. The Lefebvre article was 'Perspectives de sociologie rurale'.

dominated and undominated sectors of human experience) (I, 29). And—crucially—this awareness, born of being 'plongé dans' (plunged into) the *quotidien* rather than seeing it from the outside, is itself to some extent liberating. What Lefebvre calls 'désaliénation'—relative freedom from alienation—originates in becoming aware of alienation itself.

Turning to sociology, Lefebvre considers recent work on leisure. Against the tendency to see it as a relief from everyday life, he insists on the dialectical unity of work and leisure as elements in the wider totality of the *quotidien*. The sense of a rupture between them is then diagnosed as a symptom of alienation within everyday life itself, and poses the challenge of identifying the modes of contact or interaction between these various integral elements. Everyday life needs to become aware of itself—'il faut la révéler à elle-même' (I, 40)—since it is both infinitely rich in its potential and in actuality often infinitely poor and deprived. In seeking to understand the everyday as a total phenomenon Lefebvre seeks to redress the tendency in sociology to atomize social reality into various sectors, including leisure, thus reducing it either to a simple aggregate of juxtaposed phenomena or a negative backdrop for a range of positive activities.

Whilst acknowledging the vital contribution of sociological enquiry, Lefebvre insists on the need to fuse this with concepts derived from early Marx, and firstly that of alienation, which, he argues, can illuminate the connections between the various sectors that globally make up the everyday. But he also stresses the contribution of what he calls 'sociologie concrète', often found in literary and essayistic work, as well as surveys and investigations. Lefebvre develops both lines of argument when he switches to the 'sociologie du travail' (sociology of work) and criticizes the well-known studies of Georges Friedmann for seeing leisure in terms of the irruption of freedom into the domain of necessity, setting up a polarization whereby 'le loisir apparaît comme le non-quotidien dans le quotidien' (leisure appears to be the non-everyday in the everyday). One way of parrying this, and demonstrating that work and leisure must be seen within the 'structure globale' of everyday life, is to give close scrutiny to leisure activities—including radio and television, as well as more active pursuits such as amateur painting, and social spaces such as the café or the 'fête foraine' (I, 50)—with a view to identifying the 'interférences multiples' (multiple interconnections) between work, leisure, family life, and private life. In a chapter on the 'monde pavillonaire' of Paris suburbia Lefebvre offers an exercise in 'sociologie concrète' where he bemoans the uniformity and mediocrity that have come to overlay 'la diversité primitive de l'homme quotidien' (the primal diversity of the everyday individual), but sees this predominance of negative 'quotidienneté' as transitional, and as by no means excluding what, not without sentimentality, he calls the 'new marvels' that spring up in the midst of mediocrity (I, 61). The essential point is that grasping the everyday requires getting 'inside' it. If this is to adopt a phenomenological angle, phenomenology cannot in this instance be accused of severing reality from wider determinations since it is precisely the mark of these wider determinations, within the global totality of the everyday, that such enquiry seeks to perceive, tearing the veil with which everyday life constantly masks itself (I, 66). The process of unveiling involves starting from the simplest *donnée*, a woman buying a pound of sugar, for example, and tracking, as Brecht might have done, the networks and relationships in which this act is embedded. By identifying a 'fait social infiniment complexe' (infinitely complex social fact) in the minor, individual phenomenon, 'la recherche découvre un enchevêtrement' (research uncovers an imbrication) (I, 67). The mark of Marcel Mauss's concept of the 'fait social total' is clearly a key influence here, as it will be on later prospectors of the everyday.[9]

Lefebvre argues that in his discussion of labour Marx did not envisage the future end of the reign of necessity as a sudden leap forward when alienation would abruptly cease. Setting himself against revolutionary optimism, Lefebvre highlights in Marx the view of an 'homme total' whose advent would come about through a gradual process of appropriation. What Lefebvre calls 'another fundamental concept—appropriation' (I, 75) derives from passages in Marx's writing such as the following: 'l'homme s'approprie son essence universelle (Allseitiges) d'une manière universelle, c'est–à–dire en tant qu'homme total'[10] (man appropriates his universal essence universally, as a total man) (this is the Marx whom Agnes Heller, following Lukács, will also emulate).[11] For Lefebvre this concept serves to bring a temporal dimension to the understanding of alienation by insisting on the ineluctable nature of transitional phases: 'l'homme de transition ne peut s'éluder' (transitional man cannot be avoided) (I, 76). Revealing himself to be a thinker of transition, Lefebvre affirms here the predominance of the middle, the median and the mixture in his sense of everyday life. And indeed we witness in the 'Avant-propos' the progressive emergence of a vision of the *quotidien* as a medium, a

---

   [9] See Marcel Mauss, 'Essai sur le don', in id., *Sociology et anthropologie* (1950; Paris: PUF, 1997), 145–279 and the discussion of Augé in Ch. 8 below.
   [10] Quoted by Lefebvre, I, 75.
   [11] See above, Ch. 1.

space of process and transition, a *milieu* in which different orders of human reality merge and evolve. At the core of the process of appropriation is the 'dépassement des scissions et contradictions internes à l'humain' (overcoming the scissions and contradictions within human reality) (I, 77), which does not depend on a 'decisive, total moment' but on a process that can be facilitated by critical understanding. Lefebvre's commitment to a 'critique de la vie quotidienne' is conceived as actively contributing, through an understanding and depiction of alienation (drawing where appropriate on works of art and literature, such as the novels of Roger Vailland, which exhibit a 'conscience indirecte naissante de l'aliénation' (nascent indirect awareness of alienation) to the process of 'désaliénation').

Another way in which Lefebvre counteracts the polarization of the everyday and the non-everyday is by establishing the place of philosophy within the context of the *quotidien*. Conceived as an 'activité supérieure' (like art or religion) whose essential mission implies transcending everyday life, philosophy posits the everyday as a 'résidu', as what is left over when 'higher' activities are subtracted. But what if this so-called residue were actually the origin of the higher activities that seem to transcend it? What if the hidden richness of the everyday lay in its rightful claim to be the ground of such higher activities as philosophy?

En réalité ce prétendu résidu définit une matière humaine dont notre étude montre la richesse cachée. Les activités supérieures en naissent, elles en sont à la fois l'expression culminante, et la critique directe ou indirecte, et l'aliénation enveloppant un effort— plus ou moins conscient et victorieux—vers la 'désaliénation' (I, 97).

(In reality this so-called residue defines a human reality whose richness is revealed by our enquiry. It gives birth to higher activities that are both its ultimate expression and sources of direct or indirect critique: alienation comprises an effort—more or less conscious and victorious—towards de-alienation)

In support of this bold claim Lefebvre will develop the image of the everyday as the 'sol nourricier' (nourishing soil) of higher activities. Crucial here is apprehending the everyday as a 'matière humaine'. This is not achieved by combining the critiques and perspectives on the everyday that philosophy like other spheres (religion or art) can provide from different viewpoints. Nor is it achieved by repudiating these and proposing an 'apologie du quotidien' (apologia for the everyday) (this would be the populist or realist option). It requires a dialectical understanding of the 'rapport réciproque' of higher and lower activities. Lefebvre argues that 'activités spécialisées' are never actually separate from 'pratique quotidienne' even if they do transcend it.

But how can this dimension of the everyday be made visible? According to Lefebvre, 'les gens, en général, ne savent pas bien comment ils vivent' (in general people do not really know how they live): we do not understand our real needs; hence the failure of much sociological enquiry based on interviews. Yet in different ways philosophy, sociology, and art have the capacity to reach real lived experience ('le vécu et le réel'). Both the 'caractère polyscopique, omniprésent de l'aliénation' (polyscopic and omnipresent character of alienation) and the contradictory multiplicity or ambiguity of human reality— which is simultaneously natural and historical, biological and social, ethnic and cultural, whilst embracing the conflicts between these elements (I, 106)— confer a potentially reflexive dimension on everyday experience. For Lefebvre it is 'dans la vie quotidienne et en elle seule' (only in the context of everyday life)—that the component parts of human reality are integrated. The use of the prepositions 'dans' and 'en' here, as well as Lefebvre's pervasive use of reflexive verbs, signal the way the everyday is seen as a space of transformation and mediation.

The 'Avant-propos' ends by further amplifying the presentation of everyday life as a paradoxical combination of indigence and richness, defined not so much by its content as by the processes and relationships fostered through its hybrid and ambiguous nature, the 'in-betweenness' that enables it to be a mere residue, with nothing substantial to its name, and at the same time a totality:

En un sens résiduelle, définie par 'ce qui reste' lorsque par analyse on a ôté toutes les activités distinctes, supérieures, spécialisées, structureés—la vie quotidienne se définit comme totalité. Considérées dans leur spécialisation et leur technicité, les activités supérieures laissent entre elles un 'vide technique' que remplit la vie quotidienne. Elle a un rapport profond avec *toutes* les activités, et les englobe avec leurs différences et leurs conflits; elle est leur lieu de rencontre, et leur lien, et leur terrain commun. Et c'est dans la vie quotidienne que prend forme et se constitue l'ensemble de rapports qui fait de l'humain—et de chaque être humain—un tout (I, 108–9).

(Whilst in a sense residual, defined by 'what is left over' when one analytically subtracts activities that are distinct, superior, specialized, and structured, everyday life is nonetheless a totality. Everyday life fills the gap between higher activities considered in their specialized and technical aspects. It has a strong link with all activities and encompasses them with their differences and conflicts; it is where they meet and connect and find common ground. It is in everyday life that the collection of relationships that constitute human reality—and each individual—as a totality are formed)

Striking here is the way Lefebvre operates simultaneously at the level of concepts (or epistemology) and at the level of concrete experience. Everyday life is both an abstraction that fills a conceptual void ('vide technique'), and a concrete space in which certain things happen. But this ambiguity or duality is in fact central. If the emptiness of the everyday (its residual quality) can be reconfigured as plenitude, since it consists essentially in the capacity to be a receptacle, to create a mediating space—a 'lieu de rencontre', a 'lien', a 'terrain commun', a 'rapport', and an 'ensemble de rapports'—the content of this space is not specific to it but constituted by processes rendered here by spatial verbs (*remplir, englober, prendre forme*) and reflexive verbs (*se manifester, s'accomplir*). At once empty and miraculously full, the everyday can never be concretized because it has no specificity of its own. Nothing is uniquely of the everyday, but nothing is entirely separate from it, at least in terms of the wider economy of human reality, and the central process of appropriation which always has the everyday as its ground, its 'sol nourricier'.

But what of the relationship between the manifest contents of daily life and the role Lefebvre casts it in—as empty space of mediation and transition? From his brief concluding sketch of the planned contents of a renewed attempt at a second volume—to comprise, very disparately, a theory of needs, an analysis of 'la presse du coeur' (agony aunt columns) and a study of class attitudes in daily life (I, 111)—it is clear that this issue is far from resolved. If the ambiguity of the everyday—as concept and concrete reality—has emerged as something to be embraced rather than resisted, the scope for developing ways of understanding and experiencing it remains dauntingly vast.

THE 1961 *CRITIQUE: FONDEMENTS POUR UNE SOCIOLOGIE DE LA QUOTIDIENNETÉ*

When it finally appeared in 1961, the second volume of *Critique de la vie quotidienne* differed markedly from the projected outline given at the end of the 1958 'Avant-propos'. Lefebvre ascribes his changes of approach to rapid transformations in the sphere of everyday life at this time. But they were no doubt equally attributable to his final severance from the Communist Party in 1958, and to the evolution of his ideas in the context of the 'Groupe d'études de la vie quotidienne' he created at the Centre National de la Recherche

Scientifique in 1960, and to his exchanges with the Situationists.[12] The abandoning of a 'théorie des besoins' (theory of needs) that would have rooted the 'empirical study of social reality' (II, 11) in human physiology reflected his increasing recognition of the place of desire (the impact of Lacan's ideas is perceptible). Drawing on exchanges with the Situationists, Lefebvre sees desire as capable of expressing facets of the individual that deny the conditioning and programming of the 'société de consommation'.[13] Asserting, questionably (does consumption—however programmed—not stem very often from desire?), that 'le consommateur ne désire pas. Il subit' (consumers do not desire, they succumb), Lefebvre claims (more justifiably) that desire breaks off from actual needs and thus potentially escapes the 'colonization' of everyday life imposed by consumerism. This territory will be explored a few years later in Georges Perec's *Les Choses* (1966). Similar factors underlie Lefebvre's reasons for abandoning the projected study of 'la presse du coeur'. Whilst maintaining his view of the particular link between women and the everyday, Lefebvre now feels that this needs to be understood in terms of wider concepts such as ambiguity and the interplay of cyclical and linear time, rather than as a separate area to be explored through the prism of alienation. And the decision not to proceed with an analysis of the everyday in terms of class is also motivated by recognition that what needs to be understood is the concrete relationship between individual or group and the global sphere of the everyday.[14]

In general terms it is clear that even when backed by the idea of appropriation the concept of alienation had proved inadequate. Insisting on the necessity to sidestep ideological disputes, notably with Marxist dogmatism, Lefebvre argues that in its short history the critical study of everyday life, having encompassed a vast array of facts and documents, and demonstrated its constantly shifting nature, has amounted to an 'expérience théorique' which demonstrated the necessity for the development of radically new concepts. Hence the dominance of theory in the second volume, and also its subtitle: *Fondements d'une sociologie de la quotidienneté* (foundations for a sociology of everydayness). Faithful to the concept of alienation, the 1958 'Avant-propos' had stressed the ongoing contribution philosophy could make to the critique of everyday life. But faced with the massive rise of sociological approaches

[12] On this see Hess, *Henri Lefebvre*, 214–28.
[13] I discuss the Situationists later in this chapter.
[14] Lefebvre may also have been influenced by *Chronique d'un été*, the experimental film made by Rouch and Morin, to which he refers. Cf. below, Ch. 8.

Lefebvre saw the need for a double shift—from philosophy to sociology, and then to an 'anthropologie concrète' that would provide the basis for sociological enquiry. The structure of the book reflects these priorities. A long 'Mise au point' (Update), centred on an attempt to defend the study of the *quotidien* and to arrive at a satisfactory definition, forges new concepts that are then explored in more abstract terms in subsequent chapters.

As a prelude to the search for a definition, Lefebvre, employing one of his staple stylistic ploys, sets up an imaginary question-and-answer session with a series of opponents who reject the concept of everyday life or the interest of studying it. To the common-sense relativist who argues that the everyday is no more than the basic organic level of existence, which differs according to local conditions, Lefebvre rejoins that the everyday is not in fact confined to the sordid and humble sides of life but that its scrutiny involves the detection of 'possibilités inaccomplies' (unrealized possibilities). The everyday is 'le lieu et le temps que ne saisit pas l'activité parcellaire, spécialisée, scindée' (the place and the time that is not seized by specialized, split, and parcelled-out activities) (II, 25). The paradoxical, ungraspable aspect of the everyday—always associated with its capacity for change and its link to human possibility—emerges again and again, as various specific disciplines or 'sciences parcellaires'— including history, economics, sociology, philosophy, and psychology—seek to lay claim to it, only for Lefebvre to prise it from their grasp. To the historian ready to serve up 'Everyday life in China' or the wine-trade or ancient Greece, he argues that the *quotidien* is a dimension of human reality irreducible to historical understanding. To the existentialist who sees the everyday as the realm of inauthenticity, Lefebvre concedes that it is a 'mode du vécu' (mode of lived experience) but that 'elle définirait plutôt le milieu ou [l'authentique et l'inauthentique] se confondent' (it defines rather the milieu where [authentic and inauthentic] merge) (II, 29). Citing with approval the Merleau-Ponty of *Signes* (1961) Lefebvre argues that philosophy should take up the challenge of articulating the 'vécu'—'apporter au langage cette réalité insaisissable et prégnante, la quotidienneté' (bringing into language this ungraspable and pregnant reality, everydayness)—even if this means working with the phenomenology long discredited in Marxist circles as apolitical.[15] As to various 'sciences parcellaires', it is inherent in the everyday to lie outside the sway of any particular form of knowledge, and it is therefore essential that a 'critique de la vie quotidienne' should not aspire to be a 'spécialité nouvelle'.

---

[15] Godard also cites Merleau-Ponty's *Signes* in *2 ou 3 choses que je sais d'elle* (see Ch. 8 below).

For example, the study of consumer society evades a deeper reality—'la fabrication des consommateurs' (the making of consumers) (II, 33). If Structuralism seemed to offer an alternative to the atomization of specialized disciplines, by allowing access to the totality of experience, Lefebvre believed that the tendency to fetishize the notion of structure led to a frozen view of human reality, denying, in the field of the everyday, a capacity for metamorphosis. Politically, Lefebvre sees his critique as still faithful to Marx, whose desire for a total metamorphosis of daily life was based on a true conception of human possibility, and whose project sought not to predict the inevitable but to rectify 'la dérive de l'histoire' (the drift of history) (II, 45).

Against this background Lefebvre seeks to elaborate a definition of 'la vie quotidienne'. He begins by evoking, in terms that Blanchot found very forceful, its elusive ambivalence:

La vie quotidienne, comment la définir? De tous côtés, de toutes parts, elle nous entoure et nous assiège. Nous sommes en elle et hors d'elle. Aucune activité dite 'élevée' ne se réduit à elle mais aucune ne s'en détache. Ces activités naissent, croissent, émergent; aucune ne peut se constituer et s'achever pour et par elle-même, en quittant le sol natal et nourricier (II, 46).

(Everyday life, how should it be defined? On all sides, from all directions, it surrounds us and bombards us. We are in it and outside it. No so-called 'higher' activity can be reduced to it but none is independent of it. These activities are born, grow, and emerge; none can take form and resolution in and of itself, departing from its native and nourishing soil)

We are immersed in the everyday, yet at the same time cut off from it; nothing we do can be totally reduced to it, nor wholly be detached from it. Repeating the image from the 'Avant-propos' Lefebvre sees the everyday as the native soil of all our activities and endeavours—including 'higher' forms of knowledge. What then of the connections between everyday life and the petty things in life, its 'humble and sordid' side? (II, 47). It is important, argues Lefebvre, that we acknowledge this dimension (in which banal repetition and mundane routine should also be included), but we should not regard it as immutable. Lefebvre quotes a paper by Christiane Peyre, a member of his newly formed 'Groupe d'études sur la vie quotidienne', whose powerful description of the monotony of women's domestic work leads into a definition of everyday life as a set of elementary activities necessitated by processes of biological and social evolution and transformation. Seen this way, Lefebvre concedes, everyday life is indeed 'l'envers de toute praxis' (the obverse of all praxis) (II, 48). But,

Lefebvre asserts, his approach involves a different hypothesis—that the everyday is a sphere of creativity: it is in daily life that true creations are accomplished—'c'est dans la vie quotidienne et à partir d'elle que s'accomplissent les véritables *créations*' (II, 50)—the highest expressions of human reality derive from the everyday.

Higher activities are born from seeds contained in daily practices and the everyday provides the ground in which their validity must be proven. 'La vie quotidienne' is a 'niveau intermédiaire et médiateur' (an intermediate and mediating level):

En elle, les plus concrets des mouvements dialectiques s'observent: besoin et désir, jouissance et non-jouissance, satisfaction et privation [. . .] la part répétitive au sens mécanique du terme, la part créatrice et la part créée de la quotidienneté s'entremê-lent, dans un circuit perpétuellement reproduit' (II, 50).

(Here the most concrete dialectical movements are present: need and desire, *jouissance* and lack, satisfaction and privation . . . the element of repetition, in the mechanical sense, the creative and created elements in everydayness intermingle, in an endless cycle of reproduction)

Everyday life is not 'where it all happens'—it is not co-extensive with praxis. But it is a '*niveau* de réalité' (*level* of reality) characterized by movement rather than fixity. By virtue of its connections with growth, change, and possibility, the everyday is the level of 'mouvements dialectiques inhérents au concret humain, c'est-à-dire la quotidienneté' (dialectical movements inherent in concrete human reality, that is to say everydayness). Using spatial metaphors Lefebvre represents it as a 'zone de démarcation et de jonction' (zone of demarcation and conjunction) between freedom and constraint, and, in terms that closely echo the neo-Hegelianism of the Surrealists and Situationists, as a 'région d'appropriation non de la nature extérieure mais de sa propre nature' (region where one does not appropriate external nature but one's own nature) (II, 51).

What, asks Lefebvre, if we adopt another perspective (this is his repeated tactic) and strip human activity of that which pertains to specialized activities, removing all technical knowledge and expertise and simply leaving such everyday factors as effort, time, and rhythm? What is left? For some (scientists, structuralists, culturalists), next to nothing; for others (metaphysicians, Heideggerians), everything (because the ground of human existence—the ontological) is beneath all this. But for Lefebvre, for whom the everyday is not to be confused with the ground in Heidegger's sense, what remains is 'quelque chose' (something) that is hard to define precisely because it is not a thing or a clearly defined activity but a mixture: 'Un mixte de nature et de culture, d'historique et de vécu, d'individuel et de social, de réel et d'irréel, un lieu de transition et de rencontre, d'interférences et de conflits, bref un *niveau* de réalité (of nature and culture, history and lived experience, individual and social, real and unreal, a place of transition and meeting, interconnections and conflicts, in short a *level* of reality) (II, 52). The creative fertility of the *quotidien* as a 'niveau de réalité' can be identified with its essential hybridity, its 'in-betweenness' and self-evidence, the lack of definition that makes it at once simple and elusive, superficial and profound. How de we live? The question is clear, yet it addresses what is almost ungraspable: 'l'existence et le 'vécu' non transcrits spéculativement, dévoilés' (lived experience before it has been transcribed analytically, unveiled) (II, 52)—what must be changed, yet is most difficult to change.

One of the oppositions played out in this sphere is between two sorts of time: cyclical time, which is natural, concrete and not subject to reason, and linear time, which is abstract, rational, learnt, and unnatural. For Lefebvre a central project in the critique of everyday life is to establish how 'rhythmic temporalities' subsist within the linear time of modern industrial society, and how the interaction of these two kinds of time produces dysfunctions which, once identified, could lead to the metamorphosis of everydayness (II, 54). In terms of social reality the everyday is not associated with any specific class or income bracket but constitutes a level at which each individual can be differently situated, for example totally immersed or eerily detached. Any feature of daily life, including objects, words and gestures can give expression to it as a totality. And this may make phenomenological analysis appropriate as long as the descriptive process addresses the capacity for change within the phenomenon. It is noticeable here that Lefebvre has shifted from the view that becoming conscious of alienation leads to its being transcended, arguing instead for the need to identify—through the notion of the 'niveau'—a particular kind of creative power at work in the dialectical field of the everyday, which may be harnessed or, so to speak, tapped into, on certain conditions. And one of the sources of this creativity is located in an apparently negative feature of the everyday—its residual quality.

If Lefebvre acknowledges that the everyday is what is left when you subtract higher activities, he now also maintains that it is the product of all the activities that have the everyday as an inescapable part of their horizon. Daily lived experience is 'doublement déterminé, comme *résidu* et comme *produit* de tous les ensembles considérés (donc phénomène *total* à sa manière, à savoir un niveau dans la totalité et une totalité à son niveau)' (doubly determined, as a *residue* and as the *product* of all the 'ensembles' we can identify (thus it is in its way a *total* phenomenon, i.e. a level within totality and a totality at its own level) (II, 62). But if everyday life is produced by cross-fertilizations that do away with arbitrary separations, its residual quality is not thereby abolished. In fact this is now seen as the source of another character-istic which Lefebvre increasingly emphasizes: the power of resistance con-tained in the everyday. The irreducible residue comprises basic human rhythms and biological needs that are not simply remainders but factors which, in surviving (and resisting), struggle against the forces that oppose appropriation.

By this stage in his 'Mise au point' Lefebvre feels able to offer a 'détermin-ation détaillée et affinée de la vie quotidienne' (detailed and refined determin-ation of everyday life), and to articulate more precisely its topology. Best conceived as a level of human reality, it is in practice made up of a variety of levels, many extraneous to it. Hence a considerable widening of the 'pro-gramme critique' Lefebvre had originally envisaged. Lefebvre shows that 'la quotidienneté' again reveals a double aspect, this time as both 'l'*informel* et le *contenu des formes*' (the formless and the receptacle of forms). The everyday is 'informel' by virtue of the irreducible, residual 'matière humaine' that is its core. But if everyday life is also the product of ideologies, institutions, and discourses, it gives content to these forms through the conflict between its status as 'résidu' and its status as 'produit': 'la quotidienneté, c'est "cela", qui rend manifeste l'incapacité des formes (de chacune et de leur ensemble) à saisir, à intégrer et à épuiser le contenu' (everydayness is 'that which' manifests the inability of forms (individually and collectively) to grasp, and integrate the content). There is a 'contenu' that resists outer forms—partly constituted by that very resistance. Lefebvre develops the example of bureaucracy at some length: bureaucracy, he argues, never entirely succeeds in organizing the everyday: there is always something that escapes:

La quotidienneté proteste; elle se révolte, au nom des innombrables cas particuliers et des situations imprévues. Hors de la zone atteinte par la bureaucratie, ou plutôt en marge, subsistent l'informel et le spontané. A l'intérieur de la sphère organisée ou même sur-organisée, persiste une sourde résistance, de sorte que la forme doit s'adapter, se modifier, s'accommoder (II, 69).

(The everyday protests; it revolts in the name of innumerable particular cases and unforeseen situations. Outside the zone affected by bureaucracy, or in its margins, the formless and the spontaneous subsist. Within the organized or over-organized sphere a stubborn resistance persists, so that form has to adapt, modify, and adjust)

The idea that revolt and resistance are at the heart of the everyday, a central theme in Lefebvre's dialogue with the Situationists, later developed by Certeau, is linked to the 'double dimension du quotidien': 'platitude et profondeur, banalité et drame' (flatness and depth, banality and drama) (II, 69). The everyday is neither the inauthentic nor the 'truly' authentic; rather, 'c'est "là" que transparaît la profondeur véritable et que se pose la question d'authenticité' (it is 'here' that real depth is revealed and the question of authenticity arises). Here Lefebvre develops the idea (central to the theory Agnes Heller will develop, in order to 'rectify' Lukács) that the everyday is the arena for a 'drame de personalisation [. . .] de l'individualisation' (drama of personalization . . . individualization) (II, 71). In the everyday, by confronting the social and the individual within himself, 'l'être humain devient une personne' (the human being becomes a person). One consequence is that, far from being uniform in a given society, class, social group, or family the everyday is always subject to what Lefebvre calls 'l'inégal développement' (uneven development). The quality of everyday life is not solely determined by external factors since it is the product of a process or drama involving disparate sectors. And the drama is partly an individual one, played out through the subject's specific negotiations with the 'niveau', the 'informe', and the 'contenu' of the everyday. 'L'inégal developpement' also stems from the anachronistic temporality of everyday life where archaic forms of time (in the sphere of transportation for example) may be preserved in some quarters or where pre-technical modes of production coexist with advanced ones.

Having redefined the *quotidien* in this way, Lefebvre reviews new factors that have arisen in the 1950s. (1) Rapid technological development has created a new world of objects and gadgets, but at the expense of more natural rhythms (time is 'haché' and 'morcellé' (chopped and fragmented)) and by the encouragement of passivity: 'Sémi-technicisée la vie quotidienne n'a pas conquis un style ni gagné un rythme' (semi-technologized everyday life has not established a style or rhythm) (II, 79). There is urgent need for a 'sociologie de l'ennui' (sociology of boredom). (2) The phenomenon of 'Villes nouvelles' (on which Lefebvre began to write at this time) has encouraged the rise of functionalism: 'la vie quotidienne se voit traitée comme un emballage' (everyday life is treated like wrapping paper) (II, 83). (3) A huge upsurge in 'la presse féminine' (the female press) has promoted an ideology of the 'monde féminin' and the 'femme totale', which in its deployment of a 'pseudo-everyday', offers a crude caricature of both the real ambiguities of the everyday and its claim to totality: 'Dans ce pseudo-monde rien n'est et tout signifie' (In this pseudo-world nothing is, everything signifies) (II, 89). Here the influence of Barthes is perceptible. Firstly, in Lefebvre's handling of the topic, which draws on the style and methods of *Mythologies*. But secondly because Lefebvre, who knew Barthes well (the connections between them will be explored in the next chapter), launches a critique of the rise of the sign and of the cult of the signifier that will play a significant part in the evolution of some aspects of his theory of the everyday. (4) The question of signification arises again in Lefebvre's comments on the reinforcement of private as opposed to communal life. Private life is obviously one pole of the everyday, but where it predominates, for instance in the promotion of the 'petit groupe familial', the *quotidien* is severed from history. And this curtails its capacity to constitute a sphere of resistance to historical forces, instilling sterile individualism and the cult of material goods: 'la vie privée [. . .] creuse l'abîme entre le vécu et l'histoire' (private life . . . widens the gap between lived experience and history) (II, 97)—here Lefebvre notes Sartre's ideas in the recent *Critique de la raison dialectique*.[16] The new mass media drain everyday events of meaning: radio and TV have perfected the art of packaging the everyday by detaching it from its context 'en l'accentuant, en le colorant d'insolite ou de pittoresque, en le chargeant de signification' (accentuating it, colouring it with the bizarre and the picturesque, loading it with meaning) so that ultimately 'le signe et la signification qui n'est que signification perdent tout sens' (the sign and purely semiotic meanings lose all sense) (II, 81). Similarly, in the sphere of a defensive and manufactured 'vie privée'—where privation in the sense of spiritual impoverishment is indeed the norm—'les significations deviennent maximales et tombent dans l'insignifiance' (significations become maximal and fall into insignificance) (II, 95).

The chapter on 'Instruments formels' refines the framework Lefebvre has established. A critique of various methods of sociological enquiry highlights the difficulty of homing in on the individual as a 'nébuleuse de virtualités' (nebula of virtualities). Sociology overlooks the creative dimension of the *quotidien* and to redress this Lefebvre tries further to formalize, clarify, and extend the notion of 'niveau', insisting that it is not a static concept. As a

---

[16] A debate with Sartre's *Critique* provides a central impetus and timeliness to the second volume of Lefebvre's *Critique de la vie quotidienne*.

'niveau de réalité' the *quotidien* is not a 'champ continu' (continuous field): it is partly constituted by its interaction with other levels—that of history, for example—in a dynamic process that Lefebvre compares to musical harmony (he provides a diagram or stave demonstrating a hypothetical grid of inter-secting levels making up the everyday (II, 127)). But he rejects the idea—promoted by some sociologists—that the everyday is discontinuous, by con-trast with the continuity of history. For Lefebvre the fragmentation of the everyday is a specific historical phenomenon reflecting a time when everyday life is largely subordinate to other levels such as technology, bureaucracy, or politically oppressive leadership. Such times may be contrasted with moments of revolutionary effervescence where group praxis springs up and provides direction (Sartre is again a reference point here). In its positive aspect (its vector towards the possible) the everyday actively mediates between discon-tinuity and continuity, stagnation and change:

Le niveau de la quotidienneté en tant que 'réalité' serait donc celui de la *tactique*, intermédiaire entre le niveau où il n'y a plus d'acte, où la réalité stagne et s'épaissit, où domine le trivial—et celui de la décision, du drame, de l'histoire, de la stratégie et du bouleversement (II, 139).

(The level of the everyday as a 'reality' is therefore that of *tactics*, mid-way between the level where there is no action, where reality stagnates and thickens, where the trivial dominates, and that of decision, drama, history, strategy and upheaval)

Lefebvre stresses action and process so as to avoid the impression of a level inertly sandwiched between two others, whilst acknowledging that it is by impinging on history that the everyday achieves transformation:

La quotidienneté en tant que réalité à métamorphoser [. . .] se constate au niveau des *tactiques*, des forces et de leurs rapports, des ruses et des défiances. C'est au niveau des événements, des stratégies, et des moments historiques qu'elle se transforme (II, 139).

(Everydayness as a reality to be metamorphosed . . . can be identified at the level of tactics, forces and their relationships, ruses and challenges. It is at the level of events, strategies, and historical moments that it transforms itself)

The identification of the everyday with 'tactiques' and 'ruses'—tactical guile exercised from a position of weakness—will be of fundamental importance in Michel de Certeau's notion of 'l'invention du quotidien'. Here Lefebvre develops the idea of tactics in connection with the ambiguity of the everyday, the necessary blindness (another motif in Certeau) that denies it the dimen-sion of tragedy but associates it with play: hence the ambiguous impression everyday life often gives—'inconsistance et solidité, fragilité et cohésion, sérieux et futilité, drame profond et masque de comédie sur le vide' (lack of consistency and solidity, fragility and cohesion, seriousness and levity, profound drama and comic mask over the void) (II, 141). But he is careful to underline the active contribution that the tactical field of the everyday can make to its own self-realization even if this is partly outside its control. It is associated with another 'instrument formel', the opposition between micro- and macro-levels. Whilst associated with the 'micro' the *quotidien* is not simply subordinated to the 'macro' level: the two dimensions—that of immediate interpersonal relations (the 'micro' is the 'racine vivante du social' (living root of the social)), as opposed to relations mediated by such factors as money—interpenetrate on the same ground: The 'macro' does not determine the 'micro': 'Il l'enveloppe; il le contrôle; il le pénètre [...] Le "micro" résiste, malgré ses ambiguités ou grâce à elles' (It envelops it, keeps it under surveillance, penetrates it... the 'micro' resists, despite its ambiguities, or thanks to them) (II, 144). The resistance of the 'micro' occurs within the framework of the everyday, and its identification necessitates the capacity to interpret 'indices' which Lefebvre defines as social facts that are at first sight insignificant (the notion of 'l'insignifiant' will recur later) but have wide ramifications.

Lefebvre includes 'la réalité', as one of the categories involved in the critique of everyday life, opposing negative constructions of the real—as obstacle, contingency, the inescapable—to notions such as possibility, spontaneity, and play. Viewed dialectically, in conjunction with such notions as the present, the current, and the virtual, the real can be seen as harbouring the possibility of another dispensation: In the everyday and its ambiguous depth 'naissent les possibles et se vit le rapport du présent avec le futur' (possibilities are born and the relationship of the present to the future is lived through) (II, 198). A purely functionalist view of the real omits the lived relationship to future possibility that is woven into everyday reality: 'Nous ne partons pas d'une autre réalité extérieure à la réalité étudiée. Nous partons de son mouvement interne, et du possible' (We do not start out from a reality exterior to the one we study. We start out from its internal movement [dynamism], and from the possible) (II, 204–5). This 'mouvement interne' (a Hegelian notion, underlined in Blanchot's response to Lefebvre)[17] is associated with the 'ludic dimension' of the everyday, which functionalism—architecture and town planning would be salient examples—tends to filter out: 'Le jeu dispense avec générosité de la

---

[17] In Blanchot's 'La Parole quotidienne'—see Ch. 1 above.

présence [. . .] Le fonctionalisme intégral tend à l'éliminer' (Play generously dispenses presence . . . functionalism tends to eliminate play) (II: 205–6).

A new distinction between 'le vécu' and 'le vivre' clarifies the evolution of Lefebvre's thinking on alienation. The 'vécu' is identified with the 'focalisation de la conscience dans la pratique' (the focusing of consciousness within practice) which is compared to a patch of bright light against a wider, more diffuse background. Our lived experience is a mobile habitat ('demeure mouvante') that can rapidly alter its position in response to modifications within the wider array of 'le vivre' (II, 219). The 'vécu' is a dynamic and dramatic element, associated with play and spontaneity. This new distinction leads Lefebvre to reconsider ambiguity in social rather than ontological terms. Developing the earlier discussions of Brecht and the position of women, Lefebvre sees ambiguity as a state of inertia that engenders a drab banality based on the closing down of possibilities. Ambiguity induces diminished consciousness, encouraged by mass media, and fosters the perpetuation of outworn social forms such as those affecting women and family life. For Lefebvre, a critique of everyday life should discourage the tendency to identify the *quotidien* with this kind of ambiguity ('situations vécues à partir de contradictions étouffées, émoussées' (situations lived through via suppressed and blurred contradictions) II, 222); instead, critique should trigger the 'mouvement dialectique ambiguité-décision'. To focus attention on daily life is, he argues, to desire and thus to precipitate change. 'Etudier la quotidienneté c'est vouloir la changer' (To study the everyday is to want to change it). Changing it means articulating its confusions; revealing and thus dispersing its latent conflicts. This precipitates a decision, 'la plus générale et la plus révolutionnaire, celle de rendre insupportables les ambiguités, et de métamorphoser ce qui passe pour le plus immuable dans l'homme parce que dépourvu de contours certains' (of the most general and revolutionary kind—that of making ambiguities intolerable and of transforming what is held to be most immutable in human beings because lacking any clear definition) (II, 227).

In this light the notion of praxis, derived from Marx and Sartre, also undergoes revision. Praxis is not simply production but creation. It is the gateway to a totality, albeit a totality made up of different levels—'totalités partielles' (II, 239). Both repetitive praxis and inventive praxis are subject to considerable variation (not all repetitive activities are sterile and stereotypical but many are) and everyday life—where repetition and creation interact (II, 241)—provides many opportunities for transitions from one to the other. Creativity is thus not exclusively identified with activities that transcend the day-to-day, even if the kind of creativity that operates there may often reside in activities that break with routine: creative actions are often bizarre and aberrant (II, 241).

Lefebvre pursues the link between the creative dimension of the everyday and what is marginal or unstable in the context of language and discourse. Just as, for Sartre, the 'pratico-inerte' is anti-dialectical,[18] so, for Lefebvre, dialectical movement is to be found in 'les lacunes et ruptures du discours cohérent' (the gaps and breaks in coherent discourse). Discourse is dominated by logical order that is not attuned to the realm of change and possibility. We need to identify modes of language that resist this, where the actual and the potential, the fugitive and the transitional are at work, and where, by breaking out of its limits and tending towards the articulation of the everyday, 'le langage et le discours, faits de la vie quotidienne, expriment la quotidienneté' (language and discourse, part of the everyday, express everydayness) (II, 260). It is the capacity to embrace a wide range of tensions and contradictions that characterizes—in the sphere of language as well as life—the kind of work that engages the creativity of the everyday. Lefebvre explicitly draws the analogy between the way the artist or philosopher grapples with contradictions and 'l'effort général de l'individu dans la pratique sociale pour poser et résoudre ses problèmes' (the individual's effort in social practice to pose and resolve problems) (II, 263). Self-realization through the harnessing of possibilities is seen as akin to artistic creation on the part of the everyday subject: 'Son oeuvre, c'est sa vie quotidienne' (his creation is his everyday life) (II, 263). This perspective reveals the convergence between Lefebvre and the Situationists.

Lefebvre devotes a whole chapter to 'le champ sémantique', an aspect of the 'champ total' that can only be grasped fragmentarily (II, 275). In insisting that language itself only represents a part of the wider field where meanings are formed, Lefebvre reflects the recent broadening brought about by developments in semiotics. In positive terms, this leads him to discuss various non-linguistic signs and to develop the idea of a 'texte social'. More negatively, the focus on the semantic field affords Lefebvre the opportunity to bemoan the fetishizing of signification and language generally. He argues for the need to apprehend the workings of the 'in-signifiant' within the everyday, insisting that it must be captured 'raw': bringing everyday life 'into language' means exploring a semantic field 'qui déborde le discursif comme tel' (that overruns the discursive as such) (II, 279). Another area threatened by the inflation of the

---

[18] Jean-Paul Sartre, *Critique de la raison dialectique* (Paris: Gallimard, 1960), *passim*.

sign is the symbolic. Lefebvre argues that everyday consciousness, increasingly invaded by the multiplicity of signs in the modern environment, tends to suppress the symbolic dimension of human experience (associated with vital rhythms and impulses connected to day and night, parents, hunger, sexuality, II, 297). Driven underground, it only finds expression outside the field of articulated discourse:

le symbolisme devenu archaïque, [. . .] fuse; il crève le tissu des signes et du discours cohérent [. . .] dans le cri, dans l'interjection et l'exclamation, dans le lapsus, [Il y a] donc littéralement des trous, des cratères dans le champ sémantique, paysage volcanique tourmenté' (II, 304).

(becoming archaic the symbolic erupts . . . breaks through the web of signs and coherent discourse . . . in cries, interjections, exclamations, slips of the tongue . . . there are literally holes, craters in the semantic field, a volcanic landscape)

This emphasis on the necessity of being receptive to the wider 'champ sémantique', beyond the customary mechanisms of signification,[19] leads Lefebvre to envisage a close study of conversation and dialogue. The 'texte social' is the overall array of signifying systems at various levels, as we encounter it non-conceptually and affectively in daily life and in which we are both spectators and players. For Lefebvre, who will develop this idea massively in later writings, the city, and particularly the city street, has superseded the domestic arena to become the cardinal space of the everyday in its social aspect: 'La rue [. . .] représente la quotidienneté dans notre vie sociale. Elle en est la figuration presque complète [. . .] Comme la quotidienneté, la rue change sans cesse et se répète toujours' (II: 310) (the street . . . represents everydayness in our social life. It is its almost total figuration. Like the everyday the street is endlessly changing and endlessly repetitive) (II, 310).[20] Because it is a 'lieu de passage', a place of change, interconnection, circulation, and communication, a fundamentally theatrical space, the street reflects the inner as well as the outer aspects of the lives it links (II, 310). As participants in the social text, our relation to the spectacle of the street is that of the 'reader' (Barthes and Certeau will both develop the analogy with reading), confronted in this case with facial expression, clothes, lifestyles, objects—the 'spectacle' of the street 'enveloppe de multiples séméiologies' (embraces multiple semiologies) (II, 311). Via the social text in which it enables us to participate the street offers access to the

---

[19] See Nancy and Lyotard on *sens* and the figurality of the everyday in Ch. 9 below.
[20] See 'Street Names', in Ch. 9, below.

multiplicity of the 'champ sémantique'. This depends, however, on street life being able to maintain its character, and at the time of writing Lefebvre could already—like the Situationists—bemoan its impoverishment, epitomized on the one hand by excessive congestion, on the other by the functionalism of 'villes nouvelles'. Daily life loses its interest when the street is uninteresting: 'Or, que devient la ville, remplie à crever d'autos, réduite aux systèmes de signaux?' (Yet what does the city become when it is jam-packed with cars, reduced to signalling systems?) (II, 310).

The question of the evolution of everyday life arises in a different way in the last two chapters, both focusing on matters of time. 'Théorie des processus (cumulatif–non-cumulaif)' (Theory of processes (cumulative–non-cumulative)) provides a theoretical elaboration of the notion of 'l'inégal développement'. For Lefebvre daily life is not only susceptible of different degrees of plenitude depending on the extent to which possibilities are realized, it is also inherently located at the junction of opposed temporal forces, one progressive, the other regressive: 'à l'intersection, à la fois incertaine et tranchante, du cumulatif et du non-cumulatif. [. . .] à la frontière entre le secteur dominé (par la connaissance) et le secteur non-dominé. Frontière indécise et dangereuse . . . ' (at the intersection, at once uncertain, sharp, dangerous, of the cumulative and the non-cumulative . . . of the sectors dominated (and undominated) by knowledge) (II, 336).

In the final chapter, 'Théorie des moments', Lefebvre develops a theory closely parallel to the Situationists. It marks a return to the question with which the 1947 *Critique* had begun, namely the relationship between the special and the ordinary, 'la banalité' and 'la fête', in daily life, and raises general issues concerning poetry, epiphany, and the present. Lefebvre begins by positioning the 'moment' as a superior form of repetition based on 'la perception d'une analogie et d'une différence dans le temps vécu' (the detection of an analogy and a difference in lived time) (II, 342). The 'moment' always refers to an individual's history, and it stands out in the midst of the 'informe', through an intensity that stems from the tension between the desire for duration and the inevitability of termination. However, it is not of a different order from other instants: '[Le moment] s'insère dans le tissu de la quotidienneté qu'il ne déchire pas mais tend à transformer (partiellement et "momentanément" [. . .]). Il utilise ainsi ce qui n'est pas lui: ce qui passe à sa portée, le contingent et l'accidentel' (The moment is part of the fabric of everydayness, which it does not tear but tends to transform (partially and "momentarily" . . .). It uses what is not itself: what is near at hand, contingent, accidental) (II, 346). The moment is not a rupture in the flow of the everyday—a tear in its fabric, as Lefebvre puts it, using an image we will find later in Perec. It represents a point when the transitory and contingent take on a certain density and when an impression—like a pattern on cloth—is left. If the moment is 'désaliénant' by comparison with the triviality of daily life (II, 347), it does not come from outside its frame: the moment is born in and of the everyday (II, 350). But the moment does stem from the impulse to realize a possibility: an act that produces, from within, 'une structuration sur le fond incertain et transitoire de la quotidienneté' (structuration to the uncertain and transitory background of everydayness) (II, 348), effectively 'opens up' a moment. In implicit dialogue with the Situationists, Lefebvre explores the relationship between the moment and the situation. A more intensely 'lived' present is often produced through structuring activities—ceremonies, rituals, structured behaviour—that make a framework within which the 'creativity' of situations emerges (II, 352). The moment connects with the place of rituals and ceremonies in daily life.[21] But Lefebvre underlines how, in stemming from a free act of structuring, or destructuring, it has links with invention and discovery. Yet the moment must at some point part company with the everyday since the impulse that creates it is in effect a criticism of daily life: 'les moments critiquent—en acte—la vie quotidienne et la quotidienneté critique—en fait—les moments paroxystiques' (moments critique—actively—everyday life—and everydayness critiques—in fact—moments of paroxysm). The moment springs from the everyday and borrows its substance, yet it constitutes, in its paroxystic dimension, a tragic double of the everyday. Ultimately the brilliance of 'la fête' stands out against the ordinary run of the everyday (II, 355). Only a transformed everyday would bring resolution to the age-old conflict between the trivial and the festive (II, 357).

THE FREEDOM OF THE CITY: LEFEBVRE, DEBORD, AND THE SITUATIONISTS

As we saw in the previous section, the second volume of Lefebvre's *Critique*—seeking to establish the *Fondements d'une sociologie de la quotidienneté*—bears many traces of dialogue with the Situationists. The question of what Guy Debord and his collaborators may have owed to Lefebvre, or vice versa, has

---

[21] On this see Ch. 8 below.

often been discussed, generally in a partisan spirit by admirers on either side.[22] In the context of discourses on the *quotidien* we need to look at this more critically because some of the richest and most influential thinking on the everyday—in Lefebvre's 1961 volume, and in the writings of Debord and others in the early Sixties—emerged in a climate of exchange, rivalry, and in the end enmity, between Lefebvre and the 'Situs' as they are often called.

Lefebvre's expulsion from the Parti communiste in 1958 gave him a new freedom, and the first formulation of his 'théorie des moments', in a lengthy and unconventional intellectual autobiography, *La Somme et le reste*, published that year, may have owed something to the notion of the 'situation' which had come to the fore in the creation of the Internationale Situationniste group in 1957. At all events, the Situationists engage actively (if often critically) with Lefebvre's ideas from the first issue of their journal *L'Internationale Situationniste* in June 1958; and in the six issues between then and August 1961 there is always some reference to Lefebvre—most notably, in August 1961, a key text by Debord based on a contribution to Lefebvre's CNRS 'Groupe d'études sur la vie quotidienne'.

Between 1958 and 1961 we can identify a gradual convergence of the Situationist perspective with that of Lefebvre, evinced principally by the recognition of 'la vie quotidienne' as the prime forum of Situationist intervention. Just as striking, however, is the way Lefebvre's 1961 *Critique*, much of which, on the evidence of its references, seems to have been written in late 1961 (Lefebvre cites Debord's intervention at his seminar), with its emphasis on the creative potential of the everyday, bears witness to the stimulation of the Situationists. Although Lefebvre and Debord may have met briefly earlier, the two men spent considerable amounts of time in each other's company, initially at Lefebvre's instigation, in Paris and in the Pyrenees, between 1960 and 1962, when a fierce argument, where one bone of contention was Lefebvre's alleged plagiarism of Situationist ideas regarding the Paris Commune as an outburst of revolutionary festivity, brought the relationship to an end.

The dialogue with the Situationists is important because the second, 1961, volume of the *Critique* marked the high point of Lefebvre's contribution to

---

[22] I have found the following useful: Hess, *Henri Lefebvre: une aventure dans le siècle*; Christophe Bourseiller, *Vie et Mort de Guy Debord* (Paris: Plon, 1999); Vincent Kaufmann, *Guy Debord, La Révolution au service de la poésie* (Paris: Fayard, 2001); Peter Wollen, *Raiding the Icebox* (Bloomington, IN: Indiana University Press); Eleanor Kofman and E. Lebas (eds.), *Henri Lefebvre: Writings on Cities* (Oxford: Blackwell, 1996); Sadie Plant, *The Most Radical Gesture: The Situationist International in a Postmodern Age* (London: Routledge, 1992); Simon Sadler, *The Situationist City* (Cambridge, MA: MIT Press, 1998).

the understanding of 'la vie quotidienne', developing key ideas in the 1958 'Avant–propos' and making the original 1947 volume look crude by comparison. Subsequently, the more accessible 1968 volume, *La Vie quotidienne dans le monde moderne*, based on lecture courses Lefebvre gave at Strasbourg and Nanterre universities between 1960 and 1968, is largely a popularization of his ideas, fired by often reactionary diatribes against structuralism and the dominance of the linguistic paradigm. And the third volume of the *Critique*—subtitled *De la modernité au modernisme (Pour une métaphilosophie du quotidien)*—published in 1981—is primarily a survey of reactions and ramifications (including the place of the 'Situs'), along with an update considering new factors, such as the rise of multinationals, that had modified the conditions of everyday life. The main conceptual innovation in volume III is the notion of 'rythmanalyse', further expounded in one of Lefebvre's last publications, which develops the notion of the differential temporal rhythms constituting the lived experience of the everyday.[23]

The waning of Lefebvre's conceptual engagement with the notion of everyday life accompanies the rise, from the mid Sixties to the mid Seventies, of a set of concerns that effectively subsume and replace the *quotidien* as his main area of investigation—space, urban design, and the modern city. From his 1960 article on 'Les Nouveaux Ensembles urbains', to *Le Droit à la ville* (1968), *La Révolution urbaine* (1970) and *La Production de l'espace* (1974), Lefebvre does pioneering work on city space that earns him an enduring international reputation, particularly through the adoption of his ideas, in the Eighties and Nineties, by a new generation of post-modern geographers.[24] Whilst not absent, the *quotidien* is rarely more than implicit here, although the vulnerable rhythms of daily life remain a touchstone in Lefebvre's consistent attack on technocratic control. Yet Lefebvre's analyses of urban space tend to be highly abstract, and it is later writers—Barthes, Certeau, and Perec, for example—who integrate new ways of thinking about cities, inspired partly by Lefebvre, with the concrete experience of the *quotidien*.

The Situationists provide a significant link. Their activities began as, and to some extent always remained, a way of engaging with the city,[25] and their main ancestors, shared with Lefebvre, were the Surrealists. But where Lefebvre had seen only the 'literary' side of a surrealist text like *Le Paysan de Paris*, the

---

[23] Henri Lefebvre, *Éléments de Rythmanalyse* (Paris: Syllepse, 1992).

[24] Cf. David Harvey, *The Condition of Postmodernity* (Oxford: Blackwell, 1990); Soja, *Postmodern Geographies*.

[25] See Sadler, *The Situationist City*.

Situationists reactivated the spirit of surrealist urban *errance*, fusing it with the ideas of dissident architects, opposed to modernist functionalism. In the later perspective of the 1980s Lefebvre claimed that the shift towards the question of the city, which occurred in the context of work on rural sociology that led him to study the emergence in the 1950s of soulless *villes nouvelles* in his own region of South-West France, had been inflected by the ideas of the Dutch architect Constant, a member of the COBRA group of artists, formed in 1948, who for some years was in close alliance with Debord and the Situationist group. Citing Constant's 1953 essay, 'Pour une architecture des situations', as an inspiration, Lefebvre noted that Constant in his turn acknowledged a debt to the 1947 *Critique de la vie quotidienne*. Lefebvre was also happy to insinuate that the key idea of the 'situation' derived from Constant, and thus from COBRA (and so, circuitously, from Lefebvre himself) rather than from the 'Situs'.[26] Whatever its origin, it is the contextualization of the *situation*—through the practices of *dérive*, *détournement*, and *psychogéographie* that were the hallmark of the Internationale Lettriste group from 1954 to 1957 before this mutated into the Internationale Situationniste—which gave it substance; and it is these activities—where the city is a concrete space not an abstract issue—that provided the real basis for the rapprochement between Lefebvre and Debord. If Lefebvre's 1961 *Critique* bears the imprint of the Situationists it is in the emphasis on the fertility of moments, and on a level of reality where creativity springs from lack rather than abundance, and where resistance to conditioning is spawned in the key space of the street. But if his dialogues with the 'Situs' had a decisive effect on Lefebvre's orientation to the city, his break with Debord led him to develop his ideas in other ways.

Yet equally, after the break, the Situationists tended to downplay the ludic interactions with the city which, at the point when they make common cause with Lefebvre, were explicitly construed in terms of what Raoul Vaneigem called a 'revolution' in everyday life.[27] The dominant note in the last six issues of *L'Internationale Situationniste* (1963–72), as well as in Debord's *La Société du spectacle* in 1967, is a more explicitly political vision that focuses on mechanisms of conditioning and constraint. If the bleak picture of brainwashed consumers mesmerized by the homogeneous falsity of the 'spectacle', epitomized by television, city design, and advertising, presupposes the truly

---

[26] See 'Henri Lefebvre on the Situationist International', interview, conducted and translated by Kristin Ross (1983), *October*, 79 (Winter 1997).

[27] Raoul Vaneigem, *Traité de savoir-vivre à l'usage des jeunes générations* (1967; Paris: Gallimard Folio, 1992).

lived life that the spectacle negates, there is often little sense that positive energies are harboured within everyday life itself.

The contribution of the Situationists to ways of thinking about the everyday originated in the activities of the Internationale Lettriste, a splinter group which, in 1954, split away from the Lettristes, who were centred on the neo-Dadaist word manipulations of Isidore Isou, turned its back on the re-constituted Surrealists, and tuned in to currents emanating from COBRA and other groupings, primarily in Holland and Belgium (notably Marcel Mariën's dissident surrealist journal *Les Lèvres nues* which started up in the same year). Although they kept the Lettrist label—in the spirit of ironic appropriation they were to call *détournement*—they called their free newssheet *Potlatch*, referring to the transgressive gift economy, based on moments of pure expenditure, identified in certain tribal societies and theorized by Mauss and Bataille. What Debord, Wolman, and the rest found in COBRA were clues as to how the ground of avant-garde activity might be shifted away from the production of artworks to direct interventions in life itself. Far from being a showcase for new art or writing *Potlatch* provided a record and a stimulus for certain types of experience. Replying in July 1954 to an 'enquête' the group claimed that poetry lay in 'the power of human beings over their adventures'; 'la beauté nouvelle', they asserted, 'sera DE SITUATION, c'est-à-dire *provisoire* et vécue' (the new beauty will be that of THE SITUATION, i.e. provisional and lived); poetry for them meant the elaboration of 'conduites absolumment neuves' (new forms of behaviour).[28] It is easy to see the surrealist antecedents for these priorities. The chief difference was that where Surrealism saw experimental activity in terms of releasing the dormant energies of the unconscious Debord's group believed it was possible to bring about change through conscious volition, via particular forms of behaviour. The notion of psychogeography, later defined as the study of the precise effects of the geographical environment, natural or artificial, on the affective behaviour of individuals, arises early in *Potlatch*, as do the related activities of *dérive*, *détournement*, and, as above, *situation*. Psychogeography rests on the postulate that different environments or ambiences work directly on human feelings and are more or less conducive to desirable states of being or behaviour (*ambiance* and *comportement* are words that recur constantly).[29] A rather

---

[28] Guy Debord (ed.), *Potlatch, 1955–57* (Paris: Gallimard Folio, 1996), 42.

[29] A view anticipated in Breton's notion of the 'magique-circonstancielle' and very explicitly in 'Pont-Neuf', on which see Sheringham, 'City Space, Mental Space, Poetic Space'.

simplistic determinism or behaviourism is sometimes at work here, betraying an 'architecture and design' mindset in which a critique of modernism (pillorying the *bête noire* 'Le Corbusier—Sing Sing')[30] for overt constraint and conditioning is countered by the creation of environments designed to have a different impact, and thus effectively to condition in a different way.

Another key theme is play. In 1955 Debord praised Johan Huizinga's 1951 *Homo ludens* (which included a discussion of potlatch) although he took issue with Huizinga's argument that play depended on a contrast with the 'vie courante' it provisionally suspended. For Debord a feeling for momentariness or transience was a key component of desirable lived experience, and a playful, anti-utilitarian attitude could help foster it. Rather than a literary school, he and Wolman wrote, their group was concerned with 'une manière de vivre [...] qui tend elle-même à ne s'exercer que dans le provisoire' (a way of living that tends only to be exercised provisionally) (186). Their aim was not to suspend 'la vie courante' but to make it primordial. In 1957, at the point when the Internationale Lettriste was subsumed into the new 'théâtre d'opérations cultuelles' of the Internationale Situationniste, Debord wrote: 'Nous avons à trouver des techniques concrètes pour bouleverser les ambiances de la vie quotidienne' (we must find concrete techniques for shaking up the ambiences of everyday life) (163). New here was the use of the phrase 'vie quotidienne', marking a stronger socio-political as opposed to cultural framework, and pointing to a rapprochement with the perspectives of Lefebvre. *Potlatch* featured endless psychogeographic games, exercises, and *faits divers*. The psychogeographic propensities of particular Parisian streets, squares, and quartiers were celebrated, and suggestions for changing street names were aired.[31] *Dérive*, defined as 'une technique du déplacement sans but [qui] se fonde sur l'influence du décor' (a technique of aimless drift based on the influence of the surroundings), was commended, and some of its practical aspects (taxis are approved of since they can propel you rapidly to another part of town) and concrete achievements were debated (65). In 1955, rejecting the 'fétichisme de l'insolite' (fetishizing the bizarre) (190), the group issued a list of 'Projets d'embellissements rationnels [and not 'irrationnels' as in the case of a famous piece in *La Révolution surréaliste*] de Paris' (Projects for the rational embellishment of Paris) (203), demanding easy access to metro tunnels, which should be kept open at night after the last trains, rooftops,

---

[30] Debord (ed.), *Potlatch*, 37. Page references are cited in the text.
[31] On street names see Ch. 9 below.

via ladders and walkways, and prisons, where it should be possible to 'faire un séjour touristique'.

L'Internationale Situationniste, and its eponymous journal, maintained many of these activities and priorities, but the sense of ludic, counter-cultural avant-gardism is replaced by a more concerted effort at theorization and socio-political intervention. This is reflected in three theoretical and programmatic texts dating from the period of transition: Debord's 'Théorie de la dérive', and a 'Mode d'emploi du détournement' co-written with Wolman, both originally published in the Belgian journal *Les Lèvres nues* in 1956, but reprinted in *L'Internationale Situationniste*; and Debord's 'Rapport sur la construction des situations...' delivered at the founding conference of the Internationale Situationniste at Cosio d'Arroscia in Italy in August 1957.

The term *dérive* had first surfaced in a 1953 text 'Formulaire pour un urbanisme nouveau' by Ivan Chletligov (alias Gilles Ivain), which Debord published in the first issue of *L'Internationale Situationniste* (hereafter, *IS*). Describing cities as geological and haunted, Ivain imagined experimental spaces designed to propitiate certain forms of behaviour, for example a city where the *quartiers* would induce various feelings experienced haphazardly in everyday life (*IS*, 15–20).[32] Transposing this idea into a less visionary context, Debord's 'Théorie de la dérive' combines it with the pioneering urban sociology of Chombart de Lauwe, who had studied the relation between Parisians and their *quartiers*, identifying the micro-city each inhabitant creates by the patterns of his or her movements, and with ideas drawn from ecology. *Dérive*, redefined as 'une technique du passage hâtif à travers des ambiances variées' (*IS*, 51) (a technique of rapid passage through varied ambiences) is seen as a 'comportement ludico-constructif' based partly on play and desire, but aimed at the gathering of experimental data concerning the differential features of the 'tissu urbain', the role of micro-environments, and the powerful force exerted by certain key spots that can be seen as psychogeographical 'plaques tournantes' (turntables) (*IS*, 55).

In the Cosio d'Arroscia text, *dérive* is seen as part of a collective, organized effort aimed at 'un emploi unitaire de tous les moyens de bouleversement de la vie quotidienne' (*IS*, 696) (a unitary use of all the means of shaking up everyday life). The word 'unitaire', as in the recurrent phrase 'urbanisme unitaire', underlines the holistic aspirations of the Situationists. As in Lefebvre, the 'bouleversement' of 'la vie quotidienne' is associated with the

---

[32] References incorporated in the text are to the 1997 Fayard reprint.

overcoming of hierarchies and divisions. Situationist theory will develop what Debord called a 'critique de la séparation'.[33] And like Lefebvre Debord cites Brechtian theatrical practice, with its methods for devising ways of turning the traditionally passive spectator into an active and critical participant. The 'constructed situation', another way of intervening in the sphere of behaviour, is conceived as a kind of theatre in which there are only participants, the aim being to destroy the spectacle by making the participant an active creator of his or her own life 'provoquant ses capacités de bouleverser sa propre vie' (stirring up the capacity to transform one's own life) (*IS*, 699). Interventions in the sphere of behaviour go hand in hand with the 'action sur le décor' of unitary urbanism—spearheaded by Constant who designed labyrinths (a favourite Situationist motif) and plans for a utopian city called New Babylon where the multiple constituents of the urban milieu, including sound, refreshment, the differential fields of force represented by varying *quartiers*, are seen as an integrated totality.[34] Yet Debord insists that the Situationist view of life does not tend towards unity: but rather 'une conception non continue de la vie' (*IS*, 700). Even if it takes the combination of a wide range of factors to produce it, the currency of truly lived experience is the 'instant isolé'. Against Surrealism (and like Bataille) the Situationists oppose the shibboleths of unity and continuity, embracing what Debord called life's principal drama: the sense of 'l'écoulement du temps' (the flow of time). 'L'attitude situationniste' Debord claimed, 'consiste à miser sur la fuite du temps [avec] le pari de gagner toujours sur le changement' (consists in gambling on the flow of time, gambling on always winning change) (*IS*, 700).

From the first issue in June 1958, *IS* manifested an explicit orientation towards everyday life. The opening editorial notes the widening gap between material abundance and quality of life: the rise of the consumer society in the 1950s had not been accompanied by any real enhancement of the possibilities of everyday life (*IS*, 4). Rather, the 'domination de la nature' on which material progress rests is concomitant with a dominion exerted on human beings. And an aspect of this conditioning, abetted by art and culture, is the restriction of the field of human experience to past models which invite passive acquiescence. Refusing to be custodians of the cultural past, the Situationists

---

[33] This was the title of a film Debord made in 1961. See Guy Debord, *Œuvres cinématographiques complètes 1952–78* (Paris: Gallimard, 1994), 43–57.

[34] See Sadler, *The Situationist City*.

insist on 'la nécéssité de l'oubli' (the need for forgetting) (*IS*, 8): their terrain is the present.

Active participation in the production of daily life is at the heart of Debord's 'Thèses sur la revolution culturelle' where for the first time he explicitly engages with Lefebvre. Debord begins by rebutting the traditional role of the aesthetic realm as guardian of an immutable order, separated from the present. The aim of the Situationists is immediate participation in 'une abondance passionnelle de la vie, à travers le changement de moments périssables délibérément aménagés' (a passionate abundance of life through the transformation of transitory moments deliberately organized) (*IS*, 20). Cultural activity, therefore, viewed 'du point de vue de la totalité' (from the point of view of totality), should consist in the 'experimental construction' of everyday life, aimed less at reporting on experiences than on generating them; rather than produce artworks it should produce transformed individuals: 'Il s'agit de produire nous-mêmes' (the aim is to produce ourselves). Social progress should not simply give people more free time but access to the means of production of daily life—'Il n'y a pas de liberté dans l'emploi du temps sans la possession des instruments modernes de construction de la vie quotidienne' (there is no freedom in our daily schedules without possession of modern instruments for constructing everyday life). Although the inspiration here is unmistakably Lefebvrian, Debord goes on to criticize the very limited role Lefebvre had reserved for culture in a recent article, 'Vers un romantisme révolutionnaire', in the *Nouvelle Revue française* in 1957. Lefebvre had argued that the revolutionary role of the artist lay simply in registering the ironic disparity between the world he aspires to and the real world he lives in. Condemning the inadequacy of this 'conscience du possible–impossible' (awareness of the possible–impossible) which Lefebvre ascribes to the artist, Debord insists on the need to 'surmonter notre désaccord avec le monde [. . .] par quelques constructions supérieures' (overcome our dissent from the world . . . by some superior constructs), forgetting the past and working directly towards 'l'apparition concrète de l'ordre mouvant de l'avenir' (the concrete emergence of the moving order of the future) (*IS*, 21).

A similar criticism is levelled in issue 3 of *IS* in an editorial responding to the publication, in 1958, of Lefebvre's autobiographical *La Somme et le reste*. Lefebvre is applauded for having identified the self-destructive logic that gives rise to the rapid turnover of artistic movements and aesthetic positions, but censured for not recognizing that art, as *expression*, is itself now dead. In the place of his own very dated poems, incorporated in *La Somme et le reste*, and his conception of the Romantic revolutionary, Lefebvre should recognize the need to identify 'moyens d'action culturels' (*IS*, 72) that would work directly on life itself. What must be found are 'instruments opératoires intermédiares' that can mediate between the 'praxis globale' of social revolution and the 'pratique individuelle de la vie'—the construction of individual lifestyles through 'une planification de l'existence' where one's life takes the place of the artwork. The anonymous editorial opposes two visions of cultural activity: 'Nous ne voulons pas travailler au spectacle de la fin d'un monde, mais à la fin du monde du spectacle' (we do not work to create the spectacle of the end of the world, but the end of the world of the spectacle) (*IS*, 76).

Issue 2 of *IS* reported a missed encounter between Lefebvre and the Situationists at a meeting to debate whether Surrealism was dead or alive. Lefebvre cried off, and Debord's contribution, via a tape-recorded message, praised Surrealism for its 'essais d'intervention' (attempted interventions) in everyday life but bemoaned the tension it had always maintained between the affirmation of a 'nouvel usage de la vie' (new use of life) and a 'fuite réactionnaire' (reactionary flight) beyond the real (IS, 65). This measured view was already evident in the opening issue of *IS* which began with a discussion of the 'exigence profonde' (profound demand) that gave Surrealism its 'caractère indépassable' (definitive importance) (*IS*, 3). A few pages on, in a key essay on the construction of situations, 'Problèmes préliminaries à la construction d'une situation', a surrealist note is perceptible in the insistence that Situationist experimentation with existing and constructed ambiences, through psychogeography and *dérive*, aims at 'l'apparition confuse de nouveaux désirs' (the confused hatching of new desires) and thus necessitates a 'situationist psychoanalysis' where 'chacun doit chercher ce qu'il aime, ce qui l'attire' (each must seek out what he or she loves, is drawn to, *IS*,11);[35] collectively this will promote the elaboration of Situationist desire.

An unsigned editorial in the fourth issue of *IS* (118–9), headed 'Théorie des moments et construction des situations', was prompted by Lefebvre's first elaboration of his idea of the moment, itself possibly a response to the Situationists, in *La Somme et le reste*. The *IS* piece begins with a long quotation where Lefebvre argues that the moments he envisages, whilst not being everyday in themselves, would arise in the context of everyday life and raise it, so to speak, to a higher level, providing a richness it lacks (this view will be modified, possibly in the light of Situationist criticisms, in the 1961 *Critique*

---

[35] This was at the heart of Breton's *Nadja*—see Ch. 2 above.

de la vie quotidienne). The *IS* writer (probably Debord) then offers a densely argued parallel analysis of the Lefebvrian moment and his own, Situationist, conception of the situation. Common ground includes the fact that the moment and the constructed situation both go beyond the rapid, ephemeral instant: each combines the assertion of an absolute with a sense of passage, and points toward a unification of generic form and contingent occasion, the 'structural' and the 'conjonctural'. But where Lefebvre can talk of a plurality of 'moments privilégiés' that manifest a kind of presence, the situation must be seen as remaining *between* the instant and the moment. For where the Lefebvrian moment can be lasting and is repeatable—it is compatible with the idea of a state, a stable content, like being in love—the situation, even if it lasts for a while, is inherently contingent, particularized and unrepeatable. It is a production that is for immediate consumption; it has a 'valeur d'usage' (use value), but no 'valeur marchande' (exchange value). While instances and types of moment—love is the example Lefebvre gives—can be listed (they have a recognizable content), the situation lies in 'la praxis même' and can enter into an infinite number of combinations. Finally, if Lefebvre's moment is primarily temporal—a good patch of time—constructed situations cannot be severed from their spatial articulation: they are 'complètement spatio-temporels' and in their one-off, here-and-now quality they constitute breaks and accelerations in the individual everyday—*'les révolutions dans la vie quotidienne individuelle'* (*IS*,119).

Moments were always going to be perilous ground for Lefebvre, given his searing critique of Surrealists and others in the 1947 *Critique* for having done down the everyday through a cult of privileged experience. And, as we saw earlier, in the 1961 *Critique* he will work much harder to develop a dialectic where the moment, as a creation, emanates from the *quotidien* against whose more routine ordinariness it stands out. But the Situationist critique of Lefebvre leads to a definition of the situation—as pure praxis, pure 'valeur d'usage', bound to context—that is in fact closer to certain Surrealist positions (see Chapter 2, above) and to ideas we will encounter in Perec and Certeau. And this points to the value of the Situationist vision of the everyday which, in its consistent emphasis on city life and hence on movement in space, always resisted essentializing human experience, through its insistence on 'la valeur d'usage de la vie'. As Debord put it magnificently, in a set of theses on traffic of all things: 'les urbanistes révolutionnaires ne se préoccuperont pas seulement de la circulation des choses, et des hommes figés dans un monde de choses. Ils essaieront de briser ces chaînes topologiques, en expérimentant des terrains pour la circulation des hommes à travers la vie authentique' (revolutionary urbanists will not only concern themselves with the circulation of things and individuals immobilized in a world of things. They will try to smash these topological chains by experimenting with new terrains for the circulation of human beings in authentic life) (*IS*, 105).

There is an underlying paradox in the fertile interaction between Lefebvre and the Situationists. While Lefebvre would come to narrow his focus, in the end very productively, onto the city, Debord and his colleagues came increasingly to insist on setting *dérive*, psychogeography and the construction of *ambiances* in the wider framework of the need for a wholesale revolution in everyday life. An editorial piece in the sixth issue of *IS* criticized Lefebvre for not going far enough in his critique of a utopian project by a team of Zurich architects and sociologists because he failed to acknowledge that urbanism, however utopian, could only betray the need to 'embrasser la totalité' (embrace totality) through a 'nouvel usage de la vie' (*IS*, 205) (new usage of life). Denouncing the 'mensonge urbaniste', the Situationists declare that all attempts to 'organize' everyday life, invariably involving 'specialists', were based on alienation and constraint. Earlier, a key editorial in issue 5 of *IS* proclaimed the Situationists to be the purest example of a 'corps anti-hiérarchique d'anti-spécialistes' (anti-hierarchical, anti-specialist grouping) (*IS*, 153). Affirming that their field of action was 'la vie quotidienne'—which Lefebvre would of course define in terms of its residual status, outside all specializations—they insisted that *their* 'critique de la vie quotidienne' would be 'effectuée, et non plus souhaitée, indiquée' (enacted, no longer just wished for, pointed to) (*IS*, 153). If the idiom is that of Lefebvre, the implications are decidedly darker. Situationist critique aims to expose the 'néant' (nothingness) of daily life in modern capitalist society. To the abundance of material objects and processed images of happiness imposed by the 'terrorism' of advertising, the Situationists oppose an abundance of transient lived experiences. But such 'exercices pratiques' as the *détournement* of existing environments, like the Gothic châteaux beloved of the Surrealists, or new kinds of *dérive* accentuating the plasticity of the human subject, are now seen as laboratory experiments combating 'le conditionnement d'ensemble' (overall conditioning) by the liberation of existing desires. These activities are no more than preparatory: 'Voici donc les ultimes avant-postes de la culture' (Here then are the ultimate outposts of culture). The real struggle is beyond: 'Au-delà, commence la conquête de la vie quotidienne' (*IS*, 155).

On 17 May 1961 Guy Debord made a contribution to the Groupe de recherche sur la vie quotidienne, a section of the Centre d'Études socio-logiques of the CNRS set up by Lefebvre in 1960. Although he may have been present, Debord's voice was relayed by a tape-recorder, and at the beginning he claims that this is a Brechtian device to make the audience concretely aware of how everyday lived experience is often manipulated by technology and the discourse of experts; for those who think the everyday is a mere abstraction Debord's tactic is designed to demonstrate 'par un léger déplacement des formules, que c'est ici même, la vie quotidienne' (by a slight displacement of formulae, that everyday life is *here*) (*IS*, 218). This leads into his first main point. As the rest of the exposé will show, Debord had clearly been a regular listener at Lefebvre's seminar, and over the preceding year had heard people talk on such topics as new technologies, *faits divers*, leisure, and private life. Yet he had been surprised to find that most of the speakers tended to cast doubt on whether there was such a thing as 'vie quotidienne', and Debord takes this symptomatic scepticism as the basis for his analyses. His first move is to link it to the very idea of a 'groupe d'études' given that, in his view, the point is not to study the everyday but to change it. While the desire for transformation (not the same as organization or reform) brings the everyday into focus—if only negatively—the impulse to study it invariably involves the adoption of a specialized and partial point of view that fails to see it as a totality. As an object of study 'vie quotidienne' is liable to resemble the Yeti, dismissed in the end as a quaint joke. Or else, study 'exoticizes' the everyday, locating it exclusively 'chez les autres': notably amongst the working classes. Acknowledging Lefebvre's definition of the *quotidien* as 'ce qui reste quand on a extrait du vécu toutes les activités spécialisées' (what remains when all specialized activities have been subtracted from lived experience), Debord notes that this means that there is nothing left for the specialist. But he goes on to make a declaration that strongly echoes Lefebvre's 1958 'Avant-propos',[36] as well as anticipating and perhaps influencing some of the inflections of the 1961 *Critique*. Specialized activities clearly exist, he says, although they are in constant osmosis with the everyday. But the essential point, which Debord enounces in terms that sound like a *détournement* of Lefebvre's own idiom, is that:

Il faut placer la vie quotidienne au centre de tout. Chaque projet en part et chaque réalisation revient y prendre sa véritable signification. La vie quotidienne est la mesure

---

[36] Lefebvre, *Critique de la vie quotidienne*, I, 108–9.

de tout; de l'accomplissement ou plutôt du non-acomplissement des relations humaines; de l'emploi du temps vécu; des recherches de l'art; de la politique révolutionnaire' (*IS*, 219).

(Everyday life must be placed at the centre of everything. Every project starts out from it and every realization returns here for its true meaning. Everyday life is the measure of everything; of the fulfilment, or rather non-fulfilment of human relationships; of the way time is lived; of artistic researches; of revolutionary politics)

But why is this not recognized? The answer lies in the impoverished status imposed on the everyday by a politics of exploitation and repression. Debord argues that the logic of acceleration and accumulation that goes with industrialization depends on corresponding entropy in the sphere of everyday life. Citing the analogy developed by Lefebvre in his seminar, and later in the 1961 *Critique*, according to which the *quotidien* displays the retarded state characteristic of underdevelopment ('l'inégal développement'), Debord insists on seeing a more direct link between this 'résistance à l'historique' and the logic of advanced capitalism (and by analogy the 'specialized' sectors, like mass entertainment, that it favours). Taking the idea a step further Debord asserts that 'la vie quotidienne' can be seen as a 'secteur colonisé' (it is this idea that Lefebvre endorses when he cites Debord in the 1961 *Critique*).[37] If colonization produces underdevelopment, then similarly the manipulation and policing that work on everyday life tend to engender its depletion and alienation. Debord gives a bleak picture of everyday subjects who make the system work without understanding it. Modern society involves the agency of disconnected, specialized forms of knowledge: at the 'general' level of the everyday there is ignorance, emptiness, and passivity. Technological innovations modify everyday life but do not transform it because they operate randomly and tend to reduce individual autonomy and creativity.

Somewhat inconsistently, Debord suggests that we tend to repress a persistent sense that everyday life should possess a 'richesse profonde', and that this awareness produces the abiding sense of its current *misère*, so reinforcing the tendency to flee from it into the arms of various, more specialized, pursuits and distractions. This tendency to deny the potential richness of the everyday is important because it suppresses what would otherwise be an inclination to transform it. Debord heaps lavish praise on the *quotidien*, suggesting that the phrase 'critique de la vie quotidienne' should be interpreted to mean the 'critique que la vie quotidienne exercerait, souverainement, sur tout ce qui

---

[37] Ibid., II, 17.

lui est vraiment extérieur' (the critique that everyday life exerts, in sovereign fashion, on all that is really external to it) (*IS*, 222). And he claims that the phrase 'vie privée' should be understood as 'privée de', in other words as an area of privation where people are effectively deprived of the possibility 'de faire leur propre histoire, personellement' (of making their own history, personally). The current malaise of everyday life is a political crisis of advanced capitalist society that will only be resolved through the recognition that life is a text on which we can impose our own style. The new type of revolutionary organization to which the Situationists aspire will be based on 'nouvelles pratiques quotidiennes' (*IS*, 224), and will renounce anything that claims it is superior to everyday life. The present will dominate the past and creativity will dominate stagnant repetition. The 'social text' will be written by subjects themselves in virtue of the kind of experimentation pioneered by the Situationists. Resisting current oppression, such activities will pave the way for the perpetual renewal of the totality of everyday life that will ultimately be the lot of all.

Although Debord could hardly have gone further in endorsing the central place of 'la vie quotidienne', what is missing is a sense of the performative efficacy of critique, a sense that a 'prise de conscience' of the value of the everyday could itself, as Lefebvre supposed, have de-alienating force. The 'Perspectives de modifications conscientes' in Debord's title clearly necessitate a struggle against powerful opposition. Yet the brief recension of Situationist tactics has a perfunctory air, as Debord clearly targets the strategies of advanced capitalism and its key weapons of separation and spectacle. *Critique de la séparation*, the 'anti-documentary' film Debord made in the same year (1961), is both a declaration of defeat and, in its military images, a reflection of the need to combat repressive forces. A few years later *La Société du spectacle* (1967) will evoke 'la suppression de la rue' (the suppression of the street), and the 'autodestruction du lieu urbain' (self-destruction of urban space), identifying in urbanism a 'glaciation visible de la vie' (visible glaciation of life).[38] The same year Raoul Vaneigem's *Traité de savoir-vivre à l'usage des jeunes générations* will repeatedly proclaim the sovereignty of everyday life, stating famously that 'Ceux qui parlent de révolution et de luttes de classes sans se référer à la vie quotidienne [. . .] ont dans la bouche un cadavre' (those who talk of revolution and class struggle without referring to everyday life have corpses in their mouths).[39] Yet symptomatically Vaneigem's text is based on a

---

[38] Guy Debord, *La Société du spectacle* (1967; Paris: Éditions Champ Libre, 1971), 112.
[39] Vaneigem, *Traité du savoir-vivre*, 32.

very undialectical and Manichean opposition between the zombie-like state of subjects condemned to the 'survie' (survival) of 'la participation impossible' (impossible participation)—and to 'la vermine des contraintes' (the vermin of constraints), where the individual is subordinate to the many—and a libertarian individualism based on a dubious notion of deep subjectivity derived from Kierkegaard and Nietzsche—'la volonté subjective d'être tout' (the subjective will to be everything) (243). The domain of immediate subjectivity is the present moment which, according to Vaneigem (292), has the capacity to elude the general conditioning, even if the 'espace-temps' thus purloined is a monad cut off from the rest of life: 'l'espace de la vie quotidienne détourne un peu de temps à son profit, il l'emprisonne et le fait sien'; 'il n'y a que le présent qui puisse être total' (the space of everyday life purloins a portion of time for its own benefit, and appropriates it . . . only the present can be total) (302).

As for Lefebvre, his 1961 *Critique*, full of subtle twists and turns, gives the fullest expression of his belief in the *quotidien*, but is succeeded by a long-lasting attempt to bring a similar philosophical and methodological eclecticism to the specific question of the city. At the core of *Le Droit à la ville* (1968) is the opposition between the city as *oeuvre*, an accumulation not only of wealth but of knowledge and civilization, and the city as powerhouse. Industrialization marks the moment of a transformation where these facets of the city begin to work against each other. In the city as *oeuvre* use value, manifested in non-productive festivity, is uppermost (even in a context of repressive despotism). The rise and predominance of industrialization, and the generalization of commodities, pose a grave threat to 'urban reality'. Yet while the historical and philosophical analyses of *Le Droit à la ville*, further developed in *La Production de l'espace*, constantly emphasize the depredations of industrialization and the rise of technocratic control, a key element in Lefebvre's argument is that there is something irreducible in urban centres and that their resilience is demonstrated by the resistance articulated through the activities of city 'users'. Maintaining a belief in enlightened urbanism, Lefebvre sees sport, theatre, parks, and so on, as offering scope for the enduring place of play and creativity in the city, arguing indeed that the future of art lay in the urban. The concept of the everyday is absorbed into a debate on the city.

This chapter has underlined the rich, wayward, but quite crucial contribution Henri Lefebvre made to the twentieth century's persistent fascination with the notion of the *quotidien*. I have stressed the particular value and resonance of the 1961 second volume of the *Critique de la vie quotidienne*, where the idea of the everyday as residue, as resistance, as fountainhead of creativity is explored with exceptional conceptual vigour. Whatever the contribution the exchanges with the Situationists may have made to the crystallization of Lefebvre's most fertile ideas in this domain, the rapprochement undoubtedly helped to bring the idea of scrutinizing the *quotidien* to a wider audience. From this point on, the notion of the *quotidien*, in its particularity and irreducibility, will constitute the nucleus of a long-lasting tradition of dissidence with regard to the burgeoning fields of sociology, social psychology, leisure studies, social anthropology, and so on. Yet in the early Sixties both Lefebvre and the Situationists move away from the *quotidien* itself into more specific struggles and concerns. We therefore turn to Roland Barthes, the first of three key figures who, between the late Fifties and the early Eighties, partly by absorbing Lefebvre's analyses and the force of Situationist critique, took the exploration of the everyday in new directions.

5

All that Falls: Barthes and the Everyday

BEYOND *MYTHOLOGIES*

First published in 1957, *Mythologies* alone would give Roland Barthes an important place in the evolution of thinking about the everyday. Yet in many ways this pioneering and ever-popular account of 'quelques mythes de la vie quotidienne française' (a few myths in French everyday life) (I, 565)[1]— including steak and chips, detergent adverts, striptease, and astrology—offers a narrow view of the everyday in Barthes's overall *oeuvre*, and of his contribution to the configuration of discourses this book sets out to trace. As Diana Knight has highlighted, everyday life was one of Barthes's 'lifelong concerns' (others being history, language, literature, and sexuality), and Knight shows how the notion of utopia was both a point of convergence and a mediating agency for these interwoven strands in Barthes's thought.[2] Alluding in 1967 to the organization of space and time in the works of Sade, and allying him with the utopian thinker Charles Fourier, Barthes wrote: 'la marque de l'utopie, c'est le quotidien; ou encore: tout ce qui est quotidien est utopique: horaires, programmes de nourriture, projets de vêtement, installations mobilières, préceptes de conversation ou de communication' (the mark of utopia is the everyday; more, all that is everyday is utopian: timetables, diets, plans for what to wear, furnishing layouts, precepts about conversation or communication) (II, 1052). Even if a late work, the *Collège de France* lectures entitled 'Comment vivre ensemble', would underline Barthes's awareness that utopias harbour fantasies of control,[3] his relish for the details of everyday life and the impulses that lead human beings to lavish attention on the minutiae of daily

---

[1] All Barthes references (incorporated in the text) are to the three volumes of his *Œuvres complètes*, ed. Eric Marty.

[2] Knight, *Barthes and Utopia*, 1.

[3] Roland Barthes, *Comment vivre ensemble* (Paris: Seuil, 2002), to be discussed below.

existence, was a far cry from the largely ironic and negative posture adopted by the 'mythographer' of 1950s consumer society. Yet, as we shall see most clearly in the work of Michel de Certeau, it is precisely the desire *not* to limit the sphere of the everyday to the false consciousness of consumerism that animates the compelling and influential investigations of everydayness to be found in Lefebvre, Perec, Certeau, and Barthes himself.

As it happens, Henri Lefebvre was a lifelong friend of Barthes's, who must have been familiar with Lefebvre's 1947 *Critique de la vie quotidienne* when he started composing his 'mythologies' in the early 1950s, for publication in the review *Lettres nouvelles*. Biographers of the two men evoke regular meetings in Paris and in the Basque country where both had family attachments and summer residences.[4] Michael Kelly has argued that Lefebvre's 1947 *Critique* and Barthes's *Mythologies* display a 'shared vision of everyday Marxism', rooted in Marx's earlier writings and 'a common project... which may be described as the critical analysis of bourgeois ideology and is summed up as a strategy of demystification'.[5] But just as Lefebvre would go on, in the second, 1961, *Critique* to emphasize the ambiguity of the everyday and the creative energies that are not simply snuffed out by dominant ideology, but in fact contained dialectically within everyday life itself, so Barthes's project would evolve into a more positive and not simply denunciatory approach to the multiple modes of signification and levels of discourse at work in a wide range of phenomena, including everyday life. In the original 1957 preface to the volume that brought the 'petites mythologies' together, with the addition of a long theoretical essay, Barthes insisted that for him demystification, already an outworn notion, is not merely 'une opération olympienne' (an Olympian operation). To a significant extent, he explains, *Mythologies* exposes his own myths and his own participation in the period (whence, for Steven Ungar, the fact that *Mythologies* is itself now a 'site of memory' through which the 1950s are understood in French culture).[6] In a preamble to the 1970 edition, Barthes singles out the two 'gestures' of *Mythologies*: ideological critique, and semiological deconstruction ('démontage') which he now sees less in terms of negative critique than as the agent of 'une certaine libération du signifiant' (a certain liberation of the signifier) (I, 563). Although he would not now write mythologies in the same form, Barthes still endorses the alliance of the

    4 See Hess, *Henri Lefebvre*, and Jean-Louis Calvet, *Roland Barthes* (Paris: Flammarion, 1990).
    5 Kelly, 'Demystification: A Dialogue between Barthes and Lefebvre'.
    6 Steven Ungar, 'From Event to Memory Site: Thoughts on Rereading *Mythologies*', *Nottingham French Studies*, 36/1 (Spring 1997).

two 'gestes', where finely graduated critique is wedded to a semiology attuned to what breaks with the conventional regimes of the sign.

As Diana Knight remarks, the ferocity of Barthes's irony makes it hard to pinpoint a positive dimension in *Mythologies*. Yet Knight's account of space in these texts shows how Barthes's analyses often establish splits and fault-lines by dint of which the positive is glimpsed through the negative. The pervasive denial of historicity and alterity that Barthes diagnoses in petit-bourgeois culture, and in the media representations that sought to profit from its voracious demands, is seen to mark a denial of human possibility reflected in a predilection for enclosed and artificial spaces or regimens severed from the real world. But in Barthes's account of the Tour de France as epic, or in the 'wholly positive mythology' inspired by the photographs of Paris during the 1910 floods,[7] we encounter spaces whose mythic appeal is seen as liberating insofar as it involves imaginative appropriation and projection rather than ideological misprision and distortion. Knight's account of later mythologies, written after the 1957 volume, and notably the brilliant essay on the Eiffel Tower, dating from 1964, points to ways in which Barthesian semiology, in its evolving emphasis on the complexity of modes of signification, led in the direction of a more enthusiastic engagement with the historical present and notably the everyday. Far from maintaining a fastidious distance from a reality deemed to be irretrievably tainted by false consciousness, Barthes's semiology, for all the 'dream of scienticity' that Barthes himself would later bemoan, becomes a passionate exercise in which 'lived experience [is] constantly renourished by intelligibility'.[8]

In his last decade (the 1970s) Barthes evolved a series of notions and forms—the 'incident', the 'romanesque' (novelistic), 'haiku', the 'chronique'—reflecting an engagement with the everyday world which, more than *Mythologies*, had a strong impact on writers who were to explore everydayness in the years after his death. But to appreciate fully the nature of his contribution we must see how the *quotidien* remained a central preoccupation between *Mythologies* and *L'Empire des signes*, the book that fully crystallized Barthes's later response to the everyday. What is at stake, firstly, is the status of reference in Barthes's semiological phase, running approximately from the mid Fifties to the mid Sixties; and, secondly, what we might call the existential or lived ('vécu') dimension of the modes of signification he progressively taps into as

---

[7] Knight, *Barthes and Utopia*, 37.
[8] Ibid., 53.

he develops his analyses in various fields. At times Barthes is inclined to suggest that he is exclusively interested in the methodological dimension of his work, its 'scienticity', and in studying processes of signification in and for themselves. But more often than not he suggests that in studying systems of signs the semiologist encounters not only routine mechanisms of sense construction but a level of signification with a profounder, more unsettling character. And there will be a progressive convergence between this kind of signification and a positive if intermittent and elusive mode of everydayness. To explore this I will look first at Barthes's account of fashion, opening out the discussion to examine other theorists whose work illuminates ways of looking at the *quotidien*.

ENVISIONING FASHION: BARTHES, BENJAMIN, BAUDRILLARD, AND OTHERS

The prestige of the detail, as 'le lieu même de la signification' (the place of signification itself) (I, 833), a theme running throughout Barthes's work, connects with a range of notions including the banal, the insignificant, the object, and the fetish,[9] and features prominently in his extensive writings on fashion which, from 1957 onwards, encompass methodologies whose variety and interconnectedness are very germane to ways of thinking about the everyday. Barthes's first major essay in this field, the 1957 'Histoire et socio-logie du vêtement' (I, 741–52), published in *Annales*, aligns his enquiry with the new historical school that sought to substitute micro-history and 'la longue durée' for a historiography of major events. Dedicated to incorporating sociological and ethnological methods, *Annales* would play a significant role in fostering the empirical study of the everyday, and although after further articles on fashion and food Barthes's contributions lapsed, *Annales* methods and paradigms remained a feature of his work. Already, however, Barthes's specific contribution is to draw on his recent discovery of Saussure and to apply the *langue/parole* distinction to dress, studying how the *langue* of costume is actualized in the *parole* of individual acts of 'habillement' (I, 746). In a second major essay, 'Langage et vêtement' (1962), Barthes links the study of what he calls 'à première vue un objet banal' (at first glance a banal object) to 'cette *observation de l'évidence* qui marque aujourd'hui comme un

---

⁹ See Naomi Schor, *Reading in Detail: Aesthetics and the Feminine* (New York and London: Methuen, 1987), and Knight, *Barthes and Utopia, passim*.

tourment salutaire notre recherche la plus aiguë' (this scrutiny of what is evident, which torments our most acute research in a salutary way) (I, 793). Taken together, the phrases I have italicized underline Barthes's sense of how extraordinarily difficult it can be to zero in on what is paradoxically quite evident. As we saw in Chapter 2, the power of *évidence*, associated with pure denotation, stems from the fact that, in reversing the hierarchy of the customarily significant and insignificant, it also subverts narrative. Barthes makes this point in an interesting 1959 mythology on Chabrol's film *Le Beau Serge* where he borrows from Claudel the striking (and punning) phrase 'la détonation de l'évidence' to convey the force of the film's micro-realism, epitomizing 'toute une façon moderne de voir justement la surface du monde' (a whole modern way of just looking at the world's surface) (I, 787), sadly let down by Chabrol's pathos-laden story. Similarly, according to Barthes, in *L'Année dernière à Marienbad* Alain Robbe-Grillet ends up telling a story and thus betraying his ability to promote a mode of relation to the world that does not pass through the ideological relays of plot and theme (I, 934).

As Barthes's analyses of fashion evolve in the early 1960s, keeping pace with his theoretical development, we witness at one level the progressive eradication of content in favour of the play of structures. *Système de la mode* (1967) is, accordingly, based on textual material accompanying fashion items in magazines. But it is important to remember that the appeal of dress for Barthes was always its superficiality, insignificance, and minimalism. He does not so much progressively drain fashion of its residual 'content' as, bit by bit, apprehend the significance of what he will come to perceive as its near-nothingness. At one level, costume detail illustrates perfectly a cardinal property of all systems of signification, namely the way a minimal difference can have maximal consequences. As such, the appeal of fashion is formal: 'La Mode donne un grand pouvoir sémantique au détail' (Fashion gives detail considerable semantic power) (II, 331). But by another token the appeal of formal systems, and especially what Barthes will come to call their 'systematicity', is that they enable us to observe a wider context—that of everyday experience—where tiny details and infinitesimal differences conspire to produce multiple networks and processes of meaning in the thick of the seemingly insignificant. In a 1964 interview Barthes clearly identified the highly overdetermined nature of his interest in dress, placing it in the wider context of a class of 'good objects of communication', including food, gestures, conversation, behaviour:

d'une part, ils possèdent une existence quotidienne et représentent pour moi une possibilité de connaissance de moi-même au niveau le plus immédiat [. . .] d'autre part, ils possèdent une existence intellectuelle et s'offrent à une analyse systématique par des moyens formels (II, 453).

(they exist in the everyday and provide me with opportunities for knowing myself at the most immediate level . . . and they also exist intellectually and lend themselves to systematic analysis by formal methods)

Before looking more closely at *Système de la mode* I want to step back and examine the wider connections between fashion and the *quotidien*. Like fashion, the everyday can be viewed in at least two ways: firstly, through empirical studies of daily life—in Ancient Rome, under the German occupation, or in front of the TV. Secondly, via attempts, such as those of Lefebvre or Certeau, to grasp the everyday as a particular level of human reality, that of generic daily activities: eating, dressing, talking, working, relaxing, etc., all of which can be done in different ways, producing different patterns, rhythms and lifestyles. Fashion helps explain why at a given time groups of people are moved to do some things in roughly the same way, for example dress in black, pierce their bodies, or eat kebabs in the street, and why a year later they are all doing something else. To think about fashion is to think about how we go from one configuration of daily existence to another. The everyday is what we sally forth into when we wake, before we direct ourselves to some specific sector or more specialized activity. Fashion inheres in the everyday as part of the backdrop to our lives, accounting for the ambience of particular times and places (a point reflected in Perec's *Je me souviens*). But fashion is also one of the forces leading us to do things this way rather than that, orientating us within a wider field—pushing us to wear, eat, think about, or value certain things rather than others.

Since Baudelaire, theoretical or philosophical speculation about fashion has been closely linked to the ephemeral and the present. The author of 'Le Peintre de la vie moderne', an essay largely inspired by the success of Constantin Guys at capturing the fleeting reality of costumes and manners, endorses fashion as 'un symptôme du goût de l'idéal surnageant dans le cerveau humain au-dessus de tout ce que la vie naturelle y accumule de grossier, de terrestre et d'immonde' (a symptom of the taste for the ideal floating in the human brain above all the gross, terrestrial, and vile things that life in the raw accumulates)[10] and sees it as the expression of 'modernité' whose essence is

---

[10] Baudelaire, *Œuvres complètes*, 1184.

'le transitoire, le fugitif, le contingent' (the transitory, the fugitive, and the contingent). Fashion offers privileged access to 'the memory of the present', a dimension of experience harbouring 'the value of circumstance': 'car presque toute notre originalité vient de l'estampille que le *temps* imprime à nos sensations' (for most of our originality stems from the stamp that *time* impresses on our sensations).[11] Whence, in part, the dignity of fashion since, as Georg Simmel argued in 1911, 'la mode aiguise de plus en plus la conscience du présent' (fashion increasingly sharpens our sense of the present).[12]

The importance ascribed to fashion in Walter Benjamin's *Arcades Project* (where a substantial dossier is devoted to the topic)[13] underlines the author's sense of the overdetermined nature of fashion's cultural, social, and psychological meanings. In his usual way Benjamin gives quotations from numerous sources. The citations from Baudelaire (who of course also has his own massive dossier in the *Arcades Project*), Mallarmé, Apollinaire, Rilke, and the Surrealists (including Caillois and the Collège de sociologie, as well as Breton, and also the nineteenth-century illustrator Grandville, whose work is deemed to show in advance how fashion always has a surrealist potential) usefully underline how the topic of fashion is central to the tradition of reflection on the *quotidien*. Benjamin also indicates, as Barthes did, the wealth of interpretations to which the phenomenon of fashion had given rise in the late nineteenth and early twentieth century. Drawing on Simmel, Jhering, Fuchs, Vischer, Alphonse Karr, and others, Benjamin cites theories that account for fashion in terms of social class, hygiene, economics, political power, biology, gender difference, and other factors, drawing attention to such key parameters as materials, nature and artifice, sexual display, and so forth.

Like many commentators, including Barthes and Baudrillard, Benjamin sees constant and rapid change as central to the essence of fashion, and his own, avowedly 'philosophical' reflections underline this facet. Temporality is at the heart of fashion's unstable—yet strangely permanent—present, which is linked existentially both to the past, which it incorporates, and to the future which it anticipates. Fashions define themselves in contrast (and often violent opposition) to what went before, and this means that 'what sets the tone is without doubt the newest, but only where it emerges in the medium of the

---

[11] Baudelaire, *Œuvres complètes*, 696.
[12] Georg Simmel, *La Tragédie de la culture* (Paris: Rivages, 1988), 103.
[13] Benjamin, *The Arcades Project*, 62–81. Page references are incorporated in the text.

oldest, the longest past, the most ingrained' ('new fashions' invariably involve the recycling of old ones). Thus the 'true dialectical theatre of fashion' lies in 'the self-construction of the newest in the medium of what has been' (64). Yet at the same time, 'for the philosopher the most interesting thing about fashion is its extraordinary anticipations': the 'feminine collective' has an 'incomparable nose for what lies waiting in the future' (63). Benjamin's account of the temporal dimension of fashion gives it the 'sedimented' character, where past and present are inseparable, that Certeau will see as central to the *quotidien*. Although accelerated by modernity the tempo of fashion is intrinsic and reflects a constant need for demarcation from previous generations, a need that for Benjamin is essentially erotic (the fashions of immediately preceding generations are repellent and 'anti-aphrodisiac'), and linked to death and the lure of the inorganic. By generating the 'sex appeal of the inorganic', fashion abets the fetishistic impulse to abolish the boundary between the organic and the inorganic, life and death (79). Fashion changes quickly because it 'titillates' death (Benjamin cites Leopardi and Rilke on the links between fashion and death), challenging the decay of the mortal, time-bound body and the deadliness of tradition and ancestry (62–3). Fashion 'mocks' or ignores death (which it thereby acknowledges) by creating its own tempo, favoured by the 'new velocities' of modernity, and by taking its cue from everything—fetishistically 'enlivening' inorganic materials (cloth, stone, plastic) and 'imitating' music, landscape, moods, or works of art. Overall, whatever it is that draws or drives us to attend to it, fashion reveals, for Benjamin, a 'deep affective attitude to historical process' on the part of human beings (67). As we will see increasingly in later chapters, a feel for the historicity of existence, rooted in a sense of the indivisibility of individual and collective experience, is central to the tradition of thinking about the *quotidien*, and Benjamin's 'deep affective attitude' points to how fashion, with its link to the unfolding present, has a significant place in that tradition, as Barthes's work shows.

What, though, is 'the present' in this context? For Baudelaire, Simmel, Benjamin, and later theorists to be considered further on, the present is what is historically current—particular styles manifested concretely in dress, artefacts, and forms of behaviour that can be described and classified—but also, more diffusely yet more tellingly, the present is the 'feel' or atmosphere of what surrounds us at a given moment, the ever-changing totality we are part of but cannot see. These aspects are reflected in two approaches to fashion. Firstly, since Baudelaire, along a line running through Mallarmé (who edited a fashion magazine, *La Dernière Mode*), Apollinaire, the

Surrealists, and Benjamin, fashion serves as a conduit into the manifold present, apprehended through experiences that blur the distinction between the subjective and the objective. But, secondly, beside this avant-garde line, a steady evolution in research documenting changing styles, designers, materials, fashion institutions, or analysing the values and meanings attributed to dress, boosted by the *Annales* school, sociology, gender theory, and cultural studies, builds up an abundant historical archive and fosters major exhibitions, such as the 1998 'Art and Fashion' at London's Hayward Gallery, and journals featuring articles on the 'Carole Lombard look' or the theatricality of dress in today's shopping malls. Yet the historicizing basis of these approaches tends to deny any particular status to the present.

I want to argue that the 'Baudelairean' way of looking at the present—and the 'vécu' of everyday experience—through the prism of fashion is preserved and developed in some recent theories or philosophies of fashion, starting with Barthes's *Système de la mode*. The connections between fashion, the present, and the everyday are central to *Système de la mode* (1967). Far from being an arid exercise in methodology, applied opportunistically to an indifferent topic, Barthes's text, completed in 1964 and based on studies undertaken over a six-year period following the publication of *Mythologies*, reflects his lifelong interest in everyday life. He chose to analyse a restricted corpus—the 1958–9 issues of *Elle* and *Le Jardin des modes*—but if this narrowness of focus and method stemmed from disenchantment with diachronic approaches, it did not represent indifference to the human meaning of fashion. Indeed Barthes's approach reflects the postulate that there is a dimension of fashion—namely how it works as a 'system' at large in everyday life—that diachronic approaches fail to address. What Barthes studies in *Système de la mode* is the way fashion messages are produced and consumed. To be sure, Barthes argues that 'la mode écrite' is a purely self-contained system that could function perfectly well even if real clothes (or at least clothes of the types evoked) did not exist. As a formal system 'la mode' works through categories and oppositions that are timeless or operate in a kind of perpetual present. But rather than excluding history or the 'vécu' this reflects the fact that certain phenomena, which by dint of their modes of dissemination and consumption possess a degree of systematicity lending them to semiological analysis, exist both in the mode of history, where they change and interact with other phenomena, and in a mode that is outside history. One of the crucial insights this provides is that the everyday existence of these phenomena is more closely allied to their semiological—perpetual present—dimension than to their objective historical aspect. The everyday is of the present and of the lived ('vécu'), and fashion is apprehended both as a slowly changing evolution in real time and as a synchronic system of relationships. Fashion thus becomes a facet of the *quotidien*.

Barthes in fact argues that the pressure fashion exerts is not historical. To be a dedicated follower of fashion is of course to be in thrall to the 'latest', but in fashion the latest is not the most recent stage of a historical development, as it would be in the case of the American presidency or microprocessors, where this would refer to the latest incumbent (ontologically different from all others) or the latest model (technically different from the others). In fashion the latest simply means the most recent turn of the wheel, the most recent configuration of meaning established through subtle or gross permutations of a relatively restricted number of ingredients. What we respond to in fashion is the power of signification, which for Barthes is to be understood not as stable 'signifié', 'mais au sens actif de procès' (but in the active sense of process) (II, 170). Fashion creates powerful meanings out of tiny differences articulated in the most humdrum of media: pockets, buttons, waistlines; front/back, long/ short; silk, taffeta, cotton; pink, blue, cerise. Fashion discourse conjures up all kinds of mental pictures through its favoured scenarios of parties, travel, leisure, domesticity, and occasionally work, but these lavish meanings are all pinned to details: 'la fragilité de la Mode ne tient donc pas seulement à sa variabilité saisonnière, mais aussi au caractère gracieux de ses signes, au rayonnement d'un sens qui touche pour ainsi dire à distance les objets qu'il élit' (the fragility of fashion does not derive from its seasonal variability, but from the grace of its signs, the radiance of a meaning that works from a distance on the objects it favours) (II, 187). However nebulous the worlds it conjures up, fashion rhetoric deals at one level with the highly concrete, specific, and singular. Barthes has great fun classifying all the ingredients that are conscripted into the signifying process of the fashion system and the different ways they combine to produce meanings. But whilst he admires its creative fertility he notes the stereotyped character of the *imaginaire* articulated through fashion rhetoric, where nothing changes, and all is festive, idle, utopian. His portrait of the 'Femme de mode' is brilliant:

Féminine impérativement, jeune absolument, douée d'une identité forte et cependant d'une personnalité contradictoire, elle s'appelle Daisy ou Barbara; elle fréquente la comtesse de Mun et Miss Phipps; secrétaire de direction, son travail ne l'empêche pas d'être présente à toutes les fêtes de l'année et de la journée; elle part chaque semaine en week-end et voyage tout le temps, à Capri, aux Canaries, à Tahiti, et cependant à chaque voyage elle va dans le Midi; elle ne séjourne jamais que dans des climats francs, elle aime tout à la fois, de Pascal au cool-jazz . . . (II, 344).

(Necessarily feminine, unquestionably young, endowed with a strong identity and yet a contradictory personality, her name is Daisy or Barbara; she consorts with the Countess of Mun or Miss Phipps; her job as a PA does not stop her being at all the daily and annual festivities; she is away each weekend and travels incessantly to Capri, the Canary Islands, or Tahiti, and yet every journey is to the South; she only frequents well-defined climates, she likes everything at once, from Pascal to cool jazz . . .)

Part of *Système de la mode* involves a critique, reminiscent of *Mythologies*, of how in mass culture systems of signification work to disguise culture as nature, to naturalise meanings that are in fact produced by an arbitrary process. Barthes shows how naturalization is effected in the two main ways through which fashion creates meanings. In both cases the signifier is the concrete fashion detail. One way is referential, invoking the 'real world' through a mythology of the functional and the useful. The particular exigencies of weekends in Tahiti(!), or the contradictory requirement to be both serious and sexy at work, act as relays 'explaining' the 'need' for purple mohair, or two-tone buttons. But the 'real' here is intransitive: 'un réel vécu d'une façon fantasmatique, c'est le réel irréel du roman, emphatique à proportion de son irréalité' (a reality that is lived out at the level of fantasy, this is the unreal reality of the novel, whose emphatic nature is a reflection of its unreality) (II, 349). In the second mode—statements like 'cet été les chapeaux étonneront, ils seront à la fois piquants et solennels' (this summer hats will amaze, solemn yet at the same time piquant) (II, 352)—naturalization of the fashion phenomenon is effected by sheer assertion. Everything that is noted is deemed, or decreed, performatively, to be fashionable; what is not noted is *ipso facto* out of fashion. Fashion disguises its arbitrariness by playing up the peremptoriness of its *diktats*: 'chaque fois que la Mode admet l'arbitraire de ses décisions, c'est sur un ton emphatique, comme si se prévaloir d'un caprice, c'était l'atténuer, comme si jouer un ordre, c'etait du même coup l'irréaliser' (when fashion admits the arbitrariness of its decisions, it is emphatic, as if proclaiming a caprice attenuated it, and 'playing' a command made it unreal) (II, 351). By its use of tenses and other features fashion rhetoric creates an autarchic universe, a reality founded on its own *sagesse*. Barthes gives a subtle analysis of the temporality involved here (II, 357), concluding that if fashion is tyrannical it is because it refuses the past. Unfaithful and forgetful, fashion delivers vendettas against what went just before, but at the same time seeks to present itself as part of a stable universe (fashion is not really revolutionary), disguising its hunger for a 'présent absolu, dogmatique, vengeur' (absolute, dogmatic, and vengeful present) under a softer appearance, through a rhetoric that creates a purely fictitious, relaxing order.

A key feature of the second type of signification is that it is purely denotative and tautological. *This winter jackets are short and blue*: nothing is predicated of the items except their own existence, yet a world of meaning is created. In this purely reflexive system 'le sens n'est finalement que le signifiant lui-même' (the meaning is ultimately the signifier itself). At play here is what Barthes, in a phrase that will feature prominently in his 1970s writings, from *L'Empire des signes* on, calls 'la déception du sens' (the disappointment of meaning). For in this mode of signification it is the signifier alone that is on show. We are given to witness the spectacle of signification itself by a 'système sémantique dont la seule fin est de décevoir le sens qu'il élabore luxueusement' (semantic system whose sole aim is to disappoint the meaning it elaborates so luxuriantly) (II, 365). Meaning exists with no obvious means of support. At this point (II, 365) Barthes draws a parallel with Mallarmé's *La Dernière Mode*, a fashion magazine that ran to eight issues, entirely composed by the poet under pseudonyms such as Miss Satin.[14] Barthes notes that *La Dernière Mode* was wholly made up of 'signifiants de mode' without 'signifiés' (most of the costumes evoked did not exist), so that Mallarmé succeeded in creating a purely immanent and reflexive semantic system. The Mallarmé reference recurs in all the main interviews Barthes gave after the publication of *Système de la mode* where he insists on the poetic dimension of the modes of meaning deployed in fashion. Insofar as it combines these two kinds of meaning production, 'la mode' is a double system divided between the pull towards the referential and the purity of the signifier. This clearly aligns it with literature, as Barthes frequently observes in passing. More significantly in our context, this double nature of fashion, and the peculiar temporality it creates, will also associate it with a cluster of ideas—focused around such categories as the incident, haiku, the 'romanesque', and indeed the *quotidien*—which together constitute a way of thinking about the everyday in late Barthes.

Whilst he does underline the poverty of its basic contents Barthes does not pass a negative judgement on the fashion system. This is because, on his analysis, the ways in which meanings are produced does not depend on the

[14] See Mallarmé, *Œuvres complètes*, 707–847; Pearson, *Mallarmé and Circumstance*, and Roger Dragonetti, *Un Fantôme dans le kiosque: Mallarmé et l'esthétique du quotidien* (Paris: Seuil, 1992).

sinister manipulation of a victimized public but playful participation in a game that often has a quasi-poetic dimension. In an article on the rivalry between Chanel and Courrèges Barthes describes fashion as 'a truly poetic object', 'constitué collectivement pour nous donner le spectacle profond d'une ambiguité, et non l'embarras d'un choix inutile' (constructed collectively to give us the profound spectacles of an ambiguity, rather than the burden of a futile choice) (II, 414). It may be that Barthes idealizes fashion but if so it is by seeing it as a source of pleasure and potential liberation. Essentially poetic, through their dependence on the play of the signifier, the modes of signification at work in the fashion system are viewed positively because they liberate rather than fix meaning. Moreover, for Barthes the play of the signifier and the exemption from meaning have existential spin-offs that can be manifested in lifestyles attuned to the everyday present. In later writings Barthes will explore this idea in a number of contexts, including Japanese life, being in love, and photography. Other thinkers, including Jean Baudrillard, Gilles Lipovetsky, and Michel Mafessoli, will also develop the connection between fashion, signification, and lifestyle. Before moving on to them, however, it is worth looking briefly at negative reactions to Barthes's optimistic view of the fashion system on the part of three figures with a close interest in the everyday, Henri Lefebvre, Georges Perec, and Pierre Bourdieu.

Lefebvre's ongoing elaboration of a theory of everyday life, and his close personal and intellectual links with Barthes, led to a discussion of fashion in the book he was writing when *Système de la mode* appeared, *La Vie quotidienne dans le monde moderne* (1968). But although he seems fully to endorse Barthes's account of how the fashion system works Lefebvre takes a diametrically opposed view of the primacy of the linguistic dimension. The self-contained universe of 'la mode' is seen not as a tribute to the extraordinary richness and creativity of our sense-making capacity ('la capacité de fabriquer du sens avec rien' (the capacity to make meaning out of nothing) as Barthes puts it) but as the baleful outcome of a cancerous growth of the linguistic. For Lefebvre the excess of signifiers over signifieds brings about 'la chute des référentiels' (the downhall of reference), an 'opération scabreuse' characteristic of the damage to everyday life inflicted by the 'société bureaucratique de consommation dirigée' (bureaucratic society for directed consumption).[15]

---

[15] Lefebvre, *La Vie quotidienne dans le monde moderne*, 209. Two years earlier *Le Nouvel Observateur* printed a discussion between Lefebvre, Barthes, and Jean Duvignaud on the erotic nature of fashion. See 'La Mode, Stratégie du désir', *Le Nouvel Observateur* (23 March 1966), 28–9. I am grateful to Andy Stafford for drawing this uncollected piece to my attention.

Essentially Lefebvre sees fashion as on the side of *constraint*—factors that perpetuate the negative features of everyday life: meaningless repetition, lack of variety, atomization—as opposed to *appropriation:* factors that tend towards the positive transformation of everyday life by fostering the sense of the everyday as a totality in which human possibility can be realized. For Lefebvre, the Barthesian analysis of fashion confirms that in contemporary society the agents of *contrainte* (and enemies of appropriation) are primarily linguistic. The predominance of metalanguage leads to the rise of self-contained 'sous-systèmes'—such as fashion, sexuality, youth, cars—that work against the everyday as totality by promoting themselves as autonomous harbingers of social goods. Where for Barthes the 'tyrannical' aspect of fashion is largely rhetorical, Lefebvre's analysis chimes with the conventional view—to be vigorously opposed by Certeau in *L'Invention du quotidien* (1980)—of consumers as victims.

Although Perec denied that his 1966 novel *Les Choses* was a straightforward attack on consumer society, it is clear that his young couple, Sylvie and Jérôme, are enslaved by their addiction to advertisements, brands, and images. In a series of short pieces, usually headed 'L'Esprit des choses', written for *Arts et Loisirs* magazine in 1966–7, Perec went on to expound the view that 'la mode' was essentially a form of terrorism, a system admitting no criteria other than those it arbitrarily sets for itself.[16] Later, in a 1976 piece, entitled 'Douze Regards obliques', he offers a subtler but equally uncompromising critique of fashion. Here he begins by attacking 'la mode' for its immorality, citing the exploitation of children to advertise clothing brands, and for its social exclusivity, encouraged by the obsession with labels. Like Lefebvre he bemoans the way fashion works by making signs more important than things, thus engendering a rapid turnover without substance. If 'la mode' ought to be a 'forme de jouissance', associated with pleasure, play, and imagination, in modern society it is in practice simply loud and frenetic: 'ça casse les oreilles'. Where it might resemble the gentle fads and enthusiasms of the school playground, fashion actually exploits notions of innocence and inventiveness for its own ends. Despite what 'diverses idéologies contemporaines' may claim, fashion is not gentle, but complicit with violence: 'violence de la conformité, de l'adhérence aux modèles, violence du consensus social et des mépris qu'il dissimule' (violence of conformity, of adherence to models, of social consensus

---

[16] Georges Perec, 'L'Esprit des choses', *Arts et Loisirs*, October–December, 1966.

and the disdain it disguises).[17] Fashion expunges the present's rootedness in the past, the density that grounds it in some kind of continuity. Yet if here Perec will have no truck with fashion's forgetfulness, the inclusion of references to fashion in his book of 'micro-memories' *Je me souviens* (1978) will show his willingness to recognize that fashion, because it involves a 'deep affective attitude to historical process' (Benjamin), can be a conduit for the density of a present that enfolds the past.

Similarly negative in tenor, Pierre Bourdieu's contributions to fashion theory—in articles such as 'Le Couturier et sa griffe' (1975)—are entirely on the lines of his overall argument in *La Distinction* (1979) about individual social mobility and the accumulation of social capital. In the spirit of Veblen's classic analyses of 'conspicuous consumption' Bourdieu sees fashion purely in terms of the achievement of social distinction. By contrast, in different ways, Baudrillard, Lipovetsky, and Maffesoli, taking their lead from Barthes, will align fashion with appropriation—a way of throwing off the burden of the past and energetically embracing the new and the now.

Like Lefebvre, Baudrillard follows Barthes in seeing fashion in the context of the autonomous logic of signs. But rather than seeing this as terroristic, he rejects the opposition between *contrainte* and *appropriation* and sees 'la mode' as a defining symptom of modernity.[18] In his Barthes-inspired study of the 'system' of objects (1968) Baudrillard shows how a few basic types of car—the Simca Ariane, the Renault 4L—can generate a vast range of models via minor differences of equipment and trim, this 'seriality' constituting 'fashion'.[19] Quoting at length from Perec's *Les Choses*, Baudrillard asserts that in order to become an 'objet de consommation' the object must become a sign (277), (in Perec's novel 'tout [. . .] est signe, et signe pur') (279). Developing this argument in *La Société de consommation* (1970), he sees consumption as the 'organisation totale de la quotidienneté' (total organization of everydayness). The logic of fashion binds modern society together. The shop window is 'le foyer de convection de nos pratiques urbaines' (convector of urban practices), 'le lieu [. . .] de cette communication et de cet échange des valeurs par où toute une société s'homogénéise par acculturation quotidienne incessante à la logique, silencieuse et spectaculaire de la mode' (the place of the communi-

---

[17] Perec, *Penser/Classer*, 51.
[18] Jean Baudrillard, *L'Échange symbolique et la mort* (Paris: Gallimard, 1976), 135.
[19] Id. *Le Système des objets* (Paris: Gallimard, 1968), 99.

cation and exchange of values through which a whole society makes itself homogenous through daily acculturation by the silent and spectacular logic of fashion).[20] But this is not merely a matter of standardization or loss of individuality. For the Baudrillard of *L'Échange symbolique et la mort* (1976) fashion's imperium has a more positive consequence. Its extraordinary prowess is to blot out the empirical world by 'l'accélération du seul jeu différentiel des signifiants [qui] y devient éclatante jusqu'à la féerie—féerie et vertige qui sont ceux de la perte de tout référentiel' (the acceleration of the differential play of signifiers that becomes dazzling to the point of unreality—unreality and vertigo induced by the loss of all reference to the real).[21] Fashion signs are endlessly commutable and permutable—theirs is an 'émancipation inouïe' and this applies in the sphere of 'signes légers'—like clothes, bodies, and objects—as well as in the sphere of 'signes lourds'—politics, morality, economics, science, culture, and sexuality. For Baudrillard this represents a radical break with the whole order of representation. We can enjoy the 'liquidation du sens' (liquidation of meaning), the 'finalité sans fin' (finality without end) of fashion this engenders—especially at the level of the body—even if it may also be painful to see all values go the way of fashion, a break even more radical than that of capitalism which saw the victory of 'la loi marchande' (the law of the market).

With regard to temporality Baudrillard argues in *L'Échange symbolique et la mort* that 'la mode, c'est paradoxalement *l'inactuel*' (fashion is paradoxically the non-current) (132). Fashion presupposes that forms are already dead so that in cyclical recurrence they can haunt the present 'de tout le charme du revenir opposé au devenir des structures' (with all the charm of recurrent as opposed to dynamic structures) (133). Underlying fashion is a 'pulsion de mode'—a 'désir violent d'abolition du sens et d'immersion dans les signes purs' (violent desire for the abolition of meaning and immersion in pure signs) (141) that has clear affinities with the 'jouissance' Barthes had ascribed to 'l'exemption du sens' a few years earlier in *L'Empire des signes*. Like Barthes, Baudrillard steers his discussion round to the question of 'modes de vie'. The issue is not simply the impact of fashion on our daily lives or its link to choices of lifestyle. Following Barthes very closely, and quoting a number of passages from *Système de la mode*, Baudrillard rhapsodizes over the way 'un trait de mode circule, diffuse à une allure

20 Jean Baudrillard, *La Société de consommation* (Paris: Denoël, 1970) 264.
21 Id. *L'Échange symbolique*, 131. Subsequent references incorporated.

vertigineuse à travers tout le corps social, scellant son intégration et ramassant toutes les identifications' (a fashion trait circulates, diffusing at incredible speed through the social body, integrating it and accumulating multiple identifications) (141). The subversive power of fashion lies in its frivolity and the way that for individuals it can become a kind of 'fête' involving the staging of the body (143). And he sees this as part of a historical process, an extension of the sphere of fashion culminating in a state where 'la mode diffuse partout et devient *le mode de vie* tout simplement' (fashion diffuses itself everywhere and becomes just lifestyle) (146).

The celebration of fashion and the connection between fashion and 'mode de vie', are central themes in two further contributions to the theorization of fashion: Gilles Lipovetsky's *L'Empire de l'éphémère* (1987) and Michel Maffesoli's *Au creux des apparences* (1990). In both cases the inheritance from Barthes and Baudrillard is clear: fashion does not simply possess social, political, or economic meanings—articulating such social phenomena as youth, revolt, and money. Rather, it is the operation of fashion as a system, and particularly a regime of meaning, that is seen to have existential or ontological spin-offs. The phrase 'logique de la mode' recurs constantly in Lipovetsky who claims that, in its most recent phase, fashion has stopped being a specific and peripheral sector and has become a general principle operating in the social totality: 'On est immergé dans la mode, un peu partout et de plus en plus, s'exerce la triple opération qui la définit en propre: l'éphémère, la séduction, la différentiation marginale' (we are immersed in fashion, everywhere and increasingly we see the triple operation that defines it: the ephemeral, seduction, and marginal differentiation).[22] Lipovetsky's basic premise is that it is wrong to bemoan the progressive 'sway' of fashion or to theorize it (like Bourdieu) purely in terms of achieving social distinction. Rather, in its consummate or total phase, fashion serves the ends of democracy, enlightenment and individual autonomy. As it comes to infiltrate every aspect of our lives fashion does not so much programme us as provide an infinite range of ingredients out of which we can forge our own identities—not by conflict, emulation, or rivalry with others, but by fashioning ourselves (Lipovetsky is influenced here by Foucault's work on sexuality).[23] The increasing hegemony of the 'forme de la mode' fosters the 'hyper-individuation' of human beings, and in doing so actually pacifies social conflict. As a 'sujet

[22] Gilles Lipovetsky, *L'Empire de l'éphémère* (Paris: Gallimard, 1987), 183.
[23] On Foucault see Ch. 9 below.

ouvert et mobile au travers du kaléiodoscope de la marchandise' (a subject who keeps open and mobile within the kaleidoscope of merchandise),[24] the individual pursues his or her own personal goals through fashion, enjoying a fundamentally 'labile' form of identity that nevertheless constitutes the apotheosis of modern individualism.

For Michel Maffesoli, fashion is a particularly symptomatic indicator of a general trend towards what he sees as an aestheticization of experience. The 'creux des apparences' in the title of his 1990 volume designates a void that enables the creation of new—and again very labile—identities in a process whose ethical validity (hence a subtitle: *pour une éthique de l'esthétique*) Maffesoli seeks to establish by dint of a celebration of fashion: 'cela revient à reconnaître ses lettres de noblesse au "frivole": "mode", "design", "stylisme", etc., comme participant au terreau dans lequel va croître l'imaginaire social' (this means fully recognizing the 'frivolous': fashion, design, style, as part of the ground in which the social imaginary is grown).[25] Yet his argument differs from Lipovetsky's because a central tenet is that the reign of appearances (rooted in all the features of the fashion system) does not foster individualism but social and collective existence. For Maffesoli the dominion of fashion augments the theatricality of everyday life, where the subject, aspiring to identification rather than identity, adopts a succession of masks which favour 'la socialité' rather than leading to alienation: 'L'asservissement de l'individu [à la mode] signifie ici sa dilution dans un ensemble plus vaste dont il n'est qu'un élément [. . .] la mode [. . .] tend à privilégier le corps social en son entier' (the individual's subjection to fashion means dilution in a wider ensemble of which he is only an element . . . fashion tends to privilege the social body in its entirety).[26] The 'displayed body' does not affirm individuality—'l'apparence est rien moins qu'individuelle' (appearance is far from individual)—rather it fosters new modes of collective belonging.[27]

Alongside the jeremiads of Lefebvre and Perec, a line in contemporary theory, stemming from Barthes, but drawing on earlier phases in the theorization of fashion, including Simmel and Benjamin, sees the 'logic' of fashion as a signifying practice that is not tyrannical or enslaving but potentially liberating. Resolutely of the present, acknowledging the past only as a source of styles and looks to be recycled or rejected, fashion as process resists History's

[24] Lipovetsky, *L'Empire de l'éphémère* 207.
[25] Maffesoli, *Au creux des apparences*, 135.
[26] Ibid., 141.
[27] Ibid., 144. For further discussion of Maffesoli see Ch. 7 below.

ideological conditioning and reveals itself to be in league with an everyday historicity that offers comparable resistance to fixity and regimentation.

CHANGING SCALE, RESISTING FUNCTION

In a 1964 essay on the illustrations to the eighteenth-century *Encyclopédie* Barthes observed that these didactic images remain comprehensible even when they make the familiar seem monstrous—through techniques such as magnification, miniaturization, and the revelation of a usually invisible 'inside' —and he identifies the essence of this device as 'un déplacement du niveau de perception' (a shift in level of perception). To vary ('*varier* au sens musical du terme' (*vary* in the musical sense of the term)) the level of perception is to liberate form itself: 'La poésie n'est-elle pas un certain pouvoir de *disproportion*, comme Baudelaire l'a si bien vu en décrivant les effets de réduction et de précision du haschisch?' (Does poetry not consist in a certain power of disproportion, as Baudelaire suggested when he described the effects of reduction and precision induced by hashish?) (II, 1356).[28] The Baudelaire passage is also cited in *L'Empire des signes* with reference to how in Japan everyday things (parcels in the immediate context) appear small even when they are not, the effect of miniaturization stemming from packaging and framing which appear to give the object a hallucinatory precision (II, 778). Crucial here is the link between disruption of scale and new order of experience, anticipated in the famous mythology on the Paris floods when a 'rupture du visuel quotidien' (break in everyday vision) (I, 599) had the effect of refreshing Parisians' perception of their world.[29] More radical versions of this phenomenon occur in various texts from the 1970s where another point of reference becomes habitual. In an interview on *S/Z* Barthes noted that by his process of slowed-down reading he had changed the level of perception and thereby transformed its object (a story by Balzac) (II, 1293). In a 1973 essay on the painter Réquichot he observes that if you home in on a detail in a painting you discover a different work, so that there are as many works as there are levels of perception: 'Changer de niveau de perception: il s'agit là d'une secousse qui ébranle le monde classé, le monde nommé [...] et par

---

28 The reference is to *Les Paradis artificiels*, Baudelaire, *Œuvres complètes*, 338.
29 On this see Knight, *Barthes and Utopia*, 37–9.

conséquent libère une véritable énergie hallucinatoire' (Changing the level of perception: a jolt that shakes up the classified world, the named world ... letting loose a hallucinatory energy) (II, 1634). In support of his hypothesis Barthes cites an art historian who once claimed that the slabs of colour in Nicolas de Staël's paintings were in effect 'blow-ups' of three square centimetres of Cézanne, and the same example features in a 1976 essay, on the drawings of Saul Steinberg (to whom Perec would owe the starting point for *La Vie Mode d'emploi*), which celebrates the artist's power to challenge the meanings we think of as natural by changing scale or proportions (III, 410). In the course of the 1970s the capacity to disrupt familiar perception by a change of scale that transforms the power of attention and observation becomes central to Barthes's relationship to everyday experience.

A second motif linking the semiological work of the 1960s with 'late Barthes' is what might be called the limits of functionalism. From the Situationists onwards the opposition between functionalism and lived experience or 'habitability' becomes a central theme in discourses on the everyday. Lefebvre and Certeau often insist that the *quotidien* cannot be limited to constraints, routines, functions, or responses conditioned by wider social and political forces. For Lefebvre its 'profondeur ambiguë' resides in the fact that the everyday subject is creative as well as reactive, so that the everyday harbours dissident, unprogrammed energies. In the areas he studied Barthes often saw a tension between a functionalist view, where each element is ultimately bound by its place in an overall totality, and a view that identifies a residual area where certain 'unbound' elements constituting a 'third' position, beyond the binary oppositions that regulate the system, can be identified. In essays from the late Sixties—'Sémantique de l'objet' (II, 65–73) and 'Sémiologie et urbanisme' (II, 439–46)—Barthes identifies a functionalist level and then something that seems to exceed or outplay it.[30] Initially his commitment to systems makes him reluctant to allow the functionalist projection to be definitively thwarted by what exceeds it, and so he tends to find *in extremis* that it is precisely the *function* of the apparently 'unbound' elements to signify, by connotation, a programmed and therefore functional 'freedom'. But increasingly Barthes concedes that there is indeed free play in the system. 'Sémantique de l'objet' picks up his long-standing interest in the meaning-bearing properties of objects, both those saturated with ideology, as in the case of the toys discussed

---

[30] See also 'L'Effet de réel' (1968), II, 479–84.

in *Mythologies*, and those seemingly drained of meaning. Devoting his first seminar at the École Pratique des Hautes Études (1962–4) to an 'Inventaire des systèmes contemporains de signification: systèmes d'objets' (attended by Jean Baudrillard who went on to write *Le Système des objets*), Barthes identifies a paradox in the fact that, beyond its function, an object such as a telephone also has a meaning that exceeds ('déborde') its use—'un sens indépendant de sa fonction' (a meaning independent of its function) (II, 67). Yet despite the object's capacity to bear a host of simultaneous vectors of meaning, the split between function and meaning is never definitive. Despite the initial 'obstacle de l'évidence' (obstacle of self-evidence) (II, 68)[31]—the simple 'thereness' of the object which confronts the semiologist—objects are ineluctably constrained to have meaning. But the meanings objects accumulate always end up being recuperated as part of their inherent nature: meaning remains domesticated.[32]

'Sémiologie et urbanisme' develops a similar opposition between the realm of what Barthes now calls 'la signification'—a concept with more active connotations than 'sens'—and the functional level.[33] In the case of the city the relationship between 'fonction' and 'signification' is the despair of planners precisely because, from the point of view of the city dweller, 'la signification est vécue en opposition complète aux données objectives' (signification is lived in complete opposition to objective factors) (I, 441). For Barthes, in other words, the 'citadin' exploits the 'semantic power' of the city not by responding to the use value of such urban amenities as parks, trees, squares and transport systems, but by creating an individualized, privately planned city, constituted by the individual user's whims: 'La cité est un discours, et ce discours est véritablement un langage: la ville parle à ses habitants, nous parlons notre ville, la ville où nous nous trouvons, simplement en l'habitant, en la parcourant, en la regardant' (The city is a discourse that is truly a language: the city speaks to its inhabitants, we speak our city, the city where we find ourselves, simply by inhabiting it, moving around it, looking at it) (II, 441). This brilliant insight, with its Situationist antecedent, leads straight to one of the central tenets of

---

[31] On *évidence* and the everyday see above Ch. 2.

[32] In the case of 'L'Effet de réel' Barthes sees 'le réel concret' as one of the 'résidus irréductibles de l'analyse fonctionelle'. The pure denotation of the real 'apparaît comme une résistance au sens' (II, 483). Yet he ends up arguing that the role of seemingly insignificant details in realist novels is to *connote* the real—functionalism triumphs in the end. On this and other passages regarding denotation as 'le passage des objets dans le discours' see Andrew Brown, *Roland Barthes: The Figures of Writing* (Oxford: Oxford University Press), 236–84.

[33] A contrasting distinction between *sens* and *signification* will be discussed in Ch. 9 below.

Certeau's work on the everyday—the active transformation, rather than passive activation, of systems by their users. The identification between speech and walking, inspiring Certeau's 'le parler des pas perdus' (the chatter of idle footsteps), not only underlines Barthes's concern with the everyday but shows how it was at stake in his efforts to develop a satisfactory account of the workings of signification. A first visit to Tokyo, to which several references are made, seems to inspire Barthes to think the semiologically unthinkable and postulate a process of meaning that outruns the system within which it is generated. Crucial here is the way this potentially abstruse debate is conducted in the context of everyday experience.

Tokyo illustrates Barthes's three observations designed to show how an 'open' process of signification might work. First, the fact that it has a blank space at its centre, constituted by the closed-off Imperial Palace, suggests how signification does not require fixed terms or centres but only their simulacra. While it might seem exceptional, Tokyo in fact reveals that a 'city centre' is really only a quasi-fictional point of reference, a void that keeps the whole urban system on the move: no-one 'lives' there. Second, the symbolic dimension of urban reality is not based on fixed equivalences but on circulating signifiers and links that never come to a final resting point. Far from a neatly distributed set of functional spaces a big city is an amalgam of micro- and macro-structures. Tokyo is a 'ville polynucléé' possessing several 'centres' identified with large railway stations. The different sections of a city are not like simple nouns, but akin to the parts of a sentence, and the city 'user' is a reader who engenders the city's meanings by private itineraries: 'une sorte de lecteur qui, selon ses obligations et ses déplacements, prélève des fragments de l'énoncé pour les actualiser en secret' (a kind of reader who, depending on his obligations and movements, selects fragments of the overall message and actualizes them in secret) (II, 444). Third, the fact that there is no ultimate signifier means that the process of signification involves metaphorical chains where each signified becomes in its turn a signifier in another chain. And this process, far from being purely neutral, possesses its own 'existential' character (initially psychoanalytical since these ideas stem in the first instance, as Barthes indicates, from Jacques Lacan). At this point in his essay Barthes's paradoxical strategy becomes clearer. Having started with the city's resistance to semiological analysis, he first uses it to illustrate certain developments in semiotics. But at the same time it is clear that the pressure to remodel semiotics is generated from the outside, notably from the city, and Tokyo in particular. If Barthes's determination to keep semiology and urbanism in synch is sometimes far-fetched, it is symptomatic of his desire to open a two-way channel between experiential values and processes of signification, and it demonstrates clearly how the evolution of his semiology accompanied his ever-closer engagement with the everyday.

TOWARDS A NEW 'ART DE VIVRE'

Barthes's 1966–8 encounter with Japan intensified his fascination with the everyday, hatching a number of notions and forms that would remain 'live' for the rest of his career. In this further evolution and re-evaluation the ethical, existential, and hedonistic dimensions of Barthes's passion for the processes of signification fully emerge. And from this point the word 'vie' will play a significant role in his discourse.

In *L'Empire des signes* the everyday is called Japan. In some ways it is unfortunate that a crucial range of Barthesian ideas made their first appearance in oriental garb: the consequent drama of repatriation would occupy him for the rest of his life. Barthes trod a well-worn path: back home via an exotic land; apprehending his own predilections in the daily sphere by finding them writ large elsewhere. This is consistent with other prospectors of the everyday for whom the exotic and the utopian are snares that can never be wholly circumvented.[34] It is poignant that in some respects Barthes never surpassed *L'Empire des signes*: it remained his favourite among his own books as he sought to find other ways of exploring its insights. Yet *L'Empire des signes* displays a tension or hesitation between post-structuralist avant-gardism and a more direct engagement with the everyday, and some of the text's profounder emphases only become fully evident in its aftermath. In one strand Barthes's text promotes a salutary disruption of occidental limits, notably in the overlapping areas of writing, the body, and identity. The idiom here, often reminiscent of the avant-garde *Tel Quel* group in its inflexions, is that of a radical decentring, and the overthrow of an exhausted hegemony. But intertwined with this is another strand, featuring a mellower order of immediate experience, a gentler dislocation or displacement rooted in imaginative projection into alternative ways of living. In four consecutive chapters (II, 794–804) focused on the poetic form of haiku the opposition between 'l'effraction du sens' (the violation of meaning) and 'l'exemption du sens' (exemption from meaning) opposes one kind of

---

[34] See below, Ch. 8.

violence to another: initially the Western desire forcibly to inject haiku with meaning, opposes the Japanese way of seeing haiku as a 'pratique destinée à arrêter le langage [. . .] casser [. . .] cette récitation intérieure qui constitue notre personne [. . .] agir sur la racine même du sens' (practice aimed at halting language . . . breaking . . . the inner recitation that constitutes our person . . . working on the very root of meaning) (II, 798). Haiku then takes on another complexion when Barthes switches from the sphere of signification to that of experience, and sees the particular semantics of haiku as the touchstone of a particular quality of event, the 'incident', where it is not what happens but the very fact of happening itself, that counts. Transposed onto 'la page de la vie' (the page of life), haiku, as incident, has the quality of a 'pli léger' (light fold), a 'poussière' (dust), as it is rapidly read 'dans l'écriture vive de la rue' (in the live script of the street), rather than a violence. This switch of emphasis reflects the two senses of the phrase 'l'exemption du sens': exemption *from* meaning ('comme on l'est du service militaire' (as from military service) as Barthes put it on one occasion) (III, 161), as opposed to a process where meaning is obliterated. The two senses generally mingle in Barthes's usage, but by the fourth chapter, 'Tel', which emphasizes the 'flash' that reveals nothing but simply happens, haiku has become synonymous with 'tout trait discontinu, tout événement de la vie japonaise tel qu'il s'offre à ma lecture' (any discontinuous trait, any incident in Japanese life as it offers itself for me to read) (II, 803) and points in the direction of an equivalent way of living, 'un mode graphique d'exister' (a graphic mode of existence).

In a number of interviews Barthes stressed that Japan had inspired him to think about 'des problèmes d'art de vivre' (issues relating to the art of living) (II, 528). The phrase *art de vivre* with its source in ancient treatises on the good life (studied closely by Michel Foucault at this time)[35] and its fusion of the aesthetic, the ethical, and the hedonistic, occurs frequently in Barthes's writings from the late 1960s onwards, with reference not only to Japan but to the lifestyle of the hippies (II, 544–8), the utopian worlds of Sade and Fourier, or the philosophy of Brillat-Savarin (III, 280–94). In 1975 Barthes stated that what interested him most when he travelled were 'les lambeaux d'art de vivre que je peux saisir au passage' (the scraps of 'art de vivre' I can grasp in passing) (III, 750). Closely linked to what he called his deep-rooted 'ethnological temptation' (III, 158), the theme of *art de vivre* was also linked to possible

---

[35] See Ch. 9 below.

forms of writing closely bound up with the everyday, now reflecting Barthes's own pleasures and values rather than, as in *Mythologies*, those he deplored.

In Barthes's later treatment of processes of signification the experience of being in the everyday, of apprehending everydayness, is equated with a certain experience of meaning. In the 1970 essay on 'Le Troisième Sens' one of the sites of what Barthes calls the 'obtuse meaning' is 'une certaine façon de lire la "vie"' (a certain way of reading 'life') (II, 878), and he goes on to characterize this mode of signification in terms of haiku, the depletion of meaning, and the 'romanesque' (II, 880). Elsewhere Barthes claims to have identified an ideal 'régime of meaning' in the 'art de vivre' of Japan, at the 'niveau essentiel de la vie quotidienne [. . .] c'est-à-dire à même une certaine pellicule de vie' (the essential level of everyday life . . . on the surface skin of life) (II, 1014). It is important to note that this equation between apprehending everydayness and 'living' meaning in a particular way is wholly consistent with Blanchot, Lefebvre, Certeau, Perec, Ernaux, Réda, or Vinaver when they associate the difficulty of articulating the everyday with a resistance to meaning engendered by modes of subjectivity or subject position, corresponding to an experience of flux and anonymity that Barthes identifies with 'immersion dans le signifiant'.[36]

The constant crossovers between 'la vie' and 'le texte' in late Barthes reflect a desire to shift the arena of textual play from the book to life itself, to locate 'le bruissement de la langue [. . .] dans la vie, dans les aventures de la vie, dans ce que la vie nous apporte d'une manière impromptue' (the rustle of language . . . in life, the adventures of life, in what life brings in impromptu fashion) (III, 276). The notion of the 'texte de la vie' occurs in connection with the avant-garde writing of Sollers (III, 963) and in the context of walking in the city where, as Barthes put it in a very positive essay on advertising, 'nous promenant dans une rue, c'est nous qui écrivons ces corps, ces nourritures, ces objets, qui deviennent comme la scansion de notre marche' (walking in the street, it is we who write these bodies, these foodstuffs, these objects that become part of the rhythm of our walk) (II, 509). Barthes praised the Surrealists for recognizing that writing was not just writing: 'il y a des écritures de vie, et nous pouvons faire de certains moments de notre vie de véritables textes' (there are 'life writings', and we can make certain moments of our lives into real texts) (II, 565). In the last decade of Barthes's career the search for ways of living and forms of writing are totally bound up with one another. If

---

[36] On this see Bernard Comment, *Roland Barthes: vers le neutre* (Paris: Christian Bourgois, 1991).

the 'gestures of everyday life' are 'signes écrits sur la soie de la vie' (signs written on life's silk) (II, 1024), one possibility is to write haiku, another to look for alternatives. For Barthes the 'romanesque' (novelistic) was intended to be a form of writing, a 'régime de sens', and a way of living. An 'écriture de vie', working 'dans le signifiant' (through the signifier) (II, 1292), the 'romanesque' is also 'un mode de notation, d'investissement, d'intérêt au réel quotidien, aux personnes, à ce qui se passe dans la vie' (a type of notation, of investment, of interest in everyday reality, in people, in what is going on) (III, 327).[37] Like the other forms and projects Barthes thought up in these years the 'romanesque' constituted a form of life writing, and indeed Barthes described his self-portrait, *Barthes par Barthes* as an example of 'le romanesque intellectuel' (III, 178). The same applies to such forms as the *incident*, a type of anecdotal writing Barthes had experimented with in Morocco in the late Sixties (III, 1255–72), the *anamnèse*, a version of haiku addressed to 'la ténuité du souvenir' (the tenuousness of recollection) (III, 178), and the *biographème* based on the perception of 'trait[s] de vie signifiant[s]' (significant life traits) in the lives of other people (Fourier for example).

Barthes's commitment to writing the everyday modulated increasingly towards the pole of the *incident* as wonderfully characterized in a 1971 essay on Pierre Loti: 'l'incident est simplement ce qui tombe, doucement, comme une feuille, sur le tapis de la vie. C'est ce pli léger, fuyant, apporté au tissu des jours; c'est ce qui peut être à peine noté' (the incident is simply what falls, softly, like a leaf, on the page of life. It is this fleeting, light fold in the fabric of days, that can scarcely be noted) (II, 1403).[38] Remarkably, this formulation was anticipated as early as 1964 in an essay on the writings of 'F.B.' whose texts are described as 'non des fragments, mais des *incidents*, choses qui *tombent*, sans heurt et cependant d'un mouvement qui n'est pas infini: continu discontinu du flocon de neige' (not fragments but *incidents*, things that *fall*, without a jolt and yet in a movement that is not infinite: the continuous discontinuity of snowflakes) (I, 1440). So evanescent is the 'incident' that it can only be rendered by indirect modes of utterance of which the paradigm is allusions to 'le temps qu'il fait' (weather) discussed brilliantly in the Loti essay and in a fragment titled 'Quotidien' in *Le Plaisir du Texte* that bemoans the bowdlerization of references to the weather in an edition of Amiel's diary (II,

---

[37] On this see Marielle Macé, 'Barthes romanesque', in id. and Alexandre Gefen (eds.), *Barthes, au lieu du roman* (Paris: Desjonquères/Nota Bene, 2002), 173–94.

[38] On this see Johnnie Gratton, 'The Poetics of the Barthesian Incident: Fragments of an Experiencing Subject', *Nottingham French Studies*, 1997, 63–75.

1521). 'Donc, il se passe: rien. Ce *rien*, cependant, il faut le dire. Comment dire: *rien?*' (So, nothing happens. This nothing has, nonetheless, to be expressed. How can one express: *nothing?*) (II, 1403). With these words Barthes summed up not only the challenge which haunted him in the last decade of his life but also the challenge confronted by all investigators of the everyday.

'COMMENT VIVRE ENSEMBLE'

The most striking testimony to the evolution of Barthes's fascination with the everyday, and its key place in his work, is the course he gave in his first year at the Collège de France. From January to May 1977 Barthes's weekly two-hour *cours* was titled 'Comment vivre ensemble: simulations romanesques de quelques espaces quotidiens' (How to live together: fictional simulations of some everyday spaces). The implication that Barthes's investigation of communal living would focus on fictional renderings of everyday spaces (although, as we have seen, the word 'romanesque' had other resonances for Barthes) was borne out by the eccentric corpus of texts, each identified with a particular type of space, he outlined in his presentation: Defoe's *Robinson Crusoe* (the hut), the *Lausiac History* of the fifth-century writer Palladius, with its accounts of early monastic life in the Near East (the desert), Thomas Mann's *The Magic Mountain* (the hotel/sanatorium), Gide's *La Séquestrée de Poitiers*, a documentary account, based on legal archives, of a woman who was incarcerated in her bedroom for fifty years by her own family (the room); Zola's *Pot-bouille*, a novel in the Rougon-Macquart series centred entirely, like Perec's *La Vie mode d'emploi*, on the inhabitants of a single Parisian 'immeuble bourgeois' (the apartment building). But it soon becomes evident that the main thread of Barthes's analyses stemmed from a key word—*idiorrythmie*—that he had come across in an account of daily life in the ancient world, Jacques Lacarrière's *L'Éte grec. Une Grèce quotidienne de 4000 ans.* The word referred to the activities of a group of monks on Mt Athos who had parted company with the prevailing 'coenobitic' current where the monk's life is entirely regulated by the monastic community. Maintaining some of the characteristics of the anchorites, these monks spent the greater part of their time alone but came together on a regular basis (say two days a week). *Idiorrythmie* designates the individual rhythm, based on a free and fluctuating balance between solitude and community, which these monks preferred to both the total isolation of the anchorite and the permanent commonality of the conventional monastic community.

At the outset Barthes associates the discovery of *idiorrythmie* with the aspiration, voiced just a week earlier in his inaugural *leçon*, to offer an 'enseignement fantasmatique' (fantasmatic teaching) rather than lay down the law. When a particular word seems to hold the key to a fantasy research can proceed by 'mining' its layers and ramifications; the word, says Barthes, transmutes the fantasy into a field of knowledge. What struck him about *idiorrythmie* was the way the prefix—from *idios*—modulated the suffix, *rythmos*, allying it to another word, *ruthmos*, whose origins had been explored in a famous article by Emile Benveniste.[39] According to the linguistician, *rythmos* designated a distinctive pattern, fixed and regular, while *ruthmos* (derived from a word meaning to flow) designated the fluid, mobile form of an entity lacking organic consistency, a 'forme, improvisée, modifiable' (an improvised, modifiable form), as Barthes puts it.[40] *Idiorrythmie*, by activating *ruthmos*, points for Barthes to a rhythmicity that is 'par définition individuel' (by definition individual) and highlights the way the subject engages with the social or natural code. *Idiorrythmie* 'renvoie aux formes subtiles du genre de vie: les humeurs, les configurations non stables, les passages dépressifs ou exaltés; bref le contraire même d'une cadence cassante, implacable de régularité' (has to do with the subtle forms of the way one lives: moods, unstable configurations, phases of depression or elation; in short, the exact opposite of a brusque, implacably regular, cadence) (39).

By making his listeners privy to the unfolding of his fantasy Barthes hopes to inject into the *cours magistral* something of the spirit of the *séminaire*, seen by him—fantasmatically—as a utopian space and community based not on mastery but on the circulation of desire. In the case of 'Comment vivre ensemble' the core of Barthes's fantasy is the notion of an ideal balance between solitude and conviviality where each subject has his or her own rhythm. He calls this a 'fantasme de vie, de régime, de genre de vie, de diète' that is 'ni duel, ni pluriel ... quelque chose comme une solitude interrompue d'une façon réglée' (the fantasy of a life, a regime, a lifestyle, a diet that is neither dual or plural ... a kind of solitude interrupted in a regular manner) (37). It is all a matter of degree. Just as the work of fantasy, manifesting the

---

[39] Emile Benveniste, 'La Notion de rythme', in id., *Problèmes de linguistique générale* (1966; Paris: Gallimard 'Tel', 1976), 327–35. Lefebvre, of course, came to see rhythm as a central feature of the *quotidien* (see Ch. 4 above).

[40] Roland Barthes, *Comment vivre ensemble* (Paris: Seuil 2002), 38. References to *Comment vivre ensemble* will be incorporated in the text.

discontinuity of the human subject, acts like an unruly projector ('projecteur incertain'), highlighting fragments and details of the world, so the word *idiorrythmie*, as vehicle of fantasy, identifies the right degree or proportion of solitude as against commonality. Referring to the 'ontology' of proportion, the idea that the variations of a given phenomenon each have a different reality—some of which are more conducive to human happiness than others—Barthes alludes again to the idea that de Staël's pictorial world sprang from five centimetres of Cézanne. In this fantasy *idiorrythmie* is a variation on—or deviation from—modes of organization that impose rigid guidelines often reflected in spatial organization. In the spirit of Perec's *Espèces d'espaces*, Barthes ties the 'apartement centré' of the couple, with its 'chambre à coucher', to a fixed economy of desire. Equally abhorrent (in Barthes's fantasy) is the inevitable tyranny of communal living—whether in a monastery, a phalanstery, or a hippy commune—where the individual necessarily submits to the group, surrendering individual rhythm to one imposed from the outside. Both the bourgeois couple or family and the monastic community are seen as attempts to regulate and control, and some of Barthes's fascination with *idiorrythmie* stems from his discovery that the edict of Theodosos in AD 380 sought to impose the coenobitic communal monastery and stamp out the anchorite tendency. Through the 'enseignement fantasmatique' he brings to the Collège de France in 1977 Barthes identifies his own marginality with that of a doomed experiment in semi-communal living carried out on Mt Athos in the fourth century AD.

Again like Perec, and at the very point when the younger writer was hard at work on *La Vie mode d'emploi*, Barthes makes a strong connection between the novel and space, arguing that the basic *donnée* or armature of the novel—its 'maquette'—is often manifested spatially. Simulation of a space enables the novel to be a fictive experiment where the action consists in the exploitation of topics and situations that are, as it were, 'let loose' in the simulated environment. Barthes's corpus (outlined above), together with texts relating to monasticism, consists in works centred on particular spaces, but he makes it clear that his way of reading them will not be confined to space. Fantasmatic reading does not home in on themes but on what he calls 'traits'—discontinuous insights or perceptions which, rather than being contained in the text, are engendered in a process where one text in the corpus, or one 'trait', prompts a new perspective on one of the others.

As in Nietzsche, to whom Barthes refers here, the perspective is that of the discontinuous subject; the question being not what perspective, but whose?

Following Nietzsche Barthes insists on the connection between breaking down the fixity of language and discourse by means of fragmentary utterance (even if this is necessarily somewhat artificial) and the manifestation of 'our fundamental discontinuity' (52). Adopting the same practice as in his *Fragments d'un discours amoureux* (1977) (III, 184–215)—he was working on the published version of this seminar as he composed 'Comment vivre ensemble'—Barthes presents his traits, identified by a key word, in alphabetical order, refusing to tie them to an 'idée d'ensemble'. Later referred to as 'figures', Barthes's 'traits' are not facets of a central idea but offshoots, digressions, associations, variations. Under the aegis of Nietzsche (and Deleuze), and anticipating Certeau, Barthes opposes the straight line of method with the 'tracé eccentrique' (eccentric line) of culture, defined as a challenge or violence to thought—'un dressage qui met en jeu l'inconscient' (a training that activates the unconscious). Claiming an 'infinite right to digress', and the non-specialist's licence to draw on all fields of knowledge—'tituber entre les blocs de savoir' (to stumble among blocks of knowledge)—Barthes also identifies indirect expression with 'la vérité du sujet' (the truth of the human subject) (178) and ethics (184). Disclaiming encyclopedic knowledge, Barthes nonetheless asserts the validity of the 'geste encyclopédique' on the grounds that 'une utopie (surtout au quotidien) se construit avec des morceaux de réel empruntés ici et là avec désinvolture' (a utopia (especially an everyday utopia) is constructed with pieces of reality borrowed nonchalantly here and there) (183). As Barthes moves alphabetically through his traits—from *Akèdia*: disconnection from one's 'train de vie' (routine existence) prompted by the 'mauvais quotidien' of meaningless routine; to *Xénitea*, a more active 'dropping out'—everyday experience is always the implicit, and often explicit, context of his concern.

The central project of *Comment vivre ensemble*, with its implied question mark, is to ask whether any kind of communal living can foster rather than smother subjectivity. 'Comment décrocher le sujet de l'individu' (how to unhook the subject from the individual) (72): if the everyday is crucial here it is not simply because daily life is where we interact with others (the non-everyday being the sphere where we can escape this constraint) but because for Barthes the subject—as distinct from the defined and regimented individual, spoken for by organized knowledge—is fundamentally an everyday subject, rooted in everydayness: in transient moods, embodied desires, in likes and dislikes.

Barthes's central question is one that runs through the whole tradition of everyday discourse. Is it inevitable that the regulating systems that always threaten to make the everyday a colony where everything indigenous has been all but annihilated, should prevail over the factors that make the everyday subject ethically and existentially primordial? If everyday experience is, in Barthes's perception of it—consistent with that of Perec, Certeau, and others—attuned to the present, the uneventful, the self-evident (but not the seemingly obvious) can we imagine a form of group existence that would favour it? According to Barthes such a group would have to forgo the factor that brings most groups into existence, namely a common purpose or *telos*. Anything beyond a 'telos flottant' is incompatible with *idiorrythmie*. What the group needs is a common fantasy not a faith: something immanent not transcendent, bearing on the experience of group life itself and the myriad details of its organization. The obsession with the nitty-gritty of everyday life is what attracts Barthes to utopian thought, but utopias are invariably over-regulated. Thus, under the heading *Règle,* Barthes develops an opposition between a good term, *règle,* and a bad term, *règlement. Règlement* implies codification, prescriptiveness, power, hierarchy, and obedience. *Règle,* on the other hand, has to do with custom, tacit or oral, an enshrined but not prescribed set of habits. A *règle* invites acknowledgement not obedience, an 'acte éthique [. . .] dont la fin [. . .] est de donner à la vie, à la quotidienneté, une transparence' (an ethical act . . . whose aim . . . is to lend transparency to life and everydayness) (164). The impulse to turn *règle* into *règlement* by the adjunct of power (and hence to occlude the everyday) is all but irresistible (Barthes cites Golding's *Lord of the Flies* and Brecht's saying 'Sous la règle, cherchez l'abus'). But what Barthes makes clear here is the link between *règle, idiorrythmie,* and the everyday. Ultimately the shared fantasy (the 'telos flottant') that would be the tacit bond of a group is *idiorrythmie* itself, in other words the desire to live at the level of the everyday and everyday things.

'Chaque sujet a son rythme propre' (All subjects have their own rhythm): if this is the key to *idiorrythmie* the question of propitious space is clearly fundamental. Barthes makes a link between *règle* and territory, or habitat, the 'espace approprié' (appropriated space) where a creature is 'chez lui' (at home). But in his account of 'espaces quotidiens' and their 'simulations romanesques' Barthes shows little interest in architecture, planning, or design. 'Béguinages' reveals a fascination with the 'halfway house' religious establishments popular in the low countries; 'Rectangle' tilts at functionality. What really matters is distance. *Idiorrythmie* implies an 'éthique (ou une physique) de la distance entre les sujets' (an ethics (or physics) of the distance between subjects) (110). At the physical level the proximity of the bodies of others inspires attraction and repulsion, and Barthes makes interesting connections between the regulation of desire in monastic treatises and more recent literary and psychoanalytical references. What interests him most, however, is the question of 'la bonne distance' as it arises in the subject's relation to his or her own ambient space. For Barthes 'a room of one's own' is the *sine qua non* of idiorrythmic living, and in 'La Chambre' he surveys different versions of this 'espace du quant-à-soi' (space where I keep to myself). The key to it for him is what he calls 'la structure de chambre' (room structure) (89), a personal constellation of functional reference points: bed, table, shelves, and cupboards for keeping one's things in good order. What matters is the structure not the content. Viewed in this light, Gide's crazed, grimy, and bedridden *Séquestrée*, incarcerated, but at the same time mollycoddled by her family (for fifty years!) is almost to be envied, as is Proust's Tante Léonie, a favourite reference point for Barthes. Citing the famous scene in Zola's *Pot-bouille* where the would-be adulteress, Berthe, finds herself wandering half-naked on the stairs, Barthes suggests that the bourgeois apartment block comprises a whole range of demarcations and subterritories (Perec will exploit this in *La Vie mode d'emploi*). In 'Clôture' Barthes distinguishes, on the basis of anthropological theory, between enclosure as protection, and enclosure as a marking out of one's own space or territory, one's distance: *idiorrythmie*, he insists, does not protect 'une pureté, c'est-à-dire une identité. Son mode d'implantation dans l'espace: non la concentration, mais la dispersion, l'espacement' (a purity, i.e. an identity. Its spatial mode is not concentration but dispersal, spacing) (94).

Where one's personal rhythm is concerned (Barthes's at any rate) the key space is within arm's reach. A 'trait' entitled 'Proxémie' begins with a bulletin from Barthes's everyday experience: reaching into the drawer of his bedside table in the dark to find the handkerchief he knows will be there. Proxemics, he informs his listeners, is a neologism coined by E. T. Hall in 1966 to designate our understanding of 'les espaces subjectifs en tant que le sujet les habite affectivement' (subjective spaces as they are 'lived' affectively by subjects) (156). Citing the work of Abraham Moles in France Barthes suggests that one could establish a typology of the spaces we 'make our own' (Perec's *Espèces d'espaces*, not mentioned by Barthes, can of course be seen as an essay in proxemics). Barthes himself chooses to focus on objects he sees as 'créateurs de proxémie': the lamp and the bed. As a 'créateur de micro-espace sedentaire' (creator of a sedentary micro-space) the lamp fits historically between the fireside and the television set. If the centre light favours family space, the table lamp delivers a 'proxémie forte' isolating the writing or reading surface. The proxemic properties of the bed are most intense in the case of the sickbed: Matisse in old age, or Tante Léonie. Like Perec, Barthes makes it clear that he likes his bed; and Perec would undoubtedly have approved Barthes's aside to his audience at the Collège de France, a delicious example of an everyday reality being defamiliarized by language, and further testimony to Barthes's fascination with the everyday: 'Je me connais moi-même un être assez proxémique et gouttant [*sic*] les délices de la proxémie' (I know myself to be the kind of person who revels in the delights of the proxemic) (157).

'CHRONIQUE' AND EVERYDAY WRITING

The last two or three years of Barthes's career saw a further convergence between questions of *art de vivre* and a search for new forms of expression. This is evident in his last two books—*Fragments d'un discours amoureux*, on being 'in love', and *La Chambre Claire*, on photography—where the essay genre's author–topic symbiosis is accentuated; in his last sets of lectures, *Le Neutre* and *La Préparation du roman*; and in the 'Chronique' column Barthes supplied for three months in the weekly *Nouvel Observateur*. To conclude this chapter I want to focus on Barthes's 'chroniques', but a brief account of the late *cours* provides necessary background.

Defined as 'ce qui déjoue le paradigme' (what outwits the paradigm), 'le neutre' (the neuter or neutral) fitted in with many of Barthes's long-standing preoccupations. At the outset of the *cours* which ran from February to June 1978 Barthes slants his approach towards 'une introduction au vivre, un guide de vie (projet éthique)' (an introduction to living, a life guide (ethical project)), making clear that his mother's death some months earlier had changed his life.[41] Once again displaying a series of 'figures' that came to mind in connection with the central 'topique', his aim is to 'vivre selon la nuance' (live according to nuances): the 'désir de neutre' will be seen not as an abstract ideal but as a desired state of being. Randomizing the order of presentation even further than before, by adopting, Perec-fashion, a constraint derived from a journal of applied statistics, Barthes explores such notions as 'Délicatesse', 'Fatigue', and 'Bienveillance', injecting the material with his affective life, for example when he cites a recent experience in order to explain the importance he attaches to minutiae. Recounting a sortie at dusk, Barthes links his sensi-

[41] Roland Barthes, *Le Neutre* (Paris: Seuil, 2002), 37.

tivity to 'des détails infimes, parfaitement futiles, de la rue (un menu écrit à la craie . . . etc.)' (tiny details, totally futile, of the street (a menu written in chalk . . . etc.)), to the key perception that for him 'descendre dans l'infiniment futile, cela permettait d'avouer la sensation de la vie' (descending into the infinitely futile allowed one to admit the sensation of life) (79): life is not life force but flow or *durée*: 'l'infiniment futile devient comme le grain même de cette durée vitale' (the infinitely futile becomes the very grain of this vital temporal flow) (79). Later, Barthes suggests that the neutral escapes the rigidity of systems because it can be linked to the notion of *kairos* in Greek philosophy. *Kairos* means occasion, and thus what is contingent or opportune, and for both the Stoics and the Sceptics *kairos* opposes the normal run of thought and discourse based on logical 'development'. Like Barthes, and possibly partly influenced by his *cours* (as well as by Detienne and Vernant) Certeau will also give *kairos* and the temporality of the opportune moment a defining role in his account of the *quotidien*.[42]

In the aftermath of his mother's death, and in the course of delivering his lectures on 'Le Neutre', Barthes resolved to adopt a *vita nova*, to transform his life through a closer embrace of literature and the search for a new form of writing.[43] The category of the *romanesque*, originally forged to qualify a category of everyday experience, became more closely allied to a form of writing that would be responsive to the affective currents and nuances of present experience. Enjoying rumours that he was contemplating writing a novel, Barthes toyed with this idea in some reflections of Proust, and also experimented with the *journal intime*.[44] At the Collège de France he devoted his last two sets of lectures to 'La Préparation du roman'.[45] In the first set, in 1978–9, he looked at the author's decision to write as the adoption of a *vita nova*, involving new modes of attention to, and notation of, everyday experience, taking haiku as a model. The last *cours*, in 1979–80, used the genesis of Proust's *Recherche* to explore the nature of the decision to write, using the mutation of notes and sketches into a finished work as a basis for seeing the project of registering the present, rather than reconstituting memories, as the bedrock of the novel. 'On peut écrire le présent en le notant' (one can write

---

[42] See Ch. 7 below.
[43] See Diana Knight, 'Idle Thoughts: Barthes's *Vita nova*', *Nottingham French Studies* 36/1 (Spring 1997), 88–98.
[44] See 'Délibération', III, 1004–14.
[45] Roland Barthes, *La Préparation du roman* (Paris: Seuil, 2003).

the present by noting it): many of Barthes's late writings reflect an obsession with capturing the immediacy of the present.

This is certainly the case in the 'Chronique' column Barthes supplied between December 1978 and March 1979 to the *Nouvel Observateur* weekly magazine. Each column comprised an average of four separately titled and unconnected entries ranging from a few lines to a couple of substantial paragraphs. In each case Barthes gave his reactions to a few things that had caught his attention that week, for example, in the first column, a book about Leni Riefenstahl, an encounter at the hairdresser's, media coverage of the collective suicides of a sect in Guyana, and a rumour that Mayor Chirac planned to outlaw busking. All the main types of stimuli involve the display of attitudes enshrined in different types of discourse. Thus there are social situations such as a dinner party; *faits divers*; incidents at the doctor's or in shops; films, radio, music, and other entertainments; political events such as Khomeini's exile; advertisements and health campaigns; modern habits, mores, and situations, such as struggling with parcels. Power, isolation, and language are key themes.

In voicing his reactions week by week Barthes often casts himself in the role of an outsider unable to share the types of consensus he sees at work in the world around him. Generally dissenting, he recoils from the stereotyped misogyny of his neighbour at the hairdresser's, notes his irritation at a *faits divers* concerning the prompt action of a 'good citizen' who tripped up a street thief, or observes the way a newspaper report euphemizes the horrific death of some youths in a road accident. The items concerning politics generally lament its fusion with religion, as in Ayatollah Khomeini's fundamentalism or Jimmy Carter's Puritanism. Style and discourse concern him more than content, as when he observes that in anti-smoking campaigns, or more anodyne contexts, the imperative mood invokes the links between language and power. In some cases Barthes bemoans a reaction he at least partially shares, as when he notes his own susceptibility to rumours. In one entry, concerning a visit to the ballet when he failed to appreciate Nuryev's genius until he was sure which dancer he was, Barthes enjoys the parallel with the Proustian narrator's reaction to the actress La Berma, appreciating the interaction of text and life. But an entry inspired by the annual meeting of his 'co-propriété' (housing association) laments the way it seemed like something out of Balzac, since here the predominance of a literary grid subordinates the present to the past and to the already written. A true writing of the present needs to dismantle this structure and grasp 'flashes' of meaning.

In one entry Barthes notes the various voices (liberal, anarchist, Brechtian) he identifies in his own conflicted reaction to a *fait divers*. In other entries Barthes notes ways in which his own reactions are outlandishly aberrant and singular: for example his regret that you can now buy cherries at any time of year. By contrast, some of the entries feature more positive reactions, generally inspired by things Barthes sees as a counterbalance to the negativities that cause him such dismay. He admires the *comédienne* Zouc because her verbal dexterity, based on close observation, involves mimicking a multiplicity of discourses, creating a continuous skein of language without any fixed point of view. Noting that medical discourse is as obfuscating as it was in Molière's day, and that its enduringly comic aspect continues to conceal the power to intimidate, Barthes commends by contrast the remarkable metaphorical inventiveness of some contemporary scientific language. Devoting a whole week to a defence of Philippe Sollers against the accusation that he is unreadable, Barthes insists that there are different tempos of reading and that Sollers's project vigorously affirms literature's capacity to encompass and transcend the discourses of society. The question of tempo arises again when Barthes hears Schumann's *Abend* performed more slowly than usual and realizes that this is how it should be played. As in the case of reading a change of tempo transforms perception.

On 26 March 1978 Barthes's readers were confronted with a single entry announcing a temporary suspension of his column that would in fact prove permanent. In 'Pause' Barthes outlines very lucidly what he had been trying to achieve and then explains why he feels he failed. Scotching the rumour that he was trying to resurrect *Mythologies*, Barthes insists that his 'Chronique' was an experiment, a quest for a new form of writing that would be deliberately brief, minor, and gentle, whilst at the same time political. In fact the political and moral charge would come from this deliberate *douceur*, aimed at contrasting with the overheated clamour of surrounding discourses. For Barthes, to use the pages of a political weekly to talk about incidents that had struck him that week, 'mes *scoops* à moi' (my personal scoops), was to counteract the scale of values imposed by the press's obsession with big events. To risk talking about 'le ténu, le futile, l'insignifiant', is to change the scale, and Barthes again cited his favourite example from painting. Orthodox media treat events in the manner of official painters of the Napoleonic era, ever eager for the 'big picture'. But just as painting only evolved because it changed scale—the whole of Nicolas de Staël emerging from *one* square centimetre of Cézanne (Barthes's own hyperbolic scaling-down is symptomatic here)—so the media should make room for 'weak' events that nevertheless point to real malaises. To insist on the particularity of one's own 'small language' is to challenge the dominance of the 'grand monde'. All the more so if the micro-world one puts on view is far from monolithic and is made up of the very diverse voices that constitute us—transient moods, different strata of our subjective history, the views of others we briefly identify with. But this dialogical and theatrical aspect of his 'Chronique' induces what Barthes sees as its fatal flaw: 'Le défaut, c'est qu'à chaque incident rapporté je me sens entraîné (par quelle force—ou quelle faiblesse?) à lui donner un sens (social, moral, esthétique, etc.), à produire une dernière réplique' (The flaw is that for every incident I bring up I feel myself drawn (by what power—or weakness?) to give it a meaning (social, moral, aesthetic, etc.) to have the last word) (990). What prevents the columns from embodying the kind of writing Barthes had dreamt of is the seemingly irresistible tendency to moralize, to make a point, to have the last word, to lay down the law (even if it is one's own).

'Pause' is an important text because Barthes put his finger here on a range of issues raised by comparable attempts to place the everyday self and its observations at the centre of writing. If Barthes's criterion—the 'exemption du sens' of haiku that he had sought to emulate in his notions of the *incident* and the *romanesque*—is proper to him, the difficulty of capturing the tenuous and the unspectacular will preoccupy Perec in comparable ways, while a similar sense of how hard it is to avoid moralizing when one trains one's sights on the media and the socio-political field, with a view to isolating one's own reactions, will be conveyed in similar terms in Ernaux's *Journal du dehors*. Even if it is hard to disagree with the author's critical judgement on his 'Chronique', the lucidity of 'Pause' underlines once more the central importance of Barthes's contribution to the field of discourses on the everyday.

6

Michel De Certeau:
Reclaiming the Everyday

In 1974, Michel de Certeau, a Jesuit historian and cultural anthropologist, was commissioned by the French Ministry of Culture, on the strength of his writings on cultural activity and particularly the significance of May '68, to produce a report on future prospects and orientations.[1] The demand was for crystal-gazing rather than statistics, since the latter had been amply furnished by a recent enquiry into the cultural practices of French citizens, largely concerned with the activities of consumers. Certeau quickly created a team, including Luce Giard and Pierre Mayol, who were both to make major contributions. The results of the commission, published in 1980, were two volumes: *L'Invention du quotidien I, Arts de faire (The Practice of Everyday Life)*, written by Certeau alone, and *L'Invention du quotidien II, Habiter, cuisiner*, which consisted primarily of two monographs, based on recorded interviews, by Mayol and Giard.[2]

L'Invention du quotidien is, from start to finish, an experiment and a project. Even though the contributions of Mayol and Giard (considered later in this chapter) are more conventional than Certeau's extraordinary text, the overall impact of the two volumes derives from the multifaceted ways in which the topic of the everyday is addressed, the only obvious precedent being the pioneering work of Henri Lefebvre. In Certeau's contribution the avoidance of linear argument reflects the tactical play with systems and disciplines that is his central point. Just as narratives, he will claim, knit places together, bringing the contingencies of utterance to bear on sites otherwise monopolized by controlling discourses, so Certeau conceives his text as a series of 'récits'

---

[1] For biographical information see François Dosse: *Michel de Certeau: le marcheur blessé* (Paris: La Découverte, 2002).

[2] The current edition of both volumes was edited by Luce Giard for Gallimard Folio in 1990. References to this edition are incorporated in the text.

(stories) whose aim is to recount 'common practices', the explicit aim being to make the form of the analysis reflect its object (I, xxxiii).[3] Equally, to read or write about *L'Invention du quotidien* is to invent an order, and in what follows I will provide an overall account of Certeau's theorizations of the *quotidien*, paying particular attention to the way his diffuse text progressively elaborates an overall 'logique opératoire' (operational logic) (I, xxxvi) of everyday practices, and underlining links and parallels with Lefebvre, Perec, Barthes, and others.

CONSUMPTION AS PRODUCTION

L'Invention du quotidien is not about popular culture, nor is it a study of consumer behaviour.[4] Certeau's aim is to tease out the common logic underpinning everyday practices—the way people go about things in their ordinary lives. What interests him about the activities of consumers or users—selecting goods in the supermarket, zapping between TV channels, using local amenities, reading books, periodicals, or advertisements—is their alleged passivity in the face of the technocratic, bureaucratic and other systems that produce the goods, services, and environments in which consumption takes place. Certeau mounts a strong challenge to the portrayal of consumers as docile and manipulated subjects. His basic hypothesis is that consumption or use is in fact active and productive. If consumers are subject to manipulation, as they 'deal with' images and representations, they also manipulate the material they receive. Some TV viewers are couch potatoes, munching mindlessly on chewing gum for the eyes. But even in vacuity there is distance, if only that of indifference or disengagement. And often it makes sense to ask what the consumer *makes* ('fabrique') with the images he or she consumes (I, 53). There is a gap between the image and the 'production secondaire qui se cache dans le procès de son utilisation' (secondary production hidden in the process of its utilization) (I, xxxviii). The model here is that of *énonciation* (enunciation) (I, 56). In linguistic performances, the language user produces utterances by appropriating or reappropriating a common system.[5] Like utterances, the 'productions' of consumers are ephemeral, and tied to specific present con-

---

3 On narrative in Certeau see Ch. 1.

4 For an excellent account of Certeau's overall intellectual project see Ahearne, *Michel de Certeau*.

5 See Benveniste, 'De la subjectivité dans le langage', *Problèmes de linguistique générale*, 258–66; Catherine Kerbrat-Orrechioni, *L'Énonciation* (Paris: Armand Colin, 1999).

texts. Certeau stresses that this kind of productivity differs markedly from the rational, dominant, visible production to which it responds. The often invisible production secreted in these 'opérations d'emploi—ou plutôt de réemploi' (modes of use—or rather recycling) (I, 52) has as its characteristic features 'ses ruses, son effritement au gré des occasions, ses braconnages, sa clandestinité, son murmure inlassable' (I: 53) (its ruses, its bittiness (the outcome of circumstances), its poaching, its clandestine nature, its endless murmur) (I, 53). All these features will be recurrent, and demand further discussion. At this point the metaphor of poaching calls for comment. 'Le quotidien s'invente avec mille manières de *braconner*' (Everyday life invents itself through countless forms of *poaching*) (I, xxxvi). Poaching is a clandestine use of resources that one does not own, on a territory that is not ours. Certeau places great emphasis on the idea that the everyday has no fixed contents or characteristics, and above all no space of its own (as in Lefebvre, the *quotidien* is a specific level construed in terms of a particular mode of appropriation). The distinction between tactics and strategy, at the heart of poaching, is based on the fact that 'la tactique n'a pour lieu que celui de l'autre' (the space of a tactic is the space of the other) (I, 60). Tactics work within the constraints of a given order, bringing about 'manipulations within a system' on the basis of an '*absence of power*', a 'non-lieu' (non-place) (I, 61). Like Freudian jokes (*Witz*), the 'ways of doing' of consumers constitute 'zébrures, éclats, fêlures et trouvailles dans le quadrillage d'un système' (slashes, fragments, cracks, and lucky finds in the framework of a system) (I, 62).

   Consumption or use is a form of play that injects Brownian movement into the workings of systems. The 'ant-like' work of consumption ('travail fourmilier' (I, 52)) is reactive, insofar as it can only work with the constraints of the given, but also distortive: it alters, erodes (a recurrent metaphor), and displaces the 'quadrillages institutionnels' (institutional grids) on which it operates. 'Pratiques quotidiennes' (Everyday practices) often involve the ludic, subversive modes of appropriation for which the Situationists coined the term 'détournement'.[6] For Certeau the paradigm of a 'pratique de détournement' (I, 43) is to be found in the clandestine activity known as 'la perruque' ('the wig') where workers disguise their private work as that of their employer, affirming their own, often collective, identity, by using leftover materials and unaccounted time in the workplace to make things that are often useless and purely decorative (I, 45). 'La perruque' introduces another economy: that of

---

[6] See above, Ch. 4.

the gift and the potlatch, based on reciprocity, gratuitousness, and pure 'expenditure', thus subverting the dominant order. In making a useless object out of spare parts the worker applies his or her know-how in a way that forgoes the authority of expertise. The subject of everyday practices is not an expert but someone whose competence takes the form of tact, flair, and the aesthetic judgement identified by Kant (I, 73). Certeau sometimes uses the motif of blindness to contrast everyday 'manières de faire' (ways of doing) with strategic order where the creation of dominated space is associated with sight—scopic or panoptic mastery (I, 61). 'Sans lieu propre, sans vision globalisante, aveugle et perspicace, comme on l'est dans le corps à corps sans distance, commandée par les hasards du temps, la tactique est déterminée par *l'absence de pouvoir*' (Lacking its own place or overall view, blind yet perspicacious as in hand-to-hand struggle, subject to the possibilities of the moment, a tactic is determined by *absence of power*) (I, 62).

This is where Certeau's account of the logic or 'formality' of 'practices' differs markedly from that of Pierre Bourdieu, whose work he discusses in a chapter also concerned with Foucault. Like Certeau, Bourdieu sees practices as heterogeneous and transgressive insofar as they cut across established divisions and systems of order. His analyses are thus predicated on the disparity between the objective structures of the social world, that can be quantified statistically, and an underlying 'logique de la pratique'.[7] Yet unlike the tactics of Certeau the practices studied by Bourdieu are not free and active but serve ultimately, albeit indirectly, to bolster established structures. This mode of conformity or attunement is accounted for by the concept of '*habitus*'. For Bourdieu practice is driven by the accumulation of symbolic capital in the form of goods and heritage. However anarchic, improvisational, or adaptive they are, practices serve to generate a stable 'acquis' (acquisition) made up of internalized dispositions and modes of understanding. Bourdieu concentrates on how *habitus* is generated, and how it tends to reproduce itself in all the manifestations of an individual or group. For Certeau, there is a glaring opposition between Bourdieu's account of the way practices work in the space between subjects and systems, an account which has many affinities with Certeau's account of tactical play, and the way Bourdieu ultimately denies any freedom or control to individual subjects by his insistence on the way they act out their *habitus* unconsciously and passively—in 'docta ignorantia' (I, 50). Bourdieu's logic of practices is based on reproduction rather than production.

---

[7] See Pierre Bourdieu, *Esquisse d'une théorie de la pratique* (1972; Paris: Seuil, 2000).

THE POWER OF THE RUSE

If, for Certeau, *strategies* work through spatial domination, setting up resistance to time by asserting permanence, *tactics* derive their productiveness from time and timeliness (I, 63): a timely intervention is one that profits from circumstances, from spotting the 'right moment'; swiftness of action can affect the organization of space; a sense of the unfolding of a process can lead to ways of determining its outcome; a sense of differential timescales or rhythms can be advantageous. Certeau derives some of his thinking on the temporality of everyday practices from Marcel Detienne and Jean-Pierre Vernant's *Les Ruses de l'intelligence: la mètis des Grecs*, published in 1974. Detienne and Vernant unearthed the Greek concept of *mètis*, designating a form of practical intelligence that enables a weaker party to get the better of a stronger by seizing fleeting opportunities and exploiting blind spots in the operation of superior power. *Mètis* is not a philosophy or world view but a series of context-specific operations—ploys, scams, knacks, 'tuyaux', 'astuces'—that rejig the balance of forces. Accordingly, Detienne and Vernant build up their picture of this 'type of intelligence' by retelling numerous myths and legends, and tracing the recurrence of terms which, in the absence of an abstract body of doctrine, make up a coherent semantic field. The link between *mètis* and the practical specifics of stories, as opposed to the schemes of abstract rationality, will be of importance to Certeau.

Les Ruses de l'intelligence attracted considerable interest when it appeared in 1974, and Certeau was not alone in seeing the relevance of 'la mètis' in the wider context of social life. In 1977, the review *Cause commune*, whose editors included Georges Perec, Jean Duvignaud, and Paul Virilio, brought out a special number on 'La Ruse'. Duvignaud's editorial stressed the importance of Detienne and Vernant's work for the understanding of the ancient world as well as its more general implications:

Mais la vie quotidienne, dans ces sociétés, n'est-elle pas faite de ruse? *Une casuistique informulée ne permet-elle pas à la plupart des hommes de tourner les règles?* [...] Ces détournements ne caractérisent-ils pas la vie commune au moins autant que le rituel?[8]

(In those societies everyday life was made up of ruses, was it not? A casuistical rule of thumb probably allows most people to bend the rules. ... Don't such *détournements* characterize communal life as much as ritual does?)

___

[8] 'La Ruse' *Cause commune*, ed. Georges Perec, Jean Duvignaud, and Paul Virilio (Paris: Union générale d'éditions, 1977).

For Duvignaud and his collaborators the ethos of 'la ruse' is the avoidance of violence and direct confrontation by means of indirection, and they examine it in various fields, including politics, the logic of decision-making, anthropology and, in the case of Perec, psychoanalysis.[9] If it is associated with transgression, trickery, and dissimulation, 'la ruse' is beneficent because, through displacement and distance, it opens up spaces unforeseen by mechanistic rationality.

Published a year after *Les Ruses de l'intelligence*, Michel Foucault's *Surveiller et punir* (1975) is another key text in the gestation of Certeau's work on the *quotidien*. Certeau finds much of Foucault's account of how the operation and location of power was transformed in the nineteenth century extremely persuasive. Foucault's argument is that, through their translation into such 'disciplines' as penal reform, education, and so on, the humanistic ideas of the Enlightenment were transformed into a set of procedures dominated by the idea of keeping human bodies under control through a 'biopouvoir' exerted via panoptic surveillance. Certeau is particularly attentive to the way, in this perspective, the use or implementation of ideology can end up turning the original ideology on its head. And he is also struck by Foucault's descriptions of how the new modes of power—'une nouvelle microphysique du pouvoir'—operate essentially at the micro-level of everyday detail and embody the logic of 'la ruse'. Foucault writes of

Petites *ruses* dotées d'un grand pouvoir de diffusion, aménagements subtils, d'apparence innocente, mais profondément soupçonneux [. . .] *Ruses*, moins de la grande raison qui travaille jusque dans le sommeil et donne du sens à l'insignifiant, que de l'attentive 'malveillance' qui fait son grain de tout. La discipline est une anatomie politique du détail.[10]

(Tiny ruses that possess a considerable power of diffusion, subtle adjustments, seemingly innocent, but highly suspicious . . . Not so much the ruses of high reason that works even in our sleep and makes the insignificant meaningful, but ill-meaning attention that sticks its nose in everywhere. Discipline is a political anatomy of detail.)

Certeau will seek to identify very similar mechanisms—working in parallel with those described by Foucault—whose effect is to bring to bear on the whole apparatus of disciplinary control, whether it operates at the macro- or the micro-level—modes of subversive agency, similar to those outlined in *Surveiller et punir*, yet geared instead to the reappropriation of 'l'espace

---

[9] See Perec's 'Les lieux d'une ruse' in *Penser/Classer*, 59–72.
[10] Michel Foucault, *Surveiller et punir* (Paris: Gallimard, 1975), 165, emphasis added.

organisé par les techniques de la production socioculturelle' (the space organized by sociocultural production) (I, xl). *L'Invention du quotidien* will duly be concerned with a kind of 'anti-discipline' and in this connection Certeau acknowledges Lefebvre's work on the everyday as a 'source fondamentale' (I, 303 *n*.).

Detienne and Vernant's account of 'la mètis' provided the antidote to Foucault's insistence on the all-pervasiveness of power. But if these key works helped to shape Certeau's argument and vocabulary, many ideas were already present in 'Des espaces et des pratiques', the concluding essay of an earlier book, *La Culture au pluriel* (1974). May '68 had oriented Certeau towards contemporary culture, and for him the crucial aspect of the *événements* was the way an event that did change something in the nation consisted not in the invention of a new order, social or linguistic, but in a new way of living, using, and articulating what was already there. In May '68 the 'prise de parole' had consisted in an 'usage *différent* d'un langage *déjà fait*' (a different use of an existing language).[11] In 'Des espaces et des pratiques' Certeau identifies similar mechanisms in culture at large. He argues that culture is not a repository of customs, usages, or representations but a fluid and mobile set of practices constituted by the way we do things ('manières de faire'). If culture also exists at the level of 'ce qui permane' (what endures) it is in the form of 'lenteurs [. . .] latences [. . .] retards qui s'empilent dans l'épaisseur des mentalités, des évidences et des ritualisations sociales' (slow, latent, tardy elements that pile up in the density of mentalities, social rituals, and common assumptions) (211). Here culture is a 'vie opaque, têtue, enfouie dans les gestes quotidiens, à la fois les plus actuels et millénaires' (opaque, obstinate life, buried in everyday gestures, at once current and ancient) (211). Overall, Certeau sees culture as a 'nuit océanique' (oceanic night) that resists history, sociology, economics, and politics, either by consisting in a reuse that subverts such discourses, by denying their generality, or by drawing on a reservoir of compacted experiences accumulated outside their sway.

But he also stresses already the parallel that will play a key role in *L'Invention du quotidien*—that of 'pratique' as 'énonciation'. The trace of the act of 'énonciation' in the 'énoncé' becomes a paradigm for the agency of cultural practices seen as being capable of effecting a 'grignotement de l'inventivité dans les marges des textes légaux' (gnawing of inventiveness in the margins of legal texts) (216). This inventiveness is located in everyday lifestyles—dress,

---

[11] Michel de Certeau, *La Culture au pluriel* (Paris: Seuil, 1974), 64.

decoration, types of circulation and social activity, ways of working—and it makes the culture of the everyday as rich as the 'high' culture which, by pushing it to the margins, allows it to proliferate there. The decisive shift Certeau will make in *L'Invention du quotidien* is to focus not on the content of cultural activity but on its style or form. Having in an earlier essay delivered a swingeing critique of the notion of 'popular culture', seeing it as a 'commodity' produced for political ends,[12] Certeau now moves away from the concept of culture itself, substituting for it the more neutral notion of the *quotidien*. In *L'Invention du quotidien* the word culture is largely replaced by such terms as 'pratiques' and 'manières de faire', now located in the overall framework of the *quotidien*. In the conclusion to *La Culture au pluriel*, Certeau recommends a focus on 'cultural operations' and insists on their plurality. In *L'Invention du quotidien* he will go a step further and, while still emphasizing multiplicity, seek to identify a generic *modus operandi*, a common 'formalité', for the profusion of 'pratiques', now seen as constituents of everyday life in general, not simply that of minorities.

PRACTICAL MEMORY

A key word in the semantic field of *mètis* is another Greek term, *kairos*, used here in the sense of 'opportune moment'. For Detienne and Vernant 'La mètis est rapide, prompte comme l'occasion qu'elle doit saisir au vol, sans la laisser passer' (*mètis* is rapid, as prompt as the occasion that it grasps on the wing, without letting it pass).[13] The art of rusing (on which Certeau derives further ideas from Clausewitz, who was a favourite point of reference for the Situationist, Guy Debord) is effective and inventive not because it brings something from the outside but because it seizes opportunities located within the temporal configuration of a situation. *Kairos* is inseparable from particular occasions and circumstances. Certeau adopts and develops this concept in terms of a particular form of memory. Although 'grasping the right moment' is not dependent on a force deriving from another place, it does not quite happen *ex nihilo*. It depends on a form of unsystematic memory, inseparable from the particular occasions that have nurtured it:

12 See 'La Beauté du mort' in Certeau, *La Culture au pluriel*, 45–72.
13 Marcel Detienne and Jean-Pierre Vernant *Les Ruses de l'intelligence: la mètis des Grecs* (Paris: Flammarion, 1974), 22.

Une *mémoire*, dont les connaissances sont indétachables des temps de leur acquisition [. . .] instruite par une multitude d'événements où elle circule sans les posséder [. . .] elle suppute et prévoit aussi 'les voies multiples de l'avenir' en combinant les particularités antécédentes ou possibles [. . .] L'éclair de cette mémoire brille dans *l'occasion* (I, 125–6).

(A *memory*, whose knowledge cannot be dissociated from the time of its acquisition . . . nourished by a multitude of events among which it moves without possessing them . . . it also computes and predicts 'the multiple paths of the future' by combining antecedent or possible particularities . . . The flashes of this memory illuminate the *occasion*)

Occasions exist only insofar as they are grasped; they do not pre-exist the exercise of a faculty that identifies or creates them. But this faculty only exists at the point when it is exercised: in the conjunction with a set of circumstances that it grasps, thus transforming the situation. There is something paradoxical in Certeau's recourse to a notion of memory since it inevitably introduces connotations of cumulative experience pointing in the direction of an 'acquis' that would have some of the characteristics of a place ('lieu') from which strategies could flow. This is why Certeau is so insistent on the actual operations of this type of memory, this daily practice 'qui consiste à saisir l'occasion et à faire de la mémoire le moyen de transformer les lieux' (that consists in seizing the opportunity and making memory the means of trans-forming places) (I, 130). If this can sound like falling back on established know-how, assessing the new in the light of the old, Certeau makes sure we perceive the difference, insisting that the mechanism of what he calls '*l'im-plantation de la mémoire dans un lieu*' (the implanting of memory in a place) (I, 130), is neither 'localisée ni déterminée par la mémoire-savoir' (localized nor determined by memory-knowledge). What is implanted by practical memory is not a 'ready-made organization' but a quickly improvised 'touch', 'un petit rien, un bout de quelque chose, un reste devenu précieux dans la circonstance' (a little something, a scrap that becomes precious in these particular circum-stances) (I, 130). Even if it provides this missing detail, memory only receives its form from the external circumstance in which it comes into operation. And in the process memory is itself altered or refashioned.

Sa force d'intervention, la mémoire la tient de sa capacité même d'être altérée—déplaçable, mobile, sans lieu fixe [. . .] Bien loin d'être le reliquaire ou la poubelle du passé, elle *vit* de croire à des possibilités et de les attendre, vigilante, à l'affût (I, 131).

(Memory derives its force from its very capacity to be altered—detached, mobile, lacking any fixed position. . . . Far from being the reliquary or dustbin of the past, it *lives* by believing in possibilities and by awaiting them, vigilantly)

'Practical memory' (I, 130) involves a 'régime d'altération répondante' (system of responsive alteration) (I, 132). Rather than recording, it responds and inscribes. Certeau's model all but obliterates the traditional image of store and receptacle:

la mémoire pratique est régulée par le jeu multiple de *l'altération* [...] Elle ne se constitue que d'être marquée par des rencontres externes et de collectionner ces blasons successifs et tatouages de l'autre [...] la mémoire est jouée par les circonstances comme le piano 'rend' des sons aux touches des mains. Elle est sens de l'autre (I, 132).

(practical memory is regulated by the manifold activity of *alteration* ... It is constituted only by the successive blazons and tattoos inscribed by the other ... memory is played by circumstances as the piano 'renders' sounds via the touch of the fingers. Memory is a sense of the other)

The relation between the otherness of memory (its uncanny combination of the personal and the collective) and the experience of the everyday is also a central constituent in Perec's sense of the *quotidien*, as we shall see in the discussion of his *Je me souviens* in Chapter 7. Equally, Certeau's insistence that the responses of practical memory focus on the singular, metonymically absorbing a whole into a detail that has the force of a demonstrative: '*ce* type au loin ... *cette* odeur' (*that* person in the distance ... *that* smell) (I, 88) chime with Barthes's obsession with haiku and with the 'exemption from meaning' which positions everyday experience as a dimension made visible when customary regimes of thought are interrupted. Less paradoxical than it seems, Certeau's insistence on the operations of a certain kind of memory delivers a challenge to conventional ways of linking the everyday with cultural memory. Well away from the museum, the souvenir, and the commemorative token, everyday memory is essentially mobile, and the 'space' it creates, that of a 'non-lieu mouvant' (moving nowhere), (I, 133) might be considered the very model of the 'art of practice' he is seeking to delineate.

THE LOGIC OF EVERYDAY PRACTICES: WALKING, TALKING, READING

The central project of *The Practice of Everyday Life* is to establish 'la formalité des pratiques' (I, 23) the logic of daily 'arts de faire'. Although in their resistance to 'la loi du lieu' (the law of the place) (I, 51) '*tactiques* traversières' (transverse *tactics*) are relative, plural, heterogeneous, contingent, and oblique, their specificity may be grasped in terms of 'types' or 'operational schemas' (I, 51). What are the common properties of different 'manières de faire' or 'styles d'action' (styles of action) (I, 51) such as walking, reading, making, speaking?

At an initial level they take place in a field that is already regulated—by the layout of streets and services, the order of chapters or paragraphs, the economic targets of a factory. But as 'ways of doing' ('manières de faire') their essence lies in how, by playing according to different rules, they take advantage of what is initially laid down, and so introduce a second level 'imbriqué dans le premier' (interwoven in the first) (I, 51). Using a phrase with strong echoes of Perec, Certeau asserts that these 'ways of doing' are similar to *modes d'emploi* (instructions for use) that introduce play into the machine by pointing up different possible uses and functions (I, 51).

A second common feature of practices and the operations they engender is the way they display both heterogeneous multiplicity and metaphorical interchangeability. Certeau emphasizes again and again the sheer plurality of everyday 'manières de faire', conveyed through recurrent images of teeming and swarming, and words such as 'pullulate' and 'proliferate'. This multiplicity stems from the *ad hoc* contingency of interventions based on singular occasions rather than overarching strategies grounded in doctrine. But if this autonomy puts pressure on institutional and symbolic organization (I, 95), the power of everyday 'pratiques' stems from their interconnectedness: 'Normalités, généralités et découpages [cèdent] devant le pullulement transversal et 'métaphorisant' de ces microactivités *différentes*' (Norms, generalizations, and segmentations [. . .] yield to the transverse and 'metaphorizing' pullulation of these *differentiating* activities) (I, 95). Through various strategies of exorcism—for example by writing off 'ways of doing' as folklore or deviancy—the homogenizing thrust of the social sciences tries to resist capitulation to the heterogeneous power of 'pratiques'. But this is impeded by a proliferation that derives in part from, and is held together by, metaphorical productivity. Certeau repeatedly underlines the active force of practices, their capacity not only to elude systemic control by exploiting gaps and niches, but actively to alter and disrupt the systems within which they work. By virtue of a commonality rooted in the paradigm of enunciation, each of the everyday activities on which Certeau focuses in detail—primarily walking, talking, and reading—can be seen as metaphorically related to the others. Walking is a mode of reading the spatial environment; reading is a mode of journeying; speaking involves narrativization that links spaces together as in walking, and so on. These metaphorical links are not merely fortuitous. In fact it is this inherent metaphoricity that makes these activities—in their everyday manifestations—representative of everyday 'pratiques'. They are operations which, like metaphor, cut across established boundaries and hierarchies. It is insofar as they partake of the creative potential and mobility of metaphor itself that everyday practices are inventive.

A third general feature in the 'formality' that links together the multiplicity of 'pratiques' is the way each of them stands in opposition to an order that is monolithic, centred, strategic, universal, timeless, and spatial. In the case of walking this order is manifested by the planned city, the 'ville-concept', already in serious decline, and subject to the critiques of Henri Lefebvre and others. In the sphere of speaking, what is opposed is 'the scriptural economy'—a view of writing as an institution predicated, firstly, on the act of separation that determines an 'exteriority', a 'reste' (remainder); and, secondly, on an authority typified by the regulation and subjection of bodies. Where reading is concerned, 'la pratique liseuse' (I, 248) opposes the ideology of the book as a source of truth, consecrated information, and literal, universal meaning. In each case, of course, the 'pratique' does not exist outside what it opposes but works within it, through the way in which the dominant order is used and appropriated.

'Marches dans la ville' in the section of *L'Invention du quotidien* devoted to 'Pratiques d'espaces' (Spatial Practices)—echoing Perec's *Espèces d'espaces* (Species of Spaces)—begins with the justly famous evocation of the 'panoptic' view of the New York streets from the top of the World Trade Centre. For Certeau this vista, where the streets are a grid and humans like ants, manifests a disembodied, voyeuristic vantage point, where dominance over the visual field creates a fiction of knowledge and control—a 'Ville-concept' (I, 144). Certeau contrasts this with the level of the ordinary practitioners of the city in the streets down below. Here there is no overall view. Images of blindness, invisibility, physicality, and opacity predominate: 'Echappant aux totalisations imaginaires de l'oeil, il y a une étrangeté du quotidien qui ne fait pas surface' (Escaping the eye's imaginary totalizations, the everyday has a certain strangeness that does not surface) (I, 142). If the movements of subjects criss-crossing the city make up an urban 'text' (cf. Lefebvre's 'social text'), the multiple story composed of their 'écritures avançantes et croisées' (moving, intersecting writings) (I, 141) has no author, reader or spectator. The strangeness of the *quotidien* stems from the obscure interweaving of daily routines that always fall outside prevailing representations.

Yet the users of the city, in their daily circulation, create a second, meta-phorical city within the first. For Certeau this comes about in two distinct but complementary ways. The first relates to the paradigm of enunciation. If there is a 'parler des pas perdus' (chatter of idle footsteps) it is not because walking creates an order. The phrase 'pas perdus' (echoing André Breton's surrealist title *Les Pas perdus*) registers the random, incalculable steps of the walker.[14] What makes them into a speech or chorus is the fact of mobility itself: Certeau privileges the physicality of walking, seeing it as the key to 'un style d'appré-hension tactile et d'appropriation kinésique' (a style of tactile apprehension and kinaesthetic appropriation) (I, 147). It is through the motions of bodies, and by virtue of the 'scrambling' of established itineraries and landmarks that the city is appropriated. There is no need for the deliberate injection of the aleatory—the 'comportment lyrique' (lyrical stance) of the Surrealists, or the 'dérive' of the Situationists. For Certeau, well aware of these precedents, the operations of walking are in themselves 'multiformes, résistantes, rusées et têtues' (multiform, resistant, tricky, and stubborn) (I, 146).[15] The analogy with utterance is developed with brio, under the heading 'Énonciations piétonnières' (Pedestrian Speech Acts), and Certeau here acknowledges a debt to Roland Barthes's seminal 1967 essay 'Sémiologie et urbanisme' (Semi-ology and Urbanism).[16] Going a stage further, and benefiting from recent work on urban itineraries by Jean-François Augoyard,[17] Certeau reinforces the linguistic parallelism by suggesting that the appropriation of space through motion favours two particular rhetorical figures, synecdoche and asyndeton. This reintroduces the motif of style—that it is the style or manner of an action that makes it 'operative'. The existence of such 'rhétoriques cheminatoires' (walking rhetorics) points to the idea that walking engenders a 'métamorphose stylistique de l'espace' (stylistic metamorphosis of space) (I, 154).[18]

In addition to the act of motion and the parallel with enunciation there is another way in which circulation in urban space is creative or 'opératoire'. This overlaps with another facet of utterance: the way the unfolding of discourse (I, 155) is laced with incompleteness—on two counts. First, because it involves a relation between *these* words, being uttered now, and other words

---

[14] Cf. Eric Hazan, *L'Invention de Paris: Il n'y a pas de pas perdus* (Paris: Seuil, 2003).

[15] On walking see Rebecca Solnit, *Wanderlust: A History of Walking* (London: Verso, 2001).

[16] See Ch. 5.

[17] See Jean-François Augoyard, *Pas à pas. Essai sur le cheminement quotidien en milieu urbain.* (Paris: Seuil, 1979).

[18] Cf. Jean-Christophe Bailly on 'la grammaire générative des jambes', *La Ville à l'œuvre* (Paris: Éditions Jacques Bertoin, 1992), 23–42, and the discussion of the essay genre in Ch. 1.

somewhere beyond them; and, second, a relation between a point of origin—the context within which utterance is initiated—and the 'non-lieu' (nowhere) it produces by virtue of the parameters (link to the present moment, to others, etc.), that make enunciation itself 'une manière de passer' (a way of passing by) (I, 155). The parallel in the realm of walking is a relationship, embodied in the way a walk progresses, between *here* and an absent place that in some way impinges on, gives direction to, the walker's steps. 'Marcher, c'est manquer de lieu. C'est le procès indéfini d'être absent et en quête d'un propre'. (To walk is to lack a place. It is the indefinite process of being absent and in search of something of one's own) (I, 155). Certeau develops this idea in connection with the role of proper names in the city, and the 'semantic tropisms' they generate (see Chapter 9 below).

In Certeau's analysis speech confirms the overall 'formalité' of everyday practices by enshrining the act of enunciation and by standing in opposition to writing. But speaking is also explicitly seen to harbour other aspects of the paradigm, for example the lack of its own 'place', and a relationship with the body. Having provided a thorough survey of 'the scriptural economy', Certeau looks at speech not under the aspect of conversation but, more radically, in terms of the return of repressed orality in the field dominated by 'systèmes scripturaires' (scriptural systems) (I, 196). Voice is deemed to have been banished (Certeau points to an analogy with 'the people' in this context) under the regimen of writing. Speaking itself has been purged of the link to the singularity of the subject's body that constitutes orality for Certeau. Orality returns only as a trace or mark threaded in language, within a linguistic order that is predicated on the exclusion of this dimension. Voice has no place except in the discourse of the other where it figures as the uncontrolled dimension of enunciation that stems from the fact that '*La place d'où l'on parle est extérieure à l'entreprise scripturaire*' (*The place one speaks from is outside the scriptural enterprise*) (I, 231). Voice is therefore only present fragmentarily, as quotation from another space, that of the body and the other. Although pitched in radical form, and thus apparently remote from everyday contexts, Certeau's account of speaking is important because it introduces a field widely associated with the everyday—that of speech, the oral and the vernacular—into the framework of everyday 'ways of doing'.

Along with walking and speaking, reading constitutes a third practice derived from the paradigm of enunciation and which foregrounds an aspect of the overall model, in this case 'consumption' or 'use'. In criticizing the pervasive image of reading as a passive activity, Certeau opposes the notion of the cultural consumer as inert receptacle for material possessing the prestige of the written. Production is associated with writing, while reading is seen as pure reception: a child imbibing the catechism, or a TV viewer the latest bit of pap. A 'mission to inform' by the book accompanies educational methods that tend to deny any autonomy to the act of reading (I, 244). In fact, the suppression of the active side of reading has traditionally enabled powerful elites to preserve their status through the institution of literal meaning. For Certeau reading is not passive: 'Lire, c'est pérégriner dans un système imposé' (to read is to wander through an imposed system) (I, 245) whether it be that of the book or, by analogy, the constructed order of a city, a supermarket, or a TV show. Drawing on Barthes, Certeau shows how the reader can be a producer, and how readings can transform texts. The notion of meaning as a hidden treasure, secreted by a sovereign author, to which the reader only accedes through docile submission, is challenged by recognition of the reading process as involving the reciprocity of text and reader rather than any hierarchy. The institution of reading is founded on the fear of free and inventive readers. Citing a recent article by Georges Perec, on the 'socio-physiology' of reading,[19] Certeau observes that one only has to look at people reading to see that, even if intermittently spellbound, they are extremely active: skipping, day-dreaming, fantasizing, jumping to the end, moving or touching different parts of the body, and so forth. Attention to the reading process points to the hidden history of a practice whose characteristics match those of other everyday 'pratiques'. The active potential of reading does not need to be invented so much as recognized, generalized and mobilized. Citing the psychoanalyst Guy Rosolato, Certeau locates in reading an experience of ubiquity and 'impertinent' absence. Readers can inhabit and explore texts according to their own whims, and 'absent themselves' by creating secret spaces or 'carnavals' within its order. Readers are travellers and poachers. Yet the inventive dimension of reading does not reside in what the reader imposes on the text. To read is to expose oneself to difference and thus to be changed as well as to change. Like that of walking or speaking, the space of reading is a 'non-lieu': '(le lecteur) se déterritorialise, oscillant dans un non-lieu entre ce qu'il invente et ce qui l'altère' (the reader deterritorializes himself, oscillating in a nowhere between what he invents and what changes him) (I, 250). What makes reading a practice is the opportunity it provides for creative interaction.

---

[19] 'Lire: esquisse socio-physiologique' in Perec, *Penser/Classer*, 109–20.

NARRATIVITY, HISTORICITY, SUBJECTIVITY:
CERTEAU, WITTGENSTEIN, AND CAVELL

Beyond the paradigm of enunciation, Certeau's account of what renders everyday practices 'operative' is embedded in a wider context of spatial and temporal operations. Users introduce creative play into the rigidities of ordering systems and this results in a form of secondary production that is to a large extent ephemeral, by contrast with the aspiration to monolithic permanence characterizing the systems it subverts from within. But, as we saw in the context of *kairos* (the opportune moment), Certeau's understanding of everyday 'pratiques' also encapsulates a less ephemeral temporal order. In its way Certeau's everyday has its ancestor in the articulation of the transient and the eternal in Baudelairean modernity. At various points in *L'Invention du quotidien*, particularly in connection with narrative (récits), two principles of organization that attenuate the sheer contingency of everyday practices are perceptible.

The first is that of 'cutting across', the feature that earns practices the label 'traversières' (transverse). Certeau's account of narrative has already been outlined (Chapter 1) and requires little further comment. As we saw, he notes affinities between the tactical operations of practices and the practice of narrative (I, 121). This resides not in the objective, descriptive aspect of the novel, but in the performative activity of storytelling. Later, Certeau develops the idea that a story or narration is an 'everyday tactic' on the basis that a narrative structure is inherently a spatial trajectory (I, 170). Narrative performances link disparate spaces together, like metaphors. Stories build bridges and in so doing transgress limits. The 'formes microbiennes de la narration quotidienne' (the microbe-like forms of everyday narration) (I, 191) subvert established codes, displacing stable states in favour of 'trajectories' or narrative 'developments'.

The second feature is that of 'piling up', linked to the cumulative potential of successive 'turns' and 'détournements'. As we saw earlier, in the context of *kairos*, Certeau's discussions of practical memory posited a cumulative memory of 'occasions'. In the conclusion of *L'Invention du quotidien* Certeau develops the notion of the 'lieu pratiqué'—the *frequented* place that has therefore been a locus of practice, and hence, by dint of the layering (the imbricated strata of cumulative experience that practice brings), may constitute a bastion of resistance to the logic of functionalism

(I, 293). Thus planners prefer a *tabula rasa* to the 'illisibilités d'épaisseurs dans le même lieu' (illegibilities of the layered depths in a single place) (I, 293). Beneath the universalization of technology, and the fabrications of written authority, 'des lieux opaques et têtus permanent' (opaque and stubborn places remain) (I, 294). Where social spaces—neighbourhoods, *quartiers*, villages, apartment buildings—are made up of heterogeneous layers, they survive not just through inertia but because they are animated by constant shifts of balance: far from being immobile, such 'lieux' are marked by 'mouvements infinitésimaux, activités multiformes' (infinitesimal movements, multiform activities) that can be compared to the endless interactions of photons.

This idea connects with Certeau's remarks on the historicity of the everyday, and its implications for subjectivity: 'cette *historicité* quotidienne, indissociable de *l'existence* des sujets qui sont les acteurs et les auteurs d'opérations conjoncturelles' (this everyday *historicity*, which cannot be dissociated from the *existence* of the subjects who are the agents and authors of context-bound operations) (I, 39). This historicity, rooted in ways of doing things rather than discourses about them, and which cannot be dissociated from circumstances, is what is suppressed by knowledge, or simply preserved in the form of inert relics in museums. Yet it is intrinsic to being in the everyday, a point developed right at the outset of *L'Invention du quotidien* in a discussion of Wittgenstein and ordinary language.

For Certeau, the essence of Wittgenstein's later philosophy is the insight that the everyday world is determined by our ordinary uses of language: 'le langage [. . .] définit notre historicité [. . .] nous surplombe et enveloppe sous le mode de l'ordinaire' (language . . . defines our historicity . . . dominates and envelops us in the mode of the ordinary) (I, 25). We are immersed in the everyday and the ordinary, and despite the countless pretensions of philosophy and science there is no external vantage point from which to 'penser le quotidien' (think the everyday) (I, 26). Wittgenstein provides a radical critique of all attempts to find a place from which to articulate the everyday. 'Wittgenstein', argues Certeau, 'se tient dans le présent de son historicité [. . .] se reconnaît "pris" dans l'historicité linguistique *commune*' (stays in the present of his historicity . . . recognizes that he is caught in *common* linguistic historicity) (I, 25). We find here a criterion of historicity that is linked to a certain kind of universality, that of 'l'expérience commune' (communal experience) (I, 26), and to the coexistence, in the present, of the past layers that common usage has bestowed on language. A notion of the historicity of experience—and of the subject—can thus be seen to underpin the two complementary faces of Certeau's reflections on everyday practices: the focus on the singularity of the momentary 'hit' or 'coup', and the focus on the layers and stratifications accumulated by practical memory and communal existence.

At this point I want to sketch a brief parallel between Certeau's *quotidien* and the idea of the 'Ordinary' developed by the Wittgensteinian philosopher Stanley Cavell.[20] Both Certeau and Cavell underline the radicalism of Wittgenstein's attempts to bring words back from their metaphysical to their everyday use, making the ordinary a touchstone, and denying the authority of specialized or established knowledge. Certeau refers to the 'travail de débordement qu'opère l'insinuation de l'ordinaire en des champs scientifiques constitués' (the overspill effected by the insinuation of the ordinary into established scientific fields) (I, 18). The ordinary exceeds the bounds of all constituted fields of knowledge. Like Certeau's, Cavell's reading of Wittgenstein also brings out the subversive consequences of appealing to the ordinary. Having been marginalized by specialized knowledge, the ordinary looks strange: it returns as the odd, the uncanny. By asking 'what we say when', by making manifest the criteria governing the use of words, the appeal to ordinary language aligns us with the world and with others, and thus with that sense of lived totality which is at the heart of most attempts to 'think' the everyday (including those of Lefebvre and Certeau). Bringing words back to their everyday use is a way of declaring our commonness (acknowledging others and otherness) as opposed to our uniqueness. For Cavell, to reaffirm the ordinary is to confront the threat of scepticism: the denial (or partial denial) of the existence of others and of the world. Rooted in doubt, scepticism desires knowledge. But the desire to know fails to connect with the world as a place we inhabit; indeed the clamour for knowledge is destructive of this human world. Knowledge needs to be *disowned* if the world we live in—the ordinary, everyday world—is to be acknowledged. But acknowledgement—a key term in Cavell's account of the ordinary—is not an alternative to knowledge, or an alternative form of knowledge. It is, rather, a different alignment of and disposition towards knowledge, a different use.

It is therefore *modes of acknowledgement* that make up what Cavell calls the *practice* of the ordinary.[21] Even if Cavell often presents it in terms of turning

[20] See in particular Stanley Cavell, *In Quest of the Ordinary* (Chicago: Chicago University Press, 1988).

[21] Cavell, *In Quest of the Ordinary*, 8.

and conversion, acknowledging the everyday does not consist in the adoption of a new view or philosophy but is conceived as a task, a practice, the invention of 'an angle towards the world'.[22] We can posit spheres of acknowledgement: talking, where we accept to be subject to criteria; human relationships, which pose the challenge of accepting the separateness of others; interaction with our self, particularly with respect to our past; reading, seen as a form of writing, and writing, seen as a form of reading. But what is important—as in Certeau's insistence on the overall logic of practice—is the common element in these spheres, the connection to the ordinary that makes various modes part of one practice. As Cavell writes with regard to a passage from Thoreau: 'each calling . . . is isomorphic with every other. This is why building a house and hoeing and writing and reading are allegories and measures of one another'.[23]

What is achieved through acknowledgement? If 'the ordinary is always the subject of a quest' it is by the same token always 'the object of an inquest'; 'the everyday is what we cannot but aspire to, since it appears to us as lost to us'.[24] Wittgenstein's example shows that the practice of the ordinary is a process, a therapeutic path with no settled destination.

Wittgenstein's insight is that the ordinary has, and alone has, the power to move the ordinary, to leave the human habitat habitable, the same transfigured. The practice of the ordinary may be thought of as the overcoming of iteration or replication or imitation by repetition, of counting by recounting, of calling by recalling. It is the familiar invaded by another familiar.[25]

This passage illustrates the way many of Cavell's ideas hang together, and in so doing it points to a similar constellation or topography of concepts and concerns in Certeau. For both Certeau and Cavell, the ordinary or the everyday has been lost—overlaid or repudiated by 'savoirs constitués' (established forms of knowledge). Both thinkers are concerned with practices that unconceal the everyday, reactivating its power to make the world habitable ('l'habitable' and 'l'habitabilité' are terms used by Certeau as well as by Perec and Lefebvre). Like Cavell's, Certeau's account of 'pratiques du quotidien' revolves around a core structure common to a similar range of activities and spheres of practice—walking, organizing living space, reading, telling stories—seen as analogues of

[22] Stanley Cavell, *The Senses of Walden* (1981; expanded edn.; Chicago: Chicago University Press, 1992), 61.
[23] Ibid., 61–2.
[24] Id., *In Quest of the Ordinary*, 171.
[25] 'Wittgenstein as a philosopher of culture' in Stephen Mulhall (ed.), *The Cavell Reader* (Oxford: Blackwell, 1996), 232.

one another. *L'Invention du quotidien* seeks to construct an underlying logic of 'pratiques', and, as in Cavell, ordinary language provides the basic model. In Certeau's case Wittgensteinian procedures are replaced by ideas derived partly from them, namely theories of *énonciation*.

In Certeau, the efficacy of practice (Cavell's 'practice of the ordinary') does not stem from imitating or replicating what it opposes (that would be the way of strategy—meeting like with like: deploying similar resources of its own). But it does involve the repetition of a performance, in response to particular situations. In both thinkers this is linked to style. Certeau says that 'tactiques traversières' and 'manières de faire' can be seen as 'styles d'action' (I, 51) or 'modes d'emploi' (I, 51). At a first level they are regulated by the systems in which they are applied; but at a second level, by virtue of superimposition or stratification—creating another layer—such repetition redistributes the play of forces and changes the stakes.

What Cavell calls 'recounting' (as opposed to 'counting'—statistical calculation based on stability) has to do with a mode of identity that is given only in interaction, in narrative: what counts is what can be recounted or what is given through recounting. Cavell uses the word recounting because of its echoes of the procedures of ordinary language philosophy where 'what counts as', making a promise for example, solicits narrative performance, contextualization, stories. Recounting thus draws on recollection. This matches the way, in Certeau, the 'récit' is seen as a 'pratique traversière' linking heterogeneous spaces and contexts through 'un art de la relation' (I, 133), a metaphorical activity of superimposition. 'Le récit n'exprime pas une pratique. Il ne se contente pas de dire un mouvement. Il le fait' (a narration does not describe a practice, or content itself with expressing a motion. It performs it) (I, 123). Recounting is linked to memory, not as a stock of accumulated experience carrying weight, but as a field that can be activated in a given context, giving rise to a tactical intervention, effective because it seizes the moment.

The parallel with Cavell helps to pinpoint the level of the individual, and the model of the subject, which underlie Certeau's account of 'manières de faire'. The foregoing account of Certeau's text has deliberately sought to underline how, despite its deliberately polycentric and multidimensional qualities, a consistent logic of practices underpins the argument as it takes in a dazzling variety of fields. The metaphorical equivalences established between speaking, walking, reading, dwelling, and a host of other related activities, not only point to a general category of experience but suggest that this experience is itself inseparable from the energy of metaphor. This enables us to see that the operational logic at work in the activities of users, consumers, readers, or urban subjects, even if it is always contextualized and contingent, has wider implications. Certeau is sometimes seen as proffering small cheer to the powerless, offering them no more than the opportunity to play in the margins of the systems set in place by their masters. But Certeau's text suggests that the logic of systems creates an endless dialectic of mastery, submission, and creation that denies fixed positions. More than this, it points to a view of everyday subjects that credits them with the ability to impact on and alter the systems with which they engage. Through engagement with the other, the subject of everyday practices has the capacity to be involved in a process of appropriation or reappropriation that manifests a particular mode of identity, one predicated on the acceptance of difference, and on forgoing the imaginary self-sufficiency that plays into the hands of those agencies and media that pander to this vision of an autonomous self.

The 'ways of doing' whose logic Certeau seeks to establish articulate 'le mode individuel d'une réappropriation' (an individual mode of reappropriation) (I, 146), 'une manière d'être au monde' (a way of being in the world) (cf. Cavell's 'angle towards the world'), albeit one predicated on the recognition, incorporation, and recollection of otherness. In Certeau's logic of practice the subject's mobile, context-bound interaction with an established order creates room for manoeuvre, activates a mode of subjectivity structured by absence.[26] In the realm of place (for example the city) a glancing encounter activates memories and creates a stratified, sedimented space: 'Déjà en ce lieu palimpseste, la subjectivité s'articule sur l'absence qui la structure comme existence et la fait "être-là, *Dasein*" ' (In this place that is a palimpsest, subjectivity is already linked to the absence that structures it as existence and makes it 'be there, *Dasein*'). The mode of subjectivity that corresponds to Certeau's account of the subject of practice involves 'un être-là [qui] ne s'exerce qu'en pratiques de l'espace, c'est-à-dire en *manières de passer à l'autre*' (a being-there [that] exists only in spatial practices, in *ways of invoking the other*) (I, 163). Certeau's everyday practices all involve being displaced ('Marcher c'est manquer de lieu' (To walk is to lack a place) (I, 155)), and finding one's place in a reaction with and to the other: 'c'est parce qu'il perd sa place que l'individu naît comme *sujet*' (it is because he loses his place that the individual comes into being as a subject) (I, 204). In Certeau's everyday practices, as in Cavell's practice of the

[26] Cf. the rich account of wandering, digression, and subjectivity in Ross Chambers, *Loiterature* (Lincoln: University of Nebraska Press, 1999).

ordinary, we are dealing with what Certeau calls 'un rapport de soi à soi' (relation of oneself to oneself), a subject's self-relation and self-realization, in which the other is essential: 'un être-là [. . .] sans l'autre mais dans une relation nécessaire avec le disparu' (being-there . . . without the other but in a necessary relation to the absent) (I, 164).

Comparison with Cavell helps to underline the wider, positive implications of Certeau's ideas, and the place of the everyday subject's interactions with others (which will be crucial in some of the writers considered later on). The same is true, but in this case because of a marked contrast, when we compare *L'Invention du quotidien* with another version of the everyday that emerged in the same period: that of the sociologist Michel Maffesoli.

THE CONSERVATOIRE OF RITUAL: CERTEAU AND MAFFESOLI

Published a year before *L'Invention du quotidien*, in 1979, Michel Maffesoli's *La Conquête du présent: pour une sociologie de la vie quotidienne* can be seen as a rival manifesto. Arguing for a 'sociologie compréhensive' directed at the concrete, Maffesoli claimed that attention to the minutiae of everyday situations and practices could reveal the vital importance of the present. Drawing on such Anglo-Saxon exemplars as Richard Hoggart and Erving Goffman, Maffesoli's plea for the richness of the *quotidien*, led him, in 1982, to found a Centre d'Études sur l'Actuel et le Quotidien (CEAQ) at Université Paris V-Sorbonne. Maffesoli's own work in this field has been continued in such subsequent writings as *La Connaissance ordinaire* (1985), *Au creux des apparences: pour une éthique de l'esthétique* (1990) and *L'Instant éternel* (2000).

Maffesoli's central idea is that everyday social existence cannot be grasped by political or economic analysis. Essential to the 'socialité de base' manifested in the *quotidien* is the way it resists appropriation by abstract rationality, and manifests limited, *ad hoc* forms of creativity. In the first instance this can be understood as resistance to imposed forms of social structure and organization: 'socialité de base' involves the interplay of individual outlooks and desires rather than modes of association: as Maffesoli will argue at greater length in *Au creux des apparences* individualism is a 'facteur de socialité' rather than an impediment to it.[27] Maffesoli's profile of 'everyday man' has a number of

---

[27] Maffesoli's account of fashion was discussed in Ch. 5.

interrelated facets: cynicism towards all forms of imposed consensus or official discourse; fatalism and the acceptance of destiny; a tendency to live for the present, which can extend beyond daily pleasures and festivities to an 'enlightened' sensualism that may inspire inventiveness in dress or lifestyles (66).[28] In the everyday, the local is preferred to the national or global, spatial relationships are more important than temporal ones. With its imbricated spaces and interlocking pathways the everyday city becomes, as in Certeau, a paradigm. Yet whereas for Certeau (following Lefebvre) the 'lieu pratiqué' of the city street is a locus of accumulated, compacted histories, for Maffesoli, everyday space is associated with the attenuation or abolition of time: the *quotidien* is a haven from history.

This indicates further divergences. For Maffesoli, the sceptical detachment of everyday man is a kind of ironic dissidence, a capacity to see double, to live the present on more than one level. And this 'duplicité' reveals the existence of an irrational and 'mythic' dimension: the discontinuity engendered by the double focus, if it tears the fabric of organized experience, opens onto the continuity and density of non-linear, mythic time. Maffesoli argues that the fantastic and the cosmic are part of the *quotidien*, taking ritual behaviour as his prime concept. Repetition in daily life is linked to the acceptance of limits, and indeed tragedy, and the 'eternal return' of the present is associated with worldly melancholy. Timelessness is also seen as a facet of resistance, as is the acceptance of hierarchy, which is held to favour variety and the non-egalitarian play of differences. Maffesoli also links ritual to the cult of appearances and surfaces. The cynical detachment from past and future that stems from accepting to live in the everyday fosters masks (Nietzsche), simulacra (Baudrillard), and non-productive play (Caillois).

A clear sign of how Maffesoli differs from Certeau is his constant use of the word 'ruse'—but without reference to Detienne and Vernant. Whilst in Certeau rusing operates in the context of consumption and use, for Maffesoli 'la ruse' inheres in everyday attitudes and situations that can put up passive resistance to change (159). Certeau and Maffesoli both insist that the strength of the everyday resides in the concrete and the local: Maffesoli also often uses the word 'minuscule' —'minuscules détournements de la vie courante' (minuscule 'diversions' of everyday life (118))—and stresses the multidimensional character of social existence whose essence is in the 'petits faits de la vie

---

[28] References to Michel Maffesoli, *La Conquête du présent* (1979; Paris: Desclée de Brouwer, 1998) are incorporated in the text.

quotidienne' generally excluded from sociological analysis. The notion of accumulated layers ('sédimentation') and its connections with place and narrative are also present: 'la vie propre d'un lieu [...] est faite d'anecdotes et de faits divers, elle est cahotante et éclatée, elle a toute *l'obscurité* de la concrétude' (the life of a place . . . is made up of anecdotes and *faits divers*, it is untidy and fragmented, possessing all the obscurity of the concrete) (53). The sediment of the past nourishes the living (76), and past stories ('les micro-histoires individuelles', 121) provide a solid bastion against the dispersion of new experience. Spaces and stories can be repositories of a living past in the present. But Certeau and Maffesoli differ in their accounts of how these dormant layers can become active in everyday life. Maffesoli uses the term *kairos* once or twice, but where for Certeau ruse and resistance spring from seizing the opportune moment, the gap in the system, for Maffesoli *kairos* seems to designate a generalized view of the everyday as the sphere of 'l'occasion et les bonnes opportunités' (9, 132).

As its orientation towards myth, archetype, ritual, and the sacred attests, Maffesoli's vision of the *quotidien* is conservative, static and antihistorical. Throughout *La Conquête du présent* and subsequent works Maffesoli presents the *quotidien* as a bastion against visions of progress, whether they take the form of revolutionary action, social reform, or simply belief that improvement is possible. For Maffesoli, the essential conservatism of the everyday order of rituals is a defence against the illusion that change is possible, proof against the mendacity of 'les lendemains qui chantent' (Maffesoli twice pours scorn on this socialist expression). The everyday provides resistance not only to control but to the alleged false consciousness that spawns belief in the perfectibility of human life and institutions. The attitude of 'présentéisme' that Maffesoli anatomizes and commends resists not only the burden of the past but the lure of the future. The plural heterogeneity of the everyday is essentially synchronic. In Maffesoli, paying heed to the present provides access to un-changing atavisms that are held to be the roots of the human condition. Seeing the *quotidien* as a set of attitudes rather than 'pratiques', Maffesoli characterizes 'ruse' not in terms of inventive 'détournement', but of a *philosophia perennis* rooted in folk wisdom and based on acceptance of destiny and finitude. Where in Certeau 'faire avec' has active force, designating a way of working with what is imposed from without, in Maffesoli it means 'bearing, or putting up, with': 'ce bon peuple a toujours su composer ou ruser' (the wily common man has always known how to accommodate) (31). What Maffesoli seeks to identify is a set of ingrained attitudes, a mindset that is not context-bound but universal. In support of this, he cites Anglo-Saxon descriptive sociology—Goffman's 'presentation of self', and particularly Hoggart's 'culture du pauvre', with its accounts of working-class attitudes in post-war Britain: the stoic resignation of the socially deprived, expressed in immemorial, proverbial wisdom, sardonic humour, a conviction that things will always be the same, a lack of ambition that offers defence against inevitable failure. Here there is little sense of the temporal specificity of circumstances, the flux of time where, in Certeau's vision (as in fact in Hoggart's), opportunities exist, within the everyday, for the deadness of repetition to give way to something else, that is also part of the *quotidien.*

For Maffesoli, all belief in change or 'devoir-être' (53)—'what should be', perfectibility—is seen as injurious to the values for which the everyday is to be lauded. Certeau might concur if perfectibility were seen exclusively in terms of prescriptions imposed from without. But what of a 'devoir-être' stemming from within the individual or the community? Despite Certeau's insistence that everyday inventiveness is an *arte povera*, an *ad hoc* resourcefulness without resources, a practice with no inherent ideological content, the creative dimension of the *quotidien* in Certeau's vision, associated with such notions as habitability, believing, opening, does have aspects that transcend the specific occasions from which it springs and to which it remains linked. When and where it exists—because far from being ubiquitous, still less the universal prerogative of popular culture (a myth Certeau consistently opposed), it is erratic—'l'invention du quotidien' creates and opens.

There is then an activist, perfectionist, and future-oriented side to Certeau's theory of the everyday, even if the rejection of long-term strategy in favour of *ad hoc* tactics roots the future in the energies of the present. In Certeau, the longer term may be secreted within the short term, but the rejection of holistic, globalizing views or vectors does not confine us to the present order. Maffesoli and Certeau both see the present as a dense, polysemic, and multidimensional milieu that resists overall reduction to wholesale schemata. But for Certeau there is scope for resistance via local initiatives and ruses. The present is not a potential plenitude to be lived through intensely, in and for itself, but rather a context for *kairos*, a vantage point. For Maffesoli, the forum for the 'minuscules créations de la vie quotidienne' is 'le conservatoire du rituel' (the conservatoire of ritual) (116). The phrase is telling: a conservatoire maintains and transmits a tradition, nurturing timeless skills. To associate the creative performances of the everyday subject with the 'conservatoire du rituel' is therefore to give them a conservative rather than a truly creative role: their creativity merely preserves an immutable equilibrium. Creative play takes place only within the limits of an established order: 'rien n'est contesté [...] et pourtant, sans bruit, de minuscules détournements dans la vie courante [...] sont là comme autant de gages de la vitalité de la masse' (nothing is contested...yet, noiselessly, minuscule 'diversions' of everyday life...attest the vitality of the masses) (118). Where, in Certeau, play serves to contest and circumvent the given order, in Maffesoli it serves to make it liveable. Maffesoli is concerned with a 'natural', passive process of adaptation, where ruse loses all active sense: 'une ruse quasi organiquement liée à la vie [...] qui excuse en quelque sorte l'existence elle-même' (a ruse organically linked to life...that as it were compensates for existence itself) (163). The minor ruses of the everyday change nothing: they simply make up for what life lacks. Despite some superficial resemblances, Maffessoli's cynical hedonism is a far cry from Certeau's vision. What then of the view of the everyday that we find in the work of Certeau's fellow investigators, authors of the second volume of *L'Invention*?

L'INVENTION DU QUOTIDIEN II: HABITER, CUISINER

Even if the richness of thought, virtuosity of style, and brilliance of argument that make *L'Invention du quotidien I, Arts de faire* such a dazzling performance have tended to overshadow it, no account of Certeau's contribution to thinking about the everyday can ignore the 'second wing' of the project. Extending the range of 'pratiques quotidiennes' and developing their own methodologies, Pierre Mayol and Luce Giard underline the collective, project-based, dimension of *L'Invention du quotidien*. Working within parameters elaborated in close conjunction with Certeau, they provide valuable insights into the strengths and limitations of Certeau's approach and influence.

Outlining the genesis of the overall project Luce Giard recounts that after receiving the initial commission, Certeau sought the collaboration of a dozen young researchers in different domains (I, xvi). They were to form a 'groupe expérimental' that would select an area of Paris for close investigation. Each member would then identify a 'pratique observatrice et engagée' (a practice of engaged observation) (I, xvii) based on his or her area of interest or expertise. Certeau provided a bibliography comprising general works on culture (including Bourdieu and Hoggart) and on urban space. This initial project failed to materialize, and Certeau's seminar in anthropology at Université Paris VII became the principal forum for the intellectual elaboration of the project, while a smaller group, consisting of Certeau, Mayol, and Giard, met regularly to discuss ways of implementing the concrete dimension of Certeau's programme. Mayol, based in Lyon, chose to study the relationship between individuals and their local *quartier*, while Giard chose to concentrate on culinary practices because she felt that women's experience had not been adequately represented in the 'projet' (I, xxii).

As Giard stresses in the introduction to *L'Invention du quotidien II. Habiter, cuisiner*, the challenge for her and Mayol was to devise 'enquêtes' that would embody the spirit of *L'Invention du quotidien*—crucially, a sense of the creativity of 'pratiquants de l'ordinaire' (II, ii)—without cleaving to orthodox sociological, historical, or anthropological approaches:

Il fallait saisir sur le vif la multiplicité des pratiques, non pas les rêver [. . .] il y avait en jeu le désir d'un *retournement du regard* analytique [. . .] pour réussir, ce retournement devait s'appuyer sur une mise en évidence dans l'ordre des faits et sur une mise en intelligibilité dans l'ordre de la théorie (II, v).

(We had to capture 'live' the multiplicity of practices, not dream them up . . . A *reversal of the look* in analytical terms was at stake . . . to succeed, this reversal had to be based on 'making evident', in the domain of facts, and 'making comprehensible' in the realm of theory)

The phrase 'un *retournement du regard*', highlighted here and repeated twice later on, picks up a key element in Giard's presentation of her account of 'faire-la-cuisine', where it underlines the desire to pay heed to the ordinary concrete reality that is usually overlooked. Giard recounts vividly the way she and Mayol, in their discussions with Certeau, would elaborate hypotheses that soon proved unsustainable in practice; and conversely, she stresses the constant difficulty of generating wider perspectives from the concrete data provided by the practical side of their 'enquêtes' (II, vi). In different ways she and Mayol developed projects involving participant observation. Mayol's focuses on the working-class community in the Croix-Rousse area of Lyon and is based on interviews conducted with three generations of his own extended family. In Giard's case, evidence on culinary 'pratiques' is provided by interviews with a group of women conducted by another participant, Marie Ferrier. Just as prominent however is the role of Giard's own experience which gives her 'enquête' a significant autobiographical dimension. The difficulty for both Mayol and Giard was to observe accurately and critically practices which, far from being exotic, were a familiar part of their own world. The 'retournement du regard' meant not only diverting attention onto things that are often overlooked, but making sure the look was not deflected by the adoption of established analytical categories and procedures. And it meant determining the significance of the 'micro-différences' they identified (II, vii):

Fallait-il les imputer à la différence des générations, des traditions familiales, des habitudes locales, des groupes sociaux, des idéologies, des circonstances, relevaient-elles de l'occasion ou fallait-il les mettre au compte de régularités plus profondes, enfouies dans le secret des pratiques? (II, vii).
(Should they be imputed to differences between generations, family traditions, local habits, social groups, ideologies, circumstances, did they stem from particular occasions or were they attributable to deeper regularities, buried in the secrecy of practices?)

The way traditional modes of analysis deal with data is quickly to abandon the micro-level by reaching for the kinds of explanatory framework adumbrated here. But the challenge of what Certeau and Giard, in their 'Envoi' to *L'Invention du quotidien* (II, 353–62), call a 'science pratique du singulier' (practical science of the singular) is never to lose sight of the micro-level, and of the inherent or secret dimension of 'pratiques' themselves.

To assess the relative success or failure of Mayol and Giard in realizing this ambition I want to focus particularly on the balance of theory and practice in their 'enquêtes', and at the same time relate it to Certeau's own approach. Of course to some degree Mayol and Giard had the difficult task of applying empirically, in specific contexts, ideas elaborated by and with Certeau. Yet it is important to remember that Certeau's text did not in fact exist when they undertook their investigations. The first volume of *L'Invention*, elaborated in parallel with Giard's and Mayol's projects, is the outcome of Certeau's own 'enquêtes' into walking, speaking, and reading. But it is dominated by the articulation of an overall logic of everyday practices that deliberately avoids the application of method from the outside, and seeks instead to make 'l'interrogation théorique' a 'pratique traversière' in its own right. For Certeau, theory, as opposed to any 'science particulière', any particular discipline, avoids setting up limited criteria that isolate the phenomenon from the totality in which it is embedded. Theory, like Antigone, 'n'oublie pas [...] Elle se lie au pullulement de ce qui ne parle pas (pas encore?) et qui a, entre autres, la figure des pratiques "ordinaires". Elle est la mémoire de ce "reste"' (does not forget ... it is linked to the proliferation of what does not (yet?) speak and bears, among others, the countenance of 'ordinary' practices. It is the memory of this 'residue') (I, 98). Mayol and Giard do strive to avoid being bound by pre-existing disciplines but, as we shall see, they tend to fall into the trap of eclecticism—fusing disciplines, but remaining bound to them—that Certeau avoids.

Mayol's monograph, 'Habiter' (II, 15–185) focuses on how the inhabitants of an old silk-weaving suburb of Lyon relate to their *quartier*. Although based on first-hand knowledge, and interviews specially conducted by the author, Mayol sees his task as far more than anecdotal, historical, or descriptive. At the outset he formulates the challenge of studying 'des manières d'habiter la ville' as that of blending two existing methods—urban sociology and the 'analyse socio-ethnographique de la vie quotidienne'—into a single approach. Such a fusion of 'sciences particulières' is of course inconsistent with Certeau's views, but in any event the thrust of Mayol's overall argument seems to derive primarily from a combination of Certeau and Bourdieu. Mayol establishes that the *quartier* serves as a sort of halfway house between the private and the public spheres. From one angle it is an extension of the home—familiar spaces and faces, set routines, ease of access, etc.; from another angle, the *quartier* is an extension of the big city or the wider world: we do not possess it, others have equal rights there, public institutions govern it to some extent, and so on.

Echoing the ideas being developed concurrently by Certeau, Mayol stresses that in our own *quartier* we are involved in 'processus d'appropriation' (the word 'appropriation' with its echo of Lefebvre is recurrent). On our home turf we never lack 'lieux de repli'; we are on familiar territory that we have 'signed' and made our own in a variety of ways. We may have our 'own bench' or seat in the café, or regular banter with the grocer, and through this we 'privatize' public space.[29] Here, we usually go on foot, and our steps are often free of utilitarian constraints. This gratuitousness introduces a poetic quality into our relationship with space. Things have familiar, and often unofficial or 'pet' names, and street names may act as signatures ('on *est* de la rue Vercingetorix', II, 23).[30] All in all, the 'pratique du quartier' is tactical, not strategic (II, 24).

But having sketched out a framework on the basis of these Certeau-inspired motifs, Mayol develops his analysis in a way that is more redolent of Bourdieu than Certeau. By means of a central concept, 'la convenance', defined (II, 27) in a way that closely resembles Goffman's concept of 'self-presentation', he argues that the function of the *quartier* is to serve as an intermediate zone

---

[29] Cf. Sophie Calle, *L'Erouv de Jérusalem* (Arles: Actes Sud, 2002), referred to in Ch. 8.
[30] On street names see below, Ch. 9.

where we can adjust and adapt to the space of the other rather than subvert and customize it to our own ends. Mayol's analysis involves a kind of social calculus where the subject gauges (albeit unconsciously) the symbolic benefits to be derived from attunement to the demands of the social body. In this perspective appropriation is not subversive but adaptive. If tactical play uses the territory of the other it is the better to play the social game. For Mayol the 'efficacité sociale' and the 'fonction anthropologique' of the *quartier* lie in the social contract it offers:

La pratique du quartier—l'effort qu'elle requiert de ses usagers pour que l'équilibre ne soit pas rompu—repose tout entière sur cette hypothèse fondatrice: le quartier ne peut pas ne pas être bénéfique pour l'usager s'il joue le jeu social prévu par le contrat (II, 161).

(The practice of the *quartier*—the effort it demands of its users if the balance is to be maintained—rests entirely on this basic hypothesis: the *quartier* cannot but be beneficial to the user if he plays the social game implied in the contract).

This is much closer to Bourdieu's *La Distinction* than to *L'Invention du quotidien*. Mayol's ethnographic descriptions of the modalities of *convenance*—'le *texte* de la convenance, tel qu'un observateur attentif peut l'entendre dès qu'il se trouve affronté aux micro-événements de la vie quotidienne' (the *text* of convenance, as an attentive observer can understand it when confronted by the micro-events of everyday life) (II, 40)—consistently stress the benefits accrued by tactics geared to maintaining the right balance of distance and proximity to one's neighbours by gauging the correct doses of deference, jocularity, gossip, and so forth, to be administered on specific occasions. If the work of Erving Goffman and Richard Hoggart provides useful insights into the language and theatricality of everyday social interaction, Bourdieu's *Esquisse d'une théorie de la pratique* is cited for its account of what Bourdieu calls 'la grammaire demi-savante des pratiques que nous lègue le sens commun' (the grammar of half-known practices bequeathed to us by common sense) (II, 40). In this context Mayol endorses the insistence on the necessary ignorance of users with regard to social systems that Certeau will specifically repudiate in Bourdieu.

The most striking and perplexing feature of Mayol's work is the mixture of extremely detailed, concrete, down-to earth subject matter with consistently abstract and sometimes absurdly high-flown analytical rhetoric. He often falls into the trap of justifying the study of the banal by wrapping it up in arcane language. Since he is working out his own method, on the basis of ideas drawn from a variety of sources, Mayol does not adopt the idiom of any particular discipline. Nor does he forge a new vocabulary. But whilst remaining strongly eclectic Mayol sets great store by the need to dissect, classify, and scrutinize everyday activities with such precision that their true meaning—or function—can be elucidated.

In many respects Mayol's approach to his subject is reminiscent of the empathetic attention to the minutiae of working-class life to be found in a work such as Richard Hoggart's *The Uses of Literacy*.[31] Among the topics he treats in detail, always with an eye to rhythms and patterns, are networks of inter- and extra-familial relationships as reflected in visits to other people's houses and meals shared with others; shopping in all its aspects—economic, sociolinguistic, etc.; gender roles in such contexts as going to the market and using cafés; changes in the function of the *quartier* brought about by Saturday ceasing to be a workday, thus enabling men to visit the town centre and become full consumers. Yet there are few depictions of people going about these activities. This clearly stems from the desire to avoid static description and to emphasize the dynamic logic of practices:

Sous ses paquets d'habitudes banales, ce n'est pas l'apparence routinière qu'il faut viser, ce n'est pas l'allure paisible des jours qui suivent les jours au fil des semaines, des mois, des années; c'est le rythme produit dans le temps par cette famille, et par lequel elle pratique sa singularité (II, 77).

(Under these bunches of banal habits it is not routine appearances that must be pinpointed, nor the peaceful flow of days, months, and years; it is the temporal rhythm produced by this family, through which it performs its singularity)

But the constant drive to establish a multiple logic of social operations, to make everything meaningful, legible and functional, often leads to interpretative excess and overload. For example, in a self-indulgent chapter on the 'fonction philosophique' of bread and wine in the life of the *quartier*, a methodological mish-mash of Bachelard, Lévi-Strauss, and an already dated Structuralism, Mayol devotes inordinate space to a scheme offering customers a free bottle of wine after a certain number of purchases, and concludes:

le vin, jusque dans son ambivalence, est une dynamique socialisante. Il ouvre des itinéraires dans l'épaisseur du quartier, tisse un contrat implicite entre des partenaires factuels, les installe dans un système de don et de contre-don dont les signes articulent

---

[31] See Brian Rigby, *Popular Culture in France: A Study of Cultural Discourse* (London: Routledge, 1991); and ibid., *'Popular Culture' in France and England: The French Translation of Richard Hoggart's* The Uses of Literacy (Hull: The University of Hull Press, 1995).

l'un à l'autre l'espace privé de la vie familiale et l'espace public de l'environnement social' (II, 140).

(Wine, in its ambivalence, has a socializing dynamic. It opens routes in the density of the *quartier*, weaves an implicit contract between actual partners, installing them in a system of gift and counter-gift whose signs articulate the private space of the family with the public space of the social environment)

This is the kind of writing that gets studying the *quotidien* a bad name, and there is a great deal of it in 'Habiter'. Where in Certeau the *bricolage* of philosophy, poetry, theory, however abstract, often effectively defamiliarizes banality,[32] in Mayol the philosophical veneer often makes the phenomenon all but invisible. With Certeau defamiliarization ensues from the invention of a genuinely strange and original analytical style—itself a 'manière de faire'— while in Mayol the conventional critical languages of the period are often simply combined and applied to unfamiliar objects.[33]

In 'Faire-la-cuisine' Luce Giard, like Mayol, looks at one specific area of everyday 'pratique' and attempts to bring out the complexity and multiplicity of something apparently simple and straightforward: making a meal. Although she uses a wide range of sources and a plethora of approaches ranging across history, philosophy, anthropology, literature, and most of the human sciences, Giard does not seek to elaborate or adopt a particular methodology or approach. In the main she uses her sources (including Barthes, Braudel, Valéry, Tournier, etc.) to highlight the multiplicity of her object of study, and she writes very much in the spirit of Certeau's notion of the creativity of the *quotidien*. Even when dealing with the most humdrum aspects of her topic, Giard celebrates 'conduites alimentaires' (culinary tasks) as a 'lieu de bonheur, de plaisir, et d'invention' (locus of happiness, pleasure, and invention) (II, 214). At the same time Giard writes from a specific standpoint: that of gender and her own experience as a woman. This gives her intervention particular importance since it redresses a potentially damaging blind spot in Certeau's account of the everyday. However, Giard not only makes it clear that she does not believe in a feminine essence but she insists that the links between women and domestic activities are rooted in culture not nature.[34] Like Mayol, she

---

[32] Cf. Cavell on 'The Uncanniness of the Ordinary', in id., *In Quest of the Ordinary*, 153–80.

[33] In *Les Gens de peu* and other works Pierre Sansot is arguably more successful at describing everyday practices. Cf. Ch. 9.

[34] It is interesting to compare Giard's account of female domestic space with Marguerite Duras's *La Vie matérielle* (Paris: POL, 1987), a work which repays study in the context of writing on the

gives priority to the body as the locus of everyday 'pratique', although here it is not spatial or verbal experience but the domain of those 'techniques du corps' delineated in a pioneering article by Marcel Mauss, cited by Certeau, as well as Bourdieu (who derives some of his notion of 'habitus' from it) and, as we shall see, by Perec.[35] The gestures involved in preparing a meal are at the heart of 'Faire-la-cuisine', providing the focus for the aptly named 'Entrée' and the third of the text's four chapters. The rest of the text can in fact be seen as filling in the context and pursuing the multiple ramifications of a number of very basic and simple actions.

The autobiographical vein in which Giard's text begins is essential to its effect since it establishes a link between what writing the everyday means to Giard, and the particular 'pratique' she has chosen to investigate. She recounts how she had refused to take any interest in cookery as a child, strongly resisting her mother's lessons. But when years later as a student she had needed to fend for herself, she had found that by an 'étrange anamnèse' (strange anamnesis) (II, 216) her body remembered gestures and procedures the child had absorbed unconsciously during long hours in the kitchen. By the same token she was to discover that the secret pleasures of 'faire-la-cuisine' had in her case been invested in the activity of writing conceived as fundamentally anonymous and ephemeral. For Giard the reciprocity between these activities is linked to the anonymous transmission of experience by women through the generations. Through their interconnections, writing and cooking incarnate the pleasure of the *quotidien* which resides in an experience of anonymity and solidarity.

Giard sees her essay as a tribute to her female lineage, and to the 'peuple féminin des cuisines' (II, 219). In this she feels a strong affinity with Chantal Akerman whose 1975 film, *Jeanne Dielman 23 Quai du Commerce, 1080 Bruxelles*, focuses extensively on the domestic tasks carried out by the heroine played by Delphine Seyrig. Giard quotes approvingly some remarks made by Akerman in interviews (and later an interview with Seyrig), identifying strongly with the revalorization of gestures, the desire to 'montrer la juste valeur du quotidien féminin' (show the precise value of the feminine everyday) and the 'nécéssité de retourner à l'insignifiance pour rompre l'encerclement'

---

quotidien. Cf. Michael Sheringham, '"Là où se fait notre histoire...": L'autobiographique et la quotidienneté chez Marguerite Duras', in C. Rogers and R. Udris (eds.), *Marguerite Duras: Lectures Plurielles* (Amsterdam: Rodopi, 1998), 115–32.

[35] See Mauss, *Sociologie et anthropologie*, 365–88, cited by Certeau, *L'Invention du quotidien*, I, 303; and by Perec, *Penser/Classer*, 109, 145.

(need to return to the insignificant in order to break the spell). (II, 219). Seen in a proper light, 'pratiques ordinaires' can be sources of liberation rather than enslavement since they offer scope for inventiveness that is thwarted in other dimensions of the social order. However utilitarian in its function, any sequence of everyday gestures affords such a variety of techniques as to allow for the invention of an individual style. Equally, by a paradox with echoes in Barthes's thought, the act of attending to the 'insignifiant', of valorizing 'une activité supposée sans mystère ni grandeur' (an activity supposedly without mystery or grandeur), is seen as providing release from entrapment. This conversion of attention constitutes the 'retournement du regard' Giard was to stress in her introduction ten years later (II, 7).

Orality provides another link between the culinary and the linguistic. Giard insists on the importance of the interviews that were part of her project, but, like Mayol, who makes scarcely any direct reference to the interviews in his analysis, she seems uncertain as to their role in the final text, seeking to avoid the impression that the interviews were designed to supply scientific or statistical information. Giard stresses that the main function of the interviews was to hear women's voices: '*écouter des femmes parler*' (II, 226). The interviews attest a living communication with the reality of women's experience. Yet the refusal to cite these voices as authorities is consistent with a respect for the specificity—the alterity—of the oral. It can nevertheless look like sidelining, particularly since it accentuates the prominence of other testimonies which happen to take written (and frequently masculine) form. Where Mayol tends to supplant his interviewees by his own voice, Giard draws extensively on her reading and sprinkles her analysis with quotations from a wide range of material, often culled from publications which appeared during her work on the project (the interviews with Charlotte Akerman and Delphine Seyrig, in *Télérama*, *Le Monde*, and *Cahiers du cinéma* being a case in point). Many works of social history are cited, including childhood memoirs of country kitchens, so that the reader 'hears' la Mère Brazier, Pierre Bonte, Mary Barnes, and others.

Ultimately, Giard's valorization of culinary practices and the humble gestures at their root is effected through a counterpoint of her own personal affirmation (supported by a chorus of quoted voices), and the elaboration of a comprehensive network of historical, ethnographic, cultural, and medical material, rather than an overarching theoretical model. The longest chapter celebrates the rich diversity of the culinary field by looking at it successively from four perspectives. Firstly, a given recipe, diet, or technique is seen to be the product of such an extraordinary range of determinants as to make it a palimpsest of 'histoires empilées' (histories piled on top of one another) (II, 253). Then, synchronically, the cultural significance of ways of preparing and eating food is seen to be connected to a much wider field of social meaning, as Lévi-Strauss and Bourdieu have demonstrated in different ways. Here Bourdieu's recently published study of class and taste, *La Distinction*, is commended for its vivid accounts of 'manières de table', although the dogmatic character of Bourdieu's notion of social trajectory, and his indifference to gender, are noted. Giard then looks at the role of 'la cuisine' in cultural memory, touching on inherited patterns and rituals, prohibitions and taboos, links with childhood, and temporal rhythms. And lastly, she focuses on the body, notably the links between food and mothering, and the way eating mediates our relation to our own bodies, as demonstrated in the pathologies of various kinds of eating disorder as well as in the links between food and sex.

In a relatively small space Giard provides a remarkable distillation of culinary lore—extended in the final chapter on recipes, which provides further speculation on the links between cooking and language. Tightly organized, well illustrated, often speculative and always analytical rather than merely descriptive, her study is nevertheless a survey and a compilation. This is a strength, to the extent that it amply vindicates the key assertions about the complex multiplicity of the apparently banal; and it provides a perfect springboard for the core chapter on 'séquences de gestes' with its far-reaching reflections on the 'techniques du corps' which die as fashions and technologies change, and on the new gestures—for example, checking dates and e-numbers on supermarket packaging—that replace them. Yet the speculations and hypotheses that emerge from the accumulation and juxtaposition of data, however varied, tend for the most part to be uncontroversial and straightforward, and to inspire above all recognition and assent. If this is a considerable achievement in itself it invites some further reflections on the links with the overall project of *L'Invention du quotidien* and on the role of the other main aspect of 'Faire-la-cuisine'—Giard's personal stake and style.

In addition to the explicitly autobiographical elements, Giard's text is marked by a strikingly personal and often lyrical register involving the use of such figures as apostrophe, anaphora, and metaphor. The authorial voice articulates the cumulative cultural memory of generations of women whose experiences have gone unrecorded, and celebrates the everyday labour of the kitchen as a way of uniting 'matière et mémoire, vie et tendresse, instant présent et passé aboli, invention et nécessité, imagination et tradition, etc.'

(matter and memory, life and tenderness, present moment and vanished past, invention and necessity, imagination and tradition) (II, 313). By virtue of its very power and effectiveness, and also its strong feminist orientation, this lyrical and personal discourse raises significant questions with regard to the theoretical positioning of Giard's contribution to *L'Invention du quotidien*. Never explicitly cited, Certeau is everywhere and nowhere in 'Faire-la-cuisine'. Many passages make implicit reference to his ideas—for example, the account of tactical inventiveness in the chapter on gestures (II, 283), or the description of food protocols as 'le lieu d'empilement silencieux de toute une stratification d'ordres et de contraintes' (the locus of a silent piling up of a whole stratification of orders and constraints) (II, 261). But if Certeau's inspiration is obvious, Giard's analysis still invites one to ask whether the 'formalité' of 'la cuisine' as a 'pratique' is homologous with those at the core of Certeau's model. Does Giard—who cites the poignant reference to haddock and sausages in the last entry in Virginia Woolf's diary, just prior to her suicide—not show that the kitchen has been a haven for women, a 'room of one's own'? Is the context of necessity and constraint in which culinary gestures spring up comparable with the space of the other which for Certeau is the scene of *L'Invention du quotidien*? Is there 'braconnage' or *bricolage* of purloined or diverted resources when a woman, within the confines of her own private domestic space, prepares a meal for her loved ones? To be sure, what she does is enmeshed in the 'longue durée' of historical change and can be looked at from a host of angles, as Giard demonstrates so well. But the characteristic subversion and 'détournement', the encounter with an altering alterity, the rusing at the heart of Certeau's sense of the *quotidien* seem to be absent here. The subversive charge in Giard's vision lies in the focus on women: 'Gestes de femmes, voix de femmes qui rendent la terre habitable' (women's gestures, women's voices that make the earth inhabitable) (II, 213). In Giard what counts is the affirmation of solidarity with a living tradition incarnated by women. Of course there is potential provocation in the glorification of the seemingly menial. Like Certeau, Giard urges a change in our perception of what seems merely passive. But in placing the emphasis on this revaluation, on the 'retournement du regard', Giard makes the question of how we regard and value the activity as important as the way in which it is carried out. In the end it is the nature of our attention to the everyday that is paramount, a view that Certeau—and many other explorers of the everyday—would wholeheartedly endorse.

7

Georges Perec: Uncovering
the Infra-Ordinary

In Georges Perec the everyday finds its most resourceful explorer and indefatigable champion. The *quotidien* is a thread that runs throughout his career, cut short in 1982 when he was only 46, from *Les Choses* (1965), to *La Vie mode d'emploi* (1978) and his last projects. Absorbing, in the early 1960s, the lessons of Lefebvre and Barthes, who played a direct role in his apprenticeship; interacting, through the 1970s, with Certeau (an exact contemporary who also died young), Perec, through his remarkable inventiveness, wove together and extended ways of thinking about the everyday that would prosper in the years after his death.

In 1978 Perec likened his practice as a writer to a method of cultivation. The main 'fields' he ploughed represented 'quatre modes d'interrogation' (four types of enquiry). Interestingly, 'comment regarder le quotidien' (how to look at the everyday)—the 'sociological' field—is the first to be mentioned.[1] The others are the 'autobiographical', the 'ludic' (writing generated by fixed rules), and the 'romanesque'—a passion for narrative, for the kinds of story we devour at top speed. Each field reflected specific items in Perec's diverse output, but he insists that this eclecticism masked a set of interconnections: most of his works combine several of these 'interrogations', and in the end they all probably ask the same question. The implication is that fathoming the nature of that question (no doubt issuing from the terrible loss at the core of his life-history, his mother's death in Auschwitz) involves exploring the links between autobiography, rule-bound creativity, storytelling, and the investigation of everyday life.[2] If this interconnectedness means that the central

---

[1] Perec, *Penser/Classer*, 10.
[2] On Perec's life see David Bellos, *Georges Perec: a Life in Words* (London: Harvill, 1993), and Paulette Perec (ed.), *Portrait(s) de Georges Perec* (Paris: Bibliothèque nationale de France, 2001).

question Perec refers to cannot fully be articulated, it also fosters the fertile indirection and obliquity that are as central to his work as they were to his mentor Raymond Queneau. And it means that the strength and vitality of Perec's care for the *quotidien* stems from its indissoluble link to his personal, ethical, literary, and historical concerns.

Five years earlier, in February 1973, the fifth issue of *Cause commune*—a journal Perec had cofounded the year before with Jean Duvignaud, Paul Virilio, and others determined to undertake 'une investigation de la vie quotidienne à tous ses niveaux, dans ses replis ou cavernes généralement dédaignés ou refoulés' (an investigation of everyday life at every level, in its folds and caverns that are usually disdained or repressed)[3]—contained Perec's manifesto for a practical ethnosociology of the everyday. The daily newspapers, he says, only feature the spectacular or the abnormal. What of the rest?

Ce qui se passe vraiment, ce que nous vivons, le reste, tout le reste, où est-il? Ce qui se passe chaque jour et qui revient chaque jour, le banal, le quotidien, l'évident, le commun, l'ordinaire, l'infra-ordinaire, le bruit de fond, l'habituel, comment en rendre compte, comment l'interroger, comment le décrire?[4]

(What is really happening, what we live through, what happens every day and recurs every day: the banal, the quotidian, the obvious, the common, the ordinary, the infra-ordinary, the background noise, the habitual, how can we give some account of it, how can we interrogate and describe it?)

Perec's question marks—there is also one in the title of the piece: 'Approches de quoi?'—emphasize that the *quotidien* is indeed, as Blanchot had asserted in his commentary on Lefebvre, 'the most difficult thing to uncover'.[5] And yet, Perec insists, the *quotidien* is 'ce que nous sommes'. How can we grasp this missing dimension?

Comment parler de ces 'choses communes', comment les traquer plutôt, comment les débusquer, les arracher à la gangue dans laquelle elles restent engluées, comment leur donner un sens, une langue: qu'elles parlent enfin de ce qui est, de ce que nous sommes?[6]

(How can we speak of these 'common things', or rather how can we track them down, flush them out, prize them from the magma in which they are stuck, how can we give them a meaning, a language: so that they may at last speak of what is, of who we are?)

---

[3] *Cause commune*, 1 (1972), anonymous editorial.
[4] Georges Perec, *L'infra-ordinaire* (Paris: Seuil, 1990), 10–11.
[5] See Ch. 1, above.
[6] Perec, *L'Infra-ordinaire*, 11.

Turning to practical proposals, Perec advocates interrogating, inventorying, and describing—traditional modes of ethnographic enquiry, but here addressed to unfamiliar objects:

Interroger ce qui semble tellement aller de soi que nous en avons oublié l'origine [. . .]
Décrivez votre rue. Décrivez en une autre. Comparez.
Faites l'inventaire de vos poches, de votre sac. Interrogez vous sur la provenance, l'usage et le devenir de chacun des objets que vous en retirez.
Questionnez vos petites cuillers (12).

(Interrogate what seems so self-evident that we have forgotten where it came from . . .
Describe your street. Describe another. Compare.
Make a list of what's in your pockets, in your handbag. Ask yourself about the provenance, use, and likely future of each object you take out.
Question your teaspoons)

There are important affinities here—Surrealism, Mass Observation, the Situationists, OuLiPo—but this passage encapsulates the originality, quintessential tactics and tone of Perec's immensely influential approach to the everyday. The project or modest proposal, often apparently footling, is a stratagem designed to let something else be apprehended obliquely, something utterly serious and important: 'Peut-être s'agit-il de fonder enfin notre propre anthropologie, celle qui parlera de nous [. . .] Non plus l'exotique, mais l'endotique' (The point is perhaps to found at last our own anthropology, one that will speak about us . . . Not the exotic but the endotic) (12). A central portion of this chapter will therefore look at the practical experiments Perec devised in order to explore the *quotidien*. But to understand the coherence and continuity of Perec's multifaceted engagement with the everyday we need first to go back to his beginnings as a writer.

FABLES OF DISCONNECTION: *LES CHOSES* AND *UN HOMME QUI DORT*

In summer 1958, while Perec was doing his national service in South-West France, Jean Duvignaud introduced him to Henri Lefebvre. Then aged 22, and already determined to be a writer, Perec was invited to stay with Lefebvre at Navarrenx.[7] At this stage Lefebvre, again preoccupied with his theorization of the *quotidien*, had just written the long preface to the reprint of the 1947

---

[7] See Bellos, *Georges Perec*, 192 and *passim*.

Critique, and was now revising the foundations of the second (1961) volume. Perec found the philosopher stimulating, and Lefebvre, whilst not a close interlocutor, would play a tutelary role in Perec's development, encouraging him to read Marcel Mauss and in 1960 involving him in the activities of his newly founded 'Groupe d'études sur la vie quotidienne'.[8] Lefebvre wanted to investigate the rise of market research and Perec agreed to participate in a survey in Caen on which he reported to Lefebvre's group. This would have a significant impact on *Les Choses*. Between 1959 and 1963 Perec and a group of friends tried unsuccessfully to set up a journal, *La Ligne générale*, strongly coloured by the ideas of Lukács and Goldmann as well as Lefebvre. In 1962 Lefebvre linked the *Ligne générale* group to the Situationists, under the common umbrella of 'Revolutionary romanticism' (it is not clear whether he sought to bring the two groups together but it is likely that he discussed Debord's ideas with Perec).[9] In 1967 Lefebvre involved Perec in a colloquium on literature and the mass media held in Venice, while in 1972 Duvignaud and Perec invited Lefebvre to contribute to *Cause commune*.

Lefebvre's ideas may have contributed directly to Perec's focus on con-sumerist addiction to the dream worlds peddled by advertising images. Yet Perec's perspective on the *quotidien* was never narrowly tied to Lefebvre's. Through Duvignaud he also had an entrée into the *Arguments* group, where he encountered the sociologist Edgar Morin. The important experimental film, *Chronique d'un été*, on which Morin collaborated with the ethnographer Jean Rouch, based on interviews with Parisians in the summer of 1960, explicitly raised the question of 'le bonheur' which underlies *Les Choses*.[10] And *Arguments* also brought Perec into the orbit of Roland Barthes, whose contribution to Perec's vision of the everyday was to be equally important.

To Perec's chagrin, *Les Choses* was widely applauded as a brilliant exposition of sociological theories (including those of Morin and Lefebvre) rather than a literary work. Certainly in some of its detail and ethos, Perec's text reflects Lefebvre's *Critique*. But it differs markedly in that it lacks any desire to categorize or philosophize. Despite resembling a case study, *Les Choses* is composed with subtlety and stylistic virtuosity, plunging the reader into the imaginary universe of everyday subjects rather than viewing them exclusively from the outside. Yet if there is an important element of identification,[11] the

---

[8] Ibid., 234.

[9] Henri Lefebvre, *Introduction à la modernité* (Paris: Minuit, 1962), 337.

[10] See Introduction and Ch. 8 above.

[11] Underlined by Perec in interviews. See for example Georges Perec, *Entretiens et conférences*, ed. Dominique Bertelli and Mireille Ribière, I (Nantes: Joseph K, 2003), 51.

textual realization of this complicity between author and subject diverges from the autobiographical. In fact, to understand how Perec's first book initiates his particular slant towards the everyday we need already to identify the presence, beside the sociological and the autobiographical, of the two other fields he saw as his own, the ludic and the 'romanesque', and we also need to consider the role of Barthes, and the affinities between *Les Choses* and Perec's next two books.

A few months before he died Perec told an Italian journalist that his real mentor was Roland Barthes: 'Quand j'écrivais *Les Choses*, je suivais un de ses séminaires sur la rhétorique de la publicité. Et c'est de lui que me vient cette façon de regarder les choses un peu de biais, de manière oblique' (When I wrote *Things* I was attending his seminar on the rhetoric of advertising. And it's from him that I learnt a way of looking at things a bit sideways, obliquely) (II, 328). In 1963-4 Perec attended Barthes's seminar entitled 'Inventaire des systèmes de signification contemporains', and the following year a further seminar, 'Recherches sur la rhétorique' where Barthes sought to reinstate rhetoric as a dimension of literary work and cultural analysis. 'Rhétorique de l'image', where Barthes analysed an advertisement for Panzani pasta, displayed the convergence of rhetorical analysis and everyday life. In a talk on *Les Choses* at Warwick University in 1967 Perec surprised his audience by sidelining conventional sociological and moral concerns, insisting instead on a ludic, citational, and rhetorical approach to writing (I, 76–88). Rejecting both Sartrean 'littérature engagée' and the sterility of the 1950s *Nouveau Roman*, Perec positioned himself as a realist writer, but one for whom the relation between language and the world was far from straightforward. Alluding to Barthes's seminal account of *écriture* as 'la morale de la forme', Perec retraced his own path through Brecht (distantiation), Lukács (the role of irony in critical realism), and the discovery of rhetoric which, thanks to Barthes, he saw not as an impediment to the encounter with the real world but as a vehicle of distance, irony, and critique. Pointing to the multiplicity of ways of saying, rhetoric is at the heart of a practice which recognizes that literature produces new perceptions by working with the already written and the already felt. Perec's breakthrough came when he decided, firstly, to make his account of consumer society an exploration of the rhetoric of advertising and the fascination it engenders, rather than a realist slice of life or a clever plot; and, secondly, to take as stimuli four texts that fascinated him: Flaubert's *L'Éducation sentimentale*, Paul Nizan's *La Conspiration*, Robert Antelme's *L'Espèce humaine*, and Roland Barthes's analyses of contemporary 'myths' (in *Mytholo-*

gies) and imagery. These pre-texts contributed in different ways. The Nizan novel served as a case study of youthful delusion, and Antelme's meditation on his experiences in a Nazi camp offered a model of how literature could explore the incommensurable gap between language and experience. Flaubert and Barthes contributed more directly. *L'Éducation* not only furnished another study of youthful misprision and disillusion but also stylistic rhythms that are pastiched and directly quoted in *Les Choses* through borrowings that were to become one of Perec's trademarks. The Barthes intertext, constantly referred to in interviews, lay not only in the spirit of semiological critique but in the type of corpus Barthes had used, namely women's magazines. Perec claimed to have written *Les Choses* with a pile of magazines at his side, turning to *Mythologies* from time to time after a surfeit of *Madame Express!*[12]

If the territory of *Les Choses* is the sociology of consumer society, exploration does not proceed via traditional literary methods (Perec rejects psychology), or those of the social sciences. Perec's aim is not to create an image but to devise a mode of description that makes a certain level of reality visible, a project that is in some respects phenomenological but whose tactic is rhetorical. There is an autobiographical dimension here (Perec often indicated that he had portrayed himself and his friends), but it is impersonal rather than individual. It is not the self that writing explores and reveals but the linguistic and cultural community in which that self is a participant. There is also a ludic side: exposing oneself to the fashion features in *Madame Express*, and then writing out the fantasies this provokes, involves playing with what rhetoric calls commonplaces. For Perec, the value of rhetoric is precisely that it offers access to communal ground, to the everyday world in which we collectively live. Rhetorical play—on 'lieux communs' and 'lieux rhétoriques'—is a way of working through and towards this dimension of experience.[13]

When Perec gave his Warwick lecture he underlined the affinity between *Les Choses* and another, seemingly very disparate, work he had just completed. Where *Les Choses* manifested the rhetoric of fascination, *Un Homme qui dort*, the study of a withdrawal from life, communicated what he called 'les lieux rhétoriques de l'indifférence', the rhetoric of indifference (II, 84). Where Jérome and Sylvie sever themselves from appreciation of the ordinary and the everyday through their addiction to consumer products they cannot

---

[12] Ibid., II, 83.
[13] Perec claimed that in writing *Les Choses* he went from anger to thought to critical description, Ibid. II, 37. For a fascinating discussion of the links between rhetoric and common experience, see Anne Cauquelin, *L'Art du lien commun: du bon usage de la doxa* (Paris: Seuil, 1999).

afford, obsession with 'lifestyle' foreclosing recognition of life itself, the anonymous student of *Un Homme qui dort* deliberately experiments with passivity and inertia.

Perec conceived *Un Homme qui dort* as an antidote to *Les Choses*, exploring fantasies of self-denial rather than acquisitiveness, but once again weighing up possible stances toward the world of ordinary experience. As in many 'exist-ential' fictions (there are references to Sartre, Camus, Joyce, Lowry, and others) the text centres on a mental crisis that transforms a protagonist's relation to the world and to other people. A number of devices render his states of mind: instead of saying 'I' the nameless narrator describes his thoughts and actions through the second-person 'you', appearing to view himself from outside. As in *Les Choses*, absence of dialogue and paucity of salient incidents produce a hypnotic prose that highlights sequences and rhythms rather than specific moments. But the prevalence of intertextual echoes and rhetorical variations on basic themes maintains distance and militates against a psychological reading, drawing the reader to evaluate the narrator's relation to the world. At one level the protagonist's attitude of neutrality is itself a rhetorical and intertextual tactic. His discourse is an exhaustive inventory of the language of severance and non-participation: allowing rhetoric to dictate action involves abandoning the particular for the general. And the script of rhetoric is doubled by the script of literature: the protagonist plays out the 'I would prefer not to' of Melville's *Bartleby*, a key reference point for Perec,[14] as well as the quietist abdication from choice and volition advocated in the Kafka aphorism Perec chose as an epigraph, which begins: 'you do not need to leave your room . . . Do not even listen, simply wait . . .'[15] What is being tested in Perec's fiction is not so much a psycho-logical attitude as an approach to signification itself.

To some degree the experiment is viewed positively: radical deconditioning generates fresh perceptions. Abandoning his sociology studies, jettisoning his copy of Raymond Aron's *Dix-huit leçons sur la société industrielle* (amusingly, in Perec's film version of *Un Homme qui dort* this is replaced by Lefebvre's *La Vie quotidienne dans le monde moderne*), the narrator repudiates the ambitions, ideals, and material obsessions of modern society. A key passage identifies this as a refusal of both a functionalist ideology (where everything must serve a

[14] Herman Melville, 'Bartleby' in id., *Billy Budd and Other Tales* (New York: Signet Classics, 1961).

[15] Franz Kafka, *The Great Wall of China and Other Pieces*, ed. Edwin Muir (London: Martin Secker, 1933), 286.

goal) and self-images. The postulate ('propos') of indifference does not rest on hostility or ignorance; the aim is not to regress to some illusory innocence but to refrain from the kinds of choice that indicate taste, distinction, and 'personality'. By suspending his will, putting himself into neutral (setting himself to run on the empty generality of rhetoric), Perec's protagonist wants to stop his actions from having any kind of 'functionality' (a key word in this period, as we saw in Chapter 5), and thus (unlike the couple in *Les Choses* who crave the emblems of distinction) from 'representing' him in any particular way: 'ton habillement, ta nourriture, tes lectures ne parleront plus à ta place [...] Tu ne leur confieras plus l'épuisante, l'impossible, la mortelle tâche de te représenter' (your clothes, the food you eat, what you read will no longer speak in your place.... You will no longer give them the exhausting, impossible and deadly task of representing you).[16]

The benefits of extricating oneself from life's onward momentum are many: Perec's protagonist discovers the present, including his own embodied presence in the world of experience, as he lies in his tiny room listening to the sounds of the city outside or as he roams about noticing things he had previously overlooked. A surrealist register is explicitly invoked as he enjoys the spoils of *dérive*, perceiving patterns and laws in the micro-gestures of the street: two men with identical briefcases; series and variations of gait, colour, and purpose; a world of infinite difference. He enjoys the sufficiency of things in their simple *évidence*, encountering, within the highly specific, the open, generic quality that makes a thing a figure of itself. Accepting the given, dispensing with the restrictive aperture of one's personal tastes and ambitions, is seen as a way of simply apprehending what is.

Yet *Un Homme qui dort* also progressively mounts a critique of the protagonist's attitude, plotting a curve that passes through psychotic episodes before returning to normality. Making clever use of the 'tu' mode, which can simultaneously suggest both self-accusation and authorial judgement, Perec employs the traditional method of the French *récit* (from Gide to Camus and Duras), where an attitude to existence, in its own way valid and productive, ultimately founders on its own self-contradictions when taken too far. Thus indifference in *Un Homme qui dort* is seen to stem in part from misanthropy bred of solitude, depression, fear of others, and defensive pride. The protagonist's withdrawal reveals its pathogenic side as a protective strategy and an excuse for not really living. The freedom he achieves turns out to be another

---

[16] Georges Perec, *Romans et récits* (Paris: Livre de poche, 2002), 254.

kind of conditioning or enslavement. He has fallen into a trap: 'le piège: cette illusion dangereuse d'être—comment dire?—infranchissable' (the trap: the dangerous illusion of being—how should one say?—unreachable);[17] his mistake is to think that the new world he has discovered, beneath the patina of social conditioning, can legitimately be seen as a world without others. He needs to reflect on the terms of another Kafka aphorism that Perec saw as a vital, if paradoxical, corrective to the earlier one: 'In the struggle between yourself and the world, second the world'.[18] As the student becomes hyper-receptive to the tiniest of details, the world becomes frightening and incomprehensible.

Concerned with our participation in the everyday world, the rhythms of dailiness, *Les Choses* and *Un Homme qui dort*, are fables of disconnection. *Les Choses* suggests that we fail to engage with the everyday when we succumb to manufactured lifestyles, allowing these to dictate our patterns and responses; *Un Homme qui dort* exposes the equally illusory dream of total disengagement. It probes the temptation of reducing the everyday to a generic realm of pure experience, a perpetual present without retrospection or anticipation, a sphere of blissful repetition and minor variation, a scaled-down world of tiny gestures and anodyne things. The experiment is in some measure validated: the stance of neutrality and self-effacement does reveal what we seldom see, and does position the everyday as what is frequently lost to our ordinary perceptions. But, by associating this stance with a refusal to live, a recoil from the world, *Un Homme qui dort* also affirms the need to engage with others, and the ending suggests that the protagonist has understood the need to return to the world.

The affinity between Perec's first two major works, and the way each raises the central issue of the *quotidien*, can be linked to the dual role played by rhetoric. On one hand, through its association with style, variation, intensity, play, and performance, rather than fact and content, the 'generativity' of rhetoric—which does not deal in entities but in the diversity of expressive contexts and possibilities—articulates a dimension of experience where it is not what happens, but the way things happen, that counts; a view of the world as a stream of percepts in which we are immersed, where individual acts and impulses are secondary. On the other hand, by dealing with the virtual, the hypothetical, the infinitely variable, and the performative, rhetoric reveals the

17 Perec, *Romans et récits* , 282.

18 Kafka, ed. Muir, 266. Perec cites this aphorism in id., *Entretiens et conférences*, ed. Bertelli: and Ribière, I, 114, 170, 181.

unstable, evanescent status of this dimension, its lack of autonomy. In the context of exploring the everyday, rhetoric's duality exposes the everyday's own indeterminacy, the unstable space it occupies at the intersection of the mental and the physical, the social and the individual. As we shall see, rhetoric will continue to be at the centre of Perec's immensely varied approaches to the everyday.

THE MATRIX OF *LIEUX*

Between *Un Homme qui dort* and 'Approches de quoi?' (1973) the question of the *quotidien* in Perec's work was absorbed, firstly, by his 'contrainte'-based writings which resulted in an invitation to join the Oulipo group co-created by Raymond Queneau;[19] and, secondly, by autobiography. *Quel petit vélo au guidon chromé au fond de la cour* (1966) grew directly out of Barthes's seminar on rhetoric (the story proceeds by illustrating a string of rhetorical figures enumerated at the end). Soon dazzling his fellow Oulipians with his prowess at creating palindromes and lipograms Perec quickly delivered his tour de force, *La Disparition*, an entire novel without the letter 'e'.

Yet if 'contraintes' would remain central, he had by no means become an out-and-out Oulipian. In a letter to Maurice Nadeau, dated 7 July 1969, Perec claimed that since finishing *La Disparition* he had revived a number of projects (a word he keeps repeating) that preceded Oulipo, and reconfigured them as part of a vast autobiographical ensemble comprising four books to be written over twelve years. A project dropped from the four, 'Les *Lieux* de la trentaine', was to have been a narrative, like *Les Choses* and *Un Homme qui dort*, in which, working once more with the 'notion de "*Lieux* rhétoriques"', qui me vient de Barthes' (the notion of 'rhetorical places' I derive from Barthes),[20] Perec sought to render the states of feeling of a 30-year-old man. (Perec does not mention here 'Les Lieux d'une fugue', a short autobiographical narrative he had written in 1965 where the 'lieux' (places) are both literal and rhetorical.)[21] The four-part autobiographical ensemble Perec outlined to Nadeau comprised 'L'Arbre', based on the genealogies of his maternal, paternal, and

---

[19] Perec, *Portrait(s) de Georges Perec*, 70. On Oulipo see Warren Motte (ed.), *Oulipo: A Primer of Potential Literature* (Lincoln: University of Nebraska Press, 1986).
[20] Georges Perec, *Je suis né* (Paris: Seuil, 1989), 56.
[21] Ibid., 15–31.

adoptive families; 'Lieux ou j'ai dormi', inspired by Proust and Leiris; and an adventure novel, to be called 'W', based on a fantasy about a remote island community dominated by sport, that had arisen in the course of Perec's psychotherapy at the age of 13 (this would eventually be absorbed into the autobiography *W ou le souvenir d'enfance*, published in 1975). The fourth project (to be called *Lieux*) would last twelve years. Perec explains to Nadeau that he had chosen twelve locations in Paris, linked to memories and important moments in his life. His intention (initiated a few months earlier) was to describe two of these places each month; in one case he would write *in situ* and convey as neutrally as possible what was to be seen there, through the enumeration of shops, architectural features, or 'micro-events' (a fire-engine going past, a woman tying up her dog outside the charcuterie). The second text would be written away from the place itself (at home or in a café), and aimed to record memories of people and events connected to that particular location. In the course of each year all twelve places would be written about twice, once *in situ*, and once from memory, and in order to achieve the best distribution (avoiding, for example, visits to the same place in consecutive months) Perec asked a mathematician to provide a suitable algorithm (he would do the same later with *La Vie mode d'emploi*). When finished, each text is placed in an envelope, and sealed. By the end of twelve years Perec anticipated that he would have the contents of 288 envelopes to examine (some containing a few photographs and stray memorabilia such as bills and tickets), and would be in a position to witness a triple 'vieillissement' (ageing): the way the places had 'aged', the way his memories had evolved, and the way his manner of writing had changed. Rather than restore lost time the texts would provide concrete evidence that it had passed.

Philippe Lejeune has provided an invaluable account of how the *Lieux* project unfolded between 1969 and its abandonment, midway, in 1975, arguing that it was the matrix for Perec's radical innovations in autobiographical writing.[22] Here I propose to look at how *Lieux* also served as the matrix for Perec's invention of new ways of attending to the everyday. Having read the contents of the 133 envelopes that Perec did accumulate, Lejeune discovered that the twelve Parisian locations were not only linked to personal memories but in one case at least to the painful break-up of a recent love affair. Quoting a 'memory' text ('souvenir') Lejeune shows that one of the functions of *Lieux* was to 'justify' Perec's ongoing transactions with specific places and Paris in

---

[22] Philippe Lejeune, *Georges Perec: la mémoire et l'oblique* (Paris: POL, 1991), 141–209.

general. By pre-programming his visits, he secured opportunities to gauge the degree of preservation or obliteration of his memories. If this means that the role of the 'memory' texts is easily understandable, what of the texts (which Lejeune refers to as the 'réels' (reality texts)) produced under the constraint of simply noting what was visible on the occasion of Perec's visit? Granted that these are places where Perec or someone close to him had lived, what exactly is the role of a neutral list of the shops in the Passage Choiseul, or an inventory of the cafés and billboards of the Place d'Italie or the rue de l'Assomption?

Clearly, having a pretext for regularly visiting these outposts of one's past serves to keep them in mind, but the act of noting what one sees there in the present, and deliberately refraining from memory—the constraint of the 'reality texts'—is a different kind of exercise altogether. Lejeune accounts for this activity by arguing that it is essentially projective: the present is grafted on to the past by means of ritual exercises, with enumeration as a sort of incantation (163). This means that, according to Lejeune, the 'reality texts', whilst apparently resisting the discourse of memory, in fact function as a coded, indirect way of invoking it. Just as the twelve spaces are metonymic displacements of Perec's inner world of memory, so the 'reality texts', however apparently neutral, constitute a series of 'screen descriptions' (168). Perec's strategy pretends that the present is independent of the past whilst in fact drawing on and reinforcing a relationship of dependency.[23]

Yet the encoding of memory in the 'reality texts' is, at the very least, implicit. If it is there at all, it lies in the illocutionary force, the enunciation, rather than in what is actually stated. As Lejeunes's detailed account of the composition of an on-the-spot description indicates, there is a double displacement from the sphere of personal memory: firstly, because writing *in situ* involves a whole set of practical considerations and variables (writing on the move, or from one fixed point, or several points; writing telegraphically or in full sentences; elliptically or discursively; writing up or not); secondly, because the items recorded generally have no direct personal significance, and are in many cases ephemeral or contingent (182–9). This means that if we simply take a 'reality text' as it comes we can account for its features in a very different way. I want now to consider the evidence that Perec himself came to 'read' the process and products of the 'reality texts' in a different, non-autobiographical, way, and I want to relate this to his new-found concern with the everyday in the initial context of *Cause commune*.

---

[23] Later, discussing *Je me souviens*, Lejeune does concede that in the 'reality' texts of *Lieux* Perec was tuning in to the 'infra-ordinary' (238).

Perec had difficulty keeping to the schedule of *Lieux*, often catching up through a spate of activity in the 'wrong' months. The fifth year, 1973, was almost a total blank, which Perec 'excused' by saying he was preoccupied with the film version of *Un Homme qui dort*, where he made amends by including shots of most of his twelve 'lieux'! Since May 1971 Perec was again involved in psychoanalysis, this time with J.-B. Pontalis, who subsequently noted that Perec's principal concern was less with remembering the past than with not forgetting the present.[24] Since 1972 Perec had teamed up with Duvignaud and Virilio on the periodical *Cause commune* devoted to the *quotidien*. There are grounds, then, for linking the partial reorientation of Perec's work, around 1973, from time to space, from past to present, and from autobiography to the everyday, with his psychological as well as his intellectual evolution. Yet if we claim that his obsession with preservation shifted from the past to the present, we need to acknowledge that the object of his attention had nonetheless moved from the inside to the outside, or at least to a new conjunction of the two. Lejeune describes a ledger where, in January 1973, Perec inscribed the words: '1973. Choses communes. Espèces d'espaces.' (1973. Common things. Species of Spaces) (242). The first phrase alludes to a new method of remembering that Perec inaugurated on 21 January, namely the 'collective' memories gathered in *Je me souviens*. The second phrase records the title of the 'journal d'un usager de l'espace', commissioned by Virilio, that Perec composed over the next few months and published in 1974. *Espèces d'espaces* and *Je me souviens* both involve a fusion of personal and collective, past and present. If we see them as growing out of aspects of *Lieux* we could surmise that the notations of *Je me souviens* hive off the 'memories' channel, while *Espèces d'espaces* represents an extension of the concerns of the 'reality texts'. But rather than splitting *Lieux* into two, it seems rather that the new projects both involve a unification of what *Lieux* strove (ostensibly at least) to keep apart, namely the 'personal' and the 'impersonal'. Looked at another way, we can suggest that the 1973 projects ratified the centrality of a dimension—the everyday—whose nature is precisely to be at once individual and collective, anonymous and embodied, spatial and temporal.

Once Perec had abandoned *Lieux* in 1975, he opened some of the envelopes, and in 1977 began publishing some of the texts, selecting them exclu-

---

[24] On Perec's relationship with Pontalis see Claude Burgelin, *Les Parties de dominos chez Monsieur Lefevre: Perec avec Freud—Perec contra Freud* (Paris: Circé, 1996), 95–130.

sively from the 'reality texts' and not the 'memories'. As we shall see later, there are signs that, once he had exhumed them from *Lieux*, Perec viewed these texts differently. Just as tellingly, however, while the *Lieux* project was still ongoing, if in abeyance, Perec twice composed pieces that closely resembled the 'reality texts'. The first, which features in the chapter on the street in *Espèces d'espaces* in 1974, records observations made at the intersection of the Rue du Bac and the Boulevard Saint-Germain in May 1973. The text, headed 'Practical Exercises',[25] is largely metadiscursive, a development of the mock-didactic and hortatory style of the peroration in 'Approches de quoi?' (written at just this point). It opens with bare details of location, time, and weather, and consists of a string of imperatives and questions (observe the street, learn to see, read what's written, detect rhythms, identify what the shops are selling, scrutinize actions like parking a car), interspersed with a few, presumably 'live' observations of Perec's own, including references to a dog, of uncertain breed (Agfhan?, Saluki?), a Land Rover, and some beautiful women. Unlike the 'reality texts' in *Lieux* there is relatively little that conveys Perec's own activity of looking here; on the other hand, in a context that exactly matches the 'reality texts', Perec provides a detailed and multiple rationale for submitting the everyday to close scrutiny, a rationale very different from anything in *Lieux* even if that was the initial forum for the activity involved.

The second text is one of Perec's most famous writings, the fifty-page *Tentative d'épuisement d'un lieu parisien* (Attempt to Exhaust a Parisian Space) based on three days of 'fieldwork' in the Place Saint-Sulpice in October 1974. The *Tentative d'épuisement* is, I believe, Perec's single most significant contribution to the exploration of the *quotidien*, and I propose to examine it in some detail.

THREE DAYS IN THE PLACE SAINT-SULPICE

Context, Protocol, Metadiscourse

On each of three successive days, 18, 19, and 20 October 1974 (a Friday, Saturday, and Sunday—three different 'kinds' of day), Georges Perec spent a number of hours observing the Place Saint-Sulpice, in central Paris, from the vantage point of three cafés on different sides of the square, and on one occasion from a bench in the middle, beside the famous fountains. This was

---

[25] Georges Perec, *Espèces d'espaces* (Paris: Galilée, 1974), 70–4.

not one of the twelve *Lieux* sites, which Perec had been neglecting (his autobiographical energies perhaps channelled into the psychoanalysis with Pontalis, and the inventory/commentary on his childhood memories he had decided to add to the sporting fantasy of *W*). It is probable that the text he wrote in the course of his Saint-Sulpice watches was always destined for *Cause commune* where it appeared the following year (1975). The original publisher had reneged and the format was now a short, themed volume in the famous '10x18' series, entitled *Le Pourrissement des sociétés*. It included an anthology of editorials from the initial series, including Perec's 'Approches de quoi?', thus juxtaposing the *Tentative* (which I shall refer to as *TELP*) with a theoretical text on the investigation of the everyday.[26]

After a preamble, *TELP* consists of a written-up transcript of notes Perec took over the three days. He was most assiduous on Friday, when he stayed for eight and a quarter hours, between 10.30 a.m. and 6.45 p.m., putting in four stints that are covered in twenty-seven pages of the 1982 edition. On Saturday, when he was present for six and a quarter hours, the three stints are covered in thirteen pages. On Sunday, he was only there for two and a half hours (arriving at 11.30 a.m. and knocking off at 2.00 p.m.), and the two stints generate only eight pages. The preamble lists things that are obviously noteworthy in the Place Saint-Sulpice, and have therefore been endlessly described. Perec's aim is different: 'décrire le reste: ce que l'on ne note généralement pas, ce qui ne se remarque pas, ce qui n'a pas d'importance: ce qui se passe quand il ne se passe rien, sinon du temps, des gens, des voitures et des nuages' (to describe the rest: the things people don't generally note down, that are unremarkable, unimportant: what goes on when there is nothing going on, and nothing going by except time, people, cars, and clouds) (12). There are clear parallels with Lefebvre's 'résidu', Blanchot's 'rien ne se passe', and Barthes's fascination with the incident and the activity of notation. The emphasis on transience, and on the *way* things happen, chimes with *Lieux*. But if change is still to be identified in the interaction of a witnessing subject and an external environment, and in the media of their exchange (language and perception), the timescale is now moments, hours and days rather than months and years. And if the focus has shifted from the *longue durée* to the present, it has also moved from the autobiographical self to the everyday subjectivity of the participant in the act of observation. Enumeration and ruminative reflection based on present

---

[26] Perec, *Tentative d'épuisement d'un lienu parisien* was reissued in book form in 1982. References, incorporated in the text, are to this edition (Paris: Christian Bourgois, 1982).

perception, adumbrated in the imperatives of *Espèces d'espaces* and 'Approches de quoi?', are now seen as devices, in the context of exploration of the *quotidien*, for appropriating the space in which one lives, and of grasping experience as process. In a text he wrote the following year, about the provenance of the objects on his writing desk, Perec described the project as 'une manière de marquer mon espace, une approche un peu oblique de ma pratique quotidienne [. . .] un effort pour saisir quelque chose qui appartient à mon expérience, non pas au niveau de ses réflexions lointaines, mais au coeur de son émergence' (a way of marking out my space, a slightly oblique approach to my everyday activities . . . an attempt to grasp something that belongs to my own experience, not at the level of its distant reflections, but at the core of its ongoing emergence).[27] Ceaseless 'émergence' will be at the centre of *TELP* as Perec tries to register what is going on all around him.

As a way of flexing his muscles, Perec initially lists the fixed items in his visual field, such as words on signboards, conventional signs like P for Parking, bus numbers, types of stonework, piles of gravel and sand; and recurrent categories such as human beings, vehicles, pigeons, trees (confusingly, he also throws in one or two temporary items: a basset hound and a lettuce in a shopping basket). He then lists trajectories (principally those of the six bus routes traversing the Place) and colours, both of which will feature repeatedly in what follows. Classification then gives way to notation of what is current. More limbering up occurs at the start of the second stint where, having switched from the Tabac Saint-Sulpice to the Café de la Mairie, Perec focuses on body language, inspired no doubt by Marcel Mauss's famous account of 'Les techniques du corps' that Lefebvre had made him read, and which Perec quotes more than once in the 1970s.[28]

plusieurs dizaines, plusieurs centaines d'actions simultanées, de micro-événements dont chacun implique des postures, des actes-moteurs, des dépenses d'énergie spé-cifiques: [. . .] le mouvement des lèvres, les gestes, les mimiques expressives' (18–19).

(several dozen, several hundred simultaneous actions and micro-events, each involv-ing specific postures, motor acts, investments of energy . . . moving the lips, gestures, facial expressions)

Lower case and indentation suggest flux and profusion, and the list goes on to classify verbal exchanges, forms of locomotion, styles of carrying, degrees of

---

[27] Perec, *Penser/Classer*, 23.
[28] Ibid., 145.

animation (strolling, hurrying, hesitating, etc.), postures, before converging on individuals: three people waiting at the taxi rank.

If classification often precedes (and effectively generates) observation, priming and orientating attention, another rhythm is set up by the alternation of 'singulative' and 'iterative' (to borrow terms from Genette's narratology). Examples of the latter are remarks such as 'Des groupes par bouffées' (22), or the passage registering the paradox that the square gives the impression of being almost empty even when twenty or more people are in view (27), or the passage at the beginning of the third stint where, ensconced in a third café, the Fontaine Saint-Sulpice, Perec describes his return at lunchtime to the first establishment and enumerates things he observed, more idly, during his break (20).

The recording of things seen is also regularly punctuated by more abstract or metadiscursive reflections prompted by the experience he is undergoing. For example, in an italicized passage (26) Perec observes how limited his attention is: even when concentrating he fails to notice things a few metres away, such as cars parking. Then, he is moved to wonder what sets off the repeated movements of the pigeons since they seem not to be responding to external stimuli such as loud noises (26). Noting his tendency to register buses passing, Perec reflects that their relative regularity provides a rhythm that contrasts with the aleatory character of 'le reste': a car reversing or a man carrying a Monoprix bag (34). The way this perception focuses his attention more closely, so that he notes the extent to which the buses are full or empty, illustrates the two-way interaction between the work of attention and the generation of categories and oppositions. Language serves as a third element in this process. In this instance, identifying gradations of fullness leads to a profusion, and a rhythm, of linguistic variations—'plutôt vide/presque plein/presque vide/plein/peu [plein]/plutôt plein/absolument vide' [fairly empty/nearly full . . . etc.]—that also impact on modes of seeing (35).

The opening session on Saturday makes it clear that a particular heuristic tactic, the identification of how things differ from the day before, focuses the work of observation. Initially all looks much the same (even if the people and cars are not always identical), then a few differences are registered (for example, there are initially no pigeons). These include, significantly, differences in the character of Perec's attention, or his investment in what he sees. He remarks on a crane he had noticed but not mentioned before, and notes that although buses continue to go by he has lost interest in them (40). After half an hour or so, he feels driven to seek out differences, and composes a list: one café is closed, the other has changed its *plat du jour*, he has consumed a Vittel rather than a coffee, the bits of detritus by his table are different. Before lunch, Perec spends time on a sunny bench, in the midst of the pigeons, which he now observes more closely, while noting the different sound of the traffic (44). After a *saucisson* sandwich and a glass of red wine (Bourgueil) his observations again turn to difference. Between a motorist who parks effortlessly, and a learner who makes a hash of it, is the difference that in the latter case people watch, comment, and sometimes intervene? But if this makes the incident noticeable is it not because it is a disruption, a tear in the fabric? What of the fabric itself?: 'comment voir le tissu si ce sont seulement les déchirures qui le font apparaître: personne ne voit jamais passer les autobus, sauf s'il en attend un' (how do you see the fabric if it is only the tears that make it visible: no-one sees buses go by unless they're waiting for one) (46). The last point suggests that the decision to look itself introduces difference. Yet this is a risk Perec is clearly prepared to run, on the grounds, amply validated here, that even if experimental attention is apt to falsify, to be seduced by the exceptional, or to make things noteworthy by noting them, it is in no sense uniform and homogeneous. Indeed, Perec's enterprise makes attention an extraordinarily variegated and multiple medium. On Sunday differences are quite evident, especially since it is raining: few people about, no delivery vehicles, patisseries doing a good trade after mass.

Language and Enunciation

The abstract and metadiscursive discourse considered in the last section counterpoints the predominant mode of *TELP*, a paratactic litany of (mainly) one-off observations, relating to all phenomena in the observer's visual field:

Un homme passe: il tire une charette à bras, rouge.
Un 70 passe.
Un homme regarde la vitrine de Laffont
En face de 'La Demeure' une femme attend, debout près d'un banc (26)

(A man is going by: he is pulling a handcart, red.
A 70 goes past.
A man is looking in the window of Laffont's
Across from 'La Demeure' a woman is waiting, standing by a bench)

Perec's text is the residue of a singular *expérience* (in both senses of the word in French) from which it is hard to extrapolate since it does not produce what we usually think of as knowledge. But the text is the record, the log, of an experience, not its summation, and one of the most striking features of *TELP* is that to read this experiment in forms of attention is to reduplicate something of the experience itself.

Un 70 passe
Un 63 passe
Il est deux heures cinq.
Un 87 passe.
Des gens par paquets, toujours et encore
Un curé qui revient de voyage (il y a une étiquette de compagnie aérienne qui pend à sa sacoche).
Un enfant fait passer un modèle réduit de voiture sur la vitre du café (petit bruit)
Un homme s'arrête une seconde pour dire bonjour au gros chien du café, paisiblement étendu devant la porte
Un 86 passe
Un 63 passe (24–5)

(A 70 is going past
A 63 is going past
It's five past two.
An 87 is going past.
People in batches, ever and anon
A priest back from a journey (there is an airline label hanging from his bag).
A child is sliding a model car on the café window (faint noise)
A man stops for a moment to say hello to the café's large dog, peacefully lying by the door
An 86 is going past
A 63 is going past)

To 'take in' what we read here, we have to attune ourselves to the rhythm of things, to the way sameness is actually ever-changing, and we ourselves are part of this constant process. Perec is not interested in abstractions, except as stimuli to observation. His notations make us privy to the vicissitudes of his attention, relayed directly (as we shall see presently) by the intermittent record of bodily sensations and changes of mood, and indirectly by constant fluctuations in his way of articulating what is happening.

These fluctuations are partly stylistic. Given that the opposition between sameness and difference is central to Perec's experience, variations in his ways of registering phenomena—noting 'passe un 63' (35) as opposed to 'un 63 passe' (22) or 'Un 63' (22)—become significant. Is a thing the same if you name it differently? At the level of objective qualities a bus is a bus, but as an

event in space, time, and subjectivity, the arrival of the fifth bus is not the same
as the third, a bus that comes after ten minutes is not the same as one that
comes after three. What is the status, or medium, of such differences? Can they
be articulated? At first Perec's style seems flat and unmodulated: 'c'est ceci, c'est
cela, c'est tel', as Barthes puts it.[29] But just as Perec finds himself tuning in to
physical micro-events, so his reader become conscious of stylistic micro-
events: shifts of register, phrase structure, or sentence length which, in revealing the trace of *énonciation* in the *énoncé*, create a field of difference where all
had at first seemed the same.

As it happens, a close study of *énonciation* in *TELP* has been undertaken. In
her book on this long-neglected dimension of language, Catherine Kerbrat-
Orecchioni explores systematically, in the wake of Emile Benveniste's teaching, the marks of subjectivity in different forms of discourse. Benveniste
defined *énonciation* as the 'setting in motion' of language by the act of an
individual user,[30] and in Chapter 6 we saw how Michel de Certeau made
enunciation the paradigm of the 'arts de faire' he saw as the essence of the
everyday. Having surveyed the most evident ways in which messages bear the
trace of the individual subject's use, Kerbrat-Orecchioni uses Perec's text to
illustrate some of the more indirect manifestations of subjectivity in language.[31] Her choice is largely dictated by the assumption that *TELP* is 'un
texte à prétention purement descriptive' (a text that aims solely at description)
(135), and that even if Perec sees its impossibility his sole aim is to test the
limits of objectivity (149). Although this is highly misleading, not least
because it ignores the preamble of *TELP*, the results of the analysis are
revealing in that they demonstrate vividly the multiplicity of modes of
enunciation in Perec's text. Gently picking holes in what she takes to be his
desire to escape subjective forms of language, Kerbrat-Orecchioni stigmatizes
Perec's tendency constantly to go beyond the 'remit' of sticking to the narrowly
perceptual; in doing so she in fact pays homage to the way Perec rings endless
changes, as his words accompany, model, and interact with his perceptions.

Among indirect manifestations of subjectivity that make the enunciative
texture of *TELP* so lively, Kerbrat-Orecchioni identifies the provision of
negative information—such as the fact that a particular coachload of Japanese
tourists are *not* wearing headphones (49)—which is redundant (or illicit) in

[29] Barthes, *L'Empire des signes*, II, 804.
[30] See Benveniste, *Problèmes de linguistique générale, passim*.
[31] Kerbrat-Orecchioni, *L'Enonciation*, 144–62.

her perspective, but consistent with Perec's desire to articulate differences. She also discusses obvious features such as lists and taxonomies, or the sudden focus on phenomena such as the position of people's hands (16). She observes the use of questions and modal expressions ('seems', 'a bit like', 'sort of'), and of typifying discourse—a granny (31), a young father (59)—with its obvious (subjective) tendentiousness: how does Perec know she's a granny? (Perec concedes this point when he arbitrarily refers to the adults accompanying a rather miserable young girl as her kidnappers!) Kerbrat-Orecchioni notes the presence of self-irony, as in the comment that disposes once and for all with the fact that the traffic lights in the Place are obviously changing between red and green all the time: 'les feux passent au rouge (ça leur arrive souvent)' (the traffic lights change to red (they do this a lot)) (49). And she appreciates (though censures) his occasional use of vivid imagery and stylistic flourishes, including neologisms, alliteration, and a gratuitous pun ('des aubergines toniques') that fuses the slang term for female traffic wardens, based on the colour of their uniform, with the English 'gin and tonic'! Kerbrat-Orecchioni sees these 'excesses' as illustrating Perec's weariness at trying to maintain objectivity when in fact, as she concludes, no description is immune from subjective factors. But if we use Perec's own criterion—of trying to make the everyday visible, not as an objective reality but as something in which we participate— we can see the stylistic and enunciative richness of *TELP* as an indication of the sheer multiplicity of the channels with which we engage with the world. And if language stands exposed as the instigator as well as the interpreter of some of these ways of apprehending the world, so be it.

The constant variations that mark enunciation in *TELP* draw attention to a central feature of our everyday life, often unacknowledged, in part because we tend to polarize objectivity and subjectivity—namely, the fact that we are *immersed* in the *quotidien*, and that the endless stream of perception and utterance is the very stuff out of which the everyday (and ourselves as everyday subjects) is made. The brilliance of *TELP* as a verbal artefact lies in the fact that all the points we can make about its language turn out to be points about the matter that this act of enunciation seeks to address. And the way we discover more and more in the text, when we read it again, matches the way observing the everyday brings about a transmutation of attention, making visible some- thing that was, according to Perec, disguised by the narrowness of our habitual modes of seeing. Thus even a negative recognition—for example, the fact that we tend to notice the singular and easily nameable, such as the postman (31), a blind person (22), a man with a neck brace (46), at the expense of more featureless individuals (Perec asks at one point why two nuns are more interesting than other passers-by (46))—is as much an insight into everyday seeing as the progressive recognition of the rhythms that underlie seemingly random repetitions.

The Experiencing Subject

TELP makes us aware of the concrete presence of the experiencing subject. Although Perec's project makes him an anonymous recorder he does not disguise the process of his attention. It soon becomes clear that the ability to note at random what he sees is limited to short periods. The need to be drastically selective, given the profusion of simultaneous events, leads him to classify and analyse, diverting his attention along specific channels, away from any sense of a totality. As things surge up in his perceptual field, the work of attention and the work of expression generate categories (people stumbling (21), carrying things (50), reading as they walk (52)), and binary oppositions: calm/agitated, slow/rapid, full/empty, regular/aleatory, predictable/unpredictable, and many more. Some categorizations relate to the way things happen: one-off events, items in a potential series, elements in an unfolding narrative (on Friday a funeral takes place in Saint-Sulpice, and on Saturday a christening and a wedding). But such oppositions are far from stable, and Perec gives them no particular value except as contingent products of the process of attention itself, as it oscillates, like a pupil dilating and contracting, between a passive 'attention flottante' (Freud's 'floating attention')[32] and a more active interrogation of experience.

The alternation of passivity and activity is also perceptible in the indications of Perec's self-consciousness and the awareness of his physical and mental state. Towards the end of the first session, self-awareness is marked by a reference to the impression that he has just been photographed from a passing tourist coach. This is followed by an entry: 'Accalmie (lassitude?)' (Lull (lassitude?)) (18) that draws attention to the interaction of viewer and viewed by suggesting that the diminution of activity in the square may be an illusion fostered by the depletion of the observer's energies! He then takes his first break, and when he resumes it is noticeable that he is back on form, although now in the guise of a social anthropologist or ethnomethodologist (this is the passage on micro-events (18)).

[32] On this see Jean Laplanche and Jean-Bertrand Pontalis, *Vocabulaire de la psychanalyse* (1967; Paris: PUF, 1997), 38–40, and Ch. 9, below.

Committed to avoiding particular forms of knowledge and understanding, Perec also has to cede his customary roles and identity. He has to deprofessionalize and anonymize himself, and shift amongst a variety of discourses and subject positions, for instance those of urban planner, fashion correspondent, or detective. The terms of his experiment cut him off from normality, so that when he recognizes people he knows, they are outside the frame. At one point he thinks he spots Jean Duvignaud, and later he does see Paul Virilio (one suspects that these two colleagues from *Cause commune* came to cheer him on, rather than, as Kerbrat-Orrechioni suggests,[33] Perec hallucinating them!). On the first of two sightings of Geneviève Serreau (24) he reports gesticulating to attract her attention, as if he needed reassurance of his identity at this point. The uncanny dislocation of self-identity leads him to see a part of himself in other people; for example, a man afflicted with a nervous tic who holds his cigarette in the particular way Perec thought was *his* trademark. Another tendency, particularly towards the end of the day, is to see doubles: one man looks like Peter Sellers, another like the film critic Michel Mohrt (spotted four times). Suspended in the currents of the everyday, Perec is no one in particular: as passers-by come to look unreal (38), as the light changes, he is just a man writing, reflected in the plate glass of a café. In the last session of the first day an entry simply reads 'Fantomatismes' (Fantomatisms)(36).

As was suggested earlier, among the traces of the subject visible in the enunciation in *TELP* are signs of Perec's evolving physical and mental state. He makes the equation when, as he notes encroaching darkness, cold, and tiredness, he writes: 'Lassitude des yeux. Lassitude des mots.' (Tired eyes. Tired words.) (30). In fact his periods of lassitude feature bursts of flippancy that seem reinvigorating. Reviving his flagging spirits by playing with different ways of naming things, he seeks relief from mechanical enumeration by recourse, variously, to sociological jargon: 'Afflux de foules humaines ou voiturières.' (Bunching of human or vehicular groups.)(41); colloquialism: 'Tout plein de gens, tout plein de bagnoles' (Loads of people, loads of motors) (50); intertextual wordplay 'passent des ouatures' (39) (a wink at Queneau); and, most spectacularly, pure fantasy: 'Précédé de 91 motards, le mikado passe dans une rolls-royce vert-pomme' (Preceded by 91 police motorcycles, the Mikado goes past in an apple-green Rolls-Royce) (48). In fact apple-green crops up frequently with reference to Citroën 2CVs, and on one occasion, seemingly, to a specific 2CV, suggesting a private allusion (also hinted at by

---

[33] Kerbrat-Orecchioni, *L'Énonciation*, 161.

one reference to 'le souvenir qui flotte dans ce café'(the memory that is floating in this café, 46)).

TELP does not offer the contents of a disembodied consciousness but the record of an experiment in observing and noting the everyday. We never lose sight of the flesh-and-blood participant, whose physical needs and sensations are conveyed through details of what he eats and drinks (interestingly 1974 was the year when, as another experiment, Perec kept a scrupulous record of everything he ate and drank),[34] the atmospheric conditions, the changes of light and temperature. Perec is certainly sardonic when he asks whether drinking a Vittel rather than a coffee affects the way he sees the Place, but this does point to a crucial feature of his project, that its aim is not to arrive at abstract knowledge but to explore the lived experience of an individual subject seeking to apprehend a dimension of his own reality that is inseparable from his participation in the wider currents of the everyday.

DISPERSAL: PLACES AND MEMORIES

The Saint-Sulpice experiment seems initially to have revived Perec's commitment to *Lieux*, and he visited several of the locations in late 1974 and early 1975. Yet by mid 1975 he had abandoned the project. Over the course of *Lieux*, and in the light of *TELP*, the rationale for scrutinizing Parisian space had shifted decisively, away from personal towards cultural memory—enshrined in the present—and the experience of the everyday. Evidence for this includes the publication of material from *Lieux* after its abandonment; other projects devised by Perec at this time; and the energies he devoted, between 1973 and 1977, to another enterprise, *Je me souviens*.

When, in the aftermath of his aborted twelve-year project Perec opened some of the envelopes and started publishing texts from *Lieux*, he played down the memory dimension, choosing only sequences of 'reality texts', and associating them with his Saint-Sulpice experiment by using the collective label 'Tentative de description de quelques lieux parisiens'. The sense of generic reclassification, or declassification, was compounded by the places of publication and the choice of titles. The first batch, relating to the rue de la Gaieté, were published as 'Guettées'—which punningly transmuted the street name

---

[34] See 'Tentative d'inventaire des aliments liquides et solides...' in Perec, *L'Infra-ordinaire*, 97–106.

into a neologism based on 'guetter' (to look out)—in the February-March 1977 number of a literary magazine, *Les Lettres nouvelles*. A few months later, the texts on the Place d'Italie appeared as 'Vues d'Italie' in Pontalis's *Nouvelle revue de psychanalyse* (autumn 1977), while 'La rue Vilin', observations made on the street where Perec was born, came out in the communist newspaper *L'Humanité* (11 November 1977). Subsequently, 'Allées et venues rue de l'Assomption' (where Perec was brought up after the war) was published in *L'Arc* in 1979 and 'Stations Mabillon' in *Action poétique* in 1980. This generic plasticity, reflected in the different types of reader associated with these various periodicals, suggests that, outside the frame of *Lieux*, these texts could now be read in a variety of ways—literary, psychoanalytical, political, poetic. This testifies to the richness of *Lieux* itself, which, though possessing a provisional rationale, was nonetheless open-ended, its significance to be determined only after completion, the acts carried out in the meantime not in themselves pre-judging the outcome. And it confirms that, outside the confines of *Lieux*, these texts could take on new meanings.

This is further corroborated by a note Perec appended to 'Vues d'Italie' (and, with slight variants, to 'Stations Mabillon') where he gives a brief account of the bare ground rules of *Lieux*, making no reference to a purpose, stressing only that he had tried, on the 'reality' sorties, to write, 'simplement, platement' (simply, flatly).[35] He goes on to say that the experiment had stopped in 1975, but that other forms of description, in different media, had taken over from it, citing the poems of *La Clôture* (1976), accompanied by photographs of the rue Vilin; the eponymous film he had based in 1976 on his story 'Les Lieux d'une fugue', filming around the Place Franklin-Roosevelt; and a forthcoming 'radiophonic' project based on the Carrefour Mabillon.

By framing the offcuts from *Lieux* as a series of 'Tentatives de description', and by linking them to ongoing investigations of Parisian spaces in other media, Perec invites us to read these texts as experiments in talking about 'le reste', in perceiving a dimension of the city that relates to everyday experience. Isolating the 'reality texts' demonstrates how *Lieux* generated *TELP*, which then provided a way of interpreting some of *Lieux*'s products. As forerunners of *TELP*, the 'reality texts' of *Lieux* took Perec out into the streets, notebook in hand, even if the metadiscursive and meditative aspects of the Saint-Sulpice days are undeveloped; in the light of *TELP*, and as an extension of it, the 'reality texts', along with the projects in poetry, film, and radio, come to be

[35] Georges Perec, 'Vues d'Italie', *Nouvelle revue de psychanalyse* (Autumn 1977), 26.

seen as embodying the radical and multidimensional spirit of everyday enquiry that Perec established so substantially in October 1974. Close readings
of the 'reality texts' and the other projects, illustrating this analysis, would
obviously require considerable space and much repetition, and I will therefore
confine myself to some brief observations on Perec's radio experiment before
considering *Je me souviens*.

For his *Tentative de description de choses vues au Carrefour Mabillon le 19 mai
1978* Perec spent six hours non-stop sitting in a radio car at this busy
intersection (which had of course been one of the *Lieux*) describing through
a microphone what he saw through the windscreen. The material was then
edited down to make a programme lasting two hours, which was broadcast
and later released on a CD. For the broadcast version Perec drew up a classified
inventory of the 457 two-wheeled vehicles, 1435 cars, 407 lorries, 574 vans,
580 taxis, etc. that he had enumerated, along with a select list of some of the
many hundreds of people, including five bald men, a woman eating chocolate,
forty-three people carrying parcels, etc. The twelve lists he produced were then
read out by an actor at various points during the programme, covering but not
obliterating Perec's voice, which could still be heard underneath. Even edited
and embellished, *Carrefour Mabillon* makes strong demands on the listener.
But as we attune ourselves to Perec's observations, two things are noticeable.
Firstly, the rhythmical variations between activity (too much to report) and
quiescence (not much going on), and between a range of other factors
(colours, types of passer-by, makes of vehicle); secondly, the rhythms of Perec's
attention as reflected in his voice. As we listen, the alternation between
lassitude and animation, interest and indifference, enthusiasm and strain,
are made perceptible with extraordinary physical immediacy in the timbre,
tone, and force (or weakness) of Perec's vocal performance. Here, as in *TELP*,
the capacity to grasp something of the everyday is seen to be the prerogative of
an incarnate being, not a disembodied mind.

Je me souviens

The same is true of the acts of memory recorded in *Je me souviens*.[36] Subtitled
Les Choses communes I, *Je me souviens* is a list of 480 numbered statements
beginning with the same ritual formula, 'Je me souviens', followed by a
conjunction, usually *que* (that), or *de* (of), linking it to a remembered thing,

---

[36] Georges Perec, *Je me souviens* (1978; Paris: Hachette, 1999).

person, or event. Perec's model was the American poet Joe Brainard, but where the sentences in Brainard's *I Remember* cumulatively constructed an autobiography, Perec's aim was to home in on a type of memory that would be common to many people living in the same society in a given period.[37] The things he strove to extract from his memory bank were deliberately not private (even if Perec's own encounter with them, from which their place in his memory of course derived, was personal); rather, they consisted in 'des petits morceaux de quotidien' (little pieces of everydayness):[38] everyday things that everyone of the same age group (in this case in their teens just after World War Two) would have shared and then forgotten, since these lacked the historical importance that would have kept them in 'live' memory.

As we noted earlier, Perec inscribed the title *Je me souviens* alongside that of *Espèces d'espaces* in the same ledger in January 1973, and it appears that by June he had already accumulated 155 entries. In this period both *Lieux* and *W* (Perec's autobiography) were suspended, while he pursued, on the one hand, his analysis with Pontalis (collecting and publishing his dreams in *La Boutique obscure* (1974)) and on the other his collaboration with Duvignaud and Virilio (who commissioned *Espèces d'espaces*) in the exploration of the everyday. Lejeune rightly suggests that *Je me souviens* fuses together the two separate strands of *Lieux* (personal memories and impersonal descriptions) to produce a short circuit, a spark that illuminates an 'intermediate' level of lived experience that is not entirely private or entirely communal, but both at once.[39] But where Lejeune wants, primarily, to interpret this practice in terms of Perec's negotiations with his own memory, I wish to incorporate it into the progressive unfolding of his negotiations with the everyday. In particular I wish to underline how Perec, like Michel de Certeau, comes to identify a particular dimension of memory as a component of the *quotidien*.

Je me souviens de l'époque où il était rarissime de voir des pantalons sans revers.

Je me souviens que Maurice Chevalier avait une propriété à Marnes la Coquette.

Je me souviens de l'expédition du *Kon-Tiki*.

Je me souviens de Christine Keeler et de l'affaire Profumo.

Je me souviens de la myxomatose.[40]

---

[37] On the link between Perec and Brainard see Lejeune, *Georges Perec: la mémoire et l'oblique*, 239–42.

[38] Perec, *Je me souviens*, back cover.

[39] Lejeune, *Georges Perec: la mémoire et l'oblique*, 238.

[40] Perec, *Je me souviens*, 75, 74, 41, 97, 93.

(I remember the time when it was incredibly rare to see trousers without turn-ups.

I remember that Maurice Chevalier had a country home at Marnes la Coquette.

I remember the *Kon-Tiki* expedition.

I remember Christine Keeler and the Profumo scandal.

I remember myxomatosis.)

What sort of memory is this? The issue is not what categories of remembered things are involved (fashions, celebrity gossip, slogans, TV shows) but the *modus operandi* of the specific memory process itself. In *L'Invention du quotidien* Certeau identified a type of practical memory that was not a store or receptacle but a faculty bred of, and operative in, specific momentary occasions. Similarly, in an important interview with Franck Venaille, Perec described the kind of memory he was dealing with in *Je me souviens* as a 'pratique assez curieuse' (a curious practice) that both characterizes and reveals the everyday. He insists on the physical and performative aspects of 'Le travail de la mémoire' (The Work of Memory): memories of this kind are not simply there, waiting to be recorded, they need to be provoked, rescued from oblivion, and Perec's account of the way this is done emphasizes the difficult experience of parturition involved.[41]

Why is it so difficult? Perec suggests that memories which truly render the 'tissu du quotidien' (fabric of the everyday)—a body of experience that transcends our own individuality and yet invokes a commonality of experience—cannot be purely personal (what happened to me) or factual (what happened to be the case). If the types of memory involved are too insignificant for the autobiographer or the social historian it is because their aura is inversely proportionate to their narrative or historical significance. If in Certeau's 'régime d'altération répondante' (system of responsive alteration) it is the 'flash of the occasion' that is criterial,[42] in Perec what counts is the 'flash' of shared recognition, the certainty that what I remember would find an echo in your memory too (the flash can be compared to the Barthesian 'c'est ça, c'est tel').[43] Perec describes *Je me souviens* as a 'sympathetic' text, which sends out an 'appel de mémoire' (memory appeal) to its readers (who are provided with blank pages to play the game themselves). But the connection with the other, with the 'tissu du quotidien', is established in the process that gives birth to an

41 Perec, 'Le Travail de la mémoire', *Je suis né*, 81–94.
42 Certeau, *L'Invention du quotidien*, I, 132. See Ch. 6, above.
43 Barthes, *L'Empire des signes, Œuvres complètes*, II, 804.

item worth entering in the ledger. Perec likens the process to meditation. At his desk, or in a train, he would try to summon up one of these memories.

En général il y avait entre un quart d'heure et trois quarts d'heure de flottement, de recherche complètement vague avant qu'un des souvenirs ne surgisse. [...] cela se passe dans cette espèce d'état de suspension! Je crois qu'il y a quelque chose de l'ordre de la méditation, une volonté de faire le vide [...] au moment où l'on sort le souvenir on a vraiment l'impression de l'arracher d'un lieu où il était pour toujours.[44]

(As a rule you had from a quarter to three quarters of an hour of floating, totally vague searching, before one of the memories suddenly appeared. [...] it happens in a kind of suspended state! It's a bit like meditation, a desire to wipe out everything [...] when you bring out the memory you really feel you're dredging it up from somewhere it could have lain forever)

Perec insists that the level of lived experience ('le vécu') he is dealing with in this process belongs neither to personal psychology (autobiography) nor to ideology (doxa):

c'est un vécu qui ne sera jamais appréhendé par [...] la conscience, le sentiment, l'idée, l'élaboration idéologique! Il n'y a jamais de psychologie. C'est un vécu à ras de terre, ce qu'on appelait à *Cause commune* le bruit de fond. C'est le vécu, saisi au niveau du milieu dans lequel le corps se déplace, les gestes qu'il fait, toute la quotidienneté liée aux vêtements, à la nourriture, au voyage, à l'emploi du temps, à l'exploration de l'espace[45]

(it's experience that eludes [...] consciousness, feelings, thought, and ideology! There is never any psychology. It's ground-level experience, at *Cause Commune* we called it the background noise. It's experience grasped at the level of the setting in which your body moves, the gestures it makes, all the everydayness connected with your clothes, with food, with travelling, with your daily routine, with the exploration of your space)

The type of memory here is both physical—it relates to 'experience grasped at the level of the setting in which your body moves'—and neutral: just as Gertrude Stein wrote 'Everybody's Autobiography', so these are 'everybody's memories'. Perec's criterion is that such memories should transcend the purely individual and autobiographical whilst remaining rooted in affective experience. Hence his insistence on the state of suspension and the process of gestation that this kind of rememoration involved. A very embodied mental

---

[44] 'Le Travail de la mémoire', *Je suis né*, 88–9.
[45] Ibid., 89. For a fascinating guide to the memory territory of *Je me souviens*, see Roland Brasseur, *Je me souviens de Je me souviens* (Paris: Le Castor Astral, 1998).

process—like Zen meditation—gives access to a space that is not psychological (personal history) or ideological (official narrative), but lived experience at the level of the body, gestures, the exploration of personal and communal space.

The concerns of Perec's various 'Tentatives', and their links with *Je me souviens*, are evident in a talk he gave in July 1981.[46] A few months earlier, an architectural research group had invited him to participate in the close study of a small section of the 11th Arondissement in Paris. Perec had visited the area only once before, and having agreed to produce a description found the task extremely difficult. On the first of his two sorties the place seemed impenetrable: he didn't 'see' anything. Putting this down to the usual 'cécité' (blindness) that stops us seeing the everyday, and to his unfamiliarity with the area, he did some homework in old guidebooks and gazetteers. But the notes from his second visit—which he read to his audience—confirm the absence of any rapport. The place was meaningless for him. What was missing? Perec recalled two impulses he had felt as he tried to note down what he saw (enumerating shop signs, cafés and micro-events in his usual manner): first a need to find some object on the ground that he could take away with him; and second a desire to stray beyond the designated sector when he saw a poster in the distance with the name Tamara, which reminded him of an old girlfriend. Reflecting on this, Perec realized that for the place to 'speak to him', he needed to feel a sense of connection and participation. He needed the bearings ('repères') that familiar itineraries or memories would have provided. If he was to see, and describe what he was seeing, the place had to be, or become, part of his 'own' map of Paris.

But we need to distinguish here between personal and private. The personal link Perec lacks is in fact the element he would have in common with others present in that space. In other words it is communal rather than private. The sense of an external command rather than a personal desire is one of the factors that inhibits Perec from participating, since it tends to make his link a purely private one. The problem is one of 'relation à un espace'. In the context of his usual 'Tentatives', Perec observes, 'ce que je note c'est quelque chose qui se relie d'une manière ou d'une autre, même si c'est extrêmement lointain, à notre propre histoire' (what I note down is something linked one way or another,

---

[46] 'Á propos de la description', Georges Perec, *Entretiens et conférences*, ed. Bertelli and Ribière, II, 227–43.

even if very distantly, to our own history).[47] In this context, our (Perec writes 'notre' not 'ma') 'own' history actually consists in the range of things that link people to the spaces they inhabit or traverse, elements that together make up what Perec refers to as the 'code' through which we read a given space. But the code he lacked in this instance did not consist solely of private memories. Evocative street names, such as two—sadly just outside the designated frame!—commemorating Roussel and Verne, among his favourite writers, would have provided conduits for imaginary participation.[48] He also mentions the 'false acacia' tree that he has recently learnt to identify: the presence of this variety in the neighbourhood would have helped him acclimatize. Seeing space involves accumulated knowledge, anticipation, recognition, and also invention, since for Perec—as *La Vie mode d'emploi* demonstrates—invention starts from 'quelque chose qui vous est donné' (something given).[49] And describing (as the extension of a process of seeing that is fundamentally relational) depends on a certain kind of memory: 'devant un paysage, devant une émotion, devant une sensation: ça ne se met à exister que lorsque cela a été mémorisé. Mémorisé, cela veut dire non pas dans ma mémoire, mais dans une trace' (a landscape, an emotion, or a sensation only begin to exist for me when memorized. But here memorized does not mean in my memory, but in a trace).[50] What sort of memory is this? It seems to be above all (as in *Je me souviens*) an active 'trace-making' notation that marks a connection established in the present, but that belongs nonetheless to the field of memory because it draws on previous recognitions, conscious or unconscious, that are only personal because they pertain to such and such a person, but in all other senses have nothing particularly personal about them. Perec's multiple 'Tentatives', with the Saint-Sulpice text as their centrepiece, represent a vital contribution to the theory and practice of the *quotidien* because, in their complex genesis, growing out of *Lieux* and diversifying into different media, as well as in their dissemination in the practices of later explorers, they establish a set of connections between active participation in the everyday spatial environment and the ongoing processes of alienation and appropriation, separation and belonging, individual and collective experience, recollection and anticipation, which make up a key level of human existence.

---

[47] 'À propos de la description', Georges Perec, *Entretiens et conférences*, ed. Bertelli and Ribière, II, 234.

[48] On street names see Ch. 9, below.

[49] 'À propos de la description' Perec, *Entretiens et conférences*, ed. Bertelli and Ribière, II, 234.

[50] Ibid., 235–6.

THE EVERYDAY IN *LA VIE MODE D'EMPLOI*

At first sight, *La Vie mode d'emploi* highlights two of Perec's 'fields' at the expense of the others. The love of 'contraintes', generating text from strict ground rules, and the 'romanesque', emulating Verne and Dumas in writing a 'page-turner' to be devoured at top speed, seem to predominate over autobiography and the investigation of everydayness. Yet this soon proves deceptive. Perec enjoyed outlining the astonishing variety of 'contraintes' he used in composing his 'romans' (in the plural), insisting that they made the work a 'machine à raconter des histoires' (storytelling machine).[51] But in the same interviews he claimed that *La Vie mode d'emploi* also furthered his interest in 'l'infra-ordinaire, le contraire de l'événement' (the infra-ordinary, the opposite of events)[52] and in a descriptive, non-analytical 'sociologie de la quotidienneté'.[53] Often lacking any narrative function, the work's innumerable inventories and descriptions were, Perec observed, part and parcel of his attempt to 'repérer dans la quotidienneté quelque chose qui la révèle' (locate in the everyday something that reveals it).[54] As a project, Perec's *magnum opus* dated back to the late 1960s and it embraces, encyclopedically, the evolution of his concerns. However, the bulk of the composition took place in 1975–8, along with much of *Je me souviens*, following the termination of his analysis with Pontalis and the dispersal of *Lieux* into a multifaceted exploration of the everyday. In what follows I will consider the place of *La Vie mode d'emploi* in the wider context of Perec's account of the *quotidien*.

The two features liable to strike any reader are lists of material things, and life stories that often end tragically. The basic unit of the text (which purports to describe the contents of a Parisian apartment block at a precise moment on a June evening in 1975) is the room, and we expect to be told what it contains and to whom it belongs. Broadly speaking, the answer to the latter question derives from three initial 'contraintes'. Firstly, inspired partly by a Saul Steinberg drawing, Perec decided that the fictional 11 rue Simon-Crubellier would be viewed as if the façade had been removed, exposing a total of ninety-nine rooms (or other spaces) on the front elevation. Secondly, the order in which

---

[51] Perec, *Entretiens et conférences*, ed. Bertelli and Ribière, I, 244.
[52] Ibid., 234.
[53] Ibid., 253.
[54] Ibid., II, 56.

each space (including stairs, cellars, etc.) was described would be determined by an algorithm that applied the knight's move in chess to a 100-square grid. This meant that Perec had initially to plan out the distribution of rooms, deciding, for example, on the number of large family apartments, 'chambres de bonnes', elaborate conversions, and so forth, and establishing a basic cast of characters—including the Altamont, Moreau, Rorschash, Plassaert, and Marcia families. Thirdly, Perec decided at an early stage to take as his lynchpin the eccentric millionaire, Percival Bartlebooth, whose grandiose project, embarked on fifty years earlier, and condemned to end in failure with his death at the instant commemorated by the text, would touch the lives of many of his co-inhabitants, and notably those of two other 'old monomaniacs' (935),[55] the puzzle-maker Gaspard Winkler and the painter Serge Valène.

If these constraints furnish the work with something of its tenor, dramatis personae, and narrative unfolding, the publication, in 1993, of the ledger (known as a 'cahier de charges') that Perec established for the text's ninety-nine chapters provided a much clearer idea of his *modus operandi*, with regard particularly to the question of the contents of each room.[56] Perec had indicated that another algorithm, a 'bi-carré latin', similar to the one used in *Lieux*, had dictated much of the text's detail, by specifying, amongst other things, which items from each of forty-two lists had to be included in a given chapter. Access to these lists allows us to grasp the parameters Perec set for himself and, in the context of the present discussion, to get a clearer idea of the place of the everyday in Perec's scheme.

A World of Lists

Even a cursory glance at Perec's lists suggests a strong bias towards everyday things.[57] More than two-thirds of the forty-odd headings relate to concrete entities such as furnishings, leaving less than a third to cover plot- and character-oriented factors, and cryptic allusions to cultural phenomena of different kinds. This ratio is if anything accentuated when we look at the contents of the lists, each of which breaks down into ten subcategories, producing over four hundred specifications in all. The few headings relating predominantly to narrative organization, plot, and character are very generalized and conventional. They are 'longueur', which specifies the length of the

---

55　References, incorporated in the text, are to Perec, *Romans et récits*.

56　Georges Perec, *Cahier des charges de 'La Vie mode d'emploi'* (Paris: CNRS Zulma, 1993).

57　The unpaginated *Cahier des charges* includes Perec's overall table of the lists.

chapter, from a few lines to over twelve pages; 'Age et sexe' bearing directly on characters; 'Ressort', which includes such hoary plot lines as 'ourdir une vengeance' (wreak vengeance), 'poursuivre une chimère' (pursue a chimera) and 'appât du gain' (greed); 'époque', which includes a wide range of historical periods and thus encourages narratives concerning earlier occupants of the house; and 'lieu' which, similarly, locates action away from the building, and so fosters adventure and intrigue. If the heading 'Nombre' specifies the number of people in the room (from 0 to 5+), thus determining narrative possibilities, 'Rôle' specifies in only three cases that the protagonist(s) should be the room's occupant(s), and in the other cases specifies, apart from 'ami', a range of everyday visitors such as delivery men, workmen, and servants. 'Sentiments', squashed between 'jeux et jouets' and 'Peintures' on Perec's chart, introduces some standard touches of psychological colour, including subheadings such as 'joie', 'colère', 'étonnement', and 'haine'. Another group of headings involves cultural references: 'citation' 1 and 2 refer to quotations from twenty authors (Flaubert, Sterne, Roubaud, *et al.*) embedded surreptitiously in the text; 'livres' specifies ten books to which specific reference has to be made; 'musiques' designates types of music, 'tableaux' specific painters.

The dozen or so headings referred to in the last paragraph are thus determinants of narrative developments and buried cultural allusions. This leaves over two dozen headings, and hence over 250 subcategories, that have scarcely any functional role in the narrative but provide its density of physical detail. Little wonder that most readers of *La Vie mode d'emploi* rapidly feel overwhelmed by the sheer accumulation of material. In underlining how these ingredients give Perec's text its strong tinge of everydayness, despite the often bizarre life stories of its inhabitants, I will begin with two that are on the borderline of the broad groupings outlined so far. If 'position' and 'activité' both refer to the actions of a central character in a given chapter, the specified postures (kneeling, standing, entering), and acts (reading, mending, decorating), are very mundane and refer us to the immediate everyday world. Even if they are not dwelt on (a point I shall return to), and merely serve as the starting point for stories that are often exotic, these specifications anchor the text in the everyday. This is truer still of categories relating to food, clothes, and accessories (belts, braces, underwear), items of furnishing (small and large), fabric, jewellery, toys, and games. Not only are these headings mundane in themselves, their subdivisions generally tend to favour the ordinary and the unexotic. Thus the 'animals' are mainly pets or household pests, the drinks are tea, coffee and the like, and the food is quite routine, apart from a mysterious entry for 'zakouskis' in the tenth column. The same is true of various headings relating to decoration, including decorative styles, types of flooring, shapes (oval, octagonal, etc.), volumes (pyramid, cone, egg-shape), modes of floral display, knick-knacks, and wall-coverings. The materials listed under 'reading' are nicely varied (from school exercise books to pornography) but fairly standard.

Interestingly, one item, '3e secteur', cross-refers to the least familiar of Perec's overall headings, one that has particular relevance to the issue of the *quotidien*. 'Le 3e secteur' was a phrase coined by François le Lionnais, joint founder (with Raymond Queneau) of Oulipo, to designate the kinds of verbal material, increasingly prevalent in modern everyday life, to be found in advertising, instruction manuals, catalogues, and so forth: 'cette manière d'utiliser le langage qu'on trouve dans les graffitti, dans les épitaphes, dans les catalogues d'armes et cycles' (the ways language is used in graffiti, epitaphs, wholesale catalogues).[58] Neither literary nor paraliterary, in 'third sector' materials typography and layout are essential to the message, and Perec's numerous examples suggest that their appeal and significance lay in ubiquity and physical appearance. The ten items on this list involve copy that looks as if it had simply been 'lifted' straight from the 'real' world into the text. The subcategories include bibliographies, dictionary entries, small newspaper items ('faits divers'), invitations, recipes, pharmaceutical prospectuses, diaries and calendars, instruction leaflets, and so forth. Perec had great fun thinking up examples and designing such reading matter as the map of France left behind by Troyan, the second-hand book dealer (909), the joke visiting cards in the window of a novelty shop (958), and the substantial contents from the catalogue of Mme Moreau's DIY equipment firm, where each entry ends with the formula, 'garantie totale 1 an' (746–50).

The incorporation of such material is the most visible sign of the everyday in *La Vie mode d'emploi*, and can be linked to themes, models, and perspectives that point to different aspects of the *quotidien*: the ephemeral and the encyclopedic, the museum and the user's manual. Perhaps its most obvious characteristic is the combination of the concrete, the contingent, and the ephemeral. Here are menu cards, shop signs, and flyers that were not expected to last, and whose *ad hoc* function relates to specific short-term purposes, contexts, and occasions. This flotsam and jetsam underlines its own ephemerality by clamouring for the viewer's attention through fancy graphics and seductive

---

[58] Quoted in the Introduction to *Cahiers des charges*, 17.

language (after the publication of *La Vie mode d'emploi*, Perec began collecting such ephemera more systematically for a project called *L'Herbier des villes*, where the myriad bits of paper we encounter in any city street were to be categorized like botanical species). Yet by having been preserved (by accident or through sentimentality) these materials, like many of those itemized in the novel, also take on the character of exhibits or relics. At times *La Vie mode d'emploi* resembles a museum of curiosities, or the contents of a time capsule carefully assembled to epitomize a period in the history of a civilization, or, more darkly, the remains of a culture destroyed by some cataclysm. This feeling is partly induced by the reader's awareness that the materials are not real but fakes: rather than using 'ready mades' Perec carefully confected his ephemera, revelling in the use of dated typography and outmoded styles.

Like *Je me souviens*, Perec's novel makes cultural memory a key dimension of the everyday. The '3e secteur', along with many of the elements of decor endlessly inventoried, registers—through gestures, rituals, and short-lived fashions and crazes—a hidden history that is bound to trigger recollection in some readers. Yet the absence of an explicit act of memory in the text points to ambivalence. The nearest to a presiding consciousness is the painter Serge Valène, whose ambition to paint a picture of the house with its façade removed obviously parallels Perec's undertaking. But if Perec succeeds where Valène fails (at the end we learn that he had barely begun work on the painting) it is perhaps because he has fewer illusions. The novel's superb central chapter (LI) voices the painter's fantasy of embracing in one image the entire contents of the building—the material objects and the people with their history and legends. For the former, Perec gives two sample enumerations, while for the latter he composed a poem-litany where each of 179 lines, containing an identical number of letters, encapsulates one of the life stories in the book. Yet Valène's grandiose project is doomed because it rests on a belief in art's totalizing power. His dream of preservation and perpetuation is the obverse of his nightmare—the dark fantasy of the house's slow decline and final destruction, as it is eventually demolished to make way for a new development (818). For Perec, as for Valène, salvaging things from destruction and disaster is a key motive for homing in on the everyday. Yet Perec acknowledges that the everyday is always caught between the tangible and the intangible; it can never be preserved but, as Certeau would say, constantly reinvented. Where Valène wants to commemorate a building where he has lived, Perec constructs a description on the basis of myriad fragments of everydayness, derived from his own archive of sightings, recognitions, and memories. Totality is not a premise, but an aspiration, and also an illusion. In this regard the use of 'contraintes' is a mark of lucidity. Unlike that of narrative, the logic of 'contrainte' means that the presence of an item—a tea cosy, a recipe, a murder weapon—is not dictated by the necessities of plot or verisimilitude, but by the workings of an algorithm. The item retains its independence and a separateness underlined by the predominance of a device—enumeration—which, although it places a diversity of things into a single list, gives each item its own salience. Composing his chapters, Perec had to summon up—often no doubt through a process resembling *Je me souviens*—a specific entity belonging to a given category, regardless of the other narrative or descriptive desiderata for the chapter. As a result this entity—tea trolley, beer mat, flyer—acquires a peculiarly intermediate status: fictional, because *La Vie mode d'emploi* is a novel, but also factual because the entity is 'quoted' from a stock of real items in the author's memory. In this regard it is interesting to recall that if, like Valène, Perec included himself in his creation, he did so not by self-depiction but through two 'contraintes': that each chapter should embody an allusion to one of his earlier writings, and that it should refer to some everyday event that had occurred in the course of the chapter's composition.[59]

Communal space

When drawing up his plan, Perec paid particular attention to communal space. Of the ninety-nine chapters twelve cover the staircase, two each are devoted to the entrance hall, lift, and boiler-room, and one each to the service entrance and the concierge's lodge. In addition, five chapters relate to the cellars, which contain the accumulated possessions of various families. Overall, more than a quarter of the book's chapters (twenty-six out of ninety-nine) focus on the communal spaces and life of the building rather than specific inhabitants, even if they naturally feature here.

After its essay-like 'preamble' on puzzle-making, *La Vie mode d'emploi* opens with a staircase chapter, a fine meditation on these neutral 'parties communes' (657) that tend to be shunned, as people lock themselves away in their 'parties privatives' (both phrases are from the jargon of estate agents). Yet just as the same patterns of behaviour are mirrored endlessly on either side of the narrow dividing walls, so the staircase underlines the everyday commonality of human destinies: fetching bread, taking the dog out, calling the

---

[59] Perec, *Cahiers des charges*, n.p.

doctor, moving house—'tout ce qui se passe passe par l'escalier' (657) (everything that happens involves the stairs). Grafting a narrative extension onto his description, Perec presents the building through the critical eye of a house agent on her way up the stairs to view Winckler's empty flat; oblivious to the lives we shall soon learn about, she notes the general dilapidation. For her this is just a piece of real estate, ripe for conversion, and Perec will often use the communal chapters to develop one of the key themes of his everyday work: indictment of administrators, planners, and speculators for their indifference to the lived reality of real human beings.

Perec consistently uses the communal chapters to explore the collective life and history of the building, and in three of the more substantial staircase chapters he makes Valène—the oldest resident (since 1919), and an avatar of both Perec and Bartlebooth—the embodiment of its accumulated past. In Chapter XVII the staircase (whose prominence in the text is motivated by the fact that the lift rarely works) is seen through Valène's eyes as a memorial space haunted by the fleeting shadows of all who have ever climbed it (731). This pinpoints a hidden history of 'imperceptible details' that have 'woven together' the life of the building, so that, for Valène, climbing the stairs is like travelling though different time zones, as tiny impressions from numerous periods are fleetingly rekindled. It therefore makes sense that in Chapter XXVIII, one of the most haunting, we again find Valène on the stair, suddenly recalling, as he crosses the fifth-floor landing, his last encounter with Bartlebooth three years earlier. Valène now imagines Bartlebooth cloistered away in his flat, poring day after day over Winckler's jigsaw puzzles, which he finds ever more difficult as both eyesight and memory—of the sites on which the puzzles were based— gradually fade (813). Valène's own project—the painting—suddenly strikes him as no more than a 'grotesque mausoleum', a vain attempt to arrest the inexorable passage of time. Haunted day and night by the rush of memories it provokes, Valène now imagines the building ripped open to expose 'les fissures de son passé, l'écroulement de son présent, cet entassement sans suite d'histoires grandioses ou dérisoires' (the cracks of its past, its crumbling present, the endless pile of grandiose or derisory stories) (814). He recalls the many inhabitants who have died or disappeared, and then, in a passage with echoes of *Espèces d'espaces*, contrasts the everyday with its antithesis. Outside history and narrative, the everyday—'un quotidien sans histoire [...] irracontable' (without stories... untellable)—is conjured up through images of moving in, setting up house, and daily living—'la lente accoutumance du corps à l'espace, toute cette somme d'événements minuscules, inexistants, irracontables [...]'

tous ces gestes infimes en quoi se résuméra toujours de la manière la plus fidèle la vie d'un appartement' (the slow acclimatization of the body to space, this sum of minuscule events, non-existent, untellable... all those tiny gestures that will always sum up better than anything else the life of an apartment) (815). This is then confronted by the 'brusques cassures' (sudden breaks) that interrupt or curtail it: things that happen out of the blue: elopements, disappearances, bursts of violence. And then, finally, Valène imagines the destruction of the building, along with street and neighbourhood. However improbable it may seem to the inhabitants, as they go about their daily lives swathed in a cocoon of micro-histories, a bomb, a fire, an earthquakes, or more probably, the redevelopment of the area by a flurry of property speculation, could make the apparently indestructible disappear in short order. Mimicking the prose of an agent's leaflet (samples of the '3e secteur' are especially prominent in the communal chapters) Perec-Valène imagines a slide into terminal decline, and then the destruction visited by bulldozers, wrecking balls and steamrollers (818).

Chapter XLIX is devoted to the top landing where the traditional frontier between masters and servants is marked by a glass door beyond which lies the narrow uncarpeted staircase leading up to two floors of what were originally maid's rooms. We are provided with a substantial sociohistorical account of the progressive subversion of this line of class division, through the sale, amalgamation, and *embourgeoisement* of many of the upper rooms, and of the numerous 'micro-conflicts' (932) this has induced. For the concierge, who refuses to deliver mail beyond the glass door, and many of the bourgeois inhabitants of the lower storeys, the 'people above' are still considered socially inferior, although they include the wealthy painter Hutting who has converted eight rooms and (controversially) the adjoining corridors and attics into a sumptuous studio. For the narrator these petty rivalries and antagonisms, whilst they enliven the annual meetings of the 'co-proprietors', are part of the building's 'tranquil history' (933), broken only by a minor explosion and a fire that gutted part of one apartment. In this context Valène's dreams of cataclysms, natural disasters, or invasion by aliens are only a figment of his imagination, even if they echo the slow, hidden vengeance that Winckler plotted year after year in his room beside the glass door.

Three of the staircase chapters are used primarily to showcase striking examples of '3e secteur' materials, for example headlines and advertisements on a newspaper (866) carried by a visitor to the Altamont's; extracts from an almanac and a religious tract peddled by door-to door collectors (891); the table of contents of a learned journal in a pile outside Dr Dinteville's waiting room (989). In three further chapters, objects pertaining to a person on the landing serve to trigger exotic narratives that contrast with the banal surroundings. As the teenage son of the Bergers takes the rubbish down, we are given a full synopsis of the episode novel he is writing with his classmates at school (856); over the shoulder of another young lad, the piano-tuner's grandson, banished to the landing for bad behaviour, we read the gripping account of the life of the explorer Carl Van Loorens in a copy of *Tintin* magazine (1125–34); two large trunks lying outside the open doors of the Rorschash apartment, because Olivia is about to leave for her fifty-sixth round the world tour, are the pretext for an account of her fabulous life story, from her beginnings as a child star on the Australian stage in the 1930s (1135–9).

Two of the most striking staircase chapters occur towards the end of the book. Consisting of a list of items found over the years, the first (chapter LXVIII) begins with the very Perequian heading: '*Tentative d'inventaire de quelques-unes des choses qui ont été trouvées dans les escaliers au fil des ans*' (1068), and the second (chapter XCIV) has the same heading followed by '(suite et fin)' (1240). Typographically, each item or group of items found on a particular occasion (date unspecified) begins a new line, indented from the usual margin, so that it stands out independently, as if in a litany. Approximately two-thirds of the items are physical objects, the others printed materials of various kinds. Some are straightforward: a bottle of milk, a tin of cough sweets; others more singular: a goldfish in a plastic bag, a model in kit form of the clepsydra Haroun al-Rachid is supposed to have given Charlemagne. The printed items often lend themselves to graphic '3e secteur' treatment: the programme of a cinema (in the rue de l'Assomption—one of Perec's 'lieux') for February 1960, a postcard detailing the life of Mark Twain; or to quotation: a joke visiting-card, the first draft of a schoolchild's Latin translation covered in doodles; or to description of their physical condition: a table of logarithms with its owner's name, a crumpled issue of the *Revue du Jazz*. Care is also taken to record anything printed on the object (such as the label on a coat) or on the carrier bag in which it was found: a radio alarm (destined for the repairer?) in a Nicolas plastic bag; the lamp shade in a bag from a record shop.

What is striking about these chapters is not the objects themselves (Perec seems to have tried to avoid making them too outlandish) but their heterogeneity (which leads to surprising juxtapositions), and the way they are not simply listed but described in detail. By providing a 'Tentative d'inventaire', the first word underlining the difficulty of exactitude, Perec treats these mundane things as if they were items in the catalogue of a dealer in antiques or rare books. This act of disinterested attention (the items are never directly related to the inhabitants of the building) gives each object an uncanny salience, but also builds up a strong cumulative effect. Yet rather than suggesting objects marooned on the dusty shelves of a lost property office, Perec's inventory, which stresses finding rather than losing, makes the staircase the stage for an ongoing, living history. These unclaimed items, often belonging to visitors, show the building as a place of passage, pointing to stories that remain untold, and to a wider anonymity transcending the named identities of the building.

To some degree, the five chapters devoted to cellars contrast with the staircase's emphasis on collective or anonymous histories. The chapter on Bartlebooth's cellar (LXXII) describes his four wonderful travelling trunks and evokes the fading memories of his factotum, Smautf. The chapter on Mme de Beaumont (LXXVI) details numerous souvenirs and family photographs and leads into an account of her late husband's friendship with Bartlebooth. Three chapters focus on adjacent cellars, building up, again primarily through lists of objects, contrasts between different families. The Altamont cellar (XXXIII) is a model of order, with sections for canned foods, wine and cleaning products, while the Gratiolet's is full of the piled-up residues of several generations— unclassified photos, torn dictionaries, collections of seashells. Exhaustive inventorying is not attempted. In chapter LXVII notable items from the Rorschash and Dinteville cellars reflect what we know about these characters while providing the opportunity to link an object to further aspects of their life histories, as in the box of rusty nails regurgitated by one of Dr Dinteville's first patients. What catches the eye in the Marquiseaux cellar (XCI) are the labels on their stocks of champagne and whisky, and sixty roneotyped fascicules comprising the fruits of fifteen years spent trying to prove that Hitler did not perish in his bunker. By contrast, the cellar belonging to Mme Marcia the antique dealer, is chock-a-block with furniture and objets d'art, including a doll's bakery shop described in loving detail.

The chapters on other utility areas strongly emphasize the collective history of the building, turning it into a 'lieu de mémoire'. Itemizing the wares of five delivery men, the service entrance chapter (LXIII) underlines the place of social gatherings in the 'mythology' of the building, while the account of successive concierges, and the description of Mme Nochère's lodge, remind us of enduring continuities. The first boiler-room chapter (XXI) gives an account of the controversies surrounding the advent of central heating in the 1960s and then fills in the history of the Gratiolet family, original owners of the house; while the second (LXIV) provides a flashback to the Occupation when the room was still just part of the Gratiolet's cellarage and Olivier, the only inhabitant to join the Resistance, had installed his clandestine press and radio. One of the chapters on the entrance hall (XXI) homes in on an American writer research-ing a book on Bartlebooth's great uncle, James Sherwood. The account of Sherwood's passion for '*unicae*'—objects of which there is only one possible example—and the elaborate swindle that leads him to purchase a dud, is a brilliant piece of storytelling. In these chapters large tracts of time and space are linked to the immediate present, the here and now in which, as we discover in the second hallway chapter (XC), three women sit chatting: Mme de Beaumont's cleaner, Mme Albin back from her daily visit to her husband's grave, and Mme Moreau's ex-servant Gertrude, now employed at Lord Ash-tray's country seat in England, although she insists on a weekly shopping trip to Paris because the produce is better. The first of the two chapters on the lift (XXXVIII: as usual, the lift is not working at the novel's 'census' point) involves a flashback to a legendary mishap, dating from the first few weeks after its installation in 1925, when Valène, Mme Albin, and two other revellers, returning after midnight from Bastille Day festivities, had been stuck for seven hours. The second lift chapter (LXXIV) is quite different. Wonderfully written, it attributes to Valène's dark imagining a chthonic fantasy of a city beneath the city, where successive levels, deeper and deeper below ground, like the circles of the Inferno, are devoted to different supplies and services on which the house, and modern civilization, depend. Piranesi-like ladders go down beneath the cellars to a labyrinth of corridors leading to storage tanks, ventilators, and extinguishers; a further level down we find huge machines, attended to by an army of technicians; then a level of silos, hangars, and cold stores, followed by piles of building materials, extensive docks and canals, locks and basins, then mines, then a whole network of services, each with its own *quartier*: tanners, metal-merchants, wine-dealers, street-cleaners, and administrators, military and civil. As it turns into one long winding sentence, with dense enumerative paragraphs separated by semicolons and anaphoric phrases, Valène's fantasy makes the banal lift shaft a passage from the warm disorder of human histories to the inhuman order of bureaucratic organization and faceless authority that poses an ever-present threat to the values enshrined in the everyday.

The prominence of the *quotidien* in *La Vie mode d'emploi* confirms the central importance of this theme in the writer's overall project. Shot through with 'non-fiction', Perec's encyclopedic 'novel' chimes in three key respects with his abiding concern for ways of exploring the seemingly ordinary and mundane. Firstly, apprehending (as opposed to documenting, transmuting, or celebrating) everydayness is seen to necessitate indirection—approaches that combine elements of diverse genres, discourses, and practices: sociological enquiry, fictional inventiveness, autobiographical commitment, and formal play. Secondly, recurrent devices and themes stake out, as they do elsewhere in Perec, the territory and parameters of the everyday: rooms and living spaces, objects and lists, ephemeral inscriptions, and the commonality of cultural memory. Thirdly, and most importantly, as Valène's ruminations indicate, the *quotidien* is seen to be a dimension of experience, always collective as well as personal, which possesses an ethical value that is constantly under threat. In an interview on *La Vie mode d'emploi* Perec said that if his stories had a moral it lay in the conflict between human beings and institutions, adding that 'le rôle de celles-ci est toujours néfaste' (the role of the latter is always negative).[60] One recalls the tribulations of poor M. Réol in his attempt to secure a pay rise (1264); the way Bartlebooth's whole project is threatened by the machinations of the Marvel Houses hotel group (1189); the emblematic fate of Mme Nochère's husband who dies after swallowing too many erasers on the ends of the pencils he sucks at his bureaucrat's desk (861). Yet bureaucratic reason is only one of the masks worn by more chilling and deep-seated threats to the human, threats which, in scarring Perec's own personal history, placed a profound sense of loss at the heart of his life and work. What is under threat? Not only the profuse variety of daily activities and environments that Perec constantly affirms against the dangers of indifference and standardization. The threat is also to the fragile and hence vulnerable medium in which such activities exist, the milieu that shelters them from mere randomness, not by endowing them with transcendent meaning, but by recognizing an immanent connectedness. In Perec—as in the whole tradition with which this book is concerned—the *quotidien* (or 'le bruit de fond', 'l'infra-ordinaire', 'les choses communes') names this threatened and priceless sense of connection, which binds persons, acts, histories, and communities to each other, not in any fixed or predetermined pattern, but in that constantly fluid becoming that Perec called 'émergence'.

---

[60] Perec, *Entretiens et conférences*, ed. Bertelli and Ribière, I, 249. Cf. ibid., 223.

When we want to find the core of Perec's contribution to theories and practices of the everyday (and to the inseparability of theory and practice in this domain), we must, I think, come back to the projects he devised and the spirit that animated them. As we shall see in the chapters that follow, what has proved most seminal in Perec is not his inimitable compendium of everyday lives but the practical spirit that animated *Espèces d'espaces, Lieux,* the various 'Tentatives de description', *Je me souviens, La Vie mode d'emploi,* and many other initiatives abruptly terminated by his death. Learning from Lefebvre and Barthes, paralleling and influencing Certeau in his insistence on unofficial, 'transversal' activities that knit spaces together into places, Perec's interweavings—of space and memory, the modest proposal and the spiritual exercise, the logbook and the inventory—have provided enduring inspiration for innumerable later explorers of the everyday.

8

After Perec: Dissemination and Diversification

Cross-fertilization between the ideas of Lefebvre, Certeau, Barthes, and Perec contributed massively to the emergence of the *quotidien* as a central notion in modern culture. Initially adopted by Henri Lefebvre in the post-war period, to promote Marxist humanism via critiques of Lukács, Surrealism and Existentialism, the *quotidien* was subsequently construed, from the mid 1950s to the mid 1960s, as a sector 'colonized' by petit-bourgeois ideology (Barthes), in the context of rapid modernization and the rise of consumerism (Lefebvre, the Situationists, Perec). Following May '68, in a third phase—marked by the evolution of Perec's work from alienation to appropriation, the transmutation of Barthesian semiology into a concern for incidents and intensities, and the development of Certeau's notion of invention—the recognition of the everyday became an important facet of a wider cultural shift from systems and structures to practices and performances. Symptomatic of this transitional period was the move from grand theory (the 'grands récits' of Lyotard's *La Condition postmoderne*) to the nooks and crannies of the 'in-between', the transversal zones such as those investigated by *Traverses*, the journal of CCI (Centre for Industrial Creation) at the Centre Pompidou, where Certeau and Perec may be found side by side with Baudrillard, Boltanski, Sansot, and Virilio, in special issues on such topics as fashion, death rituals, functionalism, gardens, and 'Le Reste'.

From the early 1980s a set of discourses on the everyday ramifies into a wide range of cultural productions in a variety of contexts and media. This chapter and the following one examine how, during the 1980s and 1990s, the ideas of four key writers helped provide an array of concepts and tactics that inspired work in theatre, film, art, literature, and social theory. In this period the balance tilts from theories advocating praxis (Lefebvre, Barthes), to practice as the vehicle of theory (Certeau, Perec), and in Chapter 9 I will suggest that one way of grasping the late-twentieth-century profusion of the *quotidien* is in terms of a move from the discursive to the figural. The present chapter anticipates this by considering, firstly, the redirection of ethnographic scrutiny from the far to the near; secondly, the figure of the urban trajectory in four writers (Augé, Ernaux, Maspero, Réda); thirdly, the treatment of the everyday across a range of genres and media.

PROXIMATE ETHNOGRAPHIES

'Peut-être s'agit-il de fonder enfin notre propre anthropologie, celle qui parlera de nous [...] Non plus l'exotique, mais l'endotique' (Perhaps it's a matter of founding our own anthropology, that will talk about us ... Not the exotic but the endotic). Frequently quoted, this statement from Perec's 'Approches de quoi?' (1973) resonates through the 1980s and 1990s, and into the new century.[1] Associating a turn towards the unspectacular territory of everyday life with a repatriation of anthropological enquiry, Perec's main aim was no doubt to convince fellow literary intellectuals of the seriousness of the project he outlined, and to inspire them to train their sights on what lay all around. Yet this plea struck a chord with many contemporary anthropologists, and by Perec's death in 1982 exponents of 'ethnographie de proximité' (proximate ethnography) were adapting their professional skills to the analysis of urban styles, football matches, sitcoms and the like; in 1985 Marc Augé's *Un Ethnologue dans le métro* (to be discussed later in this chapter) would mark a full engagement between the anthropologist and his immediate everyday environs. Yet Perec's readers might have wondered whether Augé's essay, however fascinating in its own terms, fully responded to the appeal of 'Approches de quoi?'. And this raises from the outset the issue of whether or not 'ethnographie' (or 'ethnologie') 'de proximité' (or 'ethnologie du proche') should be seen as exemplifying the theory and practice of the everyday.

If it is generally agreed that, in France particularly, the rise of proximate ethnography dates from the turn of the 1980s, its possible determinants dovetail with those at play in the rise of the *quotidien*. On the socio-political front, economic prosperity in western Europe led to a huge diversification of

---

[1] Perec, *L'Infra-ordinaire*, 11–12.

products available in ever more variants.[2] Consumers were invited to distin-guish themselves by gradations of look and lifestyle, as a result of which social texture became at once more homogeneous and more variegated, the oppos-ition between high and low culture giving way to a proliferation of sub-cultures.[3] This accelerated the predominance of urban life, as mass communications brought the city into the village living room. At the same time, decolonization, and the reverse migration that brought settler popula-tions back to the mainland, as well as new waves of immigrants, led to a more diverse social body and a consequent redefinition of national identity. Mean-while, globalization, air travel, and mass tourism 'shrank' the planet and turned exotic lands into holiday destinations. In such circumstances it is hardly surprising that the anthropologist was no longer sure where to look.[4]

On another front, the post-1968 shake-up of universities favoured the exchanges between the 'sciences humaines' that flourished at institutions like Paris VIII-Vincennes (later Saint-Denis), challenging the autonomy of separ-ate disciplines. What came to be known in the Anglo-Saxon world as 'theory' was at one level a spirit that called into question the methods and assumptions of literary and social studies as traditionally conceived; in the hands of a Certeau, whose work cut across theology, anthropology, psychoanalysis, and history, this helped shape what would come to be known as cultural studies. In this context, the anthropologist, caught like the historian, the sociologist, and the literary critic between various orthodoxies (including Lévi-Straussian Structuralism), was pushed to a new self-consciousness with regard to the methods and products of his or her profession. As one would have expected, the radical questioning to which Michel Leiris had consistently subjected 'anthropological authority'—a questioning rooted in the refusal of a clear-cut opposition between the everyday and the non-everyday as well as in a searching critique of ethnography's complicity with colonialism—came to the

---

[2] Baudrillard, *Le Système des objets*; David H. Walker: 'Shopping and Fervour: Modern Literature and the Consumer Society', *French Studies*, 58 (Jan. 2004), 29–46.

[3] See Bourdieu, *La Distinction* (Paris: Minuit, 1979); Maffesoli, *Au creux des apparences*; Gilles Lipovetsky, *L'Ere du vide: essais sur l'individualisme contemporain* (Paris: Gallimard, 1983).

[4] Of course, proximate ethnography has its antecedents in Surrealism and dissenting Surrealism (Leiris, Bataille, Queneau), and in the whole tradition with which this book is concerned. In Britain it was anticipated by the remarkable Mass-Observation movement of the 1930s. On this see Laura Marcus, 'Introduction: The Project of Mass-Observation' in Nick Hubble, Margaretta Jolly, and Laura Marcus (eds.), *Mass-Observation as Poetics and Science, New Formations*, 44 (2001); and B. Highmore, *Everyday Life and Cultural Theory*, 75–112. On 'Ethnographic Surrealism' see James Clifford, *The Predicament of Culture* (Cambridge, MA: Harvard University Press, 1988); on 'ethnog-raphy envy' in modern art see Hal Foster, *The Return of the Real* (Cambridge, MA: MIT Press, 1996).

forefront. Challenged from outside by the sociologist, the psychoanalyst, and the urbanist, and from within by the diversification of their own discipline, anthropologists felt the need to redefine the scope of their activities. And it was in this socio-political and intellectual climate that the everyday—which had of course always been the object of anthropology, albeit usually in remote parts— became the prime test bed for new disciplinary combinations. For, as we have observed, from the Surrealists onwards the everyday had always been thought of, in some quarters, as possessing an inherent indeterminacy, by dint of being outside the purview of settled systems of knowledge. In the 1980s, this lack of specific qualities, an inherent elusiveness, made the everyday a guest at every feast, the bride to be escorted down the aisle of every intellectual *chapelle*, especially those indulging in a newly ecumenical spirit. As theory shifted its attention from language and psyche to power relations, social trajectories, and questions of space, application to the everyday became a litmus test of their viability. The same climate of feeling that pushes anthropology to redefine its relationship to both centre and periphery, promoted the everyday to the forefront of attention, from a variety of disciplinary viewpoints. This is one reason why it would be a mistake to annexe the rise of the everyday solely to a transmutation of ethnographic enquiry.

Introducing work on 'Ethnologie dans la ville' in the recently founded journal *Terrain* in October 1984, Alain Morel noted that urban anthropology had only taken off in the late 1970s.[5] If, since 1968 (with Lefebvre's ground-breaking *Le Droit à la ville*), various branches of the human sciences— sociology, architecture and planning, psychology—had made the city a privileged object of study, this tended to be within the parameters of separate disciplines, each carving up urban experience according to priorities generated by its own history rather than the desire to construct an integral vision. 'Ethnologie dans la ville', on the other hand—where the 'dans' (in) reflected the ethnographic principles of immersion and participant observation—was determinedly cross-disciplinary, since it involved the application of ethnology to modern and proximate phenomena rather than to archaic and distant ones, and also because in the process it adopted some of the techniques (for example, questionnaires) of other disciplines.

Morel's optimism belied the fact that urban ethnology, like other forms of anthropology 'at home', was to be fraught with difficulties. To heed Perec's injunction—study the endotic not the exotic, look at your own street—and to

---

[5] Alain Morel, 'Introduction', *L'Ethnologie dans la ville, Terrain*, 3 (Oct. 1984). 43.

claw back the ground lost to sociologists, ethnologists had to accept that a set of aims, theories, and methods evolved from the foundations of Mauss and Malinowski with the object of studying societies other than, and usually distant from, ours, should be applied to our own society. It is hardly surprising that this enterprise met strong resistance from within the professional community and from outside it, or that those inclined to take this path should often have been at pains to legitimate their undertaking within the terms of classic ethnographic practices and paradigms, including the notion of the 'great divide'. This refers to a separation often held to determine the specificity of ethnology. While other disciplines study *us,* ethnology looks at *them*: distance, exteriority, and otherness determine its objects and methods. Gérard Lenclud has traced the history of the divide, emphasizing how, since the Renaissance, it has coexisted with less categorical divisions between us and them, expressed for example in Montaigne's 'Je ne dis les autres, sinon pour d'autant me dire'[6] (If I speak of others, it is also to speak of myself). The notion of the divide was sanctioned by the Enlightenment when the word 'ethnographie' was coined to designate the Linnaean approach to the world's peoples fostered by the newly created 'Société des Observateurs de l'homme',[7] and it subsequently gave coherence and legitimacy to ethnology as an independent science. But even if nineteenth-century evolutionist doctrines could bolster the principle of otherness by insisting on the radical difference of earlier stages of human civilization, there was a growing recognition that 'exotic' societies were as different from each other as they were from ours. Lenclud observes that Marcel Mauss made this point in a 1923 letter to Lévy-Bruhl, theorist of a universal 'mentalité primitive', while Claude Lévi-Strauss insisted in *La Pensée sauvage* that the mode of thinking he analysed was not confined to 'primitives' but was also present, in kind if not in degree, in modern advanced societies; thus the historic vocation of the anthropologist is to know about 'them', but to feel how illusory it is to separate 'them' from 'us'.[8] Yet the 'partage' dies hard. If the development of a fully-fledged 'ethnologie de la France' in the twentieth century reflects a recognition that *we* could be as different as *them,* and thus ourselves subject to ethnographic scrutiny, the 'we'

---

[6] Gérard Lenclud, 'Le Grand Partage ou la tentation ethnologique' in G. Althabe, D. Fabre, and G. Lenclud (eds.), *Vers une ethnologie du présent* (Paris: Éditions de la Maison des sciences de l'homme, 1992), 9–37.

[7] See Jean-Luc Chappey, *La Société des observateurs de l'homme (1799–1804): des anthropologues au temps de Bonaparte* (Paris: Société des études robespierristes, 2004).

[8] Lenclud, 'Le Grand Partage', 31.

in question tended to be construed as our country cousins—Bretons, Basques, or Berrichons, 'colporteurs' or basket-weavers, practitioners of various rural pursuits often extremely archaic in origin—not quite 'us' after all.[9]

Introducing a special issue of *French Cultural Studies* on 'The Ethnology of Modern France', featuring the work of a number of proponents of 'ethnologie du proche', Christian Bromberger begins by summing up the arguments of those who, in the name of the 'grand partage', still fervently oppose what he calls 'anthropology at home'. But he brushes them aside to assert that the established tools and methods of ethnology can legitimately be used to study the here and now. If, between 1930 and 1950, 'ethnologie de la France' was restricted to surveys of folklore and material culture, in the 1950s it came to embrace monographs on specific village communities, and in the 1970s, in the wake of the rise of urban studies, to focus on particular areas of cities. By the 1980s, Bromberger argues, a fully-fledged ethnology of the modern world is in place, tackling a wide range of phenomena: presidential campaigns, football matches, the use of washing machines.[10] Bromberger acknowledges that established methods of ethnological enquiry and comprehension, dependent on long-term immersion, do not readily fit the empirical objects of contemporary interest such as supermarket shopping or rock concerts, and that 'ethnologie du proche' poses acutely the problem of defining the scope of any enquiry in the absence of the traditional criteria of tribal or geographical identity. But he believes that an approach combining micro- and macro-levels, deploying the specificity of ethnographic, as opposed to sociological, vision—attention to qualitative aspects, distancing, and comparison—can help clear the patina of familiarity from what seems natural, for example, eating red meat or going to the market. Yet in his insistence that the ethnology of the modern world should shun generalities and home in on the differential quality of phenomena, avoiding the excesses of analogy that arise when such concepts as tribe and ritual are applied to contemporary contexts, Bromberger rather gives the game away. For overindulgence in analogy is one of the principal criticisms levelled by those who question the validity of 'ethnologie du proche', notably with regard to such topics as football matches (the focus of a large body of work by Bromberger himself) or the uses of the washing machine.

---

[9] See Certeau's critique of this view in 'La Beauté du mort', in *La Culture au pluriel*.

[10] Christian Bromberger, 'L'ethnologie française "at home"', in *The Ethnology of Modern France, French Cultural Studies*, 18 (Oct. 1995) 289.

A few years earlier, Jean Jamin (Michel Leiris's close collaborator and literary executor) had delivered a searching critique of the whole enterprise of ethnology applied to one's own society, seeing it, in a postmodern perspective, as a development of ethnography as text rather than as method or science. The essay was the centrepiece of *Le Texte ethnographique*, a special number of *Études rurales*, a journal which in 1983, in the wake of *Terrain*, had adopted a new orientation, welcoming studies of 'le proche'. Jamin begins by introducing French readers to recent work, including that of Clifford and Rabinow featured later in the same number, which, in the context of decolonization, had drawn attention to the epistemological issues that haunt the ethnological enterprise and are reflected in the discourses of the ethnographic text, which comes under close scrutiny. To some extent, Jamin associates the recent rise of proximate ethnography with this self-conscious, reflexive spirit that leaves the ethnographer at grips with himself, rather than his terrain, observing his everyday interactions with his own society, and confronting this with the knowledge acquired in this training.[11] But he warns that this allows the textual dimension of the ethnological encounter to become paramount: as ethnography triumphs over ethnology, the text's inevitable separation from the real is augmented, running the risks of self-pastiche and of betraying the fact that the ethnographic text has perhaps always been based on an 'effet de réel' that is essentially literary (12). For Jamin, what is questionable about this shift is the failure to recognize the specificity and historicity of ethnographic practice and discourse, formed through contact between modern and archaic or primitive societies, the ethnographic text itself—as product of technology—being a symptom of modernity. Jamin subscribes in effect to the 'grand partage': 'l'ethnographie ne va pas sans une certaine dose d'exotisme [. . .] la distanciation commande le protocole d'observation' (ethnography inevitably involves a pinch of exoticism . . . Distancing governs the protocol of observation) (15). Distance and temporal disparity are part of the force of ethnography; an anthropology of the modern world can only be understood in postmodern terms of pastiche, textuality and the end of history. It may focus on the experience of the ethnographer as hero, or the play of discourses in the ethnographic text, or celebrate culture as a patchwork of styles: whichever way, the outcome is pastiche. And this is the case with all attempts to apply ethnological concepts to modern phenomena: 'le football comme religion, les

---

[11] Jean Jamin, 'Le Texte ethnographique: argument', in *Le Texte ethnographique, Études rurales*, 97–8 (Jan.–June 1985) 12.

séries télévisées américaines comme mythologie, *Dallas* comme exercice de la parenté' (football as religion, TV soaps as mythology, *Dallas* as kinship ritual)—the examples allude to recent work by Marc Augé (although he is not mentioned by name) where, for Jamin, the *comme* (as) underlines the analogical procedure, the deconstructive 'refroidissement' that breaks with the historicity on which ethnology is based, and which, in his view, can only produce ethnographic 'fictions' (16). This results in an 'epistemological solipsism' whereby what makes a phenomenon ethnological is purely the decision to study it. In anthropology of the modern world the vital 'déracinement chronique auquel conduit toute expérience ethnographique' (temporal dislocation induced by all ethnographic experience) (20) is a bogus simulation: 'À une distanciation de fait et à une identification élective (en terrain exotique) s'opposeraient donc une identification de fait et une distanciation élective (en terrain proche)'. (A real distance and a voluntary identification (on exotic terrain) is replaced by a real identification and a voluntary distancing (on proximate terrain)) (20). In the modern context, the ethnologist freely chooses to adopt a distanced perspective, as Montesquieu did by the strategy of his imaginary visitors to France in his *Lettres persanes*. But he blinds himself to the real distance that separates his language from objects to which it in fact can only be applied metaphorically, and by means of his *fiat*. Before looking at a riposte to Jamin's strictures, by Jean-Didier Urbain, let us look at a specific area of proximate ethnography, the study of ritual.

Ritual has been a rich source of parallels and continuities between modern societies and those traditionally studied by anthropologists, partly because the survival of ritual in the modern world can be seen as a link with the remote past, and partly because the concept of ritual has always transcended an exclusively religious context.[12] Whatever the context or framework of meaning, ritual refers to behaviour, acts or sequences of actions that are invested with individual and social meanings. To understand a ritual is always to establish a link between a micro- and a macro-level, a gesture, say, and a body of representations. Accordingly, it is through the application of the idea of ritual that the anthropology of the modern world has engaged most directly with the question of the everyday. But if investigation of ritual involves the nitty-gritty of ordinary life, it is by no means easy to eliminate all relics of ritual's religious heritage. The notion of secular or profane ritual remains problematic.

---

[12] Cf. the discussion of Leiris in Ch. 3 and Maffesoli in Ch. 7.

La Ritualisation du quotidien (1996), a special issue of *Ethnologie française*,
comprises an introduction by Claude Rivière, author of a study of *Les Rites
profanes* (1995), surveying work on the everyday, followed by articles on such
diverse topics as greetings ('ça va?'), the organization of domestic space,
manuals of 'savoir-vivre', the rituals of airline pilots, lorry drivers, and beggars,
rituals of locking one's home or watching pornography. In 'Pour une théorie
du quotidien ritualisé', Rivière notes that in the 1980s the *quotidien* became a
privileged area of sociological and anthropological study, and links this to the
return of lived experience, after the theoretical embargo of structuralism, and
to a desire to escape from disciplinary pigeonholes (sociology of work, sport,
etc.). Once again, the everyday is located as a cross-disciplinary area. Rivière
notes the widespread acceptance of Lefebvre and Certeau as authorities in this
sphere, adding Erving Goffman's work on *The Presentation of Self in Everyday
Life* and *Interaction Ritual*. He also notes the importance of phenomenology,
the micro-psychology of Abraham Molès, and the recent work of Lacan,
Foucault, and Bourdieu. In practice, however, Rivière's overall account of
the *quotidien* could easily be derived from Lefebvre. His view is that even if we
tend to depreciate it, everyday life is our basic touchstone of reality, on which
everything else is based. It is the level of reality conjured up by a variety of
neutral terms—the familiar, the habitual, the implicit, the banal—but it is also
the core of concrete lived experience. 'La vie quotidienne' is always already
there: a pre-existing set of situations, as opposed to such spheres as politics
ruled by decision-making that forces change.[13] But the everyday is a zone of
opposition, intersection, or interconnection—of the accidental and the permanent, imagination and affect, the personal and the social. It is constituted
by sequences of individual actions (dressing, eating, shopping, walking), but
within a context of relations and interactions where the individual is actor as
well as agent. The *quotidien* involves continuity but also change, repetition but
also variation and evolution. It is made up of routines, but major events (often
long anticipated or long remembered) are also part of its fabric, as are festive
moments, 'mini-fêtes'. It is universal (through its link to the human condition
in general) but also variable, inflected by climate, class, and gender. It is both
independent of and marked by history. Noting that the everyday embraces the
sacred and the profane, Rivière sums up the ambiguous richness of the
everyday by observing, in a memorable phrase, that 'L'erreur de beaucoup

[13] Clande Rivière, 'Pour une théorie du quotidien ritualisé', *La Ritualisation du quotidien,
Ethnologie française*, 26 (1996), 229–38. 230.

de nos dichotomies conceptuelles est d'exclure le tiers vécu' (The error of many of our conceptual dichotomies is to leave out lived experience) (230).

Despite this, Rivière's application of the concept of ritual to the everyday is ultimately narrow and functionalist. It depends, firstly, on distinguishing between ritual and habit. And, secondly, on assessing the functions of rituals in terms of the access they are said to provide to desired social values. Rivière criticizes Lefebvre for placing abstract ideas outside the everyday sphere and seeing it in terms of praxis, whereby potential plenitude is realized from within the everyday's own logic rather than by its being transcended. This is because ultimately Rivière's view (common to ritualists) is that rather than partaking of the everyday, rituals provide a means of transcending it. Arguing that it is not a matter of grafting the religious onto the profane, Rivière refers nevertheless to the benefit of ritualization as 'le réenchanement perpétuel du quotidien par un ordre des pratiques' (the perpetual re-enchantment of the everyday by an order of practices) (229). This is why he sees it as reductive simply to describe 'les occupations de la journée' (the day's occupations): they must be seen to be animated by a ritual dimension that gives them meaning. Unlike mere habits, ritualized actions (often maligned for being 'empty' ritual and so needing to be defended against this slur) have a strong symbolic meaning rooted in often unconscious adherence to social values rather than purely instrumental ends. Where, as we saw, Lefebvre and Certeau see 'pratique' itself as the agent of appropriation (rather than transformation or transcendence), the view of the ritualists can be equated with Bourdieu's 'habitus' where 'pratique' effects the often unconscious manifestation of passively internalized social values. Rivière argues that the basic function of rituals is the social and cultural integration of the individual within the group. Thus profane rituals are said to express cultural norms through more or less codified forms of behaviour. This is where the work of Goffman, with its emphasis on the functions of role playing, 'impression management', saving face, and so forth, is so important. For Rivière, rituals inevitably refer to an underlying order or tradition, although not necessarily a religious archetype. Profane rituals, which can have a dynamic function, since they stimulate action and personal develop-ment, and because they involve cognitive skills, do not, however, provide a total world view. Rather than promoting 'pan-ritualism' Rivière insists that he and his colleagues investigate 'des bribes de ritualisation dans le flux du quotidien' (fragments of ritualisation in the flux of the everyday) (234). This reduction in scope makes his account more acceptable, although it underlines how, rather than giving expression to the order of the everyday (which must always effectively be considered as a totality), rituals are in some respects at odds with its open-endedness.

Yet some of the essays in *La Ritualisation du quotidien* indicate how studies of rituals in the context of the anthropology of the modern world can illuminate the everyday, often because of their concern for the micro-level. For example, Jean-Paul Filiod looks at how, through ritualized behaviour, we appropriate our living space. On the basis of the kind of 'enquête' recommended by Perec in *Espèces d'espaces*, he asked a group of people in Lyon to describe the sorts of thing they do when they first get home, or last thing at night, or on an afternoon off. Using Certeau's notion of 'manières de faire', his discussion addresses the experiential dimension of everyday life, the non-linear 'enchaînements de micro-activités' through which we shape our time and order our space.

C'est parfois dans la subtilité de l'ordinaire, dans les interstices de la vie domestique, que s'effectuent autant d'actes d'appropriation et de réappropriation, qui, par leur lien avec le corps et ses sens et par leur répétition plus ou moins rigoureuse, marquent de manière forte les significations du chez-soi.[14]

(It is sometimes in the subtlety of the ordinary, in the interstices of domestic life that acts of appropriation or reappropriation are effected, which, through their link with the body and the senses and through their more or less rigorous repetition, strongly mark the meanings of being 'at home'.)

Filiod sees that the only way to do justice to the rich and fascinating detail provided by his interlocutors, is to appraise the kind of behaviour they describe in non-functional terms, as a kind of play. Globally, its function is to make their habitation habitable (to create habitability in Certeau's terms): to appropriate what they already have. One may therefore feel that Filiod adds little to his analysis by tacking on a more explicit function, derived from Mary Douglas: practices of purification and replenishment that supposedly fill out some of the empty spaces within everyday rhythms. Douglas's work, particularly the account of 'effective symbolic actions' in *Purity and Danger* (1966), is important to ritualists because it deliberately extends the concept of ritual from the sacred to the profane realm. By emphasizing the pragmatic effects of rituals in modifying experience, and creating and maintaining social relations, Douglas argued that they do not simply preserve traditions but create experience by making repetition meaningful. Yet the opposition between the pure

---

[14] Jean-Paul Filiod, ' "Ça me lave la tête": Purifications et ressourcements dans l'univers domestique', in *La Ritualisation du quotidien, Ethnologie française*, 2 (1996), 264–79; 265.

and the impure, at the heart of Douglas's discussion, relates of course to the opposition between the sacred and the profane. Although Douglas insists that profane ritual does not invoke a total order, and is necessarily fragmentary, in practice it is hard to detach such antinomies as clean/dirty, familiar/strange, orderly/disorderly from the sacred/profane prototype. At any rate, by importing these into his discussion, and referring to Douglas and other work on domestic space inspired by her categories, Filiod tends unnecessarily to invite accusations of the kind of analogy-mongering stigmatized by Jamin. It is interesting in this respect that Filiod feels the need to introduce the far less charged term 'ressourcement' (replenishment) to cover much of his data. Where purification implies norms, the vaguer notion of replenishment does not. If then, overall, it is possible to see ritual as taking us into the manifold reality of the *quotidien*—as we shall see further with the discussion of Marc Augé and the Paris metro in the next section—the preoccupation with methodology, and the self-consciously metaphorical approach of many contemporary social anthropologists make the results of studying, say, the anthropology of jogging less rewarding than one might have expected.[15]

Despite opposition from Jean Jamin and others, the ethnography of the modern world became an important strand in late-twentieth-century culture, at once distinct from and intertwined with the wider culture of the *quotidien* we are studying. Jean-Didier Urbain's lively 2003 polemic, *Ethnologue, mais pas trop: ethnologie de proximité, voyages secrets et autres expéditions minuscules* provides valuable insights into the complex interconnections of the two phenomena. An anthropologist by training, specializing in the study of such phenomena as cemeteries, beach culture, and travel, Urbain provides a vigorous defence of what he calls 'ethnologie de proximité' (which I shall continue to refer to as 'proximate ethnography'). Urbain partially accepts the premise of the great divide—that there has to be distance and difference—and at the same time acknowledges that distance is, in the first instance, lacking in the relation between an observer and his own contemporary environment. Yet if it follows from this, as Jamin claimed, that proximate ethnography depends on the simulation of distance, Urbain, unlike Jamin, vigorously champions and embraces such simulation, on the grounds, firstly, that the other aspect of the great divide, an obsession with the difference between the near and the far,

---

[15] There are however many interesting insights in Martine Segalen, *Les Enfants d'Achille et de Nike: Une ethnologie de la course à pied ordinaire* (Paris: A.M. Métailié, 1994), and her *Rites et rituels contemporains* (Paris: Nathan, 1988). See also, Claude Javeau, *Sociologie de la vie quotidienne* (Paris: PUF, 2003).

is no more than a prejudice (a 'mystique de l'Ailleurs'[16] which Urbain attacks with great verve); and secondly, that distance can effectively be simulated.

Basing himself on a long tradition of travel writing where the observer ventures into alien territories incognito, using stratagems (going native, keeping mum) that disguise his role as observer, Urbain delineates what he sees as the basic posture of the proximate ethnographer: someone who makes the familiar strange by pretending he is a stranger to it: 'ne pas être du monde qu'on observe ou bien en être mais en faisant *comme si on n'en était plus'* (not being part of the world one is observing, or else being part of it but *pretending that one is no longer*) (19). As we shall see, this overriding commitment to exteriority, whilst crucial to Urbain's debate with other ethnologists, elides the interactive process at work in the most interesting explorations of the everyday in the 1980s and 1990s. Urbain's broad brush approach, illustrated by his extensive and eclectic classified bibliographies (267–84), works best when it reveals the issues at stake in the basic stance he identifies in a vast range of authors. Perec and Barthes emerge as twin heroes, the first for his constant emphasis on the ordinary that we overlook, the second for adapting semiology to contemporary reality. Yet in both cases Urbain tends to oversimplify. Returning again and again to Perec's 'Approches de quoi?' he commends anthropologists who seem to have been inspired by Perec's ability to experience 'étonnement' at what is there in the everyday. Yet when he calls for a 'repotentialisation exotique de l'Ici-Maintenant' (exotic re-empowerment of the Here-and-Now) (74) Urbain falls into a trap that Perec carefully avoids. For in claiming that the function of proximate ethnography is to ' "éxotiser" l'endotique'[17] he implies that a shift of attention from the far to the near should involve maintaining a set of attitudes and tactics devised for the study of what was perceived as alien to 'us', rather than inventing new modes of attention designed to recognize 'us' where we have hitherto failed to do so. Urbain fails fully to acknowledge the need to recognize that, in this context, we are part and parcel of what we observe, and that it is precisely this participation that is at stake. Where Urbain proclaims the possibility of maintaining distance in order to see differently, Perec advocates a sideways look, one that sidesteps issues of distance and proximity in favour of questions of recognition and identification. Urbain insists that 'l'essentiel est dans le quotidien, qu'il s'agisse de l'Ailleurs ou de l'Ici-Maintenant' (what is essential is the

---

[16] Jean-Didier Urbain, *Ethnologue, mais pas trop: ethnologie de proximité, voyages secrets et autres expéditions minuscules* (Paris: Payot, 2003), 68.
[17] Ibid., 74. Cf. 187 'Exotiser le proche est chose ordinaire'.

everyday, whether it is overt here or Here-and-Now) (123) and there is much that is stimulating in his desire to identify the common ground in say Erving Goffman's accounts of interactive rituals in daily life, the viewpoint of Italo Calvino's *Palomar*, or Nicolson Baker's *The Mezzanine*, where the second-by-second perceptions of an office worker during his lunch hour are recorded in the minutest of detail. Yet although Urbain makes the welcome claim that the objects of everyday enquiry are less important in themselves than as component parts of 'le vaste eco-système auquel [ils] s'inscrivent', (the vast eco-system in which they are inscribed) (113)—and hence should not be studied as if they each required specialized techniques—his account of the ethnological 'regard' appears relatively one-dimensional, largely no doubt because it is consistently based on the model of travel and observation. This is borne out by Urbain's enthusiasm for Barthesian semiology, which is seen as a particular form of 'regard' that negotiates a middle passage between profuse detail and cold classification, brute fact and playful fiction. If semiology is said to provide the 'voyageur de l'immédiat' (traveller in the immediate) (175) with a style of vision where simulation and fiction serve heuristic ends, the true ramifications of Barthes's later engagement with the everyday are not acknowledged here.

The limitations of Urbain's identikit profile of the proximate ethnographer are clearly inevitable given the range of writers, texts and projects he insists on embracing. But the very fact that the parameters he sets often seem so questionable make them an excellent starting point for any discussion of recent practices of the *quotidien*, and in the next section they will be put to the test as we look at a range of texts that involve journeys in the everyday.

URBAN TRAJECTORIES: AUGÉ, MASPERO, ERNAUX, RÉDA

'La mort de l'exotisme est la caractéristique essentielle de notre époque'[18]
(The demise of the exotic is the essential characteristic of our epoch)

Three of the texts to be examined in this section—Marc Augé's *Un Ethnologue dans le métro*, François Maspero's *Les Passagers du Roissy-Express* and Annie

---

[18] Marc Augé, *Le Sens des autres* (Paris: Fayard, 1993).

Ernaux's *Journal du dehors*—exemplify approaches to the everyday derived from the evolving ideas of Lefebvre, Barthes, Certeau, and Perec.[19] Yet if they can also be seen as examples of proximate ethnography they all challenge Jean-Didier Urbain's notion of making the near at hand exotic.[20] As their titles suggest, all three projects involve simulation and the adoption of roles that draw attention to issues of difference and distance. Augé's title suggests that the viewpoint is not that of an ordinary passenger but a specialized observer; Maspero's title, playing on the exotic connotations of the Orient Express, casts the journey to Roissy airport on the suburban RER as an exotic voyage into the unknown; Ernaux's title suggests that an inside discourse (that of the diarist) will be firmly focused on the outside. Yet in each case the title is ironic: highlighting the relation between observer and observed, it suggests that the division, and hence the roles, may be far from clear-cut. The titles highlight assumptions that the texts will in fact hold up to question. As I shall demonstrate, the three authors will, in different ways, reject exoticism (as Perec had enjoined). If the question of the other is at the heart of each text, and thus of the sense of the everyday it communicates (as it is in the work of Certeau), the key issue in each case will turn out to be the inextricability of otherness and selfhood, the individual and the social.

A fourth text to be discussed—Jacques Réda's *La Liberté des rues*—features another kind of travelling in the everyday, and provides a further slant on issues of self and other, the exotic and the endotic, and the paradigm of proximate ethnography.[21] Once again, the title is ambiguous: the eponymous freedom turns out to be a privilege granted to the city walker by the streets themselves, in a process of reciprocity and recognition.

Marc Augé: Un Ethnologue dans le métro

An ethnologist in the metro: we might assume that Marc Augé, a distinguished anthropologist who had done extensive fieldwork in West Africa, set out to apply the methods of his profession to the Parisian metro. Yet it would be truer to say that, in closely probing his own experience, Augé in fact asks what lessons—and indeed challenges—the metro might have for ethnography as

---

[19] Marc Augé, *Un Ethnologue dans le métro* (Paris: Hachette, 1985); François Maspero, *Les Passagers du Roissy-Express* (Paris: Seuil, 1990); and Annie Ernaux, *Journal du dehors* (1993; Paris: Gallimard Folio, 1996).

[20] See previous section.

[21] Jacques Réda, *La Liberté des rues* (Paris: Gallimard, 1997).

practice, theory, and institution.[22] Like Maspero and Ernaux, Augé puts himself in an experimental situation and observes his own interaction with a given set of phenomena. As a result, his text, like theirs, is not an application of methods but a reflection on method. And, as with the travel narrative for Maspero, and the diary for Ernaux, the form Augé adopts—the speculative literary essay—is moulded and adapted to record the complex multiplicity of the encounter it stages. Augé's first foray into the everyday world, *La Traversée du Luxembourg*, published a year earlier in 1985, called itself an 'ethno-roman' because it used a single day (20 July 1984) in the life of the author's *alter ego* to explore the pertinence of ethnographic themes in daily life.[23] But the device is little more than the framework for a set of mini-disquisitions—on football as ritual, for example. In *Un Ethnologue dans le métro*, the 'romanesque' dimension does not reside in the simulation of plot and character, but in the imaginative work of empathy that teases out the varieties of lived experience fostered by the metro. These will in fact include experiences that make the metro, as the site of shifting meanings, fleeting encounters and unresolved narratives, itself inherently 'romanesque' (96),[24] in Barthes's sense. Augé's essay also draws attention to its digressions and parenthetical developments, necessitated by the multiple tracks of meaning that progressively emerge. The use of the essayistic 'I' grounds the discussion in first-hand experience, without involving autobiographical revelation as such, apart from a few touches. The perspective is consistently that of the user: focusing on 'la pratique du métro' (81) it progressively encompasses numerous facets of the metro as a social practice that tell us a good deal about the everyday.

Envisaging the user of the metro as a 'praticien ordinaire de la vie quotidienne' (ordinary practitioner of everyday life) (16), Augé progressively shows how, in their varied use of this basic facility, metro travellers engage with the multiplicity of social structures and the multiple identities at play within them. It is quite common to use the metro in many different ways—for leisure as well as work, in company as well as alone, in different frames of mind, at different times of the day, week or year, and at different stages of our lives. An individual's patterns of use are likely to reveal the multiplicity of a single life. Yet Augé will insist throughout that the metro is also always a social institu-

---

[22] On Augé see Michael Sheringham, 'Marc Augé and the Ethno-analysis of Everyday Life', *Paragraph*, 18 (1995), 210–22; Tom Conley, 'Introduction' and 'Afterword' to Marc Augé, *In the Metro*, trans. Tom Conley (Minneapolis: University of Minnesota Press, 2002).

[23] Marc Augé, *La Traversée du Luxembourg* (Paris: Hachette, 1985).

[24] References to *Un Ethnologue dans le métro* are incorporated in the text.

tion; when we take the metro, we participate in, and are to some degree shaped and constrained by, social laws and structures. At the heart of *Un Ethnologue* is a closely worked set of observations, disclosed by the example of the metro, on the imbrications of the social and the individual, the private and the historical, in everyday life, and the way these may be articulated with questions of identity, difference and community. Augé organizes his ideas into three main clusters, each of which links concrete aspects of the metro with the articulations (and ultimate indivisibility) of the individual and the social. He considers, firstly, the emblematic metro plan, and the names of metro stations (public and private memory); secondly, the activities people engage in while in the metro (privacy and sociability); thirdly, the large metro station, where lines intersect, as a physical space (parallel codes and dimensions of experience).

On his or her regular journey, the *habitué(e)* instinctively knows where to wait on the metro platform in view of the position of exits at his or her destination, when to quicken or slacken the pace, how to brace the body as the train takes a bend, how to avoid physical contact with other passengers. In a brilliant passage Augé shows how this know-how ('art de faire' would be Certeau's term, 'tacit knowledge' that of Polanyi) is fully embodied in routines and gestures, and he uses this as part of his account of how the individual user appropriates the metro. For many Parisians the metro plan can readily serve as an aide-memoire for their own life histories and personal trajectories, indicating routes and changes that marked particular periods of their lives, or stations that have particular connotations because of the years in which they lived, worked, socialized, or shopped. But the parallel of metro lines and lifelines, with their overlaps, doublings back, and repetitions, suggests that the mode of identity the metro reveals is not singular but plural. For it points less to signal events than to the divergences, convergences, coalescences, and disproportions between the various dimensions of our professional, sentimental, medical, historical, and political lives. The metro points to the way that the individual is really plural (17), while suggesting that our plurality is one thing we have in common with everyone else. And from there we can surmise that our difference from ourselves is perhaps not so different from our difference from others. Throughout his investigation of the metro Augé will find evidence that difference is not what divides selves from others; rather, alterity figures right across the space of relations (with self and others) engendered by the social practice of metro travel.

This is where the issue of exoticism comes in. Proponents of the great divide insist that anthropology depends on the difference between we and they. But who are we and who are they? Augé's point is that modernity has brought about a redistribution or relocation of alterity. In certain respects we may be as different from (or as similar) to our fellow metro travellers as we are from members of a given African tribe. The Alterity (with capital A, as in Lacan's 'Autre') that separated us from them, in the exotic dispensation, has been largely superseded by minor alterities (as in Lacan's 'petit a'), and it is imperative that we locate the latter—which Augé calls 'alterité immédiate'—just as much within our self as between ourselves and others around us, both here— in the metro—and in distant parts. My metro life/line is never coterminous with yours, but stretches of it will be common, and overall the difference between us is not absolute but stems from the relative distribution of things that are the same and things that are different. Yet the differences are real: they do not need to be imported (or simulated) in a strategy that exoticizes the familiar in order to unveil it. As the diverse populace of the metro shows at a glance, generational, class, sexual, cultural, and even physical difference can work just as much as agents of differentiation (or affinity) as ethnicity.

A consideration of the names of metro stations suggests that history is an important component of the difference within and between individuals. Stations bearing the names of famous people or historic events indicate the possibility of shared bearings and collective memory; our own past is intertwined with that of the city, the nation, and beyond. Yet if history gives individual identity a collective dimension there is nothing uniform about this. One type of difference between individuals is the nature and degree of collective memory that forms part of their make-up. And if the metro provides some occasions for communing in shared memory, it tends rather to illustrate how the collective dimension of individual experience is generally lived through at a private level.

As Augé shows in the central part of his discussion, the 'practice' of the metro illustrates the central paradox of ritual experiences, which are necessarily social and collective, but are nevertheless lived through individually and subjectively. The metro is a system: a regular, ordered, and functional space, and when we travel by metro we participate in its codes, whether we conform to them or violate them. Participation does not deny subjectivity, it defines the conditions of subjectivity in the everyday world. Useful here is Augé's distinction between solitude and isolation. By and large, what we do in the metro is what everyone else does: doze, read, listen to music, stare into space, observe others whilst avoiding eye contact, etc. In the constrained circumstances of metro travel, people act in a fairly stereotypical and circumscribed range of ways, which suggests that they do not act in isolation but as part of a social body. Yet the absence of isolation does not mean the absence of solitary individuality. To engage in behaviour that could be classified as average does not make one a cipher—a Mr or Mrs Average.

Yet the limitation of traditional anthropological theory is that it views social behaviour in ways that deny solitude, autonomy, and subjectivity. If the metro is potentially an example of what Marcel Mauss called a total social fact—a phenomenon (like gift exchange) that implies the totality of social processes (e.g. religious, economic, linguistic, symbolic)—the drawback of Mauss's approach is that it filters out the concreteness of individual experience. Augé develops this point at length in a 'detour' where he offers a close analysis of Mauss in the light of Lévi-Strauss's famous commentary.[25] Augé shows how Lévi-Strauss subtly reworks the theory of the 'total social fact' to introduce, in principle, individual subjectivity (and not just the 'average' person) into the relation between person and social ritual. Lévi-Strauss argues that the ethnographer needs to grasp the social fact from both outside and inside, apprehending the 'subjective understanding (conscious or unconscious)' involved in 'living the fact'. In practical terms this involves identifying and probing the innumerable ways in which subjective understanding or participation is objectified in behaviour. Yet for Augé the value of Lévi-Strauss's notion of 'le processus illimité d'objectivation du sujet' (the subject's endless process of objectification) is undermined when, confronted with the reality of ethnic difference (and hence inter-ethnic comprehension of subjectivity), he chooses to locate subjective participation in the supposedly universal dimension of unconscious structures, thus again, like Mauss, subsuming the concrete into the general. If Augé believes the metro can be seen as a 'total social fact' it is because it bears out the central intuition articulated, but qualified, by Mauss and Lévi-Strauss, that the human being's own self-consciousness as an individual only arises in the context of consciousness of others, 'bref, qu'ils ne prennent conscience d'eux-mêmes qu'en prenant conscience des autres, qu'il n'y a de conscience individuelle que sociale' (they only become conscious of themselves when they become conscious of others, individual consciousness is social) (69). This implies the need to relativize the notion of the other, recognizing that 'il y a de l'autre dans le même, et la part de même qui est dans l'autre est indispensable au moi social' (there is other in the same, and the

---

[25] Claude Lévi-Strauss, 'Introduction à l'œuvre de Marcel Mauss', in Marcel Mauss, *Sociologie et Anthropologie* (1950; Paris: PUF, 1997).

portion of sameness in the other is indispensable to the social self) (70). As we shall see, a similar perception is at the heart of both Maspero's and Ernaux's forays into the *quotidien*.

For Augé, then, to see the metro as a 'total social fact' is not to establish an overall 'culture' of the metro, and its local variations, but to home in on the interactions of users and systems. Useful here is Mauss's emphasis on contract. As is suggested by the various categories of ticket, the metro is a contractual system. The fact that metro users display their differences through the clothes (or badges) they wear, their reading matter, and so on, implies awareness of others. This is further borne out if we consider deviant forms of behaviour like thieving ('la fauche') and cheating ('la triche'). Hopping over the ticket barrier with youthful agility, the cheat acknowledges the contract he flouts. Different types of beggar and performer impose additional forms of contract with other passengers, especially when they invade the carriage and demand reciprocity for their services. Avoiding such invasiveness, musicians in the metro corridors tacitly invite reward for their talents; while some beggars also adopt a minimalist approach by indicating their predicament on a bit of card and confronting the passer-by with their physical appearance, sometimes theatrically enhanced (Ernaux too will pay close attention to styles of begging in the metro). In their parading of abjection, such beggars incarnate 'what we are not' (86). Mauss described beggars as representatives of the gods and the dead, and Augé sees them as 'black holes in our everyday galaxy', symbolizing the totality of the social system of which they are the outer edge. In the spectacle of the metro we gauge our similarities with and differences from others, drawing wider inferences from dress, gestures, and other details, which we see as 'objectivations' of subjective existence. And at the same time we measure ourselves against the overall view of us that the metro as a whole seems to promote through its notices to users and the imagery that festoons its walls.

In the third chapter, Augé looks at another feature of the metro that makes it a 'total social fact'—the 'correspondance'. The social practice of the metro is also a symbolic practice because its 'parcours' and 'itinéraires' (key words in the text) often link different dimensions of an individual's life: for example, public and private, economic and sexual, political and convivial. This is emblematized by overground stretches, where the metro suddenly emerges from below, and above all by the switching between lines in the many stations that offer 'correspondances'. To change lines is often to shift between roles and identities, negotiating the transitions between the different lives a single person leads. An intermediate space, the metro station, with its corridors and concourses, is 'romanesque' because those who traverse it are in transit between disparate 'symbolic systems' (Lévi-Strauss is again invoked). And this further illustrates how, as the concretization of 'a total social fact', the metro is not a circumscribed system but a necessarily open and mobile totality of relationships within which no two participants ever fully coincide. Thus an ethnographic study of the metro would have to engage with this mobile multiplicity, and Augé ends with some suggestions as to how one might proceed. He commends a close study of a single station, Franklin-Roosevelt for example, based not on statistics or interviews but on minute observations, and offers various guidelines, dealing at length with the ways in which advertising images could be analysed, with the presence of retail outlets and officialdom that extend the economic and juridical dimensions of the metro, and with the convergence of classes from different lines.

Augé's reinterpretation of the Maussian 'total social fact', in the light of his progressive evaluation of the parameters that make up the social space of the metro, brings it into harmony with concepts of the everyday. The emphasis throughout is on the practice and experience of metro users, and the central insight is that the constraints, limitations, and regulations of social existence do not annul freedom and individuality but constitute the framework in which they are exercised. The fact that every 'parcours' depends on the system does not mean they are identical. We discover ourselves through our discovery of others, and in so doing we come to acknowledge that part of what is 'us' is as other as 'they' are. The ghosts of Perec (quoted three times) and Certeau can be detected in Augé's metro, whilst in Augé's subsequent 'ethno-analyses' of the contemporary world, Certeau and Barthes will be prominent, along with Lefebvre's account of space. *Domaines et châteaux* (1989) draws on Barthes's account of fashion to study glossy advertisements for luxury houses in upmarket magazines. *Non-Lieux* (1992) investigates the 'non-places' that are a feature of 'surmodernité' (supermodernity). A prologue introduces them by imagining a motorway journey to Roissy airport and then, via cash points, check-in desks and other interchangeable public areas, to the airline passenger's sense of anonymous well-being. Like Certeau, Augé attaches considerable importance to the backlash against uniformity wielded by the individual user of systems. Traditionally, the 'anthropological place' is the cornerstone of stable identity, social relations and historical continuity. Supermodernity clearly imperils all this, yet, as Augé insists, places (or non-places) still exist, and subjective experience survives. To locate this, we need to see how the organisation of space reveals the relationship between shared and individual identity in a given collectivity. This means that the ethnologist has to put himself in the place of those he studies and become 'le plus subtil et le plus savant des indigènes' (the most knowledgeable and subtle of the natives),[26] seeking to empathize with the way a member of a collectivity understands, if indirectly, the anthropological reality of his own existence. Augé emphasizes that the non-places produced by supermodernity are not monopolistic but coexist with other more stable and relational spaces in a sort of palimpsest or patchwork. Following Certeau (from whom the expression 'non-place' is adapted), Augé sees space in terms of spatial practices, notably travel, ethnic migration, and new technologies which upset the traditional relation between place and identity. Where the traditional place bears the imprint of its inhabitant, the non-place produces the identity of passenger, client, migrant, or Sunday tripper. Or rather, in loosening the grip of socialized identity, the non-place provides an experiential zone where new modes of freedom and identity, grounded in solitude rather than communality, come into view: 'C'est dans l'anonymat du non-lieu que s'éprouve solitairement la communauté des destins humains' (It is in the anonymity of non-places that the solitary individual experiences the communality of human destinies).[27] In *Le Sens des autres* (1993) Augé explores at length the links between the transformation of space and the transformation of alterity. The demise of exoticism is seen as a cardinal feature of the late twentieth century, and the need to engage with 'l'autre proche'—starting with the ways in which modern experience makes us other to ourselves—is a task of paramount importance that should not be left to ethnologists.

Marc Augé's defence and illustration of proximate ethnography, in a range of works, makes a key contribution to discussions of the *quotidien* because it consistently wrestles with the ways in which everyday life in the modern world both invites and resists ethnological scrutiny. Recognizing his debts to Barthes, Perec, and Certeau, Augé develops a style that combines first-hand experience, empathetic projection and essayistic rumination, and foregrounds the tensions between anthropological doctrine and the concrete reality of the everyday world. If Augé is sometimes inclined to over-emphasize his abstract conclusions, the way he engages with his own hands-on experience of the metro or the motorway heralds the adventures of subsequent investigators.

---

[26] Marc Augé, *Non-Lieux: Introduction à une anthropologie de la surmodernité* (Paris: Seuil, 1992), 58.
[27] Ibid., 150.

François Maspero: Les Passagers du Roissy-Express

Les Passagers du Roissy-Express records a journey through the Paris suburbs. In May-June 1989, as France prepared to celebrate the freedoms of the French Revolution, and while student ferment in China turned into the tragic massacre of Tianamen Square, the writer-broadcaster (and erstwhile left-wing publisher and bookseller) François Maspero, accompanied by his friend Anaïk Frantz—whose photographs of people and places he had long ad-mired—spent a month on the Ligne B of the RER. Having said goodbye to their sceptical families and friends, the two companions travelled to Roissy-Charles de Gaulle airport, the end of one of the northern branches of the line (which traverses Paris on a roughly NE to SW axis) and then, rather than jet off to a distant destination, began to wind their way back, with the rough aim of devoting a day to each stop on the line, finding modest bed and board on the way, and talking to as many of the local inhabitants as possible. Going over the motivating factors behind the journey, Maspero recalls one particular moment when, returning from the airport on a rainy January day, he had been struck by how little he knew of the suburbs he could see through the window of the train. Here, he mused, were the truly uncharted spaces, now that charter flights have made Peru and China relatively familiar. Yet rather than relocating the exotic, Maspero, like Augé, seems more concerned to question presup-positions (including his own) about the 'otherness' of the suburbs. When he outlines his project, friends either think he is crazy or believe he has a mission: they see the 'banlieues' as a problem area, a 'magma informe' (24) that needs sorting out. Maspero's perception is more ambivalent.[28] Seen from the train, the suburbs do seem to lack any coherence—'incompréhensibles espaces désarticulés' (incomprehensible shapeless spaces) (14) he calls them—yet, as he slowly hatches his plans, Maspero realizes that his desire to explore the *banlieue* stems partly from the recent transformation of his own quarter in central Paris, where the traditional residents have slowly been forced out by rampant commercialization and cultural packaging. If the centre has become empty, a 'centre bidon', perhaps the periphery, the 'tout autour' to which the old inhabitants have migrated, is now 'le vrai centre'—a decentred centre, but

---

[28] References will be incorporated in the text. On *Les Passagers* see Max Silverman, *Facing Postmodernity* (London: Routledge, 1999); Jean-Xavier Ridon, 'Un Barbare en banlieue', *Nottingham French Studies*, 39/1 (Spring 2000), 25–38; Kathryn Jones, 'Voices of the Banlieues: Constructions of Dialogue in François Maspero's *Les Passagers du Roissy-Express*, *Contemporary French and Francophone Studies*, 8/2 (Spring 2004), 127–34.

nevertheless something possessing a life—'la vraie vie'—that the capital has lost (25)?

These conflicting images of disarticulation and plenitude, linked to specific historical processes, will continue to haunt Maspero throughout his journey in the suburbs, and they inspire the ground rules which, from its inception, give the project its flavour. The central rule, which will determine the way Maspero and his companion go about things, is to be travellers rather than investigators, amateurs rather than professionals. The journey will be a 'balade' (jaunt) not an 'enquête' (investigation) (20). They will not *pretend* to be travellers, they *will* be travellers, doing exactly what travellers usually do: using maps and guides to plan the daily itinerary, looking out for suitable places to stay and to visit, and then taking pot luck. The aim will be to enjoy and learn, profiting from any encounters along the way. They will not consult specialist works (in sociology, demography, economics, social policy) or conduct surveys, but nor will they be empty-headed tourists simply out for a good time. After all, travellers often make sure they are well informed, so as to get the most out of a trip and appreciate the sights. The main thing is to keep an open mind, to look rather than to judge or diagnose. This does not mean becoming anonymous or neutral: but being onself. 'Ce n'était pas une enquête. C'était juste un regard, le leur, et rien d'autre, un regard attentif' (It wasn't an investigation. It was just a look, and no more, an attentive look) (22). And in this context, an attentive look is not external and objective, but one that seeks to establish a connection: 'Plutôt que de regarder, dire ça me regarde' (rather than look, say this concerns me) (20). An attentive look does not interrogate, it prompts one to ask things; rather than hurrying, it observes the rhythms of the everyday: 'Ils ne feraient rien que de très ordinaire. Ils laisseraient couler le temps, celui de tous les jours, et ils suivraient son rythme' (they would do nothing out of the ordinary. They would let everyday time pass, and follow its rhythm) (23).

These considerations explain why Maspero invites Anaïk Frantz to go with him. Although she has carried out numerous photographic projects, she works as a supermarket demonstrator because her pictures lack the obvious picturesque or shock features that would make them commercial. Anaïk takes pictures of people on the margins, in their own surroundings, often studying the progressive demolition of an area or community. What Maspero likes about her pictures is their commitment to an ongoing history: 'une histoire à suivre [...] C'étaient des photos qui prenaient leur temps' (a history to be pursued ... They were photos that took their time) (18). The travelling companions bring different things to the journey. Maspero deals with the written word: maps, guides, books, pamphlets, and inscriptions revealing the histories of the various localities. He attempts to keep notes as they go along, and to write them up in the evenings, and he is responsible for the final text which takes the form of a diary in which he generally refers to himself in the third person, as 'François'. 'Anaïk' takes photographs, but since she is averse to snapshots, and always asks people if she can take their picture, her role is also to break the ice and engage people in conversation.

From the moment they set off, François and Anaïk discover how complex and fragmented the northern suburbs are, with their endless motorways, slip roads, tunnels, railway lines, factories, hangars, and so on. This jumble of juxtaposed vertical and horizontal bits is not a continuous space, but 'des espèces d'espaces' in Perec's vivid phrase, gratefully acknowledged by Maspero ('merci Perec' (30)), making up a puzzle where there always seems to be a piece missing. Usually you just whizz past, but what if instead you slow down and try and experience it 'on the ground'? Would it be possible to get a sense of what it is like to live in these 'species of spaces'? Clearly, to test this out you need to talk to the people who do live there, but the richness of Maspero's project lies in his recognition that to understand people's first-hand experiences you need also to understand the socio-political, economic, and broadly historical processes in which those experiences are embedded. In Certeau's terms you need to see the *lieu* as an 'espace pratiqué', a sedimented space made up of accumulated narratives. History, then, plays a key role in *Les Passagers*, and before coming on to the interactions with individuals I want to focus on this aspect.

The first thing to note about the place of history in Maspero's project is its plurality and profusion. He is interested in the ways the past still impinges on the present—in the past's traces, or their absence (attempts to obliterate the past are of course abundant here). Real history, he notes, is 'accumulation, mélange, confusion et même bric-à-brac' (33). Deliberately eclectic, his sources include: old guide books, such as the 1921 Blue Guide, that retain a sense of the traveller's itinerary rather than picking highlights; pamphlets and guides written by local historians and available only *in situ*; monuments and museums; the schedules of major building projects; and perhaps above all the testimony of those who live there. These multiple histories feature in *Les Passagers* alongside other ingredients that give its pages, already enlivened by Anaïk's photos, an agreeably cluttered and populated feel. For example, transcriptions of innumerable notices, posters, stickers, graffiti, and 'tags' (echoes of Perec's '3 secteur'); references to writers like Nerval and Dumas, associated with the Plaine de France; and excerpts from numerous conversations, some of them derived from the recordings François makes on his small Sony tape recorder. Such abundance constantly gives the lie to the prevailing idea that there is nothing to see in the suburbs, as does the humorous pastiche of picaresque travel fiction in the form of chapter digests in bold italics that summarize the day's adventures.

Maspero pays particular attention to the way historical factors, now generally forgotten, have shaped the human geography through which he is travelling, particularly as regards questions of housing. Like Lefebvre, Barthes, Certeau, and Perec, he is acutely aware of the role played by urban planning in determining the everyday conditions of people's lives. Delving into the background of such huge housing developments as the 3000 at Aulnay or the 4000 at La Courneuve (where the reference in the chapter digest reads 'barre implosée, racines perdues' (imploded block, lost roots)(193)) he discovers political and economic factors that have left lasting scars on their residents. Guided round Villepinte by Gilles, a young postman who had studied with Maspero's friend, the geographer Yves Lacoste (who will himself be visited later in the journey), François learns to 'read' the built environment by understanding its layers: 'il y a là presque un siècle de conceptions successives d'habitats venus s'agglomérer. Traverser Villepinte, c'est comme opérer une coupe dans des stratifications géologiques' (here is an agglomeration of nearly a century of conceptions of habitation. Crossing Villepinte is like cutting through geological strata) (113). At Drancy, François is surprised to find that the Cité de la Muette, which had been the location of the notorious transit camp for Jews rounded up in Paris during the Occupation and sent to their deaths in the Nazi camps, has reverted to being a 'grand ensemble', as it had been when the architects Lods and Beaudoin designed it in 1935. Yet in some of the most haunting pages of the book Maspero delves into the history of this site, splicing an account of the visit with a collage of documents; and he comes to perceive an affinity between the enduring emptiness and soul-destroying banality of this architecture and the 'banality of evil' perpetrated here. The Cité de la Muette could go seamlessly from being a supposedly enlightened housing project to a transit camp, and then house people again, because it had always been an essentially inhuman space (187).

Drancy survives because, despite some plaques and an ugly monument that everyone ignores, its history has been forgotten. In *Les Passagers* the absence or erasure of history emerges progressively as an essential criterion of 'non-habitability', as it is in Perec. On the negative side, the Plan Delouvrier and

other *démarches* of post-war planning have been responsible for vast developments that obliterate local histories; and some of Maspero's efforts to redress
this, with recourse to his pamphlets and old guides, can seem whimsically
antiquarian. At times the reader may feel François has been carried away by his
enthusiasm for historical detail for its own sake, as in the lengthy accounts of
Aulnay or Pierre Laval's Aubervilliers. Yet, on the positive side, Maspero finds
much to be heartened by in his meetings with such 'native informants' as
Gilles, or Akim, who shows him round Aubervilliers, or Rachid, or Gérard
who is the guide in Arcueil, as well as with the many encounters with
inhabitants who display a keen awareness of the factors shaping their everyday
lives.

   Anaïk's photographs (around sixty in all—one every five or six pages) are
not only a record of the travellers' many encounters, but mementos of real
exchanges where the ritual of having one's picture taken played a part. Anaïk
does not take snapshots, she is sensitive to people's suspicions—she and
François are constantly taken for journalists (61) or inspectors from the
town hall—and like her companion she is well aware that, in these suburbs
with large immigrant communities, racial tensions are legion. She always seeks
permission to photograph, and when on one occasion there is a misunder-
standing, she is not at all surprised by the hostile reaction of a group of Malian
youths, and their concern for the 'respect de l'autre' (127). But her motives for
asking are essentially positive, since inviting people to choose how they would
like to be depicted produces pictures that reveal a felt relationship to their
everyday environment. This is palpable, for example, in the wistful image of
an old man at his window in Roissy-Ville (in fact a still rustic village blighted
by the airport) (34); two women, with a baby and a husky conversing in front
of a high-rise (48); two black youths posing in front of a magnificent 'tag' (51);
M. Salomon and his dog Mickey sunbathing by the Canal de l'Ourq (82); a
group of schoolchildren striding across a *terrain vague* towards a cluster of
tower blocks in the distance (95); Mme Bernadette at her desk in the run-
down Chinese hotel at Aulnay. The photographs often commemorate encounters where Anaïk and François were given vivid and moving insights into
the life stories of very varied individuals and families: one man remembers the
Great War, but also his childhood amidst memories of 1870; another recol-
lects the column that set out from Aubervilliers to join the peaceful demonstration by Algerians in 1961 that ended in a savage massacre by Paris police;
Mme Marie-José remembers rag-pickers in the 'zone' round the old fortifica-
tions, while Daoud tells them about his participation in a film.

Anaïk found little to photograph on the second leg of the journey, when after sixteen days she and François crossed Paris under ground and emerged in the much wealthier southern suburbs. If everyone in the north aspires to an individual 'pavillon', in places like Sceaux, Fontenay, and Robinson most people actually live in one, and street encounters can be infrequent. The 'banlieue sud' is François's patch, and the journey will end at his family house in Milon. This is just beyond the terminus of the Ligne de Sceaux (subsequently incorporated into the Ligne B, with a branch line to Robinson), and François is able to serve as native informant here, quoting his own testimony verbatim between inverted commas (275–83). Thanks to Gérard, François is able to realize his childhood dream of ascending the Arcueil aqueduct as he helps out the organizers of a vast municipal banquet that forms part of the bicentennial celebrations. The book's concern with the opposition between real histories and the fake history of modern commemorative culture comes to a head here, underscored by the remnants of the mayor's pompous speech transcribed from Fançois's Sony.

François ascribes the relative meagreness of the second part of his account to the growing disorder and incoherence of his notes. Yet after covering the fourteen stops of the northern half in sixteen days he and Anaïk could have devoted at least an equal amount of time and space to the South, whereas in fact they cover twenty-four stops in ten days, and end their journey after being away somewhat less than the anticipated month. After a fairly detailed account of the communist suburb of Arcueil, the text condenses the whole of the last week (4–10 June) into a mere twenty pages, employing the phrase 'on les a vus' anaphorically to introduce some isolated scenes. A predominant note here is indeed isolation: by contrast with the northern suburbs, the travellers feel cut off, remote from actuality, including the breaking news of real historical developments in China.

Yet Maspero shows a reluctance to make any general observations or to draw conclusions. And this underlines a key feature of *Les Passagers*: the adherence to its own ground rules. Throughout the diary of the journey we are given glimpses of François anxiously marshalling his scrappy notes in fly-blown hotel bedrooms, at odds with the dynamic executives he sees arriving for their daytime seminars. As in Perec's experiments, the metatextual dimension provides regular updates on the physical and mental conditions of the protagonist, and François increasingly reports on his inability to order his material. Yet his difficulties testify to two related issues: the desire to maintain a spirit of openness, receptivity, and reciprocity (to look rather than judge, to exchange rather than interrogate) and the sheer profuse richness of the sights, sounds, voices, and lives encountered. It is hardly surprising that François runs out of steam in the southern suburbs: already an *habitué*, he sees mainly what he already knows, and surrenders to the temptation of pastiche (composing odes to dogs and trains). Does this mean that there really was more to see in the stricken North, or did the spectacle of deprivation turn Maspero, despite himself, into a nostalgic dealer in the exotic, in the tradition of Doisneau and Prévert? The question is valid, and it is a tribute to the honesty of *Les Passagers* that it remains unresolved. Yet this honesty, and the genuine discoveries, about themselves as well as others, that he and Anaïk make, are a tribute to the invention of a mode of enquiry where the everyday is given a space to breathe, without being pressed into existing moulds.

Annie Ernaux: Journal du dehors

Five years after original publication in 1993, on its second appearance in the 'Folio' series, *Journal du dehors* featured a preface, dated 1996, where Annie Ernaux discussed the motives behind the book.[29] No doubt designed to counteract the disorientation many readers had experienced, this preface has the disadvantage of playing down one of the work's most striking features: the hesitant, exploratory nature of the project, and the way, without the preface, readers must respond piecemeal to the book's fragments, absorbing along the way the rare metatextual statements that seem to emerge at specific points in the evolution of the project.[30] Setting aside the preface, I want initially to consider the sparser paratextual material provided for the 1993 reader—title, epigraph, and a two-sentence back-cover text, signed 'A.E.' The title seems to point to a deliberate paradox: a form generally devoted to recording inner experience—the 'journal intime'—will be used to record the 'outside': specifically, according to the first sentence on the back cover, scenes and conversations 'transcribed' in the RER, hypermarkets, and the shopping centre of the Ville nouvelle at Cergy-Pontoise where the author lives. But if this suggests a wholesale switch from subject to object (the verb 'transcribe' might imply this), the epigraph from Jean-Jacques Rousseau offers a corrective: 'Notre *vrai*

---

[29] Page references, to the 1996 Folio edition, will be incorporated in the text.

[30] On *Journal du dehors*, see Siobhahn McIlvaney, *Annie Ernaux: The Return to Origins* (Liverpool: Liverpool University Press, 2001), 117–52, Nancy Miller, 'Autobiographical Others: Annie Ernaux's *Journal du dehors*', *Sites* (Spring 1998), 127–39.

moi n'est pas tout entier en nous' (our *real* self is not entirely within us) implies that the true self, which the 'journal intime' traditionally seeks to express, may lie outside rather than inside; and thus that a 'social' self, linked to collective experience, and often held to be inauthentic, is in fact 'true'. The second sentence on the back cover suggests that this self is revealed through fleeting human encounters that provoke an emotive reaction—disquiet, anger, or pain—and make us feel that our life is 'traversed' by others. The revelation does not stem from the analysis of feelings but from the transcription of the event in its specificity.

How are these parameters reflected in the text we are given to read? *Journal du dehors* consists of one hundred and twenty 'entries' covering an eight-year period, from 1985 to 1992. Although each records a specific experience, the texts, unlike most diary entries, are not individually dated but simply grouped in years. Distribution is very uneven, as a result either of selectivity or intermittent commitment to the project (as in Perec's *Lieux*): for example, there are forty-two entries for 1986 and only twelve altogether for the last three years. The focus on outer events is consistently maintained: we glean very few biographical details about the author, and nothing about her own residence, but we learn a good deal about the social spaces of her daily life: the suburban train that takes her regularly to the Gare Saint-Lazare, and then, when the Ligne A of the RER opens in 1988 (75), into one of the big Parisian stations such as Auber; the Paris metro and fashionable clothes stores; the motorway; the big supermarkets of the Ville-Nouvelle and the retail outlets and services of its main square and shopping centre: butcher, post office, hairdresser, chemist, ironmonger, and so on, as well as the taxi queue, the orthopaedist, and the dentist. Other manifestations of the 'outside', which impact on the author, are newspaper articles (*Le Monde* and *Libération* are cited), radio and TV programmes, popular songs, graffiti, advertisements, and flyers (including posters and small ads), and snatches of overheard dialogue. The list underlines the diversity of contexts where, in the course of her daily life, and without practising introspection, Ernaux finds herself engaged in encounters that simultaneously reveal the age she lives in and aspects of her own identity. Grasping this imbrication of self and other, and pursuing the ramifications of identity it implies, do not involve turning inwards, however, but 'homing in' on the encounter, for it is the outside that reveals the self, not the inside. For Ernaux, transcription does not therefore involve playing up the subjective component in the event so much as playing back its objective unfolding in a way that will reveal—through inference—the elements within it that provoked a reaction. What is being explored is less a psychological reaction, a characteristic way of responding to certain types of event, than the way in which a dimension of one's identity is, as it were, held in suspension in the outer world.

Transcribing, then, does not mean accentuating the personal but locating what Ernaux, in a short essay, 'Vers un Je transpersonnel', written the same year as *Journal du dehors*, calls the 'transpersonal'. Recounting her earlier shift from autobiographical fiction to the 'family ethnography' of *La Place* and *Une femme*, where she had explored the lives of her mother and father, Ernaux notes that, in adopting the first-person singular in these works, her aims had been objective not subjective. In these hybrid texts, combining literature, sociology, and history, the 'je' becomes impersonal, or rather transpersonal, as it fuses self and other, seeking not to bolster an identity but to grasp, in the field of Ernaux's own experience, the signs of a wider collective reality.[31] This is carried a stage further when a form of writing, the diary, where we expect the 'I' to be prominent, is used, 'transpersonally'. For a striking feature of *Journal du dehors* is the attenuation of the 'I', totally absent from more than two-thirds of the individual fragments. 'Transcribing' for Ernaux means using a wide range of strategies to render the way the subject's participation in the event (generally that of an onlooker in whom it provokes a tacit reaction) does not point to more or less familiar psychological traits, that could help build up a portrait, but to less individualized regions of identity relating to class, gender, cultural status, economic power, consumerism, language, education. Among the most prominent of these writing strategies are the use of neutral language such as 'on' or 'il faut', and the narration of events in the historic present, using direct quotation and obviating contextualization. When it is used, the 'Je' refers, by and large, to the subject of verbs of action (who did this, or went there), the recipient of 'impressions', or else the author, rather than the protagonist. Thus, in the nine entries for 1985, the first of only two instances of 'Je' conveys actions in a supermarket car park (12), while, in the second, Ernaux reports reading her horoscope and wondering all day which of various men is the promised 'homme merveilleux'. This prompts a metatextual aside on the impact of using the first person, in an ostensibly 'literary' work where the reader is likely to have a lofty image of 'the author', to register trivial daily acts and responses. Encapsulating the reader's imagined censure, Ernaux remarks that ' "Je" fait honte au lecteur' ('I' makes the reader embarrassed) (19).

---

[31] Annie Ernaux, 'Vers un Je transpersonnel', *Cahiers RITM*, 6 (Paris: Université Paris X-Nanterre, 1994), 219.

By blurring the distinction between inner and outer, private and public, Ernaux's experimental observations look at how the dimensions of identity we often think of as private (as pertaining only to ourselves), are in fact inseparable from the occasions and interactions in social space—i.e. everyday space— that reveal them. I want now to focus on how Ernaux's text enacts the plurality of our everyday identities. As already noted, the individual entries that make up *Journal du dehors* transcribe, explicitly, a moment in an urban trajectory where Ernaux has observed something that caught her attention, and, implicitly, the nature of her reaction to the scene or event. The core of the text lies in the multiplicity of both the occasions and the reactions, and this makes the fragments difficult to classify since each gives, so to speak, a different slant to the self–other, public–private relationship, providing a further angle at which the indivisibility of the social and the personal in everyday life is refracted.

One broad cluster of fragments relates to questions of gender. Given the important dynamic of positive and negative identification which *Journal du dehors* uncovers in social space, it is unsurprising that reactions to women and 'female' behaviour are prominent. For example, as in the case of the horoscope, Ernaux notes how strongly she feels the power exerted by both popular songs and new fashions. In a big department store the rapid sequence of desire triggered by different styles and colours is compared to an assault (55), while the intense but unresolved desire provoked by a song blaring out in a supermarket is able to conjure up a period in her past more effectively than any work of literature (63). Sexuality, as well as gender, is often an important component in Ernaux's reactions. Reading an item about a museum displaying Imelda Marcos's wardrobe, she speculates on the different fantasies the vast collection of luxurious underwear would inspire in women as opposed to men (23). In another fragment a woman chewing gum in the metro is 'read' in terms of the male fantasy Ernaux imagines this sight would inspire (43). Interesting here is the way Ernaux's approach draws on and diverts the semiological analysis of modern culture and media inaugurated by Barthes. The frequent use of the word 'signes' draws attention to the way Ernaux acts as a detached observer of urban codes and sign systems. But when she describes a lesbian pick-up (83), a woman at the butcher's ordering 'un bifteck pour mon homme' (a steak for my man) (17), a charismatic male voice tempting housewives with special offers over a supermarket sound system, which turns out to belong to an unprepossessing man (18), or checkout girls reversing gender roles when they push a man round the aisles in a wheelchair (50), there is an added level provided by a complex play of identification and subjective reaction. Inflected by issues of gender, class, sexuality, and personal identity, the semiological gaze is conscripted into a wider textual network. The relations between gender and filiation are clearly at play in several entries centred on the interaction of mothers and daughters.

Class is a central preoccupation in *Journal du dehors*, and many fragments reflect the way Ernaux's reactions to people and events are affected by her own social trajectory from rural working-class origins to the cultivated and economically comfortable middle classes. Ernaux often reports occurrences when her response clearly derived from an enduring solidarity with working-class or culturally deprived people. This sometimes takes the form of indignation at middle-class condescension, as when Jacques Chirac refers to 'les petites gens' (39), or the historian Jacques le Goff implies that he finds the metro exotic (47). In more complex cases Ernaux, now conscious of being a middle-class teacher and writer, is surprised by reactions that reveal her instinctive sympathy with and understanding of working-class mores. In one fragment the censorious reaction to a silly hit song about 'Pernod and saucisson' is initially one Ernaux clearly shares, yet she views such censure as stemming from a failure to see anything positive in working-class culture (65). At the chemist's, the expressions used by a woman purchasing medicines for 'her man' remind Ernaux of her own 'original' culture (70). Similarly, in the RER, Ernaux is struck by the verbal exchanges of a jovial group on a works outing (74), and in the metro by a working-class girl telling her friend that her boyfriend had not informed his best mates that she was pregnant (71). Ernaux often responds to scenes where social classes are juxtaposed or opposed, as when a middle-aged woman at the supermarket checkout is publicly humiliated by an irate customer who calls in the supervisor to check the till receipt (24). Several entries observe the tactical interaction between beggars and commuters, noting for example (78) the success of a down-and-out whose play-acting distances him from his abject condition, making it more 'acceptable', and in another case the advent of a new form of 'manche' where the beggar, with ironic cynicism, asks for money 'to get pissed' (87).

The theatricality of social exchange in public space is a consistent theme in *Journal du dehors*, which Ernaux links to the experience of living in a Ville nouvelle, created *ex nihilo*, and where social structure has no long-term antecedents but is affirmed through behaviour. One entry focuses on the accumulated detritus on a piece of land 'behind the scenes', which contrasts with the show of civic tidiness generally promoted in the new suburb (29). At the hairdressing salon, in the post office, in the metro and the RER, Ernaux is a keen observer of what Goffman called 'impression management'—people forging identities by dress and gesture and above all 'talking to the gallery'.[32] Two entries (41, 92) carefully study the behaviour of people at the butcher's, including a middle-aged, middle-class couple, whose double act, choosing meat in loud voices and showing off their 'valued customer' status, reinforces their sense of social superiority. In the train, a mother and daughter, just back from holidays, 'make a spectacle' of their intimacy (49), whilst, on another occasion (45), a woman tells her friend, in endless detail, a complicated story about her mother, revelling, as Ernaux sees it, in the 'erotic' power of narrative. In the metro (91) a young couple alternate aggression and canoodling, giving the appearance of insouciance but in fact eyeing the other passengers from time to time. On another occasion, two tramps create embarrassment by loud expostulations. At a cheap discount store a checkout girl parades her indifference to the customers by engaging in conversation with a couple of her friends (91).

As we acclimatize ourselves to the modes of social understanding at work in *Journal du dehors*, we are likely, as readers, to have a sense that the reaction underlying many scenes is based on identification, and that Ernaux discovers bits of herself in the people she sees. The recurrent figure of the boy who rounds up trolleys in the supermarket car park (12, 16, 39, 56), disappears for a while, and is then glimpsed out of uniform, as a paying customer in the company of his girlfriend, can perhaps be seen as an avatar of Ernaux whose double vision often induces her to imagine what she would have been like if she had not broken away from her origins. Similar currents are present in the entry that notes the way a young beautician, taken on at the hair salon in the run-up to Christmas, is reduced to making coffee and sweeping up hair when the festive season is over (34). The various scenes involving checkout girls, whose status is sometimes ambiguous, since this may be a temporary expedient, tend to have the aura of a key scene at the end of *La Place* where Ernaux reports an encounter, at the checkout, with one of her own pupils, whose failure to find a way out of the working class via education could have been Ernaux's own destiny.[33]

In the course of *Journal du dehors*, this experience of partial self-recognition is increasingly acknowledged to be central to the project's *raison d'être*. In an

[32] Goffman, *The Presentation of Self in Everyday Life*, 203–47.

[33] Annie Ernaux, *La Place* (Paris: Gallimard, 1984), 113–14. See Michael Sheringham, '"Invisible Presences": Fiction, Autobiography, and Women's Lives: Virginia Woolf to Annie Ernaux', *Sites*, 2 (1998), 5–24.

entry for 1986, Ernaux asks herself why she records these scenes of everyday banality, and wonders if, rather than analytical meaning, what she is looking for is some sort of proximity with those she sees, a proximity that might hold something of herself —'je cherche quelque chose de moi à travers eux' (I am seeking something of myself through them) (36). Later, on hearing a man on a train ply a woman with questions about where she lives and what she does, Ernaux finds herself approving this desire to know 'comment les autres vivent pour savoir comment, soi, on vit' (how others live so as to know how one lives oneself) (56). The impulse she comes to locate behind her seizing on these moments of experience is not the desire to make them serve literary ends—descriptive or narrative—but to record them simply for their own sake, as what she calls 'ethnotexte' (64), a point she reiterates later by noting her desire to transcribe things 'hors de tout récit' (independently of any narrative) (85). This does not exclude literature, since a desire to seek out the 'signs' of the literary in daily life is identified by Ernaux as one of her characteristic responses to experience (46)—a point beautifully exemplified in an entry where she seeks out the hotel where Nadja—the alter ego Breton had pursued in his own diary of the outside—had stayed (79).[34] But Ernaux, like Breton, seeks to explore the interactions between literature and life, rather than transmute life into art. And this means adopting a mobile and responsive approach to urban experience, a stance Ernaux—echoing Baudelaire this time—compares to prostitution: 'Je suis traversée par les gens, leur existence, comme une putain' (I am traversed by people, their existence, like a tart) (69). The metatextual strand in *Journal du dehors*, which we have been retracing in this paragraph, culminates with the text's last entry where the 'transpersonal' experience of feeling traversed by the lives of others finds its most arresting formulation. In the same carriage of the RER, a chubby adolescent and a young mother remind Ernaux of different moments in her life, and this prompts her to recollect other times when she had caught something of her mother's gestures and phrases in a woman at the checkout, and to assert that it is thus 'au-dehors', in fellow RER passengers or people spotted on escalators in Galeries Lafayette or Auchan, that her past existence is deposited:

Dans des individus anonymes qui ne soupçonnent pas qu'ils détiennent une part de mon histoire, dans des visages, des corps, que je ne revois jamais. Sans doute suis-je moi-même, dans la foule des rues et des magasins, porteuse de la vie des autres (107).

---

[34] Cf. the discussion of *Nadja* in Ch. 2 above.

(In anonymous individuals who do not realize they hold a part of my history, in faces and bodies I never see again. No doubt I myself, in the crowded street or shops, am a carrier for other people's lives)

To see others, fleetingly observed in the street, as 'carriers' of our own life history is to challenge many traditional assumptions of autobiographical writing, but more importantly in our context, it is to identify a crucial dimension of identity at the level of the anonymous banality of everyday existence.

One of the strengths of *Journal du dehors* in its original form (without the 1996 preface) is that the reader initially has to work at a series of disconnected perceptions, with no stated rationale, slowly refining the pitch and pace of reading in the light of the intermittent metatextual asides just considered. In the later edition, the 'Avant-propos' summarizes these tentative findings— which match the reader's adjustment to 'reading' the everyday—and places them at the start. Ernaux recounts the disorientation she had first felt in the anonymous Ville nouvelle, a place without memory, and how this had led her to pay attention ('prêter attention') to everyday experience, and to record things that prompted emotion, unease or anger. In terms that closely echo Maspero, she insists that the resulting 'journal' is *not* a piece of reportage or an 'enquête de sociologie urbaine' (8). And although there are no photographs like those of Anaïk Frantz, Ernaux cites photography as the basis of her method and style. The emotional response at the origin of each fragment is played down in favour of an 'écriture photographique du réel' (photographic writing of the real) which aims, as in Paul Strand's images of an Italian village, to preserve the enigmatic opacity of the existences encountered—for Strand, 'ces êtres sont là, seulement là' (these people are there, simply there) (9). Yet in a final paragraph Ernaux acknowledges that there is much more of herself than she had originally bargained for in these texts, and this leads her to articulate what, as we have seen, is the project's ultimate discovery: we find out far more about ourselves when we look outwards rather than inwards. It is other people, encountered anonymously in public space, and who prompt a reaction that *traverses* us, who reveal us to ourselves (10).

Jacques Réda: La Liberté des rues

Jacques Réda's urban and suburban explorations, starting with *Les Ruines de Paris* in 1977, seem initially to have little in common with the projects of Augé, Maspero, and Ernaux (different as those already are from each other).

Yet in reinvigorating a poetic tradition of writing about Paris, running from Baudelaire, through the Surrealists, to Queneau and Roubaud, Réda has also progressively refreshed its links with the investigation of everyday experience.[35] More discursive than the often dense prose poems of *Les Ruines*, or the verse poems of *Hors les murs* (1982), the short essay narratives of *Châteaux des courants d'air* (1986) reflected a shift towards the itinerary, the catalogue, the (ironic) treatise, and the experimental project, thus betraying sympathies with the spirit of Perec (and Certeau). Proceeding more systematically than before, the *promeneur* takes soundings in the 15th Arrondissement, then the 14th, before looking at samples of a Parisian garden, a church, a bridge, and an arcade, and then embarking on a circular visit to the capital's railway termini (not forgetting those on the now derelict *petite ceinture* line). As in *Les Ruines*, his posture is never fixed—he is once again 'tour à tour (ou ensemble) nuageux, curieux, inquiet, hilare, furibond, tendre, ahuri . . .' (in turn (or all at once) hazy, curious, anxious, amused, worked up, tender, perplexed . . .'); his 'furtive step' is still that of a 'heretic', whose aim is not control but dispossession; and he retains his passion for 'terrains vagues', those vacant lots where the city both forgets its past and anticipates its future.[36] Making his own mind a 'lieu de passage mental' (place of mental passage) where the city is described, x-rayed, and subjectively transmuted, Réda conceives his work as a space of ongoing metamorphosis, reflecting the endless interactions of the city and its inhabitants.[37] Yet the encounter with Paris in *Châteaux* is inflected by the very leisurely prose of *L'Herbe des talus* (1984), where Réda evokes in more anecdotal and autobiographical fashion his travels in various parts, often interspersing his accounts with segments in verse. And he had written two other works in this vein, *Recommendations aux promeneurs* (1988) and *Le Sens de la marche* (1990)—where he further refined his idiosyncratic style of travel writing—by the time he composed another concertedly Parisian work, *La Liberté des rues* (1997), quickly followed by *Le Citadin* (1998).

Intermittent self-interrogation, with regard to the aims, motivations and conduct of his peregrinations, is a consistent feature of Réda's Parisian writing, but in *La Liberté des rues* this is taken a stage further, particularly in the eponymous second section I wish to focus on.[38] Here Réda explicitly applies inductive reasoning to his characteristic *modus operandi*. Referring back to the

---

[35] See Sheringham, 'City Space, Mental Space, Poetic Space . . .', 85–114.
[36] Jacques Réda, *Les Ruines de Paris*, (Paris: Gallimard, 1977), back cover and 45.
[37] Jacques Réda, *Châteaux des courants d'air* (Paris: Gallimard, 1986), back cover.
[38] Id., *La Liberté des rues*, 47–82. Quotations from *La Liberté* will be incorporated in the text.

prose pieces in the opening section, which focus on the city at nightfall, he starts out from the state of nervous excitation that dusk induces (famously treated by Baudelaire), prompting him to sally forth, or, if he is already in motion, to stop and take stock. The imminent prospect of darkness, which he associates with the theft of a precious object, induces a sense of expectancy and duty, yet what is primal, he surmises, is not retrieval or possession but the 'élan pur de commencement' (pure impulse to begin)—the desire to keep possibilities open when closure threatens.

The following text, which links this forward momentum to a simple drive to 'pursue' space, introduces a connection between open space, lateral extension—the key word here is 'l'étendue' (the sense of 'le monde en extension latérale')[39]—and freedom. When he allows his itinerary to be dictated by a logic apparently inherent in the succession of spaces he traverses, Réda can find himself in quite unexpected locations, for example peering into the window of a smart shop selling ties (which he rarely wears). And in such cases the impromptu objects of his attention, whilst lacking any transcendent meaning, seem to act as relays for the non-stop flow of impressions in which he finds himself immersed. Noting that a young woman beside him is also looking at the ties, Réda wonders if for her as well, and potentially for any other passer-by, the ties are merely a provisional receptacle or point of intersection for the multiple connections that make up the 'ensemble en perpétuel mouvement qui nous contient' (constantly shifting ensemble that contains us) (52). The sense of being contained within a total 'ensemble' is fundamental to Réda's sense of the *quotidien*. Figured by the city, this totality is associated with anonymity—the dissolution of the self as it becomes part of this wider 'field'—and with freedom: 'un sentiment dilatant de liberté dans l'infini, vivant possible' (a feeling of dilation and freedom in the infinite and living realm of the possible) (52). Réda's prose consistently alternates first-person comments about his moods with a marked use of the impersonal, anonymous 'on'. From *Les Ruines* onwards his texts record numerous moments of 'dilation' when the walker feels that he becomes an emanation of the spaces he frequents. The back cover of *Le Citadin* (1998) notes: 'on dirait pourtant que sa véritable ambition est de disparaître, pour devenir un des éléments de l'étendue qu'il parcourt infatigablement' (you would think that his real ambition was to disappear, to become a constituent of the expanse he tirelessly traverses).

---

[39] Réda, *Les Ruines de Paris*, 15.

Returning to the 'besoin de sortir' (need to go out) that leads him into the Paris streets, Réda observes that, even when a specific errand makes him go out against his will, this practical purpose by no means excludes receptivity to stray impressions induced by the tiniest of events (57). However liminal, his attention to such phenomena is constant (Réda later compares it to the kind of all-round vigilance urban cyclists develop to survive (58)). When, on the other hand, he feels impelled to go out for no particular reason, he is motivated by a desire to find something that in some way links with, and so assuages, the obscure desire that has animated him (such as the aforementioned ties). In deciding on a route, he relies initially on an inner mechanism that determines his changes of direction, and when this gives out (as often happens) he resists the application of any rigid artificial formulae and tries instead simply to put himself under the control of space itself, hoping to come upon the 'bon signe', however minor, that may be in store for him. The logic here is always of finding what he was *not* looking for: 'Trouver ce qu'on ne cherchait pas' is the title of another section of *La Liberté des rues*, echoing the sequence in *Les Ruines de Paris* entitled 'On ne sait quoi d'introuvable' (the thing you can't find) where Réda recounts a series of errands and purchases he makes on a Saturday morning.[40] In Réda, the *quotidien* becomes a space of potentiality not when it is the site of any definitive revelation or transformation but when its most banal constituents impress themselves on the attention as displacements for a desire that only the *quotidien*—as the milieu, the 'tout-ensemble' of basic existence—can inspire or allay.

With its clear echoes of surrealist 'errance' and automatism, and its relation to a long tradition of poetic epiphany, Réda's perception of urban perambulation could be seen to imply faith in some sort of transcendent reality, or at least in a vision where the everyday becomes transmuted into a poetic realm. But, in addition to the consistent humour and irony of his tone, his doggedly factual and practical bent, and his own self-questioning, a further factor that gives Réda's perspective a wider resonance with regard to the question of the everyday is the insistence on interaction between the walker and his environment, a transaction where the physical layout of the streets, the circumstances of his presence on any occasion, and the vicissitudes of his attention as well as his physical relationship to space all have a role to play.

In the core text of 'La Liberté des rues' Réda claims that when out in the streets his path is dictated neither by his private whims nor by a 'higher' power,

---

[40] Réda, *Les Ruines de Paris*, 67–76.

but engendered rather by his participation in an 'activity' fomented by the streets themselves. Such an idea could obviously be seen as purely fanciful, as outrageous anthropomorphism, yet closer examination reveals its basis in the phenomenology of urban walking, and the paradigmatic status (as in Certeau) of 'marcher dans la ville' with respect to the experience of the everyday. In what sense are the inanimate streets the 'active' partner in the type of spatial transaction called a walk in the city? Of course the physical and mental mobility of the human participant is primal; nonetheless, Réda suggests, it is conditioned by a reciprocal mobility that it generates. Naturally, streets may be, as one says, 'animated'—in other words, full of ever-changing activity, things going on; and other contingent features, notably weather, light, sky, colours, contribute to their 'mouvement incessant' (60); but other factors, more intrinsic to the streets themselves, are in play here. Above all, for Réda, what makes the street an active agent (at least with regard to its effect on him) is the way its infinitely varied and quite specific spatial physiognomy presents itself—by virtue of its contrast and variation, and actual contiguity with other streets (into which it debouches, from which it splits off, or with which it intersects)—as a kind of proposition or axiom delivered in response to a challenge. The challenge facing any street (initially via its architect) is to articulate space: to link A to B, or provide a setting for X or Y; yet this cannot be done without taking into account the lie of the land, the dimensions of the terrain, the disposition of other streets, the materials at hand, the functions of the buildings that will furnish it. As a result, a street's physiology can be interpreted as an attempt to corral or coerce space into a particular configuration; it is to this that the pedestrian—and the writer—responds, and in so doing he ventriloquizes the street's propositions, becoming the medium of its utterances and the stage for its particular spatial performances. As is borne out again and again in *La Liberté des rues* and its companion volumes, a city street, vista, or itinerary is an enigma that prompts interrogation: 'what are you getting at?', 'what are you saying?'. The response occurs at a physical, a verbal, and then more broadly an ontological level. To walk in the streets is to apprehend physically, through the body's engagement with gradient, proportion, ratio (of breadth to length, building to sky, stone or brick to vegetation), uniformity or variety, the wholly particular feel or imprint of a specific spatial environment; yet the fact that this is necessarily at an arbitrary, contingent moment means that one can never feel sure that on this occasion the 'essence' of the space has been patent. For Réda, the walker's symbiosis and affinity with the streets spring from the fact that motion requires orientation, bifurcation, constant adaptation to local conditions; this basic spatiality will often determine the wavelength on which we tune in to an urban itinerary on a given occasion, as when Réda remarks on the 'fort lien d'harmonie' (strong harmony) that links the Avenue Trudaine to its pedestrians via the 'proportions de leurs corps en mouvement' (proportions of their bodies in motion) (64).

The role of language as a medium for the transaction between walker and treet rests on a double affinity. Where Certeau (following Barthes) saw the pedestrian's itineraries as speech acts, a *parole* drawing on the rigid *langue* of the planned city grid, Réda sees the streets themselves, in their endless variety—bifurcations, widenings and narrowings, links (passages), aporia (impasses)—as constituting a *parole* to which walking (and then rationally articulating the 'logic' of one's path) can serve as echo or reply. Through his steps, the walker engages in dialogue with the city. And just as the *parole* of the streets, whilst possessing a huge range of historical, socio-economic, and aesthetic determinants, cannot be limited to any of these (partly because a street cannot be isolated from its physical context—where it leads, what runs into it, parallel streets), so a 'parcours' that seeks to respond to what the streets propose, invariably ends up, in Réda's experience, not as an ordered, analytical discussion, but as a 'parcours disloqué' (60), where writer (and reader) never know where the next paragraph, or page, will land them.

Of course, a city street is also full of words, from its name (street names will be discussed in the next chapter), the names of shops and buildings, and inscriptions relating to architecture and utilities, to the whole realm of transient bits of writing that Perec called 'l'herbier des villes', and for which Réda (an avid consumer of such '3e secteur' material) provides a loving checklist that includes signboards on demolition sites, by-laws regulating parks or metro stations, auction posters, small ads on drainpipes offering babysitting or alternative therapies, and so on (77–8). Then there are the even more transient bits of language on passing vehicles—which, as Réda notes, with regard to removal lorries, often seem to occur in series, and then disappear. Réda sees his urge to absorb all these 'street' writings as the sign of a persistent delusion that the streets bear messages for him, a delusion that is in fact simply testimony to the endlessly circulating energies in which he feels he participates (79).

For Réda, 'la liberté des rues' is the privilege of neither *promeneur* nor street, but of their interaction. Undertaken in the spirit he consistently displays, and reflects on, urban walking becomes a creative performance that opens up a free zone, at a certain remove from the constraints of individual psychological routine, and from the utilitarian configuration of the urban environment. This zone has clear affinities with Certeau's *quotidien*—the product of performative invention rooted in enunciation, and also with Perec's emphasis on *étonnement* and *émergence*. And it also links back to the surrealist city and questions of chance. Yet, as in the dimension of Surrealism we highlighted in Chapter 2, Réda does not aspire to escape from the real but rather, to encounter and hence perhaps uncover what is there. Yet, does the emphasis on liberation, on what Réda calls 'désobstruction' (120), make his *quotidien*, and the urban trajectories that reveal it, incompatible with those of Augé, Maspero, and Ernaux? In particular, does its apparently private motivations mean that it lacks connection to the social and collective realm (and to proximate ethnography)?

Certainly we do not find in Réda an explicit equation between the space of the *quotidien* and the collective historicity of experience that is so significant in Perec, and modulated in different ways in the writers just mentioned. But it would be wrong to suggest that Réda's work is exclusively focused on the isolated individual. Indeed, as we have seen, the emphasis on escape from self into anonymity points to a shared, generic dimension of experience, where lives are no longer strictly demarcated by the context of a specific curriculum vitae, but participate in a commonality—and a freedom from biographical isolation—that is rooted in the multiple histories of which the ever-changing fabric of the urban environment (on which Réda never ceases to comment and to thrive) is the daily manifestation. Like Ernaux, Réda constantly finds bits of himself in others; like Augé, he sees the city as a space of non-tragic dis-individuation (there are numerous encounters with doubles). The personal slant and the specific uses he gives to his endless desire to participate in this common dimension (and to partake of the movement, the endless renewal and beginning of street life—what Barthes called 'l'écriture vive de la rue') should not be confused with this dimension itself. The same applies of course to Augé's abiding professional obsessions as an anthropologist, or Ernaux's fixation with her class origins. In Réda's case, the identification of *quotidienneté*, as evinced in the city street, with resistance and freedom, chimes with a persistent penchant in *quotidien* writing: to see this dimension of human life, or rather this way of apprehending and processing existence, as a way of combating destructive and dehumanizing forces.

THE PROLIFERATION OF THE EVERYDAY: MUTATION, ENUNCIATION, AND GENRE

The word 'mutation' in French often refers to a process of transformation. Pursuing analysis of works drawing on theories and practices of the *quotidien*, I wish now to focus on the interplay between different genres and media, and to highlight interactions linked to the perception of 'mutations' in the field of everyday life. In key works to be considered here—Jean-Luc Godard's film-essay, *2 ou 3 choses que je sais d'elle*, Michel Vinaver's chamber-play, *Les Travaux et les jours*, Sophie Calle's compendium of projects, *Double-jeux*, the novels of Jean Echenoz, François Bon's monologue, *Parking*, the poet Anne Portugal's *définitif bob*, Pierre Sansot's *Les Gens de peu*, Roger-Pol Droit's *101 Exercices de philosophie quotidienne*—the impulse to home in at the micro-level inspires a generic bricolage that reflects the everyday's resistance to codification and its connection with change as much as with stability. In the discussion that follows I will suggest that the connections between generic, social, and existential 'mutations' are exhibited at the level of *énonciation*. Thus, the relational, performative aspects of the *quotidien*—a dimension that emerges through the act of being apprehended—are enacted in the way a film, play, or artwork 'stages' an interaction between human subjects and social structures. The enunciative situation created by the 'crossing' of genres and media reflects a fusion of theory and practice that demonstrates how change is not simply an objective fact but above all something that is lived through, in a continuous process of alienation and appropriation.

In its unusual use of the first person, the title of Jean-Luc Godard's 1967 film, *2 ou 3 choses que je sais d'elle*, foregrounds personal enunciation, and makes a strictly limited claim to knowledge. The opening titles identify 'elle' as 'la région parisienne' (19),[41] and Godard's starting point was a magazine article on the new high-rises—the *grands ensembles* that sprang up rapidly as Paul Delouvrier implemented de Gaulle's policies—claiming that women were resorting to part-time prostitution in order to afford the benefits of the new consumer society. This fitted with Godard's conviction that living in modern society necessarily involved prostituting oneself (a metaphor developed in his

---

[41] References are to the published script, which is preceded by 'Le film vu par Jean-Luc Godard', 11–17.

earlier film *Vivre sa vie* (1964), which contains the famous scene where Anna Karina receives a disquisition on 'la vie quotidienne' from the philosopher Brice Parain). Yet he insisted that his real objective was not sociological commentary but the wish to register change: 'observer une grande mutation' (11). For Godard, what counts is the lived experience of social transformation: the remarkable formal strategies he deploys in the film reveal the oppositions and ambiguities that pertain to this level of experience. In particular, the conflict between subjectivity and objectivity is explored through a set of polarities between text and image, image and sound, documentary and fiction, politics and domesticity, knowledge and ignorance, language and silence.

In seeking to apprehend change, rather than describe or judge society, Godard locates the act of meditative scrutiny within the film itself, replacing the confident authority of the documentary film-maker with his own whispering 'authorial' voice, which the viewer strains to catch above the insistent noises of cranes, bulldozers and cars: 'je me regarde filmer, et on m'entend penser' (I observe myself filming, and you can hear me thinking) (12). Similarly, the central protagonist is doubly split. She is presented both as a fictional character, Juliette, and as the actress Marina Vlady, and at the same time she performs in two registers: objectively, by carrying out the actions of a housewife, consumer (we see her shopping, and reading a magazine in a café), mother, and amateur prostitute; and subjectively, by responding to questions emanating from the authorial *voix-off*, outside diegetic space, as well as by monologues reporting on the mechanisms of her consciousness in relation to the external world. This phenomenological slant, picked up in references to Merleau-Ponty and Ponge, ties in with Godard's theoretical reflections on combining subjective and objective perspectives, with a view to establishing a 'sentiment d'ensemble': in a phrase that foreshadows Perec, Godard asserted that the film's 'mouvement profond' (wellspring) lay in a 'tentative de description d'un ensemble (êtres et choses)' (attempt to describe an ensemble (people and things)) (16). But if *things* are omnipresent in the shape of consumer articles, clothes, cars, and so forth, the investigation into ways of articulating their meanings takes in a multiplicity of competing media and modes of knowledge, ranging from philosophy, linguistics, psychology, the visual image, politics, economics, literature, and ethnology (one shot shows the book cover of an *Introduction à l'ethnologie* (55)). Even though visual images are submitted to a thoroughgoing critique, it appears at times that cinematic language, when handled in this all-embracing and multi-generic way, is credited with the ability to create the kinds of 'dialectical image' Benjamin spoke of, that are capable of articulating a complex set of relationships in one frame or sequence.[42] The famous shot of a cup of coffee, overlaid with quotations from Wittgenstein and others (49–51), or the later sequence involving the sky reflected in the roof of a red Austin Mini (65), certainly have some claims in this regard. If it would be inappropriate to regard such moments as positing definitive truths, we may acknowledge that Godard's polycentric tactics of enunciation convey a compelling sense of the multiple channels that make up everyday life, and of a *quotidienneté* in the throes of endless mutation. If Godard compared making *2 ou 3 choses* to writing a sociological essay in the form of a novel, whilst only having musical notes at his disposal (16), the generic 'mutations' this involved helped him gain some purchase on the hybrid layerings of the everyday.

Gilles Deleuze's theory of cinema provides a wider framework for understanding how and why film can serve as an instrument for probing and revealing the everyday. Deleuze argues for example that Godard's 'pedagogy' eliminates the distinction between real and imaginary, fiction and truth, yet cannot be equated with documentary or the 'enquête' (322).[43] Through 'unnatural' cuts, the mixing of genres, the use of colour, sound, objects and many other devices, Godard creates a stratified, archeological viewing experience that makes the spectator 'read' each image rather than wonder (as in classic cinema) what is coming next (356). The fundamental shift, from 'movement-images' to 'time-images' (225), which defines modern cinema in Deleuze's scheme, occurred in France when the Nouvelle Vague took Italian neorealism on to a further stage. Significantly, this shift was closely bound up with ordinariness, banality, and the quotidian, because the new regime of the 'time-image' exploits the way film consists in a series of images that are in themselves 'quelconque' (unexceptional). Breaking with motor-sensory perception, modern cinema creates purely optical (or sound) situations, disconnected from one another and possessing an autonomy reflected in the act of 'reading' the image. Deleuze argues that the Japanese director Yasujiro Ozu developed this mode of cinema precisely in order to apprehend everyday ordinariness in the context of family life. In Ozu's films 'Tout est quotidien' (all is everyday) (25): time is made visible through the attenuation of both narrativity and any hierarchy between significant and insignificant moments.[44]

---

[42] Benjamin, *Arcades Project*, 462–3 and *passim*.

[43] References are to Gilles Deleuze, *Cinéma, 2, L'Image-temps* (Paris: Minuit, 1985).

[44] See also Andrew Klevan, *Disclosure of the Everyday: Undramatic Achievement in Narrative Film*, (Trowbridge: Flicks Books, 2000).

Yet the 'pure' image does not preclude critique: for Deleuze it instils a type of vision that is subjective and objective, critical and compassionate; indeed the etiolation of narrative linkage is particularly suited to grasping social disintegration or 'mutation'. According to Deleuze, Ozu, and subsequently Rossellini and Godard (Deleuze cites the latter's desire to observe 'mutations' (31)), recorded seismic shifts at the level of their tremors in the everyday.

Emerging in Europe after the war, Deleuze's new regime of the image is linked to historical 'mutations', including decolonization and rapid urbanization. The *cinéma-vérité* of Jean Rouch evolved from his ethnographic film-making in Africa, and led, in the 1960s, to experiments, including *Chronique d'un été* (discussed in the Introduction) that anticipated proximate ethnography and focused, like *2 ou 3 choses*, on the city (Rouch and Godard would later collaborate on the collective film, *Paris vu par...*). For Deleuze, Rouch's example helped Godard evolve a cinematic discourse that 'operated' in and on the real (202). In Rouch's *cinéma-vérité* truth is not depicted, it is constructed and interrogated through techniques (including the use of unobtrusive cameras) and modes of enunciation. Other key film-makers of the Nouvelle Vague can be placed in this lineage. In Agnès Varda's film-making, often non-fictional, 'description'—the representation of 'real' people and places—does not 'presuppose reality' (176), and a protagonist's 'disconnected gestures' can explore (as in her *Documenteurs*, or in the fictional experiment in real time, *Cléo de 5 à 7*) the temporality of the female body's gendered experience of space and time. This emphasis on body, gesture, and temporality (reflecting another important 'mutation') is also a key feature in the work of Chantal Akerman, notably in her *Jeanne Dielman, 23 Quai du Commerce, 1080 Bruxelles* (an important reference point for Certeau and Giard) where the themes of domesticity and part-time prostitution are pursued through microscopic attention to everyday domestic tasks.[45] In a different register, the films of Eric Rohmer use improvisation and other devices to explore conversational exchange in a way that does not simply construct a fictional world but creates a reality which, through its mode of enunciation, apprehends the mores of a society in crisis (315–6). Deleuze's reading of the Nouvelle Vague and its aftermath, in terms of a non-descriptive 'invention' of everyday experience, dates from the 1980s, when its emphases chimed with the orientations we have been pursuing, particularly in this chapter. If the tendencies he highlights

---

[45] On Akerman see Ivone Margulies, *Nothing Happens: Chantal Akerman's Hyperrealist Everyday* (Durham, NC: Duke University Press, 1996).

emerged in the 1960s, accompanying the constitution of discourses on the *quotidien*, Godard, Varda, Akerman, and Rohmer have continued making films into the twenty-first century (and thus through the period when everyday works diversify and proliferate), challenging the boundaries of genre, particularly fiction and documentary, and often exploring the experience of the everyday. At the same time, new directors have emerged, whose work further pursues film's capacity to engage with *quotidienneté* and social 'mutation', as in Erick Zonka's exploration of class and female friendship, *La Vie rêvée des anges*, Cédric Klapisch's study of urban community, *Chacun cherche son chat*, the Dardenne brothers' *Rosetta* or Bruno Dumont's *La Vie de Jésus*. Women directors, like Claire Denis and Catherine Breillat have, like Akerman and Varda, continued to explore gendered experience and the body.[46]

The exploration of the *quotidien* is central to Michel Vinaver's work, and his 1979 play, *Les Travaux et les jours*, demonstrates that it is at the level of language, and through the act of writing, that the playwright seeks to grasp everydayness in its inchoate immediacy, whilst exposing its relationship to socio-political and economic 'mutations'.[47] Although associated with the 1970s 'Théâtre du quotidien' movement, influenced by Lefebvre, Perec, and others, Vinaver's own concerns go back to the 1950s, paralleling those of Barthes who had enthusiastically received his first play *Aujourd'hui, ou les Coréens* (a poster for which can be seen in one of the scenes in *Chronique d'un été*).[48] Vinaver insists that his aim was never to view the *quotidien* from the outside, but to convey what it is like to be '*dans* le quotidien'.[49] In 1978, he recorded his abiding perception that the everyday is a precarious 'territory' that needs to be discovered.[50] Often likening the *quotidien* to a formless 'magma', a fragmentary, disconnected zone, that is nevertheless full of virtual possibilities that can either be ironed out, by the adoption of a fixed view, or probed through 'micro-description' and other techniques (including the collage of verbal fragments)[51] Vinaver consistently attempts to locate this material in its state of fusion by starting with fragments, and then pursuing the patterns,

---

[46] On cinema's exploration of the 'everyday body', see Deleuze, *Cinéma 2*, 249, 255.

[47] On Vinaver see David Bradby, *The Theater of Michel Vinaver* (Ann Arbor: University of Michigan Press, 1993).

[48] See Barthes, *Œuvres complètes*, I, 646–9.

[49] Michel Vinaver, *Écrits sur le théâtre*, I (Paris: L'Arche, 1998), 291. In discussing his work Vinaver generally talks of a 'théâtre ancré dans le quotidien', *Écrits sur le théâtre*, 128 and *passim*.

[50] 'Pièce jointe' (afterword) to *Les Travaux et les jours*, 74.

[51] Vinaver, *Écrits sur le théâtre*, 287–96.

conflicts, and discharges of energy that emerge. Theatre came to predominate because for Vinaver listening is more important than seeing, and conversation is the area where the emergence of the everyday can be captured.[52] In Barthes's Collège de France lectures in 1978, Vinaver recognized affinities with the concern for the challenge of noting the present, and the fascination with the discontinuous flow of incidents that provoke the response 'c'est ça' or 'c'est tel'.[53] For Vinaver, such 'instants d'évidence'—when patterns, fissures, and complexities become visible in the opacity of boring and repetitive experience—are not linked to the revelation of individual psychology or destiny, but to the relation between the individual and collective forces. Working exclusively with words and phrases uttered in extremely humdrum circumstances, and then juxtaposing them, Vinaver attempts to go beyond realism in order to apprehend how the 'tout-venant' of the *quotidien* is shot through with political resonances. The 'environnement historique dans lequel baigne le quotidien' is discovered in, and not beyond, everyday experience itself (284). Meaning is not achieved by rising to a higher level but by grasping the process at work in the fragments he assembles—Vinaver's remarks on his 'théâtre ancré dans le quotidien' abound in such phrases as 'connaissance à tâtons', 'acte de fouille' or 'tentative de saisie d'un vécu brut' (287, 300). In 'Une écriture du quotidien' he provides a glossary of words that seem to him to capture facets of the everyday. In quest of a 'quotidien non-hiérachisé', Vinaver argues that the everyday is something we constantly 'put together' through our ways of living (134).

The economic sphere (with which Vinaver, who was chief executive of Gillette in France, is very familiar) has a particular pertinence since, with the rise of the consumer and then with globalization, our relationship to the wider world increasingly occurs at an economic level. And for Vinaver the ironies that condition the individual's relation to both the micro- and the macro-economic levels, found a new kind of tragedy rooted in the social body's adherence to an order that transcends it, a situation explored in *Par-dessus bord*, his 1969 play about the fortunes of a company with an excess stock of lavatory paper, as well as in *La Demande d'emploi* (1973). The perception that an individual can at the same time be ground down ('broyé') by a system, and

---

[52] Like Blanchot (see Ch. 1) and Deleuze, *L'Image-temps*, Vinaver sees conversation as a key feature of the everyday.

[53] Vinaver, *Écrits sur le théâtre*, I, 130. Further references are incorporated in the text. Citing other phrases from Barthes's late work, Vinaver notes that he seeks 'le quotidien de l'incident. Ce qui tombe' (134).

in heartfelt communion with it (286), is also at the heart of *Les Travaux et les jours*.

The play is set in the after-sales service of Cosson, a company making coffee grinders. Three women, Anne (aged 40), Nicole (aged 30), and Yvette (aged 20) tend the phones, while Guillermo, an artisan, does repairs and servicing, and Jaudouard, the departmental manager, spouts bureaucratic clichés. The play's nine scenes compress an indeterminate amount of time (each scene may in fact encompass more than one day, and the time gap between scenes is highly variable and covers several months overall) into a seamless continuum of utterances involving the characters as well as unheard customers on the phone. Rather than dialogue, we are presented with discontinuous and intertwining streams of speech (written without punctuation, so that the actor or reader has to find the articulations) that juxtapose family life, relationships, office gossip, employment worries, fashion tips, current affairs, and so forth. Bit by bit, we gather that Cosson is an old-fashioned family firm that has traded on brand loyalty and a clearly outmoded paternalistic and sexist treatment of its employees. As rumours of a takeover lead to a prolonged strike in the factory, the members of the after-sales team respond very differently according to age, personal history, and future prospects. The youngest, Yvette, is amoral, pragmatic (she is willing to sleep with the boss to get up the ladder) and will ultimately be 'kept on' whilst others are 'let go'. Yet she too has her fantasy life, which leads her to seduce Guillermo—son of a Spanish Civil-War *immigré* whose traditionalist loyalties to Cosson turn out to be focused on the grinders themselves rather than the company—despite the fact that Nicole, who left her husband for Guillermo, will be desperately unhappy. Anne, the oldest woman, reassures Nicole that Yvette's crush will blow over, and worries about her own daughter who keeps running away, hoping that Yvette might be a positive influence. Anne gets the low-down about the company from her friend Cécile and sees the management point of view— she is more tolerant of Jaudouard than Nicole, who sides with the strikers— and will in fact be responsive to overtures from him towards the end, after he has had his way with Yvette. Jaudouard's speech is peppered with bureaucratic jargon, euphemisms, and subservience, and he frequently reports on the activities of the top brass whilst citing company missives, including an absurd decree regarding the employees' right to brighten up their workspace with posters.

The title of the play is derived from the ancient Greek writer Hesiod, whose cosmogony provides two epigraphs contrasting an equable vision of dignified labour with a nightmarish evocation of accursed toil. A third epigraph cites a recent speech by a government minister claiming that the advent of information technology will usher in a new epoch (as in Hesiod's 'ages'). Vinaver's play approaches these themes obliquely, via a concern for the way they are lived through in the context of the 'tout-venant' of the everyday. His protagonists are not passive victims of extraneous forces: if he shows that they are complicit with the order that grinds them down like coffee beans, his aim is not to decry but to explore the ironies, conflicts, and interactions that permeate our daily lives, to show how the 'mutations' of the late-twentieth-century world—including the impact on individual lives of corporate takeovers by multi-nationals—are played out in the enunciation of everyday subjects. Yet it is by avoiding realism and description that Vinaver achieves his ends. The world he progressively builds up through the juxtaposition of verbal fragments does not pre-exist the creative process, and the everyday he seeks to uncover is charged with ambivalence because, whilst it bears the marks of history, it is also constantly invented in the present, and thus harbours dissident energies.

This verbal exploration of the *quotidien* from within may be contrasted with the approach characteristic of playwrights like Wenzel, Kroetz, Kalisky, Deutsch, and Grumberg, associated with the 'Théâtre du quotidien' group established by Wenzel in 1975. A play like Wenzel's *Loin d'Hagondage*, about a working-class couple who retire to the countryside to escape the world of the factory, but find themselves repeating the internalized gestures and discourses of their previous way of life, seeks to avoid naturalism through a combination of hyperrealist minimalism and a découpage in short scenes. This is effective in suggesting pressures beneath the surface, but in the end the characters are viewed externally. As in Vinaver, the world of work or physical activity is often directly staged, for example in Kalisky's *Scandalon*, about a cyclist, Grumberg's *L'Atelier*, or Deutsch's *Dimanche*, where we see the gym sessions of a young girl obsessed with being a majorette. Deutsch skilfully parallels Ginette's desire to achieve bodily harmony and freedom with the manual labour of the local coal miners, but whilst their strike is (provisionally) successful, her utopian desire to sublimate the regularities of her body, associated with virginity, leads to isolation and exhaustion. Influenced by Foucault, Deutsch makes the actor's body the site of conflicting pressures and develops an undramatic everyday situation with a range of mythical resonances (including parallels with Büchner). In a subsequent 'epitaph' for the 'Théâtre du quotidien', where he discusses his own conception of the everyday, starting out from Heidegger, and his aims—'plutôt que de viser le quotidien, s'ouvrir à lui' (rather than target the everyday, expose yourself to it)[54]—Deutsch notes that whilst everyday alienation can be staged, it is immensely difficult for theatre to capture the essential ambivalence and indeterminacy of the *quotidien* and he laments the way so many attempts to explore the everyday theatrically, rather than succeeding in capturing 'des micro-événements invisibles' (invisible micro-events) (32) have simply led to 'le retour débile d'un naturalisme' (the feeble return to naturalism) (51).

Whilst as a movement the 'Théâtre du quotidien' quickly faded, Vinaver has continued to explore the everyday, embracing such areas as television and the terrorist attack on the World Trade Centre. At the same time, through the 1980s and 1990s, the Paris stage played host to many attempts to explore the everyday by theatrical means, including productions of Perec's *L'Augmentation*, where an office worker seeks a raise,[55] and stage versions of his plays and texts (for example, the marvellous adaptation of *Je me souviens* with the actor Sami Frey). The ambitions (and inevitable limitations) of a theatre of the everyday become a persistent current in French theatre, apparent in approaches to earlier classics as well as new writing; the theatregoer, attuned to Vinaver, is unlikely to be surprised if an evening in the theatre involves being plunged into the currents of an everyday life that is, in principle at least, not simply represented but apprehended through its rhythms and layers.

Sophie Calle's 'La Filature' and Christian Boltanski's 'Les Abonnés du téléphone' encompass many of the orientations through which the visual arts in the 1980s and 1990s contributed to investigating the everyday.[56] In April 1981 Calle asked her mother to hire a private detective to 'tail' her in the course of a day, setting up a highly ambiguous situation where Calle was hyperconscious of the everyday activities she conducted for her witness, yet did not know who he was; while the detective was oblivious of the fact that she knew she was being followed. For an exhibition in 2000, Boltanski painstakingly ordered and assembled a vast library of telephone books from all over the world, and exhibited them in alphabetical order of country in a public space where visitors were at liberty to make practical use of them if they wished. In

---

[54] Michel Deutsch, *Inventaire après liquidation* (Paris: L'Arche, 1990), 32.

[55] Vinaver, *Écrits sur le théâtre* I, 9–59.

[56] See Calle's seven-volume *Doubles-jeux* (Arles: Actes Sud. 1998). ('La Filature' is in vol. IV, *À suivre*, 110–49. For Boltanski see the catalogue *Voilà—le monde dans la tête* (Musée d'art moderne de la ville de Paris, 2000). For overall perspectives see Lyn Gumpert (ed.), *The Art of the Everyday: The Quotidian in Postwar French Culture* (New York: New York University Press, 1981).

both cases the artwork is essentially a project: its traces or residues can be exhibited in a gallery as an 'installation', but the viewer's response is directed not so much at these as at the implications and unfolding of the experiment that produced them.[57] If Calle and Boltanski draw on the mechanisms and mixed media of conceptual and minimalist art, the content of their work, and the nature of their projects, point less in the direction of art itself than towards a range of issues we have encountered in work on the everyday. In fact, both artists are frequently associated with Perec (to whom they allude).[58] In addition to projects, they share with Perec a fondness for inventory and enumeration, a love of constraints, and a fascination with objects, space, and identity (in an essay on Calle the novelist Olivier Rolin underlines her resemblance to Perec).[59] Moreover, both Calle and Boltanski home in on familiar realms of experience—using a phonebook, moving around the city— and then prompt us into seeing its wider ramifications or resonances. For both artists the project fits into a string or nexus of other projects that complement, complicate, and qualify it. Repetition, minor variation, parallels, and echoes are essential, and their multiplicity contrasts with the otherwise laconic character of these works, whose textual ingredients often feature a deliberately plain and deadpan style. Elements from different genres and media are combined, and this is partly what engenders a constant play on the border of fiction and reality (although they constantly use their own image and life histories, we are never sure to what extent the Calle or Boltanski we encounter in these projects coincides with the real person, and indeed this indeterminacy is crucial to what is being explored and illuminated).

Displayed in a gallery, or published in book form, 'La Filature' consists of three texts and two sets of photographs. Calle's own narrative reveals how her 'day' is influenced by the detective's gaze, and thus induces awareness of the identities her actions produce for others; the detective's report, accompanied by the photographs he was asked to take, betrays inferences he drew from the 'surveillée's' encounters. We are also given a brief report by a friend of Calle's, who was asked to identify, and photograph, her pursuer. The interplay of text and image is central here: in theory, the photos should corroborate the written account, but the existence of two (or three) versions of 'events' may give us

---

[57] On artworks as projects see the introduction by the co-editors in Johnnie Gratton and Michael Sheringham (eds.), *The Art of the Project* (Oxford: Berghahn Books, 2005); on everyday projects specifically see below, Ch. 9.

[58] See Lyn Gumpert, *Christian Boltanski* (Paris: Flammarion, 1994).

[59] Sophie Calle, *Sophie Calle: m'as-tu vue* (Paris: Centre Pompidon, 2004), 137–40.

pause. The suspicion is not so much that the camera can lie, but that there may not be any truth for it to record: not merely because the whole set-up could be a simulation, but because identity itself may be seen to be a function of interactions, fantasies, and double-takes.

In the major retrospective, *Doubles-jeux*, inspired by a fictional appropriation of her persona by the novelist Paul Auster, Calle places 'La Filature' alongside other projects where it is she who follows unknown people in the streets.[60] I want however to mention briefly two other strands in her work that engage with labile identities and the everyday. 'Le rituel d'anniversaire' probes the ritual of birthdays and the metaphorical relationship between the two parties involved in present-giving.[61] By (ostensibly at least) preserving and displaying all the gifts she received on a succession of birthdays—including one from Boltanski—Calle explores the links between people and objects. Similar themes are broached in 'De l'obéissance', where, this time at Auster's instigation, she temporarily regulates her daily life according to constraints relating to colours or letters of the alphabet (including the letter W, which enables her to pay homage to Perec).[62] Some of Calle's projects are designed to explore areas of common experience and memory, testing the borders between what can and cannot be shared. Like other everyday explorers she subverts the techniques of scientific sociology, devising simple yet telling situations and questions (like those at the origin of *Chronique d'un été*). For 'Les Dormeurs' she invited a succession of experimental subjects to take a turn in her bed, and be photographed while asleep; in *L'Erouv de Jérusalem* she asked people to show her a place in their everyday environment where public space was the forum for private emotion. For the large-scale project *Douleur exquise* Calle set out to exorcise a painful episode in her own personal life by asking others to tell her about the moment when they experienced the greatest suffering. Exposed to these narratives, sumptuously exhibited with gleaming photographs and fine typography, the viewer is drawn into a space where experience is seen as both individual and, to borrow Annie Ernaux's word, 'transpersonal'.

Like Calle's, Boltanski's work is multifaceted and based on a consistent set of interests, obsessions and strategies. Whilst photography plays a part (more usually through 'found' images), Boltanski's installations are generally three-

---

60 Including her *Suite vénitienne*, originally published in 1983 (Paris: Éditions de l'Étoile) with an essay by Jean Baudrillard, 'Please follow me'.

61 *Doubles-jeux*, II.

62 *Doubles-jeux*, I.

dimensional, and the public history he interweaves with his own biography (or self-inventions) is often related to the Holocaust (Boltanski's complex relation to Jewishness parallels Perec's). Torn from their usual context, the telephone directories mutate into an archive of humanity, and we can dwell on the many different ways in which a living person can be represented by (or reduced to) a line or two of letters and numbers. Like Perec, Boltanski is fascinated by the act of classification and many of his projects consist in accumulations of materials (especially clothing, identity photographs, personal possessions) constituting real or fake archives. Like Calle, Boltanski explores the relation between identity and personal possessions, buying large quantities of bric-à-brac in flea markets and then exhibiting them as the imaginary relics of a once–living community.

Boltanski's archive of telephone directories was originally featured in a massive exhibition, *Voilà—le monde dans la tête*, held at the Musée d'art moderne de la ville de Paris in 2000, featuring more than sixty artists whose work involves archiving, classification, and the accumulation or inventorying of everyday materials. As the catalogue clearly indicates, Perec is a presiding source of inspiration both for individual artists and for the idea of assembling this cornucopia of memory traces—always collective as well as personal: life histories, real and imaginary, spatial trajectories, documents, projects, and exercises. Whilst the photographic series (not the individual shot, but a planned sequence, usually produced over a significant period of time),[63] and the installation, consisting of accumulated materials, clearly emerge as the prime instruments through which visual artists participate in the exploration of everyday experience, their efficacy is often related to the ways in which they combine and play with existing models and situations such as photographic reportage, the urban walk, the preservation of souvenirs, or the display of new technologies. Subverting media and genres, often by injecting the quirkiness of individual style or obsession into a seemingly objective context, such artworks direct attention to the processes that are endlessly remodelling daily experience.

It is clear, then, that film, theatre, and the visual arts accompany and interact with explorations of the *quotidien* in written texts. We saw earlier how, in the wake of Barthes and Perec, writers like Augé and Ernaux developed interdisciplinary forms attuned to the hybrid indeterminacy of the *quotidien*. In the course of the 1980s and 1990s we see an increasingly widespread tendency for

---

[63] Cf. the discussion of surrealist photography in Ch. 2 and Ch. 3.

everyday writings to evolve modes of enunciation that signal a crossing of generic boundaries, and in so doing reflect 'mutations' in the everyday world and the way it is perceived. Symptomatic here is the common ground between two different modes of reorientation towards everydayness that can both be associated with Perec: autobiographical excavation and ludic fictionalizing. The radical reworking of autobiographical practices that placed life-writing at the centre of the cultural field from the late 1970s was part of a major shift where the structuralist displacement of subjectivity was succeeded by a cautious and questioning 'return' of the subject. However, as Barthes insisted, the 'subject' that returns had jettisoned much of its former psychological 'baggage', and, rather than laying claim to sovereignty, now displayed its multifaceted and dependent character. If Perec's own work was of major importance here (the publication of both *W ou le souvenir d'enfance* and *Roland Barthes par Roland Barthes* in 1975 made this a turning point in life-writing), it can be argued that a key aspect of his contribution was to show that the recovery of everyday experience could have a stake in the refashioning of autobiography. Thus, alongside the invention of new modes of autobiographical *récit*, and the ludic spirit of *autofiction* with its blurring of fact and fiction (to both of which Perec is of course germane), there is an important strand of life-writing, often involving the interface between autobiography and biography, and between individual and collective memory, that gives primacy to the relationship between self and other in the context of ordinary and banal experience. The painstaking reconstruction of a lost archive of family or community experience, reflecting the orientations of ethnographic enquiry, characterizes such works as Pierre Michon's *Vies minuscules*, Pierre Bergounioux's *Miette*, and Annie Ernaux's *La Honte*, just as it underlies Perec's *W*. If it is legitimate to speak of the 'return' of the subject, it is essential to link this to the return of the 'referent' (a problematized and precarious 'reality') and of memory as a perturbed and perturbing realm of experience. And these new priorities often tend to produce a convergence on seemingly mundane or unspectacular realities. The general disposition of life-writing in the Eighties and Nineties makes this one of the many sites of the rehabilitation of the *quotidien*.

Within the literary field, the same period saw another 'return', with apparently opposed inclinations. The 'retour du récit', associated in part with a new group of writers published (and collectively promoted) by Éditions du Minuit, including Jean Echenoz, Jean-Philippe Toussaint, and later Christian Oster and Christian Gailly, was frequently hailed as a refreshing restoration of reader-friendly wit and quirky inventiveness to the literary novel.[64] Yet, as in Perec's *La Vie mode d'emploi*, and its antecedents in Queneau's work, the ludic profusion of the 'romanesque' had less obvious effects and ambitions. A characteristic feature is the disparity between narrative voice and fictional world. Echenoz's novels play with such genres as the detective or spy novel and therefore include exotic locations and bizarre situations. Oster and Toussaint devise narratives that develop in surprising directions. But the laconic, self-ironic narrating voices devised by these writers constantly deflect reading from narrative ends, frequently offering highly detailed explanations and depictions of very ordinary actions and perceptions. Creating protagonists with an inclination to observe their interaction with the world, and placing them in circumstances where they are disposed to pay attention to what is happening around them, the Minuit writers of the 1980s and 1990s fill their novels with accounts of everyday objects like cigarette lighters and vacuum cleaners, and mundane activities like driving a car or making a phone call. Attention to the ordinary does not stem from any declared inquisitiveness but from a basic tendency to register whatever the protagonist notices. The everyday is made visible not by being the manifest carrier of narrative meanings, but by being noticed. If everyday objects and actions are there it is not primarily because they are deemed to be noteworthy but because they are noticeable. Of course what makes everyday things and situations noticeable is usually the way we find ourselves embroiled with them—when keys can't be found, the car breaks down, or an effort at seduction goes awry. Such happenings are the stuff of micro-narratives and of the 'incidents' that constitute the 'romanesque' for Barthes. Writers like Echenoz and Toussaint have a place in the field of the *quotidien* because their fictional techniques, like Perec's, serve to subvert the poetics of the realist novel, playing down narrative functionalism, and releasing the energies of a 'romanesque' linked, as we saw in Chapter 1, to the realm of practice. Whilst it would be wrong to exaggerate the extent of their engagement with the everyday, given the other concerns of these writers (for example, with parodying genre) and the inherent limitations of fiction, these works reveal, at the very least, the way the cultural sphere, and contemporary French fiction in particular, is permeated by awareness of, and commitment to, the everyday world.

---

[64] See Fieke Schoots, *'Passer en douce à la douane': L' écriture minimaliste de Minuit: Deville, Echenoz, Redonnet, Toussaint* (Amsterdam-Atlanta: Rodopi, 1997); and Paul Pelkmans, and Bruno Tristsmans (eds.) *Écrire l'insignifiant: dix études sur le fait divers dans le roman contemporain* (Amsterdam-Atlanta: Rodopi, 2000).

Many other writers could be added to those already mentioned, including novelists from earlier generations whose work has been reappraised in the light of a realigned *quotidien*, such as Eugène Dabit, Emmanuel Bove, Georges Simenon, or Leo Malet, and new exponents of detective or *polar* writing, including Didier Daeninx and Jean-Patrick Manchette who have imported everyday elements into genre fiction. François Bon, another Minuit author, whose projects will be discussed in the next chapter, drew on his background as an electrical engineer, and his acquaintance with the world of industrial plants and factories, to develop a powerful strand of fictional writing increasingly nourished by his experience of running writing workshops in communities such as prisons and rehabilitation centres. Like other contemporary writers (Leslie Kaplan, Emmanuel Carrère, Richard Millet), Bon often takes *faits divers*, including crimes, as his starting point. And as in Ernaux and Vinaver, attention to everyday speech is one of the key ways through which he tunes in to the everyday worlds of his protagonists. This led Bon to explore the possibilities of monologue or vociferation and, in *Parking* and *Impatience*, to bring about, at least at an imaginary level, a fusion between the fictive space of the 'récit' and the virtual space of the theatre stage. In these hybrid texts, Bon's aim, indicated through a marked metadiscursive dimension, is to devise means (his word is 'dispositifs') of giving expression to radical 'mutations', notably in the sphere of the city. The novel is found wanting: 'non plus le roman mais le dispositif même des voix qui nomment la ville et tâchent de s'en saisir' (no more novels but the the articulation of voices that name the city and try to grasp it).[65] Writing—rooted in direct engagement with the lives of the city streets—should aim to collect and broadcast the shattered words that bespeak a *quotidienneté* in crisis: 'Non, plus de roman jamais, mais cueillir à la croûte dure ces éclats qui débordent et résistent' (No, forget the novel: instead, collect on the hard crust those shards that stick out and resist).[66]

The interplay of orality and fragmentation is also central to the ways contemporary French poetry has absorbed and disseminated a concern with writing the everyday. As we saw earlier, Queneau was fascinated with everyday spoken language.[67] Combining with his passion for mathematical harmony, formal repetition, resemblance, and variation, this led to *Exercices de style*, where the same banal incident in the city street is rendered in dozens of styles,

---

[65] François Bon, *Impatience* (Paris: Minuit, 1996), 23.

[66] Ibid., 67.

[67] See also the everyday autobiography in verse, *Une Vie ordinaire*, by Georges Perros (1967; Paris: Gallimard-Poésie. 1988).

language serving to generate multiple ways of apprehending the same event. The mission of the Oulipo group, created in 1961, was to devise formal constraints that could recycle and generate texts, and through Queneau, and then such recruits as Perec, Jacques Roubaud, and Jacques Jouet, Oulipian experimentation continued to prospect the *quotidien*.[68] Moreover, the post-humous publication of Queneau's diaries revealed that the quest for peace and transcendence, achieved though immersion in the rhythms of the every-day world, and often drawing on oriental philosophy, was a constant strand in his personal life.[69] In *Morale élémentaire* (1975)[70] Queneau devised a fixed poetic form particularly attuned to the ungraspable, indeterminate quality of the everyday, experienced as a flow of perceptions and reflections.[71] Written at the rate of one per day, after a walk in the streets, each text consists of an identical pattern of word combinations (initially three 'stanzas', each com-prising four pairs of words) consisting of a noun plus an adjective ('Journée commençée') or present participle ('Chiens trottant'), followed by a brief poem of seven short lines, and ending with another 'stanza' of noun–adjective combinations. In the absence of any 'je', the recurrence of words in different combinations and positions creates patterns of repetition and rhythmical variation that enact an anonymous subject's immersion in the everyday world. The 'mutation' here is in the endless streaming of present experience, and the interplay of transience and permanence: 'Ça a bien changé et ça changera encore' (it's really changed and it'll change again) as Queneau wrote elsewhere.[72]

Both Perec and Roubaud paid homage to *Morale élémentaire* by writing poems of their own in this fixed form.[73] Roubaud, a poet and mathematician who, like Perec, saw Queneau as his mentor, found formal models in Japanese poetry as well as in numbers. Roubaud's first book was called Σ: (*Epsilon, le signe d'appartenance*), since this is the symbol, in set theory, for 'belonging' to a larger 'ensemble'. (The key motif of *quotidienneté* as totality recurs in

---

[68] See, e.g., Jacques Jouet's *Poèmes du métro* (Paris: POL, 2000).

[69] Raymond Queneau, *Journal 1914–1965* (Paris: Gallimard, 1996). See Michael Sheringham, 'Raymond Queneau: The Lure of the Spiritual', in David Bevan (ed.), *Literature and Spirituality* (Amsterdam: Rodopi, 1992), 33–48.

[70] Queneau, *Œuvres complètes*, I, 611–99.

[71] See Ibid., 611–61.

[72] Ibid., 282.

[73] Georges Perec, 'Deux "Morales élémentaires"' in *La Clôture et autres poèmes* (Paris: Hachette, 1980), 69–72; Jacques Roubaud, *La Forme d'une ville change plus vite, hélas, que le coeur des humains* (Paris: Gallimard, 1999), 186–9.

Ensembles, a collaboration between Roubaud and Boltanski, based on the Perequian practices of list-making and classification.) Roubaud's second book, *Mono no aware*, a canonical Japanese phrase he translates as 'le senti-ment des choses', reflected the desire to make poetry a spontaneous emanation of ambient reality.[74] Since then, it is by emulating Queneau (and Réda), in devising systematic pathways through the streets of Paris, London, New York, or Tokyo—that Roubaud has continued to ally poetic exploration and the everyday, composing sonnets in his head as he pounds the pavements, then logging them on his computer when he gets back to base. Inspired by Perec, *Tokyo infra-ordinaire* also sees Roubaud attempting a poetic form devised by a fellow Oulipian, Jacques Jouet, where the constraint is to write a poem with as many lines as the stops on one's journey in the metro, mentally composing a line while the train is in motion, and then writing it down in the interval when the train is stationary.[75]

Roubaud provides a direct link to a new generation of poets, including Olivier Cadiot, Pierre Alferi, Nathalie Quintane, and Anne Portugal, who, whilst not participants in Oulipo, have responded to Roubaud's eclectic fascin-ation with form, and the way his poetic writing involves collecting and organ-izing verbal fragments of diverse origins. In their manifesto for a new lyricism, Alferi and Cadiot rejected inspiration in favour of the manipulation of bits of language, a 'mécanique lyrique' that often draws on texts for its source material but tends to exploit the heteroclite, pell-mell amalgams of immediate percep-tual experience, and thus, whilst rejecting description or thematic consistency, tends, via language, to stay in the orbit of everyday immediacy (poetic tran-scendence of the ordinary is emphatically not envisaged).[76] The small square poems of Alferi's *Kub Or* (alluding to soluble soup and Rubik's Cubes) provide compact, *ad hoc* 'definitions' of stray sights and sounds wafting in the everyday environment. Nathalie Quintane's *Chaussure* focuses on the micro-world of footwear, while in *Les Commodités d'une banquette* Anne Portugal makes poems out of the innumerable written signs and notices (Perec's '3ᵉ secteur') that feature in daily life. The eponymous 'hero' of Anne Portugal's *définitif bob*, with his reversible lower-case name, is a homunculus, inspired by video games, whose 'missions serrés horizontales' (tight horizontal missions), whilst taking

---

[74] On this see Jacqueline Pigeot, *Questions de poétique japonaise* (Paris: PUF, 1997).

[75] Jouet, *Poèmes du métro*.

[76] See Pierre Alferi and Olivier Cadiot (eds.), *Revue de littérature générale*, I (*La Méchanique lyrique*) and II (*Digest*) (Paris: POL, 1995–6).

place strictly in the virtual world of words, explore ambient everyday reality. Each of this poem-novel's twenty-four chapters feature episodes from bob's investigations: he appears to survey a house, test the countryside, try out various media, assay cultural allusions and myths, while donning successively the guises of a spy, film director, scientist, ethnographer. The computer game motif, with its idiom of quick-fire appearances and disappearances, miniaturization, microscopic detail, fantasy, prowess, and compulsive forward momentum, figures, in the first instance, the infinite resources of language. But the idea of a reality consisting in a range of co-extensive possible worlds (in *La Pluralité des mondes de Lewis* Roubaud drew attention to the branch of post-Wittgensteinian philosophy that uses this concept), determined by different sets of rules applied to the same elements—bob shifts from one scenario to another with amazing alacrity— provides a vivid metaphorical enactment of the immediacy and multiplicity of ordinary experience. A recurrent formula, stemming from the *énonciation* of spoken language, 'et bob il peut comme ça' (and bob can, like this (or in this fashion)), followed by an infinitive—for example: 'pousser une porte', 'se comporter en retrait' (open a door, hang back)—makes a connection between the activity of negotiating one's passage through the everyday, and what Certeau called 'arts de faire': context-bound, *ad hoc*, improvised aptitudes that turn the given our way, as we use our accumulated know-how to grasp opportune moments.[77]

By the 1990s, the word 'minuscule', and the cult of the 'micro', the 'peu', and the 'mineur', noted in a special feature in the *NRF*, devoted to a group of writers (including Delerm and Jouanard) labelled 'Les Moins-que-rien', became ubiquitous signals of the widespread turn to the near at hand that we have identified in a variety of genres and media.[78] In concluding our survey with the protean mode of the essay, a first observation is that the set of concepts, discourses, and examples whose constitution we located in the interactions between Lefebvre, Barthes, Certeau, and Perec, has not been superseded by subsequent theoretical or analytical contributions. Since Perec's death in 1982 numerous books with *quotidien* in their titles, or which, across a wide range of areas and disciplines, clearly touch on this area, generally tend to

---

[77] Cf. Michael Polanyi on 'tacit knowledge' (id., *Personal Knowledge: Towards a Post-Critical Philosophy* (1958; Chicago: University of Chicago Press, 1974). See Michael Sheringham, 'Dans le quotidien: immersion, résistance, liberté (Raymond Queneau, Anne Portugal)', in E. Cardonne-Arlick and Dominique Viart (eds.), *Ecritures contemporaines*, 7 (Paris: Minard, 2003), 205–20.

[78] *NRF*, no. 540 (Jan. 1998), 3–54.

cite (or allude to) these increasingly canonical figures, and to illustrate, consolidate, or query existing perceptions and approaches rather than offer new paradigms (even if originality is usually claimed). Looking at the over-looked, learning to attend to the traces of a seemingly 'residual' dimension of experience, developing ways of homing in on the present, identifying the performative character of everyday 'manières de faire'—these and other recurrent motifs (micro-gestures, the 'romanesque', the 'tout-ensemble', etc.) that we have identified in this book, prove durable.

The two main strands I want to pick out—sociological-ethnographic, and philosophical-aesthetic—whilst in themselves quite varied, co-exist and intertwine with other modes of essayistic writing that reflect the rehabilitation of the everyday (and the link just noted with the rise and modulation of life-writing in the 1980s and 1990s). One example is the *chronique*, a regular column where the writer reports in a non-specialized way on a particular activity (like gardening) and voices what is on his mind. In the hands of the psychoanalyst Daniel Sibony, the philosopher Jean Baudrillard, or the gay writer Renaud Camus, the *chronique*, (of which Ernaux's *Journal du dehors* is a version, and Barthes's 'Chronique' a precedent) comes not only to articulate an oblique slant on current affairs, as in say Mauriac's *Bloc-notes* in the 1950s, but to focus explicitly on contingent aspects of the writer's daily existence.[79] Moreover, in Baudrillard's *Amérique* or Camus's *Le Département de la Lozère*, the *chronique* is also a form of travel or topographical writing, which, in writers like Jean Rolin, Michel Chailloux, or Gil Jouanard (as in Réda) is often strongly tinged with the *quotidien*.[80] The writing of history is another notable area. Just as *Annales* had a part in Lefebvre's early work, and historiographical reflection in Certeau's thought, new styles of historical writing have pursued agendas where the impact of *quotidien* discourse is felt. This is a vast area, encompassing developments (from Philippe Ariès onwards) in the history of private life, micro-history pioneered by Carlo Ginzburg and Robert Darnton, monographs on particular regions (Thuillier on the Nièvre), Alain Corbin's histories of the senses, Michel Pastoureau on colours.[81] A central motif here is

---

[79] Cf. Daniel Sibony, *Evénements*, I *Psychopathologie du quotidien* (Paris: Seuil, 1995).

[80] See Jean Rolin, *Zones* (Paris: Gallimard, 1995); Michel Chailloux, *La France Fugitive* (Paris: Fayard, 1998); Gil Jouanard, *Mémoire de l'instant—nouvelles ordinaires de divers endroits* (Lagrasse: Verdier, 2000).

[81] On 'nouvelle histoire' see François Dosse, *L'Histoire en miettes. Des Annales à la nouvelle histoire* (Paris: Pocket, 1997); see Carlo Ginzburg, *The Cheese and the Worms: The Cosmos of a Sixteenth-Century Miller* (1976; London: Routledge and Kegan Paul, 1980); see Alain Corbin, (1982; Paris: Flammarion, 1998) *Le Miasme et la jonquille*; see Michel Pastoureau, *Bleu: Histoire d'une couleur* (Paris: Seuil, 2000).

that of the archive. In *Le Goût de l'archive* Arlette Farge locates her work on crime and street life in eighteenth-century Paris in the context of a passion for the 'minuscule' traces of ordinary lives to be found in long-forgotten documents. Citing Certeau, along with Foucault, Ricoeur, and others, Farge shows how reflections on the everyday are closely bound up with the restoration of lost histories, and points to how everyday life has become an important category in feminist and post-colonial work, and generally in Anglo-Saxon cultural studies. Some of the writings of the Italian philosopher Giorgio Agamben, a disciple of Benjamin, whose thought is also imbued with Bataille and Blanchot, and whose writings have been widely read in France, pursue a line where the historical, the archival, and the everyday interpenetrate— sometimes, as in *La Communauté qui vient*, in the mode of the *chronique*.

Another field of investigation deserving mention for the way it conjoins ethnography, autobiography, and the *quotidien*, is the study of 'écritures ordinaires'—transient bits of writing, such as shopping lists, graffiti, notes, postcards, aides-mémoires, holiday diaries, that have come to attract people working in a variety of disciplines.[82] Also to be noted are periodic attempts to update Barthes's *Mythologies*. In 2000, the psychoanalyst Serge Tisseron's *Petites Mythologies d'aujourd'hui* analysed new gestures, rituals, and rhythms induced by such technological innovations as mobile phones, plastic bags, disposable cameras, and computer games. In 2004, the *Nouvel Observateur* marked the fiftieth anniversary of Barthes's first 'mythology' (published in the *Lettres nouvelles* in 1954) with a special supplement on *Mythologies d'aujourd'-hui*: thirty-two items, covering reality TV, greenhouse gases, Formule 1 hotels, body-piercing, thongs, Harry Potter, disposable cameras, and DIY, scrutinized by a range of sociologists, ethnographers, and philosophers including Jean-Didier Urbain and Serge Tisseron. The six contributors of introductory essays (including Jean Baudrillard) concur in the view that the spirit, if not always the letter, of Barthes's enterprise is still valid, enlightening, and applicable, and that the need to locate ideological operations in the discourses surrounding the objects, celebrities, and institutions of daily life is as pressing as ever. Philippe Mesnard notes that Barthes's work should now be seen in the wider context of Lefebvre, the Situationists, Perec, Baudrillard, and Tati.[83] On the whole, however, the contributors write in the idiom of their own speciality on fairly predictable topics that can be seen as 'signs of the times'. Another trend in the

---

[82] See Daniel Fabre (ed.), *Écritures ordinaires* (Paris: POL, 1993).
[83] *Mythologies d'aujourd'hui*, *Le Nouvel Observateur*, hors-série no. 55 (July–Aug. 2004), 10.

essayistic writing of the everyday that should be mentioned is the trend for cultural studies books on single topics such as cod, cigarettes, chewing gum, or walking. This can further be linked to the rise of interest in material cultures which has led to many new museums devoted to everyday artefacts and related rituals.

Pierre Sansot's *Les Gens de peu* (1991) shows how, as in the case of 'écritures ordinaires', the impact of *quotidien* thinking on social anthropology led away from norms and statistics to 'thick' descriptions (Clifford Geertz's term) of practices and lifestyles.[84] Working initially on the phenomenology of the imagination, in the line of Bachelard, Durand, and Dufrenne, before teaching anthropology, Sansot began by studying the 'poetics of the city', looking at concrete urban spaces in terms of their imaginary and mythic potential.[85] Extending the range of phenomenological description, he went on to develop a theory and practice of the 'sensible'[86]—implying the observer's sensuous interaction—which he applied to various components of Frenchness, from landscape to (in later books) primary-school books, public parks, and rugby.[87] In *Les Gens de peu* Sansot set out to break the mould of sociological studies of popular culture, generally preoccupied with class stratifications and statistical norms, and to capture the essence of an outlook: that of modest folk who find contentment in ordinary pleasures. Echoing Maspero, he refers to himself as an observer of social life whose method is *promenade* rather than *enquête* (26).[88] The book consists of short essays on representative figures, such as the house-wife, the DIY enthusiast ('le petit bricoleur'), the local drunk, and institutions or pastimes such as camping holidays, street football and community celebra-tions. Notions of ritual and of the 'legendary' are intermittently invoked (reference is made to Eliade's distinction between sacred and profane (46)), but the focus is primarily on detailed evocations of behaviour. The introduc-tion ends with an approving reference to Henri Calet, a post-war autobio-graphical essayist and 'chroniqueur' with a strong sense of place and *quotidienneté*, whose works have, symptomatically, been rediscovered in recent years.[89] In their emphasis on describing such attitudes as *débrouillardise* and

---

[84] Clifford Geertz, *The Interpretation of Cultures* (New York: Basic Books, 1973).

[85] See Pierre Sansot, *Poétique de la ville* (Paris: Klinksieck, 1973).

[86] See id., *Les Formes sensibles de la vie sociale* (Paris: PUF, 1986) and id., *La France sensible* (Paris: Champ Vallon, 1985).

[87] See id., *Cahiers d'enfrance* (Paris: Champ Vallon, 1990); *Jardins publics* (Paris: Payot, 1994); *Le Rugby est une fête* (Paris: Payot, 2002).

[88] References to Sansot, *Les Gens de peu* (Paris: PUF, 1992) are incorporated in the text.

[89] Henri Calet, *De ma lucarne: chroniques* (Paris: Gallimard, 2000).

day-to-day hedonism Calet's writings have affinities with Albert Camus's descriptions of French Algerians in *Noces* and *L'Été*, which can also be seen as models for Sansot's enterprise. Like Michel Maffesoli, to whom he does not refer, but whose works were published in the same 'Sociologie aujourd'hui' series, Sansot alludes to Hoggart's *La Culture du pauvre*, but if, like Hoggart, he celebrates minor virtues, unlike Hoggart and Maffesoli he is not concerned with stoic endurance but with pleasure. The moral or existential posture Sansot wants to make visible (since 'les gens de peu' leave few traces) may consist in not putting oneself forward, in restraint, lack of fuss and anonymity, but it is expressed in the way people derive enjoyment from ordinary activities (13).

The slant towards life's small pleasures, and to the ethics of the everyday, may underline the circumspect attitude Sansot adopts towards Perec in his methodological discussions. Keen to distance himself from the sociology of leisure pioneered by Dumazier (as well as, implicitly, Bourdieu's account of social reproduction), Sansot is also anxious to suggest that he has not fallen prey to the by then (1991) pervasive 'cult' of the *quotidien*, which, somewhat caricaturally, he associates with the transubstantiation of Adidas trainers and Coca-Cola into ersatz religious icons. With more justification, after citing Perec's exercises and exhortations in 'Approches de quoi?', Sansot notes that deliberate enumeration is not a natural activity and that the 'infra-ordinary' is closer to the extraordinary than the ordinary (12). Yet, as his descriptions will show, Sansot's reservations reflect not only unawareness of the deeper springs of Perec's attachment to the everyday, but Sansot's own reluctance to question the polarity between the everyday and the exceptional that Perec had sought to deconstruct: the attitudes and aptitudes of Sansot's ordinary folk create regular, but exceptional, diversions from the daily grind.

The importance of creativity, however, allies Sansot with Michel de Certeau, not cited yet arguably omnipresent. Indeed one might think Sansot had set out to apply Certeau's model—consumption, or use, as creative *détournement* and self-affirmation—to the everyday leisure activities of unexceptional French citizens. He explicitly states his desire to 'privilégier la consommation [...] l'usage que nous faisons de notre vie' (foreground consumption ... the uses we make of our lives) (14), and to highlight processes of 'collective reappropriation' (18), albeit underlining the relative autonomy of each 'pratique', whilst seeking to divine a particular overall attitude (that of 'modestie'). In clarifying the place of minor pleasures in his sense of an ethics of the *quotidien*, Sansot alludes to Michel Foucault's recent work on the 'souci de soi' (to be discussed in Chapter 9 below), but in referring constantly to 'pratiques' (and once to 'ruse'(58)), in unveiling 'façons de faire' (57), such as the *bricoleur*'s pride in diverting (*détourner*) materials from their original use, or in celebrating the way his subjects do not simply reproduce dominant culture (*pace* Bourdieu) but 'reinvent' their ways of living (214), he is firmly in the line of *L'Invention du quotidien*. In fact, it often seems as if Sansot provides a better defence and illustration of Certeau than Mayol and Giard were able to do. At one point Sansot notes that a single 'pratique' can often be seen to mark both consent to an order that constrains and engagement in an activity that fosters self-realization (24). And this dialectic of submission and creation (noted earlier in Vinaver's plays) finds expression in the banal object to which Sansot devotes the conclusion of *Les Gens de peu*: the 'pliant', or folding stool, beloved of fishermen, which, he hastily adds, has not been assimilated into the cult of the everyday—unlike the ill-sited benches and ugly flower boxes that make many 'rues piétonnes' into 'non-lieux'—a veiled reference to Marc Augé (222). The humble 'pliant' symbolizes compliant patience and the pleasures of dogged resistance.

Sansot's emphasis on simple pleasures is heightened in Philippe Delerm's *La Première Gorgée de bière et autres plaisirs minuscules* (1995) and its sequels, whose huge popular success was noted in Chapter 1. In fact, the theme of pleasure is predominant in the second main strand of essayistic writing on the *quotidien*. The question of happiness, of how we should live, has always been at the heart of writing on the everyday—since *quotidien* discourse usually summons us to attend to a dimension we have forgotten. However, if philosophers (for example, Wittgenstein and Cavell) have often taken the ordinary as a touchstone, the analytical discourses of philosophy have rarely provided appropriate vehicles for the exploration of concrete *quotidienneté*. Yet if, as Adorno suggested, the vocation of the essay has been to weigh up common experience in the scale of general human needs, philosophical essayism has had a significant place in the *quotidien* tradition. In the 1980s and 1990s, the prominence of the everyday is at once the context for and instigator of styles of philosophical reflection, essayistic in spirit, where everyday experience is examined in the light of questions of 'mode de vie'. The popularity of André Comte-Sponville's *Petit traité des grandes vertus* (1995), and the 'new' hedonism of Michel Onfray's *La Sculpture de soi* (1991) can be seen in the light of this general trend. Yet more often than not the encounter between philosophy and the *quotidien* is skewed by preoccupations which, rather than opening up ordinary experience itself, tend to see such scrutiny as a way of transcending it: attention to the everyday becomes a way of escaping its clutches.

A notable example is Herman Parret's *Le Sublime du quotidien*. Combining semiotics with analytical and aesthetic philosophy, and autobiography theory, Parret insists on the need to cherish everyday activities, albeit essentially as the framework for sudden 'reorientations' or 'resemanticizations' of experience. It is by dint of its lack of distinct form and substance that the everyday has the merit of virtuality, which makes it the gateway to the 'sublime'. *Quotidienneté*, asserts Parret, is only 'pertinent' because it is the setting for sublime experience, associated with beauty.[90] We miss out on such experience when we give our lives direction, adopting goals and ambitions that deliver us from the *quotidien* (168). Only by lingering in the sphere of everyday experiences will we find pathways that lead, through the *quotidien*, to the sublime. Parret provides accounts of the 'little ontologies' to be found in such domains as music, gardens, caresses and kisses, seeking to demonstrate that if we attend to it the *quotidien* is constantly 'fractured' by the tremors of the sublime. Parret's aestheticization of the everyday is a current that can be identified elsewhere: for example, in Patrick Drevet's *Huit petites études sur le désir de voir* and its sequel. These volumes comprise finely nuanced meditations on the act of reading, the metro, window cleaners, bodily gestures, and so forth, which seek to elucidate the sense of self-evidence which, as we saw earlier (Chapter 2), is a familiar touchstone of everyday experience. This kind of writing has an earlier exemplar in Jean Grenier, Albert Camus's mentor, whose *La Vie quotidienne*, published in 1968, develops strands in his (and Camus's) earlier essayism, linked to the celebration of the Mediterranean, and applies them to a dozen realms of experience, ranging from walking and sleeping to tobacco, perfume, silence, and reading. In his presentation Grenier says that these everyday activities disclose 'ways of being' that go beyond their apparent functions, and that if we analyse them closely we can see how 'la vie courante' secretes styles of living that can be associated with art.[91] In practice, analysis draws out this aesthetic dimension of everyday experience by weaving into it numerous threads from a wide range of literary and philosophical traditions. (As Barthes's work on Japan and Perec's championing of Sei Shonogon indicate, writing on the everyday often involves a convergence of European and Eastern traditions.)

With its Perequian motif of practical experiments, the work of another contemporary philosopher-essayist, Roger Pol-Droit, looks set to avoid

---

[90] Herman Parret, *Le Sublime du quotidien* (Amsterdam: John Benjamins, 1988), 20.
[91] Jean Grenier, *La Vie quotidienne* (1968; Paris: Gallimard, 1982), back cover.

aestheticization and abstraction. Yet despite an emphasis on concrete experience the vector of *101 Expériences de philosophie quotidienne* runs through the everyday to forms of awareness that transcend it. The book's novelty, which no doubt explains its huge success (comparable with Delerm's), lies in its format. Each short essay outlines a practical experiment which, by inducing a sideways step, a change of perspective, is supposed to bring about a 'petit déclic' (little jolt) that will open our mind to the true mystery of daily existence (the brief introduction promises 'everyday adventures'). Often resembling the thought experiments of Eastern philosophy, especially Zen Buddhism, the exercises are strictly non-utilitarian and usually humorous. Each entry starts by specifying a recommended duration, any materials needed, and a brief statement of the effect it is supposed to produce. Listed in one of three indexes—another Perequian touch—these effects range from 'calming' and 'dreamlike' to 'floating' and 'Jurassic'. Thus, for the first exercise, 'S'appeler soi-même', where we are instructed to call out our own name, the recommended time is about twenty minutes, the only equipment needed is a quiet place, and the desired effect is feeling 'double'. Unsettling all sense of fixed identity is one of the book's main ambitions, and the 'petit décollement de soi par rapport à soi' (slight detachment from oneself), aimed at here, is echoed in many other exercises (for example, showering with one's eyes shut, or imagining one is invisible (80)).[92] Pol-Droit insists that the starting point should be as banal as possible and that the essence of the experiments is the 'mutation' (for example, in our sense of identity) brought about by the channelling of attention (95). Sometimes the exercise does return us to ordinary reality, rather than foster estrangement. Imagining a planet of tiny gestures (the motif of possible worlds is recurrent) draws attention to the power of barely perceptible actions, like placing someone else's hand on one's forehead, or certain ways of waving goodbye (189). The piece on emerging from a cinema into broad daylight does summon up a common experience of *dépaysement* (197). In theory, experiments like phoning people at random are meant to initiate 'micro-adventures' (48) in the enigmatic opacity of the human world; gratuitous actions, such as taking the metro just for the sake of it (97), break with functional routine and launch us on journeys of initiation into the infinitely variegated worlds of ephemeral details in the manner of Nicholson Baker's *The Mezzanine* (215). Yet this may lead to anticlimax, as in the piece on going to

---

[92] Roger Pol-Droit, *101 Expériences de philosophie quotidienne* (Paris: Odile Jacob, 2001). References are incorporated in the text.

the barber where we are initially instructed to imagine all kinds of counter-factual scenario, albeit based on real anxieties, for example that we will come out looking unrecognizable. For we are then instructed to dismiss such fantasies, and thus to gauge the gap between our 'fantasmagories' (116) and reality which, we are now told, is in fact nearly always banal, simple, uniform, and reassuring.

The weakness of Pol-Droit's book, which makes it no more than a *jeu d'esprit*, is that in reality the author has little interest in the everyday. The point of stirring readers to indulge in philosophical speculation is not to explore and illuminate the banal but, through artifice, to make the banal seem interesting. For Pol-Droit, the ordinary world is boring; philosophy can enliven it by augmenting the mind's power to alter and embroider given reality. The pleasures on offer here are those of a mind that detaches itself from the ordinary world, rather than those in store if we try to tune in to our everyday surroundings. For all its ludic gestures *101 Expériences de philosophie quotidienne* is profoundly anti-Perequian. Whilst Perec's tactics have inspired many people to explore their surroundings, it is hard to imagine many people bothering to spend an hour imagining they are rowing across their living room, or drinking while they urinate. By very simple means, Perec convenes us to authentic *étonnement*, while the philosophical wonder laboriously engineered by Pol-Droit seems trivial and unenlightening.

9

Configuring the Everyday

Should we pay attention to the everyday? If so, how should we do it? Our concluding chapter starts out from four parameters identified in earlier discussion. First, while many things are commonly identified with the *quotidien*—eating, phoning, shopping, objects, and gadgets—everydayness is not a property or aggregate of these things; it inheres rather in the way they are part of manifold lived experience. Secondly, the ensemble in which we are immersed comprises other people: *quotidienneté* implies community. Thirdly, while the everyday is not the place of the event (always exceptional), and is therefore in tension with history, it has a historicity that is embodied, shared and ever-changing (repetition does not have to be stale). Fourthly, *quotidienneté* dissolves (into statistics, properties, data) when the everyday is made an object of scrutiny. Everydayness lies in practices that weave contexts together; only practices make it visible. Overall, this summary points to two lines of approach that rise to the challenge of the everyday. Both are implicit in the evolution of thinking on the *quotidien*, and in the works in different media which, as we have noted, bear the imprint of such thought. One approach centres on the *figure*, the other on the *project*. In practice they intertwine, as will be seen when we consider three areas: the day, the street and the project itself.

If the everyday is the site of a struggle between alienation and appropriation, critical reflection is inevitably involved in a similar dynamic. The factors that make the everyday alien to us are themselves bound up with the project of rationality. The foreclosure induced by most ways of thinking about the everyday is of a piece with the alienation wrought in the sphere of the everyday through its 'colonisation' (Guy Debord) by abstract and technocratic reason. Attempts to theorize the everyday that use the methods of individual 'sciences parcellaires' (Lefebvre) are in complicity with the segmentation and rationalization that threaten the everyday in the first place. Thus the ways of rethinking the everyday with which this book is concerned—Lefebvre, Debord,

Blanchot, Barthes, Certeau, Perec, Augé, Cavell—acknowledge its resistance to thought, the indeterminacy that makes for its paradoxical strength.

The everyday cannot be reduced to its content. It is not just repetition that makes daily activities part of everydayness, but the endless variation and sedimentation which, according to Réda or Certeau, turn the *quotidien* into a sphere of invention. Driving to work, getting the groceries, talking to friends are all objective phenomena—instances of which can be analysed in a wide variety of ways—but the everyday invokes something that holds these things together, their continuity and rhythm, or lack of it, something that is adverbial, modal, and ultimately therefore ethical, because it has to do with individual and collective *art de vivre*. Just as the early modern shift in sensibility towards ordinary life identified by Charles Taylor was encapsulated in Joseph Hall's phrase 'God loveth adverbs',[1] so, in a more secular dispensation, the challenge of the everyday has to do with how things are done, with appropriation. The everyday as lived reality only exists modally, through the slant or impetus we impart to particular iterations. How can we grasp this modal dimension of daily actions?

One line of thought is suggested by the philosopher Jean-Luc Nancy when he invites us to home in on the plain fact, the simple *évidence*, of existence. If, he argues, rather than seeing it empirically, in terms of conditions of possibility, or transcendentally, as possessing a meaning beyond itself, we envisage existence in its 'factuality'—as possessing, here and now, its own reason—then we must, according to Nancy, identify it with freedom. Existence, freedom, and thought converge in 'la libre dissémination de l'existence' (the free dissemination of existence), which does not consist in 'la diffraction d'un principe, ni l'effet multiple d'une cause, mais [...] l'an-archie [...] d'un surgissement singulier, et donc par essence pluriel' (the diffraction of a principle or the multiple effects of a cause, but... the an-archy... of a springing forth that is singular, and thus essentially plural).[2] To apprehend existence in this way—as freedom—requires a mode of thinking that Nancy elsewhere refers to as the '*praxis* de la pensée',[3] in which meaning (*sens*) exceeds—or outruns—discourse and *signification*. And like Jean-François Lyotard, who makes the same distinction in *Discours, figure*,[4] Nancy identifies such thought, and such praxis, as 'figural'.

[1] Taylor, *The Sources of the Self,* 211–33.
[2] Jean-Luc Nancy, *L'Expérience de la liberté* (Paris: Galilée, 1988), 16–17.
[3] Id., *Le Sens du monde* (Paris: Galilée, 1993), 37.
[4] Jean-François Lyotard, *Discours, figure* (Paris: Klinksieck, 1971), 91–100 and *passim*. References are incorporated in the text.

In fact, Lyotard's account of 'le figural' also suggests ways of understanding and grasping how the everyday is configured. The kind of participation in the world Lyotard identifies as the figural avoids polarizing figure and discourse, seeking instead to show how the figural, whilst associated with seeing, is in fact at work in discourse (just as discourse is at work in the figure). What does the figure bring to the process of meaning? Firstly, a remainder, a residual opacity or density that resists discourse's transparency and functional instrumentality by virtue of its connection to space, to what is out there, 'en vis-à-vis', an externality that makes it inassimilable to the interior, and hence to interiority (just as the everyday is always the 'dehors', never wholly the 'dedans'). The figure is 'une manifestation spatiale que l'espace linguistique ne peut pas incorporer sans être ébranlé, une extériorité qu'il ne peut pas intérioriser en *signification*' (a spatial manifestation that linguistic space cannot incorporate without disturbance, an exteriority that it cannot interiorize as *signification*)(13). The figural is a perspective we can adopt, a subject position in the process of meaning, a mode of enunciation that produces or discloses 'sens' rather than 'signification'. *Sens* is a kind of meaning, or an experience of meaning, that is closer to the opaque exteriority and otherness of things, but it cannot be divided from the *signification* that transcends it, in which it is an immanent residue (this residual opacity links with the everyday): 'le sens ne se révèle qu'à l'encontre des significations' (meaning only reveals itself in opposition to significations)(382). The figural is neither an ornamental excrescence nor a property of things, like a function or a definition; it is not a regular pattern that can consistently be read in a particular way, by means of an established semiotics. As a linguistic or discursive event, the figural, which renounces 'l'armature du logos scientifique' (the framework of scientific reason) is a one-off, an undoing of codes: '[il s'agit de] défaire le code, sans pourtant détruire le message' (it is necessary to undo the code without destroying the message). Constructing 'sens' means deconstructing 'signification' (19). Resistant to standard narratives and functions, and thus eluding 'la vraisemblance sociale, psychologique, éthique' (social, psychological, or ethical verisimilitude), the figural requires a mode of attention that Lyotard compares to the 'attention flottante' (free-floating attention) Freud recommended to the analyst: attention that closes an eye to the 'secondary revisions' through which the analysand's discourse conforms to established models, and maintains the vigilance needed to spot the primary processes of desire.[5]

---

[5] Lyotard, *Discours, figure*, 17, 379–82. On 'attention flottante' see Laplanche and Pontalis, *Vocabulaire de la psychanalyse*.

Figurality, resistance, *évidence*, attention, enunciation, and practice. I am suggesting that Nancy's account of existence as freedom, and Lyotard's category of the figural, dovetail with ways of seeing the *quotidien* as resistant to codification, as dependent on forms of attention that grasp it as a totality that only exists modally, at the level of practice or usage. That is why it is difficult to approach the everyday thematically, via its attributes. We can certainly make lists of objects, situations, activities, and other attributes that seem to typify the everyday, but they will not tell us anything about lived everydayness until we grasp their part in a wider configuration, the ensemble or process from which they are inseparable. The notion of the figural helps us understand the conditions on which a particular feature of daily life can disclose something of the everyday in general, and thus to see why certain aspects or characteristics of the everyday, which crop up recurrently in the kinds of work we have been studying, do so by virtue not so much of their typicality as their figurality, in other words their capacity to resist knowledge and foster understanding of a wider set of lived relationships.

Think of the street in Certeau, the metro in Augé, the 'ville nouvelle' in Ernaux, the apartment block in Perec, Japanese cuisine in Barthes, workplace conversation in Vinaver, the houses explored by Duras in *La Vie matérielle* or Savitzkaya in *En vie*.[6] What releases the figural dimension of these realities, their *sens* rather than *signification*, is the way they are seen not in terms of a descriptive system but as the sites of practice, of things being done—in time as well as space, in community as well as solitude. Figurality depends on modes of perception where lived experience involves being at grips with the real, processing it and attending to it, albeit obliquely. Temporality and intersubjectivity are vital. To be figures of the everyday, pathways into the apprehension of everydayness, the house, the conversation or the object must be mobilized and modalized, grasped through such parameters as the interplay of the individual and the collective, the significant and the insignificant, the singular and the plural, identity and difference, the cumulative and the noncumulative. Thus, for example, if the everyday is always connected to the short term, because it has to do with iteration, regular returns of the similar, it is not restricted to the instant. Embracing the archive of previous occurrences that make an activity generic, habitual, or regular, the *quotidien* is also the terrain of

---

[6] The figure of the house, and domestic space in general, merit close consideration in connection with the everyday. In addition to these texts by Duras and Savitzkaya, both of which are steeped in thinking about the *quotidien*, one would want to consider Bourdieu's ethnographic studies of the 'Maison kabyle' in *Esquisse d'une théorie de la pratique*, 61–82, as well as Perec.

resurfacings, recognitions, and connections. As a result, the everyday partakes of that aspect of phenomena that becomes the stuff of nostalgia. The present-ness of everyday things stems from their belonging to a communal flow, to a time that washes around historical events, leaving the kinds of flotsam and jetsam Perec so memorably enumerated in *Je me souviens*. There, in Perec's book of erstwhile, everyday matters, we are reminded of how things are constantly replacing each other in our affections, in the living space we share with others, and in the living time of day-by-day experience.

THE SPACE OF THE DAY

The first figure I want to consider is that of the day. What sort of vantage point does the *journée*, the span of a single day, provide for scrutinizing everyday experience? To what extent is it a paradigm, and what sorts of thinking about days make the day a figure of everydayness? It is an obvious point of depart-ure—*quotidien*, after all, has the Latin *dies* as its root: the everyday pertains to the day. Yet in some respects a particular day is the antithesis of the everyday: the *quotidien* ignores the difference the calendar marks, it belongs, indiffer-ently, to the day after day, to repetition rather than difference. Still, we will not catch hold of everydayness if we sever it from given days. Dailiness both transcends particular days and partakes of the day. A day is a microcosm. Whether defined as the interval between sunrise and sunset, or as one com-plete rotation of the earth, thus comprising a day and a night, a day can be experienced as a continuous flow of consciousness or bodily awareness. The day is crucial to the currency of lived experience. Smaller denominations (minutes, hours, seconds) can be intensively scrutinized, but they are deriva-tives, the small change of the day, while larger denominations (weeks, months, years) are multiples of a smaller unit. A day is a temporal structure related to the movement of the sun: morning, noon, and night; morning, afternoon, evening; *métro, boulot, dodo*. Change and process are imprinted in human physiology, in the circadian rhythms of the body.[7]

The literature of the day in western culture is extensive, ranging across prescriptions for a regulated existence in classical antiquity, the books of hours of medieval Christianity, the *journal intime* which arose in the context of

---

[7] In his late work Henri Lefebvre came to see rhythm as a fundamental property of the *quotidien*, see id., *Éléments de Rythmanalyse* (Paris: Syllepse, 1992).

Romanticism, and such modern classics as Joyce's *Ulysses*, Woolf's *Mrs Dalloway*, Apollinaire's 'Zone', Lowry's *Under the Volcano*, Claude Simon's *Histoire*, as well as the many variations on the 'One Day in the Life' theme, from Solzhenitsyn to the *Sunday Times* magazine and, more recently, Olivier Rolin's *L'Invention du monde*, a novel drawn from the events of a single day as reported in newspapers from all round the world. Jean Starobinski has shown how, as a 'forme porteuse de sens'[8]—a meaning-bearing structure—the span of the day can articulate many themes. In Rousseau, for example, descriptions of *journées* in their unfolding, as in the famous 'idylle des cerises' scene in *Les Confessions*, are linked with states of happiness where the inner world of feeling and the outer world of nature fuse harmoniously through the medium of an unbroken succession of experiences. Rousseau talks of 'ma journée'—'le posessif marque une appropriation', notes Starobinski (236)—when, paradoxically, he escapes from his usual identity, and the day serves as a mediating agency linking self to cosmos through a 'mouvement de totalisation' (237). In Joyce, a single day in the life of an individual encompasses the whole of human history and culture. In Woolf, 'an ordinary mind on an ordinary day' makes visible the labyrinthine motions of consciousness. In Claude Simon, the twenty-four hours of a day are capacious enough to contain an infinite number of temporal gradations, including numerous links with the past.[9]

Much of the literature of the *journée* has a bearing on the rendering of everyday experience. Marc Augé used the 'day in the life' structure in the first of his essays in everyday ethnography.[10] Starobinski's work suggests, however, that the figure of the day is most illuminating, with regard to the figural dimension of everydayness, when the day becomes the framework for an act of individual self-enquiry concerned with *art de vivre*. In this mode, attention to the hour-by-hour unfolding of one's day becomes a means not only of self-discovery but of self-transformation. The day becomes the instrument of an ongoing process of self-fashioning, albeit one that often moves away from individuation towards recognition of commonality. This orientation in Starobinski's writings on the *journée* derives in part from Michel Foucault's work and it underlines the contribution made by Foucault's notion of the 'souci de soi' to the range of discourses on the everyday. Starobinski's 'L'Ordre du jour',

---

[8] Jean Starobinski, 'Jean-Jacques Rousseau/La Forme du jour', in *Jean Starobinski: Cahiers pour un temps* (Paris: Centre Georges Pompidou, 1985) 201 (this comprises four articles on Rousseau envisaged as part of a wider study (as yet unpublished) on 'la forme du jour').

[9] Id., 'La Journée dans *Histoire*', in R. Dragonetti (ed.), *Sur Claude Simon* (Paris: Minuit, 1987).

[10] See Ch. 8.

to which I shall return, makes specific reference to Foucault's 1983 article
'L'Écriture de soi',[11] part of his ongoing work on the history of sexuality and
the aesthetics of existence.

Observing a new accent on the regulation of pleasure in the first two
centuries AD, Foucault notes that it focused on inner regulation rather than
outer control or legislation. He highlights a new consciousness of the 'rapports
de soi à soi' (relation of oneself with oneself),[12] a 'culture de soi' where the
notion of an 'art of existence' is dominated by the idea of 'care for oneself'.
'Application à soi' involved not only adopting a general attitude, but working
on the self (practices Foucault calls 'technologies de soi'), and this is where the
day comes in: 'Il y faut du temps. Et c'est un des grand problèmes de cette
culture de soi que de fixer, dans la journée ou dans la vie, la part qu'il convient
de lui consacrer' (It takes time. And one of the great problems of this culture of
the self is determining, in a day or a life, the share it should be allotted) (65).
There are many different formulae: morning or evening 'recueillement',
examination of the day to come, or the one just spent, and many kinds of
exercise, practical tasks, diets, bodily cares, and forms of meditation, including
reading and observing. But the common objective of these various 'pratiques
de soi', often using the form of the day, is 'la conversion à soi' (conversion to
oneself), which involves a 'déplacement du regard' (81) but also a 'trajectory':
conversio ad se 'est aussi une trajectoire [. . .] grâce à laquelle, échappant à
toutes les dépendances et à tous les asservissements, on finit par se rejoindre
soi-même, comme un havre à l'abri des tempêtes' (a trajectory... thanks to
which, escaping all dependency and enslavement, we return to ourselves, as to
a harbour sheltered from storms) (82).

In 'L'Écriture de soi' Foucault traced the emergence of an 'écriture
éthopoétique' through which the subject learns 'l'art de vivre'.[13] Focusing on
correspondence, he sees letter-writing as a performative mode that works on
the sender as much as on the addressee: the efficacy of the 'récit de soi' derives
less from self-analysis than from making oneself manifest, to oneself and to
others. Foucault observes a tendency to present oneself to one's correspondent
'dans le déroulement de la vie quotidienne' (in the unfolding of everyday
life)(1247), not because of the importance of the events that may have marked
it out, but precisely because it has no other quality than that of being

---

[11] In Foucault, *Dits et écrits*, II, 1234–49.

[12] Id., *Histoire de la sexualité*, III, *Le Souci de soi* (Paris: Gallimard, 1975), 57. References are
incorporated in the text.

[13] Foucault, *Dits et écrits*, II, 1235. Subsequent references are incorporated in the text.

'semblable à toutes les autres journées, attestant ainsi non l'importance d'une activité, mais la qualité d'un mode d'être' (the same as all the other days, thereby attesting not the importance of an activity but the quality of a mode of being)(1247). Thus Lucilius asks Seneca to recount his day, hour by hour, and Seneca accepts because it obliges him to 'vivre sous le regard d'autrui' (live under the scrutiny of the other), recounting the day just past, 'la plus commune de toutes' (the most common day possible), whose 'valeur tient justement à ce que rien ne s'y est passé qui aurait pu le détourner de la seule chose qui soit pour lui importante: s'occuper de lui-même' (value lies precisely in the fact that nothing happened that could divert from the only important thing for him: to occupy himself with himself), laying claim to 'une journée à soi' (a day of one's own)(1247). A 'récit de la banalité quotidienne'—things we ate, the physical and mental exercises we performed, the things we did wrong or got right—can play a role in the 'culture de soi'. Foucault quotes a letter from Marcus Aurelius to Frontonius containing vivid details of health and hygiene, sensations, and an account of a day that ends in an evening 'examen de conscience' where the minutiae of the day are recapitulated. Recounting the day in its 'quotidienneté' (1249), the letter repeats this recapitulation bringing about a convergence between the look of the other and our own self-scrutiny when we weigh up our 'actions quotidiennes' in terms of the rules of a 'technique de vie' (a technique for living)(1249).

Foucault's developing concern with 'biopouvoir'—power relations wrought by a multiplicity of structures, institutions, and agencies, operating on individual lives—brought his work increasingly into the orbit of discourses on the everyday, notably through Certeau's dialogue with Foucault's ideas in *L'Invention du quotidien*. More strikingly, however, as in the context of the uses of the day, Foucault's late work displayed a marked shift 'from the power exercised on, and forming, individuals to the power individuals exercised upon, and through which they formed, themselves'.[14] Drawing on a number of strands, including Pierre Hadot's work on the importance of 'spiritual exercises' in the culture of antiquity,[15] Foucault developed an 'aesthetics of existence' where the everyday subject is credited with a capacity for evolving an

---

[14] Alexander Nehamas, *The Art of Living: Socratic Reflections from Plato to Foucault* (Berkeley: University of California Press, 1998), 179. It is interesting to observe Foucault writing in 1984 that, for him, the subject is constituted by both 'pratiques d'assujetissement' (practices of subjection) and 'd'une façon plus autonome, à travers des pratiques de libération' (more autonomously, through practices of liberation), *Dits et écrits*, II, 1552.

[15] See Pierre Hadot, *Exercices spirituels et philosophie antique* (Paris: Études augustiniennes, 1981).

individual 'art de vivre' through conscious self-fashioning. Yet, importantly, Foucault does not see the 'souci de soi' as the expression of individualism: the 'subjectivation' achieved through 'techniques de soi', where the emphasis is always on 'pratique', involves interaction with others and a weaving together of individuality and collectivity.[16]

In 'L'Ordre du jour' Starobinski pursues Foucault's line of argument by exploring further how the topos of the day well spent—running through the 'littérature de la journée', from Seneca and Horace, through monasticism, Petrarch and Rabelais, Rousseau, Fourier and the 'journal intime'—articulates an opposition between constrained time (Lefebvre's 'temps comprimé') and the ideal of a life free of constraints. In Horace's *Satires* the city, where time is never your own, is opposed to the country where, as in Rousseau's idylls, the daily round is determined by the spontaneous motions of desire rather than the 'horaire impérieux' (tyrannical schedule) of urban occupations.[17] Yet Starobinski notes a central paradox. Escape from constrained time can take opposing forms: one is hedonistic and involves the relaxation of all 'contraintes' in a generalized *fay que voudra*. Whilst in the second, escape from constraints imposed by others is effected by the imposition of even more rigorous constraints on oneself (106). This is the essence of the regulation of monastic life as formulated for example in the Rule of Saint Benedict, and also of Petrach's *De vita solitaria* where 'l'astreinte quotidienne à laquelle se plie l'homme sorti du monde est infiniment plus exigeante que celle que lui eût imposée la loi ou la coutume de la cité profane' (the daily constraint that the man who retreats from the world imposes on himself is infinitely more demanding than the laws or customs of the profane city).[18] At various points Starobinski's discussion echoes the account of monasticism (and also Fourier) in Barthes's 1977 course, 'Comment vivre ensemble', where the organization of the day is constantly implicit despite the predominance of spatial paradigms.[19] And throughout this discussion one should of course bear in mind the connections between 'contrainte' and the recovery of the *quotidien* in the work of Perec.

Starobinski broaches another topic, the 'journal intime',[20] also explored by Barthes in his later writings, in connection with self-transformation.[21] In its development through the nineteenth century, the 'journal intime' was not just

[16] Cf. Foucault, *Dits et écrits*, II, 1472.
[17] Jean Starobinski, 'L'Ordre du jour', *Le Temps de la réflexion*, 4 (1983), 101–26: 103.
[18] Ibid., 105.   [19] See Ch. 5 above.   [20] Ibid., 117–20.
[21] See Roland Barthes, 'Délibération', *Œuvres complères*, III, 570–89.

the expression of Romanticism's glorification of the self but the instrument of what Pierre Pachet, in his study of the birth of the genre, calls 'un retour dubitatif sur soi' (a questioning retrospect on the self). Like Starobinski, Pachet emphasizes how the personal diary can be an instrument of moral perfectionism, marking a desire to 'work on the self' within 'l'ordre des jours'. A diary can be seen as a form where someone manifests 'un souci quotidien [. . .] considère que le salut ou l'amélioration de son âme se fait au jour le jour, est soumis à la succession, à la répétition des jours' (a daily concern . . . considers that the fate or improvement of his soul is determined day by day, is subject to the succession or repetition of days).[22] Pachet notes that early proponents of the *journal intime*, as opposed to the chronicle diary, sought to track down the minute differences between one day and the next, making the diary a 'baromètre de l'ame' (barometer of the soul), an instrument for registering its ever-changing 'weather'.[23] The relation between theories and practices of the *quotidien* and the practice of diary-keeping or regular notation (as in Barthes or Ernaux) is a topic that would repay thorough investigation, a notable case being Queneau whose posthumous *Journal* reveals many links between his fascination with the everyday in all its forms and his enduring aspiration to spiritual peace through a daily 'souci de soi' manifested in his diary-keeping, and also in the poems of *Morale élémentaire*.[24] Moreover, the fixed form or 'contrainte' applied in these poems, noted in Chapter 8, can also be seen as emblematic of the shape of a day, the three parts suggesting morning, afternoon, and evening.[25]

To make the unfolding of a day the instrument of an act of self-fashioning is to apprehend the day as a figure of the everyday *in its figurality*, in other words as possessing a *sens* over and above its descriptive or statistical *significations*. It is to make 'l'ordre du jour'—the regular, cyclical unfolding of the hours, which is at the same time endlessly changing and made up of an infinity of minor gradations—a touchstone for a particular relationship to experience, everyday experience, and to locate this as a dimension of subjectivity that one seeks to uncover and cultivate. The version of this conjunction of day and self-fashioning that we find in Foucault in the early 1980s chimes with a more widespread turn, in the 'littérature de la journée', noted by Starobinski in the context of

---

[22] Pierre Pachet, *Les Baromètres de l'âme: naissance du journal intime* (Paris: Hatier, 1990), 13.

[23] Cf. Barthes's objection to the suppression of references to the weather in an edition of Amiel, *Œuvres complètes*, II, 1522.

[24] Queneau, *Journal 1914–65*.

[25] See Sheringham, 'Raymond Queneau: The Lure of the Spiritual'.

modern poetry, that was further transformed when the *quotidien*, in the wake of Certeau, Perec, and others, came increasingly to the fore.

The 'carnets' of the poet Philippe Jaccottet provide an illustration. Jaccottet's writings consist in observations culled from his daily experience of a specific landscape in northern Provence.[26] Often mixing prose and verse, whether in the form of the diary or the meditative essay, he attempts to elucidate particular passages of experience where the natural world prompted a work of intense attention. What makes Jaccottet (like Réda and Queneau) a poet of the *quotidien* is the insistence on anonymity and self-effacement and the constant sense of the inextricability of the ordinary and the extraordinary. One of his recurrent preoccupations, also shared with Réda, and with many other explorers of the *quotidien*, including Perec, is colour, a field closely linked to that of the day because both are characterized by minute variegation.[27] As Merleau-Ponty observed, a colour is not a thing, one and indivisible, to be apprehended or not, it is always part of a range that belongs to both the outer world and the inner world of memory and fantasy. To pursue an experience in terms of colour is also to locate it in the historicity of one's own experience, giving it a layered, sedimented quality. To focus on a colour is not to home in on some pure quality or essence but to enter a field of resonance. If this means shifting attention away from the colour itself to a field of associations, the move is not away from the particular but towards the specificity of a particular moment, 'une modulation éphémère de ce monde' (an ephemeral modulation of this world).[28] To attend to an occasion with regard to the dimension of colour is to attend to what makes it this occasion and not another. Often drawing attention to the unfolding of a day, as in *Autres journées*, Jaccottet's essays start off from something that has arrested his attention, the sight of cherry blossom, for example, or three flowers of different hues, and then proceed to explore the ramifications of this experience.[29] As is also often the case in Réda, the attempt to seize the nuances of colours is a way of holding on to an elusive experience whilst avoiding pinning it down definitively, for it is precisely the open-endedness, subjectivity, and

[26] See, e.g., Philippe Jaccottet *La Semaison: Carnets 1954–79* (Paris: Gallimard, 1984); id., *Cahier de verdure* (Paris: Gallimard, 1990), etc.

[27] On this see Michael Sheringham, 'Language, Color and the Enigma of Everydayness', in M. Syrotinski and I. MacLachlan (eds.), *Sensual Reading: New Approaches to Reading in its Relation to the Senses* (Lewisburg, PA: Bucknell University Press, 2001), 127–52.

[28] Maurice Merleau-Ponty, *Le Visible et l'invisible* (Paris: Gallimard, 1964), 174–5.

[29] See Philippe Jaccottet, *Autres journées* (Montpellier Fata Morgana, 1987) and id., *Cahier de verdure, passim*.

connectivity of the experience that is at stake. The pursuit of colour maintains this openness. Being contingent on atmospheric conditions, on light, weather, and other situational factors, the perception of colour links subjectivity to temporal process, to the momentary, but also to duration, and thus to the unfolding rhythms of the day.

Starobinski observes in modern poetry a laicization of the religious notion that the cycle of hours includes 'moments de vérité'—enshrined in the prescription of prayers for different times of day. As in Heidegger's notion of Aletheia (Truth), where truth involves uncovering or unveiling,[30] the moment of truth—Rimbaud's 'Matin', Valéry's 'Midi je juste', Baudelaire's 'Crépuscule du soir' or 'À une heure du matin'—involves a self-revelation that is achieved through attunement to one of the day's major articulations, but also, as in Perse or Bonnefoy, through attention to passage and duration, the unfolding of the hours of a day.[31] Starobinski nonetheless sees that there is often a tension between the moment of truth and the 'cours total de la journée', and he suggests that the evocation, often detailed, of slow unfolding, underlines the 'écart différentiel' (differential gap) between privileged moment and simple duration. The moment of truth, he claims, contrasts with 'une durée de niveau ontologique inférieur. Le jour est comme l'ecrin du moment de vérité' (a duration of a lower ontological level. The day is like the jewel-box for the moment of truth).[32] Yet the *quotidien* tradition we have been tracing, from Lefebvre onwards, refuses to prize the instant, and thus to polarize the ontological and the ontic, and rejects the separation between background banality and momentary illumination.

There could be no better exemplification of the difference this makes than Peter Handke's *Versuch über den geglückten Tag* (1991), translated into French as *Essai sur la journée réussie* (1994). This merits inclusion in our discussion because Handke has lived for many years in the Paris *banlieue*, and his work, widely translated and read in France, is informed by the spirit of the contemporary *quotidien*, whilst also being imbued with mystical and pietistic currents in German thought. Exemplifying Adorno's account of the essay form,[33] Handke's *Versuch* (a word also meaning trial or experiment) weaves styles

---

[30] See, e.g., Martin Heidegger, 'On the Essence of Truth', *Existence and Being* (Chicago: Gateway, 1949).

[31] Jean Starobinski, 'Le Cycle des heures et le moment de vérité', *Bulletin de l'Institut Collégial Européen* (1986), 110–18.

[32] Ibid., 113.

[33] See Ch. 1.

together in meandering sentences, switches of pronoun, dialogue between narrating voices. In its windings, the essay itself becomes an emblem of the successful day that it seeks to define, which is progressively seen not as the perfect day, but as one when 'the weight of the world', to cite another work by Handke, is fully apprehended and negotiated.[34] The sinuous line is itself a key bridging motif, represented by various talismans including the 'line of beauty and grace' in Hogarth's Tate Gallery self-portrait, and curving railway lines on the 'ligne de banlieue' that runs through Suresnes in the hills above Paris, a sudden glimpse of which provokes an awakening, experienced as emergence from constriction into bodily ease. As the essay evolves, the idea of the successful day mutates as it is apprehended in different ways, endlessly reformulated in both abstract and concrete terms. A review of past versions of the good day, ranging across the Greek *kairos*, Christian models of fulfilment, and the modern notion of success through accomplishments, is interrupted by the memory of a Van Morrison song, 'Coney Island', about a Sunday ride through the Northern Irish countryside. The song's authenticity derives from the fact that the singer is a balding man on the brink of middle age, that it is spoken rather than sung, and that it breaks off after barely a minute. This fragility contrasts with Hogarth's confident line of beauty: if unity and totality are still the aim, Van Morrison's voice befits an era when the successful day has no pretension to eternity, but is, rather, an aspiration rendered in the song by forward momentum underlined by the repeated word 'on' and the sense of a trajectory towards the self—a *conversio ad se* (in Foucault's phrase)—via the unfolding of a particular day.

Handke's essay constantly asks if the idea of a successful day should be held up as an antidote to the curse of distraction, or whether it must incorporate the struggle with what threatens it: not external forces, but something within oneself—Foucault's 'mouvements intérieurs entre soi et soi' (inner movements between me and myself)—that prevents one seeing in 'chaque instant une possibilité à saisir' (each moment a possibility to be grasped).[35] Yet this could imply that the success or failure of the day always hangs on a single moment, a view promptly acknowledged to be inconsistent with the growing recognition that the 'instant isolé' does not stand for the whole day: on the contrary, 'seul

[34] Peter Handke. *Le Poids du monde* (Paris: Gallimard, 1979).
[35] Id., *Essai sur la journée réussie: un songe d'un jour d'hiver*, trans A. Goldschmitt (Paris: Gallimard, 1994) [*Versuch über den geglückten Tag*, 1991], 26. Page references are incorporated in the text.

compte justement la journée entière'. (29) Perhaps the successful day is one
that sounds the same note throughout: responding to it would be a matter of
listening, of catching its rhythm—like burglars sounding out a safe—and then
living through subsequent experiences in consistency with its wavelength.
Does that mean the day would be spoilt if something discordant happened?
No, pipes up another voice, a successful day is one that admits of our foibles
and failings, and acknowledges 'ce qui est quotidiennement là, même dans les
circonstances les plus favorables' (what is there on a daily basis, even in the
most favourable circumstances) (33). The successful day does not require us to
be better than we actually are, to change our nature. A key sequence at the core
of the essay recounts a day that gets off to a good start but soon becomes a
struggle. The narrator tries to saw some logs but the blade meets resistance and
sticks. He then drops a log on his toes, and when he tries to light a fire it won't
start. Yet in retrospect he had understood that these 'avanies' (setbacks) had
not necessarily annulled the day's capacity to be successful. Indeed, had he
approached these moments of adversity in another way he might have seen
them as opportunities to make this a successful day. Instead of giving up he
might have found another way of making the saw bite, got a rhythm going,
and then known when to change rhythm by being in harmony with the wood
(38–40). The key is attention. Sawing the wood the right way by paying close
heed to its knots and fibres would have been at the same time a process of self-
attunement, providing the opportunity to put into practice an essential skill—
akin to the mode of *kairos* discussed by Certeau: that of being able to tweak the
moment the right way. What counts, in the 'tentative de journée réussie'
(attempt at a successful day)—the choice of phrase echoes Perec—'c'était à
l'instant de la déconfiture, de la douleur ou du mécompte—du dérangement
et du déraillement—de montrer la présence d'esprit nécessaire pour jouer
autrement de cet instant, pour le transformer par cette prise de conscience qui
le libérerait en un tournemain du rétrécissement' (what mattered was that—at
the moment of upset or adversity—one should have the presence of mind to
play this moment a different way, transforming it by an awareness that would,
in a jiffy, get it out of its narrow groove) (40). Progressively constructed by the
twists and turns of the *Essai* itself, from which it is inseparable, the 'journée
réussie' is an idea sustained by the play of thought—a midwinter's dream, as
the essay's subtitle indicates. The successful day is one that is attended to; it has
no fixed qualities but only a certain kind of performativity. Like the *Versuch*, it
is the product of using, putting together, living through, and appropriating
what the succession of hours throws our way.

For a last instance of the day as an instrument of self-fashioning, let us consider a justly successful movie fable, Harold Ramis's *Groundhog Day* (1993). A Scrooge-like misanthrope, Phil the TV weatherman, played by Bill Murray, is condemned to relive, again and again, the events of a single day. Deliverance is achieved only through progressive modifications in his attitude to the ordinary, everyday world, registered through the different ways in which he seeks to handle the central relationship in the film, with Rita, played by Andie McDowell. When his alarm rings early each morning (a scene we see numerous times) Phil has a chance of awakening to the world. He is stuck in the same day as long as he sees every day as necessarily the same. The future starts existing again when he acknowledges that it can bring difference. Initially, rather than try and reflect on his situation, he sees it as an intellectual problem to be coldly analysed, and he tries to cheat himself out of it. In one phase he is obsessed with constructing a perfect day, yet gradually, like Handke's essayist, he comes to understand that the criterion of the 'good day' is not one that fits a preordained pattern, but a day 'lived through' in the unpredictability of its unfolding, attended to in its moment-by-moment imperfection and potential.

Despite a sometimes cloying sentimentality and rather glib Hollywood Kierkegaardianism, *Groundhog Day*'s championing of the everyday is redeemed by its details, and the way they emphasize process and practice. By repeatedly showing us the same sequence of events, modified only by Phil's different tactics, the film manifests—like Handke's essay, or the letters of Foucault's Romans—the variousness of a single day, the endless possibilities it offers for appropriation and invention. One could read the film as an exemplification of Stanley Cavell's perfectionist and communitarian philosophy where the 'practice of the ordinary', operating at the level of the day, recognizes that knowledge (and its mastery) needs to be disowned if the world we live in, the ordinary universe and the human community, are to be acknowledged.[36] The fact that the film is a fable or tale is not irrelevant, if we recall Benjamin's view that the tale, unlike the novel, retains a link to practice, community, and performance.[37] The same applies to the genres of the letter and the meditative essay. Like Handke's essayist, Foucault's Roman correspondents, or Jaccottet's poet, Phil the weatherman learns to treat the day as the framework for a work on the self based not on precepts but on an *art de*

36 See Ch. 6.   37 See above, Ch. 1.

vivre rooted in understanding how the figure of the day can provide access to the totality which is the everyday.[38]

STREET NAMES

For Henri Lefebvre 'La rue passagère [. . .] représente la quotidienneté dans notre vie sociale. Elle en est la figuration presque complète' (the street artery. . . represents everydayness in our social life. It is its almost total figuration).[39] The figure of the street—'lieu de passage, d'interférences, de circulation et de communication' (place of passage, of interconnections, of circulation and communication)—is the spatial counterpart of the *journée*. It runs right through *quotidien* writing, from the 'rue assourdissante' of Baudelaire's 'À une passante' to the present. From Hausmann onwards, attempts to contain and control its energies are met with new manifestations of street life, and new cultural forms to publicize and celebrate them.[40] The street is prominent in Decadent and Naturalist writing—Huysmans, the Goncourts, Zola—and Impressionist painting, and central to French, as to other European modernisms: Romains and Proust, and crucially Apollinaire's poetry, where the 'jeune rue' in 'Zone', and the seminal 'Lundi rue Christine', herald the Surrealists.[41] For Breton and his companions 'la rue' is, along with language, the crucial terrain of the surrealist adventure. Aragon noted: 'Il y a des possédés que tient la hantise de la rue: là seulement ils éprouvent le pouvoir de leur nature' (There are people who are haunted by the street: only there do they experience the power of their being).[42] Surrealism's visual archive includes de Chirico's *Mystère et mélancolie d'une rue*, the scenography of the 1938 Surrealist Exhibition, conceived as a series of streets, and the marvellous photographic archive of Brassaï, Kertesz, and their many descendants, who made photography an art of the street. Situationist psychogeography rekindled the surrealist spirit in the 1950s and 1960s, combating the functionalist agenda of the 'urbanistes' in ways that were absorbed into new theorizations by

[38] Cf. Jacques Réda: 'n' importe quel jour est toute une histoire, même quand on croit qu'il ne s'y est rien passé', (any day is quite a business, even when you think nothing really happened), *Accidents de la circulation* (Paris: Gallimard, 2001), 15.

[39] Lefebvre, *Critique de la vie quotidienne*, I, 309.

[40] Cf. Adrian Rifkin, *Street Noises: Parisian Pleasures 1900–1940* (Manchester: Manchester University Press, 1993).

[41] See Ch. 1.

[42] Aragon, *Le Paysan de Paris*, 66.

Lefebvre, Barthes, Certeau, and others. Perec's ongoing rapport with the street where he was born, the ever more desolate rue Vilin, is at the heart of *Lieux* and *Espèces d'espaces*, and its fate after his death, buried under a new public garden, then resurrected nearby as the 'Rue Georges-Perec', encapsulates the role of the street as an emblem of the everyday.[43] By the late twentieth century, the street is a point of convergence for new currents in ethnography, history and geography, conceptual art, and many other strands.[44]

In this tradition the street is a stage that produces events: political, socio-logical, and psychological. Blurring the line between public and private space, it 'publishes', according to Lefebvre, what is otherwise hidden away, producing a collective 'social text'.[45] For recent historians, including Arlette Farge, author of *Vivre dans la rue à Paris au 18e siècle*, the street is itself a 'social actor' engendering modes of behaviour.[46] Jacques Réda's sense of being the plaything of the streets, to which he subjugates his will, expresses a widely shared perception. Yet, what makes the street a figure of the everyday is the import-ance of participation, interaction, and appropriation. To underline this I want to approach the street obliquely, via an apparently peripheral feature—its name. For Walter Benjamin the name distils the essence of the street's performative capacities. As we shall see, his account of the 'unconquerable power' of street names, echoed by that of Certeau, centres on the interaction between the everyday urban subject and the potency of the proper noun. In connection with Proust, whose remarks on the Rue du Bac were among Benjamin's sources, Barthes observed that the name was both a biological 'milieu' to be entered and explored, and a densely reticulated object to be carefully opened like a flower.[47] For Julien Gracq, the names of Nantes, especially those without any historical connotations, conjure up, better than any visual image, the spool-like network of his 'vagabondages quotidiens' (daily wanderings), which are for him the essence of the city where he spent his adolescence.[48] Celebrating what Gracq calles 'le sortilège des noms'[49] Jean-Christophe Bailly talks of the 'ricochets à la surface de la langue' (ricochets on

---

[43] See the film by Robert Bober, *En remontant la rue Vilin* (1992).

[44] See *La Rue, Tracés*, 5, (2004).

[45] Lefebvre, *Critique de la vie quotidienne*, II, 306–12.

[46] 'Entretien avec Arlette Farge', *Tracés, La Rue*, 5 (2004) 143–8.

[47] Barthes 'Proust et les noms', *Œuvres complètes*, II, 1368–76.

[48] Julien Gracq, *La Forme d'une ville* (Paris: José Corti, 1985), 2–3, 200–8. See also Jacques-François Piquet, *Noms de Nantes* (Paris: Joca Seria, 1992).

[49] Ibid., 210.

the surface of language) engendered by toponyms, by virtue of their being at once extremely localized and packed with echoes and connotations.[50]

Daniel Milo has retraced the history of street-naming in France in a chapter of Pierre Nora's *Les Lieux de mémoire*. Street names were originally local, unofficial, and anecdotal (until the eighteenth century there was still a 'Rue de l'enfant qui pisse' in Lyon). The idea of using names officially and commemoratively, as a 'biographical dictionary' of the nation, originated with Sully in 1600, was then implemented to a limited extent, and boosted in the eighteenth century by the cult of 'les grands hommes'. The French Revolution brought sharp awareness of the ideological and pedagogical potential of street names, and the politically charged nature of semantics: 'le milieu linguistique dans lequel nous évoluons a des effets idéologiques incalculables' (the linguistic milieu we live in has incalculable ideological effects).[51] The potential for ideological manipulation leads to a key feature of street-naming—expedient name-changing ('la débaptisation massive par éclairs' (waves of wholesale renaming))[52] becomes a constant. The Revolution suppresses the 'Saint-' prefix in numerous names (a gesture repeated unofficially by the Situationists, who were surprised to find that their post was still delivered!).[53] Then Napoleon restores the Saints, but purges old names and creates new streets and monuments to celebrate his victories. The Restoration 'debaptizes' with a vengeance, reinstating numerous pre-revolutionary names. The pantheon of Republicanism (Thiers, Gambetta, Jaurès) and two world wars (Foch, Leclerc) produce massive renaming. In the later twentieth century, the construction of 'villes nouvelles' leads to what Jacques Réda calls 'la toponymie de fin de conseil municipal' (end of council meeting toponymy)[54]—bland bunches of Impressionist painters, flowers, and lesser authors.

Milo is justly sceptical about whether official naming ever really succeeds in 'immortalizing' people and events by preserving them in living memory. Walter Benjamin would have concurred: yet for him the recurrent failure of schemes for ideologically based reform—for instance Pujoulx's proposal that Paris street names should be reorganized to represent an educational map of France (implemented much later in the Parisian satellite town of Maurepas,

---

[50] Bailly, *La Ville à l'œuvre*, 126–7.

[51] Daniel Milo, 'Les Noms de rues', in Pierre Nora (ed.), *Lieux de mémoire*, II (Paris: Gallimard, 1997), 283–315; 295.

[52] Ibid., 301.

[53] Debord (ed.), *Potlatch*, 69.

[54] Jacques Réda, *Le Citadin* (Paris: Gallimard, 1998), 176.

and doubtless elsewhere)[55]—underlines the wayward, anarchic 'magic' of
names, which are neither ideological nor educational. One of the dossiers of
Benjamin's *Arcades Project*, Konvolut P, headed 'The Streets of Paris', concentrates more or less exclusively on 'the unconquerable power in the names of
streets'.[56] What are the constituents of this power? Like that other cardinal
Parisian reality, the arcade, street names enfold the past in such a way that,
within the field of experience, 'present and far-off times interpenetrate'. (518)
Traces of realities that have vanished, like ancient springs or markets, still act
on us via the name: 'what gives the name its potency is this strange capacity for
distilling the present, as inmost essence of what has been' (833). The active
dynamism that works on the mind of the city-dweller also derives from the
intersection between personal history and the collective history and creativity
enshrined in the name. And for Benjamin the tendency for names to change
underlines their mobile energies, partly because change often engenders a
contradiction between a street's look or character and its name.

Benjamin also insists that street names do not exist in isolation: their
contrasts and juxtapositions make up 'a vascular network of imagination'
(901), the 'linguistic network of the city'. (84) Whilst the names of metro
stations remain separate from one another other, exuding a sacred aura (84),[57]
street names, by raising hundreds of ordinary words to the higher level of the
proper noun, make the city a cosmos:

What was otherwise reserved for only a very few words . . . the city has made possible
for all words, or at least a great many: to be elevated to the noble status of name. This
revolution in language was carried out by what is most general: the street. Through its
street names, the city is a linguistic cosmos (522).

Constantly foregrounding the encounter with the name, seeing it as sensual
and even voluptuous because it brings us into contact, vicariously, with the
physical 'knowledge' possessed by those who go barefoot or bed down on the
pavements, Benjamin sees street names as 'intoxicating substances' (518).
A source of their evocative energy, the intense mental energy they generate,
is the 'interpenetration of images'. The name 'Place du Maroc', with its
associations, induces 'topographic vision' that is then intertwined with alle-
gorical meaning, yet has a physical dimension (518). As the name links here
and there, now and then, a dialectical energy is produced: 'in the inmost

---

[55] I am grateful to Morgane Beaumanoir for giving me a plan of Maurepas.
[56] Benjamin, *The Arcades Project*, 516. Page numbers are incorporated in the text.
[57] Cf. Augé, *Un Ethnologue dans le métro*, 40–7.

recesses of these names an upheaval takes place, and thus we retain a world in the names of old streets, and to read a street name at night is like a transmigration' (833; translation modified). Here we have an experience of the 'Architectural Uncanny' in Anthony Vidler's phrase,[58] where the street name, like the sight of a swan in the gutter in Baudelaire's 'Le Cygne', takes us on a mental journey into our past lives and imaginings.

Benjamin's passionate theorizing and his urban nominalism ('Only the meeting of two different street *names* makes for the magic of the "corner"' (840)—a view enshrined in Paris where neighbourhoods and metro stations like Faidherbe-Chaligny take their names from intersections) make it less surprising that Michel de Certeau should place a similar emphasis on street names in his account of walking in the city. It will be recalled that in *L'Invention du quotidien* Certeau makes a parallel between the act of walking, *vis-à-vis* the imposed order of the city, and the act of speech, *vis-à-vis* the linguistic system.[59] In a section on 'Names and symbols' he elaborates on their mediating role. Street names do not simply provide personal memory with a social framework, in the manner of Augé's *Un Ethnologue dans le métro*. Rather, like Benjamin, Certeau argues that the encounter with the name can have active force, giving rise to 'tropismes sémantiques' (semantic impulsions or tropisms) (I, 156) capable of determining urban itineraries. But rather than seeing this in terms of plenitude, he sees the process of displacement that occurs when we respond to the name—by virtue of its associations, historical and personal (and fundamentally the fusion of the two)—as opening a space, creating a vacancy:

Dans les espaces brutalement éclairés par une raison étrangère, les noms propres creusent des réserves de significations cachées et familières. Ils 'font sens'; autrement dit, ils impulsent des mouvements, à la façon de vocations et d'appels qui tournent ou détournent l'itinéraire en lui donnant des sens (ou directions) jusque-là imprévisibles. Ces noms créent du non-lieu dans les lieux; ils les muent en passages (I, 156).

(In the spaces brutally lit by an alien reason, proper names carve out pockets of hidden and familiar meanings. They 'make sense'; in other words, they are the impetus of movements, like vocations and calls that turn or divert an itinerary by giving it a meaning (or a direction) that was previously unforeseen. These names create a nowhere [non-lieu] in places; they change them into passages)[60]

---

[58] Anthony Vidler, *The Architectural Uncanny* (Boston: MIT Press, 1992).

[59] Certeau, *L'Invention du quotidien*, I, 148. Cf. above, Ch. 6.

[60] Translation from Certeau, *The Practice of Everyday Life*, trans. Rendall, 104.

As they sponsor itineraries based on affect and whim, the names of the city create clearings in the urban jungle. Losing their original, functionalist *raison d'être*, linked to hierarchy, classification, administrative tidiness and convenience, historical legitimation, or official commemoration, toponyms provide citizens with polysemic material for a 'géographie nuageuse' (I, 157) (cloud-like geography) where journeys and rendezvous can be generated by the 'pouvoirs magiques' (magical powers) of the proper noun. Certeau insists on the negativity of this subversive 'géographie seconde, poétique' (I, 158) (secondary, poetic geography): it does not fill a void, it opens a space, introducing play (in both senses)—'un espace de jeu' (I, 159)—into the urban system which strives to create a saturated plenum. (Marc Augé will later develop the ambivalence of the 'non-lieu' as connoting both emptiness and freedom.)[61] This negative, indigent process creates habitability by infiltrating the local into the universality of 'le totalitarianisme fonctionnaliste' (functionalist totalitarianism), which always seeks to eliminate the 'autorité locale' (local authority) enshrined in the *lieu-dit* (hence the bureaucratic obsession with name-changing).

Certeau goes on to discuss 'récits de lieux': narratives of peregrination where toponyms are often vestiges or verbal relics—'les débris du monde'—that combine in a bricolage which subverts the homogeneous order of narrative. Such narrative itineraries activate a dispersed memory that is the opposite of the museum since it invokes the presence of what is absent 'les lieux vécus sont comme des présences d'absences. Ce qui se montre désigne ce qui n'est plus: "vous voyez, ici il y avait . . . ", mais cela ne se voit plus' (in lived places absences are present. What you see points to what no longer exists. 'You see, here there was . . . ', but it is no longer visible)(I, 162). This echoes Benjamin's comment that 'what the name preserves is the habitus of a lived life',[62] and his (Heideggerian) reference to 'indwelt spaces' (very close to 'lieux vécus') based on the idea that 'to dwell' can be a transitive verb and living in a place like 'fashioning a shell'.[63] Certeau outlines a view of the 'lieux vécu' as a palimpsest, a 'lieu hanté' made up of fragmentary and layered stories. And at the end of *L'Invention du quotidien* he stresses how the layering, the archaeological stratification of place—epitomized in the compacted density of the proper name (its resemblance to a cosmos (Benjamin), or a flower (Barthes))—creates opacity and ambiguity that may constitute resistance to 'la rationalité fonctionnaliste'. In a later essay, on the restoration of old city *quartiers* and the

---

[61] See above, Ch. 8.   [62] Benjamin, *The Arcades Project*, 868.   [63] Ibid., 865.

'legendary' dimension of the everyday, the 'historicités exogènes'[64] which, like Benjamin, he believed were accessible via the encounter with names, Certeau talked of the need to awaken 'les histoires qui dorment dans les rues et qui gisent quelquefois dans un simple nom, pliées dans ce dé à coudre comme les soieries de la fée' (the stories that lie dormant in the streets, and are there sometimes in a simple name, folded up as in a thimble like the silk dresses of the fairy).[65]

It would be nice to learn that Certeau was aware of the crossword puzzles Georges Perec set for *Télérama* in 1980–1, twenty-one in all (one for each *arrondissement* and one for the metro), where the clues and additional games and exercises all related to Parisian phenomena, with street names especially prominent.[66] Perec's model was probably 'Connaissez-vous Paris?', the daily quiz column Raymond Queneau wrote for *L'Intransigeant* from November 1936 to October 1938, where he taxed his readers' knowledge of the most minute details of Parisian history as exhibited in its buildings and names.[67] In this case it is more than likely that one of Queneau's readers was Walter Benjamin.

Queneau took to the pavements again in the 1960s, conscious of the rapid changes Paris was undergoing, this time recording his findings in a deliberately prosaic collection of poems.[68] *Courir les rues* is not nostalgic or resistant to change. As Queneau noted philosophically in the title of a poem written slightly earlier (which reports on a walk round a *quartier* being rebuilt), 'Ça a bien changé et ça changera encore' (I, 282–3). He claimed that *Courir les rues* was not about 'Paris inconnu' or 'Paris mystérieux' but about comings and goings in a Paris of 'petits faits quotidiens' (little everyday facts) (I, 1328), like the one he took as the basis for the multiple variations of *Exercices de style*. Of course Queneau lamented some contemporary developments, above all the massive growth of traffic and the volume of noise that had done away with most of Paris's traditional street cries (except for the 'Aye aye' of pedestrians being run over!) (I, 430), but one poem observes how every decade had its 'conneries' (idiocies) (I, 422), and overall Queneau is more interested in feeling the constant flux and dynamism of the everyday city than lamenting its transformation. The Paris he cherished was unnoticed rather than un-

---

[64] Certeau, *L'Invention du quotidien*, II, 192.   [65] Ibid., II, 203.
[66] Republished in Georges Perec, *Perec/rinations* (Paris: Zulma, 1997).
[67] See Raymond Queneau, *Œuvres complètes*, I, (Poésie) (Paris: Gallimard Pléade, 1989), 1326.
[68] Ibid., I, 348–431. Subsequent references are incorporated in the text.

known and he saw himself as performing a task like that of the road sweeper who picks up what everyone leaves behind (I, 1328).

Street names are everywhere in *Courir les rues*. The match between streets and the person they are named after often arises: Cauchy is hard done by (I, 377), as is the Abbé Grégoire whose principled refusal of regicide merited a less noisy setting (I, 419). A poem about the way the city forgets its past refers to 'les rues débaptisées' (I, 358). A poem about going from the rue Capron to the rue de Capri plays with the semi-homophonic sounds of these names (I, 393), underlining what Benjamin called the 'voluptuous' aspect of street names, the linguistic colour of the signifiers.[69] The stories lying dormant in street names are 'unfolded' as Certeau would urge: thus we learn that the man commemorated in 'Rue Flatters' was killed by Touareg tribespeople (I, 400), and that Jules Simon was not the minister's original name: he changed it from Jules Suisse because seemingly, as the poem's title wryly has it, 'Il ne voulut pas d'un nom helvète' (He didn't want a Swiss name) (I, 417). A poem on a 'petite échoppe ancienne' (ancient little shop) in the rue Volta contrasts the antiquity of the street with the modern connotations of the 'pile Volta' (volta battery), 'dont le nom s'égara là' (whose name landed up here) (I, 352). If streets are often named after people, the link between person and street may be arbitrary or incongruous. And the street or edifice may have developed new associations that eclipse the fading memory of past historical personages, a point doubly made in a two-line poem called 'Rue Pierre-Larousse' which reads:

> MIRABEAU: Orateur français (1749–1791)
> *Encycl.* Sous son pont coule la Seine[70]
>
> (MIRABEAU: French orator (1749–91)
> *Encycl.* The Seine flows under his bridge)

If Larousse conjures up an encyclopedia entry for Mirabeau, the name Mirabeau, in the context of Parisian toponyms, now chimes more with Apollinaire's famous line than with the eighteenth-century statesman. Arbitrary collocations and striking coincidences abound in the field of Parisian nomenclature. In wiping the name Waterloo off the Paris street map, the bulldozers that demolished the Passage Waterloo were as effective as Wellington's fire-

---

[69] Benjamin closely identified with the *chiffonier*, and Réda also compares himself to a street cleaner, *Les Ruines de Paris*, 32–3.

[70] Queneau, *Œuvres complètes*, I, 361.

power. Yet in the same area near the Porte de Vanves the Gaulish chief Camulogène—'qui avait déjà un nom bien parisien' (who already had a very Parisian name)—still has his street, whose intersection with the 'Impasse de Labrador' prompts a poem titled 'Canada' (I, 368).

Queneau's poems conjure up a Paris of words. 'Le Paris de paroles' lists all the Parisian references in Prévert's famous collection of poems, but also celebrates the huge variety of things that feature in Parisian names: 'des innocents des blancs manteaux | un roi de Sicile des rosiers' (innocents and white habits | a king of Sicily and some rose plants), etc. (I, 374). Another poem, inspired by the Musée Carnavalet which houses material relating to the history of Paris, sees both words and streets as offering mute (the word 'mutes' is appropriately an oral archaism) testimony to historical change: 'histoires mutes et silence bu | boire à la source des histoires | source des mots source des rues' (mute stories and silence drunk | drink at the spring of stories | spring of words spring of streets) (I, 421). The connections between streets, words, and stories confirm how, as Benjamin and Certeau insisted, street names—at once indispensable and utilitarian, prosaic and poetic, tangible and verbal—keep cultural memory alive in the everyday and at the same time, as the tools of daily practices and rituals, stand more widely as a figure of everydayness itself.

In 'Recourir les rues', a section of his 1999 collection *La Forme d'une ville change plus vite, hélas, que le coeur des humains*, Jacques Roubaud reports on how, thirty years later, he revisited many of the places Queneau had referred to in *Courir les rues*. Playing with the forms and sonorities of Queneau's original verses, he notes, for example, that there is no longer a 'petite échoppe ancienne' in the rue Volta.[71] Thereafter, many poems and three distinct sections are given over to a ludic celebration and exploitation of street names. In 'Lisant les rues' the poems are based on categories of thing found in street names. Thus 'Un peu de sociologie' lists the professions of those commemorated (155 saints, 8 cardinals, 1 Lord, etc.)(178), while 'L'Invitation au voyage' lists the names of cities, rivers, and other geographical features found in Paris toponyms (175). Other poems are based on street names referring to numbers, colours, and classical authors (190, 191, 184). In a homage to Perec's *Les Revenentes* (a novel written with only the vowel 'e') one poem enumerates alphabetically all the Parisian street names containing only this vowel (195). In another homage to Perec, Roubaud composes three poems in the 'morale élémentaire' form, rounding up street names consisting

[71] Roubaud, *La Forme d'une ville*, 15. Further references are incorporated in the text.

of noun plus adjective (186–8). A beautiful poem, 'L'Heure', links the figures of the day and the street name: each line evokes a particular hour in a particular street, beginning with early morning and, after sixty lines, ending at dead of night (201–2).

'Hommage à Sébastien Bottin' (the compiler of the first phone directory, commemorated by a street famous for being the headquarters of Gallimard) consists of poems about the relation between street names and the people who live in the street. Thus 'Tout naturellement' (Quite naturally) notes that Bruno Petit lives in the Rue Petit and Colette Meunier in the rue des Moulins (205), while 'Complications' worries that Jacqueline Lenoir should reside in the rue Blanche and Christian Marin in the rue du Sahel (208). In a third series, Chansons des rues et des rues, rhyming is the basis of playful and often irreverent ditties. One poem asks why a Place rather a Boulevard honours General Brocard (218), a second makes up a story from words rhyming with the rues Custine and Caulaincourt (221), while a third composes a story about a man and a woman who live in the rues Madame and Monsieur respectively (223). 'Ah!' parodies the notion that every street has its individual character by finding an attribute based simply on rhyme: 'quel vacarme | Dans la rue de Parme!' (220). In 'Orage à neuf' Roubaud plays with street names containing allusions to wetness and produces a deluge of wet weather (225). In strong contrast to this light-hearted tone, two haunting poems in a later collection focus on names that have disappeared (preserved at best on those secondary plaques, which give the old name preceded by the word 'anciennement' (formerly) or 'autrefois' (before), through which municipal authorities try to atone for their destructiveness). 'Promeneur des rues mortes' imagines a walk through 'rues débaptisées',[72] while 'D'un plan' imagines a map of Paris where the 'voies disparues' would be superimposed on tracing paper, creating a 'palimpseste de nominaux' enabling us to 'chercher les cicatrices de son coeur' (seek the scars on its heart).[73]

Why do street names hold such fascination for explorers of the everyday? If the street is the heartland of the *quotidien*, why play with street names rather than describe actual streets? Whilst description may tend to cut us off and position us outside, the appeal of the street name is that it draws attention to our participation in everyday space. The encounter with the name has a

---

[72] Jacques Roubaud *Churchill 40 et autres sonnets de voyage 2000–2003* (Paris: Gallimard, 2004), 132.
[73] Ibid., 168.

strongly practical orientation (even when it is confined to the street map) because it invokes a practice of space: not a desire to describe but a desire to circulate, to be drawn through space. For another devotee, Jacques Réda, street names often act as stimuli: he refers to featureless, lifeless streets as 'lugubre-ment amnésiques [...] malgré leur nom, lui, qui se souvient—rue de la Fontaine-au-roi [etc.]' (lugubriously amnesiac... despite their names, which remember).[74] Elsewhere, in the rue des Feuillantines, the last syllable in the name is one factor that induces a disorientating experience of *déja-vu*, making the moment a palimpsest and projecting Réda into an intermediate space and time, between Paris and Dublin.[75]

Always both mental and physical, the encounter with the street name is a 'bodily practice' as well as a cognitive one,[76] not only because it induces mobility but because the sounds and graphic shape of street names (as in the famous bells of Saint Clement's) have a physical impact and produce their own associations and vectors. The virtue of the encounter with the street name is that it is always ambiguous and double. Unlike other attributes (passers-by, shops, monuments) it is metonymically minimal, a simple plaque. As a synecdoche (an aspect) it is elusive because it is in fact a piece of language (a street would retain its name even if it did not have a plaque). What we are drawn to when we dwell on a street name, in other words when a name strikes us, amuses us, or grabs our attention (or eludes us—Queneau's poem 'Rue chose' is about having a street name on the tip of one's tongue)[77] is both signifier and signified, mental and physical, tangible and intangible; what it invokes is both absent and present, visible and invisible. The street name is on the cusp of the remembered and the forgotten, the obvious and the recondite, the ordinary and the extraordinary, the serious and the frivolous, the public and the private (we all have a private map of our familiar space, including its names). This ambiguity and duality ally it with the everyday. The inseparable mental and physical journeys induced by street names arrest and redirect our attention. The fact that they offer an oblique route to grasping the realities of the street befits the way the everyday is a vulnerable, evanescent dimension of our ambient reality, a dimension that is not simply there, but depends on our inventive interaction to come into being.

[74] Réda, *Les Ruines de Paris*, 65.

[75] Id., *La Liberté des rues*, 113.

[76] Cf. Paul Connerton, *How Societies Remember* (Cambridge: Cambridge University Press, 1989), 72–104.

[77] Queneau, *Œuvres complètes*, I, 409.

PROJECTS OF ATTENTION

It is easier to talk about a special *journée*—Virgil's *summa dies* or the 'Perfect Day' of Lou Reed's hit song—than about an ordinary, everyday sort of day, and easier to make the street a symbol or microcosm than see it simply as a street. Think all day, observes Queneau, and you may convince yourself that a street is a cavern; think for a year and you may decide it is a grotto; just give it the odd thought from time to time and you will no doubt recognize that 'toute rue est une rue'.[78] What needs 'factoring in' if one is to apprehend the everyday street is not something extra—aesthetic, subjective, or intellectual—added from the outside, but our lived experience of it, our participation and immersion in its fields, the ways in which we make it part of our world and recognize it as such. For Certeau this is the dimension of *pratique*. The difference between a *lieu* and an *espace* is that 'un espace est un lieu pratiqué' (a space is a place appropriated by practices). Practice makes a difference through vectors, velocities, and timing.[79] The everyday exists through the practices that constitute it, the ways in which times and spaces are appropriated by human subjects and converted into physical traces, narratives, and histories (of the kinds Maspero encounters in the Paris suburbs, or Perec invents for his apartment block). Thus, in Foucault's Roman letter-writers, in Benjamin and Roubaud, we encounter practices—of the day and the street. The figural dimension of the day, the street, the conversation, the gadget, the *fait divers*, which connects with everydayness as *sens*, over and above (or prior to) *significations* that can be objectified, stems from practice.

Yet surely, one may object, the activities of Maspero and Queneau, like the 'exercices pratiques' Perec advocated in *Espèces d'espaces*, and executed in *Lieux*, are self-conscious, artificial, and experimental. How may they relate to what we actually do in our everyday lives? In the terms of Pierre Bourdieu's account of *pratique* the difference would be radical. For Bourdieu, 'C'est parce que les sujets ne savent pas, à proprement parler, ce qu'ils font, que ce qu'ils font a plus de sens qu'ils ne savent' (It is because subjects do not, strictly speaking, know what they are doing, that what they do means more than they know).[80] Bourdieu's theory of practice does link *pratique* with a synthesizing *sens* that

---

[78] Queneau, 'Une Facilité de pensée', *Œuvres complètes*, I, 422.
[79] Certeau, *L'Invention du quotidien*, I, 173.
[80] Bourdieu, *Esquisse d'une théorie de la pratique*, 273.

exceeds objectified *significations* (in fact he placed a dictionary entry for the word 'sens' as the epigraph to the ethnographic studies that accompany the *Esquisse*), and with 'stratégies'. But in Bourdieu the subject of 'le sens pratique' is debarred from self-knowledge and volition. Ultimately, as Certeau points out, the logic of practice in Bourdieu fetishizes *habitus* and unconscious reproduction rather than creation.[81]

Certeau rebuts this view of *pratique*. For him, people know more than we imagine: doing is a kind of thinking. In his logic of practice,[82] what makes *pratiques* operative and efficacious is the level and context of their application. It is not a matter of knowledge or power but of local, pragmatic flair. In Certeau *pratique* does not possess its own content or space: it is a secondary production that exists only through the way it uses what is already in place, but it does thereby have a projective, dynamic aspect: it produces by reusing rather than reproducing. And this creative, indigent, ludic dimension is what gives Certeau's *pratique* an affinity with the more deliberate ruses of Breton, Queneau, Perec, Ernaux, or Roubaud. For Certeau, we invent our own unofficial everyday through the improvised ways in which we go about our daily activities (inhabiting, shopping, reading, conversing)—'le quotidien s'invente avec mille manières de braconner' (the everyday is invented in a thousand ways of poaching).[83] Whether we recognize it as such or not, everydayness is what we invent through the way we conduct our activities: 'art de faire' pertains to 'art de vivre' (Certeau's emphasis on style chimes with Foucault's 'art of existence'). Hence the possibility that if we want to draw attention to and acknowledge the everyday we need to simulate and thus stimulate the dynamic creativity that is inherent in the practices that constitute it, yet are generally hidden in the 'opacity' of gestures and local contexts. If the explorer of the everyday—Aragon, Certeau, Perec, Augé, Ernaux, or Calle—seeks to grasp a dynamism that springs from *pratique* it makes sense that it should be by inventing practices of his or her own.

Outlining *Lieux* and many other enterprises in his 1969 letter to Maurice Nadeau, Perec repeatedly uses the word *projet*,[84] an appropriate general term for the types of activity through which he and other explorers make themselves—at a second degree—what Certeau calls practitioners of the everyday. Semantically, the difference between *project* and such cognates as plan,

---

[81] Certeau, *L'Invention du quotidien*, I, 96.
[82] Ibid., I, xl.
[83] Ibid., I, xxxvi.
[84] Perec, *Je suis né*, 51–66, *passim*.

scheme, undertaking, task, or endeavour is that, although it points towards an end, a project makes the end less defined, more hypothetical. Compared to a plan, a project is less determined by a specific goal that is known in advance and is to be achieved in a set way. Although it has a 'projected' outcome, on the horizon, the notion of the project focuses on steps to be taken during a stretch of future time. In a project the relation between the activities in the foreground or midterm and any eventual issue is uncertain: to talk of a project is to invoke the hazards of that relationship. To outline a project is not so much to focus on an achievement as to invoke, on the one hand an idea, a mental postulation, and on the other hand a range of actions conducive—in theory—to its realization. A project—a commitment to midterm actions—implies a pre-occupation with the domain of practice.

As many developments in twentieth century culture attest, the notion of the project has come to occupy a central place in aesthetic and broadly cultural activities, shifting attention from outcomes (for instance, a finished artwork) to processes, practices, constraints, and durations.[85] Dada and Surrealism played a key role in favouring these developments. Of central importance in this cultural appropriation of the project is the way it accentuates the gap between action and result, mental and physical, the theoretical and the practical, whilst underlining their inextricability. Here the hatching of a project generally involves an ironic attitude to both systematic knowledge and utilitarian attitudes. Under the aegis of the project, the product of cultural practice is, on the one hand, a report on the conduct of the project itself (as we see clearly in Perec) and on the other hand a redirection of attention and a change in awareness brought about by the progressive implementation (or non-implementation) of the project. Projects are about practices and the differences they make, but also about the limits of orthodox, abstract thought: hence the strong affinity between the project and the everyday. The agency of practices in the constitution of the everyday—the projective dimension through which practices 'invent' the *quotidien*, not as an objective statistical reality but as lived experience that has its own bearings—finds its counterpart in the project. What the project figures is the active, performative dimension of the everyday, the way it inheres in 'arts de faire'. Thus I would like to probe further how the everyday finds its articulation in *ad hoc* grass-roots projects, involving both a marked practical dimension and an ample pinch of salt; a

---

[85] Cf. Gratton and Sheringham, 'Introduction' to *The Art of the Project*.

specific example, François Bon's project, recorded in his *Paysage fer*, will then highlight which aspects of the everyday are illuminated by the figure of the project.

Embarking on a project means avoiding the limitations of particular frames of understanding: a set of *ad hoc*, provisional, yet rule-bound actions and procedures provides a neutral framework within which experience can be freely addressed and received (constraints help regulate the balance between activity and passivity). Three examples may briefly be added to the list of projects already encountered in previous chapters. In May 1982 Julio Cortazar and Carol Dunlop devoted a month to travelling from Paris to Marseilles on the Autoroute du Soleil in a Volkswagen camper van.[86] The key rule was that they would stop in service areas (two per day), eat and sleep there, but never leave the immediate environs of the motorway. Accompanied by numerous photographs and a logbook of their daily activities (including details of what they ate and the flora and fauna of various car parks), the narrative of their 'voyage intemporel' (timeless journey)—as the book's subtitle puts it—pays particular attention to the progressive 'mutation' of their awareness as they floated free of customary purposes and preoccupations. Cortazar's project influenced Maspero's *Les Passagers du Roissy-Express*,[87] which was in turn emulated by Jean Rolin. Rolin's *Zones* (1995)—a title evoking existential as well as geographic terrain—reports on three journeys, each of approximately two weeks' duration, round the fringe areas of Paris (either side of the Périphérique). Leaving on a Sunday in June 1994 (he will strive throughout to be a 'Sunday' traveller) Rolin took the metro towards Pont de Sèvres, alighted at the Marcel-Sembat station and checked in to the modest Hotel Phénix (signalling rebirth?), the first of many establishments, similar to those frequented by Maspero and Frantz, where he will rest fitfully over the next two weeks, often ruminating 'la lancinante question de ce que je pourrais bien faire, en voyage à Paris, qui ne soit pas du journalisme pittoresque ou de la sociologie de comptoir' (the pressing question of what I was up to, travelling round Paris, if not picturesque journalism or bar-room sociology).[88]

---

[86] Julio Cortazar and Carol Dunlop, *Les Autonautes de la cosmoroute, ou un voyage intemporel Paris-Marseille* (Paris: Gallimard, 1983).

[87] Cf. Maspero's 'Postface 1993' in the English translation of *Les Passagers*. For a discussion of Maspero and Cortazar, see Charles Forsdick 'Projected Journeys: Exploring the Limits of Travel', in J. Gratton and M. Sheringham (eds.), *The Art of the Project* (Oxford: Berghahn Books, 2005), 51–65.

[88] Rolin, *Zones*, 37. On Rolin see Catherine Poisson, 'Terrains vagues: *Zones* de Jean Rolin', *Nottingham French Studies*, 39/1 (Spring 2000).

Like Maspero, Rolin frequently insists that his aim was to look, not to carry out a survey: everyday projects are interrogative rather than assertive. Jacques Réda's *Le Méridien de Paris* (1997) logs the author's attempt to follow the line of the Paris meridian, established by the scientist Arago (1786–1853) when he was director of the Bureau des Longitudes, then superseded when Greenwich was adopted. Armed with a brochure giving approximate directions, Réda tries to 'walk' the line, even though it 'traverses' boulevards, parks and buildings of all kinds, and even 'crosses' the Seine (Réda wonders if, in keeping with the logic of his project, he should swim across!). Although the activity involved is simple and physical, the hypothetical nature of the meridian locates the project at the interface of the abstract and the concrete, the material and the intangible, testing the parameters of different kinds of understanding or participation. Réda's account of his forced deviations makes his narrative comically digressive and rich in speculation, nuance and variation, thereby communicating the experience of Paris in arresting and unfamiliar ways.

In the sphere of everyday life, the project 'allows for' everydayness by suspending abstract definition and creating a breathing space, a gap or hiatus that enables the *quotidien* to be apprehended as a medium in which we are immersed rather than as a category to be analysed. Projects (like Aragon's, Roubaud's, Maspero's, or Rolin's) often originate in curiosity or anxiety about something in the field of everyday experience. An impulse grows into a project when it hatches a possible *modus operandi*, a sequence of thoughts or actions that generally consist in putting oneself (or someone else) into a particular concrete situation: cruising round the Buttes-Chaumont park at night (Aragon), visiting twelve chosen places once a year (Perec), following a stranger to Venice (Calle). Once under way, the project highlights the conditions of the experiment, the rules of the game, the practical steps to be taken. At the core of the experimental situation are factors designed to maintain openness and avoid pre-judgement. If there is a gap between mental impulse and practical execution, there is a further gap between the activities that thematize or concretize the project and any outcomes or conclusions. These must wait on events, they 'remain to be seen'. The deviation into practice is designed precisely to suspend judgement and 'see what happens'.

How does the project's practical dimension enact this suspension? When Perec spends three days in the Place Saint-Sulpice, or Sophie Calle works as a hotel chambermaid and photographs the guests' possessions, or Christian Boltanski assembles photographs of missing children, we note an insistence on the hands-on, grass-roots level, on practical steps geared to the accumulation of data. One of the defining features of the everyday project is that it neutralizes purpose by displacement from the long-term macro-level, to the short-term micro-level, through a proliferation of rules, constraints, provisos, and methodological niceties. In most projects the specifications (usually self-imposed ordinances) bear on both space (location, itinerary) and time (duration, frequency), as well as on mental and physical 'acts' to be performed. Codified as a set of instructions, such specifications are often ironic because their precision accompanies a strong sense of the gratuitous. The elements of irony or play suggest that the project involves parodic simulation, that 'scientificity' is being debunked to some degree, that collecting data is less important than the process of gathering. Yet the gratuitousness that neutralizes scientific enquiry also redirects attention.

There is a characteristic myopia of the project. Repetition of a sequence of actions according to a set procedure is often central and one of its effects is to neutralize the teleology of continuous narrative. But repetition has its positive aspects as it focuses attention on minute variations. This allies the project to a kind of knowledge linked to process—Perec's 'émergence' (emergence).[89] Repetition fosters a different sort of attention by numbing customary activities. Its temporality is that of progressive 'tuning in' to a particular level of existence, a new mode of attention that is responsive to the uneventful, to what is initially hidden by habit. Projects often succeed in making visible what is already there, not hidden but lying on the surface. By diverting attention from a goal to the carrying out of a repeated, preordained programme, the project creates its own intermediate spatio-temporal zone. In so doing, it generates attention to the present, to the unresolved matter of what is still in process (the process may be the spectator's current flow of awareness). The project is a frame, but nothing that comes to fill that frame can be said to complete or realize the project, which always remains open and unfinished. Yet within its framework a shift, essentially a shift of attention, takes place. The project brings us into proximity with something that might have seemed familiar, but which we now acknowledge more fully. In this sense we can see at work in the project the interface of alienation and appropriation that is central to thinking about the everyday.

As noted in Chapter 8, François Bon is a writer who has consistently explored the impact of social and economic change on French everyday life after the end of the 'trente glorieuses' (the three decades of prosperity that followed post-

---

[89] Perec, *Penser/Classer*, 23.

war reconstruction). The project dimension stems from his work with local communities (including institutions such as prisons, youth clubs, and hostels for the homeless). He is a leading exponent of 'ateliers d'écriture' (writing workshops) that help people develop creative awareness of their lives (Bon regards Perec's *Espèces d'espaces* and other texts as an indispensable source of ideas for practical exercises).[90] *Paysage fer*, a book based on observations made on train journeys, is the offshoot of a project with 'sans-abris' (homeless people) in Nancy, but in this case the writer-observer and the world he tries to capture are the sole protagonists.

For five winter months in 1998–9 Bon took the train every Thursday morning, leaving Paris-Est at 8.18 and arriving in Nancy at 11.22. Soon to be superseded by the high-speed TGV, the line goes via Vitry-le-François, Château-Thierry, Toul, and many smaller places—Commercy, Foug, Révigny. From the window he could see waterlogged sports fields, breakers' yards, cement works, cemeteries, and deserted factories. The speed of the train made description difficult so Bon thought of another approach. Adopting a fixed protocol of looking and noting, he would rely on the rhythms of attention induced by repetition and variation. He would sit in the same seat each week, in the front carriage, look out of the same side, and in the notebook on his knee he would note strictly what he saw, while it was visible. In the following weeks he would do the same: not revising or embellishing but plunging back and trying to see more: how many windows are broken on the dilapidated wireworks near Vitry; whether it is the same shade of pink on the signs for the Dance Hall and the Café de la Gare at Foug; how far you can see up the deserted main street of Liverdun or Cheppes. In writing up the notes, he would make the text match its origin: having made himself a pure receptor, he would use the pronoun 'one' rather than 'I'.

Central to *Paysage fer* is the insight that it is the 'travail du regard' (work of looking),[91] the process of attention induced by rules and constraints, which

---

[90] See François Bon, *Tous les mots sont adultes* (Paris: Fayard, 2000).

[91] Ibid., *Paysage fer* (Lagrasse: Verdier, 2000), back cover. References to this work are incorporated in the text. It would be interesting to compare Bon's project, and that of Maspero in *Les Passagers du Roissy-Express*, with Pierre Bourdieu's *La Misère du monde* (Paris: Seuil, 1993), a fascinating compendium of interviews with individuals and families suffering from every kind of social deprivation. In his methodological conclusions Bourdieu's stress on the dissident character of the techniques used by his team of collaborators, underlining *contrainte*, anonymity, and the transformation of attention, echoes Perec, Bon, Maspero, Certeau and the whole tradition of the *quotidien* project: 'Ainsi au risque de choquer aussi bien les méthodologues rigoristes que les herméneutes inspirés, je dirais volontiers que l'entretien peut être considéré comme une forme *d'exercice spirituel*, visant à obtenir, par *l'oubli de soi*, une véritable *conversion du regard* que nous portons sur les autres dans les circonstances ordinaires de la vie' (1406).

produces insights into 'cela qui est nous, tellement nous' (this, which is us, so much us). The train, with its company of busy executives and school students, is on the move, but the world it traverses is in terminal slowdown: the fleeting glimpses afforded by the train, the limited knowledge this allows, are attuned to a condition of poverty. Yet fleetingness and suddenness—as things sighted, however much anticipated week after week, go by in a flash—are profoundly germane to what the project makes visible: not only loss and abandonment, but a rich profusion of details still residually there in the midst of decline. Avoiding nostalgia, Bon makes us aware of the mournful beauty of dereliction. If the 'steelscape' is a territory largely without figures, it is because modern society is abandoning a world, a type of community, whose signs are still so legible along the track.[92]

Beginning with the words 'récurrence et répétition' (recurrence and repetition) (9), Bon's text reflects the way his project involved progressive accumulation and combination of different sets of writings: notes produced 'in motion', consisting largely of discontinuous images, lists of items seen, and so forth; ideas and self-exhortations generated in the process of writing up the notes, relating both to what has been noted and the conduct of the project itself; a tidied-up version where the material is presented in sixteen untitled and unnumbered sequences, often unified by a repeated phrase or rhetorical device. The text we read recreates the overall development of the project, respecting the way it involved submitting a brief interval of time—the three-hour train journey on the same route each week—to an intense scrutiny that severed it from everyday time, and yet, through the compressed temporality of the project, squeezed out of it a variety of perceptions and insights. Constraints and ground rules operate at these two levels, specifying and refining the relation between them. In the train, the basic rule is to synchronize writing and seeing. It would have been impossible to write non-stop for three hours, and Bon varies the points of the journey when he takes out his notebook; but in the conduct of a particular week's task—sometimes to concentrate on a particular type of building, or to look more closely at a given item—the obligation to note it in the process of its appearance and disappearance remains constant. Speed is a crucial element in the project because it under-

---

[92] It is clear that Bon's project has affinities with the photographic practices of Bernd and Hilda Becher who, over four decades, since the 1960s, have produced an extraordinary archive of images of industrial buildings, displaying them, usually in rows and sequences, in ways aimed at inducing an act of attention—in this case comparative—that is heuristic. See *Bernd et Hilda Becher* (Paris: Éditions du Centre Pompidou, 2004).

lines transience; the speeding train makes what is near look far away (80). Writing constrained by the race to capture something that lasts only as long as the brain retains impressions on the retina—at one point Bon calculates the maximum number of discrete images that a 'retinal flow' of three hours' duration might contain (17)—is infused by a strong sense of anxiety and urgency stemming from the fear of letting things go by unrecorded. The project makes an ethical demand on its experimental subject—the anonymous 'one' whom Bon strives to become—since he must try and rescue what he strives to see from the oblivion by which it is already threatened. 'Ici [. . .] le visible est à reconstruire' (Here . . . the visible is to be reconstructed) (37).

The constant use of infinitives as imperatives is central to the discourse of 'contrainte'. All through the project Bon issues, reiterates, and revises instructions to himself: to collect all the names and other inscriptions he sees (11, 24, 34); to keep going without rereading or revising, if necessary just making lists; to note specific types of building such as boiler houses on the edges of towns (33); to look up the names of factories in Vitry-le-François in the phone book as an aid to identification (34); to respect a regular sequence of rituals, including programmed visits to the train's refreshment car where the windows are larger and the view different (45); to decide in advance (at the weekend) what is to be looked out for next time, 'ce sur quoi il faut s'acharner' (what must really be worked on (79)), so that one week he concentrates on a particular house near Révigny (73); to look out for books and old postcards so as to compare what he sees now with its appearance in the past (he reports finding a photograph of one of the level crossings he passes, taken a century earlier (82)). Ultimately, all the instructions foster the same end: to make the sheer process of looking—and of holding on to images—incrementally transformational, so that, by training one's eyes to see and retain more, one is also understanding, and hence preserving, more of what one sees. The inferential process is often indicated by the use of 'donc' (therefore). At the heart of *Paysage fer* is the understanding that the real discloses itself fleetingly in the process of its sudden appearance ('surgissement') and equally sudden disappearance from view. The act of concentration that this induces, imparted to the optical nerves, is also transmitted to the act of verbal formulation. Writing under pressure makes writing, through its rhythms and repetitions, reveal the truth harboured in the visible through the process of appearance and disappearance. At one point, Bon formulates the constraint that the text should obey the same rule as the look (36), and elsewhere he urges: 'que l'image quand elle surgit puis cesse impose avec elle un mot comme un emblème' (as it rises up, then vanishes, the image should leave behind a word as a kind of emblem) (62). Bon then uses some of these key words to structure a portion of his text. By writing again and again what one sees, we constrain both the text and ourselves to transmute attention and to intensify our relation to the seen: 'contraindre le récit à parvenir par seule répétition à gagner sur le réel répété [. . .] nous contraindre à densifier dans l'instant le rapport visuel qu'on en a' (constrain the narration solely by dint of repetition to get some purchase on repetitive reality. . . and constrain ourselves to thicken our visual connection to it) (50). Towards the end, Bon is struck by how much five months of Thursdays have changed his perception (84). And as we read the text, noting the recurrence of cemeteries, houses, cement works, allotments, and canals, we notice how they become more distinct, how their specificity, whilst still fleeting and vulnerable, is progressively recognized and honoured.

Insofar as it turns looking into a task (that one can perform well or badly), the project induces a sense of responsibility, providing occasions for self-reproach and anxiety (39). The project makes the act of looking both hermeneutic and ethical: the compositional imperatives in the text point to moral imperatives. If *Paysage fer* establishes a grammar and phenomenology of the visible, of the ways phenomena can briefly explode onto the retina, it also locates what is seen fleetingly as requiring to be salvaged (18). For the way phenomena appear to proffer themselves briefly but repeatedly (week after week), before being eclipsed by other things, points to a potential that is in the process of being destroyed. Another recurrent word in Bon's text, linked to 'surgissement', is 'profusion', and he refers in the same sentence to 'le surgissement à sauver, la profusion saturante d'un détail qu'on ne peut attraper suffisament vite' (the sudden appearance to be saved, the saturating profusion of a detail one cannot grasp quickly enough) (18). If the sense of profusion is largely an effect of the conditions of the journey—so many water towers, stations, factories, and so on—it also suggests a rich commonality that is then belied by the mournful emptiness of the places the train passes by. The social meanings generated in *Paysage fer* are linked to the way the project lays bare the tension between profusion and dereliction: potential life and living death. Over its 352 kilometres the train journey furnishes all the elements of a sad scenario, providing clear evidence of how one world has obliterated another (35), as lorries bear the spoils of the countryside to a voracious capital. There may be industrial plants, new buildings, stockyards, and stores, but those who bring them into being are nowhere to be seen: 'tout est mort ici d'un coup' (everything round here died overnight) (30). The eerie unreality of the deserted countryside, and the sad little towns with their old-fashioned signs, reflect a world 'qui se défait' (that is crumbling) (21). From the train, we see signs of a transfusion whereby the blood of the rural organism has been sucked up by the city (the motif of the 'saignée' (bloodletting) occurs on pages 37 and 74).

The train puts the passenger in an ambiguous situation: privy to what you do not see if you go by car (80), yet still cut off from the surroundings. The conditions of the project make the twin experiment—firstly, traversing the landscape in a hermetically sealed compartment, with only vision as a link to the outside; secondly, making a cargo of mental images the substance of a written text—into an experience where the train window becomes the frontier between two worlds (80). Through a paradoxical conjunction of distance and uncanny proximity, underlined by repetition and progressive acclimatization, the project creates conditions that make things visible (84). By becoming pure image (the word occurs numerous times), and thus tinged with the imaginary, the world outside the train reveals its haunting air of unreality, and this becomes a sign of its precarious vulnerability, as it succumbs to the effects of socio-economic change. But Bon emphasizes that the world-as-image engendered by the effects of compression and speed (84) is a human world. The rhythm of something being proffered to us, but then withdrawn, and the sense that the more strenuously we look the more we will see, bring out the way the lingering humanity of the afflicted world depends on our recognition. Paradoxically, Bon comments (84), the sense of being brought close to a hidden reality (underscored by the way the train line often gives us glimpses of the backs and hidden sides of places and buildings) is amplified by the way the desire to see occurs in specific artificial conditions. The strange beauty of the moribund world, that draws one to it as to something we may cherish yet are powerless to hold on to, is a tribute to the dimension of our identities—our social past and genealogy—that the threatened countryside still harbours. Yet far from encouraging nostalgia for a fading world, Bon's project points to the processes, the tensions and contradictions between competing worlds, laid bare along the tracks. Hence the epigraph to *Paysage fer*: a quotation from Michel Foucault that expresses the desire to restore to 'notre sol silencieux et naïvement immobile [...] ses ruptures, son instabilité, ses failles' (our silent and apparently motionless territory... its ruptures, instabilities, and cracks).

On 28 March 2003, when America and its allies had just gone to war with Iraq, the philosopher Jean-Luc Nancy devoted one of the monthly 'philosophical chronicles' he was then delivering on the French radio station France Culture to the concept of the *quotidien*.[93] Nancy observed that turning to the topic of everyday experience would provide a necessary corollary to his previous chronicle which had considered the failure of major twentieth-century ideologies, left and right, adequately to respond to the crisis of history induced by modernity. Martin Heidegger's flirtation with Nazism, Nancy claimed, should be understood in terms of the German philosopher's acute sense of what Walter Benjamin would call the 'atrophy of experience' brought on by technological progress. If Heidegger's recourse to the category of the 'people' chimed for a while with Nazi ideology, and was then reiterated in his later thought via notions of 'the gods' or poetic 'dwelling', it enacted, however waywardly, a desire to maintain that sense of historically grounded experience which, in Nancy's view, had fallen victim as much to Marxist-Hegelian ideas of endless progress as to fascist mythologizations. Even when it was wrong-headed, Heidegger's stubborn refusal to give up on the historicity of existence (denied by the 'ruse of history') pointed to a knot that still needed untying. Nancy notes the important if ambiguous place of the *quotidien* in *Being and Time*. If, as we saw in Chapter 1, Heidegger sees *Alltäglichkeit* as the indispensable pre-ontological ground for the experience of Being, true *Dasein* involves transcending the ordinary averageness of the everyday. Thus, whilst constantly keeping everydayness in view and affirming its importance as a route towards Being, Heidegger's thought ultimately depreciated the everyday. Yet Nancy points out that, partly in response to Heidegger, later thinkers, including Lefebvre, the Situationists, Michel de Certeau, and Michel Foucault, had sought to 'apprehend' the everyday differently. And he notes that Maurice Blanchot had grappled with the central 'difficulty' of the everyday: the fact that, if its defining quality is *insignificance*—resistance to the canons of the significant—the *quotidien* almost invariably ceases to be itself the moment we pay heed to it, since 'paying heed' usually invokes historical, aesthetic, or religious values and criteria that are extraneous to the everyday. But this very difficulty suggests something precious and compelling in the *quotidien*, when it succeeds in resisting the sway of the spectacular and the eventful: a dissidence that might pertain specifically to a dimension of experience whose value we relinquish at our peril.

---

[93] Jean-Luc Nancy, *Chroniques philosophiques* (Paris: Galilée, 2004).

Nancy's timely meditation testifies both to the key importance of *quotid-ienneté* in French thought since the 1980s, and to the genealogy of this concept through the twentieth century as a whole. Alluding to Perec he emphasizes the 'inapparence' of the *quotidien*, in opposition to the spectacle and the event, and he argues that to think (and to salvage) the everyday is not to make it apparent, but to grasp the modes of its persistence, and the way it is manifested in the textures of a time that unfolds. When human beings simply keep on going in the face of death, war, and disaster, neither heroically nor indifferently (Nancy cites Abbas Kiarostami's film 'La vie continue'), the everyday is fleetingly affirmed, and reveals itself not as the seat of shoulder-shrugging empiricism or resignation but of what Nancy calls '[une] sourde ressource pour penser autrement' (a stubborn resource for thinking otherwise).[94]

My aim in this book has been to retrace and celebrate the remarkable richness of a tradition of doing, thinking, and writing. Yet just as in this tradition the everyday cannot be defined or demarcated, sociologically or in terms of any fixed content, so it would be a mistake to narrow it down intellectually to specific acts of thought or, thematically, to limited sectors and activities. I hope to have shown how wide-ranging the dimension of the everyday really is, and how versatile its explorers have been, as they scotch the differences between thought and practice, literature and theory (all the major works we have studied—and strikingly those of the Surrealists, Lefebvre, Barthes, Certeau, and Perec—are as literary as they are theoretical, and vice versa). As well as resistance and resilience one should associate the *quotidien*, above all perhaps, with the act and process of attention. Inherently performative, the everyday comes into view—is appropriated (Lefebvre), invented (Certeau), acknowledged (Cavell), affirmed (Nancy)—when it receives attention. And attention to the everyday, as Georges Perec never ceased to observe, is not attention to the niceties of individual psychology but to a commonality of experience that is endlessly forming and reforming in human activities and encounters—if only we deigned to notice it.

[94] Jean-Luc Nancy, *Chroniques philosophiques* (Paris: Galilée, 2004). 51.

Bibliography

Adair, Gilbert, 'The Eleventh Day: Perec and the infra-ordinary', *Review of Contemporary Fiction*, 13/1, (1993), 92–103.

Ades, Dawn, 'Photography and the Surrealist Text' in Rosalind Krauss, Jane Livingston, and Dawn Ades, *L'Amour fou: Photography and Surrealism* (New York: Abbeville Press, 2002), 153–89.

Adorno, T. W., 'The Essay as Form' (1958), trans. B. Hullot-Kentor and F. Will, *New German Critique*, 32 (Spring-Summer 1984), 151–71.

Agamben, Giorgio, *La Communauté qui vient* (Paris: Seuil, 1990).

Ahearne, Jeremy, *Michel de Certeau: Interpretation and its Other* (Cambridge: Polity Press, 1995).

Akerman, Chantal (dir.), *Jeanne Dielman, 23 Quai du Commerce, 1080 Bruxelles* (Film; Belgium/France, 1975).

Alferi, Pierre, *Kub Or* (Paris: POL, 1994).

—— and Olivier Cadiot (eds.), *Revue de littérature générale*, I (*La Mécanique lyrique*) and II (*Digest*) (Paris: POL, 1995–6).

Alquié, Ferdinand, *Philosophie du surréalisme* (Paris: Flammarion, 1955).

Althabe, Gérard and Jean-Louis Comolli, *Regards sur la ville* (Paris: Centre Georges Pompidou, 1994).

—— D. Fabre, and G. Lenclud (eds.), *Vers une ethnologie du présent* (Paris: Éditions de la Maison des Sciences de l'homme, 1992).

L'Amour fou: Photography and Surrealism: Hayward Gallery, London, July to September 1986. See also Krauss.

Apollinaire, Guillaume, *Œuvres poétiques* (Paris: Gallimard Pléiade, 1959).

—— *Œuvres en prose complètes*, III (Paris: Gallimard Pléiade, 1993).

Aragon, Louis, *Le Paysan de Paris* (1926; Paris: Gallimard Folio, 1972).

Ariès, Philippe, 'Pour une histoire de la vie privée', in P. Ariès and G. Duby (eds.) *Histoire de la vie privée*, 5 vols., III (Paris: Seuil, 1986), 7–19.

Arrouye, Jean, 'La Photographie dans *Nadja*', *Mélusine*, 4 (1982), 123–51.

Auclair, Georges, *Le Mana quotidien: structures et fonctions de la chronique des faits divers* (2nd edn., Paris: Éditions Anthropos, 1982).

Augé Marc, *La Traversée du Luxembourg* (Paris: Hachette, 1985).

—— *Un Ethnologue dans le métro* (Paris: Hachette, 1986); *In the Metro*, trans. Tom Conley (Minneapolis: University of Minnesota Press, 2002).

—— *Domaines et châteaux* (Paris: Seuil, 1989).

—— *Non-Lieux: Introduction à une anthropologie de la surmodernité* (Paris: Seuil, 1992).

—— *Le Sens des autres* (Paris: Fayard, 1994).

Augoyard, Jean-François, *Pas à pas. Essai sur le cheminement quotidien en milieu urbain* (Paris: Seuil, 1979).

Bachelard, Gaston, *La Poétique de l'espace* (Paris: PUF, 1961).

Bailly, Jean-Christophe, *La Ville à l'œuvre* (Paris: Éditions Jacques Bertoin, 1992).

Baker, Nicholson, *The Mezzanine* (1988; London: Penguin, 1990).

Barthes, Roland, *Œuvres complètes*, ed. Eric Marty, 3 vols. (Paris: Seuil, 1993).

—— *Comment vivre ensemble* (Paris: Seuil, 2002).

—— *Le Neutre* (Paris: Seuil, 2002)

—— *La Préparation du roman* (Paris: Seuil, 2003).

Bataille, Georges, 'Le Bas Matérialisme et la gnose', in Denis Hollier (ed.), *Documents*, II (Paris: Jean-Michel Place, 1991), 1–8.

—— 'Le Gros orteil', in Denis Hollier (ed.), *Documents*, I (Paris: Jean-Michel Place, 1991), 297–302.

Baudelaire, Charles, *Œuvres complètes* (Paris: Gallimard, 1961).

Baudrillard, Jean, *Le Système des objets* (Paris: Gallimard, 1968).

—— *La Société de consommation* (Paris: Denoël, 1970).

—— *L'Échange symbolique et la mort* (Paris: Gallimard, 1976)

—— *Amérique* (Paris: Grasset, 1986).

—— 'Please follow me', in Sophie Calle, *Suite vénitienne* (Paris: Éditions de l'Étoile, 1983).

—— (with Marc Guillaume), *Figures de l'altérité* (Paris: Éditions Descartes, 1999).

Bellos, David, *Georges Perec: A Life in Words* (London: Harvill, 1993).

Benjamin, Walter, *Illuminations*, trans. H. Zohn (London: Jonathan Cape, 1970).

—— *One-Way Street and Other Writings*, trans. E. Jephcott and K. Shorter (London: New Left Books, 1979).

—— *The Arcades Project*, trans. H. Eiland and K. McLaughlin (Cambridge, MA: Harvard University Press, 1999).

Benveniste, Emile, *Problèmes de linguistique générale* (1966; Paris: Gallimard 'Tel', 1976).

Berger, Peter and Thomas Luckmann, *The Social Construction of Reality: A Treatise in the Sociology of Knowledge* (London: Penguin, 1967).

Bergounioux, Pierre, *Miette* (Paris: Gallimard, 1995).

Berman, Marshall, *All That is Solid Melts into Air* (London: Verso, 1983).

Bernd et Hilda Becher (Paris: Éditions du Centre Pompidou, 2004).

Blanchot, Maurice. 'La Parole quotidienne' (1962) and 'Le Demain joueur' (1966) in id., *L'Entretien infini* (Paris: Gallimard, 1989), 355–66 and 597–619.

Bober, Robert, *En remontant la rue Vilin* (Film: INA, 1992).

Boltanski, Christian, see *Voilà-le monde dans la tête* (Paris: Musée d'art moderne de la ville de Paris, 2000).

—— and Jacques Roubaud, *Ensembles* (Paris, 1997).

Bon, François, *Impatience* (Paris: Minuit, 1996).

—— *Parking* (Paris: Minuit, 1996).

—— *Paysage fer* (Lagrasse: Verdier, 2000).

—— *Tous les mots sont adultes* (Paris: Fayard, 2000).

—— (with Jérome Schlomoff), *La Douceur dans l'abîme: vies et paroles des sans-abri* (Strasbourg/Nancy: Nuée bleue/Éditions de l'Est, 1999).

—— (with Jérome Schlomoff), *15021* (Coaraze: L'Amourier, 2000).

Bonnefoy, Yves, *Breton à l'avant de soi* (Tours: Farrago, 2001).

Bourdieu, Pierre, *Esquisse d'une théorie de la pratique* (1972; Paris: Seuil, 2000).

—— 'Le Couturier et sa griffe: contribution à une théorie de la magie', *Actes de la recherche en sciences sociales*, 1 (1975), 7–36.

—— *La Distinction* (Paris: Minuit, 1979).

Bourseiller, Christophe, *Vie et mort de Guy Debord* (Paris: Plon, 1999).

Bowie, Malcolm, *Psychoanalysis and the Future of Theory* (Oxford: Blackwell, 1993).

Bradby, David, *The Theater of Michel Vinaver* (Ann Arbor: University of Michigan Press, 1993).

Brasseur, Roland, *Je me souviens de Je me souviens* (Paris: Le Castor Astral, 1998).

Breton, André, *Le Surréalisme et la peinture* (Paris: Gallimard, 1965).

—— *Manifestes du surréalisme* (Paris: Pauvert, 1972).

—— *Oeuvres complètes*, ed. Marguerite Bonnet *et al.*, 3 vols., (Paris: Gallimard Pléiade, 1988, 1992, 2000).

Bromberger, Christian, 'L'ethnologie française "at home"', in *The Ethnology of Modern France, French Cultural Studies*, 18 (October 1995), 287–92.

Brown, Andrew, *Roland Barthes: The Figures of Writing* (Oxford: Oxford University Press, 1992).

Buchanan, Ian, *Michel de Certeau: Cultural Theorist* (London: Sage, 2000).

Buisine, Alain, *Eugène Atget ou la mélancolie en photographie* (Paris: Jacqueline Chambon, 1994).

Burgelin, Claude, *Georges Perec* (Paris: Seuil, 1988).

—— *Les Parties de dominos chez Monsieur Lefebvre: Perec avec Freud—Perec contre Freud* (Paris: Circé, 1996).

Burger, Peter, *The Theory of the Avant-Garde* (Minneapolis: University of Minnesota Press, 1984).

Butor, Michel, *Passage de Milan* (Paris: Minuit, 1954).

Cadiot, Olivier and Pierre Alferi (eds.) *Revue de littérature générale*, I, *La Mécanique lyrique* (1995), II (*Digest*) (1996)

Caillois, Roger, *L'Homme et le sacré* (1939; Paris: Gallimard Folio, 1992).

Calet, Henri, *De ma lucarne: chroniques* (Paris: Gallimard, 2000).

Calle, Sophie, *Suite vénitienne*, with essay by J. Baudrillard (Paris: Éditions de l'Étoile, 1983). The text is included in *Doubles-jeux*, IV.

—— *Doubles-jeux*, 7-vol. boxed set (Arles: Actes Sud, 1998).

—— *Les Dormeurs* (Arles: Actes Sud, 2001).

—— *Douleur exquise* (Arles: Actes Sud, 2003).

—— *L'Erouv de Jérusalem* (Arles: Actes Sud, 2002).

—— *Sophie Calle, m'as-tu vue* (Paris: Centre Pompidou, 2004).

Calvet, Jean-Louis, *Roland Barthes* (Paris: Flammarion, 1990).

Camus, Albert, *Noces, suivi de l'Été* (Paris: Gallimard, 1952).

Camus, Renaud, *Le Département de la Lozère* (Paris: POL, 1996).

Cauquelin, Anne, *La Ville, la nuit* (Paris: PUF, 1977).

—— *L'Art du lieu commun: du bon usage de la doxa* (Paris: Seuil, 1999).

Cause commune, ed. Georges Perec, Jean Duvignaud, and Paul Virilio, 7 issues, 1972–3, followed by 3 vols., 1975–7, 10×18 series (Paris: Union générale d'éditions).

Cavell, Stanley, *In Quest of the Ordinary* (Chicago: Chicago University Press, 1988).

—— *The Senses of Walden* (1981, expanded edn.; Chicago: Chicago University Press, 1992).

—— *The Cavell Reader*, ed. Stephen Mulhall (Oxford: Blackwell, 1996).

Caygill, Howard, *Walter Benjamin: The Colour of Experience* (London: Routledge, 1998)

Certeau, Michel de, *La Prise de parole* (Paris: Desclée de Brouwer, 1968).

Certeau, Michel de, *La Culture au pluriel* (Paris: Seuil, 1974).

—— *L'Invention du quotidien*, I, *Arts de faire* (1980; Paris: Gallimard Folio, 1990); *The Practice of Everyday Life*, trans. Steven Rendall (Berkeley: University of California Press, 1984).

—— with Luce Giard and Pierre Mayol, *L'Invention du quotidien*, II, *Habiter, cuisiner* (1980; Paris: Gallimard Folio, 1990); *The Practice of Everyday Life, 2: Living and Cooking*, trans. Timothy J. Tomasik (Minneapolis: University of Minnesota Press, 1998).

Chacun cherche son chat, see Klapisch.

Chailloux, Michel, *La France Fugitive* (Paris: Fayard, 1998).

Chambers, Ross, *Loiterature* (Lincoln: University of Nebraska Press, 1999).

Chappey, Jean-Luc, *La Société des observateurs de l'homme (1799–1804): des anthropologues au temps de Bonaparte* (Paris: Société des études robespierristes, 2004).

Clifford, James, *The Predicament of Culture* (Cambridge, MA: Harvard University Press, 1988).

Cohen, Margaret, *Profane Illumination: Walter Benjamin and the Paris of Surrealist Revolution* (Berkeley, London: University of California Press, 1993).

Cohn, Dorrit, *Transparent Minds: Narrative Modes for Presenting Consciousness in Fiction* (Princeton: Princeton University Press, 1978).

Comment, Bernard, *Roland Barthes: vers le neutre* (Paris: Christian Bourgois, 1991).

Comte-Sponville, André, *Petit traité des grandes vertus* (1995; Paris: Seuil, 2001).

Conley, Katherine, *Robert Desnos and the Marvellous in Everyday Life* (Lincoln, NE: University of Nebraska Press, 2003).

Conley, Tom, 'Introduction' and 'Afterword', in Marc Augé, *In the Metro*, trans. Tom Conley (Minneapolis: University of Minnesota Press, 2002).

Connerton, Paul, *How Societies Remember* (Cambridge: Cambridge University Press, 1989).

Construire pour habiter (Paris: Éditions L'Équerre-Plan Construction, 1981).

Corbin, Alain, *Le Miasme et la jonquille* (1982; Paris: Flammarion, 1998).

Cortazar, Julio and Carol Dunlop, *Les Autonautes de la cosmoroute, ou un voyage intemporel Paris-Marseille* (Paris: Gallimard, 1983).

Danto, Arthur C., *The Transfiguration of the Commonplace* (Cambridge, MA: Harvard University Press, 1981).

Darnton, Robert, *The Great Cat Massacre and other Episodes in French Cultural History* (New York: Basic Books, 1984).

Debord, Guy, *La Société du spectacle* (1967; Paris: Éditions Champ Libre, 1971).

—— *Œuvres cinématographiques complètes 1952–78* (Paris: Gallimard, 1994).

—— (ed.), *Potlatch (1955–57)* (Paris: Gallimard Folio, 1996).

De L'Ecotais, Emanuelle and Alain Sayag, *Man Ray, Photography and its Double* (New York: Gingko Press, 1998).

Deleuze, Gilles, *Cinéma 1, L'Image-mouvement*, and *Cinéma 2, L'Image-temps* (Paris: Minuit, 1983, 1985).

Delerm, Philippe, *La Première Gorgée de bière et autres plaisirs minuscules* (Paris: Gallimard, 1997).

—— *La Sieste assassinée* (Paris: Gallimard, 2001).

—— *Enregistrements pirates* (Monaco: Éditions du Rocher, 2003).

Desan, Philippe, *Montaigne: Naissance de la méthode* (Paris: Nizet, 1987).

Deshimaru, Taisen, *Zen et vie quotidienne* (Paris: Albin Michel, 1985).

Detienne, Marcel and Jean-Pierre Vernant, *Les Ruses de l'intelligence: la mètis des Grecs* (Paris: Flammarion, 1974).

Deutsch, Michel, *Inventaire après liquidation* (Paris: L'Arche, 1990).

—— *Dimanche* (Paris: L'Arche, 1994).

Didi-Huberman, Georges, *La Ressemblance informe ou le gai savoir visuel de Georges Bataille* (Paris: Macula, 1995).

Documents, see Hollier (ed.).

Dosse, François, *L'Histoire en miettes. Des Annales à la nouvelle histoire* (Paris: Pocket, 1997).

—— *Michel de Certeau, le marcheur blessé* (Paris: La Découverte, 2002).

Douglas, Mary, *Purity and Danger: An Analysis of Concepts of Pollution and Taboo* (1966: London: Routledge, 2002).

Dragonetti, Roger, *Un Fantôme dans le kiosque: Mallarmé et l'esthétique du quotidien* (Paris: Seuil, 1992).

Drevet, Patrick, *Huit petites études sur le désir de voir* (Paris: Gallimard, 1991).

—— *Petites études sur le désir de voir*, II (Paris: Gallimard, 1996).

Droit, Roger-Pol, *101 Exercices de philosophie quotidienne* (Paris: Odile Jacob, 2001).

Duhamel, Georges, 'Guillaume Apollinaire: *Alcools*', *Mercure de France*, 16 (June 1913).

Dumont, Bruno (dir.), *La Vie de Jésus* (*The Life of Jesus*) (Film: France, 1996).

Duras, Marguerite, *La Vie matérielle* (Paris: POL, 1987)

Eluard, Paul, *Œuvres complètes*, 2 vols. (Paris: Gallimard Pléiade, 1968).

Ernaux, Annie, *La Place* (Paris: Gallimard, 1984).

—— *Une Femme* (Paris: Gallimard, 1988).

—— *Journal du dehors* (1993; Paris: Gallimard Folio, 1996).

—— 'Vers un Je transpersonnel', *Cahiers RITM*, 6 (Paris: Université Paris X-Nanterre, 1994), 218–21.

—— *La Honte* (Paris: Gallimard, 1997).

—— *La Vie Extérieure* (Paris: Gallimard, 2000).

'The Ethnology of Modern France', *French Cultural Studies*, VI, 3, no. 18 (1995).

Everyday Life, ed. Alice Kaplan and Kristin Ross, *Yale French Studies*, 73 (1987).

Fabre, Daniel (ed.), *Écritures ordinaires* (Paris: POL, 1993).

Farge, Arlette, *Le Goût de l'archive* (Paris: Seuil, 1989).

—— *Vivre dans la rue à Paris au 18e siècle* (1979; Paris: Gallimard Folio, 1992).

—— 'Entretien avec Arlette Farge', *La Rue, Tracés*, 5 (2004), 143–8.

Feher, Ferenc, 'Lukács in Weimar', in A. Heller (ed.), *Lukács Revalued* (Oxford: Blackwell, 1983), 75–106.

Felski, Rita, 'The Invention of Everyday Life', *New Formations*, 39 (1999–2000), 15–31.

Filiod, Jean-Paul, '"Ça me lave la tête": purifications et ressourcements dans l'univers domestique' in *La Ritualisation du quotidien, Ethnologie, Français*, 2 (1996), 264–79.

Forsdick, Charles, 'Plonger dans un milieu réel: Edgar Morin in the Field', *French Cultural Studies*, 8 (1997), 309–31.

—— *Victor Segalen and the Aesthetics of Diversity: Journeys between Cultures* (Oxford: Oxford University Press, 2000).

—— 'Projected Journeys: Exploring the Limits of Travel', in J. Gratton and M. Sheringham (eds.), *The Art of the Project* (Oxford: Berghahn Books, 2005), 51–65.

Foster, Hal, *Compulsive Beauty* (Cambridge, MA.: MIT Press, 1993).

—— *The Return of the Real* (Cambridge, MA: MIT Press, 1996).

Foucault, Michel, *Surveiller et punir* (Paris: Gallimard, 1975).

—— *Histoire de la sexualité*, III, *Le Souci de soi* (Paris: Gallimard, 1984).

—— *Dits et écrits*, 2 vols. (Paris: Gallimard Quarto, 2001).

Freud, Sigmund, *The Psychopathology of Everyday Life* (1901; London: Penguin Classics, 2002).

Friedmann, Georges, *Le Travail en miettes* (Paris: Gallimard, 1956).

Garfinkel, Harold, *Studies in Ethnomethodology* (1967; Cambridge: Polity Press, 1984).

Geertz, Clifford, *The Interpretation of Cultures* (New York: Basic Books, 1973).

Genette, Gérard, 'Vraisemblance et motivation', *Figures, I* (Paris: Seuil, 1966).

Giard, Luce, 'Histoire d'une recherche' in M. de Certeau, *L'Invention du quotidien*, I, *Arts de faire* (1980; Paris: Gallimard Folio. 1990), i–xxx.

—— 'Faire-la-cuisine' in M. de Certeau, Luce Giard and Pierre Mayol, *L'Invention du quotidien*, II, *habiter; cuisiner* (1980; Paris: Gallimard Folio, 1990), 213–352.

Giard, Luce (ed.), *Michel de Certeau* (Paris: Centre Georges Pompidou, 1987).

Gide, André, *Les Faux-Monnayenrs* (1926; Paris: Gallimard Folio, 1986).

Gifford, Paul and Johnnie Gratton (eds.), *Subject Matters: Essays on Subject and Self in French Literature from Descartes to the Present* (Amsterdam: Editions Rodopi, 2000).

Gil, Fernando, *Traité de l'évidence* (Grenoble: Jérôme Millon, 1993).

Ginzburg, Carlo, *The Cheese and the Worms: The Cosmos of a Sixteenth-Century Miller* (1976; London: Routledge and Kegan Paul, 1980).

Godard, Jean-Luc, (dir.), *2 ou 3 choses que je sais d'elle* (Film: France, 1967). Découpage intégral (Paris: Seuil, 1971).

Goffman, Erving, *Interaction Ritual: Essays on Face-to-Face Behaviour* (1967; London: Allen Lane, 1972).

—— *The Presentation of Self in Everyday Life* (1959; London: Penguin, 1990).

Goldmann, Lucien, *Lukács et Heidegger* (Paris: Denoël, 1973).

Goncourt, Edmond and Jules, *Journal* (1851–96; Paris: Laffont, 2004).

Good, Graham, *The Observing Self: Rediscovering the Essay* (London: Routledge, 1988).

Gouldner, Alvi, 'Sociology and Everyday Life', in Lewis A. Coser (ed.), *The Idea of Social Structure* (New York: Harcourt, Brace, Jovanovich, 1975), 417–32.

Gracq, Julien, *La Forme d'une ville* (Paris: José Corti, 1985).

Gratton, Johnnie, 'The Poetics of the Barthesian Incident: Fragments of an Experiencing Subject', *Nottingham French Studies* (1997), 63–75.

Gratton, Johnnie, and Michael Sheringham (eds.), *The Art of the Project: Projects and Experiments in Contemporary French Culture* (Oxford: Berghahn Books, 2005).

Grenier, Jean, *La Vie quotidienne* (1968; Paris: Gallimard, 1982).

Groundhog Day, see Ramis, Harold.

Grumberg, Jean-Claude, *L'Atelier* (Arles: Actes Sud, 1985).

Gumpert, Lyn, *Christian Boltanski* (Paris: Flammarion, 1994).

Gumpert, Lyn (ed.), *The Art of the Everyday: The Quotidian in Postwar French Culture* (New York: New York University Press, 1997).

Guzzetti, Alfred, *Two or Three Things I Know About Her: Analysis of a Film by Godard* (Cambridge, MA: Harvard University Press, 1981).

Hadot, Pierre, *Exercices spirituels et philosophie antique* (Paris: Études augustiniennes, 1981).

Hamon, Philippe, *Introduction à l'analyse du descriptif* (Paris: Hachette, 1991).

Handke, Peter, *Essai sur la journée réussie: un songe d'un jour d'hiver*, trans. A Goldschmitt, (*Versuch über den geglückten Tag*, 1991) (Paris: Gallimard, 1994).

—— *Le Poids du monde* (Paris: Gallimard, 1979).

Harvey, David, *Consciousness and the Urban Experience* (Oxford: Blackwell, 1985).

—— *The Condition of Postmodernity* (Oxford: Blackwell, 1990)

Hazan, Eric, *L'Invention de Paris: Il n'y a pas de pas perdus* (Paris: Seuil, 2003).

Heidegger, Martin, *Being and Time*, trans. J. Macquarrie and E. Robinson (*Sein und Zeit*, 1926) (Oxford: Blackwell, 1978).

—— 'On the Essence of Truth', *Existence and Being* (Chicago: Gateway, 1949).

—— 'Building, Dwelling, Thinking', in id. *Poetry, Language, Thought*, trans. A. Hofstadter (New York: Harper Colophon Books, 1971).

Heller, Agnes, *Everyday Life* (1970; London: Routledge, 1984).

Heller, Agnes (ed.), *Lukács Revalued* (Oxford: Blackwell, 1983).

Hess, Rémi, *Henri Lefebvre: une aventure dans le siècle* (Paris: A. M. Métailié, 1988).

Highmore, Ben, *Everyday Life and Cultural Theory* (London: Routledge, 2002).

—— *The Everyday Life Reader* (London: Routledge, 2002).

Hoggart, Richard, *The Uses of Literacy* (1957; London: Penguin, 1958).

Hollier, Denis (ed.), *Documents*, 2 vols. (repr., Paris: Jean-Michel Place, 1991).

Hollier, Denis, *Les Dépossédés (Bataille, Caillois, Leiris, Malraux, Sartre)* (Paris: Minuit, 1993).

Hollier, Denis (ed.), *Le Collège de sociologie 1937–1939* (Paris: Gallimard Folio, 1995).

Hubble, Nick, Margaretta Jolly, and Laura Marcus (eds.), *Mass-Observation as Poetics and Science, New Formations,* 44 (2001).

Huizinga, Johan, *Homo ludens* (1951; London: Temple Smith, 1971).

Huysmans, Joris-Karl, *Croquis parisiens* (Paris: Vaton, 1880).

Internationale Situationniste, 1958–1969, édition augmentée (Paris: Fayard, 1997).

Jaccottet, Philippe, *Paysages avec figures absentes* (Paris: Gallimard, 1970).

—— *La Semaison: carnets, 1954–79* (Paris: Gallimard, 1984).

—— *Autres journées* (Montpellier: Fata Morgana, 1987).

—— *Cahier de verdure* (Paris: Gallimard, 1990).

James, Henry, 'Preface', in id. *The Tragic Muse, Novels, 1886–1890* (New York: Library of America, 1989).

James, Ian, 'Jean-Luc Nancy: The Persistence of the Subject', *Paragraph*, 25/1 (March 2002), 125–41.

Jameson, Fredric, *Marxism and Form* (Princeton: Princeton University Press, 1972).

—— *Post-modernism, or the Cultural Logic of Late Capitalism* (Durham, NC: Duke University Press, 1992).

Jamin, Jean, 'Quand le sacré devint gauche', *L'Ire des vents*, 3–4 (1981), 98–120.

—— 'Le Texte ethnographique: argument', in *Le Texte ethnographique*, *Études rurales*, 97–8 (Jan.-June 1985), 9–24.

Javeau, Claude, *Sociologie de la vie quotidienne* (Paris: PUF, 2003).

Jay, Martin, *Marxism and Totality: The Adventures of a Concept from Lukács to Habermas* (Oxford: Blackwell, 1984).

Jones, Kathryn, 'Voices of the Banlieues: Constructions of Dialogue in François Maspero's *Les Passagers du Roissy-Express*', *Contemporary French and Francophone Studies*, 8/2 (Spring 2004) 127–34.

Jouanard, Gil, *Mémoire de l'instant—nouvelles ordinaires de divers endroits* (Lagrasse: Verdier, 2000).

Jouet, Jacques, *Poèmes du métro* (Paris: POL, 2000).

Kalisky, René, *Scandalon* (Paris: L'Arche, 1982).

Kaplan, Alice, and Kristin Ross, 'Introduction' in *Everyday Life*, *Yale French Studies*, 73 (1987).

Kaufmann, Vincent, *Guy Debord, La Révolution au service de la poésie* (Paris: Fayard, 2001).

Kelly, Michael, 'Demystification: A Dialogue between Barthes and Lefebvre', *Yale French Studies*, 98 (Fall 2000), 79–97.

Kerbrat-Orecchioni, Catherine, *L'Énonciation* (Paris: Armand Colin, 1999).

Klapisch, Cédric (dir.), *Chacun cherche son chat* (Film; France, 1996).

Klevan, Andrew, *Disclosure of the Everyday: Undramatic Achievement in Narrative Film* (Trowbridge: Flicks Books, 2000).

Knight, Diana, *Barthes and Utopia: Space, Travel, Writing* (Oxford: Oxford University Press, 1997).

—— 'Idle Thoughts: Barthes's *Vita nova*', *Nottingham French Studies*, 36/1 (Spring 1997), 88–98.

Kofman, Eleanor and E. Lebas (eds.), *Henri Lefebvre: Writings on Cities* (Oxford: Blackwell, 1996).

Krauss, Rosalind, 'Photography in the Service of Surrealism' and 'Corpus delicti' in id., Jane Livingston, with an essay by Dawn Ades, *L'Amour fou: Photography and Surrealism* (New York: Abbeville Press, 2002), 12–53, 54–111.

—— *Le Photographique: pour une théorie des écarts* (Paris: Macula, 1990).

Lacarrière, Jacques, *L'été grec. Une Grèce quotidienne de 4000 ans* (Paris: Plon, 1976).

Laforgue, Jules, *Poésies complètes* (Paris: Livre de poche, 1970).

Langbauer, Laurie, 'Cultural Studies and the Politics of the Everyday', *Diacritics*, 22 (Spring 1992), 47–65.

—— *Novels of Everyday Life: The Series in English Fiction 1850–1930* (Cornell: Cornell University Press, 1999).

Laplanche, Jean and Jean-Bertrand Pontalis, *Vocabulaire de la psychanalyse* (1967; Paris: PUF, 1997).

Laugier, Sandra, *Du réel à l'ordinaire* (Paris: Vrin, 1999).

Lefebvre, Henri, *Critique de la vie quotidienne*, I: *Introduction* (1947, 2nd edn. with new 'Avant-propos'; Paris: L'Arche, 1958); *Critique of Everyday Life*, trans. J. Moore (London: Verso, 1991).

—— 'Perspectives de sociologie rurale', *Cahiers internationaux de sociologie*, 14 (1953), 122–46.

—— 'Vers un romantisme révolutionnaire', *Nouvelle Revue Française* (1957), 644–53.

—— *La Somme et le reste* (1959; Paris: Bélibaste, 1973).

—— 'Les Nouveaux ensembles urbains', *Revue française de sociologie*, 1 (1960), 28–67.

—— *Critique de la vie quotidienne*, II: *Fondements d'une sociologie de la quotidienneté*, (Paris: L'Arche, 1961); trans. J. Moore (London: Verso, 2002).

Lefebvre, Henri, *Introduction à la modernité* (Paris: Minuit, 1962).

—— *Le Droit à la ville* (Paris: Anthropos, 1968).

—— *La Vie quotidienne dans le monde moderne* (Paris: Gallimard 'Idées', 1968).

—— *La Révolution urbaine* (Paris: Gallimard, 1970).

—— *La Production de l'espace* (Paris: Anthropos, 1974); trans. Donald Nicholson Smith, *The Production of Space* (Oxford: Blackwell, 1991).

—— *Critique de la vie quotidienne*, III: *De la modernité au modernisme (Pour une métaphilosophie du quotidien)* (Paris: L'Arche, 1981).

—— 'Henri Lefebvre on the Situationist International', interview conducted and trans. 1983 by Kristin Ross, *October*, 79 (Winter 1997).

—— *Éléments de rythmanalyse* (Paris: Syllepse, 1992).

—— (ed.), *Morceaux choisis de Karl Marx* (Paris: Gallimard, 1934).

—— (ed.), *Morceaux choisis de Karl Marx* (Paris: Gallimard, 1934).

Leiris, Michel, *L'Age d'homme* (1939; Paris: Gallimard Folio, 1979).

—— *Miroir de la tauromachie* (Montepellier: Fata Morgana, 1981).

—— *Langage Tangage ou ce que les mots me disent* (Paris: Gallimard Œéiade, 1985).

—— *Journal 1922–1989*, ed. Jean Jamin (Paris: Gallimard, 1992).

—— *La Règle du jeu (1946–66)*, ed. Denis Hollier (Paris: Gallimard Pléiade, 2003).

—— 'Le Sacré dans la vie quotidienne' in id. *La Règle du jeu (1946–66)*, ed. Denis Hollier (Paris: Gallimard, 2003).

Lejeune, Philippe, *Georges Perec: la mémoire et l'oblique* (Paris: POL, 1991).

Lenclud, Gérard, 'Le Grand partage ou la tentation ethnologique' in Gérard Althabe, D. Fabre, and G. Lenclud (eds.), *Vers une ethnologie du présent* (Paris: Éditions de la Maison des Sciences de l'homme, 1992), 9–37.

Leonard, George C., *Into the Light of Things: The Art of the Commonplace from Wordsworth to John Cage* (Chicago: University of Chicago Press, 1994).

Lévi-Strauss, Claude, 'Introduction à l'œuvre de Marcel Mauss', in Marcel Mauss, *Sociologie et Anthropologie* (1950; Paris: PUF, 1997).

—— *La Pensée sauvage* (Paris: Plon, 1962).

Lipovetsky, Gilles, *L'Ère du vide: essais sur l'individualisme contemporain* (Paris: Gallimard, 1983).

—— *L'Empire de l'éphémère* (Paris: Gallimard, 1987).

Lomas, David, *The Haunted Self: Surrealism, Psychoanalysis, Subjectivity* (New Haven and London: Yale University Press, 2000).

Lüdtke, Alf (ed.), *The History of Everyday Life* (Princeton: Princeton University Press, 1995).

Lugon, Olivier, *Le Style documentaire. D'August Sander à Walker Evans, 1920–1945* (Paris: Macula, 2001).

Lukács, G., *Soul and Form* (1911; London: Merlin Press, 1994).

—— *History and Class Consciousness* (1923; Cambridge, MA: MIT Press, 1971).

—— *Discours, figure* (Paris: Klinksieck, 1971).

Lyotard, Jean-François, *La Condition postmoderne* (Paris: Minuit, 1979).

Macé, Marielle, 'Barthes romanesque', in id. and Alexandre Gefen (eds.), *Barthes, au lieu du roman* (Paris: Desjonquères/Nota Bene, 2002), 173–94.

McHoul, Alec and Toby Miller, *Popular Culture and Everyday Life* (London: Sage, 1998).

McIlvaney, Siobhan, *Annie Ernaux: The Return to Origins* (Liverpool: Liverpool University Press, 2001).

Maffesoli, Michel, *La Conquête du présent: pour une sociologie de la vie quotidienne* (1979; Paris: Desclée de Brouwer, 1998).

—— *La Connaissance ordinaire* (Paris: Klinksieck, 1985).

—— *Au creux des apparences: pour une éthique de l'esthétique* (1990; Paris: Livre de poche, 1993).

—— *L'Instant éternel* (Paris: Denoël, 2000).

Mallarmé, Stéphane, *Œuvres complètes* (Paris: Gallimard Pléiade, 1945).

Marchal, Bernard, *Paris: histoire d'une ville, 19e–20e siècle* (Paris: Seuil, 1993).

Marcus, Laura, 'Introduction: The Project of Mass-Observation', in Nick Hubble, Margaretta Jolly, and Laura Marcus (eds.), *Mass-Observation as poetics and science*, *New Formations*, 44 (2001).

Margulies, Ivone, *Nothing Happens: Chantal Akerman's Hyperrealist Everyday* (Durham, NC: Duke University, Press, 1996).

Marx, Karl, *Economic and Political Manuscripts of 1844* (London: Lawrence and Wishart, 1970).

—— *Capital*, trans. Ben Fowkes (1867; London: Penguin, 1992).

Maspero, François, *Les Passagers du Roissy-Express* (Paris: Seuil, 1990).

—— 'Postface, 1993', in id., *Roissy-Express: A Journey through the Paris Suburbs*, trans. Paul Jones (London: Verso, 1994), 261–8.

Mathews, Timothy, *Reading Apollinaire* (Manchester: Manchester University Press, 1987).

Maubon, Catherine, '*Documents*: une expérience hérétique', *Pleine Marge*, 4 (Dec. 1986), 55–65.

—— 'Michel Leiris: des notions de crise et de rupture au "Sacré dans la vie quotidienne"' in C. W. Thompson (ed.) *L'Autre et le sacré: Surréalisme, ethnographie, cinéma* (Paris: L'Harmattan, 1998).

Mauss, Marcel, 'Essai sur le don', in id., *Sociologie et anthropologie* (1950; Paris: PUF, 1997), 145–279.

Mayol, Pierre, 'Habiter', in M. de Certeau, Luce Giard, and Pierre Mayol, *L'Invention du quotidien, II, Habiter, cuisiner* (1980; Paris: Gallimard Folio, 1990), 15–188.

Melville, Herman, 'Bartleby', in id., *Billy Budd and Other Tales* (New York: Signet Classics, 1961).

Merleau-Ponty, Maurice, *Signes* (Paris: Gallimard, 1960).

—— *Le Visible et l'invisible* (Paris: Gallimard, 1964).

Michon, Pierre, *Vies minuscules* (Paris: Gallimard, 1984).

Miller, Nancy, 'Autobiographical Others: Annie Ernaux's *Journal du dehors*', *Sites* (Spring 1998), 127–39.

Milo, Daniel, 'Les Noms de rues', in Pierre Nora (ed.), *Lieux de mémoire*, 3 vols., II (Paris: Gallimard, 1997), 283–315.

Molès, Abraham and Elisabeth Rohmer, *Psychosociologie de l'espace*, (Paris: L'Harmattan, 1998).

Montfrans, Manet van, *Georges Perec: la contrainte du réel* (Amsterdam-Atlanta, Rodopi, 1999).

Morel, Alain, 'Introduction', *L'Ethnologie dans la ville, Terrain*, 3 (Oct 1984), 43.

Morin, Edgar, *L'Esprit du temps* (1962; Paris: Livre de poche, 1991).

—— and Jean Rouch, *Chronique d'un été* (Filmscript; Paris: Inter Spectacles, 1962).

Motte, Warren, *The Poetics of Experiment: A Study of the Work of Georges Perec* (Lexington: French Forum Monographs, 1984).

Motte, Warren, (ed.) *Oulipo: A Primer of Potential Literature* (Lincoln, NE: University of Nebraska Press, 1986).

Motte, Warren, *Small Worlds: Minimalism in Contemporary French Literature* (Lincoln, NE: University of Nebraska Press, 1999).

Mulhall, Stephen, *Stanley Cavell: Philosophy's Recounting of the Ordinary* (Oxford: Oxford University Press, 1994).

—— (ed.), *The Cavell Reader* (Oxford: Blackwell, 1996).

Mythologies aujourd'hui, *Le Nouvel Observateur*, hors-série no. 55 (July–Aug., 2004).

Nancy, Jean-Luc, *L'Expérience de la liberté* (Paris: Galilée, 1988).

—— *Le Sens du monde* (Paris: Galilée, 1993).

—— *Chroniques philosophiques* (Paris: Galilée, 2004).

Nehamas, Alexander, *The Art of Living: Socratic Reflections from Plato to Foucault* (Berkeley, CA: University of California Press, 1998).

Nesbit, Molly, *Atget's Seven Albums* (New Haven and London: Yale University Press, 1992).

Nora, Pierre (ed.), *Les Lieux de mémoire*, 3 vols. (1984–92; Paris: Gallimard Quarto, 1997).

Nys-Mazure, Colette, *Célébration du quotidien* (Bruxelles: Desclée de Brouwer, 1997).

Onfray, Michel, *La Sculpture de soi: la morale esthétique* (1991; Paris: Livre de poche, 1996).

Otto, Rudolph, *The Idea of the Holy* (*Das Heilige*, 1917) (Oxford: Oxford University Press, 1923).

Pachet, Pierre, *Les Baromètres de l'âme: naissance du journal intime* (Paris: Hatier, 1990).

Paquot, Thierry (ed.), *Le Quotidien urbain* (Paris: Éditions La Découverte, 2001).

Parret, Herman, *Le Sublime du quotidien* (Amsterdam: John Benjamins, 1988).

Pastoureau, Michel, *Bleu: Histoire d'une couleur* (Paris: Seuil, 2000).

Pearson, Roger, *Mallarmé and Circumstance: The Translation of Silence* (Oxford: Oxford University Press, 2004).

Pelkmans, Paul and Bruno Tristsmans (eds.), *Écrire l'insignifiant: dix études sur le fait divers dans le roman contemporain* (Amsterdam-Atlanta: Rodopi, 2000).

Perec, Georges, *Entretiens et conférences*, ed. Dominique Bernelli and Mireille Ribière, 2 vols (I: 1965–78, II: 1979–81) (Nantes: Joseph K, 2003).

—— *Les Choses* (Paris: Julliard, 1965).

—— 'L'Esprit des choses', *Arts et Loisirs* (Oct.–Dec. 1966).

—— *Quel petit vélo au guidon chromé au fond de la cour?* (Paris: Denoël, 1966).

—— *Un Homme qui dort* (Paris: Denoël, 1967). Film version by Bernard Queysanne and Georges Perec (France, 1974).

—— *La Disparition* (Paris: Denoël, 1969).

—— *La Boutique obscure* (Paris: Denoël, 1973).

—— *Espèces d'espaces* (Paris: Galilée, 1974).

—— *Tentative d'épuisement d'un lieu parisien* (1975: Paris: Christian Bourgois, 1982).

—— *W ou le souvenir d'enfance* (Paris: Denoël, 1975).

—— 'Guettées', *Les Lettres Nouvelles* (Feb.–March 1977).

—— 'Vues d'Italie', *Nouvelle revue de psychanalyse* (Autumn 1977).

—— 'La rue Vilin', *L'Humanité* (11 Nov. 1977).

Perec, Georges, *La Vie mode d'emploi* (Paris: POL, 1978).

—— 'Allées et venues rue de l'Assomption', *L'Arc* (1979).

—— 'Stations Mabillon', *Action poétique* (1980).

—— *La Clôture et autres poèmes* (Paris: Hachette, 1980).

—— *Théâtre I* (Paris: Hachette, 1981).

—— *Penser/Classer* (Paris: Hachette, 1985).

—— *Je suis né* (Paris: Seuil, 1989).

—— *L' Infra-ordinaire* (Paris: Seuil, 1990).

—— *Cahier des charges de 'La Vie mode d'emploi'* (Paris: CNRS Zulma, 1993).

—— *Perec/rinations* (Paris: Zulma, 1997).

—— *Tentative de description de choses vues au Carrefour Mabillon le 19 mai 1978*, 2 CDs, (Marseille: André Dimanche éditeur, 1997).

—— *Species of Spaces and other Pieces*, trans. John Sturrock (London: Penguin, 1997).

—— *Je me souviens* (1978: Paris: Hachette 1999).

—— *Romans et récits* (Paris: Livre de poche, 2002).

Perec, Paulette (ed.), *Portrait(s) de Georges Perec* (Paris: Bibliothèque nationale de France, 2001).

Perros, Georges, *Une Vie ordinaire* (1967; Paris: Gallimard-Poésie, 1988).

Pfeiffer, Jean, 'Breton, le moi, la littérature', *Nouvelle Revue Française*, 172 (1967), 855–62.

Piette, Albert, *Ethnographie de l'action: l'observation des détails* (Paris: A.M. Métailié, 1996).

Pigeot, Jacqueline, *Questions de poétique japonaise* (Paris: PUF, 1997).

Piquet, Jacques-François, *Noms de Nantes* (Paris: Joca Seria, 1992).

Plant, Sadie, *The Most Radical Gesture: The Situationist International in a Postmodern Age* (London: Routledge, 1992).

Poisson, Catherine, 'Terrains vagues: *Zones* de Jean Rolin', *Nottingham French Studies*, 39/1 (Spring 2000), 28–42.

Polanyi, Michael, *Personal Knowledge: Towards a Post-Critical Philosophy* (1958; Chicago: University of Chicago Press, 1974).

Pol-Droit, Roger, *101 Expériences de philosophie quotidienne* (Paris: Odile Jacob, 2001).

Portugal, Anne, *Les Commodités d'une banquette* (Paris: POL, 1985).

—— *définitif bob* (Paris: POL, 2002).

Potlatch (1954–1957), see Debord, Guy.

Queneau, Raymond, *Œuvres complètes*, I, *Poésie* (Paris: Gallimard Pléiade, 1989).

—— *Œuvres complètes*, II, *Romans*, I (Paris: Gallimard Pléiade, 2002).

—— *Exercices de style* (Paris: Gallimard, 1947).

—— *Journal 1914–1965* (Paris: Gallimard, 1996).

Quintane, Nathalie, *Chaussure* (Paris: POL, 1995).

Ramis, Harold (dir.), *Groundhog Day* (Film: USA, 1993).

Raymond, Marcel, *De Baudelaire au surréalisme* (1940; Paris: José Corti, 1966).

Révolution surréaliste, La, 1–12 (1924–19; repr., New York: Periodicals Service Company, 1974).

Réda, Jacques, *Les Ruines de Paris* (Paris: Gallimard, 1977).

—— *Hors les murs* (Paris: Gallimard 1982).

—— *L'Herbe des talus* (Paris: Gallimard, 1984).

—— *Châteaux des courants d'air* (Paris: Gallimard, 1986).

Réda, Jacques, *Recommendations aux promeneurs* (Paris: Gallimard, 1988)

—— *Le Sens de la marche* (Paris: Gallimard, 1990).

—— *La Liberté des rues* (Paris: Gallimard, 1997).

—— *Le Citadin* (Paris: Gallimard, 1998).

—— *Le Méridien de Paris* (Montpellier: Fata Morgana, 1998).

—— *Accidents de la circulation* (Paris: Gallimard, 2001)

Richman, Michèle, 'L'Altérité sacrée chez Durkheim', in C. W. Thompson (ed.), *L'Autre et le sacré: Surréalisme, ethnographie, cinéma* (Paris: L'Harmattan, 1995).

Ricoeur, Paul, *Temps et récit*, 3 vols. (Paris: Seuil, 1983–5).

Ridon, Jean-Xavier, 'Un Barbare en banlieue', *Nottingham French Studies*, 39/1 (Spring 2000), 25–38.

Rifkin, Adrian, *Street Noises: Parisian Pleasures, 1900–1940* (Manchester: Manchester University Press, 1993).

Riffaterre, Michael, 'L'illusion référentielle' in Gérard Genette and Tzvetan Todorov (eds.), *Littérature et réalité* (Paris: Seuil, 1982), 91–118.

Rigby, Brian, *Popular Culture in France: A Study of Cultural Discourse* (London: Routledge, 1991).

—— *'Popular Culture' in France and England: The French Translation of Richard Hoggart's The Uses of Literacy* (Hull: The University of Hull Press, 1995).

Rimbaud, Arthur, *Oeuvres complètes* (Paris: Gallimard Pléiade, 1946).

Rivière, Claude, *Les Rites profanes* (Paris: PUF, 1995).

—— 'Pour une théorie du quotidien ritualisé', *La Ritualisation du quotidien, Ethnologie française*, 26 (1996), 229–38.

Roberts, John, *The Art of Interruption: Realism, Photography and the Everyday* (Manchester and New York: Manchester University Press, 1988).

Rolin, Jean, *Zones* (Paris: Gallimard, 1995).

Rolin, Olivier, *L'Invention du monde* (Paris: Seuil, 1993).

Ross, Kristin, 'Two Version of the Everyday', *L'Esprit créateur*, 24 (Fall 1984), 29–37.

—— 'Henri Lefebvre on the Situationist International', interview conducted and trans. 1983 by Kristin Ross, *October*, 79 (Winter 1997).

—— *Fast Cars, Clean Bodies: Decolonization and the Reordering of French Culture* (Cambridge, MA: MIT Press, 1996).

—— and Alice Kaplan (eds.), *Everyday Life, Yale French Studies*, 83 (1987).

Roubaud, Jacques, *Σ (Epsilon, le signe d'appartenance)* (Paris: Gallimard, 1967).

—— *Mono no aware: Le Sentiment des choses (cent-quarante-trois poèmes empruntés au Japonais)* (Paris: Gallimard, 1970).

—— *La Pluralité des mondes de Lewis* (Paris: Gallimard, 1991).

—— *La Forme d'une ville change plus vite, hélas, que le coeur des humains* (Paris: Gallimard, 1999).

—— *Tokyo infra-ordinaire* (Paris: Éditions Inventaire, 2003).

—— *Churchill 40 et autres sonnets de voyage 2000–2003* (Paris: Gallimard, 2004).

—— and Christian Boltanski, *Ensembles* (Paris: Éditions Florence Loewy, 1997)

Rousset, David, *L'Univers concentrationnaire* (1946; Paris: Hachette, 1993).

La Ruse, Cause Commune, 1977/1 (Paris: Union générale d'éditions, 1977).

Sadler, Simon, *The Situationist City* (Cambridge, MA: MIT Press, 1998).

Sami-Ali, M., *Le Banal* (Paris: Gallimard, 1980).

Sanouillet, Michel, *Dada à Paris* (Paris: Pauvert, 1965).

Sansot, Pierre, *Poétique de la ville* (Paris: Klincksieck, 1973).

—— *La France sensible* (Paris: Champ Vallon, 1985).

—— *Les Formes sensibles de la vie sociale* (Paris: PUF, 1986).

—— *Cahiers d'enfrance* (Paris: Champ Vallon, 1990).

—— *Les Gens de peu* (Paris: PUF, 1992).

—— *Jardins publics*, (Paris: Payot, 1994).

—— *Le Rugby est une fête* (Paris: Payot, 2002).

Sartre, Jean-Paul, *Critique de la raison dialectique* (Paris: Gallimard, 1960).

Savitzkaya, Eugène, *En vie* (Paris: Minuit, 1995).

Scholem, Gershom, *Walter Benjamin: The Story of a Friendship* (New York: New York Review Books, 2003).

Schoots, Fieke, *'Passer en douce à la douane': L'écriture minimaliste de Minuit: Deville, Echenoz, Redonnet, Toussaint* (Amsterdam-Atlanta: Rodopi, 1997).

Schor, Naomi, *Reading in Detail: Aesthetics and the Feminine* (New York and London: Methuen, 1987).

Sebbag, Georges, *Le Masochisme quotidien* (Paris: Le Point d'Etre, 1972).

Segalen, Martine, *Rites et rituels contemporains* (Paris: Nathan, 1998).

—— *Les Enfants d'Achille et de Nike: Une ethnologie de la course à pied ordinaire* (Paris: A.M. Métailié, 1994).

Sheringham, Michael, 'Raymond Queneau: The Lure of the Spiritual', in David Bevan (ed.), *Literature and Spirituality* (Amsterdam: Rodopi, 1992), 33–48.

—— *French Autobiography: Devices and Desires* (Oxford: Oxford University Press, 1993).

—— 'Éros noir, éros blanc: l'interrogation du désir dans la poésie d'André Breton: 1931–33', *André Breton, Revue des Sciences Humaines*, 237 (1995), 11–27.

—— 'Marc Augé and the Ethno-analysis of Contemporary Life', *Paragraph*, 18 (1995), 210–22.

—— 'City Space, Mental Space, Poetic Space: Paris in Breton, Benjamin and Réda', in id. (ed.), *Parisian Fields* (London: Reaktion, 1996), 85–114.

—— ' "Invisible Presences": Fiction, Autobiography and Women's Lives—Virginia Woolf to Annie Ernaux', *Sites*, 2 (1998), 5–24.

—— ' "Là où se fait notre histoire...": l'autobiographique et la quotidienneté chez Marguerite Duras', in C. Rogers and R. Udris (eds.), *Marguerite Duras: Lectures plurielles* (Amsterdam: Rodopi, 1998), 115–32.

—— 'Attending to the Everyday: Blanchot, Lefebvre, Certeau, Perec', *French Studies*, 14 (2000), 187–99.

—— ' "Plutôt la vie": Vitalism and the Theory and Practice of Subjectivity in Breton's Writings', in Ramona Fotiade (ed.), *André Breton: The Power of Language* (Exeter: Elm Park Books, 2000), 9–22.

—— 'Language, Color, and the Enigma of Everydayness', in M. Syrotinski and I. MacLachlan (eds.), *Sensual Reading: New Approaches to Reading in its Relation to the Senses* (Lewisburg, PA: Bucknell University Press, 2001), 127–52.

—— 'André Breton et l'écriture du lieu', in C. Bommerz and J. Chénieux-Gendron (eds.), *Regards/mises en scène dans le surréalisme et les avant-gardes* (Leuven: Peeters, 2002), 133–48.

—— 'Dans le quotidien: immersion, résistance, liberté (Raymond Queneau, Anne Portugal)', in E. Cardonne-Arlick and Dominique Viart (eds.), *Effractions de la Poésie, Écritures contemporaines*, 7 (Paris: Minard, 2003), 205–20.

—— 'Le Romanesque du quotidien', in Michel Murat and Gilles Leclerq (eds.), *Le Romanesque* (Paris: Presses de la Sorbonne Nouvelle, 2004), 255–66.

—— and Johnnie Gratton, *The Art of the Project* (Oxford: Berghahn, 2005).

Shields, Rob, *Henri Lefebrre: Love and Struggle—Spatial Dialectics* (London: Routledge, 2000).

Shorley, Christopher, *Queneau's Fiction: An Introductory Study* (Cambridge and New York: Cambridge University Press, 1985).

Sibony, Daniel, *Événements:* I and II (*Psychopathologie du quotidien*); III (*Psychopathologie de l'actuel*) (Paris: Seuil, 1995–99).

Silverman, Max, *Facing Postmodernity* (London: Routledge, 1999).

Silverstone, Roger, *Televison and Everyday Life* (London: Routledge, 1994).

Simmel, Georg, *La Tragédie de la culture* (Paris: Rivages, 1988).

Soeffner, Hans-Georg, *The Order of Rituals: The Interpretation of Everyday Life* (New Brunswick: Transaction Publishers, 1997).

Soja, Edward, *Postmodern Geographies: The Reassertion of Space in Critical Social Theory* (London: Verso, 1989).

Solnit, Rebecca, *Wanderlust: A History of Walking* (London: Verso, 2001).

Stafford, Helen, *Mallarmé and the Poetics of Everyday Life* (Amsterdam: Rodopi, 2000).

Starobinski, Jean, 'L'Ordre du jour', *Le Temps de la réflexion*, 4 (1983), 101–26.

—— 'Jean-Jacques Rousseau/La Forme du jour', in *Jean Starobinski, Cahiers pour un temps* (Paris: Centre Georges Pompidou, 1985), 199–269.

—— 'Le Cycle des heures et le moment de vérité', *Bulletin de l'Institut Collégial Européen* (1986).

—— 'La Journée dans *Histoire*', in R. Dragonetti (ed.), *Sur Claude Simon* (Paris: Minuit, 1987).

Suzuki D. T., *Zen Buddhism: Selected Writings of D. T. Suzuki*, ed. W. Barrett (1956; New York: Doubleday, 1996).

Taylor, Charles, *The Sources of the Self: The Making of Modern Identity* (Cambridge: Cambridge University Press, 1989).

Thompson, C. W., (ed.), *L'Autre et le sacré: Surréalisme, ethnographie, cinéma* (Paris: L'Harmattan, 1995).

Thuillier, Guy, *Pour une histoire du quotidien au XIXème siècle en Nivernais* (Paris: Mouton, 1977).

Tisseron, Serge, *Petites mythologies d'aujourd'hui* (Paris: Aubier, 2000).

Todorov, Tzvetan, *Éloge du quotidien* (1993; Paris: Seuil Points-Essais, 1997).

—— *La Vie commune* (Paris: Seuil, 1995).

Tomkins, Calvin, *Ahead of the Game* (1962; London: Penguin, 1968).

Trebitsch, Michael, 'Preface', in Henri Lefebvre, *Critique of Everyday Life, I* (London: Verso, 1991) and *Critique of Everyday* Life, II (London: Verso, 2002).

Traverses (Journal; CCI (Centre de création industrielle), Centre Pompidou, 1975–86).

Ungar, Steven, 'From Ephemera to Memory Site: Thoughts on Rereading *Mythologies*', *Nottingham French Studies*, 36/1 (Spring 1997), 23–33.

Ungar, Steven, 'In the Thick of Things: Rouch and Morin's *Chronique d'un été* Reconsidered', *French Cultural Studies*, 14/1 (2003), 5–22.

Urbain, Jean-Didier, *Ethnologue, mais pas trop: ethnologie de proximité, voyages secrets et autres expéditions minuscules* (Paris: Payot, 2003).

Vaneigem, Raoul, *Traité de savoir-vivre à l'usage des jeunes générations* (1967; Paris: Gallimard Folio, 1992).

Vidler, Anthony, *The Architectural Uncanny* (Boston: MIT Press, 1992).

Vinaver, Michel, *Par-dessus bord* (Paris: L'Arche, 1969).

—— *La Demande d'emploi* (Paris: L'Arche, 1973).

—— *Les Travaux et les jours*, (Paris: L'Arche, 1979).

—— *Écrits sur le théâtre*, I, (Paris: L'Arche, 1998).

Virilio, Paul, *Esthétique de la disparition* (Paris: Balland, 1980)

Voilà—le monde dans la tête (Musée d'art moderne de la ville de Paris, 2000).

Walker, David H., *Outrage and Insight: Modern French Writers and the 'fait divers'* (Oxford: Berg, 1995).

—— 'Shopping and Fervour: Modern Literature and the Consumer Society', *French Studies*, 58 (Jan. 2004), 29–46.

Walker, Ian, *City Gorged with Dreams: Surrealism and Documentary Photography in Interwar Paris* (Manchester and New York: Manchester University Press, 2002).

Warehime, Marja, *Brassaï: Images of Culture and the Surrealist Observer* (Baton Rouge, LA; London: Louisiana State University Press, 1996).

Watson, Janell, *Literature and Material Culture from Balzac to Proust: The Collection and Consumption of Curiosities* (Cambridge: Cambridge University Press, 2000).

Welch, Edward, 'Experimenting with Identity: People, Place and Urban Change in Contemporary French Photography', in Michael Sheringham and Johnnie Gratton (eds.), *The Art of the Project* (Oxford: Berghahn, 2005).

Weil, Simone, *La Condition ouvrière* (1951; Paris: Gallimard 'Idées', 1976).

Wenzel, Jean-Pierre, *Loin d'Hagondage* (1975; Paris, Actes Sud, 1995).

Willis, Susan, *A Primer for Everyday Life* (London: Routledge, 1991).

Wollen, Peter, *Raiding the Icebox* (Bloomington, IN: Indiana University Press, 1993).

Woolf, Virginia, *Moments of Being* (2nd edn; San Diego: Harvest Books, 1985).

Zonka, Erick (dir.), *La Vie rêvée des anges* (*The Dreamlife of Angels*) (Film: France, 1998).

Index